REAL V
ILLUSTRATOR 8

Deke McClelland

Revisions
Daniel McClelland

Peachpit Press

REAL WORLD ILLUSTRATOR 8

Deke McClelland, Revisions Daniel McClelland

Peachpit Press
1249 Eighth Street
Berkeley, CA 94710
510/524-2178
800/283-9444
510/524-2221 (fax)

Find us on the World Wide Web at:
http://www.peachpit.com

Peachpit Press is a division of Addison Wesley Longman

Project Editor: Marjorie Baer
Copy Editors: Gail Nelson and Lisa Theobald
Production Coordinator: Kate Reber
Cover design: Lynn Brofsky
Cover art and part opener art: Ron Chan
Interior design: Michele Cuneo and Mimi Heft
Compositor: Margaret Copeland, Terragraphics

ISBN 0-201-35387-3

9 8 7 6 5 4 3 2 1

Printed and bound in the United States of America

ACKNOWLEDGMENTS

The creation of this book has generally been a modest affair, involving myself and a few friends sniffing processing chemicals as we ground out the pages. But I needed the help of some earnest and capable professionals to wrench the book apart and reassemble the pieces to create this most recent edition. I owe a sincere debt of gratitude to these wonderful folks.

Thanks first to my most excellent editor Marjorie Baer, who excelled at comprehending my mutterings. The net result would have been a sprawling mess of gook without the considerable help and talents of the rest of the crew at Peachpit Press. Also, thanks to Andrei Herasimchuk at Adobe for his technical expertise and bearing with all my questions.

Thanks to the invaluable encouragement and advice of super-agent Matt Wagner. Thanks also to Ron Chan, the singularly gifted artist who created the cover and parts pages. Rarely have I encountered such a pleasant blend of killer aptitude and affable modesty.

Finally, thanks to the folks I conned into quotes, including David Pogue, Sandee Cohen, and Linda Liddell, and newly christened international correspondent Jeanette Borzo. Thanks also to the many readers and user group reviewers who have contributed comments and valuable insights over the years.

Elizabeth Pheasant is in a class all by herself, which is why I married her. Life is a dream, sweetheart.

CONTENTS AT A GLANCE

TABLE OF CONTENTS

Chapter 3

Objects, Images, and the File Formats that Love Them 63

Chapter 5

Chapter 6

How to Handle Typical Type 193

Chapter 7
Some of Your Wackier Text Effects 233

Chapter 8

Chapter 10

Chapter 11

Traditional Homespun Transformations 443

Chapter 12

Hog-Wild Special Effects 491

Chapter 16
Strokes and Brushes 639

Chapter 17
Blends, Masks, and Special Inks 681

Chapter 18
Printing Your Illustrations 727

INTRODUCTION

Although I'm in my mid-thirties, a phase that's sadly unlikely to last too much longer, I sometimes feel like a crusty old codger who's witnessed more than anyone cares to hear recounted. For instance, I might venture that where computer graphics are concerned, you are spoiled rotten. Adobe Illustrator is a prime example of a professional-quality application that—despite any problems you may or may not have with it—performs without crashing and prints like a champ. You can get up in the morning, start working in the program, and expect to make substantial progress. The darn thing works.

It's quite a different story than when I was a boy. I don't think I could have endured desktop publishing back in 1986—before Illustrator hit the market—if I hadn't been a kid. When I began working as artistic director for a small service bureau, our world consisted of a laughably inept collection of software and hardware. We used PageMaker 1.2 to lay out pages. Sure, the files corrupted regularly and the program took an extra 15 minutes to print a page with a downloadable font on it, but it was better than facing the customer and admitting that desktop publishing was a cruel joke.

We used a program called FullPaint to create black-and-white bitmapped graphics because it could rotate a selection (an operation that MacPaint couldn't handle). We scanned images using a ThunderScanner, which boasted photocopier quality when it wasn't stretching and slanting photos as it curled them around its roller. Less than 100 fonts were available in all the world, most of which were clumsily executed by folks still learning their trade. For printing, we had a Linotronic 100 imagesetter—the number of which coincidentally corresponded to the thousands of dollars it cost—and a film processor that looked and acted like it had fallen off the back of a truck. And our best computer was a supercharged Macintosh 512K with a whopping 2 MB of RAM and two 400-K floppy drives. There wasn't such a thing as a hard drive.

The following year, we purchased better machines, upgraded PageMaker, and continued to pour expensive chemicals into our increasingly frightening processor. But the event that most changed how *I* worked was the arrival of Illustrator 1.0. It was the first drawing program that worked worth a hill of beans. MacDraw was nearly unusable; you couldn't get two lines to properly align. And though CricketDraw permitted gradations and type along a curve—both missing from Illustrator at the time—it crashed on the hour and absolutely refused to print to our imagesetter. Frankly, that program went a long way toward helping me loosen my fragile grasp on reality.

But Illustrator was an entirely different kind of program, unlike anything I had used before. Other programs supplied more features, but Illustrator had exactly what I needed, implemented in the most logical fashion. Most important, I could actually depend on the program. Call me a sentimental fool, but I have no memory of it ever once crashing or failing to print. It has always come through.

The new Illustrator is far more capable than its distant ancestor. And though nostalgia may cloud my judgment, it's frequently less logical and less streamlined. But it remains the most reliable application for printing computer-generated graphics that I've ever used. After nine years of writing, designing, and reworking this book, I have yet to conceive of a graphic that I couldn't manage one way or another. I can still open every illustration just as I originally created it, with no line, shape, or character of text missing or moving on the page. (I'd love to see *any* version of PageMaker do that.) And I know that everything I draw will eventually print, even if it requires some minor modifications. Mind you, I don't like everything about Illustrator—in fact, I would change quite a few features if I could—but this is an important program that has *never* been absent from any of my hard drives. Heck, I'd still be using Illustrator 1.0 if Adobe hadn't upgraded it.

Now, tell me honestly. I sound like I'm at least 86, don't I?

Illustrator and You

Adobe Illustrator 8 is a drawing program that exists both for the Macintosh and Windows compatible computers. That's right, Illustrator 8 is a cross-platform program. The same CD-ROM will install Illustrator 8 on a Mac or a Windows machine and it looks and functions (well almost) the same. The differences are few and are mostly related to things that are unique to a particular platform, such as the look and function of a palette's close box. The biggest of these differences is that the Illustrator you see on a Mac employs the ⌘ and Option keys whereas the one you see on a Windows machine uses the Ctrl and Alt keys. This difference reflects the varying structure between Macs and other PCs. Where Mac people would press the ⌘ key, Windows folks would press the Ctrl key. This same relationship holds for the Option and Alt keys. For the sake of simplicity, I've chosen to use the Macintosh convention throughout the book. I do so since most of Illustrator's users are Mac owners (in the 80 to 90 percent range) and to list both forms of key combinations is cumbersome and unnecessary. This means that if you're running Illustrator under Windows 95 or 98 and you're told to "⌘-click" or "press ⌘-Option-B", you'll instead need to Ctrl-click or press Ctrl-Alt-B.

Regardless of your platform, you can use Illustrator to draw high-contrast graphics with perfectly smooth edges. You can also edit the outline of any shape long after you create it. You see Illustrator graphics every day in newspapers, magazines, and other print media; they're even turning up in large numbers on the World Wide Web. Artists use Illustrator to create diagrams, info-art, maps, logos, posters, photo-realistic renderings, and all sorts of other illustrations that defy categorization. You can even integrate photographs corrected and enhanced in Adobe Photoshop or a similar application.

Illustrator is a graphics workshop; it's as expansive, elaborate, and perplexing as any traditional workshop on earth. Like any powerful collection of tools, Illustrator demands your attention and rewards your understanding. That's why this book guides you through every feature of the program as if you've never seen a drawing application in your life. Regardless of your level of experience, you'll find yourself easily graduating into the advanced topics that consume most of the pages in this book. Every section explains not only how to perform a technique but also provides enough background so you know why you'd want to. Most important, there isn't a single detail in any of the several hundred illustrations that I don't tell you how to create yourself. Though I hope they're pleasing to look at, my figures aren't meant to amaze; they're included to educate. I want you to amaze yourself.

The Structure of This Book

If you've seen the previous edition of this book, you're gonna feel right at home with this one. Now on the other hand, if you haven't seen this book since 5.0 appeared in the title, don't expect to find much of anything where it was before. I've pretty much dumped the old book on the floor, sorted out and thrown away 95 percent of it, and reassembled the remaining 5 percent with a tremendous amount of new stuff.

Real World Illustrator 8 contains a total of 18 chapters organized into four distinct parts. Each part explores a simple concept in exhaustive and engaging detail. My hope is that at the end of every part, you feel sufficiently confident with the material that you begin to see the gaps in my explanations. "Oh, sure, you can do *that*, but how about *this*, and *this*, and *this*?" Once you understand the topics, you can invent techniques on your own without the slightest hesitation.

- **Part One, Starting**: The first part's three chapters introduce the fundamental issues in Illustrator 8. I explain how Illustrator differs from other graphics programs. I introduce you to Illustrator's network of tools and palettes. And I tell you everything there is to know about the new file formats included with Illustrator 8. If you're familiar with previous editions of Illustrator, this part will get you up and running in no time at all.

- **Part Two, Creating**: These five chapters tell you how to create the basic type and graphic elements in Illustrator. I explain all the tricks you need to know to get the most out of the new polygon, star, and spiral tools. I make sense out of the pen tool and Bézier curves. Chapters 6 and 7 devote close to 100 pages to the topic of creating and editing text. And I close the part with a look at one of Illustrator's most overlooked features, charts and graphs.

- **Part Three, Changing**: In sculpture, a substance like clay is considered "forgiving" by comparison to, say, marble, because clay permits you to modify your mistakes. By this standard, Illustrator provides the most forgiving environment possible. Nothing in Illustrator is permanent; everything you create is subject to adjustment. In Chapters 9 through 13, I tell you how to cut apart lines and shapes and how to put them back together again. I spend more pages discussing such essential features as compound paths and Pathfinder filters than any other book. I also make sense of Illustrator's transformation and special effects capabilities. And this book alone spends an entire chapter showing you how to exploit the new relationship between Illustrator 8 and Photoshop.
- **Part Four, Coloring**: To keep the cover price as low as possible, no color was used in this book. And yet, I devote more than 200 pages to showing you how color works, how to use color, and how to print grayscale and color illustrations. If you want to see color, more colorful books are available. But if you want to master and manage color, this book contains everything there is to know. Chapter 14 simplifies the science of color and shows how it applies to Illustrator 8. Later chapters cover gradations, tile patterns, strokes, blends, masks, and the new Ink Pen patterns. I wrap up with printing in Chapter 18. Though you certainly don't need to know everything in this perhaps overly thorough chapter, I can't be accused of leaving anything out.

I've written the chapters so you can read them from beginning to end without finding the information either repetitive or overwhelming. If you prefer to read when you're stumped, you can look up a confusing topic in the index. Or you can simply browse through the pictures until you come to something that looks interesting. But no matter how you approach the text, I hope that it snags you and teaches you more than you bargained for. If you look up from the book at your watch and think, "Dang, I've got to get back to work!" then I've done my job.

Meet the Margin Icons

Throughout this book, we've designed two kinds of special text elements to attract your attention and convey fast information. The first are the figure captions. A caption is worthless unless it tells you something about the figure that you don't already know. Between the graphic and the caption text, an experienced user should be able to glean enough information to perform a similar effect in Illustrator. If you need to know more, the text contains the full story, including additional hints and details. But you shouldn't *have* to read if you don't want to.

The second special text element is the icon text. If a paragraph contains very important information or an offhanded aside that you can feel free to skip, I include an icon next to the paragraph to distinguish it from the surrounding text. If you already know Illustrator, you can get up to speed in Illustrator 8 by just reading these paragraphs.

Here are the four icons that you can expect to jockey for your attention:

This icon points out features that are new to Illustrator 8. Sometimes, the paragraph tells you everything you need to know about the new feature. Other times, the icon introduces several pages of text. Either way, you'll know it's something you didn't have in Illustrator 7 or earlier.

It seems like every book offers a tip icon. So I try to steer clear of the boring old tips that every Illustrator user hears a million times, and I concentrate on the juicy stuff that most folks don't know. But keep in mind, these are fast tips. For the more involved killer techniques, you have to read the text, too.

This icon explains an action to avoid. Few operations are hazardous in Illustrator, but many are time wasters. And you can bet that after I tell you what not to do, I include a preferable alternative as well.

I've been using Illustrator and other programs for a long as they've been out, so I occasionally feel compelled to share my thoughts on a variety of subjects. Sometimes it's a bit of history, other times it's a thoughtful observation, and every once in a while it's just me complaining. Whatever it is, you can skip it if it gets on your nerves.

Contacting the Guy Who's Responsible for All This Gibberish

I have close to ten books on the market at any one time. These plus my magazine and speaking commitments keep me busier than I care to admit—not to mention my newfound love for off-track Shetland pony racing simulations for UNIX-based machines. With one thing and another, I regret that I can't talk to every reader. But I do invite you to submit your comments, questions, and general observations to my electronic mail account, which is accessible from my Web site, at http://www.dekemc.com.

I'm not very regular about checking and responding to my e-mail, so you can expect a delay of a week to a month, depending on what the current deadline situation is like. But you have my word. One day, when you least expect it, you'll hear back from me.

PART ONE
STARTING

CHAPTER 1

ILLUSTRATOR 8: WHAT IT IS

Illustrator—what is it, and what's new with version 8? That's the stuff of Chapter 1. This chapter provides a general overview of Illustrator, specifically the most recent version.

If you've never used Illustrator before, I'll tell you what it is and why you've probably heard its name bandied about. I'll show you where it fits into the world of computer graphics. Along the way you'll find out about Illustrator's relationship to its more popular sibling, Photoshop—a graphics program with an entirely different purpose.

If you're a longtime Illustrator enthusiast, this chapter provides some amusing—if not terribly insightful—analyses along with a practical assessment of Illustrator 8's new capabilities. I even tell you which chapters to turn to for more information on Illustrator's new features.

Adobe, the "Microsoft of Graphics"

To understand Illustrator, you have to know the company behind it, Adobe Systems. One of the five largest software companies in this quadrant of the galaxy, Adobe is widely considered to be the one software developer that Microsoft cannot destroy. Adobe knows electronic graphics and design, and Microsoft never will. It's that simple.

Case in point: Photoshop, Adobe's phenomenally successful image-editing program, is widely considered the most powerful personal computer application for mucking around with computerized photographs. Photoshop is equally revered by expert and novice, young and old, educated and self-taught, primate and bottom-feeding slimefish. Photoshop isn't altogether perfect, but it has a universal appeal.

Microsoft, meanwhile, has squat. No image editor now, and none planned for the future.

Adobe also sells Premiere, the number one program for editing computerized video sequences. Premiere needs a fast computer and an awfully big hard disk to run, and you need special hardware to capture the movies and then send them back out to videotape. But there's absolutely nothing like it for messing around with moving images and creating simple animated effects.

Microsoft is currently unaware of any need for a video editing package among the populace at large.

Are you beginning to see the trend? Adobe is absolutely steeped in the world of professional artistry and business graphics, and Microsoft hasn't even begun to compete. And perhaps it never will.

In the mind of your everyday, average industry analyst, Adobe is the "Microsoft of graphics." Like Microsoft, Adobe is a dominant force that not only lords over an entire discipline of computing with an iron fist, but it also manages to consistently churn out quality software. Lesser companies regard Adobe with a combination of envy, respect, and fear. For better or worse, Adobe is currently where the artwork is.

Where Illustrator Fits In

Illustrator is important because its creation set current events in motion. Prior to Illustrator—back in the mid-1980s, when the world was learning to pronounce Mikhail Gorbachev and Scritti Politti—Adobe was a small company that had invented the PostScript printing language. PostScript revolutionized the world of typesetting and jump-started the career of at least one computer author, but it didn't exactly make Adobe a household word (except in New Mexico, where adobe houses are quite common).

The problem with PostScript was its inaccessibility. In theory, PostScript let you design incredibly ornate, twisty-curvy lines and fill them with any of several million color options. But unless you wanted to resort to PostScript programming—the equivalent of instructing a friend to draw an object by reciting numerical coordinates over the phone—your options were limited to text surrounded by a few straight lines and rectangles.

Illustrator single-handedly changed all this. One of the few programs designed from start to finish by Adobe employees (Photoshop, Premiere, PageMaker, and other top titles started out as non-Adobe products), because Illustrator was so far-and-away better than anything that had previously blessed the Macintosh computer, artists started moving to the Mac strictly to use this one program. Before Illustrator, Macintosh graphics looked blocky and turgid; after Illustrator, most folks couldn't tell Mac graphics from those drawn with pen and ink. The transition couldn't have been more abrupt or more welcome.

Close, But Not Kin: Illustrator Versus Photoshop

Now in its twelfth year, Illustrator is often seen as a kind of support program for Photoshop, thanks to the latter's dramatic and overshadowing success. Mind you, Illustrator's growth has been consistent and commendable over the years, and to this day it remains the world's most popular PostScript drawing program. But Photoshop manages to sell roughly twice as well as Illustrator, despite being nearly three years younger.

Truth be told, Adobe has tried to piggyback Illustrator on Photoshop's success. Since Photoshop was first released, Illustrator's popularity has mushroomed and the two programs have become more closely related. In fact, beginning with Illustrator 7, Adobe took this marriage one step further. Illustrator now has the look and feel of Photoshop. It still functions like Illustrator should, but the physical layout and the interface is similar to that of modern-day Photoshop. Adobe is simply trying to make Illustrator more accessible to the numerous Photoshop users.

Illustrator Does Smooth Lines; Photoshop Does Pixels

The easiest way to help you understand how Illustrator works is to start off by explaining how it *does not* work—which is precisely how Photoshop *does* work. As its name implies, Photoshop's primary purpose is to edit photographs. When you scan a photograph into a computer, the software converts it to a collection of tiny colored pixels. Each pixel is perfectly square, and one is perfectly adjacent to the next with no wiggle room between them. The purpose of Photoshop's hundred or so functions is to adjust the colors of these pixels.

Although you can force Illustrator to edit pixels in a comparatively crude fashion, the main purpose of the program is to create line art. Each line, shape, and character of text is altogether independent of its neighbors. These independent elements are known collectively as *objects*, which is why Illustrator is sometimes called an *object-oriented* application. Illustrator keeps track of each object by assigning it a separate mathematical equation. (Don't worry, there is no math in this book. Well, none that's important, anyway.) Illustrator later prints the lines, shapes, and text by sending the equations to the printer and letting the printer figure it out. The result is uniformly smooth artwork with high-contrast edges and crisp detail.

The Right Tool for the Right Job

As you might imagine, this difference in approach leads to a difference in purpose. Pixels are great for representing continuous color transitions, in which one color gradually changes into another. Such color transitions are the norm in real life, which is why pixels are so well suited to photographs. (Experienced/pretentious computer artists have even been known to call photographs *continuous-tone images*, but for our purposes, just plain *image* will suffice.)

Likewise, Illustrator is perfect for high-contrast artwork, which can vary from schematic or cartoonish to just barely stylized. This kind of computer art is known as a *drawing* or *illustration*.

Take as examples the two graphics in Figure 1-1. Both depict a sea lion in an attitude of aquatic grace, to be sure. But while the first is a photograph snapped by Marty Snyderman and distributed on CD-ROM by Digital Stock Professional, the second is a line drawing created in Illustrator. To achieve the left-hand image, I converted the color image to grayscale, corrected the brightness and contrast, and sharpened the focus, all in Photoshop. To achieve the right-hand illustration, I had to meticulously trace the photograph in Illustrator and fill each shape with a different shade of gray.

Figure 1-1: A photographic image enhanced in Photoshop (left) compared with a line drawing created in Illustrator (right).

The first image looks like a photo. But while the second is a recognizable member of the wildlife community, it is obviously executed by human hands, not snapped with a camera. This is the most significant difference between Photoshop and Illustrator.

Flexible Resizing

Another difference is in the details. Photoshop's details can be grainy, but Illustrator's are forever smooth.

As you increase the size of a Photoshop image, the square pixels likewise grow and become more obvious. On the left side of Figure 1-2, for example, I've enlarged the sea lion image to 200, 400, and 800 percent. At each level of magnification, your eye is better able to separate the pixels into individual colored squares. As a result, a photograph looks great when printed at high resolutions, that is, when a lot of pixels are packed into a small space. But it begins to look coarse, jagged, and out of focus when printed at low resolutions, with fewer pixels per inch.

Illustrator art isn't like that at all. As shown on the right side of Figure 1-2, the drawing looks great no matter how much you enlarge it. Every line is mathematically accurate regardless of size. The downside, of course, is that it took me about five minutes to adjust the sea lion photo in Photoshop, but almost three hours to draw the sea lion in Illustrator. Apart from the photography process itself, illustrations typically require a more sizable time investment than photographic images.

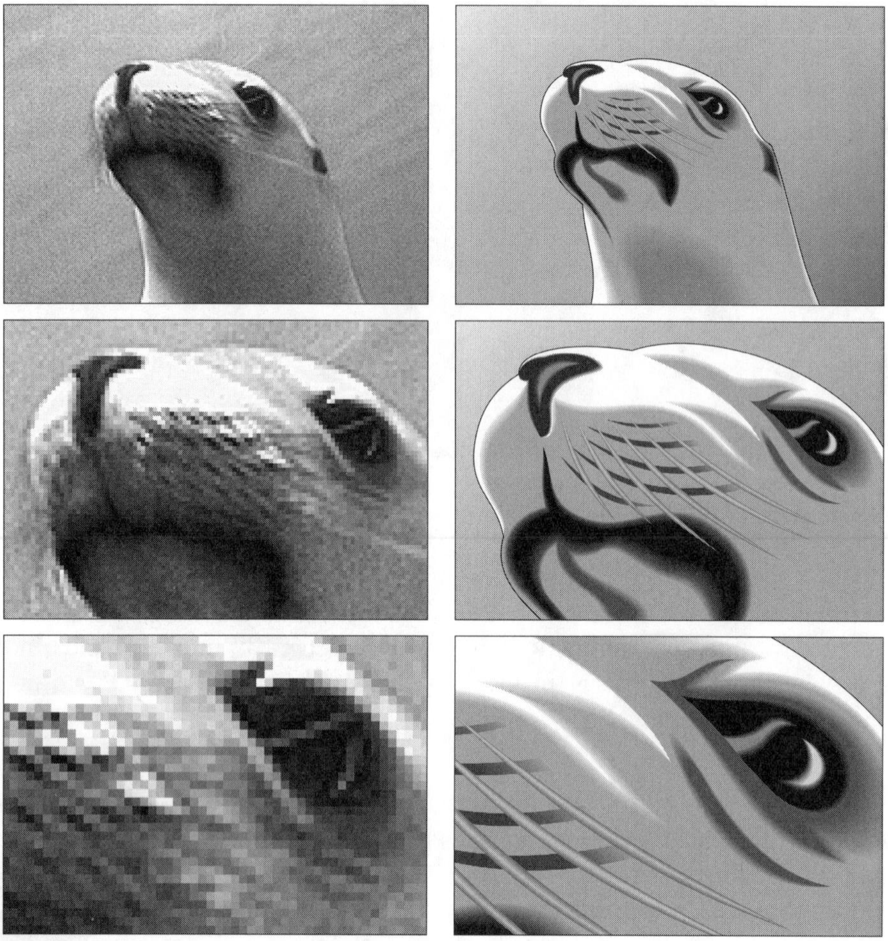

Figure 1-2: The result of magnifying the Photoshop image (left) and Illustrator drawing (right) to 200, 400, and 800 percent.

Objects and Pixels Together

The final difference between Photoshop and Illustrator is that Photoshop can handle only pixels, while Illustrator accommodates both. Don't get me wrong, Photoshop is several times more capable than Illustrator where pixels are concerned, but Photoshop doesn't do anything except pixels. With Illustrator, you can draw objects as well as import images from Photoshop or some other pixel editor. Figure 1-3 shows the object-oriented sea lion layered in front of the original Photoshop image, so that the image serves as a background.

Figure 1-3: This inspiring creature is the product of Photoshop and Illustrator working together.

But to interpret Illustrator's acceptance of pixels as an advantage over Photoshop's ignorance of objects misses the point. Illustrator and Photoshop are designed to work together, more now than ever before. There may even be times when you prefer to convert an entire illustration to pixels inside Photoshop to apply special effects that only Photoshop can handle or merely to simplify the printing process so the printer has to solve fewer equations. Illustrator and Photoshop are two halves of the artistic process, each taking up where the other one leaves off, each making up for the other one's weaknesses. It's the perfect marriage, and you're the happy beneficiary.

The Lowdown on Illustrator 8

If you're familiar with previous versions of Illustrator, you probably already know the stuff I've told you so far (although it never hurts to revisit the basics every now and then). What you may not know are the features that the new Illustrator 8 has to offer that its predecessors did not. I provide the following quick but riveting list, designed to get you up and running with little pain and lots of potential. Note that I also indicate which corresponding chapter spells out the new feature in detail, so you know where to turn when you need more information.

- **Blends get thrown a curve (Chapter 17):** Illustrator's old blending capabilities have always trailed those of FreeHand. In previous versions of Illustrator you could blend between two and only two paths and the blend would follow a straight line. On the other hand, in FreeHand you could blend between numerous paths and join the blend to a curve, resulting in a blend that followed the curve. With this latest version, the scales now tip in Illustrator's favor. Just as in FreeHand, you can now use as many paths as you want in a blend and have that blend curve any which way. Moreover, Illustrator now lets you blend in ways unheard of in FreeHand. You can blend between open and closed paths, blend between compound paths, and even blend between a number of grouped paths.
- **Smart Guides (Chapter 10):** Instead of being limited to traditional guides and grids that require you to set them up before you use them, smart guides are a system of guidelines that temporarily spring to life as you need them. Smart guides help you precisely construct and exactly align objects on the fly. Smart guides are more accurate than traditional guides and grids because smart guides are in effect from the moment you start your drag. Smart guides also provide a number of labels that appear on screen to inform you of the cursor's position relative to the various elements of your artwork.
- **Free transform tool (Chapter 11):** The free transform tool lets you perform any transform that each of the four traditional transformation tools do and a lot more. You can both transform and distort paths using the free transform tool. Unlike the old Free Distort filter that it replaces, the free transform tool is not limited to the confines of a dialog box.

Instead, you can quickly manipulate paths almost as easily as you can create them. You may find that this tool is the only transformation tool you'll ever use again.

- **Brushes (Chapter 16):** For the longest time, paths have consisted of fills and strokes, and over the years, the interiors of paths have received most of the attention. Now, with brushes, the outline of the path can take center stage. With a brush you can convert a regular path into graceful calligraphy or replace the path with another object that stretches to fit every curve of the path.
- **The Navigator palette (Chapter 3):** The Navigator palette gives you a diminutive overall view of your artwork. You can quickly see what objects lie on your artboard and which objects fall onto the nonprinting pasteboard. With a single click you are whisked away to an area of your artwork that would take multiple drags to reach with the hand tool.
- **The Action palette (Appendix):** Find yourself repeating the same set of tasks over and over to different paths? Now you can have Illustrator record your actions and repeat them with other paths. For example, you may need to reduce 40 paths by 20 percent and darken each of their fills by 50 percent. You can make these changes to each individual path yourself or you can show Illustrator all the steps once and have it apply the actions to all the paths, saving you time and ensuring you that each path receives the same modifications.
- **The Links palette (Chapter 3):** Often when you have linked several graphics into a document, it becomes rather difficult to keep track of each file and to know exactly where they are in your file and where they reside on disk. The Links palette takes a lot of the effort out of this task by both organizing all your placed files and showing you thumbnails of each file. It lets you quickly find important file information, such as a linked file's size and origin and the stability of the link, as well as letting you center the illustrator window around the linked graphic so that you can locate it in you artwork.
- **More absorbent eyedropper (Chapter 6):** In addition to picking up the color attributes of the objects on which you click with the eyedropper, you can now also pick up the character and paragraph formatting of the text block on which you click. This means that any formatting changes you make to one text block can be easily transferred to as many other text blocks as you want with a click.

- **Gradient mesh tool (Chapter 15):** It seems like just yesterday that Illustrator started offering traditional gradient fills. These gradients were either linear or radial in nature. Although competent, these standard gradients can give paths a very rigid appearance. With a gradient mesh, you can now add a gradient that flows more naturally with the outline of a path. Reticulate a path with as many lines as you want, and choose a different color at every intersection. This tool allows you to add a very organic coloring to even the most complicated shapes.
- **Bounding Box (Chapter 5):** Illustrator has always been a very independent program, often doing things differently from the competition. Whereas every other drawing program lets its users scale objects with simple bounding boxes, Illustrator has forced its users to use a specific tool for these modifications. In Illustrator 8, Adobe has decided to offer you this convenience. Now, with a preference setting, you can opt to use bounding boxes.

For those of you who are not familiar with the previous version of Illustrator—being that it has been available only for about a year—and for you Windows users who may not have seen an Illustrator upgrade since Perot was thought to be a viable candidate, here's a quick list of features that highlight the major implementations to Illustrator over the last few years.

- **Overall physical appearance (Appendix):** Before version 7, Illustrator had its own distinctive look. It offered a menu bar, a toolbox, and the work area. This was sufficient. But it meant that if you used both Illustrator and Photoshop, you had to learn the environments of both programs, and since they did not share many common user controls such as keyboard shortcuts, this required more learning than Adobe felt was necessary. To streamline this process, Illustrator 7 was made to look very much like Photoshop 4 and to share many of its keyboard shortcuts. So if you are familiar with Photoshop you should feel comfortable with Illustrator and be ready to dive in. The downside is that if you are proficient with Illustrator 6 you will need to learn a number of new keyboard shortcuts and menu layouts. The first part of the Appendix is devoted to comparing the old Illustrator versions to that of the new version 8.
- **Palettes more pal like (Chapter 2):** In the spirit of making Illustrator 7 look and feel like Photoshop 4, a number of option boxes were redesigned as palettes. Palettes, simply put, are option boxes that stay open as long as you want and allow you to change the attributes of your

art on the fly. Now, not only is a palette's presence on the screen your choice, you also have far more control over the palette's appearance. Instead of palettes containing only a limited number of functions, one palette may now contain as many or as few functions as you want. Illustrator even outdoes Photoshop in this respect by allowing you to dock individual palettes to form larger palettes.

- **The Mr. Fantastic tool (Chapter 5):** Although it's dubbed the reshape tool, I can't help feel that it should be called the stretch tool. With a single drag, this tool lets you deform an open path in a manner that, if you tried to duplicate it with the direct selection tool, would require you to alter many line segments individually.
- **Grids (Chapter 11):** One function that preceding Illustrator versions obviously needed was the option of adding grids. Grids give you more control over the precise placement of the objects in your artwork, much like the grids on graph paper. The advantage of Illustrator's grids is that they appear on screen only and do not print.
- **Keyboard shortcuts for all the tools (Chapter 2):** Although the mouse is an ideal implement for moving around inside a program, it needs only one of your hands to work—leaving your other hand flapping in the wind. With the expansion of keyboard shortcuts in Illustrator 7, your non-mouse hand has a greater role. For example, as you finish creating a line with the pencil tool you can easily switch to the pen tool by pressing the P key. The advantage here is that you never have to move the cursor to select a new tool from the toolbox and can continue creating your artwork with the new tool at the same point that you left off with the last tool.
- **RGB and HSB join CMYK (Chapter 14):** Of the three color schemes—CMYK, RGB, and HSB—only CMYK was supported by the past versions of Illustrator. Now you can use any one of these schemes in your illustrations. You can even use all three in the same illustration, although it's doubtful that you'll ever need to. Also, when opening artwork in Illustrator that you created in some other graphics program, such as Photoshop, Illustrator will preserve the color scheme that you originally used. Furthermore, Illustrator 7 provided new filters that allow you to change a CMYK color to a RGB one or a RGB color to its corresponding CMYK color.
- **Left to right goes up and down (Chapter 7):** To make Illustrator more internationally friendly, text that once could be displayed only

horizontally can now also be displayed vertically to accommodate Japanese script. Three new tools have been added that will help you create text blocks in this fashion.

- **Color libraries (Chapter 14):** Opening and using colors from color libraries—independently constructed libraries of predefined colors—is easier in the new Illustrator. Color libraries take up less room in RAM, and you can close the unused portion of a library without affecting your illustration.
- **Creating new tile patterns (Chapter 15):** Creating an original tile pattern is now just a click and drag away. Throw a few shapes together, select them all, and drag the whole mess onto the swatches palette. Whoa, Nelly, you got yourself a new tile pattern.
- **Adding a URL address (Chapter 3):** With the Internet becoming increasingly accessible and more and more people experimenting with creating Web pages, Illustrator now allows you to directly add URL addresses to your graphics.
- **Support for more formats (Chapter 3):** Illustrator 5.5 and previous versions supported the EPS and PDF (Adobe Acrobat) formats, and that's about it. It was very sad and the programmers were thoroughly ashamed of themselves. Version 6 redeemed itself by supporting such popular and essential file formats as TIFF (yes TIFF!), CompuServe GIF, Windows formats BMP and PCX, Kodak Photo CD, and more. Illustrator 6 even went so far as to allow you to colorize black-and-white TIFF images, just as you've been able to do in rival program FreeHand since 1988.
- **Improved compatibility with Photoshop (Chapter 13):** Illustrator 6 allowed you to trade low-resolution images and objects with Photoshop 3.0.5 as effortlessly as sisters trade culottes. You simply dragged objects into Photoshop and converted them to pixels on the fly or dragged images from Photoshop directly into Illustrator. Though System 7.5 has permitted dragging and dropping between applications for some time, Illustrator and Photoshop were two of the earliest programs to put the technique into practice.
- **Lift colors from imported images (Chapter 14):** New to Illustrator 6, you could lift colors from an imported image—or from a background image opened inside Photoshop!—by clicking on the color with the eyedropper tool. Illustrator 6 would automatically convert the color to CMYK, even if it was grayscale. Illustrator 7 took this one step further

by preserving the color scheme of the color you lift. In other words, if the imported color is RGB, Illustrator will recognize the color as RGB.

- **Change objects into pixels (Chapter 13):** In the past, if you wanted to convert a handful of objects into pixels—a technique known as *rasterizing*—you had to save the illustration as an EPS file and open the file in Photoshop. Now you can rasterize objects inside Illustrator. Nothing earth shattering, just a convenient feature, but useful nonetheless.
- **Photoshop filters (Chapter 13):** After selecting an imported or rasterized image in Illustrator 6, you could apply a Photoshop-compatible filter to it. Now Photoshop isn't the only program that does Radial Blur. Adobe even went so far as to throw in 12 filters from its three-volume Gallery Effects collection.
- **Dialog box previews (Chapter 3):** Not to be outdone by Photoshop, Illustrator 6 allowed you to add previews to your Illustrator files, which are visible inside the standard Open dialog box. So if the name of a file doesn't ring a bell, just click on it to see what it looks like. You can also view previews of Photoshop files. It's these little features that warm my heart.
- **More logical plug-in organization (various chapters):** As in Illustrator 5.5, plug-ins are little mini-programs that enhance Illustrator's core capabilities. In the past, all plug-ins manifested themselves as commands under the Filter menu—even though most of them were completely unrelated—but life became more logical with Illustrator 6.
- **The transform palette (Chapter 10):** Illustrator 6 included a Control palette like the one in PageMaker, which lets you position objects numerically and scale and rotate them without using tools. In Illustrator 7, the Control palette was renamed the Transform palette but continues to behave the same except that the Transform palette allows you to also shear an object numerically.
- **The knife tool (Chapter 9):** In addition to the standard scissors tool, which lets you sever a line at a point, Illustrator 6 introduced a knife tool. Drag to slice an object apart in an irregular, knifelike fashion.
- **Improved special-effects filters (Chapter 12):** In Illustrator 5.5, you could distort objects using a series of special-effects filters, similar to those found in Photoshop. But to make them work, you had to add anchor points to your objects, increasing their complexity and ensuring

some downright ugly results. Illustrator 6 included curve-fitting technology that made distortion filters smarter.

- **Stroke lines with custom path patterns (Chapter 16):** Just as you can fill objects with custom tile patterns, you can now create patterns that follow the outline of a line or shape. You design a base pattern and then create variations for the inner and outer corners. Illustrator stretches and rotates pattern elements to fit the object.
- **Gradients (Chapter 15):** Illustrator 5 introduced gradients, the ability to smoothly transform one color into another. A feature unheard of for Windows users until Illustrator 7, gradients can accommodate up to 32 key colors and you can independently set the beginning and ending as well as the mid-point of each gradient. Both linear and radial gradients are supported.
- **Expand gradients to blends (Chapter 17):** Ever wished you could make slight adjustments to an automated gradation? Well, now you can. Choose the Expand command to convert a gradation into a blend with as many steps as you want. You can also convert tile patterns to objects, a great way to avoid printing errors.
- **Let Illustrator do the math (Chapter 10):** If you want to adjust a value, but you can't do the math in your head, have Illustrator do it for you. To add a smidgen or subtract a mite, just enter the math—say, *4 – 1* or *3 + 2*—into an option box, hit the Return key, and Illustrator will perform the calculation.
- **Print color separations from inside Illustrator (Chapter 18):** For reasons that no one quite understands, Illustrator has long required you to use a separate utility to print color separations. No more. Illustrator 6 introduced a single command, Separation Setup, that provides access to the revised color printing operations. This is the way it should have been since day one.
- **Undo up to 200 times(Chapter 5):** As mind-boggling as it may seem, Illustrator 4 limited the number of undos and redos to the incredibly useful amount of one. Joy, joy. Now through one of the many Preference dialog boxes you can set up to 200 undos and redos.
- **Layers upon layers (Chapter 10):** Illustrator allows you to create and manipulate objects on separate drawing layers that overlap one another. These layers can then be manipulated independently. You can lock, hide, and alter the display mode of each layer separately.

- **Pathfinder operations (Chapter 9):** The Pathfinder palette offers a number of useful ways to combine two objects. Select two overlapping circles and the Minus Back filter and you form a crescent moon. Choose the Unite filter with the two original circles selected and a peanut-like shape results, which is, of course, perfect for all your peanut-like shape needs.
- **Expanded text handling (Chapter 6):** You can now spellcheck all text in your illustrations just like a word processor. Although it is sometimes easier to import text from some other application, it is no longer necessary to do so simply to ensure that the phrase "mi purtty piture" is spelled correctly. Also, Illustrator now sports search and replace capabilities. Life is just a bit easier.
- **Tabs, rows, and columns, oh my (Chapter 6):** For some unknown reason, Illustrator did not support the use of tabs in early versions. If you tried to use the Tab key, you would be advanced to the next line as though you had pressed the Enter key.
- **Select by attribute only (Chapter 14):** The arrow tool allows you to select one, two, or as many objects as you wish, but sometimes it's some quality of the one or more objects that you want to select. The Select submenu in the Edit menu gives you the option to choose an object by six different attributes as well as the ability to select all objects not presently selected. Say that you have a number of vermilion shapes that you know would be just dreamy in a light violet. Simply choose the Same Fill Color command and choose the new color from the Swatches palette. Oh, life is good.
- **Align and distribute (Chapter 10):** Illustrator offers a number of different options for arranging selected objects. From the Align palette, you can, for example, align objects such that the rightmost point of each object is aligned with the rightmost point of the rightmost object. Right-on. Also from that palette, you can control how selected objects are distributed from top-to-bottom and from left-to-right.

The Illustrator 8 package also includes a few hundred fonts, lots of clip art and stock photography, and a collection of path patterns to help get you started. There's a lot here to learn, so let's get going.

CHAPTER 2

WITNESS THE SPLENDOR THAT IS ILLUSTRATOR

Whenever I hear folks speak about Illustrator, someone always seems to drop the word "elegant" into the conversation. And truly, it fits. Despite its occasional flaws, Illustrator has always delivered a rare combination of a logical interface and extremely reliable performance. And what, I ask you, could be more elegant than that?

But even an elegant application can bewilder and vex the user it has sworn to serve. The biggest strike against Illustrator is that it doesn't always work like other programs. You can't resize an object by dragging a corner handle—unless you've activated the necessary preference option—as you can in every other drawing program on the planet. Illustrator provides three different arrow tools where all other programs manage to make do with one. You change the performance of many tools by clicking *with* them rather than double-clicking *on* them. The pen tool takes some getting used to with its Bézier control handles.

The end result is that the elegant Illustrator is hard to learn. Once you come to terms with it, you'll never go back. But coming to terms with it takes some concentrated and patient effort.

This chapter is my way of introducing Illustrator to new users, reminding casual users how it works, and bringing longtime users up to speed. I'll explain the interface, briefly describe the tools and palettes, and examine every single one of the preference settings in excruciating detail. I'll round off the chapter with a comprehensive list of keyboard equivalents and other shortcuts that should save you a lot of time over the long run. Bear in mind that since most of these have changed, if you are familiar with an older version of Illustrator you will want to pay particular attention to the list.

There is nothing that says you have to read this stuff sequentially. Feel free to skip around, read bits and pieces over the course of several weeks, or cut out the pages and fold them into paper airplanes. Follow whatever learning style makes you smart in the shortest amount of time.

Getting Illustrator Up and Running

Most folks are pretty clear on how to start up a program with the Mac OS or Windows system software, and Illustrator is no exception. For example, you can double-click on the Adobe Illustrator icon, which looks as though someone dolled up her thumb to look like Venus. Or you can double-click on an Illustrator file. Or you can drag some other file onto the Illustrator application icon. Some folks call this technique *launching* a program, others call it *running* a program—but whatever you call it, you have to do it before you can use Illustrator.

Setting Aside Memory

TIP: For you Mac users, prior to starting up Illustrator you may want to adjust the amount of memory (called *RAM*, like the sheep) that your Mac assigns to the application. To do this, first select the Adobe Illustrator application icon and choose the Get Info command from the File menu (or press ⌘-I while the icon is highlighted). This brings up the dialog box shown in Figure 2-1. Change the Preferred Size value to assign more or less RAM to Illustrator. (Even though you can also change the Minimum Size value, don't do it! Lowering this value can wreak havoc on Illustrator's performance and may even prevent the program from running.)

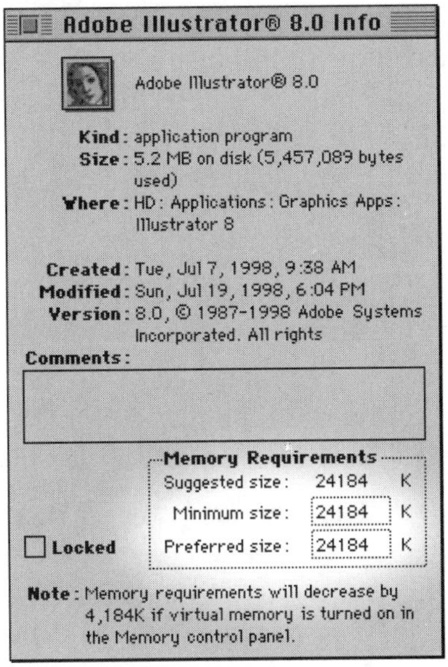

Figure 2-1: You can change the Preferred Size value, but leave Minimum Size alone.

The Splash Screen

After you launch Illustrator, the splash screen shows you that your computer is obeying your instructions. Little messages tell you that Illustrator is loading fonts or reading plug-ins. This is a perfect time to get a cup of coffee.

If you ever want to look at the splash screen again, choose About Illustrator from the Apple menu if you are on a Mac or from the Help menu on a PC. There's no practical reason you'd ever want to do this, but there are a couple of silly features that you might find mildly amusing.

- Wait a while to see a list of credits. Whoopee.
- Press the Option key to see the credits roll by quickly. Super whoopee.
- Click or press any key to make the splash screen go away.

There you have it, a bunch of silly information that won't do you a lick of good, except to clog your mind when you're in your dotage. I wouldn't blame you if you tore this page out of the book, ripped it up, and used the fragments to pick your teeth, though please be aware that this author refuses to take any responsibility for possible dental impairments that may result.

On-line Resources

Click the icon at the top of the toolbox to open the Adobe Online dialog box. This screen provides access to Adobe's Internet-based resources, which include technical support, tips and tricks and information about upgrades and related products. If you have Internet access, launch your browser and switch back to Illustrator. Click the icon atop the toolbox and then click on the Update button inside the Adobe Online dialog box.

After the splash screen goes away, the Illustrator desktop takes over the screen, as in Figure 2-2. Illustrator automatically creates a new illustration window so you can start drawing without wasting another fraction of a second.

If you've been working on the Mac or Windows system for any amount of time, you're probably familiar with the basic desktop elements labeled in Figure 2-2. If you're new to the world of microcomputing or new to Illustrator, go ahead and read the descriptions. (Labeled items from the figure appear in italic type.)

- The *menu bar* provides access to Illustrator 8's seven menus. Click on a menu name to display a list of *commands* that perform various operations. To choose a *command,* drag on top of it so it becomes highlighted, then release. *Keyboard shortcuts* appear to the right of commands. If a command is dimmed (as Create Gradient Mesh is in Figure 2-2), it isn't applicable to the current situation and you can't choose it.

  If a right-pointing arrowhead follows a command name, choosing the command displays a submenu of additional commands. To choose Object » Masks » Release, for example, you would drag from the Object menu down to the Masks command, then drag over to the submenu and down to the Release command.

- The *toolbox* includes 20 default tools and 31 alternate tools. To select a tool, click on its icon. I introduce all 51 tools in the "Using Tools" section later in this chapter. The bottom portion of the toolbox offers three sets of controls. The *color controls* let you change the colors of an object's stroke and fill as well as interchange colors. The *paint styles controls* let you select a solid color, a gradient, or none (that is, transparent) for your

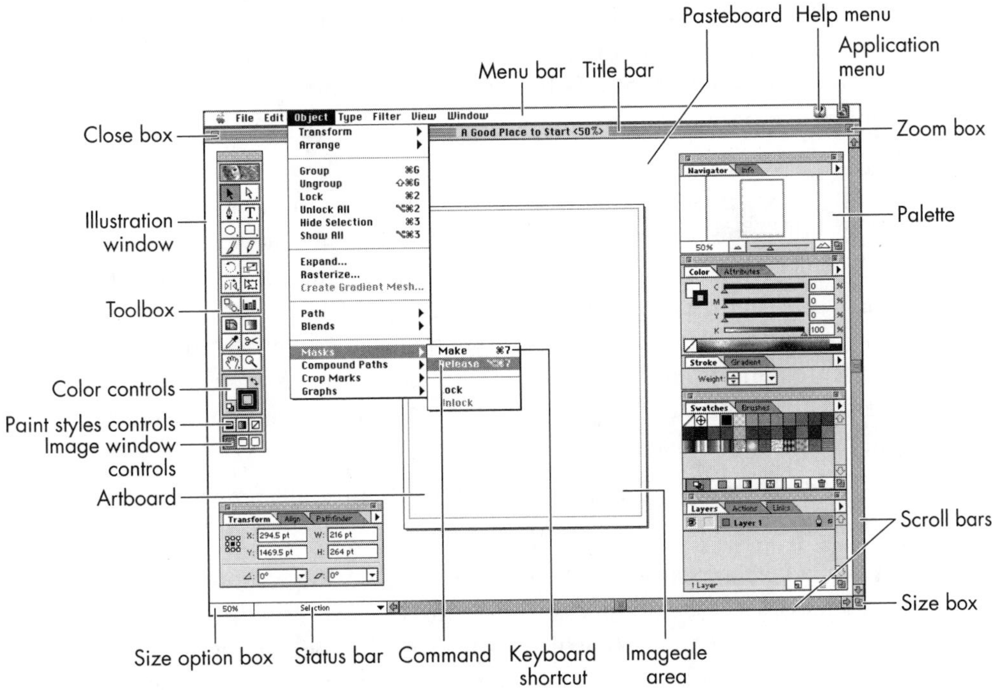

Figure 2-2: The fully annotated Illustrator 8 desktop.

fill or stroke. And in the final row, the *image window controls* give you control over the display of the foreground window.

The toolbox is known generically as a *palette*. In addition to the toolbox, Illustrator provides a number of other palettes, all of which I detail in the "Using Palettes" section of this chapter.

The *illustration window* is the large window in the middle of the desktop. A window appears for every open illustration. A title bar that lists the name of the drawing and the relative viewing size tops off the illustration window. If the illustration has not been saved, the name appears as "Untitled art," followed by a number.

You can move the illustration window by dragging the *title bar*. Close the illustration by clicking in the *close box* in the upper left corner (or in the upper right corner in the Windows environment). Drag the *size box* in the bottom right corner of the window to enlarge or reduce the size of the window manually. Click the *zoom box* on the right side of the title bar to expand the window to fill the entire screen. Click the zoom box again to reduce the window to its previous size. For you Windows users, this corresponds to the *maximize/restore box* and sits just to the right of the close box. Windows provides one additional box, *minimize*, which reduces Illustrator to a button on the Windows taskbar without quitting the program.

- The page with the drop shadow in the middle of the window is the *artboard*. This represents the size of the drawing you want to create. Surrounding the artboard is the *pasteboard*. You can move objects out into the pasteboard if you like and these objects will be saved with your illustration, but they will not print. Experienced artists typically use the pasteboard as a storage area for objects they can't quite bear to delete. The dotted line around the *imageable area* shows the portion of the artboard your printer can actually print. Most printers can't print to the extreme edges of a page.

  Together, the artboard and pasteboard are generically known as the *drawing area*.

- The *scroll bars* appear along the right and bottom edges of the illustration window, as they do in most Mac and Windows applications. They allow you to move your drawing with respect to the window to better see various portions of your illustration. Click one of the arrows on either end of a scroll bar to nudge the drawing a small distance; click in the gray area of a scroll bar to move the drawing a greater distance. Drag the tab in either scroll bar to move the drawing manually.
- The *size bar* in the lower left corner of the illustration window lets you change the view size of your artwork. Simply click on the size bar, enter any permitted value, and hit Enter. You can reduce the view to as little as 3.13 percent of the actual size, allowing you to easily see the largest possible artboard size that Illustrator permits. Going to the other extreme, you can expand a square inch to a respectable 6⅓ square feet by choosing 6400 percent.
- The *status bar* just to the right of the size bar lists all kinds of moderately useful information about the program. Click the status bar to display a pop-up menu of status bar options, as shown in the top example of Figure 2-3. You can have the status bar list the active tool, the date and time, the amount of RAM going unused inside Illustrator, and the number of available undos and redos.

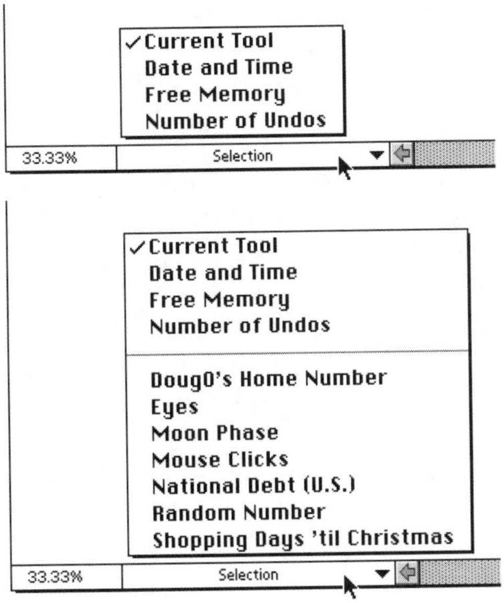

Figure 2-3: The pop-up menus that appear when you click (top) and Option-click (bottom) on the status bar.

TIP

Press the Option key (or the Alt key for Windows users) as you click the status bar to access the additional options shown in the bottom example of Figure 2-3. Most of these options are very silly—Random Number and Shopping Days 'til Christmas—but two are actually useful. If you use Illustrator on a PowerBook, you might appreciate the Eyes option, which brings up a pair of eyes that follow your cursor around the screen. No more lost cursor! And if you can't get Illustrator to work correctly, then Option-click Doug O's Home Number. You won't really get Doug, Illustrator engineer and product manager—you'll get Adobe's technical support line.

Using Tools

The toolbox, like any other palette, is entirely independent of all other desktop elements, so if you reduce the size of a drawing window the toolbox remains unchanged, with 20 tools visible and easily accessible. The toolbox serves, and is positioned in front of, any and all open illustrations. You can move the toolbox by dragging its title bar and hide it by choosing the Window » Hide Tools command. To redisplay the toolbox, choose Window » Show Tools.

TIP

You can hide the toolbox and all other palettes by pressing the Tab key. Press Tab again to bring all the palettes back. To get rid of all palettes except the toolbox, press Shift-Tab (that is, press the Shift and Tab keys simultaneously).

As with other graphics and publishing programs, you select a tool in Illustrator by clicking on its icon in the toolbox. Illustrator highlights the active tool so it stands out prominently. Even folks in the next cubicle can't help but know which tool you're using.

The toolbox contains 20 tool *slots*. In addition to the default tools occupying these slots, Illustrator offers 31 alternate tools that are initially hidden. For example, of Illustrator's 9 graph tools, only the column graph tool appears in the toolbox by default. To use one of the other 8, you have to drag on the column graph icon to display a pop-up menu of alternates, as demonstrated in Figure 2-4. Select the desired tool as you would a command—that is, by highlighting the tool and releasing the mouse button. Slots that offer alternate tools have tiny right-facing arrowheads in their lower right corners.

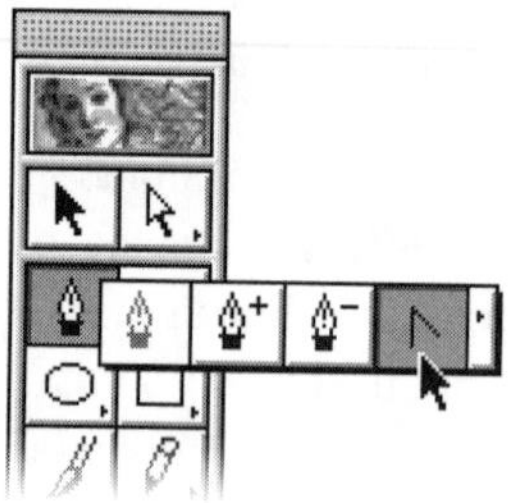

Figure 2-4:
To select an alternate tool, drag on a toolbox icon that features a small arrowhead.

All 51 default and alternate tools appear in the composite screen shot in Figure 2-5. These tools, aside from the new ones, work just as they did in Illustrator 7. Illustrator 8 adds four new tools to the list.

NEW 8

Illustrator 8 brings two brand-new tools and two not-so-new tools. The smooth tool and the gradient mesh tool are new in both form and function. The erase tool and the free transform tool are both new as independent tools, but neither provides new functionality. Illustrator 7 allowed you to perform the same tasks these two tools handle, but not in quite the same way. Three old tools that never needed to be independent tools in the first place no longer appear in the new version's toolbox: the centered ellipse, the centered rectangle, and the centered rounded rectangle. Illustrator still provides the ability to create basic shapes drawn from the center outward; it just doesn't clutter up the toolbox with them.

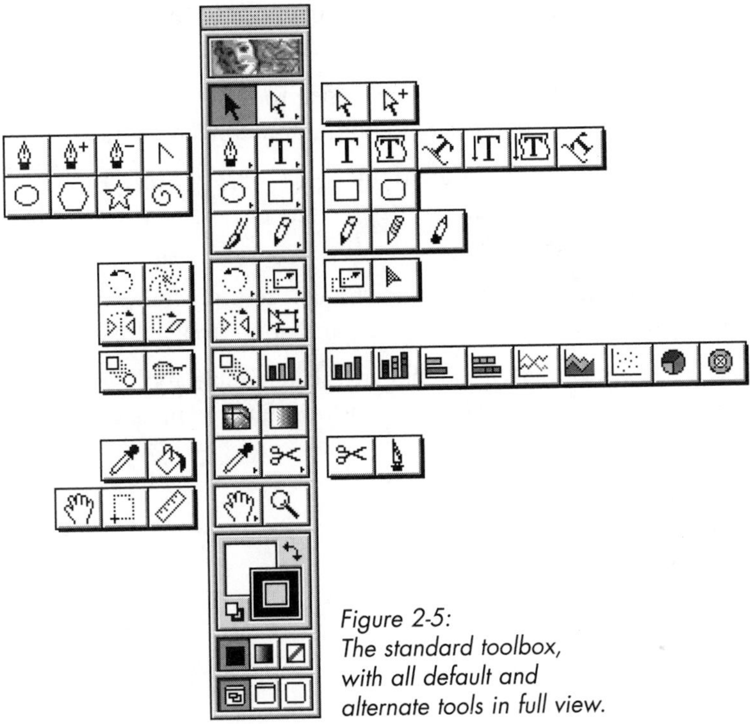

Figure 2-5: The standard toolbox, with all default and alternate tools in full view.

Illustrator allows you to switch to any of the tools, or access the controls in the toolbox, by pressing the appropriate key, as shown in Figure 2-6. Many of these are the same shortcuts Photoshop uses. They don't all make sense on first glance, but there are only so many keys to choose from. After all, the R key can't be assigned to the rectangle, rotate, and reflect tools simultaneously.

NEW 8

It used to be the case that the keys that appear in bold in Figure 2-6 served not only to switch between the various tool slots but also to toggle through the tools that shared the same slot. That is, pressing the J key switched you to the graph tool you last used; pressing it again cycled you to the next graph tool. In Illustrator 8, things have changed slightly. Pressing one of these keys still switches you to the last used tool in a particular slot. Once there, to cycle through the other tools in that slot, you now need to press the Shift key in addition to the original key. These keys work as follows:

- **A** takes you to the last used tool in the direct selection tool slot. **Shift-A** switches you between the direct selection and the group selection tools.
- **P** takes you to the last used tool in the pen tool slot. **Shift-P** cycles you through the pen, add point, delete point, and convert point tools.
- **T** takes you to the last used tool in the type tool slot. **Shift-T** cycles you through the type, area type, path type, vertical type, vertical area type, and vertical path type tools.
- **L** takes you to the last used tool in the ellipse tool slot. **Shift-L** cycles you through the ellipse, polygon, star, and spiral tools.
- **M** takes you to the last used tool in the rectangle tool slot. **Shift-M** switches you between the rectangle and rounded rectangle tools.

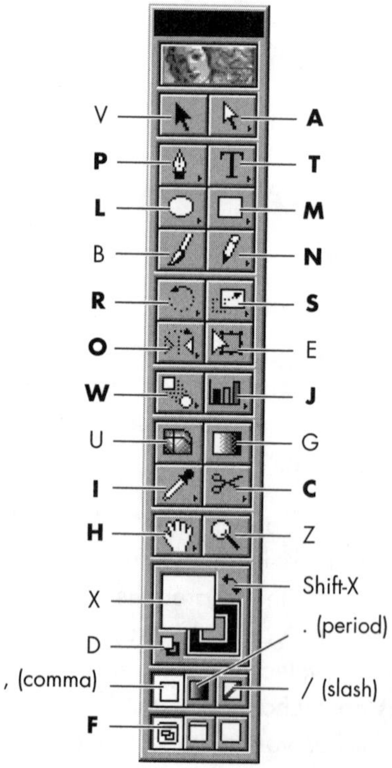

Figure 2-6: These keys let you access the different tools and toolbox controls in Illustrator 8.

- **N** takes you to the last used tool in the pencil tool slot. **Shift-N** cycles you through the pencil, smooth, and erase tools.
- **R** takes you to the last used tool in the rotate tool slot. **Shift-R** switches you between the rotate tool and twirl tool.
- **S** takes you to the last used tool in the scale tool slot. **Shift-S** switches you between the scale and reshape tool.
- **O** takes you to the last used tool in the reflect tool slot. **Shift-O** switches you between the reflect tool and shear tool.
- **W** takes you to the last used tool in the blend tool slot. **Shift-W** switches you between the blend and autotrace tool.
- **J** takes you to the last used tool in the graph tool slot. **Shift-J** cycles you through the nine graph tools.
- **I** takes you to the last used tool in the eyedropper tool slot. **Shift-I** switches you between the eyedropper and paint bucket tool.
- **C** takes you to the last used tool in the scissors tool slot. **Shift-C** switches you between the scissors and knife tool.
- **H** takes you to the last used tool in the hand tool slot. **Shift-H** cycles through the hand, page, and measure tools.
- **F** cycles you from one window mode to another.

The following paragraphs explain how to use each of Illustrator's 51 tools in the illustration window. For example, if an item instructs you to *drag*, click on the tool's icon to select it and then drag inside the drawing area; don't drag on the icon itself.

These are intended as introductory descriptions only. If a tool name appears in italics, that indicates that the tool's description appears later in the list. For you Windows users, please remember that when you see the Option key or the ⌘ key mentioned, you must use the Alt key or the Ctrl key respectively. Subsequent chapters contain more info, which is why I include chapter numbers in my descriptions.

Selection (Chapter 5): The selection tool—which I usually call the *arrow tool* in deference to its appearance—is active when you first start Illustrator. Use this tool to select objects that you've created so you can manipulate them. Click on an object to select the entire object. Drag an object to move it. You can also use the selection tool to select text blocks.

Direct selection (Chapters 5 and 10): Click with this hollow arrow to select individual anchor points and segments in a line or shape. This is also the perfect tool for editing the Bézier control handles that govern the curvature of segments. Option-click to access the *group selection* tool.

Group selection (Chapters 5 and 10): Click with this tool (or just Option-click with the direct selection tool) to select whole objects at a time. Though it frequently acts the same as the standard arrow tool, the group selection tool lets you select individual objects inside groups, whereas the arrow tool selects *all* objects in a group. Option-click to access the direct selection tool.

Pen (Chapter 5): This is Illustrator's most powerful drawing tool, the one that's most responsible for Illustrator's success. Use the pen tool to draw a line as a series of individual points. Click to add corners to a line, drag to add arcs. You can also Option-drag on an arc to change it to a cusp. Illustrator automatically connects your points with straight or curved segments. Option-click to access the *convert direction* tool.

Add point (Chapter 5): Click on a segment with the add point tool to insert a new point into a line. Option-click to access the *delete anchor point* tool.

Delete point (Chapter 5): Click on a point with this tool to remove the point while leaving the line intact. That's why I prefer to call this tool the *remove point* tool—"deleting" a point would create a hole. Option-click to access the add anchor point tool.

Convert point (Chapter 5): Use this tool to change a corner in a line to an arc or vice versa. Click on an arc to make it a corner, drag on a corner to make it an arc.

Type (Chapter 6): Click with this tool and then enter text from the keyboard to create a line of type in the standard left-to-right format. To create a text block with type that automatically wraps from one line down to the next, drag with the type tool and then start banging away at the keyboard. You can also use this tool (or one of the other five type tools) to highlight characters in a text block to edit or format them. Shift-click or drag to access the *vertical type* tool.

Area type (Chapter 7): Click on a line or shape to create text that wraps inside an irregular boundary. Option-click to access the *path type* tool, and Shift-click to access the *vertical area type* tool.

Path type (Chapter 7): Click on a line or shape to create text that follows the contours of the object, better known as text on a curve. Option-click to access the area type tool, and Shift-click to access the *vertical path type* tool.

Vertical type (Chapter 7): Very similar to the type tool, this tool arranges text vertically, the way Japanese script appears. Click with this tool and then enter text from the keyboard to create an ascending column of type. To create a text block with type that automatically wraps from one column to the next (from right-to-left), drag with the type tool and then start them magic fingers fluttering. Shift-click or drag to access the type tool.

Vertical area type (Chapter 7): Click on a line or shape to create text that fills an irregular boundary column. Option-click to access the vertical path type tool, and Shift-click to access the area type tool.

Vertical path type (Chapter 7): Click on a line or shape to create text that follows the contours of the object. As you probably guessed, one letter will stack upon the next to form a column that follows the curve. Option-click to access the vertical area type tool, and Shift-click to access the path type tool.

Ellipse (Chapter 4): Drag with this tool, previously called the oval tool, to draw an ellipse. You can also Shift-drag to draw a circle or Option-drag to draw an ellipse from the center outward. Click with the tool to enter numerical dimensions for your ellipse.

Polygon (Chapter 4): When you drag with this tool, you draw a regular polygon, like a triangle or pentagon. Click with the tool to change the number of sides.

Star (Chapter 4): Drag with this tool to draw a star with symmetrical points. Option-drag to constrain the star so opposite arms are perfectly aligned, as for a five-pointed American star or a Star of David. Click with the tool to change the number of points.

Spiral (Chapter 4): Drag to draw a spiraling line, like a stylized pig's tail. To change the number of times the line twists inside itself, click with the tool in the drawing area.

Rectangle (Chapter 4): This tool works just like the ellipse tool, except that it makes rectangles and squares. Option-drag to create a rectangle from the center outward.

Rounded rectangle (Chapter 4): If you want your rectangles to have rounded corners, use this tool. To adjust the roundness of the corners of future shapes, click with the tool in the drawing area. As you may have guessed, you can Option-drag to create a rounded rectangle from the center outward.

Paintbrush (Chapter 4): Referred to as the brush tool in previous versions of Illustrator, it creates a closed shape that resembles a brushstroke when you drag with it. If you own a pressure-sensitive tablet, you can use the paintbrush tool to draw shapes that vary in thickness depending on how hard you press.

Pencil (Chapter 4): Formally known as the freehand tool, the pencil tool makes a freeform line when you drag with it, much as if you were drawing with a pencil. If you are not satisfied with the final result, simply drag over the part of your path you wish to correct and the offending snippet toes the line.

Smooth (Chapter 4): Use the smooth tool to reposition points and reshape paths quickly. After you drag with this tool, Illustrator will add or remove points (or even move points) in an attempt to streamline the path and smooth it out.

Erase (Chapter 4): With the erase tool, you drag over a segment of an entire path to remove it. This allows you to open closed paths and delete unnecessary paths easily.

Rotate (Chapter 11): This tool lets you rotate selected objects. Click with the tool to determine the center of the rotation, and then drag to rotate the objects around this center. Or just drag right off the bat to position the center of the rotation smack dab in the center of the selected objects. You can also Option-click with the tool or double-click the rotate tool icon in the toolbox to specify a rotation numerically.

Twirl (Chapter 12): This tool lets you twirl selected objects as if the objects were in a whirlpool. Click to set the center of the twirl and then drag to twirl, or just start dragging to twirl around the objects' exact center. To twirl numerically, Option-click with the twirl tool or choose Filter » Distort » Twirl.

Scale (Chapter 11): This tool and the two other transformation tools, *reflect* and *shear*, work just like the rotate tool. The only difference is that the scale tool enlarges and reduces selected objects.

Reshape (Chapter 5): Click and drag with this tool on an open path to deform the path in a freeform manner. The result of the deformation is entirely dependent on which points of the object were selected.

Reflect (Chapter 11): Use this tool to flip objects across an axis. Usually it's easiest to just drag with this tool, or Option-click to flip horizontally or vertically.

Shear (Chapter 11): Drag with the oddly named shear tool to slant selected objects. The effects of Shift-dragging are generally easier to predict; when the Shift key is down, the shear tool slants objects horizontally or vertically.

Free Transform (Chapter 11): In Illustrator 7, to perform a free transformation on a path you used the Free Distort filter. The filter let you distort paths in the confines of a dialog box with a limited preview. It was, to say the least, the most boneheaded implementation of four-point distortion ever. Adobe has corrected the problem and more than made-up for the mistake. The free transform tool allows you to scale, rotate, reflect, and shear as well as properly four-point distort selected paths, all right on screen. No lame dialog box needed.

Blend (Chapter 17): The blend tool allows you to create custom gradations. After selecting two objects with one of the arrow tools, use the blend tool to click on a point in one object, then click on a point in the other object. Illustrator creates a collection of intermediate shapes between the two objects and fills these with intermediate colors.

Autotrace (Chapter 4): Click within 6 screen pixels of an imported black-and-white template to trace a line around the image. This tool is easily Illustrator's worst; you're almost always better off tracing images by hand.

Column (Chapter 8): Drag with this tool to specify the rectangular boundaries of a standard column graph. Shift-dragging constrains the boundary to a square and Option-dragging forms rectangular boundaries from the center out. Illustrator then presents you with a spreadsheet in which you can enter your data. Double-click on the graph tool icon in the toolbox to specify the options for the graph you want to create.

Stacked column (Chapter 8): This tool and the seven other graph tools that follow work just like the column graph tool, except that dragging with this tool specifies the boundaries of a stacked column graph.

Bar (Chapter 8): Drag with this tool to specify the boundaries of a standard horizontal bar graph.

Stacked bar (Chapter 8): Drag with this tool to specify the boundaries of a stacked horizontal bar graph in which each graph entity appears farther to the right.

Line (Chapter 8): Drag with this tool to specify the boundaries of a line graph—you know, your basic dot-to-dot with a few labels to make it look official.

Area (Chapter 8): Drag with this tool to specify the boundaries of an area graph. It's the color-within-the-lines evolution of the line graph.

Scatter (Chapter 8): Drag with this tool to specify the boundaries of a scatter graph, one in which only the points are plotted.

Pie (Chapter 8): Drag with this tool to specify the boundaries of a pie graph. Enough said.

Radar (Chapter 8): Drag with this tool to specify the boundaries of a radar graph. This is the ideal graph for confusing anyone attending your presentation.

Gradient Mesh (Chapter 15): Click inside a selected object to add a gradient mesh point and convert the it to a gradient mesh object. Click inside a gradient mesh object to add a gradient mesh point. Option-click on a gradient mesh point to delete it.

Gradient (Chapter 15): Drag inside a selected object that's filled with a gradation to change the angle of the gradations, as well as the location of the first and last colors. Shift-drag to constrain your drag to 45-degree increments.

Eyedropper (Chapter 14): Click on an object to copy its fill and stroke attributes to the toolbox. You can also double-click on an object to copy the colors from that object to all selected objects.

Paint bucket (Chapter 14): Click on an object with the paint bucket tool to apply the fill and stroke from the toolbox to the object.

Scissors (Chapter 9): Click on a line to cut it into two. Illustrator inserts two points at the spot where you click, one for each line.

Knife (Chapter 9): Drag with the knife tool to slice shapes into new shapes, just as if you had dragged through them with a real knife. This tool cuts through any objects in its path, whether they're selected or not.

Hand (Chapter 3): Drag with the hand tool to scroll the drawing inside the illustration window. It is much more convenient than the scroll bars. You can also double-click on the hand tool icon in the toolbox to fit the entire artboard into the illustration window.

Page (Chapter 3): Drag with the page tool to move the imageable area within the artboard. Unless the artboard is larger than the printed page size, you don't have to worry about this tool.

Measure (Chapter 10): Drag with this tool to measure the distance between two points. Alternatively, you can click in one spot and then click in another. Illustrator displays the measurements in the Info palette.

Zoom (Chapter 3): Click with this tool to magnify the size of the illustration. (This doesn't affect the printed size of the drawing, just how it looks on screen.) Option-click to zoom out. You can also draw with the tool to surround the exact portion of the illustration you want to magnify. Double-click on the zoom tool icon to view your drawing at the very same size it will print.

Using Dialog Boxes

When you choose any command whose name includes an ellipsis (...)—such as File » Save As... or Type » Find/Change...—Illustrator has to ask you some questions before it can complete the operation. It asks you these questions by displaying a dialog box.

A *dialog box* is a window that comes up on screen and demands your immediate attention. You can sometimes switch to a different application while a dialog box is on screen, but you can't do any more work in Illustrator until you address it, either by filling out a few *options* and clicking on the OK button or by clicking on the Cancel button.

Options naturally vary from one dialog box to the next, but there are eight basic kinds of options in all. Figure 2-7 shows examples of these option types as they appear in two of Illustrator's dialog boxes. Also labeled is the title bar, which tops just about every Macintosh dialog box these days. If the dialog box is blocking some important portion of your illustration, just drag the title bar to move it to a more satisfactory location.

Here's a quick run-down of the eight kinds of dialog box options:

- **Radio buttons:** When you can select just one option from a group of options, a round radio button precedes each option name. To select a radio button, click either on the button itself or on the name of the option following the button. This deselects all other radio buttons in the group. A radio button filled with a black dot is selected; a hollow radio button is not.

- **Check boxes:** When you can select several options in a group, square check boxes come before the option names. To turn a check box on or off, click either on the box itself or on the option name. An *x* indicates a selected check box; a deselected check box is empty.

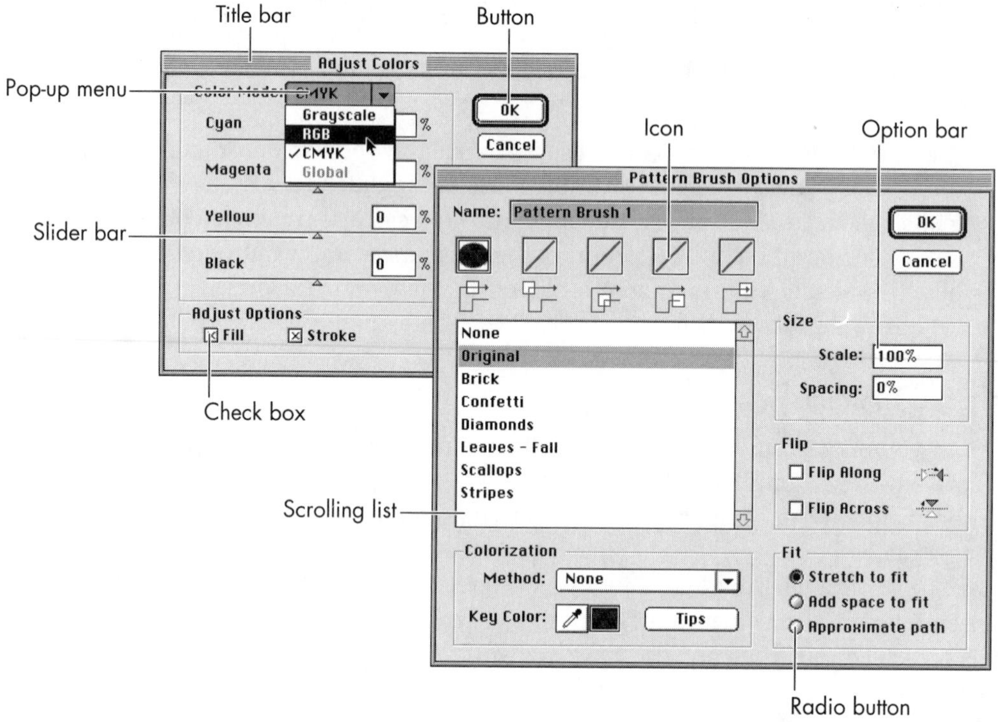

Figure 2-7: Two dialog boxes with the basic elements and options labeled.

- **Pop-up menus:** A pop-up menu looks like a word in a box. Click on the word to display a menu of options, as shown in Figure 2-7. Select the desired option from the menu just as you would a command from a menu.

- **Option boxes:** If a dialog box were a test, radio buttons, check boxes, and pop-up menus would be multiple-choice questions; while option boxes (also called *numerical fields* by the nerd faction) are fill-in-the-blank questions. Option boxes are typically reserved for numbers, such as dimensions or color percentages. To select the current value in an option box, double-click on it. Enter a new value from the keyboard.

TIP If a dialog box contains lots of option boxes, you can advance from one to the next by pressing the Tab key. To go in the other direction, press Shift-Tab.

- **Scrolling lists:** When Illustrator really wants to pack in a lot of options, it presents them inside a scrolling list. Use the scroll bar on the right side of the list to check out more options. Then click on the option you want to use. You can only select one option from a scrolling list.

TIP In most cases, you can select a specific option from a scrolling list by typing the first few letters of its name. For example, pressing the P key selects the first option whose name begins with a P. You may want to first make sure the list is active by clicking on it. If an option box is active, typing replaces the value instead.

- **Icons:** In a few rare cases, Illustrator just doesn't feel like being locked into all the other options it has at its disposal, so it resorts to small graphic icons. These icons are like radio buttons in that you can select just one icon from a group. Illustrator either highlights or underlines the selected icon.
- **Slider bars:** If you come across a horizontal line or colored bar with one or more triangles underneath it, you've encountered a slider bar. Drag the slider triangle back and forth to lower or raise the value, which is usually displayed in an option box. (You can also enter a different option box value if you prefer.)
- **Buttons:** Not to be confused with radio buttons, standard dialog box buttons look like words inside rounded rectangles. Click on a button to make something happen. Two of the most common buttons are OK, which closes the dialog box and applies your settings, and Cancel, which closes the dialog box and cancels the command. Some dialog boxes offer Copy buttons, which apply settings to a copy of a selected object. And a couple dialog boxes include Apply buttons, which let you apply your settings without closing the dialog box.

TIP

Instead of clicking on the OK button, you can press the Return or Enter key. Press Escape or ⌘-Period to cancel the operation.

A dialog box that conveys information rather than requests it is called an *alert box*. As its name implies, the purpose of an alert box is to call your attention to an important bit of news. Some alert boxes warn you about the consequences of an action so you can abort it and avert a hideous outcome. Others are just Illustrator's way of whining at you. "I can't do that," "You're using me wrong," and "Don't you think I have feelings, too?" are common alert box messages. (Okay, that's an exaggeration, but it's not far from the truth.)

Using Palettes

A palette is nothing more than a dialog box that can remain open while you fiddle about inside the software. You can gain access to every one of Illustrator's numerous palettes (including the toolbox) by choosing the appropriate command. In some cases, different commands bring up the same palettes. For example, you can display the Character palette by choosing any of three commands.

TIP

To hide all palettes, including the toolbox, press Tab. To redisplay them, press Tab again. Illustrator displays only those palettes that were on screen before you pressed Tab the first time.

Figure 2-8 shows a couple of typical palettes from Illustrator. As you can see, palettes offer many of the same kinds of options that you find inside dialog boxes, including check boxes, scrolling lists, and the like. A title bar likewise tops off each palette. Drag the title bar to move the palette on screen. Illustrator's palettes snap into alignment with other palettes; they also snap into alignment with the edges of the screen.

Options vary more widely in palettes than they do in dialog boxes. Some are so unusual there's no point in explaining them here. So for now, I'll just cover the ones that you see quite a bit in Illustrator and other applications (including Photoshop).

- **Close box:** Mac users click in the close box in the left corner of the title bar to close the palette. Windows users will find their close boxes in the right corner.
- **Zoom box:** Palettes offer zoom boxes, known as minimize buttons in Windows, on the right sides of their title bars. When you click in the

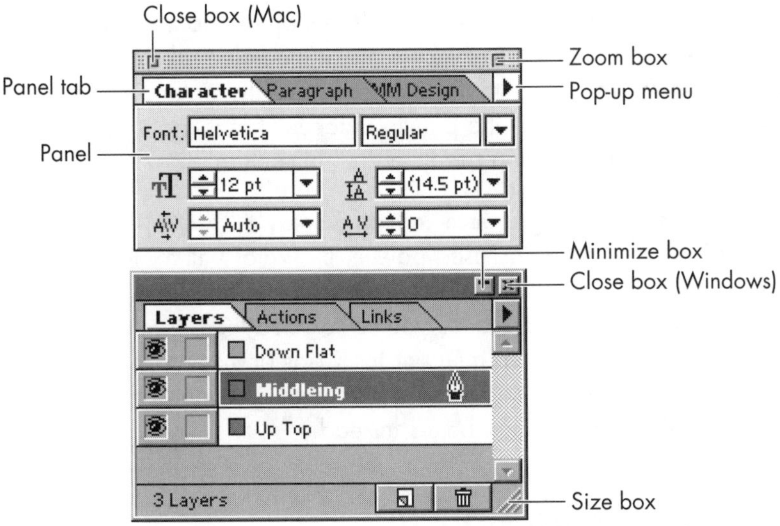

Figure 2-8: Two palettes with their strange little options labeled.

zoom box, Illustrator changes the size of the palette, either making it larger to show off more options or reducing its size to show fewer options. In the case of the Tabs palette, clicking in the zoom box aligns the palette with the active text block.

- **Palette pop-up menu:** Click on the right-pointing arrowhead located at the top right of any palette to display the pop-up menu, then drag to choose the desired command.

TIP: If you have Apple's WindowShade control panel running on your Macintosh, you can collapse a palette so only its title bar is visible. In most cases, you do this by double-clicking on the title bar. (If double-clicking doesn't work, choose Apple » Control Panels » WindowShade to see how many clicks are required. You may also have to press ⌘, Option, or Control.) Double-click (or whatever) the title bar again to display the palette in full.

- **Size box:** Drag the size box to change the size of particular palettes.
- **Pop-up menu:** If you see a little down-pointing arrowhead in a box, this indicates a pop-up menu. Drag from the arrowhead to display the menu and select your favorite option.

TIP

After you enter a value into a palette's option box, you can press the Return or Enter key to make the value take effect and to return control to the drawing area. To make a value take effect and keep the palette in focus (that is, not return control to the drawing area), press Shift-Return.

TIP

When the drawing area is in focus, press ⌘-tilde (~) to return focus to the last-used palette. Illustrator will try to activate the last option you used in that palette. Since not all options remain active once you've selected them (such as the Gradient Type pop-up menu or the Caps and Joins buttons in the Stroke palette), sometimes it will highlight one of the palette's nearby option boxes instead.

Customizing a Palette's Appearance

Palettes allow you to change the attributes of your artwork on the fly, but they can also clutter up the screen and considerably limit your view. With this in mind, Illustrator gives you a couple of different ways to customize the look and construction of palettes.

Most of the palettes in Illustrator contain more than one *panel*. For example, the color palette contains both the color panel and the attributes panel. A panel consists of a panel tab, stating the name of the panel, and the body of the panel, which lists its options. Bear in mind that there is no real difference between panels and palettes. Panels are essentially subpalettes.

TIP

Double-click on any panel's tab to reduce the palette and cycle through its different sizes. You will eventually shrink the palette to its smallest size, just as though you had clicked on the palette's zoom box. This is an especially useful function when you have meta-palettes, as described later in this section.

To take advantage of a panel's design, merely click and drag on a panel's tab and move the panel to its new location. One of three things will happen. First, if you end your drag on an empty portion of the screen, an area free of palettes, Illustrator will construct a new palette containing only that panel. Second, if you move a tab onto another panel in a different palette, the panel you move will join the other panels in the destination palette as the newest and rightmost member of that palette. When you drag a panel onto a new palette, Illustrator will indicate that it is ready to let the panel join the destination palette's little family by ringing the palette with a strip of gray, as shown in Figure 2-9.

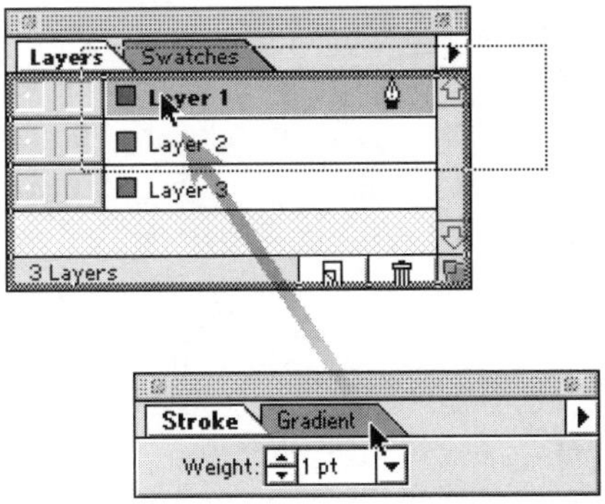

Figure 2-9:
The destination palette is ringed with gray when Illustrator is ready to join a new panel to it.

The third result of dragging a panel is that you will *dock* the panel on a new palette. Docking a panel, in which you drag a panel to the bottom of a different palette, results in a *meta-palette,* as shown in Figure 2-10. OK, meta-palette is a term I just made up, but you have to admit it sure sounds technosorific. (Yes, I just made-up technosorific. Here's the definition: **technosorific** *adj* **1**. of or pertaining to cool and sophisticated technical stuff. **2**. soft and mushy, especially in connection with the brain: *My, that technosorific gray matter of yours sure gives you an interesting slant on world issues, Mr. Gingrich.* Please feel free to share it with your friends and, above all, do use it in a sentence the next chance you have.)

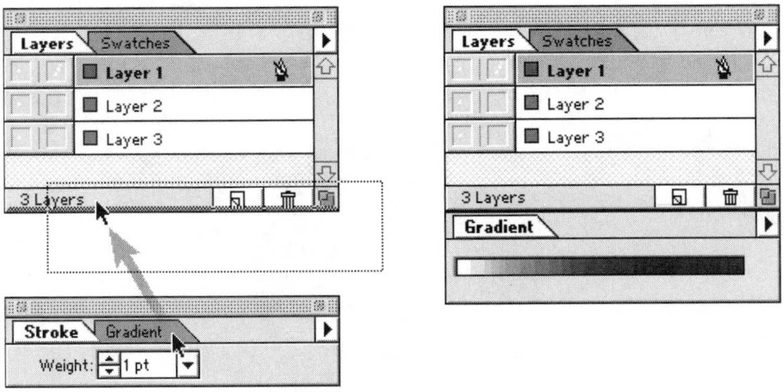

Figure 2-10: The destination palette appears with a gray bar at the bottom when docking is possible. A docked meta-palette appears on the right.

TIP

Once you have formed a meta-palette, be sure to try double-clicking on all the tabs. In a regular palette, double-clicking on a tab changes the size of the whole palette; but double-clicking in a meta-palette changes the size of only the portion where that tab resides. The rest of the palette remains unchanged.

Sorry, where was I? Oh yeah, I was talking about docking. Illustrator indicates that docking is possible by lining the bottom of the destination palette with a thin gray line. Once you have formed a meta-palette, you have the option of adding panels to either the new or old palette, as described above, or even of making an *ultra-meta-palette* by dragging another panel onto the bottom of the meta-palette, as shown in Figure 2-11.

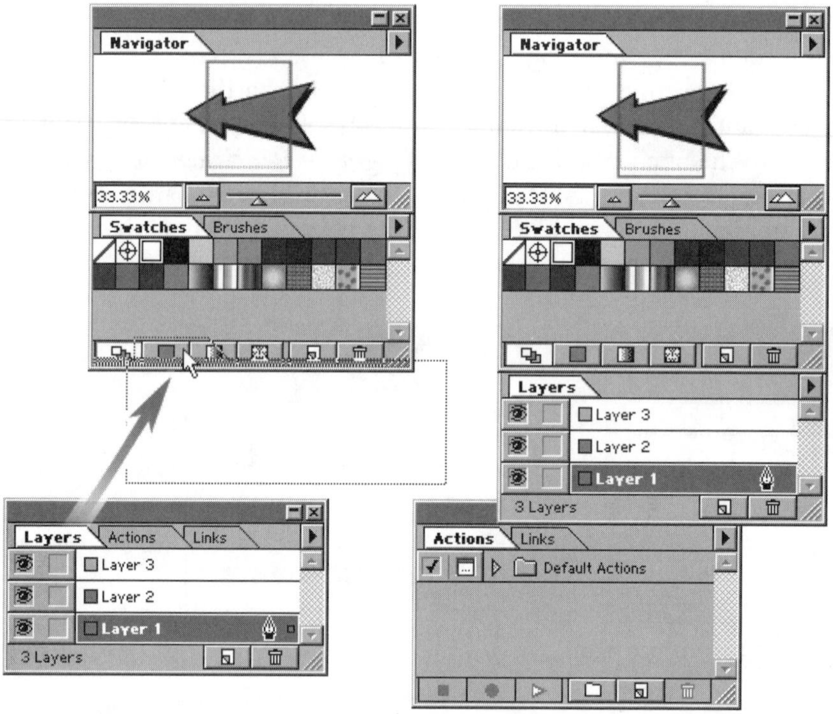

Figure 2-11: You can add to a meta-palette by dragging additional panels on top of it, as shown on the left, or by dragging additional panels onto the bottom, thus forming the legendary ultra-meta-palette.

So what does all this mean? It means that you have considerably more freedom in designing your workspace. If you find that, for the most part, you use only the color, stroke, and layers palettes, then combine them into a single palette, a meta-palette, or even an ultra-meta-palette and close all the other palettes. With your single palette, controlled by a single zoom box, you have considerably more unobstructed space to create your artwork.

Accommodating Your Personal Style

No two folks draw alike. It's a cliché, but it happens to be true (except in the case of very close twins). For those who draw to a different drummer—in other words, all of us—Illustrator provides the File » Preferences submenu, which provides seven commands that allow you to edit a variety of attributes controlling Illustrator's performance. All of these commands affect Illustrator's *global* preferences—that is, preferences that affect every single illustration you create or edit in the future. (In the next chapter I discuss Document Setup and other commands that affect one illustration at a time.)

Choosing any of the six commands in the File » Preferences submenu displays the corresponding dialog box; all of these boxes share a few identical elements. A pop-up menu appears at the top, and four buttons line the right side of each preference dialog box. The pop-up menu allows you to switch quickly to any of the other preference dialog boxes. The four buttons include both the standard OK and Cancel, which implement or ignore your changes while also closing the box, and the new Prev and Next. As you have probably surmised, clicking on Prev takes you to the previous preference dialog box, and clicking on Next advances you to the next box. Admittedly, Adobe hasn't reinvented the wheel, but this makes changing preferences a bit more efficient.

General Preferences

Choosing File » Preferences » General or pressing ⌘-K displays the General Preferences dialog box, shown in Figure 2-12. Here you can control the way some tools behave—the sensitivity of the pencil and autotrace tools, whether dialog boxes display warnings, plus much, much more.

The following list describes each option available in this dialog box. Naturally, at this early stage I haven't provided the background you need to understand many of these options. But have no fear, I cover each option in context in one or more chapters, as the descriptions indicate. For now, content yourself with the certain knowledge that these pages contain an invaluable resource you can refer to over and over throughout your happy and productive illustrating years.

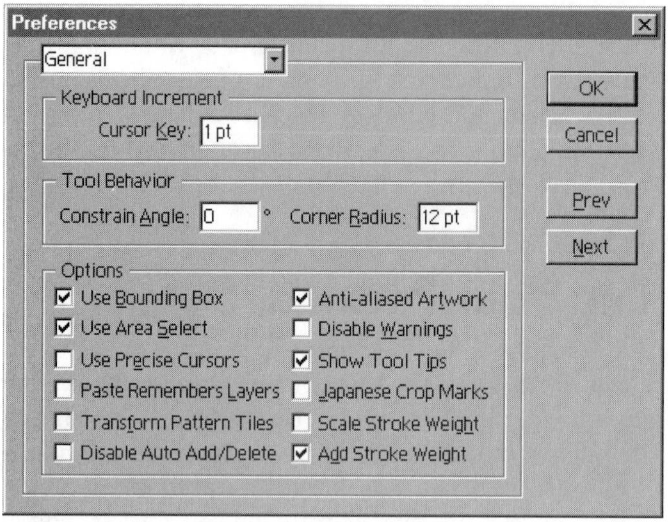

Figure 2-12: Here's where you make Illustrator conform to many of your idiosyncratic whims.

Here are the options, in their order of appearance in the General Preferences dialog box:

- **Cursor Key (Chapter 10):** Illustrator allows you to move selected objects from the keyboard by pressing one of the four arrow keys. Each keystroke moves the selection the distance you enter into this option box. The default value is 1 point, equivalent to one screen pixel at the 100 percent view size. That's a subtle nudge.
- **Constrain Angle (Chapters 4, 11, and others):** If you press the Shift key while dragging an object, you constrain the direction of its movement to a multiple of 45 degrees; that is, straight up, straight down, left, right, or one of the four diagonal directions. These eight angles make up an invisible, er, thingamabob called the *constraint axes*. You can rotate the entire set of constraint axes by entering a value—measured in degrees—in the Constrain Angles option box. This value affects the creation of rectangles, ellipses, and text blocks, as well as the performance of transformation tools.
- **Corner Radius (Chapter 4):** This option lets you round off the corners on shapes drawn with the rounded rectangle tool. A value of 0 indicates perpendicular corners; larger values make for progressively more

rounded rectangles. This value does not affect regular rectangles drawn with the rectangle tool.

- **Use Bounding Box (Chapter 5):** With the advent of Illustrator 8, you now have the option to scale paths via their bounding boxes—the smallest rectangle that encloses a path. With this option active, you can scale selected paths on the fly whenever you're using the arrow. This is very similar to scaling with the scale tool, but you do not have the ability to set the center point of the transformation arbitrarily, as you can with the scale tool.
- **Use Area Select (Chapter 5):** This option controls how you go about selecting filled objects in the preview mode. When it's checked, you can click anywhere inside an object to select the object, so long as the object is filled. When the option is off, you can select an object only by clicking on its points and segments. I recommend that experienced users leave this option off so they can select objects behind other objects easily without the fills getting in the way.
- **Use Precise Cursors:** When this option is checked, Illustrator displays crosshair cursors in place of the standard cursors for all drawing and editing tools. These special cursors let you better see what you're doing, but they're not so fun to look at.

TIP: In truth, there's no reason on earth to select this check box. Just press the Caps Lock key to access the precise cursors when the check box is off. If the check box has been mysteriously turned on, pressing Caps Lock displays the standard cursor.

- **Paste Remembers Layers (Chapter 10):** Select this check box if you want to paste objects back onto the layers from which they were originally copied. When this option is turned off, Illustrator pastes all objects onto the current layer, regardless of where they came from.
- **Transform Pattern Tiles (Chapters 11 and 15):** When an object is filled or stroked with a tile pattern, you can specify whether the pattern moves, grows, shrinks, or rotates as you move, scale, or rotate the object. By default, the tile patterns remain impervious to transformations, but you have only to turn on this check box to make them a little more flexible.

- **Disable Auto Add/Delete (Chapter 5):** By default, the Illustrator 8 pen tool will automatically change to the add point tool or delete point tool as the situation demands. For example, if you position the pen tool over a point of a selected path, the pen tool will temporally transform into the delete point tool, ready to out the damn spot. If you prefer the pen tool to limit its personalities to only its old path creation nature, check this box.
- **Anti-aliased Artwork (Chapter 13 and 18):** With this option on, your document will have a smoother on-screen appearance. This gives you a better idea of what your vector artwork will look like when printed on a PostScript printer since your final hardcopy will not have all the jagged imperfections that show up on-screen. This option doesn't affect placed graphics but it does impact the appearance of artwork you rasterize inside of Illustrator.
- **Disable Warnings:** Checking this box commands Illustrator to resist its temptation to tell you incessantly that you don't know what you are doing. For instance, clicking even slightly off an object's point with the convert point tool will by default result in Illustrator's scolding you. Disabling this warning won't correct the problem—you will still have to repeat the operation from the beginning—but you won't have to close the warning box first.
- **Show Tool Tips:** This option is responsible for those little balloons that pop up displaying the name of the tool or palette option when you position your cursor over it. In the beginning, it's probably a good idea to leave this option selected. It helps beginners become accustomed to Illustrator's different features. Even experienced users can profit from it, since Illustrator now shows icons instead of names in some palettes. This is especially true of the Character and Paragraph panels. Once you're acclimated to Illustrator 8, feel free to turn it off.
- **Japanese Crop Marks (Chapter 17):** Instead of the typical crop marks you get when you choose Cropmarks » Make, you'll get the Japanese-styled ones when this option is active. With this option selected, trim marks will also conform to Japanese styling. Japanese crop marks are a bit more involved and provide an additional center mark along each side, but they function just the same as the regular old crop marks.

- **Scale Stroke Weight (Chapters 11 and 16):** When you scale an object proportionally—so that both height and width grow or shrink the same amount—Illustrator can likewise change the thickness of the stroke assigned to the object. Check the box to scale the stroke; turn it off to leave the line weight unchanged.

- NEW 8 **Add Stroke Weight (Chapter 10 and 11)**: By default, both the Transform and Info palettes display a selected path's physical attributes without considering the path's stroke weight. For example, the Info palette would normally list a 40 point by 20 point rectangle with a 10 point stroke as having a width of 40 points and a height of 20 points. With the Add Stoke Weight option on, the Info palette would list this same rectangle with a height of 50 points and a width of 30 points. The 10 point stroke would add 5 points to each side.

Type & Auto Tracing

The next preference command, File » Preferences » Type & Auto Tracing, displays the lovely and functional dialog box shown in Figure 2-13. In this box you will find options related to text manipulation.

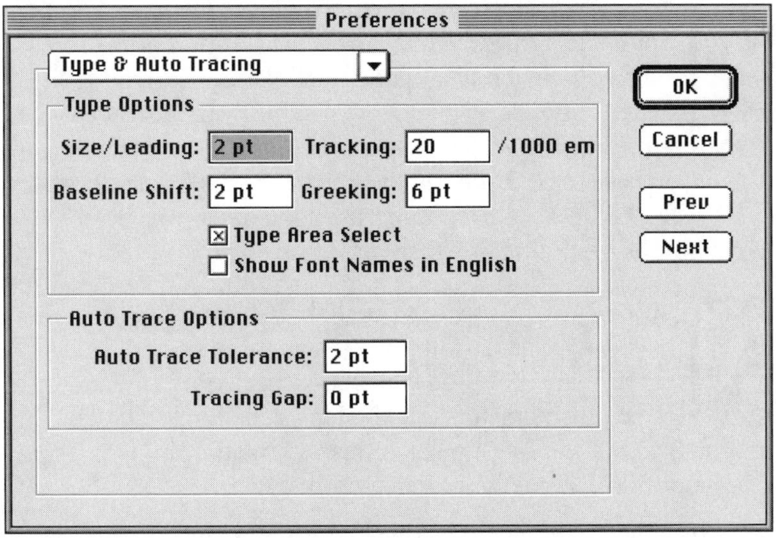

Figure 2-13: Fear not this dialog box, for it is your friend—for setting arrow key options and some text preferences.

- **Size/Leading (Chapter 6):** Just as you can nudge objects from the keyboard, you can likewise adjust the size and leading of selected text with keystrokes. To define the increment of each keystroke, enter a value in this option box.
- **Baseline Shift (Chapter 6):** Baseline shift raises and lowers characters relative to the baseline, ideal for creating superscript and subscript type. To define the increment for raising and lowering selected type, type a new value into this option box.
- **Tracking (Chapter 6):** To keep large text looking good, you may want to adjust the amount of space between neighboring characters, called *kerning* or *tracking*. You can modify the kerning from the keyboard by the increment you enter in this option box. This value is always measured in 0.001 em space. (An em space is as wide as the current type size is tall.)
- **Greeking (Chapter 3):** If text gets smaller than this value Illustrator shows the text blocks as gray bars, an operation called *greeking*. Both type size and view size figure into the equation, so that 6-point type greeks at 100-percent view size and 12-point type greeks at 50 percent. Greeking speeds up the screen display because gray bars are easier to draw than individual characters.
- NEW 8 **Type Area Select (Chapter 6):** Just as the Area Select option of General Preferences gives you control over how you go about selecting filled paths, the Type Area Select option lets you choose just how careful you have to be when you're trying to select text and text blocks. When this option is deactivated, you have to click the path in which the type resides. With this option checked, you have a bit more freedom, since you need to click only within the bounding box that envelopes the type.
- NEW 8 **Show Font Names in English (Chapter 6):** If you have fonts loaded on your system that use alphabets other than the Latin alphabet, check this option to force Illustrator to show the font in its English equivalent. This assumes that the font contains this information in its code; Illustrator cannot translate the fonts' names on its own.
- **Auto Trace Tolerance (Chapter 4):** This complex little option controls the sensitivity of *both* the pencil and the autotrace tools. Any value between 0 and 10 is permitted, and it is measured in screen pixels. Low

values make the tools very sensitive, so that a pencil path closely matches your cursor movements or an autotrace path closely matches the form of the imported template. Higher values give Illustrator license to ignore small jags and other imperfections when creating the path. Quite contrary to any semblance of logic, this value has no effect on the performance of the paintbrush tool.

- **Tracing Gap (Chapter 4):** Black-and-white tracing templates frequently contain loose pixels and rough edges. Using the Auto Trace Gap option, you can instruct Illustrator to trace over these gaps. A value of 0 turns the option off, so that the autotrace tool traces rough edges as they appear in the template. A value of 1 allows paths to skip over single-pixel gaps; a value of 2 (the highest value allowed) allows paths to hurdle two-pixel gaps.

Units & Undo

The File » Preferences » Units & Undo command focuses on the units that Illustrator uses in different dialog boxes, as well as the number of undos that are at your disposal. Please take a moment to revel in the glory that is Figure 2-14.

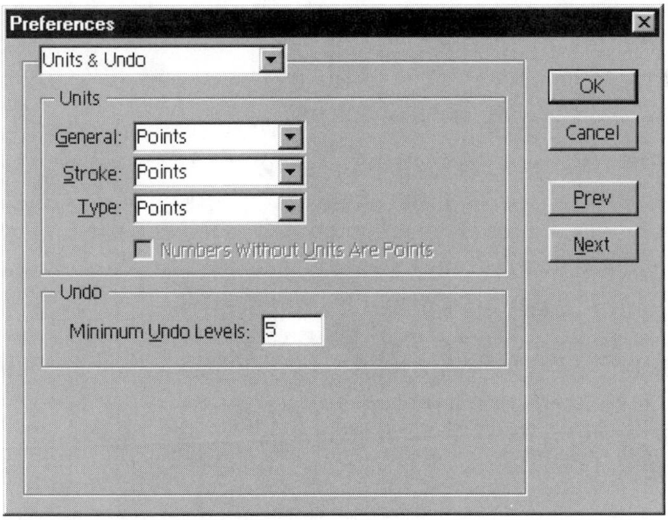

Figure 2-14: Release your inner child all over this dialog box featuring unit and undo options.

- **General (Chapter 10):** Select Points/Picas, Inches, Centimeters, or Millimeters from this pop-up menu to specify the system of measurement to use throughout all dialog boxes (including this one) as well as in the horizontal and vertical rulers. Unlike the similar option in the Document Setup dialog box—which affects just the one drawing you're working on—this option applies to *all* future illustrations in addition to the one you're working on.

- **Stroke (Chapter 16):** In previous versions of Illustrator, you chose the units to associate just as you decided the units to use throughout the program—via the General pop-up menu just mentioned. Now you can set the stroke units independently of the rest of the general riff-raff. As you've probably guessed, this is not one of the cutting-edge innovations of Illustrator 8.0.

- **Type (Chapter 6):** You *could* select an option from this pop-up menu to specify the measurement system used specifically for type. But no one in his right mind *would* do this, since points are the standard for measuring type in nearly every corner of the globe—the only exception to this rule is that a unit called Q (equal to .25 millimeters or roughly 1.4 points) has a strong foothold in Japan. Honestly, leave this option set to Points/Picas, the default. (Incidentally, this option controls the units used by three options in the General Preferences dialog box—Size/Leading, Baseline Shift, and Greeking.)

- **Numbers Without Units Are Points (Chapter 6):** Though this may sound like a nonsensical mantra, it's meant to explain that, provided you've chosen picas as your general units, you have more freedom with the way you enter numbers into dialog boxes. With this box checked, Illustrator will assume that any number you enter into an option box without specifying a unit, such as 72 instead of *72 pt*, should be in points and not picas. Otherwise, Illustrator will convert unitless numbers to picas—72 becomes 6p0 (6 picas and no points).

- **Minimum Undo Levels (Chapter 5):** Here you enter the minimum number of undos and redos that Illustrator can perform in a row. If you set the value to 7, you can back up through the last seven consecutive operations, or possibly more, depending on their complexity. (Note that changing the value to a higher number will not allow you to undo operations that you couldn't undo prior to changing the value.)

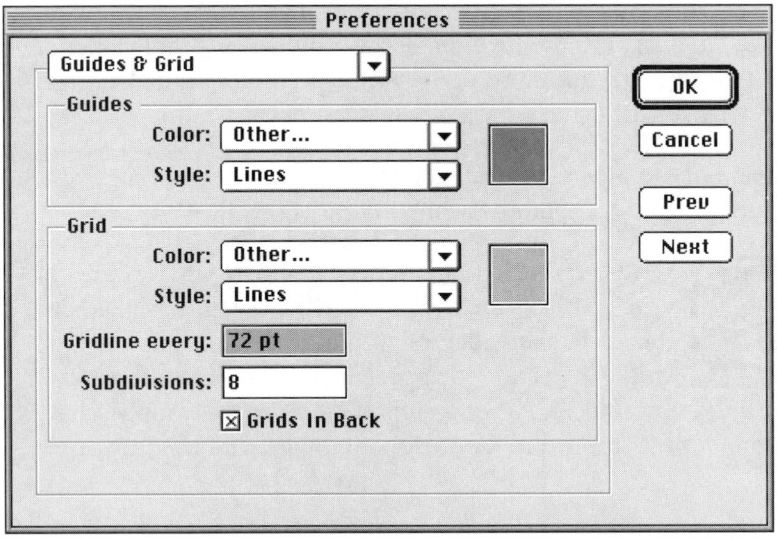

Figure 2-15: You can access even the most sublime details through Illustrator's Guides & Grid dialog box.

Guides & Grid

Descending the list, we find the File » Preferences » Guides & Grid command. This dialog box, shown in Figure 2-15, allows you to choose the color and style of both guides and grids. You can also set the size and spacing of a grid. To see the actual guides and grid, you must choose the corresponding Show command in the View menu.

- **Color (Chapter 14):** From this pop-up menu, choose from eight predefined colors for your guides and grids. If you prefer to define your own color, then either choose Other from the pop-up menu or double-click on the color box just to the right of the menu. The Color dialog box will display, where you construct your own color by clicking on the spectrum in the upper right portion of the box. Also, if you become quite smitten with your creation, you can save it by clicking the Add to Custom Color button.
- **Style (Chapter 10):** From these pop-up menus, you decide whether your guides and grid will appear as dashed or solid lines. If you select the Dots option, you will see only the major gridlines and not all the additional subdivisions.

- **Gridline every (Chapter 10):** Enter the size that you want your square grids to be. You can specify the units of this number or simply enter a number and have Illustrator use whatever units you set in the Units & Undo Preferences dialog box.

- **Subdivisions (Chapter 10):** Here you state the number of times you want to divide your grid both horizontally and vertically.

- **Grids in Back (Chapter 10):** When you're using a grid, you have the choice of having the grid overlaid on the pasteboard, partially obscuring parts of your artwork, or having it appear in the background, giving your work the appearance of lying on top of graph paper. Simply select this option to place the grid in the background where it's less intrusive.

Smart Guides

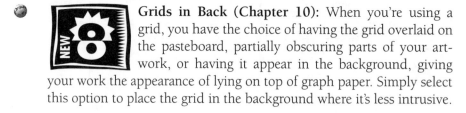

In an attempt to make it easier for you to determine where your cursor is when you're dragging various tools around the screen, Adobe has added a "smart guides" feature. Provided you have selected the command (View » Smart Guides or ⌘-U), additional information and path outlines appear and disappear as you move your cursor over the different elements of your artwork. Smart guides are meant to help you align paths as you transform and move them by showing you when your transformation coincides with different intersection points within your artwork. Note that you must select the View » Smart Guides command to take advantage of the options in the Smart Guides Preferences dialog box (shown in Figure 2-16).

- **Text Label Hints (Chapter 5):** With this option selected, several different labels (including path, anchor, align, intersect, and page) may pop into view as you move your cursor or drag paths around the screen. They indicate that your cursor is over a special point of interest, aiding you in determining whether you have found the right spot. I would suggest that you use this option sparingly. Artwork consisting of many paths is complex enough without the additional muddling these labels can add.

- **Construction Guides (Chapter 5):** One of the main functions of smart guides is the alignment guides that pop up as you move or transform paths. True to intuition, these guides spring forth to tell you when the present location is in alignment with your starting point. You use the

Angles option (discussed below) to decide where to position these guides. If you want Illustrator to display even more alignment information, select the Construction Guides option. In addition to telling you when your present location is aligned with respect to your starting point, Illustrator also alerts you when you are in alignment with respect to various aspects of the other paths in your artwork. This allows you to position paths relative to two separate points.

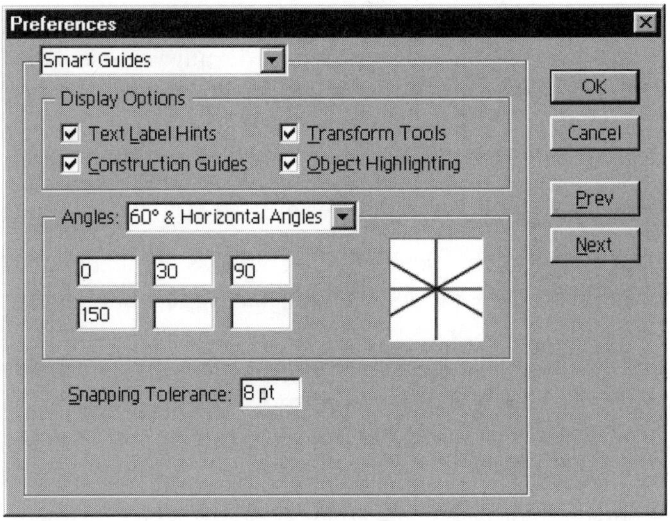

Figure 2-16: Revel at the splendor of the options determining the behavior of Illustrator's new smart guides.

- **Transform Tools (Chapter 5):** Illustrator's alignment guides appear when you are manipulating a path with one of the arrow tools or transforming a path with one of the four traditional transformation tools. If you want the alignment guides to appear only when you're using one of the arrow tools and not when you're using one of the transformation tools, simply deactivate this option.
- **Object Highlighting (Chapter 5):** When this option is on, Illustrator highlights the outline of a path, making it appear to be selected as long as you position an arrow or transformation tool over the path. This is helpful when you're dealing with a number of overlapping paths, some of which are very small or just barely exposed. Otherwise, this option is better left off.

- **Angles (Chapter 5):** With these six option boxes, you decide at what angles Illustrator will inform you whether your present on-screen position aligns with either your initial position or one of the points of some other path in your artwork—that is, provided Construction Guides is selected. You can choose from one of seven predefined sets of angles or enter the angular values that best suit your needs.
- **Snapping Tolerance (Chapter 5):** Here you decide within how many points (ranging from 0 to 10) you must position your cursor (that is, how close you must come to the various points of interest) before the alignment guides and text labels appear. The default value is 4 points and unless you really need to change it, you might as well ignore this option.

Hyphenation Options

Moving right along, you can choose File » Preferences » Hyphenation Options to exclude words from Illustrator's automatic hyphenating capabilities (covered in Chapter 7). Though most Illustrator users go their entire careers without ever giving a second thought to automatic hyphenation, you may feel compelled to rule out the occasional proper noun, so that Johnson never appears as John-son. Here's how:

1. Choose File » Preferences » Hyphenation Options to display the dialog box captured for time immemorial in Figure 2-17.
2. Select a language from the Default Language pop-up menu to determine which set of rules Illustrator uses to hyphenate your words. For example, you wouldn't want Hungarian hyphenation if you were writing in Finnish.
3. Enter the word you want to protect from hyphenation harm into the New Entry option box.
4. Click on the Add button. The word appears in the scrolling list of Exceptions.
5. If you decide you've added a word in error, select it from the scrolling list and click on the Delete button.
6. Click on the OK button to exit the dialog box.

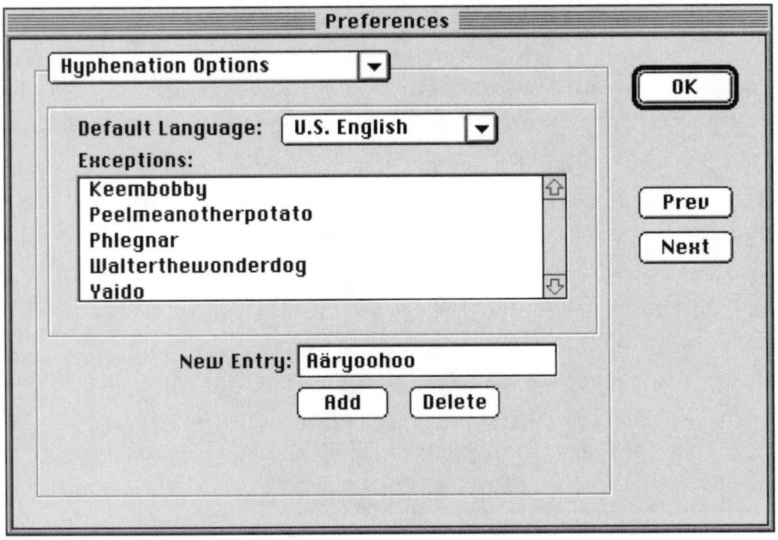

Figure 2-17: The Hyphenation Options dialog box lets you specify words that Illustrator should never hyphenate.

Plug-ins & Scratch Disk

The final item in the File » Preferences submenu is the Plug-ins command, which allows you to tell Illustrator the location of the folder that contains the plug-ins you want to use. By default, all Illustrator plug-ins are installed in the Plug-ins folder inside the same folder that contains the Illustrator application. But because plug-ins consume a large amount of RAM, you may want to organize your plug-ins into a series of separate folders. This may make Illustrator perform faster or get it to work better on Macs with little memory. Then you can use the File » Preferences » Plug-ins command to tell Illustrator which set of filters you want to use the next time you start the program.

1. Choose File » Preferences » Plug-ins. The dialog box shown in Figure 2-18 will appear.
2. Click on the Choose button and locate the folder that contains the set of plug-ins you want to use next.
3. Click on the OK button.
4. Quit Illustrator by pressing ⌘-Q.
5. Launch Illustrator again to load the program as well as the new set of plug-ins.

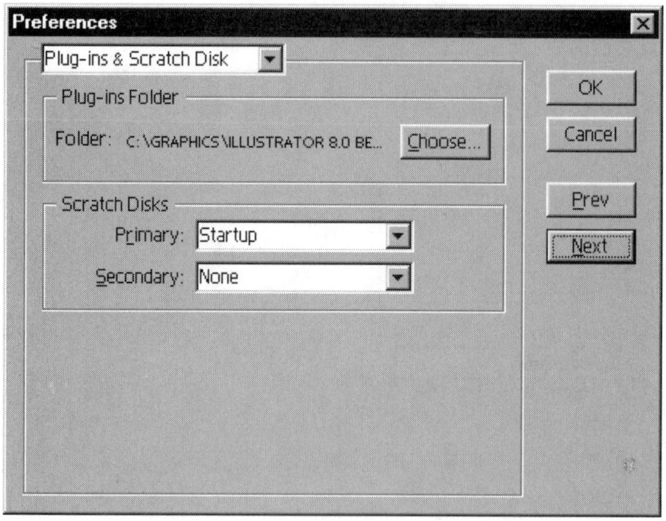

Figure 2-18: The Plug-ins & Scratch Disk dialog box enriches the body and mind.

You also have the option of specifying the location of a primary and secondary *scratch disk*—the virtual memory that Illustrator will use when all of your RAM is full. Since virtual memory resides on your hard drive, reading and writing to virtual memory will slow Illustrator considerably. Choose the location of the first place that you want Illustrator to use for virtual memory from the Primary pop-up menu shown in Figure 2-18. From the Secondary pop-up menu you select the location of the scratch disk that supplements Illustrator's memory when the first scratch disk is full. If you have a second hard drive or another form of storage media, you can use this as your secondary scratch disk.

Color Settings

Another command that affects all the illustrations you will create or edit in the future is the File » Color Settings command, which lets you *calibrate* your monitor so that the colors you see on screen match your printed output. But before I go any further, I should mention two things:

- First, calibrating consumer-grade monitors is nearly impossible. Monitors project color as a combination of red, green, and blue light. (Your eyes similarly read colors using red-, green-, and blue-sensitive cones in the retina.) Printed colors for the most part are made up of a combination of cyan (light blue with a hint of green), magenta (hot pink), yellow, and black inks. These two very different color models (RGB versus CMYK) are exceedingly difficult to reconcile.

- Second, Illustrator's brand of color matching is not nearly as well implemented or (thankfully) as essential as Photoshop's. Photoshop uses monitor and printer information to convert colors from the RGB world of scanners, through the RGB world of monitors, to the CMYK world of printers. In Illustrator, you can define *all* colors in terms of CMYK; therefore, no color space conversion is necessary.

In fact, the only reason Illustrator provides the Color Settings command is to accommodate Photoshop images and to ensure that you see your drawing on screen in roughly its true colors. But even given these limited goals, the command doesn't work particularly well.

If you're serious about producing predictable colors—some folks are more concerned about this than others—here are some better solutions than File » Preferences » Color Matching:

- Spend a few thousand bucks on a calibrated monitor. The only professional-quality Macintosh monitors currently available are the PressView series from Radius (408/541-6100, http://www.radius.com). Available in 17- and 21-inch sizes for roughly $2,500 and $4,000 respectively, these excellent screens ensure the closest thing to an exact color-for-color match. I'm using one right now, and I can't stress enough how much I value it. If you don't already own a video board that can handle 24-bit color at large screen sizes, add another $1,000 to the expense.

  On the Windows side, there's the Mitsubishi SpectraView monitor at about $2,700. Be aware that it does not come bundled with all the amenities that ensure color matching.

- Obviously, the previous suggestion is reserved for those relative few who are sufficiently interested in good color to invest until it hurts. If the mere idea of saving $3,000 makes you feel better about your crummy color already, then you can at least predict what you're going to get by purchasing a Colorfinder swatch book or Trumatch Printer Software from Trumatch (212/302-9100, http://www.trumatch.com). The swatch book, $85, demonstrates hundreds of CMYK color combinations in smooth, logical progressions, and every one of them is printed from a personal computer just like yours. The software, $50 to $100, allows you to print your own color guide from whatever printer you most often use. There simply are no better guides to color than these two. (Incidentally, Illustrator includes the entire Trumatch color library on disk, as described in Chapter 14, but you really need to buy or make your own swatch book to gauge the printed results accurately.)

Where imported images are concerned, Photoshop offers better color conversion controls, so be sure to convert all images to the CMYK color space inside Photoshop before importing them into Illustrator. If an image looks different in Illustrator than it did in Photoshop, trust Photoshop. (Not that Photoshop is altogether accurate; it's simply more likely to approach the truth than Illustrator.)

If after all my warnings you still want to use the Color Settings command, then I suppose I had better explain how it works. These steps expressly affect the printing of imported Photoshop images, so you need to set up Photoshop 5 and Illustrator 8 identically so you don't have color shifts when trading images and objects between the two programs. Here's how

1. In Photoshop 5, choose File » Color Settings » RGB Setup. The RGB Setup dialog will display. Adjust all the settings to you liking. (If you need guidance on how to set up the Color Setting related commands, you'll need to get a good Photoshop book. If I may be so bold to suggest, go buy either the *Macworld Photoshop 5 Bible* or the *Photoshop 5 Bible for Windows.* I wrote them both. So, on second thought, go buy a copy of each.) Click on the Save button to save an RGB profile as an ICC file. If you're on a Mac, save the file in the ColorSync Profiles folder found in the Preferences folder nestled in the System folder. If you're using a PC, save it in the Color directory that's in the System directory which is in the Windows directory. If you're using Windows NT, the path is WinNT/System32/Color. Be sure to give it an appropriate name that you'll easily recognize.
2. Choose File » Color Settings » CMK Setup. With the Built-in radio button selected, adjust all the options to suit your needs. Next, click the Tables radio button. Although, it might seem that you should click the ICC radio button, you want to select the Tables radio button and not, repeat not, click the ICC profile button. Now, save your CMYK in the same folder in which you just saved the RGB profile. Again, give the profile a name you'll recognize.
3. Launch Illustrator. If the program is already running, quit and relaunch.
4. Choose File » Color Settings to display the Color Settings dialog box shown in Figure 2-19.

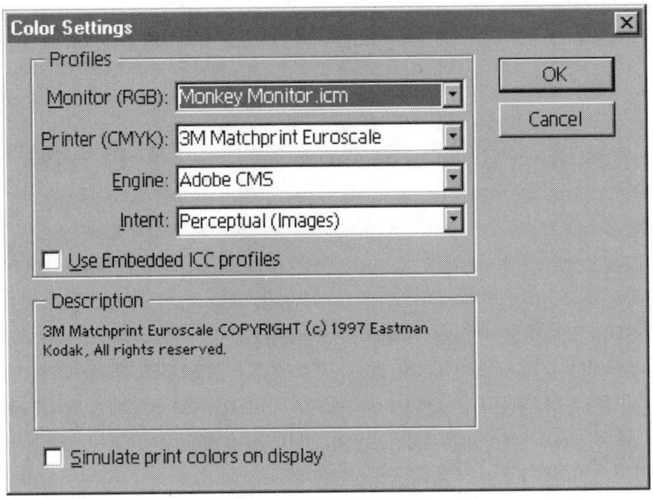

Figure 2-19: This dialog box contains the options that are useful for matching screen colors to printed output for a Photoshop image opened in Illustrator.

5. Select the RGB and CMYK settings you just saved in Photoshop from the Monitor and Printer pop-up menus, respectively.
6. Set the Intent option to Perceptual (Images).

Automatic Color Conversions

One other option—the Use Embedded ICC Profiles check box—is a little more complicated and very dangerous. Since your copy of Photoshop and Illustrator are set the same, Illustrator won't have to convert colors from Photoshop images when importing. But what about when importing images from another Photoshop user? Or from some application other than Photoshop?

When importing CMYK images that are set up exactly the way you want them, be sure to turn off the Use Embedded ICC Profiles check box! Otherwise, Illustrator converts CMYK values from Photoshop's color space to Illustrator's color space. (If two programs are set up the same, no conversion is needed. Otherwise, the colors are changed.) This means CMYK specified in Photoshop as, say, C70 M0 Y30 K0 may change to some other CMYK color when imported into Illustrator. If you turn off the Use Embedded ICC Profiles check box, you don't have that problem. CMYK colors don't shift.

In fact, you could probably live a long and happy life without ever finding a reason to turn on the Use Embedded ICC Profiles check box.

The only time you would want to check the Use Embedded ICC Profile option is if you're importing an RGB image directly from something like a scanning utility into Illustrator and you can't send it through Photoshop or some other image editor with competent color handling skills because the machine you're using doesn't have it. With the option on, Illustrator converts RGBs to its CMYK color space. As to how well Illustrator succeeds at a making a plausible conversion is entirely speculative. This is not a condemnation of Illustrator. It's just that most monitors are incapable of displaying accurate color, and Illustrator's methods of correcting this problem aren't very substantial. So, the moral here is that if it's at all possible, first open the image in Photoshop and then export the file to Illustrator.

The Benefit of EPS

The absolute safest solution is to import a CMYK image saved from Photoshop (or some other image editor) in the EPS format. When saving, Photoshop asks you if you want to use PostScript Color Management. Say no. (Again, with this option on, you run risk of color conversion occurring and messing up CMYK values.)

The downside is that colors from imported EPS image won't look right when viewed in Illustrator. (On-screen view is based on PICT [Mac] or TIFF [PC] preview, so it's not accurate.) The good news is that the EPS colors will print exactly as specified, with no chance of conversion.

The Prefs File

All global preference settings—including those specified in the General Preferences, Hyphenation Options, Plug-ins, and Color Settings dialog boxes—are saved to a file called Adobe Illustrator 8.0 Prefs, located in the Preferences folder inside the System folder (or AIPrefs in the folder where you installed Illustrator on your Windows system). Illustrator also saves a list of open palettes, as well as the physical location of the palettes on screen, in the preferences file. These settings affect every file that you create or modify from this moment on (until you next change your preferences).

To reset all preferences and related dialog boxes to their original settings, quit Illustrator and drag the Adobe Illustrator 8.0 Prefs file (or the AIPrefs file) into the Trash. Then choose Special » Empty Trash (or double-click on the

Recycle Bin icon and choose File » Empty Recycle Bin) to get rid of it for all time. This can be a particularly good thing to do when Illustrator starts flaking out on you. In fact, I recommend that you throw away your preferences file once every three months or so to avoid long-term problems. This goes for other Adobe programs such as Photoshop as well.

Keep in mind, Illustrator updates the Adobe Illustrator 8.0 Prefs file *every* time you quit the program, and *only* when you quit the program. If you crash or force-quit Illustrator (by pressing ⌘-Option-Escape on a Mac or Ctrl-Alt-Delete on a PC), Illustrator leaves the Prefs file untouched. Therefore, if you want to force Illustrator to save your preferences, quit the program by pressing ⌘-Q.

TIP

If you're the adventurous type, you may want to try your hand at editing the Adobe Illustrator 8.0 Prefs file (or the AIPrefs file) in a word processor, such as Apple's SimpleText or Windows Notepad. After quitting Illustrator, double-click on the Adobe Illustrator 8.0 Prefs (or the AIPrefs file) to open it in SimpleText. You'll see a list of items in code. There's an item to turn off the splash screen (/showSplashScreen); you can even change the default typeface and size (/faceName and /faceSize). Limit your changes to numerical values and items within parentheses. In most cases, 0 means off and 1 means on. (If you totally muck things up, you can always throw away the Prefs file and let Illustrator create a fresh one.)

The Startup File

The other method for changing Illustrator's global preferences is to edit the Adobe Illustrator Startup file contained in the Plug-ins folder (or Startup.ai, located in Illustrator's Plug-ins folder for Windows users). You can change the custom colors, gradients, tile patterns, and path patterns available to every illustration. Perhaps more alluring, you can change the illustration window size, the view size, and the position of the artboard inside the window. These are minor adjustments, of course, but if you hate the way Illustrator always fills your screen with the illustration window or the way it zooms the artboard out so it fits inside the window, minor adjustments can go a long way toward creating a more comfortable environment.

1. Open the Adobe Illustrator Startup file (or Startup.ai).
2. The file contains all kinds of patterns, gradients, and colors. Read Chapters 14 through 16 for information about editing these or creating your own. Placement is not important; just fill a shape with whatever color, pattern, or gradation you want to add.
3. Size the illustration window as desired by dragging the size box.
4. Magnify the window to the desired view size using the zoom tool, as explained in Chapter 3.
5. Use the hand tool to scroll the artboard to the desired position (also described in the next chapter).
6. Use File » Document Setup and press the Page Setup button to make any desired changes to the size and shape of the artboard and imageable area. (For the third time, see Chapter 3.)
7. Choose View » Show Rulers or press ⌘-R if you want the rulers to come up every time you start Illustrator.
8. Close the file (⌘-W) and press the Return key to save it to disk.

From now on, every new illustration you create will subscribe to these adjusted settings.

CHAPTER 3

OBJECTS, IMAGES, AND THE FILE FORMATS THAT LOVE THEM

When you first start Illustrator, the program rewards you with an empty illustration window. It's Illustrator's way of saying, "Come on, champ. Don't just sit there; get drawing!" Like any ultrapowerful graphics software, Illustrator is anxious for you to get the show on the road. And this chapter will show you how.

At this juncture, you have the following options:

- Modify the artboard to meet your needs, then start drawing your new masterpiece.
- Close the empty illustration (⌘-W) and create a new one (⌘-N).
- Open an illustration that you've previously saved to disk (⌘-O).
- Just sit there and stare with mute horror at the empty window.

I explain all but the last option in this chapter. (After all, every person must deal with artist's block in his or her own fashion.) I also tell you everything you need to know about placing graphics, magnifying your drawing and otherwise changing the way it looks on screen, and saving your artwork so you can come back to it later. As if that's not enough, I describe how computer graphics are stored on disk and examine why in the world you should care.

By the time you finish this chapter, you'll be saying to yourself, "Whelp, looks like that's it for Chapter 3." It's that kind of incredibly meaningful chapter.

Preparing a New Illustration

Some programs require you to address a dialog box full of options before you create a new document. What size are your pages? Do you want to create tall pages or wide ones? How big are the margins? And on and on.

To its credit, Illustrator doesn't make such a big deal about new document settings. As I mentioned in Chapter 2, the program simply assumes you want to use the settings stored in the Adobe Illustrator Startup file. This doesn't mean you have to accept the settings—you can modify the page size and orientation for an illustration any time you want—it's just that you don't have to worry about it up front.

The reason Illustrator soft-pedals page setup is that it isn't necessarily important. Sometimes you care about page setup; sometimes you don't. It depends on what kind of document you want to create:

- If you're creating a drawing, logo, or other graphic that you intend to place into a layout program such as PageMaker or QuarkXPress, then you aren't interested in what the page looks like in Illustrator. When you import an Illustrator drawing into PageMaker or XPress, all empty portions of the artboard are cropped away, leaving just the graphic itself. Heck, you can create the entire graphic in the pasteboard if you like. Therefore, the graphic is all that matters.

- But issues such as page size, orientation, and placement become very important when you're building a small document or slide. Although touted as an illustration program, Illustrator is well suited to full-page flyers, double-sided mailers, and even multipage newsletters. After all, what's the point of using a page-layout program that lacks drawing tools when you have all the tools you need for small-document production right here inside Illustrator?

For you page-conscious folks, Illustrator provides two dialog boxes—Document Setup and Page Setup—as well as one tool—the page tool. The following sections explain how these features work.

The Artboard Versus the Printed Page

In Illustrator, you specify the size and orientation of the printed page in one step and the size and orientation of the artboard in another. This may seem flat-out bizarre—aren't the artboard and the printed page the same thing?—but it makes sense given Illustrator's flexible approach to pages. See, in Illustrator, you can create humongous pages, just shy of 19 by 19 feet, larger than many bedrooms. Since very few printers can handle this extreme page size, Illustrator lets you divide your artwork onto several printed pages if you so desire.

Now, I know you probably aren't looking to print 19-by-19-foot artwork, but you still might find a use for an artboard that's larger than the printed page.

- Say that you want to create a 17-by-22-inch poster in Illustrator. Although this size is rather small for a poster—most are twice that large—it's awfully large for a printer. Office printers, for example, top out at 11 by 17 inches. This means you'll probably have to print your poster onto several pages and paste the pages together by hand (at least in the proofing stage).
- Illustrator gives you one artboard—no more, no less. So if you want to create a multiple-page document such as a newsletter, you have to compose the entire document on a large artboard and subdivide the artboard into pages. For example, to create an eight-page newsletter, you'd want to set the artboard to 34 inches wide by 22 inches deep, big enough to hold four pages horizontally and two pages vertically.

In most cases, you'll want to specify the size of the printed pages first and then adjust the size of the artboard. You don't have to work in this order—you can keep adjusting the two back and forth until the dogs come home—but this is frequently the most logical order. It's also the order in which I discuss the commands in the following sections.

Setting Up the Printed Page

To specify the size of the pages Illustrator prints, you first need to make sure you have the proper printer selected. Mac people will need to select the Chooser command from the Apple menu. On the left side of the Chooser dialog box you'll see a scrolling list of icons. These icons are *printer drivers*.

Select the proper driver for your printer:

- If you're using a PostScript-compatible printer, select the PSPrinter icon. If PSPrinter is not available, select LaserWriter 8. (The two are virtually identical. PSPrinter comes from Adobe and is therefore probably more recent; LaserWriter 8 comes from Apple.)
- If you own a non-PostScript printer, select the icon named after your printer. It may even look like your printer.

After you select the proper driver, click in the close box or press ⌘-W to close the Chooser dialog box.

You Windows folks can change printers by clicking the Start button on the Windows Taskbar and then choosing the Settings » Printers shortcut. Double-click on the Add Printer icon and follow the instructions in the Add Printer Wizard. You will have the opportunity to select a printer driver from a slew of drivers that come with Windows or to add one that comes from your printer's manufacturer on a separate disk. After choosing a printer and finishing with the Add Printer Wizard, return to Illustrator.

Next, choose File » Document Setup (⌘-Option-P) and click the Page Setup (called Print Setup on the Windows side) button in the Document Setup dialog box. Assuming that you're using a Mac and a PostScript printer, this displays the standard PSPrinter (or LaserWriter) Print Setup dialog box. If you're using a non-PostScript printer, the dialog box will look a little different, but the important options are the same. On a Windows system, the Print Setup dialog box appears. It looks quite different from its Mac equivalent, but the important options are easy to recognize.

For the time being, only two options in this dialog box matter. These are Size and Orientation. (For descriptions of the others, read Chapter 18.)

- **Paper Size pop-up menu:** From this menu—which goes by different names depending on which platform and operating system you're using—select the paper size on which you want to print. As you might imagine, it's important to make sure your printer can handle the paper size you select. Don't select Tabloid (11 by 17 inches), for example, if your printer maxes out at Legal (8.5 by 14 inches). A4, B5, and others are European page sizes.

- **Orientation:** You can create an upright page (portrait) or turn it over on its side (landscape), depending on whether you want a page that's taller than it is wide (the default) or one that's wider than it is tall.

After you respond to these two options, click on the OK button or press the Return key in both the Page or Print Setup and the Document Setup dialog boxes. Illustrator automatically redraws the dotted outlines inside the artboard. One outline represents the border of the printed page, and the other represents the size of the imageable area (the portion of the page Illustrator can print).

Configuring the Artboard

To change the size of the solid-bordered artboard in the drawing area, choose File » Document Setup or press the magic key combination ⌘-Option-P. Most of the options in the Document Setup dialog box (shown in Figure 3-1) control the size and orientation of the artboard, as well as the relationship between the artboard and the printed page. But a few are simply preference settings that Adobe saw fit to put in a dopey location. The difference between these preferences and those available from the File » Preferences submenu are that these affect the single foreground drawing, while those affect *all* open drawings.

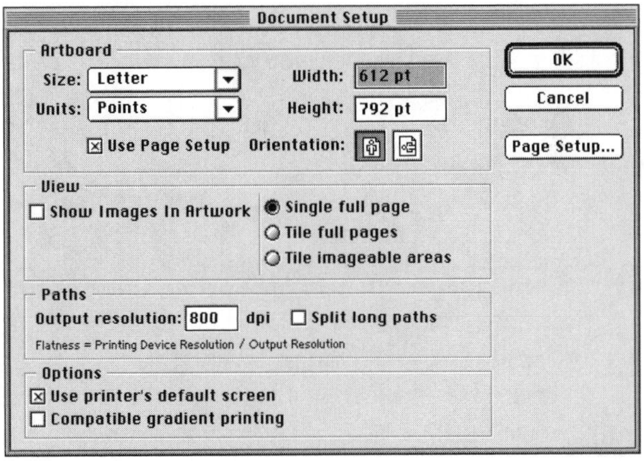

Figure 3-1: Use the Document Setup options to change the size and orientation of the artboard.

Whatever their purpose, here is how the Document Setup options work (in their order of appearance in the dialog box):

- **Size:** This pop-up menu lets you choose from a bunch of predefined artboard sizes.
- **Units:** Select an option from this pop-up menu to change the measurement system for the current drawing only (as opposed to the identically

named option in the General Preferences dialog box, which affects all drawings from now on).

- **Use Page Setup:** If you want to match the artboard to the printed page size, select this check box.
- **Width and Height:** If you don't want to use one of the predefined settings, specify the width and height of the artboard by entering values into these option boxes. It doesn't matter which value you enter first and which second—by default, the smallest value is treated as the width and the largest as the height. To change this, you have to select a different Orientation icon.

TIP: Unless you've changed the measurement systems in the Units & Undo Preferences dialog box (using the General Units pop-up menu), the Dimensions values are probably listed in points. While this is a good unit for precise measurements, few of us think in terms of points for larger measurements. To enter values in inches, just enter the value, followed by *in*. Illustrator automatically converts the measurement to points. You can also enter values in millimeters (*mm*) or picas (*p*). For example, *55p6* stands for 55 picas plus 6 points, which is 666 points or 9.25 inches. When working in inches or millimeters, you can enter *pt* for points.

- **Orientation:** Here you specify whether your artboard is taller than it is wide or vice versa. Be sure to select an option. Regardless of how you enter values in the Dimensions option boxes, Illustrator conforms to the selected orientation.
- **Show Images in Artwork:** When this preference setting is turned off, a placed image does not display properly in the artwork mode. Instead, it appears as a rectangle, twice bisected by diagonal lines. When the check box is selected, Illustrator shows a monochrome version of the image in the artwork mode. Placed images of all varieties *always* show up in the preview mode—not to mention print—regardless of the Show Images in Artwork check box.
- **Single Full Page:** The three radio buttons next to the Show Images in Artwork check box determine how Illustrator prints oversized artboards. This is the default setting. It instructs Illustrator to display just

one set of dotted lines and print just one page, regardless of the size of the artboard. Some artists like to use this option with a slightly oversized artboard so they can adjust the way the illustration fits on the page using the page tool.

- **Tile Full Pages:** Select this option to display as many whole pages as will fit in the drawing area. No partial pages are allowed.

TIP: This is the option to select when creating a multipage document such as a newsletter. Illustrator numbers the page boundaries inside the artboard so you know the order in which the pages will print.

- **Tile Imageable Areas:** By selecting the Tile Imageable Areas radio button, you tell Illustrator to chop up the artboard into as many imageable areas as will fit, thus ensuring no gap between an object printed half on one page and half on another.

TIP: In other words, select this option when subdividing poster-sized artwork onto many printed pages.

- **Output Resolution:** Set this value to reflect the resolution of the printer you want to use to produce your finished illustration or small document. This option affects Illustrator's automatic path-splitting function (described next) and the accuracy at which curves print.

WARNING: This is one of two options inside the Document Setup dialog box that affect all artwork created in Illustrator, whether printed from Illustrator or some other application. (The other is the Split Long Paths check box.) Do *not* lower this value below the default 800 unless you are encountering printing problems! And then, be sure to first consult the "Flatness and Path Splitting" section of Chapter 18!

- **Split Long Paths:** This check box automatically breaks up complex paths with gobs of points into smaller paths in an attempt to eliminate printing errors. Illustrator determines which paths are split and to what degree, based on the Output Resolution value.

WARNING

Illustrator automatically splits paths whenever you save or print a file! Do *not* select this check box unless you are experiencing printing problems and you have read the "Flatness and Path Splitting" section of Chapter 18! There is no automatic way to reassemble paths that have been split apart; you have to join paths manually, which is a major pain in the butt.

- **Use Printer's Default Screen:** With few exceptions, a printer has to convert the various colors and shades of gray in your illustration to small dots called *halftone cells*. If you turn this check box off, Illustrator automatically optimizes the halftone cells to print the best possible illustration. Leave the check box on to use your printer's built-in halftone scheme, which generally works faster. See Chapter 18 for more information.
- **Compatible Gradient Printing:** When Illustrator 5 introduced its automatic multicolor gradients, many folks had problems printing them. Adobe claims the culprits were out-of-date or nonstandard PostScript interpreters—the code readers built into the printers—but whatever the scapegoat, this option is the solution they implemented in version 6. If gradations give you fits, just select this check box. Illustrator automatically converts gradations to blends on the fly, greatly slowing the printing process but also avoiding irritating printing errors.

Once you exit the Document Setup dialog box (by pressing Return, naturally), you'll see the altered page boundaries against the altered artboard. To adjust the position of the page boundaries, read on.

Positioning the Pages on the Artboard

You can't move the artboard. (That is, you can scroll it around inside the illustration window, but you can't actually change its location.) The artboard is always positioned smack dab in the center of the pasteboard. However, you can move the page boundaries with respect to the artboard using the page tool.

The page tool is the first alternate tool in the hand tool slot. Select this tool and then click or drag inside the artboard to set the location of the lower left corner of the imageable area of a printed page. If you selected the Tile Imageable Areas or Tile Full Pages option in the Document Setup dialog box, a network of page boundaries emanates from the point at which you release the mouse button.

(If just one page boundary appears even though you selected the Tile Full Pages radio button, it's because this is the only whole page that fits at this location. Drag again with the page tool or increase the size of the artboard to see more pages.)

TIP: Always use the page tool to change the placement of an illustration on a page. It's generally easier and always faster than trying to move a huge squad of graphic objects and text blocks with the arrow tool. If you need more wiggle room, increase the size of the artboard one or more inches all around.

Hiding the Page Boundaries

If the dotted page boundaries get in your face, choose View » Hide Page Tiling to make them go away. This is, of course, merely a temporary measure. You can make the page boundaries reappear at any time by choosing View » Show Page Tiling.

Opening and Placing

Illustrator lets you have multiple illustration windows open at a time. To create another empty illustration window, for example, you can choose File » New or press ⌘-N. You can also open an illustration saved to disk by choosing File » Open or pressing ⌘-O, all without closing any open windows.

You can open four kinds of files in Illustrator:

- Drawings previously created in Illustrator.
- Drawings created in FreeHand or some other drawing program and saved in either the Illustrator file format or the format native to the other drawing program.
- Documents created in PageMaker, QuarkXPress, or FreeHand and exported in EPS format or in their native format.
- Images saved as TIFF, JPEG, or some other compatible format.

If you open an illustration (a line drawing saved in any of a number of different formats, including both the Illustrator and the FreeHand native formats), it pops up on screen in a new illustration window. You can edit any line, shape, or word of text as explained in the myriad chapters that follow. You can also edit graphic objects and text inside opened PDF files, although it is possible that you may lose some objects in the PDF conversion.

When you open a TIFF file or another image, Illustrator displays the images in a new illustration window. You can move or transform (scale, rotate, flip, or skew) images, as well as apply Photoshop filters (as described in Chapter 13). But you can't edit them in the same way that you edit object-oriented illustrations.

If you want to add an illustration or image to the illustration you're working on, choose File » Place. Rather than creating a separate illustration window, Illustrator places the graphic in the foreground window. The graphic appears selected so you can begin working on it immediately. You can move or transform a placed graphic, but you can't edit it, even if the graphic was created using Illustrator. You can also apply Photoshop filters to placed images (unless the placed image is an Illustrator EPS, as this chapter explains later).

I discuss individual file formats and the special ways to deal with them later on in the section "Those Crazy, Kooky File Formats." But first, I want to briefly go over the basics of opening or placing a file from disk. If you already know all about opening files, feel free to skip this section.

Using the Open Dialog Box

When you choose File » Open or File » Place, Illustrator displays the Open dialog box (shown in Figure 3-2) or the Place dialog box. These boxes are identical in form and function except for their names, of course, and the Place dialog box contains one additional option box, discussed below. Whichever box you choose will request that you locate and select the drawing that you want to open or place. The dialog box lets you search through all folders on all available hard drives, CD-ROMs, and floppy disks. Sometimes you can even preview what the file looks like before you open or place it.

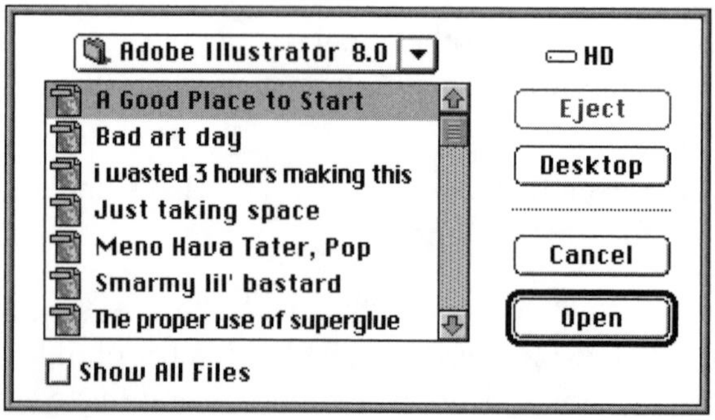

Figure 3-2: The Open dialog box is nothing more than a tool for locating graphics stored on disk.

The Folder Bar

The top of the Open dialog box sports a *folder bar,* which tells you where you are inside the folder hierarchy. The name that appears in the bar matches the current folder. Drag from the folder bar to display all the *parent folders* in the folder hierarchy—that is, all the folders in which the current folder is nestled, including the folder that contains the current folder.

The Scrolling List

Below the folder bar is a scrolling list that contains the names of all the folders inside the current folder as well as all the graphics that you can open inside Illustrator. You can use the scrolling list as follows:

- **Select a document or folder:** Select a document or folder by clicking on its name.
- **Select by key entry:** To locate a specific document or folder name quickly, enter the first few letters of its name from the keyboard. The first item in alphabetical order whose name begins with these letters becomes selected.
- **Scroll through the list:** Press the up arrow or down arrow key to advance one name at a time through the scrolling list. On an extended keyboard, press the Page Up or Page Down key to scroll up or down several names at a time. Press the Home key to scroll all the way to the top of the list; press the End key to scroll all the way to the bottom.
- **Open an item:** Open a file or folder by double-clicking on its name or by selecting it and pressing the Return key.
- **Open a folder:** If a folder name is selected, press ⌘-down arrow on a Mac or the Enter key in Windows to open that folder and display its contents.
- **Exit a folder:** To exit the current folder and display the contents of its parent folder, press ⌘-up arrow on a Mac or the Backspace key in Windows. You can also close the current folder by clicking on the disk icon above the Eject button.

The Preview Options for Macs

Illustrator 6 revised the Open dialog box slightly. It includes a thumbnail preview of the selected illustration or image on the left side of the scrolling list as well as a couple of check boxes under the scrolling list.

The beauty of the preview is that you don't have to open the graphic in order to remember what it looks like. But in order to see a preview, you must have QuickTime loaded (this popular Apple multimedia extension is finding more and more acceptance in Windows applications), *and* you have to have specifically saved a thumbnail along with the file inside either Illustrator 6 or later (previous versions didn't support previews) or Photoshop 2.5.1 or later. Illustrator can also display the PICT previews included with some EPS files.

I'll explain how to save thumbnail previews later in this chapter. In the meantime, here's how the new Open dialog box options work:

- **Create:** Let me start by saying this button is darn near useless inside Illustrator. It theoretically allows you to create a preview of a selected graphic on the fly. However, QuickTime must be running for this button to function, and even then the button applies only to PICT graphics. It doesn't work for any other files—including Illustrator drawings.
- **Show Preview:** When selected, this check box instructs Illustrator to display the thumbnail preview image on the left side of the dialog box. If you turn the option off, the preview disappears and the Open dialog box collapses to save screen space.

  Keep in mind that the preview depends on QuickTime. So if the preview is missing and the Show Preview check box is dimmed, chances are QuickTime did not load when you started up your computer.
- **Show All Files:** Select this check box to see all files in the current folder, whether Illustrator can open them or not. It lets you force Illustrator to at least make an attempt to open a graphic that it doesn't recognize as compatible.

The Extra Place Options

The Place dialog box has three additional options missing from the Open dialog box: the Link, Template, and Replace check boxes.

- **Link:** When this box is checked, Illustrator will tag the physical location of the image or illustration without integrating it into the file and the file's size therefore does not increase. Images so placed are considered linked. If you turn off this check box, the placed file will be integrated into your artwork. This means Illustrator will save the placed item as part of your artwork—resulting in a larger file. These images are called "embedded images."
- **Template:** If you choose this check box, the image that you're placing will act as a template, ideal for tracing. Illustrator will automatically create a new layer (directly below the current layer) expressly for this image. The layer and everything on it will be visible, locked, and nonprinting. To help you distinguish it from the rest of your work, the image will be dimmed by 50 percent. (For more information on layers, see Chapter 4.)

- **Replace:** Instead of simply placing an image, you can replace a previously placed image with a new one. First select the image that you want to replace in your artwork. Then choose File » Place, select the new image from the scrolling field, check the Replace check box, and press the Return key.

The Links Palette

Illustrator now offers a palette devoted to the organization and keeping of all your placed images, linked and embedded. For each image you place in a document, Illustrator creates a *link* in the Links palette—this term is used for both linked and embedded images. The link includes the image's name and a thumbnail preview of the image, as shown in Figure 3-3.

The link may also include one of three small informational icons, labeled in Figure 3-3.

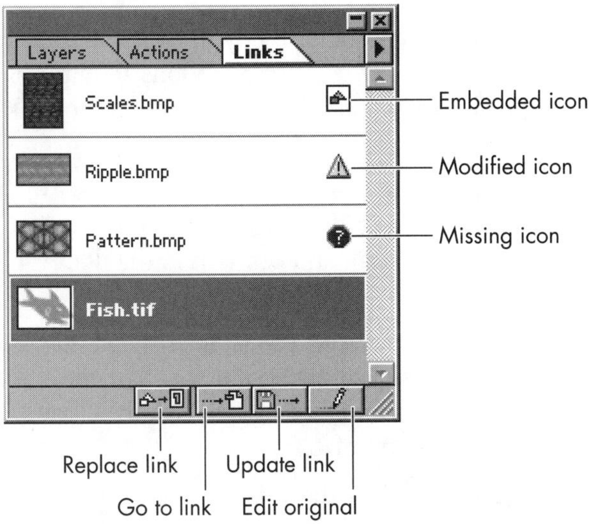

Figure 3-3: Within the confines of the new Links palette, you can organize, find, and change the embedded status of all the placed images in your document.

- **Embedded icon:** If you originally placed the image without checking the Link check box inside the Place dialog box or you embedded a linked image inside Illustrator after you placed it, you'll see this icon. You transmute a linked image to an embedded image via the Embed Image option from the Link Palette's pop-up menu or by rasterizing the image with the Object » Rasterize command.

- **Modified icon:** If you apply a filter to a linked image, this icon will pop into existence. This is Illustrator's way of telling you that if you decide to go with these changes, Illustrator will have to embed the image. If you save your document when a link shows this icon, Illustrator will automatically embed the image. The next time you open the file, the link will show an embedded icon.
- **Missing icon:** This icon never shows up when you first place an image. It appears when you open a file that originally contained a linked image that Illustrator can no longer locate. It also displays if you do something odd such as delete an image from your hard drive while it's still in use inside Illustrator. Whatever the case, Illustrator will alert you that the original is no longer available and ask you if you want to replace it with another image.
- **No icon whatsoever:** This lack of icon tells you that you have a linked image in proper working order.

The Link palette's pop-up menu contains options that let you view and modify the images associated with the different links. The first six options require that either an image is selected in you document or that a link is selected in the Links palette. These options work as follows:

- **Go to Link:** With a link selected, choose this option (or click the second icon from the left along the bottom of the palette) and Illustrator will select the image associated with the link and center it in the document window.
- **Update Link:** If you make changes (and save then) to the original file of a linked image currently open in Illustrator, Illustrator will do its best to reflect those changes in the image. If you find that this isn't the case, select the image's link and choose this option.
- **Edit Original:** Choose this option to open the original image in the application in which it was created. If the original image wasn't created on your computer, the image will open in the most appropriate application (as dictated by your operating system and the image's format). This option affects only linked images since embedded images, an integrated part of your document, no longer have an original.
- **Replace:** If you decide that an image is wrong for your document, select its link from the Link palette and choose this option. The standard Place dialog box will display. Select the image that you'd prefer in the place of the original. As with when you placed the original image,

you'll have the option of linking or embedding the new image via the Link check box.

- **Embed Image:** Choose this option to encode a linked image's information into you document. This embeds the image, just as though you had deactivated the Place dialog box's Link check box when first placed the image.
- **Information:** With a link selected, choose this option (or simply double-click on the link) to display the Link Information dialog box. Here you'll find information about the image including its name, location on disk, size in bytes, kind (that is, its file format), creation and modification dates, and any changes you that made to its scaling or angular orientation.
- **Show:** You can opt to show all links in the Links palette or just those in which you are interested.
- **Sort:** Choose the appropriate option to sort the links by name, kind or status. Sorting links by status groups the links

Those Crazy, Kooky File Formats

Prior to version 6, Illustrator was a program in a bubble. It relied on PostScript file formats and expected every other graphics application to support PostScript in kind. Thankfully, Adobe decided that with version 6 Illustrator should broaden its horizons and join the real world. Illustrator has gone from supporting three graphic file formats to supporting five times that many.

For the record, *file formats* are different ways to save or export a file to disk. Just as Betamax and VHS are different videotape formats, TIFF and PCX are different image formats. By supporting a wider variety of formats, Illustrator can accept graphics from all kinds of Macintosh and Windows applications.

The following sections explain many of the formats Illustrator 8 supports, starting with the native Illustrator format and continuing through the others in alphabetical order. I will tell you how the format works and what good it is, and I'll offer additional instructions as needed.

Native Illustrator

The native Illustrator format—the one Illustrator likes best—is a pure PostScript file. If you know how to program in PostScript, you can even open the file in a word processor and edit it line by line.

The great thing about an Illustrator file is that you can import it into just about any program that supports PostScript. If you import a PostScript file into

PageMaker, for example, you won't be able to view the illustration accurately on screen—it just looks like a gray box—but you can print it to any PostScript printer. Many other drawing programs, including FreeHand and CorelDraw, can open and even save Illustrator files.

There are seven variations on the basic Illustrator format, each corresponding to a different version of the software:

- **Illustrator 8.0:** This format saves every little thing you can do in Illustrator 8.
- **Illustrator 7.0:** This format does not support the extended blend capabilities, gradient meshes, and specialized brushstrokes.
- **Illustrator 6.0:** This format does not support grids, the expanded template abilities, and some file formats. Otherwise, it is identical to the Illustrator 8 format.
- **Illustrator 5.0/5.5:** The Illustrator 5 format does not support imported image files or thumbnail previews.
- **Illustrator 4.0 (for Windows):** From a Macintosh user's perspective, this Windows-only version of the Illustrator format is identical to the Illustrator 3 format. Illustrator 4 also supported grids and TIFF templates—neither of which was possible on the Mac side until Illustrator 7—but this hardly matters formatwise. The only thing to remember is, if you encounter an Illustrator 4 file, it comes from the Windows platform.
- **Illustrator 3.0/3.2:** This format doesn't support gradients, layers, large artboard sizes, tabs, and columns or rows. It converts gradient fills to blends and combines all objects onto a single layer. Objects in the pasteboard may be lost.
- **Illustrator 88:** This format does not support compound paths, area and path text, text blocks with more than 256 characters, custom guides, and charts. All paths remain intact, but they may not serve their original function. Text blocks are divided into pieces; area and path text may be broken up into individual letters.
- **Illustrator 1.0/1.1:** This format supports only paths and small text blocks. What it doesn't support could fill a book: tile patterns, masks, placed EPS images, and colors (that's right, colors)—in other words, just about everything that fills this book.

Acrobat PDF

Adobe's Acrobat is a paperless office program that lets you print to the screen instead of wasting precious scraps of Oregon forest. The suite of Acrobat utilities acts as a PostScript interpreter, much like the one built into your printer. You can trade PDF (*Portable Document Format*) files with other Mac and Windows users, and regardless of which program you used to create the original file or which fonts you used to format the text, all anyone needs to view the file is the Acrobat reader. Illustrator goes one better, letting you edit text and graphic objects within the Acrobat document itself.

If you export an illustration as a PDF file and intend your audience to open it in Acrobat, you can associate a separate Web address with each and every object in your document. Simply select an object in your illustration, click on the Attributes palette, and enter the http://www.whatever.something into the URL option box. As soon as your Acrobat-using friends—provided that they also have a Web browser up and running—click on said object, they will be whisked away immediately to some fanciful location of your choosing.

Amiga IFF

The Amiga was a failed experiment in desktop computers pioneered by Commodore. One of the first computers to ship with a color monitor, it never caught on with mainstream developers. But despite the fact that Commodore bowed out of the computer market more than two years ago, Amiga fans are adamant that their systems live on.

Although there aren't many Amigas around anymore, Adobe recognizes that there still may be many files originally saved in this format. To this end, Illustrator lets you open and save IFF (Interchange File Format) files. IFF is the Amiga's all around graphic format, serving much the same function as PICT on the Mac.

Encapsulated PostScript (EPS)

The EPS format combines a pure PostScript description of an illustration with a PICT preview so you can see what the image looks like on screen. It is far and away the best format for saving Illustrator drawings so that you can import them into PageMaker or XPress.

Illustrator has been able to save EPS files since its first version in 1987. In fact, it was the first program I ever saw that could produce reliable EPS files. And it has long been able to open its own EPS files, no matter when (that is, in which version) they were produced.

Up until Illustrator 6, the program didn't stand a chance of opening EPS files created in other programs such as FreeHand. Illustrator 6 included a new EPS *parser*, which is a program that reads code and converts it to editable objects and text. Personally, I've never had trouble opening a single FreeHand EPS file since this implementation, including illustrations containing gradations and special PostScript fill patterns.

If you use FreeHand, or you know someone who does, you have two ways to swap files. On the one hand, you can save to the Illustrator format from inside FreeHand, but you may lose placed TIFF images, special text effects, custom halftone dots, and other fill patterns. To avoid these oversights, save the illustration as an EPS file inside FreeHand and open the file in Illustrator 8.

You can also store images in the EPS format. Though generally an inefficient format for images (EPS offers no compression, plus it has a lot of header info), the benefit of EPS is that you can save special PostScript routines such as halftoning information. EPS images also print faster, which is why high-end service bureaus favor the format.

FilmStrip

Adobe Premiere is the foremost QuickTime movie–editing application for the Mac. The program is a wonder when it comes to fades, frame merges, and special effects, but it lacks frame-by-frame editing capabilities.

If you want frame-by-frame editing, you can export the movie to the FilmStrip format and modify the frames inside Photoshop or Illustrator. FilmStrip organizes frames into a long vertical strip. A gray bar separates each frame. The number of each frame appears on the right; time codes appear on left. Though Photoshop is a far more useful program for editing FilmStrip files, you can open and add to these files in Illustrator.

Graphics Interchange Format (GIF89a)

Originally designed for transferring compressed graphics with a modem, GIF is an extensively used format that supports up to 256 colors and LZW compression, as does TIFF (mentioned below). The conventional wisdom on GIF is that it is on its way out to make way for the up-and-coming PNG.

When you export to GIF, Illustrator presents you with a dialog box containing this assortment of options:

- **Palette:** Since GIF supports only up to 256 colors, you have to choose how you want Illustrator to reduce the number of colors in your image. If your artwork contains less than 256 colors, then the Exact command appears in the pop-up menu and no reduction is necessary. It's best to choose the number of colors in images intended for display on your system (such as wallpaper) using the corresponding System command. The Web command reduces the number of colors to fit the palettes of the most popular Web browsers, but probably your best choice is the Adaptive command. This tells Illustrator to select only the 256 most frequently used colors and to replace all the others with the closest match.

- **Interlace:** With this option selected, the image will appear bit by bit in horizontal blocks when you open it. This is a popular option for Web graphics.
- **Transparent:** If you want the transparent portions of your image to stay that way, choose this option. Otherwise all transparent pixels will save as white.
- **Anti-alias:** You can choose to have any text that appears in your image anti-aliased (see Chapter 6 for more information on anti-aliasing). The font and size of the text affect its on-screen appearance, so if you are ever in doubt, export your artwork twice (once with anti-alias on) and see which looks better.
- **Image map:** If your image is destined for the Web and has built-in hot spots (places where you can click to access a different Web address), you will need to choose whether the file should be client-side or server-side in nature. Client-side files contain all the hot spot information—they are therefore more convenient and faster—and do not require an additional file. You will need to specify all the necessary URL information via the Attributes palette and specify the file as the Anchor. Unfortunately, client-side image maps are not as widely supported as server-side. If you choose the server-side option, you will need to have a separate HTML file containing all the hot spot information.

JPEG

Named after the folks who designed it—the Joint Photographic Experts Group—JPEG is the most efficient file format available to image editors. An image saved in JPEG almost always takes up less room on disk than if it were saved in any other format. To achieve these savings, JPEG uses a "lossy" compression scheme, which means that it sacrifices image quality to conserve space on disk. You control how much data is lost when saving the image.

JPEG is best used for compressing photographs and other *continuous-tone* images, in which the distinction between immediately neighboring pixels is slight. Any image that includes gradual color transitions qualifies for JPEG compression.

JPEG is not well suited to screen shots, line drawings, and other high-contrast images. Therefore, you should avoid at all costs saving an illustration to the JPEG format. Illustrator supports JPEG so it can place images, not export them.

Kodak Photo CD

Photo CD is the affordable photographic scanning technology that leaves flatbed scanners in the dust. You can take a roll of undeveloped film, color negatives, or slides into your local Photo CD dealer and have the photos scanned onto a CD-ROM at 2,048 by 3,072 pixels for $2 per photo. Each CD holds 100 images, allowing you to acquire a library of images without taking up a lot of room in your home or office. Better yet, Photo CDs are designed to resist the ravages of time and last well into the twenty-second century (longer than any of the people that use them).

WARNING

The only problem is, Kodak's software is a nightmare. If you installed the Kodak Photo CD software when installing Illustrator, you added about 20 files to your hard drive, none of which are named logically and all of which you must leave absolutely alone. Rename a file, move it, or turn it off with an extensions manager, and you may very well crash your computer when trying to open a Photo CD image.

When you open or place a Photo CD image—found inside the Images folder in the Photo_CD folder on the CD—Illustrator displays the dialog box shown in Figure 3-4. Here you can select the resolution of the image you want to place and specify options so that Kodak's software can adjust the colors of the image to suit your screen.

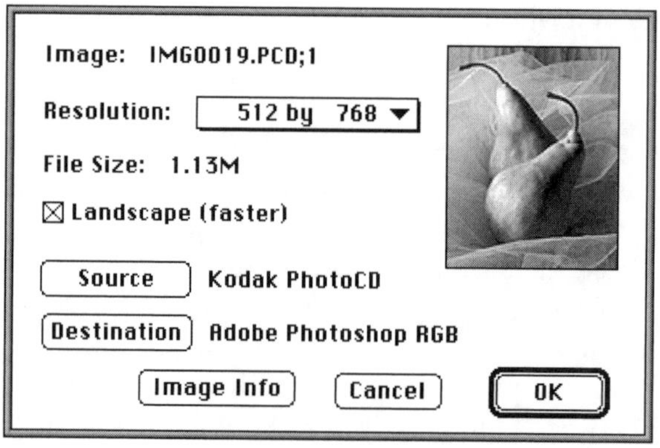

Figure 3-4: When you open a Photo CD image, Illustrator follows the standard Open dialog box with this one.

Here's how the Photo CD options work:

- **Resolution:** Select from five resolution options, from a dinky 128 by 192 pixels to 2,048 by 3,072 pixels. A sixth option, 4,096 by 6,144 pixels, is dimmed unless you are working with a superdeluxe Pro Photo CD. The larger the image you open, the longer it will take, but the better the image will look when printed.
- **Landscape:** Leave this check box selected. When turned on, it opens a vertically oriented image on its side. That's okay, because you can rotate the image with the rotate tool (as described in Chapter 11) in far less time than it would take Kodak's software to make the calculations.
- **Source:** Click on this button to specify the kind of film from which the original photographs were scanned. You can select from two specific Kodak brands—Ektachrome and Kodachrome—or settle for the generic Color Negative Film option. Your selection determines how the Kodak software transforms the colors in the image.
- **Destination:** After clicking on this button, select an option from the Device pop-up menu to specify the color model you want to use. The Adobe Photoshop RGB option is the most compatible with Illustrator.

NOTE

You can also open images from the folders inside the Photos folder on a Photo CD. But these images are converted to the PICT format by the Macintosh system software, which involves a middleman and doesn't permit you to take advantage of Kodak's automatic color corrections.

PC Paintbrush (PCX)

PCX doesn't stand for anything. Rather, it's the extension that PC Paintbrush assigns to images saved in its native file format. PCX is one of the most popular image file formats in use today, largely because PC Paintbrush is the oldest painting program for DOS. PCX images can include up to 16 million colors.

Photoshop 5

Illustrator can open and place images stored in Photoshop's native format, but this is largely a waste of time. Photoshop already supports every image format under the sun—more than Illustrator supports—so why bother with the native format? After all, Illustrator 8 doesn't support Photoshop layers. In fact, Illustrator won't properly display a Photoshop image that contains layers. Instead, it displays it with all layers flattened one to one layer.

PICT

The PICT (*Macintosh Picture*) format is a graphics exchange format Apple designed more than ten years ago and has updated irregularly over time. You can save both object-oriented illustrations and photographic images in the PICT format, but the format isn't ideally suited to either. Frankly, TIFF is better for images and EPS is better for illustrations.

In any case, you can open PICT illustrations—from MacDraw, Canvas, and the like—and edit the graphic objects and text blocks as if they were created inside Illustrator. Illustrator's PICT conversion isn't perfect—bitmapped patterns and other oddities may get lost in translation—but you'll probably find it preferable to redrawing the objects and reinputting the text from scratch.

Pixar

Pixar recently became a household word when the company went public shortly after the release of its monumentally popular movie *Toy Story*. But the company has been creating terrific computer animation for some time, from the father-and-son desk lamps in *Luxo, Jr.* to the run-amok toddler in the Oscar-winning *Tin Toy* to the commercial adventures of a Listerine bottle that boxes gingivitis one day and swings Tarzan-like through a spearmint forest the next.

In its spare time, Pixar managed to create a few 3-D graphics applications for the Mac, including MacRenderMan, ShowPlace, and Typestry. The company works its own 3-D magic using mondo-expensive Pixar workstations. Illustrator can now open a still image created on a Pixar machine.

Portable Network Graphics (PNG)

Designed to outperform and eventually replace GIF, PNG permits compression that doesn't sacrifice quality and supports both 24-bit and 48-bit images. Thus, PNG files are larger than GIF, JPEG, or TIFF files (unless you are exporting a grayscale image), and are generally best suited for smaller images.

When you export to PNG, you can specify the image's resolution. Choose among the standards—Screen, Medium, or High (72, 150, and 300 dpi, respectively)—or enter an unorthodox value in the Other option box.

Once you've decided on a resolution, Illustrator asks you to set the Interlace and Filter options:

- **Interlace:** This is the same option that appears when you export to GIF, though it's presented a bit differently. Choose None if you want the image to draw line by line when it's opened. Choose the Adam7 option if you prefer the image to draw in seven passes (hence the name).

- **Filter:** Here you specify whether you wish to use the *zlib* compression and, if so, which particular scheme. You can experiment with the options to see which will give you the best results, but since they can save you only a few hundred bytes at most, I recommend that you stick with the None option and avoid the hassle.

Targa

TrueVision's Targa and NuVista video boards let you overlay computer graphics and animation onto live video. The effect is called *chroma keying* because typically a key color is set aside to let the live video show through. TrueVision designed the Targa format to support 32-bit images that include so-called *alpha channels* capable of displaying the live video. Illustrator doesn't know a video from a rodeo, but it can place a still Targa image.

Tag Image File Format (TIFF)

Developed by Aldus to standardize electronic images so you could easily import them into PageMaker, TIFF (*Tag Image File Format*) is one of the most widely supported formats across both the Macintosh and Windows platforms. Unlike PICT, it can't handle object-oriented artwork, but it is otherwise unrestricted, supporting 16 million colors and virtually infinite resolutions.

Photoshop lets you apply so-called LZW (Lempel-Ziv-Welch) compression to a TIFF image, which substitutes frequently used strings of code with shorter equivalents. This makes the files smaller on disk without altering so much as a single pixel. Imaging professionals call this kind of compression *lossless*, because it preserves the integrity of each and every scanned color.

Illustrator 8 likewise supports LZW compression. It also opens both the Mac and Windows varieties of TIFF, so you never have to worry about your Photoshop images' compatibility with Illustrator.

Windows BMP

BMP (*Windows Bitmap*) is the native format for the cheesy little Paint utility that ships with Windows. When Microsoft says, "Jump," software vendors respond, "How high?" so naturally BMP has become a standard over the years. BMP is the equal of PCX, supporting 16 million colors and high resolutions. If you get a BMP image, rest assured that you can place it into your illustration.

Getting Around in Illustrator

Illustrator works a lot like other graphics programs. You can zoom in and out to take a closer look at a detail or view your illustration in its entirety. You also can scroll the illustration to bring different bits and pieces into view. And if you own an older, slower machine, you can view objects in a special wireframe mode that speeds up screen display.

The next few sections explain how to get around quickly and expertly. If you don't know the keyboard shortcuts already, pay special attention to these. Using navigational shortcuts rather than selecting tools and commands expedites the artistic process more than any other single factor.

Fit-in-Window and Actual Sizes

Illustrator provides 23 preset *view sizes*, which are the magnification levels that Illustrator uses to display your drawing in the illustration window. Illustrator actually allows any view size between 3.13 and 6400 percent, provided that you manually enter the value into one of the size boxes, but both the zoom tool and the Navigator palette's Zoom In and Zoom Out buttons give you access to only 23 discreet views. Magnified view sizes provide great detail but show smaller portions of the illustration at a time. Reduced view sizes show you a larger portion of the drawing area but may provide insufficient detail for creating and manipulating objects. Because Illustrator makes it easy to switch quickly between view sizes, you can edit your artwork accurately and still maintain compositional consistency.

Assuming that you haven't altered the Adobe Illustrator Startup file, Illustrator displays every new illustration at *fit-in-window size*, which reduces the artboard so it fits inside the illustration window. The specific magnification level required to produce the fit-in-window size depends on the size of your monitor and the size of the artboard. In Figure 3-5, for example, the artboard fits in the window at 50 percent magnification.

TIP

You can return to fit-in-window size at any time by choosing View » Fit In Window or pressing ⌘-0 (zero). Because this key equivalent doesn't necessarily remind one of anything, most folks just double-click on the hand tool icon in the toolbox. (To help you remember this shortcut, think of using that hand tool to push back the illustration.)

Another useful view size is *actual size*—or 100 percent view—which shows the visible details of your illustration on screen more or less as they will print. Figure 3-6 shows an example.

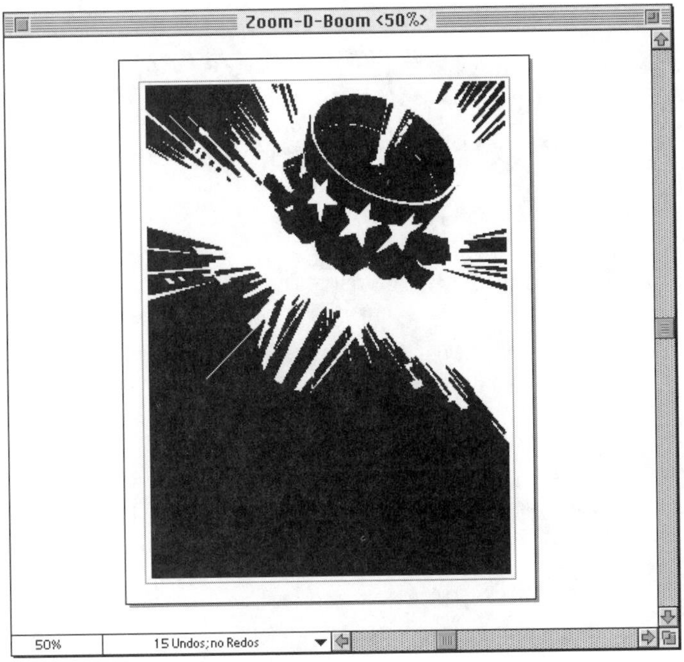

Figure 3-5:
A typical illustration viewed from far away at fit-in-window size.

NOTE

Actual size is not an *exact* representation of your illustration, and even approximate accuracy assumes your monitor displays 72 pixels per inch. Many monitors can pack in more pixels, causing an illustration viewed at actual size to appear quite a bit smaller than it prints. If you want to get a truly accurate feel for how your illustration will print, then print it (as described in Chapter 18).

TIP

You can switch to actual size by choosing the View » Actual Size command or pressing ⌘-1. But your intelligent, right-minded artist is more likely to double-click on the zoom tool icon in the toolbox (the one that looks like a magnifying glass). Just remember this handy poem:

Two clicks on the glass shows you blades of grass;
Two clicks on the hand gives you lay of land.

Figure 3-6: Switch to actual size to see your illustration as it will print.

Magnifying as the Mood Hits You

You can access each of Illustrator's 23 preset view sizes using the zoom tool. Select the zoom tool and click in the illustration window to magnify your drawing to the next-higher view size. For example, when you're viewing an illustration at actual size, clicking with the zoom tool takes you to 150 percent size. Clicking again takes you to 200 percent. Each view affords greater detail but shows off less of your artwork.

Drag with the zoom tool to surround the portion of the illustration that you want to magnify with a dotted rectangle called a marquee. Illustrator zooms in until the surrounded area fills the entire screen, as demonstrated in Figure 3-7. Whereas clicking with the zoom tool lets you step through the 23 preset view sizes, the marquee takes you to the view size that most closely reflects the exact area you drag on. Notice that in the lower portion of Figure 3-7, which shows the result of dragging with the zoom tool, the size box indicates a view size of 305.15 percent. If I were to click with the zoom tool or click the Zoom In button inside the Navigator palette, the view size would step up to the next size, 400 percent.

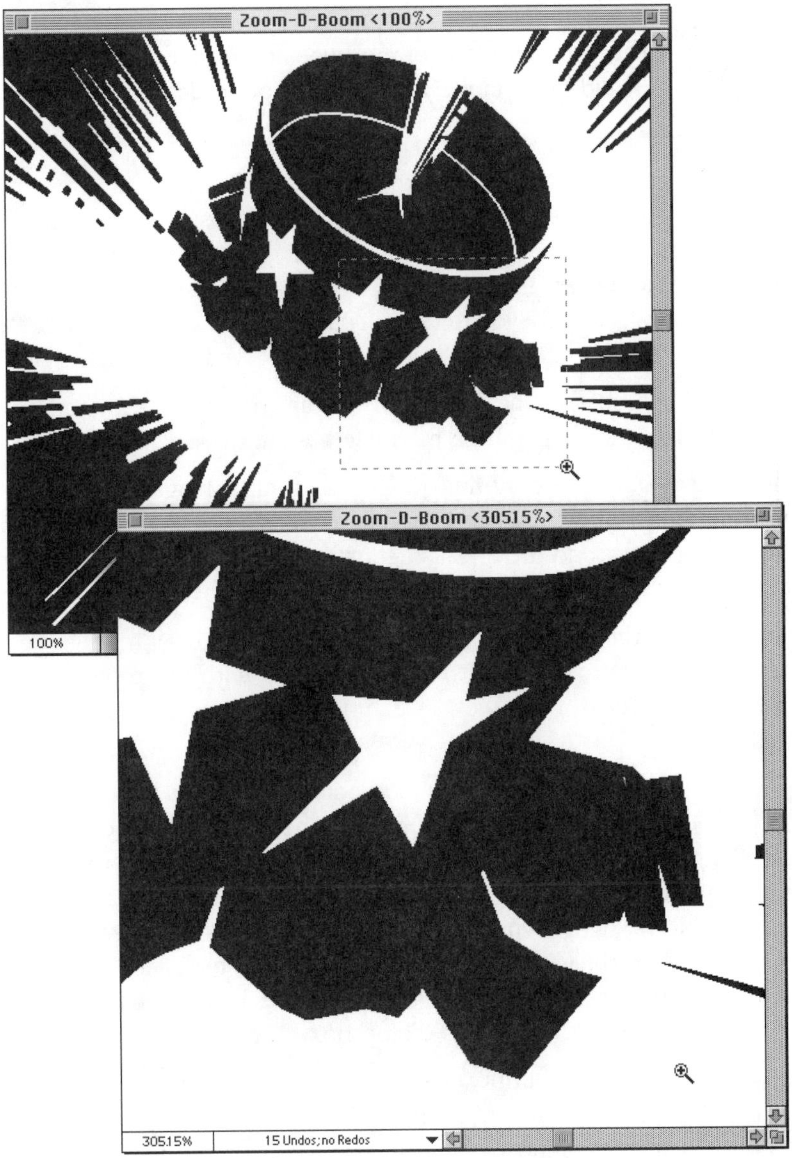

Figure 3-7: Drag with the zoom tool to surround an area with a marquee (top). Illustrator then magnifies that area to fill the window (bottom).

TIP Once you get a feel for marqueeing, try out these techniques in mid-drag to make your zooms more precise:

- Mac users can press the Control key while dragging to create your marquee from the center outward—you Windows users simply need to marquee as you normally would (depress the left button and drag with the mouse) and then, in addition, press and hold the right mouse button. (Most tools require you to Option-drag to draw out from the center; but with the zoom tool, the Option key is reserved for zooming out.)
- Press the spacebar in the middle of a drag to move the marquee. To again change the shape of the marquee, just release the spacebar.
- If you decide in mid-drag that you don't want to magnify the illustration after all, drag back to the spot where you started so the dotted marquee disappears, and then release. Illustrator knows you chickened out and leaves the view size unchanged.

When you press the Option key, the cursor displays an inset minus sign, showing you that it's all set to zoom out. Option-clicking with the zoom tool reduces the view size to the next lower view size. You can see more of your artwork but less detail.

TIP As you zoom out, you may notice text blocks turning into gray bars. This is the greeking phenomenon I alluded to in Chapter 2, which is designed to speed up screen redraw. As far as Illustrator is concerned, you can't see such small text anyway, so why bother drawing it? If you disagree, you can instruct Illustrator to display the text as tiny letters by pressing ⌘-K and lowering the Greeking Type Limit value inside the Keyboard Increments dialog box.

The zoom tool cursor is empty when your current view size is at either the maximum (6400 percent) or minimum (3.13 percent) level of magnification. At that point, you can zoom in or out no further.

TIP You can also zoom in and out using a whole mess of keyboard shortcuts:

- To access the zoom tool temporarily when some other tool is selected, press and hold the ⌘ key and spacebar. I know, it's a weird shortcut, but it's very common; PageMaker, Photoshop, and FreeHand all use it. Releasing the two keys returns the cursor to its previous appearance.
- You can also zoom in one level by pressing ⌘-+ (plus sign), the shortcut for View » Zoom In.
- Press ⌘-Option-spacebar to get the zoom out cursor. Again, all the best applications use this shortcut.
- Or zoom out by pressing ⌘-– (minus sign), which selects the View » Zoom Out command.

Zooming by the Navigation Palette

Illustrator 8 gives you a whole new way look at you document. By default, the Navigator palette displays the active illustration's entire artboard and a red rectangular *window boundary*. This window boundary represents the current display of the illustration window. As shown in Figure 3-8, the window boundary is shorter and wider than the artboard that it overlaps. This means that the corresponding illustration window shows only this portion of the artboard and a bit of the pasteboard that flanks it on either side.

The palette provides three ways to change the illustration window's view size:

- Click the zoom in button to magnify to the next larger preset view size. Click the zoom out button to reduce the view to the next smaller preset size.
- Click along the zoom slider to change the view size. Click all the way to the left to zoom in all the way to the smallest view size, 3.13 percent. Click all the way to the right to zoom out the maximum level of magnification, 6400 percent.
- Click the zoom option box and enter any value between 3.13 and 6400 to change the view size to that percent.

The Navigator palette offers a few other useful features:

- Click in the palette's window to reposition the boundary window such that it's centered on your click. Drag in the palette's window to move around the window boundary. As you drag, Illustrator will automatically update the illustration window to reflect you movements.

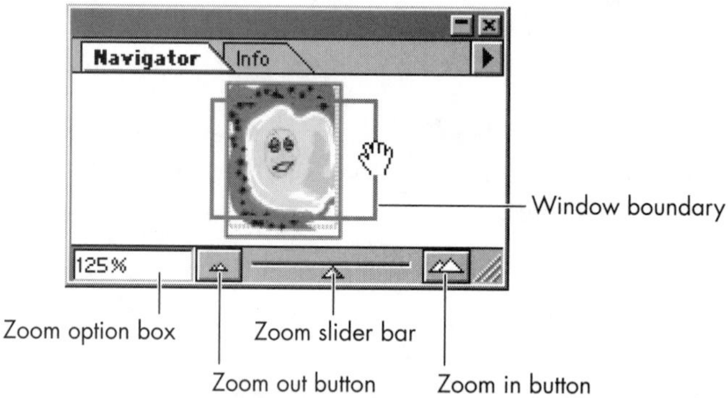

Figure 3-8: With the new Navigation palette, you can easily switch to any view size, including one of the 23 preset values. The palette also allows you to scroll quickly to any location on your pasteboard.

- Press the ⌘ key while the cursor is over the Navigator palette's window and it changes to a magnifying lens. ⌘-drag to change the size of the window boundary. This is similar to dragging with the zoom tool in the illustration window, except that the window boundary will always remain proportional to the dimensions of the illustration window.
- By default, the Navigator palette displays all the paths that will fit in its window at the current view size, including those that reside on the pasteboard outside the boundaries of the artboard. To see only those paths that appear on the artboard, choose View Artboard Only from the palette's pop-up menu. If any paths straddle the edge of the artboard, this option will truncate their appearance in the Navigator palette's window.
- Select Palette Options from the palette's pop-up window to change the color of the window boundary. You can choose from a list of predefined colors or create your own by double-clicking on the color box.

Dragging the Drawing

Since most screens aren't as large as a full page, you probably won't be able to see your entire illustration at actual size or larger. Therefore, Illustrator lets you move the artboard inside the illustration window, a technique known as *scrolling*. It's like looking through a pair of binoculars, in a way. You can see the action more clearly, but you can see only part of the action at a time. To look at something different, you have to move the binoculars (and your head) to adjust your view. This is what happens when you scroll in Illustrator.

One method for scrolling the drawing area is to use the two scroll bars, located at the bottom and right side of the window. But only saps use the scroll bars, because Illustrator provides a better tool, the hand tool.

The hand tool allows you to drag the drawing area inside the window. As you drag, the hand cursor changes to a fist to show you that you have the illustration in your viselike grip.

TIP: To access the hand tool temporarily when some other tool is selected, press and hold the spacebar. Then drag as desired. Release the spacebar to return the cursor to its previous appearance.

When a text block is active, pressing the spacebar results in a bunch of spaces. You can get around this by pressing the ⌘ key, pressing the spacebar, and then releasing the ⌘ key. As long as you keep the spacebar down, the hand tool is yours and the text block remains active.

Changing the Display Mode

Another way to control what you see on screen is to change the *display mode*—that is, how you see individual objects on screen. You can select from two basic modes in Illustrator:

- In the *preview mode*, you see objects and text in full color, more or less as they will print. (Again, Illustrator does its best with this what-you-see-is-what-you-get stuff. It's only software, after all.) Illustrator displays your drawing in the preview mode by default, and you can return to it at any time by choosing View » Preview or pressing ⌘-Y.
- If you own a slowish computer, you may grow impatient with the lethargic speed at which Illustrator draws objects on screen. To speed things up, choose View » Artwork or press ⌘-Y again. Illustrator's *artwork mode* is what other programs call a *wireframe* or *keyline* mode: text appears in black, graphic objects have thin outlines and transparent interiors, and there's not a color in sight. Figure 3-9 shows how artwork and preview modes compare.

The artwork mode is very fast, because Illustrator doesn't have to spend time displaying complicated visual effects. However, it takes some time to get used to. You basically have to imagine how the colors, strokes, gradations, and other effects are going to look. That's why most experienced artists switch back and forth between the artwork and preview modes by pressing ⌘-Y.

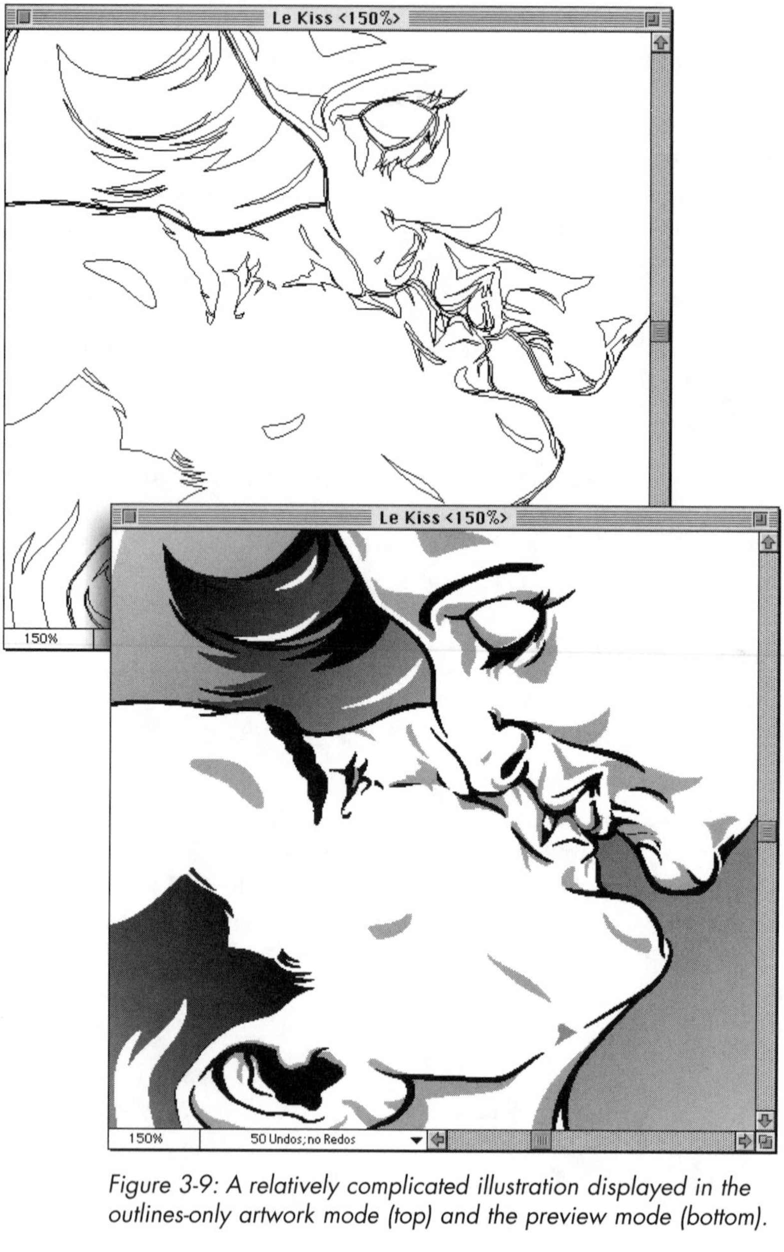

Figure 3-9: A relatively complicated illustration displayed in the outlines-only artwork mode (top) and the preview mode (bottom).

Illustrator also lets you preview some objects while viewing others as wireframes. This can be useful for gauging how objects will print without dramatically slowing down screen redraw, or for examining a few objects out of context. For example, you might want to see through a few objects to some other objects in the background.

To do this, select the objects you want to view accurately with the arrow tool, then choose View » Preview Selection or press ⌘-Shift-Y. Objects that are not selected appear as wireframes whether you start out in the artwork or preview mode. (To learn how to select objects, read the beginning of Chapter 5.)

TIP

Whether they instigated a screen preview using the Preview or Preview Selection command, Macintosh folks can cancel one that's taking too long by pressing ⌘-period. Illustrator immediately returns you to the artwork mode.

Creating a View You Can Come Back To

Do you find yourself switching back and forth between two or three views over and over again? First you zoom in on an individual leaf in a tree, then you scroll down and zoom out a little to examine the trunk, and next you zoom out two or three increments to take in the whole tree. Then you magnify the leaf again and start the process over. This kind of zooming and scrolling back and forth between key locations in your illustration can eat up all kinds of valuable drawing time.

Luckily, Illustrator has a solution. You can save specific views of your illustration and then return to them at the press of a key. When you choose View » New View, Illustrator asks you to name the current view of your illustration. Enter a name and press the Return key. Illustrator saves the view size, the relative location of the page in the illustration window, and even the display mode.

Illustrator appends the view name to the bottom of the View menu. From now on, you can return to this exact view size, page position, and display mode just by choosing the view name or by pressing ⌘-Shift-Option along with a number. (Illustrator numbers views in the order of their creation.)

You can create more than ten views, but only the first ten are assigned keyboard shortcuts. All views are saved with the illustration and change from one illustration to the next. That is, the views saved with one drawing will not necessarily be the views that are saved with any other drawing.

To change the name of a view, or delete one or more views, choose View » Edit Views. Then select a view from the scrolling list in the Edit Views dialog box and enter a new name, or press the Delete key to get rid of it. If you want to delete many views at a time, you can Shift-click on a view name to select consecutive views or ⌘-click to select one view here and another there.

Two Windows into the Same Illustration

You can create multiple views in a single illustration by choosing Window » New Window. Illustrator doesn't create a copy of the artwork, but rather a second illustration window to track your changes. Here are a couple of ways in which this strange-seeming technique might be useful:

- Set one window to fit-in-window size and zoom in on the other so you can see some really tiny detail. Now edit the detail. It changes in both windows. It's like looking at your illustration simultaneously at normal size and through a microscope.
- You can look at two different portions of your artwork by scrolling to one location in one window and another location in the other window. This way, you can edit one object so it looks like another or make other comparative decisions without scrolling back and forth like a madman.

Once the additional window outgrows its usefulness, you can close it. Illustrator doesn't ask you to save changes, because the illustration is still open; it's just a view that you have closed.

Saving Your Work to Disk

Whenever the topic of saving files comes up, I'm always tempted to jump on a soapbox and recite broken-down slogans:

- Save your illustration early and often!
- The only safe illustration is a saved illustration!
- An untitled illustration is a recipe for disaster!
- If you're thinking of switching applications, hit ⌘-S! If you hear thunder, hit ⌘-S! If a child enters your room, hit ⌘-S!

If you see a man running down the streets screaming "⌘-S! ⌘-S! ⌘-S!" at the top of his lungs and shaking his hands in the air, you'll know that I've come to visit. I'm absolutely despotic about saving, and with good reason. In my many years of writing and creating artwork on computers, I've lost more work than I can measure, and all because I didn't save in time.

So save, for crying in a bucket. The file you lose might be your own!

Saving Versus Exporting

You may have noticed that Illustrator offers both a Save and an Export command. On first glance this may seem redundant, but there is an important difference.

Saving implies that all the information associated with an illustration created in Illustrator will show up the next time you open the file inside Illustrator. This is simply not the case with the other file formats discussed above in the "Those Crazy, Kooky File Format" section, especially those that convert your elegant line drawings to a pixeled facsimile. So to say that you can save your file in one of these formats is a bit misleading.

To correct this problem, Illustrator includes both the File » Save and the File » Export command. Saving lets you choose from only three formats (Illustrator's native format, Illustrator's EPS, and Acrobat PDF), all of which will preserve your file just as it appears on screen. Exporting a file is the same as saving a file, except that the formats you can export to are the formats that will not preserve, to some degree, the information that constitutes your illustration.

Illustrator assumes that when you use the File » Export command, you understand that you're modifying your illustration, and the program doesn't warn you about the loss of information. Other than the different formats each dialog box supports, the File » Save and File » Export commands are the same.

Using the Save Dialog Box

If the foreground image is untitled, as it is when you work on a new image, choosing File » Save or pressing ⌘-S displays the Save dialog box, shown in Figure 3-10. This is Illustrator's way of encouraging you to name the illustration, specify its location on disk, and select a file format. After you save the illustration once, choosing the Save command updates the file on disk without bringing up the Save dialog box.

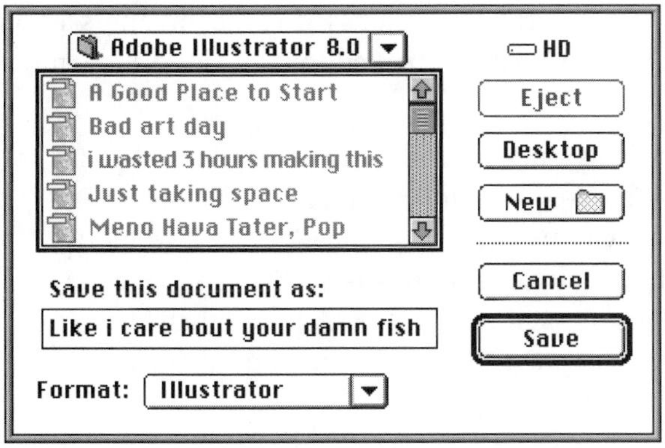

Figure 3-10: The Save dialog box lets you save a document from the current application.

Choose File » Save As or press ⌘-Shift-S to change the name, location, or format of the illustration. Choosing the Save As command always brings up the Save dialog box.

The Save dialog box is very much like the Open dialog box, with a few exceptions. For example, when you first display the Save dialog box, the option box in the lower left corner is active. Here's where you enter a name for the drawing, up to 31 characters long.

If you click on the scrolling list or press the Tab key, you activate the scrolling list and deactivate the option box. You can then scroll through document and folder names by pressing keys from the keyboard. To reactivate the file name, press Tab again.

The navigation buttons—Eject, Desktop, and Cancel—work just like their counterparts in the Open dialog box. But two buttons are unique to the Save dialog box:

- **New Folder (⌘-N):** Clicking on this button creates a new folder inside the current folder. The system software displays an alert box asking you to name the prospective folder.
- **Save (⌘-S):** This button saves the drawing to disk. If you haven't entered a file name, the Save button is dimmed. If you activate the scrolling list and select a folder, the Save button temporarily changes to an Open button. To access the Save button again, press Tab to deactivate the scrolling list. You can also select the Save button by pressing the Return or Enter key.

Selecting a File Format

The last option in either the Save or the Export dialog box is the Format pop-up menu. This option lets you specify the file format you want to use to preserve your illustration. These are the same formats I discussed earlier in the section "Those Crazy, Kooky File Formats," but I feel compelled to pass along a few more tidbits of wisdom:

- The only safe formats—the only ones that save every shred of information in your illustration—are native Illustrator and Illustrator EPS. These formats even save the window size, magnification level, scrolling, and display mode, and they include thumbnails so that you can preview the file inside Illustrator's Open dialog box. All the other formats sacrifice or reorganize objects in ways that make them more difficult or even impossible to edit.
- Use one of the older Illustrator formats to make an illustration compatible with a previous version of Illustrator or with a drawing program that supports only old Illustrator formats. FreeHand 5, for example,

supports the Illustrator 5 format, but not Illustrator 6. FreeHand 4 supports Illustrator 3, but nothing later.

- Adobe is trying like crazy to promote the Acrobat PDF format, so it's only natural that Illustrator permits you to export your drawing in this format. Theoretically, it allows you to share the drawing with other folks who could view it on their screens without owning Illustrator or some other graphics application. But Acrobat isn't quite as pervasive as Adobe would like you to believe, so it's unlikely you'll ever want to use PDF.

WARNING: If you save an illustration in any format other than Illustrator 8 or Illustrator EPS, make sure you have created a backup version of the illustration first in the Illustrator 8 format! (You can do this by choosing File » Save or File » Save As.) Otherwise, you are needlessly and deliberately throwing away some amount of your hard work.

Saving an EPS Illustration

To use an illustration in PageMaker or QuarkXPress, select Illustrator EPS from the Format pop-up menu. After you click on the Save button or press Return, Illustrator displays the EPS Format dialog box depicted in lifelike detail in Figure 3-11. You can probably figure out the majority of these options on your own, but I might as well run through them, if only to eliminate all possible confusion.

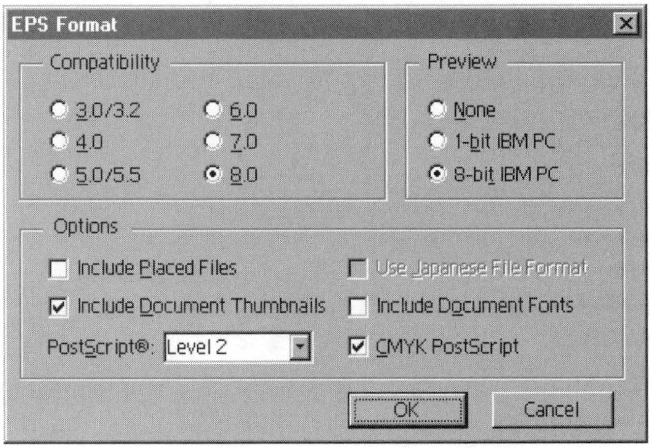

Figure 3-11: Illustrator presents you with a world of options when you're saving an EPS file.

- **Compatibility:** These radio buttons are identical to the different Illustrator formats I discussed earlier. The basic deal is this: Previous versions of Illustrator can't read an Illustrator 8 EPS file unless you select the option that corresponds to its version number. If you don't care about previous versions of Illustrator, leave the 8.0 option selected so you don't lose anything.

- **Preview:** These options control the PICT screen preview that Illustrator attaches to an EPS file. Unless the program that you want to import the illustration into doesn't support color, leave the 8-Bit Macintosh (or the 8-Bit IBM PC) option selected.
- **Include Placed Files:** This check box is usually dimmed. It's available only if you placed an EPS image or illustration, as discussed back in the "Encapsulated PostScript (EPS)" section. When checked, this option includes placed EPS code in the new EPS file. To bag the code, turn this check box off. (Frankly, I can think of no reason on earth why you'd want to do this.)
- **Include Document Thumbnails:** Always select this check box. It creates a thumbnail of the illustration so you can preview it from the Open dialog box inside Illustrator, Photoshop, and an increasing number of other programs.
- **Use Japanese File Format:** Before version 6, there was the Illustrator that we knew and loved here in America, and there was the Illustrator equally loved in Japan. If you wished to construct a drawing for your friends in the land of the rising sun, you had to save it in the Japanese format (you still do if your friend is using a version of Illustrator older than 6). This is not the case for present day Illustrator, since now the Illustrator format is universal.
- **Include Document Fonts:** If you use a font in your illustration that you're not sure is as popular with your audience as it is with you, check this option. The file will be a bit larger (depending on the size of the font file), but you ensure that your document will appear with the font you intended.
- **CMYK PostScript:** With this option selected, Illustrator will automatically convert the document's colors to their CMYK equivalents as needed.

In most cases, you can ignore this dialog box and just press the Return key to tell Illustrator to do its stuff. The default settings ensure there's no loss of illustration integrity even if you aren't paying a lick of attention to what you're doing. It's the kind of service any decent program is all too happy to perform.

PART TWO
CREATING

CHAPTER 4

DRAWING THE SIMPLE STUFF

Heaven help the experienced artist who encounters Illustrator for the first time. If you've drawn with pencil and paper, or sketched inside a painting program such as Photoshop, but you've never used Illustrator before, now is a good time to open your skull, remove your brain, and replace it upside down. Drawing with an illustration program is a very different adventure, and though it pains me to say it, your previous experience is as likely to impede your progress as to expedite it.

Drawing in Illustrator is actually a three-part process: You draw lines and shapes, you manipulate these objects and apply special effects, and you stack the objects one in front of another like pieces of paper in a collage.

This means the lines and shapes are forever flexible. You can select any object and edit, duplicate, or delete it, regardless of its age or location in the illustration. I'm still playing around with drawings I created ten years ago, and every object responds exactly as it did the day I drew it. Pencil and paper does not give you this degree of control.

But Illustrator's flexibility comes at a price. It takes a lot of time and a fair amount of object-oriented savvy to create even basic compositions. There are no two ways about it—Illustrator is harder to learn and more cumbersome to use than conventional artists' tools.

In this chapter, I'll explain how to use Illustrator's most straightforward drawing tools. If you're feeling a little timid—particularly after my pessimistic introduction—have no fear. With this chapter in front of you, you'll be up and running within the hour. If you're the type who prefers to dive right in and investigate basic functions on your own, you can discover how these tools work, largely without my help. For you, I explain options, suggest keyboard tricks, and point out small performance details that many novice and intermediate users overlook.

But before I start, I want to take a few brief paragraphs to explain how lines and shapes work inside Illustrator. You'll better understand how drawing tools work if you first understand what you're drawing.

Everything You Need to Know about Paths

Any line or shape you create in Illustrator is called a *path*. (That way, you don't have to say "lines or shapes" all the time; the one word comprises both.) Conceptually, a path is the same as a line drawn with a pencil. A path may start at one location and end at another, as in the case of an open line. Or it may meet back up with itself to form a closed shape. Paths can range in length and complexity from tiny scratch marks to elaborate curlicues that loop around and intersect like tracks on a roller coaster.

The cartoon face in Figure 4-1 contains 12 paths. Of the paths, 10 are open (lines) and 2 are closed (shapes). So that you can clearly distinguish open from closed, I've given the lines thick outlines and the shapes thin ones. The closed paths surround the face, with the white shape mostly covering the gray one. The open paths represent the face's features.

Figure 4-1: A simple cartoon composed of open paths (thick outlines) and closed ones (thin).

All paths—whether open or closed—are made up of basic building blocks called *anchor points* (or just plain *points*). The simplest line is a connection between two anchor points—one at each end. (Anyone familiar with a little geometry will recognize this principle: a minimum of two points are needed to define a line.) But Illustrator can just as easily accommodate paths with hundreds of points, one connected to another like dots in a dot-to-dot puzzle.

Points and Segments

Figure 4-2 shows the points required to create the cartoon face. I've applied thinner outlines to the lines and made the shapes transparent so you can better see the square points. The most complicated path contains 11 points; the least complicated contains two.

The bits of line between points are called *segments*. A segment can be straight, as if it were drawn against the edge of a ruler. A straight segment flows directly from one point to another in any direction. A segment may also curve, like the outline of an ellipse. Curved segments connect two points in an indirect manner, bending inward or outward along the way.

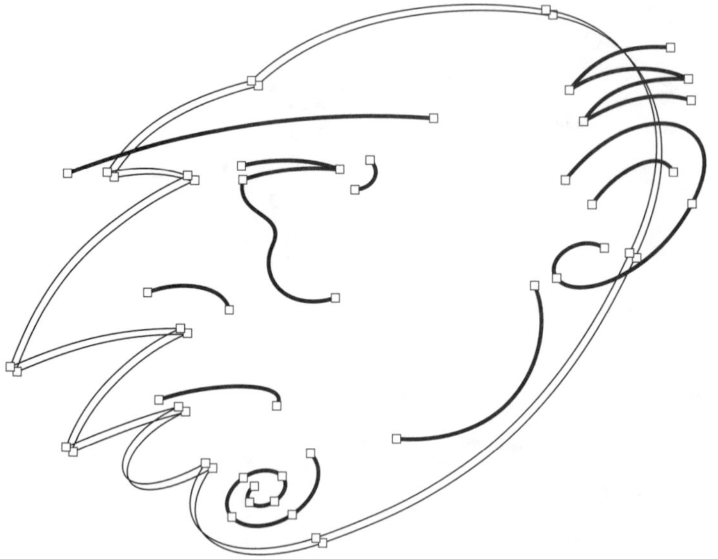

Figure 4-2: The small white squares represent the points needed to create the cartoon in Illustrator.

Strokes and Fills

Although a line drawn with a dull pencil is heavier than a line drawn with a sharpened one, the thickness of any line fluctuates depending on how hard you press the pencil tip to the page. In Illustrator, the thickness (or *weight*) of an outline is absolutely consistent throughout the course of a path. In other words, different paths can have different weights, but the weight of each path is constant (as Figure 4-1 shows).

The thickness of an outline is called the *stroke*. In addition to changing the weight of the stroke, you can change its color. Strokes can be black, white, gray, or any of several million colorful variations.

You can also color the interior of a path by assigning it a *fill*. Like a stroke, a fill may be black, white, or any color. In Figure 4-1, the shapes that encircle the face are filled with white and gray. You can even assign a transparent fill, as in the case of the shapes in Figure 4-2.

Seeing What You Draw

I explore strokes and fills in amazing detail (if I do say so myself) in Chapters 15 through 18. But because these two attributes are so important to the way you see paths on screen, I need to impart a bit of basic info in the meantime. Here's the problem: By default, Illustrator applies white fills and black strokes to each path you draw. Although this is a great improvement over the default colors of previous Illustrators (in which fills were black and strokes were transparent), the white fill can be a hindrance if you're not careful about the order in which you stack your objects.

There are two solutions, either of which is acceptable:

- Switch to the artwork mode by pressing ⌘-Y (or choosing View » Artwork). The fills disappear and the strokes become black hairlines.
- Change the fill to transparent and—if necessary—the stroke to black in the toolbox. If you haven't changed the stroke color from the default black, you needn't worry about the first step.

To change the fill and stroke, follow these steps:

1. Return Illustrator to its default colors by clicking on the Default Color button in the toolbox or by pressing the D key.
2. To assign a transparent fill, click on the Fill icon or press the ⌘ key if the Stroke icon overlaps the Fill icon. Then click on the None paint style button—the one with the red diagonal line—or press the / (forward slash) key.

Figure 4-3 shows how the toolbox should look when you've finished modifying the fill and stroke settings. These settings will affect every path you draw until the next time you change the fill or stroke.

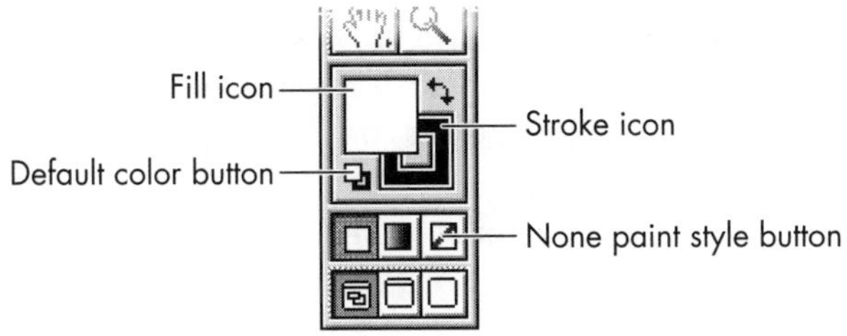

Figure 4-3: To best experiment inside Illustrator, change the fill to transparent and the stroke to black.

The Simplest of Simple Shapes

Illustrator offers three tools for creating rectangles and ellipses. The standard rectangle and ellipse tools appear by default in the third row from the top of the toolbox. The rounded rectangle is the alternative tool in the rectangle tool slot. You select it by clicking and holding on the rectangle tool slot, as shown in Figure 4-4. Now simply drag to the right until the rounded rectangle tool is highlighted.

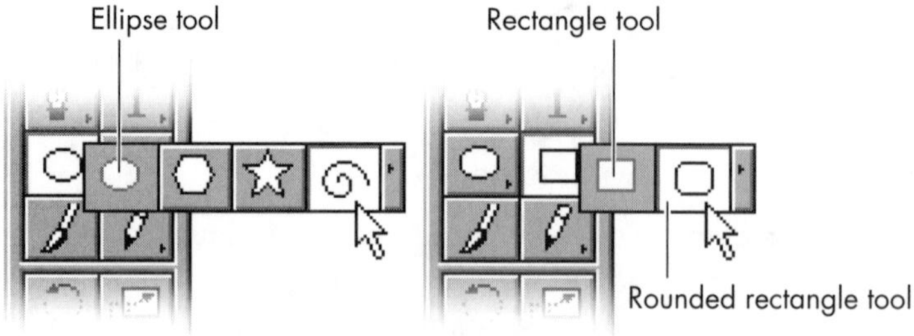

Figure 4-4: Illustrator 8 offers only three basic shape tools, having shed the archaic and superfluous basic shape tools of ye olde Illustrator 7.

Illustrator previously had three additional basic shape tools: the centered ellipse, the centered rounded rectangle, and the centered rectangle tools. These tools appeared as alternative tools in either the ellipse or the rectangle tool slots. They allowed you to draw the respective shapes from the center outward instead of from corner-to-corner as the non-centered basic shape tools do. But, as it turns out, the ellipse, the rectangle, and the rounded rectangle tools were capable (and still are) of drawing their shapes from the center outward provided you held the Option key while drawing with them. Since the centered basic shape tools didn't provided any additional functionality, they no longer appear as independent tools in Illustrator.

Drawing a Rectangle

To draw a rectangle, select the rectangle tool and drag inside the drawing area. The point at which you start dragging sets one corner of the rectangle; the point at which you release sets the opposite corner, as shown in Figure 4-5. The two remaining corners line up vertically or horizontally with their neighbors.

Illustrator creates a fifth point called the *center point* in the center of the shape. This special point floats free of the shape; it is not connected to any other point by a segment. If you move the rectangle, change its size, or completely mess it up, Illustrator repositions the center point so it remains in the center of the shape. You can use the center point to align the rectangle to another shape; I explain how to take advantage of this feature in Chapter 10.

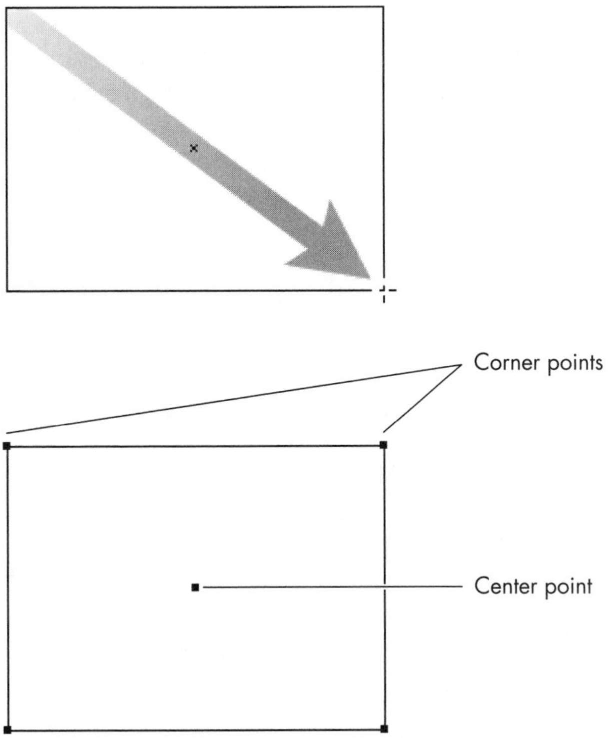

Figure 4-5: Drag from one corner to the opposite corner to draw a rectangle.

TIP: In the preview mode, you can see the center point only when the rectangle is selected. To see the center point of a deselected rectangle, switch to the artwork mode by pressing ⌘-Y.

You can also use the rectangle tool as follows:

- If you press the Option key while drawing with the rectangle tool, the beginning of your drag marks the center of the rectangle. As before, the release point becomes a corner point.

TIP: You can press and release Option in mid-drag to switch between dragging from corner to corner and from center to corner. Give it a try.

- Shift-drag with the rectangle tool to draw a perfect square. You can press and release the Shift key in mid-drag to switch between drawing a rectangle or a square. Isn't it great how Illustrator lets you change your mind?
- Shift-Option-dragging with the rectangle tool creates a square from center to corner.
- Press the tilde (~) key while dragging with the rectangle tool to create a series of rectangles, all of which border on a common point. Press Option-~ while you drag to create a series of concentric rectangles.
- Press the spacebar while dragging to move the rectangle rather than change its size. When you get it positioned properly, release the spacebar and continue dragging or release.

Drawing by the Numbers

You can also enter the dimensions of a rectangle numerically. Click with the rectangle tool—that's right, just click inside the drawing area—to display the dialog box shown in Figure 4-6. Here you can enter values for the Width and Height options. After you press Return or click on OK, Illustrator creates a rectangle to your exact specifications.

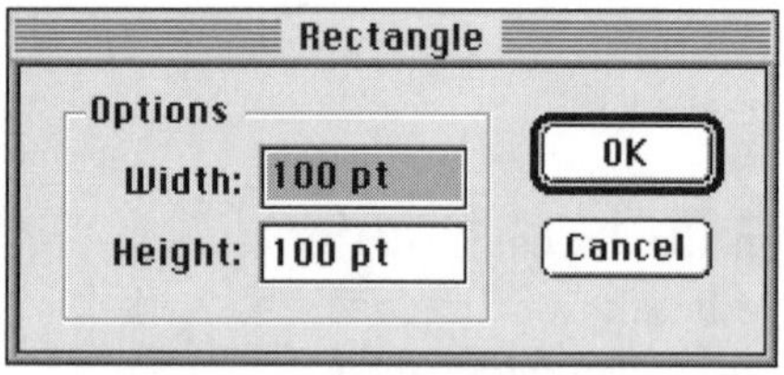

Figure 4-6: Click with any rectangle tool to enter the exact width and height of your rectangle.

TIP: Want to create a square? You could enter the same value in both option boxes, but that's frankly too much effort. Just enter the desired size into the Width option box, then click on the word Height to duplicate the value. You can likewise duplicate the Height value by clicking on the word Width.

TIP: Since the Rectangle dialog box doesn't give any placement options, the point at which you clicked with the tool serves as the upper left corner point of the shape. If you want the click point to be the center of the shape, Option-click.

Notice that both option boxes in Figure 4-6 includes the letters *pt*, an abbreviation for points ($1/72$ inch). This refers to the unit of measure you set using the General Units option in the Units & Undo dialog box. The unit of measure can alternatively be inches (*in*) or millimeters (*mm*).

TIP: If you don't like the current unit of measure, enter your own abbreviation. For example, by entering *2in* into the Width option box, you create a rectangle 2 inches wide, regardless of the active unit of measure. Illustrator automatically converts the measurement to the unit of measure (2 inches converts to 144 points) when you tab to the next option box. To enter a value in picas, enter the value followed by *p* and then the points. For example, *2p3* means 2 picas and 3 points, or 27 points.

You can enter spaces between the number and the measurement abbreviation, but you don't have to. If you enter a value without an abbreviation, Illustrator assumes the active unit of measurement—points by default.

The exception to this is when you have selected picas for the General Units option and then elected to activate the Numbers Without Units Are Points checkbox—also found within the Units & Undo dialog box. Illustrator will then assume that any numbers you enter into the Rectangle dialog box (or any other dialog box for that matter) should be interpreted as points and not as picas.

You can use the Rectangle dialog box only to create new shapes. If you want to change the size of a rectangle you've already drawn, you have a number of different options (all of which Chapter 11 discusses). One such option is to use Illustrator's Transform palette (shown in Figure 4-7). Make sure the rectangle is selected so that its points are visible. (Use the arrow tool to click on the shape if it is not selected.) Then, if the Transform palette is hidden, choose Window » Show Transform. Next, enter new values in the W and H option boxes. Illustrator will update your rectangle automatically.

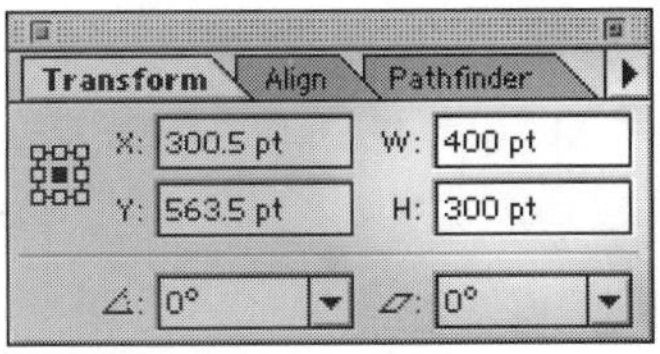

Figure 4-7: You can now change the dimensions of an existing rectangle by modifying the W and H values in the Transform palette.

Rounding Off a Rectangle's Corners

To draw a rectangle with rounded corners, select the rounded rectangle tool from the rectangle tool slot and drag away. Illustrator creates a shape with eight points—two along each side with a curved segment around each corner—as in Figure 4-8.

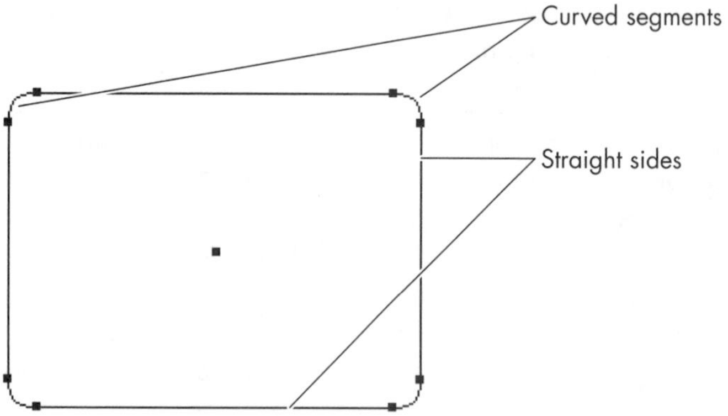

Figure 4-8: Illustrator uses curved segments to join straight sides in a rounded rectangle.

You can change the roundness of a rectangle's corners in one of three ways:

- Change the Corner Radius value in the General Preferences dialog box.
- Click with the rounded rectangle tool and enter a value into the Corner Radius option box.
- While drawing with the tool, press one of the arrow keys. Press ↑ or press ↓ to increase or decrease the rectangle's corner radius by one point. Press → to change the corner radius to 0 points. Press ← to set the corner radius to half of the rectangle's shorter side.

NOTE: In each case, you change the roundness of all future rectangles. There is presently no way to change the roundness of an existing rectangle, except to edit it by hand. (Honestly, in its 12 years, you'd think Illustrator would have resolved this problem!)

Just how does the Corner Radius value work? Well, as you may recall from your school days, the *radius* is the distance from the center of a circle to any point on its outline. You can think of a rounded corner as being one quarter of a circle, as shown in the first example of Figure 4-9.

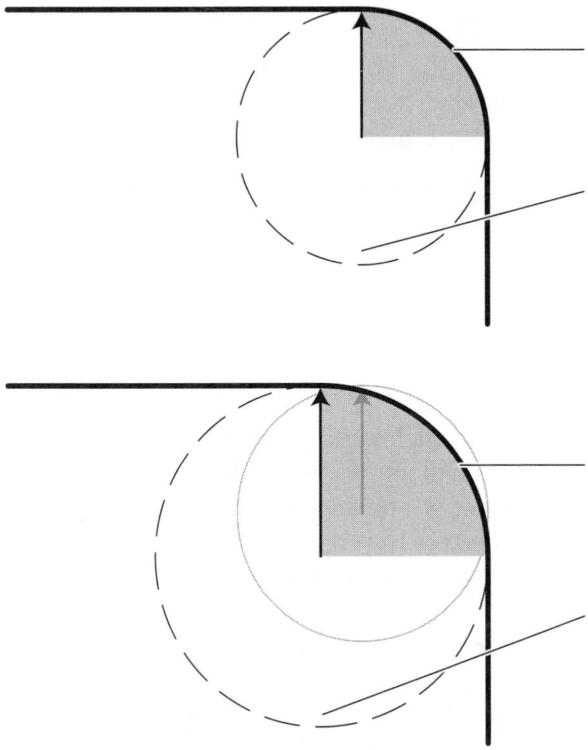

Figure 4-9: A small corner radius (top) results in a less pronounced rounding effect than a larger radius (bottom).

The size of the circle increases as the radius increases, so a large Corner Radius value rounds off the corners of a rectangle more dramatically than a smaller value. To demonstrate this idea, the second example in Figure 4-9 shows the result of increasing the radius. I've included a grayed version of the radius from the first example for comparison.

A corner radius of 0 indicates a sharp, perpendicular corner. If you click with the rounded rectangle tool and enter a Corner Radius of 0, Illustrator will create a square-cornered rectangle.

Other than the rounded nature of the rounded rectangle toll, it behaves just like the rectangle tool:

- Press the Option key while drawing with the rounded rectangle tool to draw a rounded rectangle from the center outward.
- Shift-drag with the rectangle tool to draw a rounded square.

- Shift-Option-drag with the rounded rectangle tool to create a rounded square from center to corner.
- Press either the Shift or Option key while saying "rounded rectangle" ten times quickly to produce severe tongue cramps.
- Use the tilde (~) key to form a series of rounded rectangles or press Option-~ to form a series of concentric rounded rectangles.
- Use the spacebar while drawing with the rounded rectangle to reposition the rounded rectangle without resizing it.

Drawing an Ellipse

When it comes to drawing ellipses and circles, the ellipse tool is the one for the job. Simply click and drag to form graceful and sublime rings of drawing excellence. Nothing could be more perfect—nothing, that is, except for the perfectly misguided way that the behavior of this tool has changed in Illustrator 8.

In past versions of Illustrator, when you drew an ellipse, you changed the size and shape of the ellipse directly as you dragged with the ellipse tool. In other words, the points at which you started and released your drag were opposite points along the arc of the shape, as the top example of Figure 4-10 illustrates. Imagine that the dotted rectangle forms the boundary inside the drag.

NEW 8

Now when you draw with the ellipse tool, you begin and end your drag well outside the ellipse you create. The bottom example of Figure 4-10 shows how the ellipse tool now works in Illustrator. In this case, the shape fits inside the rectangular boundary of your drag. The upper left corner of the rectangle marks the initial drag point. The drag ends at the bottom right corner of the rectangle.

Why the change? I can only guess that Adobe figured, since almost every other major application that provides ellipse-making capabilities (including FreeHand, Photoshop, Word, and PageMaker) employs this method of creation, Illustrator might as well toe the line. It's somewhat disappointing that Adobe has opted to make this change. After all, the old approach made a more efficient tracing tool. Sure, some new users found the tool's behavior a bit confusing initially, but most came around to view it as the more reasonable technique. Tracing an elliptical or circular template shape used to be a simple matter of dragging from the middle of one arc to the middle of the opposite arc. There is considerable less guesswork this way, since you begin and end your drag on portions of the template shape. With the new implementation, you must estimate where the vertical and horizontal extremes of the ellipse intersect.

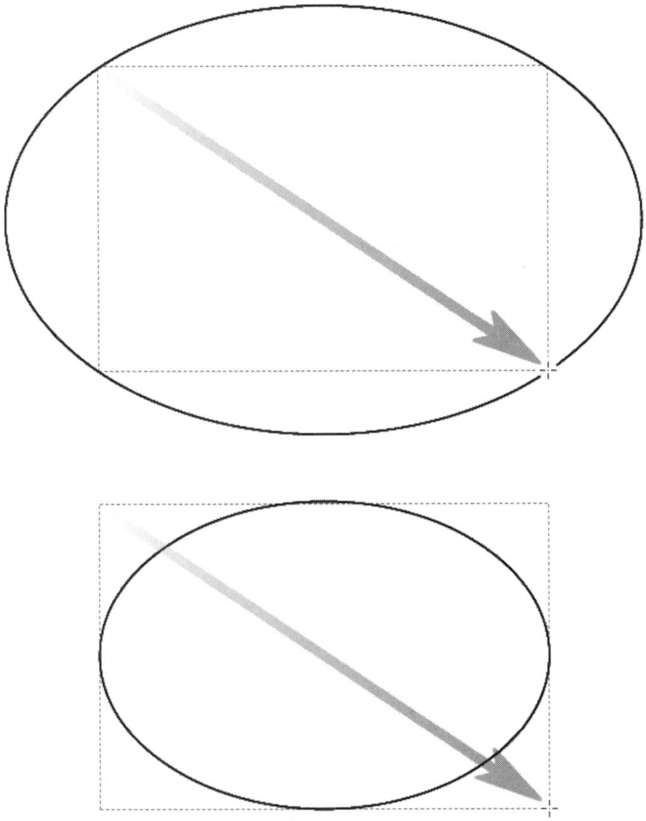

Figure 4-10: In Illustrator 7, you created an ellipse by dragging from arc to opposite arc (top). With the Illustrator 8 default method, you create an ellipse by defining the area that bounds its outer limits (bottom).

On the bright side, creating an ellipse in the Illustrator 7 fashion is still an option: Start your ellipse as you would normally—by dragging with the tool. Once you're into the drag, press the ⌘ key. The ellipse will resize in accordance. Be sure to hold the ⌘ key through the completion of the drag.

Personally, I'd have made the new corner-to-corner method for ellipse creation the alternative way (the one requiring use of the ⌘ key) and left the old arc-to-arc standby as the default choice. Or, better yet, why not make this choice a preference setting?

In most other respects, the ellipse tool works much like the rectangle tool:

- Option-drag with the ellipse tool to create an ellipse outward from the center. As always, the release point becomes the middle of an arc, determining the size and shape of the ellipse.

- Shift-drag to draw a perfect circle. Shift-Option-drag to draw a circle from the center point outward.
- Press the tilde (~) key while dragging with the ellipse tool to create a series of ellipses. Press Option-~ while you drag to create a series of concentric ellipses.
- Press the spacebar while dragging to move the ellipse rather than change its size. When you get it positioned properly, release the spacebar and continue dragging or release.
- Click in the drawing area to bring up the Ellipse dialog box. It contains Width and Height options for specifying the width and height of the shape. The shape aligns to your click point by the middle of the upper left arc. If you Option-click with the ellipse tool, the ellipse aligns by its center.
- Use the W and H values in the Transform palette to change the width and height of an ellipse that you've already drawn.

Simple Shapes at an Angle

When drawing a shape with the rectangle or ellipse tool, you may find that your path rotates at an odd angle, as demonstrated in Figure 4-11. Don't worry, you aren't misusing the tool and Illustrator isn't broken. Someone has gone and changed the Constrain Angle value in the General Preferences dialog box.

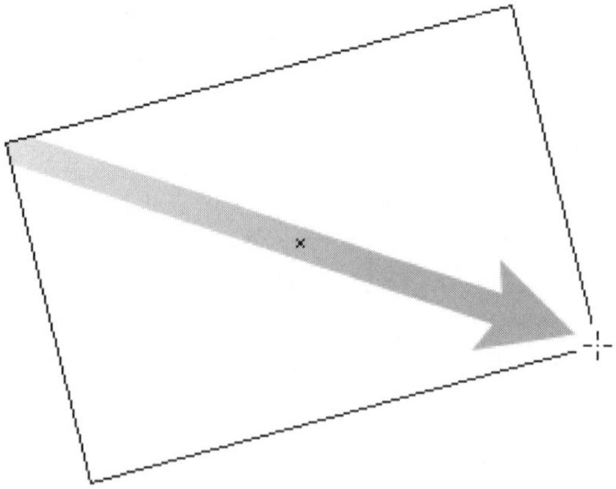

Figure 4-11: The result of drawing a rectangle after rotating the constraint axes by 15 degrees.

The *constraint axes* control the angles at which you move and transform objects when pressing the Shift key. But they also control the creation of rectangles, ellipses, and text blocks. If the Constrain Angle value is set to anything besides 0,

Illustrator rotates a rectangle or an ellipse to that angle as you draw. The Constrain Angle value has no impact on the creation of stars, polygons, or spirals whatsoever—even if you hold down the Shift key while drawing one of these shapes, they will still align to the horizontal despite the option box's value.

If someone has indeed reset your Constrain Angle, press ⌘-K (or choose File » Preferences » General). Enter 0 into the Constrain Angle option box and press Return.

Polygons, Stars, and Spirals

Illustrator offers three tools that let you draw polygons, stars, and spirals by dragging in the drawing area. The new functions still leave a thing or two to be desired, particularly when it comes time to edit the paths (for example, you can't automatically change the number of points assigned to a star after you create it). All three of these tools are alternates in the ellipse tool slot.

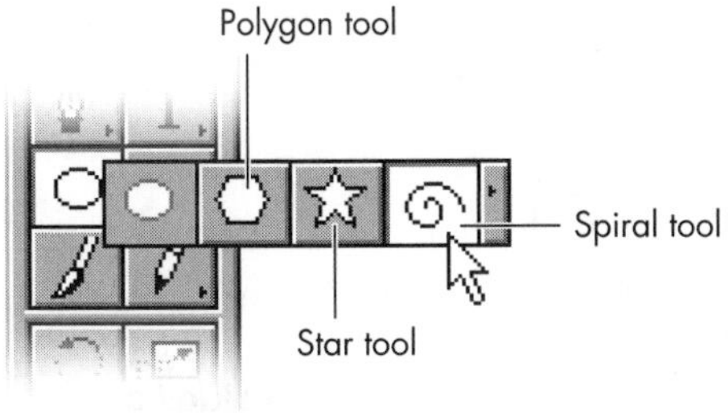

Figure 4-12: Illustrator offers three tools for drawing polygons, stars, and spirals.

Drawing a Regular Polygon

A regular polygon is a shape with multiple straight sides—each side is identical in length and meets its neighbors at the same angle. An equilateral triangle is a regular polygon, as is a square. Other examples include pentagons, hexagons, octagons, and just about any other shape with a *gon* in its name. Figure 4-13 shows a few regular polygons for your visual edification.

To draw a polygon, select the polygon tool and drag in the drawing area. You always draw a polygon from the middle outward, whether you press the Option key or not (so there's no point in pressing Option). The direction of your drag determines the orientation of the shape.

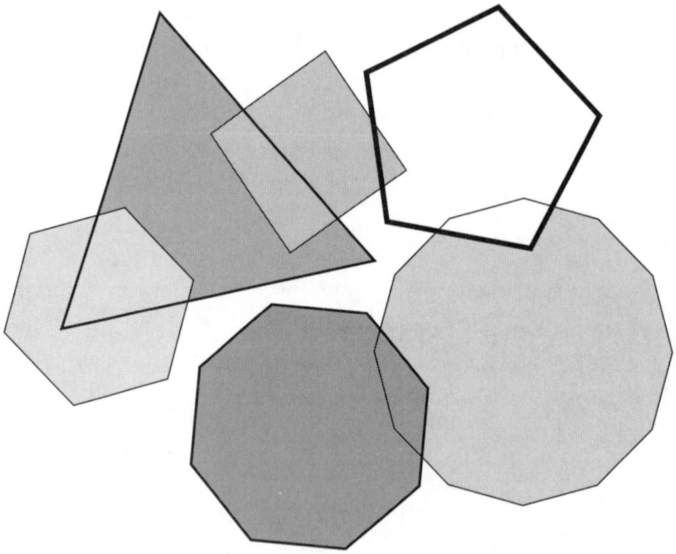

Figure 4-13: A whole mess of regular polygons, ranging from 3 to 12 sides.

By default, Illustrator draws hexagons (six-sided shapes) with the polygon tool. You can change the number of sides while dragging with the polygon tool by pressing the up and down arrow keys. The up arrow key adds a side; the down arrow key deletes one. You can also add or delete many sides at a time by holding down the arrow key.

Another way to change the number of sides is to click with the polygon tool in the drawing area. Illustrator displays the Polygon dialog box, which lets you specify a Radius value and a number of sides.

- The Radius value is the distance from the center of the shape to any corner point in the shape. Therefore, a regular polygon with a radius of 100 points would fit entirely inside a circle with a radius of 100 points.
- You can enter any number of sides from 3 to 1000. Shapes with more than 20 sides tend to look like circles with bumps.

As always, the values you enter into the Polygon dialog box affect all future polygons you create. You cannot make changes to an existing polygon using the Polygon dialog box. If you want to change the size of a polygon, use the scale tool, as discussed in Chapter 11. To change the orientation of a polygon, use the rotate tool, also covered in Chapter 11. But if you want to change the number of sides, you have to delete the polygon and redraw it.

TIP: Here are a few more (marginally useful) things you can do with the polygon tool:

- Shift-drag with the tool to constrain a polygon's orientation so the bottom side is horizontal. (This is the same way Illustrator draws a shape when you click with the polygon tool.)
- Press the spacebar while dragging to move the shape rather than change its size. When you get the polygon positioned properly, release the spacebar and continue dragging or release.
- Press the tilde (~) key while dragging to create a series of concentric polygons. This is a singularly bizarre technique. It's great for getting oohs and ahs from your friends, but it's rarely practical.

Drawing a Star

Illustrator lets you draw regular stars, in which each spike looks just like its neighbors. To draw a star, drag with the star tool, which is the fourth alternative tool in the ellipse tool slot. Illustrator draws the shape from the center outward.

You can modify the performance of the star tool by pressing the ⌘ and Option keys. But to explain adequately what you're doing, I need to conduct another small geometry lesson. A star is made up of two sets of points, one at the points where the spikes meet and one at the tips of the spikes. These points revolve around one of two circles, which form the inner and outer radiuses of the star, as pictured in Figure 4-14.

NOTE: Radius is one of those darn *us* words that doesn't sound right when you make it plural. Scholarly folks who wear mortarboards prefer the Latin *radii*, in which you pronounce one *i* as *long e* and the next as *long i*. Most editors go with *radiuses*, which sounds vaguely pejorative. I'd just as soon avoid talking about more than one radius at a time, but this inner and outer thing really forces my hand.

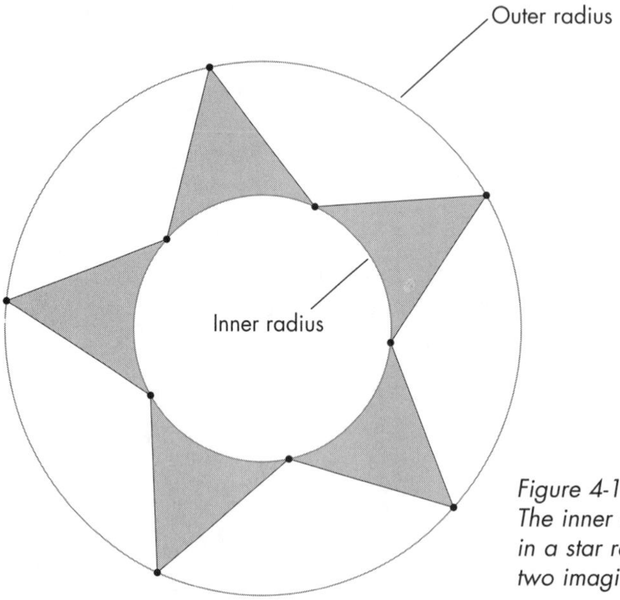

Figure 4-14: The inner and outer points in a star revolve around two imaginary circles.

When you drag with the star tool, Illustrator scales the two radiuses proportionately, so that the inner radius is exactly half the outer radius (as in Figure 4-14). If you don't like this particular arrangement, you can gain more control in the following ways:

- Press ⌘ while dragging to scale the outer radius independently of the inner radius. So long as the ⌘ key is down, the inner radius remains fixed. You can even drag the outer radius inside the inner radius to make the outer radius the inner radius. Then you can adjust the inner radius while the outer one is fixed. To resize both radiuses proportionally again, release ⌘ and keep dragging.

Say you used the ⌘ key in conjunction with the polygon tool and went way too far with the outer radius, so that you could draw only stars consisting of a number of spindly arms emerging from the center. You would probably have a heck of a time correcting this problem with just the ⌘ key. Here's the solution: Click and drag with the polygon tool. While dragging, tap both the ⌘ key and the Option key simultaneously. The star will return to a more regular shape.

- Option-drag to snap the inner radius into precise alignment so that opposite spikes align with each other. The top sides of the left and right sides of a five-sided star, for example, form a straight line.
- Because ⌘ and Option have mutually exclusive effects on a star, they cannot be in effect at the same time. If you do hold down both the ⌘ and Option keys, Option takes precedent.

TIP As with the polygon tool, you can add or delete spikes from a star by pressing the up or down arrow key in mid-drag. You can also move a star in progress by pressing the spacebar or orient the star upright by pressing Shift. And—lest I forget the least important tip of all—you can press the tilde (~) key to create concentric stars.

Probably the funkiest of all the hidden tool tips is that in addition to creating the regular star, the star tool lets you draw a double star; a star-within-a-star—not that there's a huge demand for such a shape, but it is an interesting variation on the traditional star.

To draw a double-star, here's what you need to do:

1. Drag with the star tool and hold down the mouse button throughout these steps.
2. Press the ↓ key until you have a three-sided star, the least number of sides permitted.
3. Tap both the ⌘ and Option keys.
4. Press the ↑ key until you've reached the desired number of sides. Once you're at four sides, you'll see the double star configuration.
5. Adjust the double star's size, placement, and orientation as you would a regular star's—with the ⌘ key, Shift key, and spacebar, respectively.

To take full advantage of its duality, be sure to press the ⌘ key while you're drawing a double star. This allows you to vary the size of one star independently of the other. Once you've drawn a double star, add a fill (with the aid of the Color palette), and try applying either the Intersect or Exclude filter. Both of these are part of the Pathfinder palette (which Chapter 11 explores fully). If you tire of the double star configuration and wish to return to drawing more traditional ones, you simply need to tap both the ⌘ and Option keys once again. The star tool will then draw stars as usual.

Click in the drawing area with the star tool to bring up the Star dialog box. As shown in Figure 4-15, this dialog box permits two Radius values, one for the outer radius and one for the inner. You can also specify the number of spikes. (Illustrator calls these "points," so don't confuse them with the points between segments. There are twice as many points as spikes—for example, a path with five spikes has ten points.)

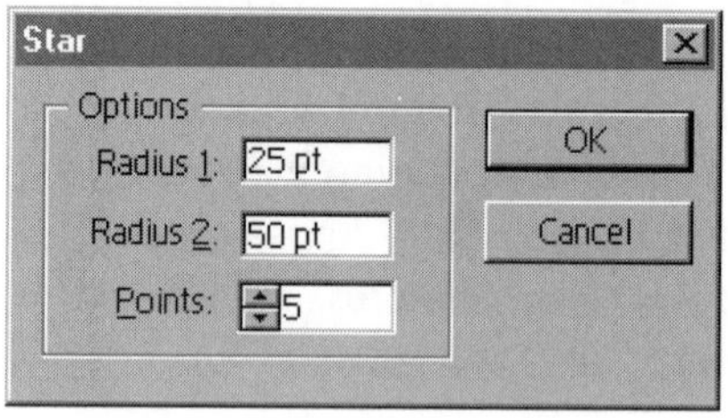

Figure 4-15: You can specify the precise inner and outer radius values by clicking with the star tool.

Drawing a Spiral

Most folks look at spirals and think, "Why in Tarnation would I want to draw that?" Spirals don't exactly lend themselves to a wide range of drawing situations, but I must admit, I've become something of an enthusiastic spiralist since their introduction in Illustrator 6. You can create text on a spiral (Chapter 7) or use a spiral as a guideline (Chapter 10). And naturally, a spiral is the perfect ornament for a pig's rump. But I find myself adding spirals to all kinds of illustrations, the most recent example being the chin dimple in Figure 4-1.

But wouldn't you know it, spirals are one of the most difficult things to create in Illustrator. Oh sure, you can draw them easily enough; just drag with the spiral tool and the spiral grows outward from its center. But controlling the number of times the spiral wraps around itself requires a fair amount of dexterity and reasoning.

Let's start with the Spiral dialog box, shown in Figure 4-16. To access this dialog box, click with the spiral tool inside the drawing area. The Spiral dialog box contains these options:

- **Radius:** Enter a Radius value to specify the size of the spiral. This represents the distance from the center of the shape to the last point on the spiral.
- **Decay**: The Decay value determines how quickly the spiral loops in on itself. Figure 4-17 demonstrates the effects of several decays. As you can see, small values result in short loops. Larger values—up to 99.99 percent—result in more tightly packed spirals.

So far so good; but here's where things get weird. If you enter a value of 100 into the Decay option box, the spiral coils on top of itself, creating a circle. Values above 100 (up to 150 percent) turn the spiral inside out, looping it in the opposite direction and outside the radius, as in the bottom two examples of Figure 4-17.

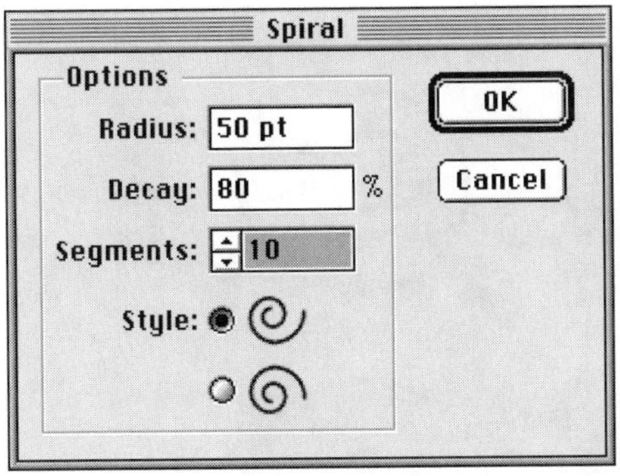

*Figure 4-16:
The Spiral dialog box allows you to specify the Radius and Decay of the spiral.*

- **Segments:** Enter the number of curved segments between points into the Segments option box. Each segment represents a quarter coil in the spiral. Figure 4-18 shows the results of six Segments values.
- **Style:** Select a radio button to coil the spiral counterclockwise or clockwise. (As I said earlier, this assumes a Decay value of less than 100 percent. If the Decay is higher than 100, the spiral coils in the opposite direction.)

By itself, an increased Segments value may not result in more coils. Strange, but true. You have to raise both the Decay and Segments values to wind the coils more tightly. This is because Illustrator drops segments when Decay is too low to accommodate them.

For example, the Segments value is set to a constant 100 in Figure 4-19. But as you can see, by upping the Decay value I give Illustrator more room to draw segments, and thus increase the number of coils in the path.

If Decay is set higher than 100 percent, Illustrator adds segments to the spiral's outside. This means it actually gets larger as you increase the Segments value. Beware, however—a Decay value as small as 105 combined with a high Segments value can completely take over your artwork. I prefer to play it safe and set Decay to less than 100.

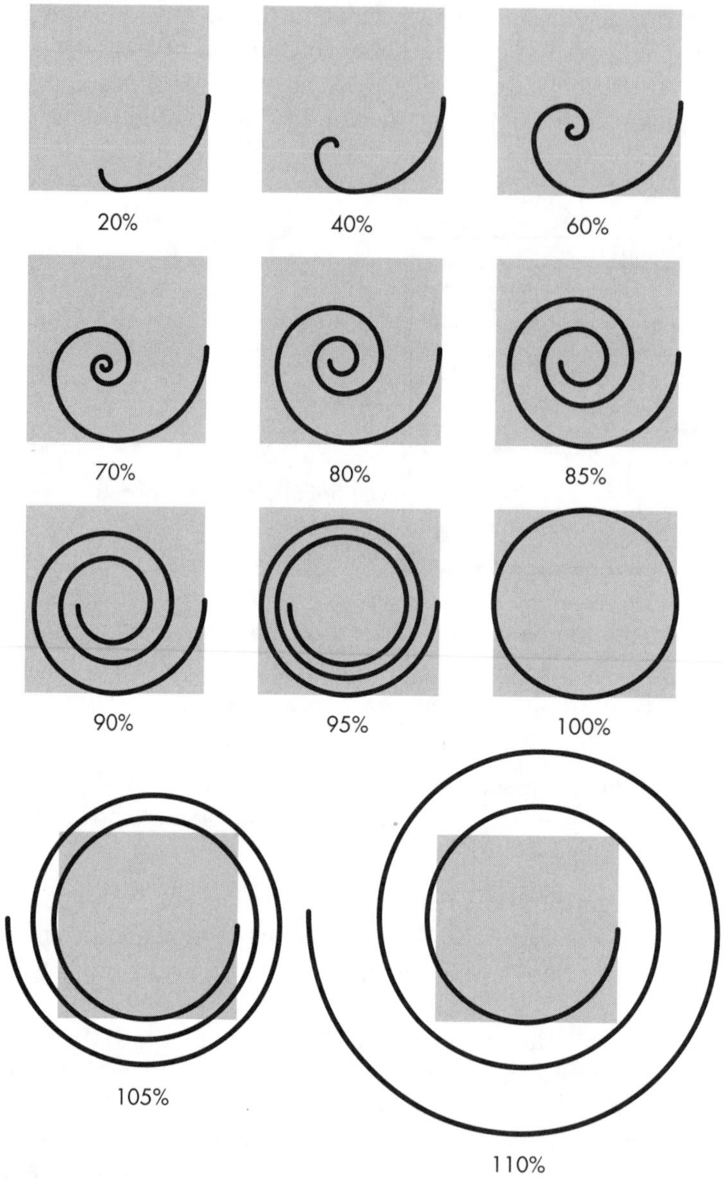

Figure 4-17: The results of changing the Decay values with Radius set to 35 points and Segments set to 10.

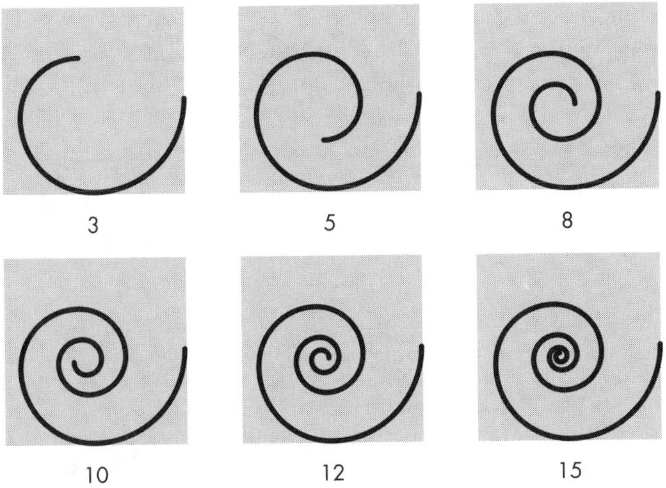

Figure 4-18: The results of several Segments values, with Radius again set to 35 and the Decay value at 80 percent.

By now you're probably thinking, "Whelp, that's it for spirals." But wait, there's more. As luck would have it, you can modify coils without resorting to the Spiral dialog box. It takes a little getting used to, but it works. Here's how:

- When you drag with the spiral tool, you're changing the radius and rotating the spiral around. I just want to get that straight before I go any farther.

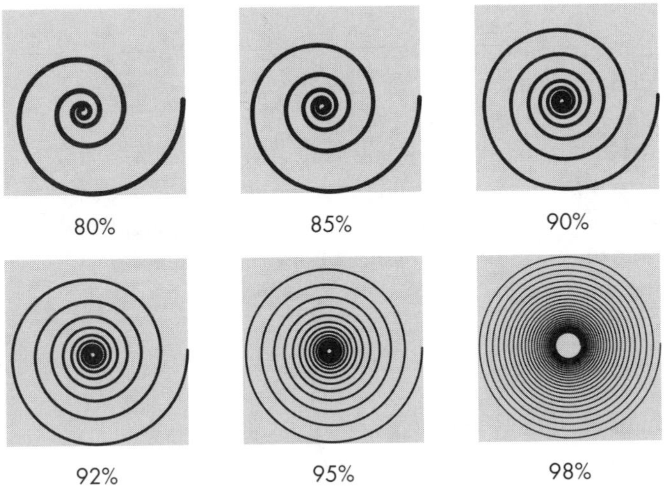

Figure 4-19: Though the Segments value for every one of these spirals is set to 100, only by raising the Decay value can I reveal all the segments I've requested.

- Press the ⌘ key while dragging to modify the decay. Drag outward to lower the decay; drag inward to raise it. If you drag inward past one of the coils, the spiral flips on itself, indicating a decay of more than 100 percent.
- Don't press the ⌘ key the moment you start dragging or you'll pop the Decay value to some ridiculously low number such as 7 percent. Start dragging, then press ⌘ in mid-drag. Release the key to modify the radius again.
- Press the up and down arrow keys while dragging with the spiral tool to raise and lower the number of segments in a spiral.
- You can also change the number of segments by pressing the Option key. Option-drag toward the center of the spiral to delete segments and reduce the radius. Drag outward to both add segments and increase the radius, thus better accommodating the new coils.
- If you press both ⌘ and Option simultaneously, ⌘ takes precedence (unlike with the star tool, where Option is dominant).
- You can also press the spacebar while dragging with the spiral tool to reposition the path. Shift-drag to constrain the spiral to some 45-degree angle.
- As if it's not goofy enough to be able to create concentric polygons and stars, you can create a series of spirals by pressing the tilde (~) key as you drag. Just the thing to embellish the next annual report.

NOTE

If you haven't seen Illustrator since version 5, you'll notice something right off the bat about how Illustrator now draws spirals: they look better. As you can see in Figures 4-17 through 4-19, the spirals curve smoothly. In Illustrator 5, spirals were blocky, almost as if they were made of rounded rectangles. This is a result of Illustrator's curve fitting (improved back in version 6), a largely invisible but wonderful enhancement to the program.

Drawing Free-form Paths

The tools I've discussed so far are all well and good. But Illustrator's true drawing power lies in its ability to define free-form lines and shapes. Such paths may be simple shapes like zigzags or crescents, or they may be intricate polygons and naturalistic forms. It all depends on how well you can draw.

Known as the freehand tool in previous versions of Illustrator, the pencil tool works much like a real pencil and lets you draw anything you want. Heck, the pencil cursor even looks like a pencil.

When you first use the pencil tool, the pencil cursor displays with a small *x* in the lower right corner. This indicates you are drawing a new, independent path. As you drag with the tool, Illustrator tracks the cursor's motion with a dotted line. After you release the mouse button, Illustrator automatically assigns and positions the points and segments needed to create your freehand path (even though the name has changed, the pencil tool still draws a path most aptly called a freehand path). The paths created adopt traditional fill and stroke characteristics as dictated by the values set in the various palettes (including the Color and Stroke palettes). For more information on fill and stroke, read the way-fab and truly meaty Chapters 14, 15, and 16.

Adjusting the Tolerances

Alas, automation is rarely perfect. (If it were, what need would these machines have for us?) Try as it might, Illustrator doesn't always do such a hot job of drawing freehand paths. When the program finishes its calculations, a path may appear riddled with far too many points, or equipped with too few.

Fortunately, you can adjust the performance of the pencil tool to accommodate your personal drawing style using the Fidelity and Smoothness Tolerances options found in the Pencil Tool Preferences dialog box. To access the Pencil Tool Preferences dialog box (shown in Figure 4-20), double-click on the pencil tool icon in the toolbox. In the Fidelity option box, either enter any value between 0.5 and 20, or if you prefer, use the slider bar to select a value within the same range. Illustrator measures the Fidelity value in screen pixels. Fidelity determines how far from the path the individual point may stray. A value of 2.5, for example, instructs the program to ignore any jags in your cursor movements that do not exceed 2.5 pixels in length or width. Setting the value to 0.5 makes the pencil tool extremely sensitive; setting the value to 20 smooths the roughest of gestures.

A Fidelity value of 2 or 3 is generally adequate for most folks, but you should experiment to determine the best setting. Keep in mind that Illustrator saves the Fidelity value, and it remains in force until you enter a new value into the Pencil Tool Preferences dialog box.

Smoothness is the other tolerance value that affects the pencil tool's behavior. This dictates how many points are needed to complete the path. Smoothness ranges from 0 to 100 percent, a value you can enter into the Smoothness option box or set via the slider bar. The higher the value, the smoother the freehand path.

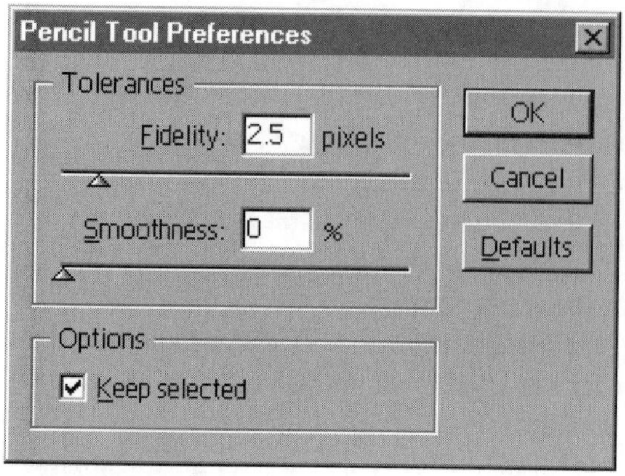

Figure 4-20:
In the Pencil Tool Preferences dialog box, you specify exactly how Illustrator mimics your mouse movements when you're dragging with the pencil tool.

TIP

Want to draw smoother freehand paths? Swap your mouse for a drawing tablet. They're inexpensive and they work like a dream. My favorites are the ArtPad II and ArtZ II from Wacom Technology (360/896-9833, http://www.wacom.com). They run $150 and $350 respectively (the ArtZ II includes a transparency for tracing and programmable buttons) and are available for both Mac and Windows These diminutive tablets are roughly the size of a mouse pad, but provide sufficient resolution to register the subtlest gestures. The wireless stylus (the name for the electronic pen) is lighter than many mechanical pencils, and it even includes an eraser you can use with Photoshop and other image editors. (Okay, it's a gimmick, but sometimes it comes in handy.) Your drawing can't help but improve.

You can't alter either the Fidelity or the Smoothness value for a path after you've drawn it because Illustrator calculates the points for a path only once, after you release the mouse button.

Two other features of this dialog box are worth mentioning. First is the Keep Selected checkbox. When you select this option, a path remains selected just after creation, allowing you to extend or close it. You can even edit the path right away, as discussed in Chapter 9. The second is the Defaults button, which sets the Fidelity and Smoothness options to 2.5 pixels and 0 percent respectively and activates the Keep Selected checkbox.

Extending and Closing a Path

Normally, when you drag with the pencil tool, the result is an open path. This is true even if the starting point of your draw coincides perfectly with the final point. In this case, Illustrator will create two points so that the initial point overlaps the final point. This is not the limit of its capabilities, however: You can also use the pencil tool to create closed paths or extend any open path, lengthening it or even closing it.

To create a closed path from scratch, press the Option key while dragging with the pencil tool and hold it through the completion of the drag. As you do this, the pencil cursor changes slightly. It still looks like a pencil, but now the eraser end is filled and a small *o* replaces the *x* that usually appears to the right, as shown in Figure 4-21. Upon your drag's completion, Illustrator automatically adds a segment that connects the first and last points. The right side of Figure 4-21 shows how Illustrator adds this segment. If the two endpoints coincide, holding the Option key creates a single point that marks both the beginning and the end of the closed path.

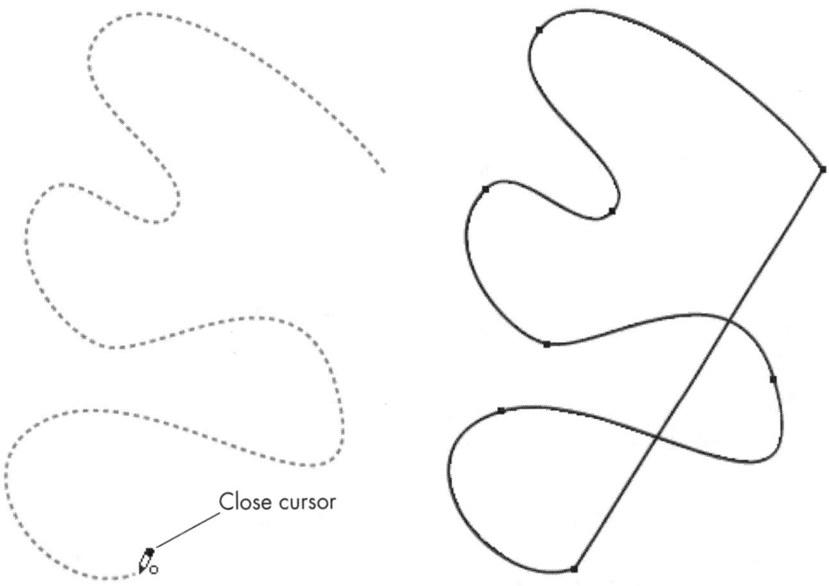

Figure 4-21: Hold down the Option key while you drag with the pencil tool, and Illustrator automatically closes your path regardless of where you start and end your drag.

On the other hand, if you want to extend an existing open path, select the path and position the pencil cursor over either end of the line. You'll know you're ready to go when you get the connect cursor (the standard pencil cursor without the little *x*, as seen in Figure 4-22). Drag away—Illustrator treats your cursor movements as an extension of the existing path.

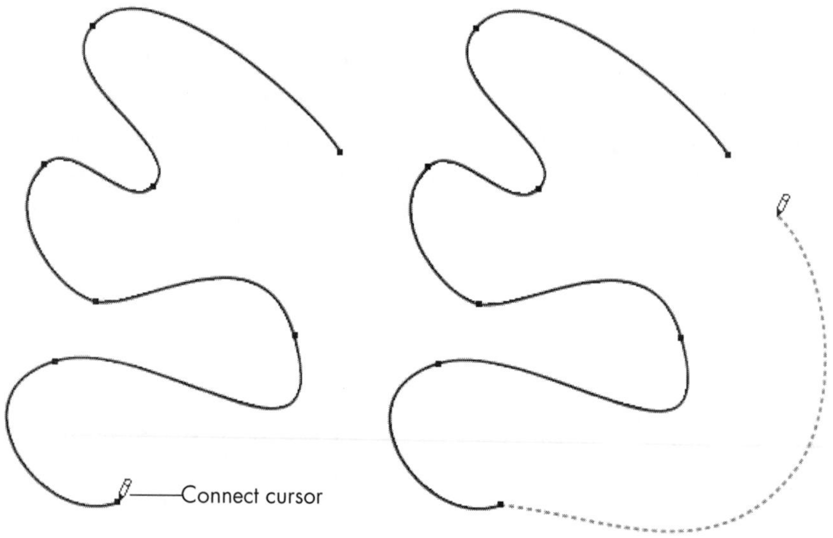

Figure 4-22: Drag from an endpoint to extend a path (left). Drag back to the other endpoint to close it (right).

NOTE

Extending a path with the pencil tool can have seemingly unpredictable results. This is because the pencil tool, in addition to creating and extending paths, can also edit existing paths. In Figure 4-22, to extend the path shown on the left, I started by dragging in a direction that would result in a smooth transition from the old path to the new portion. I then continued the path, making sure that the rest of the extension was sufficiently far from the original path. This extended the path while preserving its original shape.

Conversely, had I strayed too close to the original path anytime during my drag, I would have changed the shape of the original path instead of extending it. If you find that in trying to extend a path with the pencil tool, you instead edit its original shape, simply choose File » Undo (⌘-Z) and try again.

And finally, to close a selected open path with the pencil tool, drag from one of its endpoints as if you were extending the path. Then, while you're still dragging, press the Option key and hold it down until you have released the mouse button. Illustrator automatically connects the last point you create and the original path's other endpoint. As in the case of creating a closed path from scratch, if these two points coincide, Illustrator closes the path with a single point.

Painting Paths

The paintbrush tool—formally known as the brush tool—is the other free-form path creation tool. The paintbrush tool lets you draw lines with substance, like strokes laid down with a conventional paintbrush. As you drag with the paintbrush tool, a line flows from the end of the cursor. As with the pencil tool, Illustrator automatically assigns and positions points and segments after you release the mouse button.

The paintbrush you see here in Illustrator 8 is a very different tool from the one in older versions of Illustrator. Previously, the paintbrush produced only closed paths. Figure 4-23 shows an example of how the paintbrush tool used to work in Illustrator 7. The top portion shows how the path first appeared when I created it in Illustrator 7. Upon completion, Illustrator 7 converted the open path into a closed path, as shown in the bottom part of Figure 4-23. Typically this was an extremely complicated path, with lots of overlapping segments. The edges of the original open path defined the boundaries of the closed path. The final path's fill and stroke attributes were set via the Colors and the Stroke palettes. Using a light stroke and matching fill, the closed paths of the old paintbrush tool would give at best a mediocre approximation to its real-world counterpart.

Illustrator 8 has completely overhauled the paintbrush tool. Seasoned users may not even recognize it. The newly redesigned tool initially creates paths just as the pencil tool does. Drag with it to create open paths. Press the Option key once you've started the drag to force Illustrator to close the path automatically. Drag from the endpoint of a selected open path—one also created with the paintbrush tool—to extend it, either lengthening it or closing it.

The options that affect the paintbrush tool's behavior are the same as the pencil tool's. The Paintbrush Tool Preferences dialog box (which appears when you double-click on the paintbrush tool), looks almost exactly like the Pencil Tool Preferences dialog box and contains the same options. The Fidelity and Smoothness Tolerances have the same range (0.5 to 20 pixels and 0 to 100 percent, respectively) and impact the paintbrush tool just as they impact the pencil tool (see the Adjusting the Tolerances section above). The Keep Selected option also appears in both dialog boxes. The only differences are that the Paintbrush

Tool Preferences defaults are slightly higher and the Fill New Brush Strokes checkbox also appears. When you select this option, the active fill shows up in paths you create with the paintbrush tool. When it's off, paintbrush-created paths are automatically assigned no fill. For more about fills, sojourn to Chapters 14 and 15. As with the Pencil Tool Preferences dialog box, the options in the Paintbrush Tool Preferences dialog box only affect future paths. You cannot edit an existing path using any of these options.

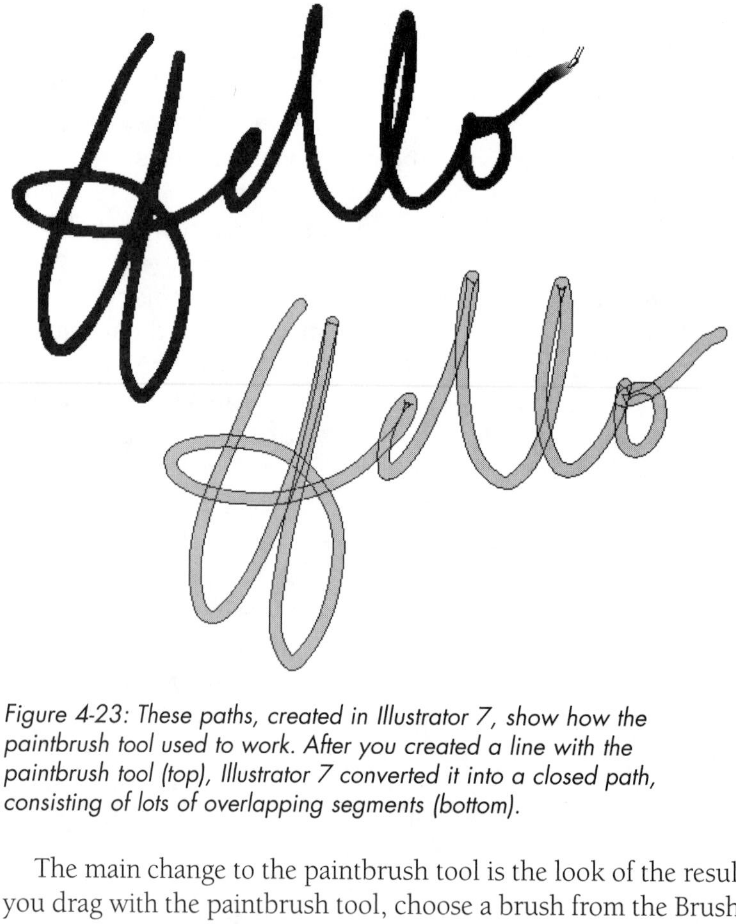

Figure 4-23: These paths, created in Illustrator 7, show how the paintbrush tool used to work. After you created a line with the paintbrush tool (top), Illustrator 7 converted it into a closed path, consisting of lots of overlapping segments (bottom).

The main change to the paintbrush tool is the look of the resulting path. Before you drag with the paintbrush tool, choose a brush from the Brushes palette. These brushes are special objects that combine characteristics of both a stroked open path and a filled closed path to create unique hybrids. These new brushes are very similar to the old Path Pattern filter, which appeared in Illustrator 7, but have considerably more capabilities.

After you drag with the paintbrush tool, the selected brush stretches and bends along the path. Figure 4-24 shows two different brushes applied to the path from

Figure 4-23. In the second example, I chopped the path into several pieces and then applied the same brush to each. This is just a brief introduction to brushes. For the full lowdown on brushes and all the paintbrush tool's unique ways (including using it in conjunction with a pressure-sensitive tablet), jump ahead to Chapter 16.

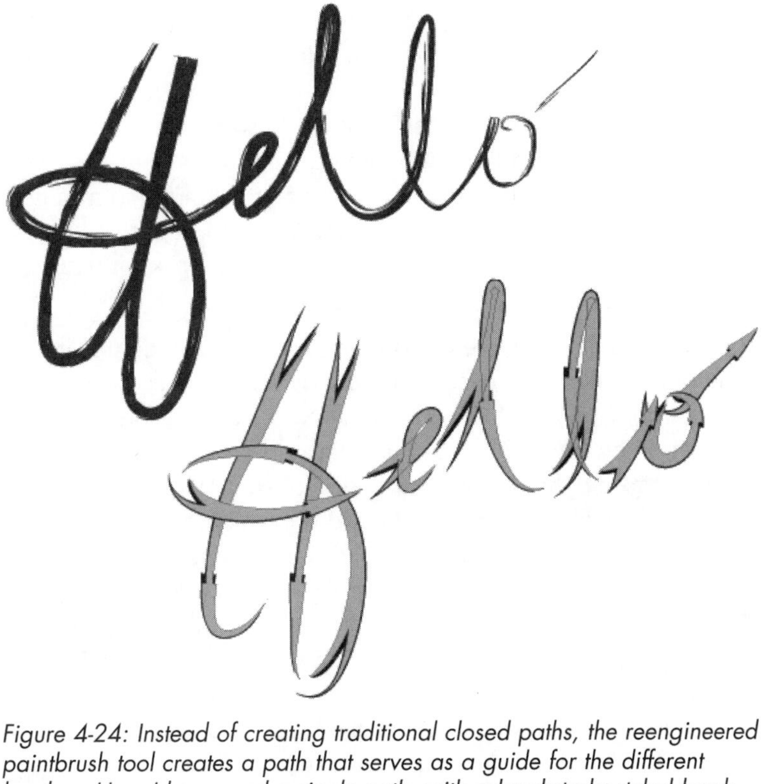

Figure 4-24: Instead of creating traditional closed paths, the reengineered paintbrush tool creates a path that serves as a guide for the different brushes. Here I have used a single path, with a brushstroke-styled brush (top) and many paths, each with a picture-styled brush (bottom) for two very different effects.

Tracing Templates No Longer a Black-and-White Issue

If version 8 is your first experience with Illustrator, then I need to tell you something of the olden days—a time when schoolchildren walked 12 miles through waist-high snow to get a copy of Windows 95, when people could see the

Star Wars trilogy only on video, and when Illustrator's template capabilities were about as comprehensive as a 1950s high school class on human sexuality.

In the past, templates could handle only black-and-white images and two formats, PICT and, of all things, MacPaint. You could have only one template in an illustration at a time, and you could neither move nor manipulate it inside your illustration.

Adobe revamped the template capabilities back in Illustrator 7. You can place or open a template saved in any of the image formats that Illustrator supports. The template may be black-and-white or color. Once in Illustrator, you can move and manipulate the template just as you can any placed or opened image. Essentially, if you have added an image to Illustrator, then you have also added a template.

Though unfortunately you still can't scan images directly into Illustrator, you should be able to scan in some line art and make it into an illustration in minutes. Sure, you have to go in and clean up the paths—you can't expect automation to eliminate artistic effort—but Illustrator does most of the grunt work for you.

TIP

If you want to trace an image (especially a color one), it's best to have the template on its own layer. You can do this in one of two different ways: the hard way and the easy way. For the hard way, first ⌘-click on the New Layer button at the bottom of the Layers palette. Illustrator adds a new layer and places it below the active layer in the Layers palette. Next, use the File » Place command to add a template to the new layer. Then double-click on the layer in the Layers palette and select the Dim Images check box in the Layer Options dialog box. Diffuse the colors to about half their original luster (by entering 50 percent into the Dim Image option box), permitting you to distinguish the image from your paths. Drag the image to its proper location, lock the layer, and switch back to your original layer. You can now trace the image contours with the autotrace tool or trace them manually with any other drawing tool. For more on layers, see "Working with Independent Drawing Layers" in Chapter 10.

NEW 8

Here's the easy way: Inside the Place dialog box (File » Place), click on the image you want to place, then select the Template check box. Once you've clicked the OK button (or hit the Return key), Illustrator places the image on its own new layer, centered in the current document, and automatically dims and locks that layer. You may wish to unlock the template's layer, reposition the template, and then lock it again. I wonder where Adobe ever came up with such a wonderful idea.

Using the Autotrace Tool

After placing or opening a template in your illustration (as described in the "Opening and Placing" section of Chapter 3), you can trace the edges manually using any of Illustrator's drawing tools. But if you want Illustrator to do the work for you, your only choice (and it makes me gnash my teeth just to think of it) is the autotrace tool. After all this time, Illustrator's tracing capabilities haven't changed one iota since they were introduced more than eight years ago.

If this were FreeHand, I could assure you that you possess an adequate tracing function that creates multiple paths at a time without a whimper. But alas, this is Illustrator and Illustrator's tracing tool is about as up-to-date as a poodle skirt and as capable as a hammer without a handle.

NOTE: To some Illustrator users, the suggestion that FreeHand might in some way be superior to Illustrator amounts to fighting words. Naturally, I don't have any desire to raise the dander of hardcore Illustrator fans. No, I prefer to irritate Adobe. My hope is that some programmer or product manager will turn to this page and become sufficiently embarrassed by my caustic critique to fix this tool.

Considering all the effort Adobe has put into improving Illustrator's template capabilities, you would think that the company could have improved the autotrace tool's capabilities. Ironically, we've, in fact, lost a convenience: we can no longer use the autotrace tool in Artwork mode at all. Admittedly, this problem stems from Illustrator's newly implemented handling of templates, but it does go to show just how much time Adobe invested in upgrading the autotrace tool. As far as I can tell, Adobe simply forgot that Illustrator had this tool and figured that anyone interested in this function would go out and buy some other program like, oh, I don't know, Adobe's own Streamline.

If you're really serious about tracing and like to scan your own handiwork or do batch tracing (that is, do a lot of tracing), you'll want to check out Adobe Streamline. This dedicated tracing program is reasonably easy to use. Choose the Open command, select the image you want to trace, and enter a name for the trace. Streamline's tracing abilities are superior to Illustrator's in a number of ways. Here are just a few nifty things about Streamline:

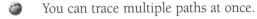

- You can trace multiple paths at once.

- It's capable of recognizing colors and automatically fill shapes.
- It lets you control the amount of straight lines and curves it uses in tracing images.
- You can select the amount of noise (random marks) that you want Streamline to recognize.
- It lets you choose whether traces will consist of open or closed paths. Streamline is also smart enough to set stroke weight.
- It allows you to do batch processing. You can take a folder of images and, in one fell swoop, have Streamline trace all the images it contains.

Chapter 13 explains how to trace paths around a scanned image—black-and-white, gray-scale, or color—inside Photoshop and then copy the paths into Illustrator. Photoshop's tracing capabilities are superior to Illustrator's, and they're really easy to use. So if you have Photoshop 3 or later, you can skip the rest of the chapter. If you don't, curse Adobe a couple of times and read on.

Select the autotrace tool (the alternative tool in the blend tool slot) from the toolbox. Figure 4-25 shows me doing just that, with a tracing template all ready to go in the background.

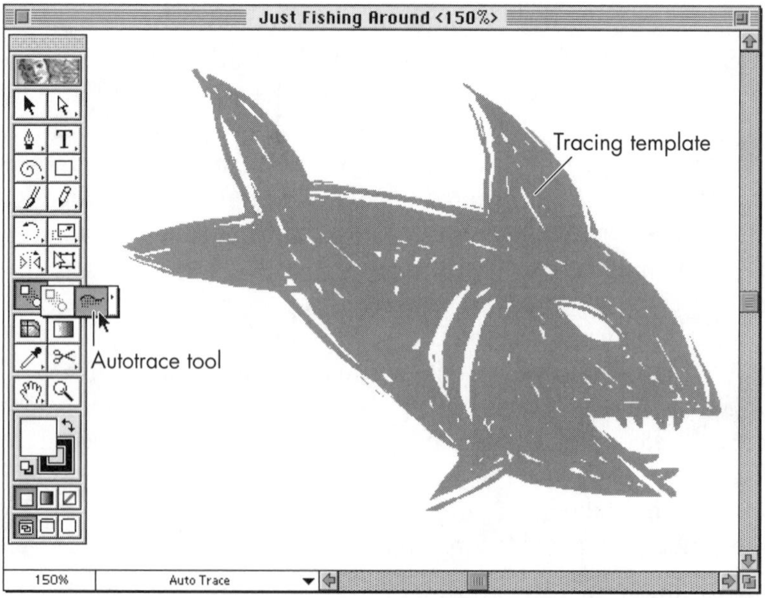

Figure 4-25: Select the autotrace tool, then click or drag within six pixels of the template.

You can use the autotrace tool in one of two ways:

- Click within six pixels of an edge in the tracing template. Illustrator automatically encircles that edge with a closed path.
- Drag from within six pixels of an edge to within six pixels of some other portion of that same edge. Illustrator traces an open path between the point at which you click and the point at which you release.

For example, to trace around the outside of the fish, I clicked at the top of the fin, as in the top example of Figure 4-26. (Illustrator always creates a point at the spot on the template nearest your click, so it's best to click near a corner.) To trace the eye, I clicked just to the right of its edge, as shown in the lower example.

Figure 4-26: I clicked above the fin to trace the outside of the fish (top). Then I clicked beside the eye to trace inside its edge (bottom).

Dragging is a less common way to trace shapes, but it can be useful if you want to trace one portion of the template automatically and the rest manually. After you complete your drag, Illustrator traces a portion of the image, tracing clockwise around exterior edges, as demonstrated in Figure 4-27, and counterclockwise around interior edges. This is true even if it's tracing the longer of the two distances between where you started your drag and where you released.

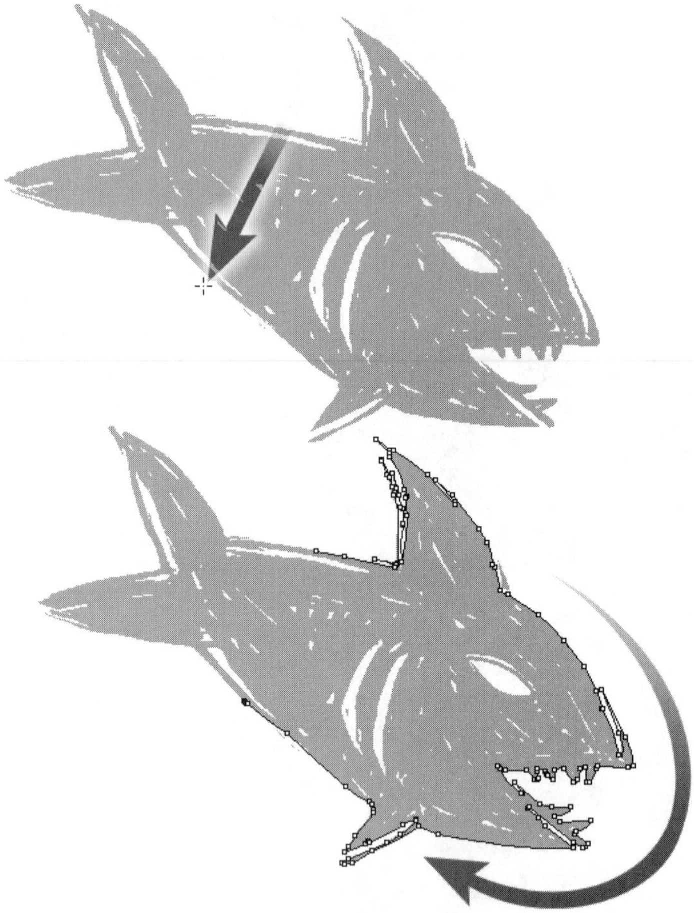

Figure 4-27: When you drag from one side of an exterior surface to another (top), Illustrator traces between the two points in a clockwise direction (bottom).

TIP

If you have placed your template on its own separate layer (as explained above in "Tracing Templates, No Longer a Black-and-White Issue"), you can temporarily hide the layer and everything on it, including the template, to get a better view of your artwork. Click on that layer's Visibility button—the leftmost checkbox—in the Layers palette. The template disappears. To bring the template back into view, again click on that Visibility button.

Adjusting Autotracing Sensitivity

If you are dissatisfied with Illustrator's tracing accuracy, you can adjust the autotrace tool's sensitivity by changing the Auto Trace Tolerance value in the General Preferences dialog box. An Auto Trace Tolerance value of 0 instructs Illustrator to trace every single pixel of a bitmapped template. If you raise the value to 10, the software ignores large jags in the outline of a template and smooths out all kinds of details.

Generally speaking, it's better to have too many points than too few. After all, you can always delete points later, as discussed in the next chapter. So for the most reliable autotracing, set the Auto Trace Tolerance value no higher than 2.

Tracing across Gaps

The autotrace tool is most effective in tracing the borders between the black and white areas in a template. But it can also trace gray areas and areas with broken or inconsistent outlines. To accommodate such rough spots, Illustrator provides a Tracing Gap option in the General Preferences dialog box.

You can set this value to any value from 0 to 2 in 0.01-pixel increments (though it's hardly worth the effort to enter a decimal point value).

- The default value of 0 instructs Illustrator to trace around a template image from one black pixel to the next. If even a single white pixel separates one black area from another, the traced path does not pass over the gap.
- A Gap value of 1 permits Illustrator to jump one-pixel gaps in order to incorporate more areas from the template into a single path.
- If you raise the value to 2, Illustrator can jump a two-pixel gap. This is an especially useful setting when you're tracing photographic images and other templates with loose pixels.

Adding to a Traced Line

Illustrator lets you extend an open path with the autotrace tool. The rules are a little stricter than they are with the pencil tool; you can't extend just any old line. A template image must exist within six pixels of the line's endpoint to qualify for autotrace extension. (This makes the feature practically useless, of course, but a feature is a feature, and I'm sworn to leave no stone unturned.)

Drag from the endpoint to another point along an edge of the template to extend a path. (Unlike the pencil tool, the autotrace tool doesn't offer any special cursor icon to show you when you have the cursor positioned correctly.) To close the path, drag from one endpoint to another. The second endpoint does not have to be anywhere near the template—a small touch of flexibility.

The autotrace tool connects and closes paths with smooth points by default. This is true even when the point appears to be a corner. To create a true corner point (which is much easier to edit), Option-drag from the first endpoint and press Option when releasing onto the second endpoint.

Yet One Tools Beats Them All

Before I close this chapter, I want to leave you with a parting bit of wisdom. We've tackled all but one of Illustrator's drawing tools, and that remaining tool—the pen tool—is far and away the best of all. It is infinitely more flexible than the rectangle, ellipse, and other shape tools, and more precise than the pencil, paintbrush, and autotrace tools. (The pen tool is also mightier than the sword tool, but that's another story.) It is, in fact, the only tool you really need. In fact, there was a time when the pen, rectangle, and ellipse tools were all Illustrator offered—yet there wasn't a thing you couldn't draw.

That's why the next chapter is so important. It shows you how to edit the paths you create with the tools in this chapter, and how to create more exacting shapes with the pen. These features require more work, but they'll reward your effort several times over.

CHAPTER 5

EXACT POINTS AND PRECISION CURVES

Much as the $375 Illustrator tries, it just can't live up to the 25¢ pencil when it comes to smooth, real-time drawing. Whether you use the pencil, paintbrush, or autotrace tool, you still get the same thing—clunky paths. A drawing tablet helps, but only to communicate smoother lines to Illustrator; it doesn't help Illustrator better interpret your beautiful work.

There is hope for the future, of course. Illustrator 8 does a much better job of interpreting freehand paths than did Illustrator 88 (the first version to offer the tool). So one might expect Illustrator 2001 to perform even better and Illustrator 2525 to be right on the money. But in the meantime, we can either suffer with clunky paths, or we can fix them.

That said, it would be a sin if fixing paths wasn't what this chapter was all about. We'll explore a whole mess of path-editing theories—you'll see how to move anchor points and bend segments to get lines as smooth as water droplets and as organic as flower petals. I'll also cover the pen tool, the only tool in all of Illustrator that lets you draw paths correctly the first time out. And just when you think Illustrator couldn't be any dreamier, I'll throw in some pointers for adding, deleting, and converting points.

If Illustrator is nothing else, it's the most excellent path creation and manipulation tool the world has ever enjoyed. This chapter tells why.

NOTE

By the way, if you are a Windows user who is just now upgrading from Illustrator 4, you will probably find this a pleasant surprise: You can reshape any kind of path, whether it was created using the flexible pencil tool or the rigid rectangle tool. Illustrator used to lock rectangles and ellipses so you couldn't get to their points without first ungrouping them. No more—rectangle, ellipse, regular polygon, star, spiral, or whatever, you manipulate them all the same way. Once you lay a path down on the page, Illustrator cares not how it originated. All paths are alike in its eyes (bless its equal opportunity heart).

Selecting Like a House on Fire

The job of sprucing up paths rests on the shoulders of three very sturdy tools. These are the selection tools, available from the top two slots in the toolbox, as shown in Figure 5-1. Clicking on a point or segment with one of these suckers selects all or part of a path. The tools differ only in the extent of the selection they make.

You can't create a darned thing with a selection tool. But you can do all kinds of stuff to objects that you've already created using one of the tools from the previous chapter. Just click on a path and start dragging its points and segments.

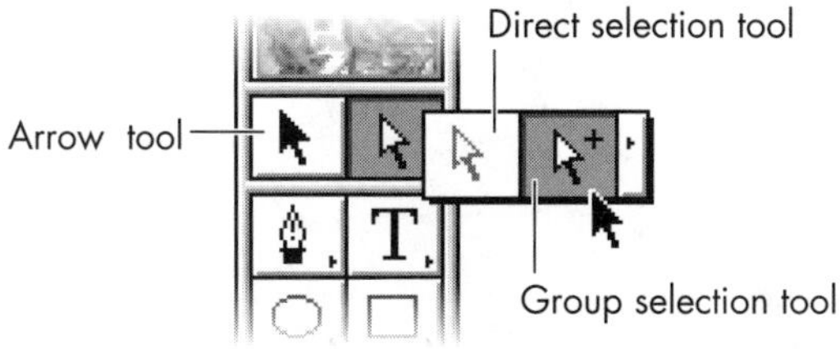

Figure 5-1:
The three selection tools are all you need to move anchor points, bend segments, and otherwise whip paths into shape.

NOTE

New with the advent of Illustrator 8 is the eight-handled bounding box (or rectangle) that by default automatically surrounds any path you select. This bounding box lets you scale selected paths and has nothing to do with selecting paths, other than to give another visual clue that a path is selected.

For this reason, the bounding box is not discussed here (you'll see it in Chapter 11), and for the sake of clarity it will not appear in any of the figures in this chapter. To toggle the bounding box on and off, use the Display Bounding Box check box in the General Preferences dialog box—File » Preferences » General or ⌘-K.

NOTE

Another addition to version 8 is smart guides. Their main function is to aid you in creating and positioning paths with perfect accuracy. Although some of their secondary functions are related to selecting paths I don't discuss their role until Chapter 10, a chapter devoted to Illustrator's precise nature.

The Plain Black Arrow Tool

The selection tool—which I call the arrow tool to distinguish it from its selection pals—is the most straightforward of the bunch. When the arrow tool is active, you can click anywhere along the outline of a path to select the path in its entirety. If the path is filled and the Use Area Select check box is turned on inside the General Preferences dialog box, you can also click inside the path to select it, provided the path has a nontransparent fill as discussed in Chapter 14. All points become visible as filled squares, as Figure 5-2 demonstrates.

After selecting a path with the arrow tool, you can move it, apply a transformation, or perform any other manipulation that affects the path as a whole. You cannot move points or bend segments. If the path has been grouped with other paths (as explained in Chapter 10), the arrow tool selects the entire group, prohibiting you from altering one grouped path independently of another.

Figure 5-2: Click on any part of a path with the arrow tool (left) to select the entire path (right).

Here are a few other ways to select paths with the arrow tool:

- When you click on a path, you not only select the path on which you click, you also deselect any previously selected path. To select multiple paths, click on the first path, then Shift-click on each additional path you want to select. The Shift key prevents Illustrator from deselecting paths as you click on new ones.
- Another way to select multiple paths is to *marquee* them. Drag from an empty portion of your drawing area to create a dotted rectangular outline, called a marquee. You select all paths that fall even slightly inside this outline when you release the mouse button. In Figure 5-3, for example, I drag midway inside the apple and the leaf to select both shapes.
- You can combine marqueeing with Shift-clicking to select multiple paths. You can also drag a marquee while pressing Shift, which adds the surrounded objects to the present selection.
- If you Shift-click on an object that is already selected, Illustrator deselects it, as I discuss in the upcoming "Deselecting Stuff That You Want to Leave as Is" section.

To access the arrow tool temporarily when some other tool is active, press and hold the ⌘ key. Release the key to return to the last tool you used. If pressing ⌘ gets you one of the hollow selection cursors instead, press ⌘-Tab and then press ⌘ again. To switch to the arrow tool, press the V key.

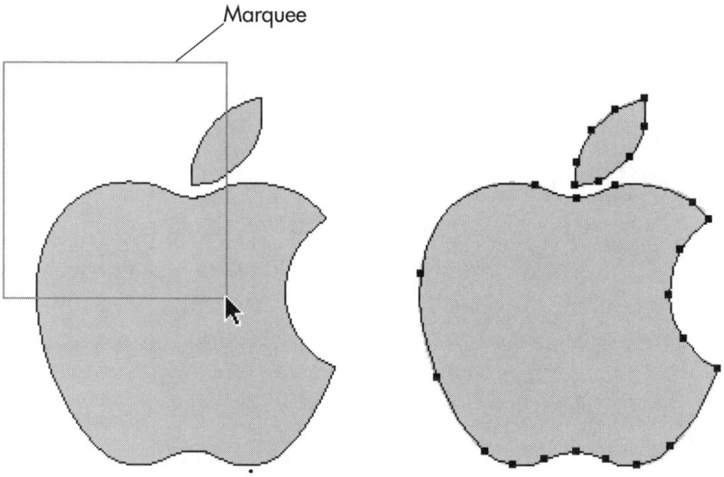

Figure 5-3: By marqueeing partially inside two shapes (left), I select them both (right).

The Hollow Direct Selection Tool

The direct selection tool is the hollow arrow in the upper right corner of the toolbox. Click with the direct selection tool to select an individual point or segment in a path. If you click on a point, you select the point; if you click on a segment, you select the segment. This works even if the path that contains the point or segment is part of a group.

Illustrator 8 has added two smart cursors to the direct selection tool's cursor category. As you move the direct selection tool around the screen, its cursor will change slightly depending on its position relative to different path elements. When the direct selection tool hovers over an empty portion of the screen, you see just the standard cursor. When the cursor is over any point, selected or not, a small hollow square joins the hollow arrow, as shown in the left two examples of

Figure 5-4. Move it over a segment of a deselected path and a filled square joins the cursor, as you can see in the top right example of Figure 5-4. These smart cursors are there to inform you that if you click with the mouse, you will select the intended element.

There are two additional things about these smart cursors that I'd like to mention. First, once you've selected a path, the direct selection cursor doesn't change when you move it over one of the path's segments. In the lower right example of Figure 5-4, notice that the small filled square has disappeared now that the path is selected. Second, if you have the Use Area Select option selected, positioning the direct selection tool over the fill of a deselected path will result in the display of the filled square appearing alongside the hollow arrow. This is a small point, but I thought I had better mention it.

Now that you know how the direct selection tool appears when you are selecting path elements, you might as well know how those path elements appear when you select them with the direct selection tool. Different elements have different ways of showing that they are selected. For example, when you select a point, it appears as a small filled square, as shown in the bottom left example of Figure 5-4. If the point borders a curved segment, you can also see a Bézier control handle connected to the point by a thin lever.

NOTE

For those of you reading aloud to loved ones, Bézier is pronounced *bay-zee-ay*. Named after Pierre Bézier—the French fellow who designed this particular drawing model to expedite the manufacture of car bodies, of all things—Bézier curve theory lies at the heart of both Illustrator and the PostScript printing language. I would be unforgivably remiss if I didn't tell you how Bézier control handles work later in this chapter in the "Dragging Control Handles" section.

When you select a path, Illustrator shows you both selected and deselected points. The deselected points appear as hollow squares, showing that they are part of a partially selected path, but are not themselves selected.

When you click on a segment with the direct selection tool, Illustrator shows you the Bézier control handles for that segment—if there are any—as in the lower right example of Figure 5-4. Unless some point in the path is also selected, all points appear hollow. Because Illustrator shows you the control handles only, you may find it a little confusing when selecting straight segments, which lack handles. You just have to click on the segment and have faith that it's selected. (Frankly, I wish Illustrator thickened the segment to provide a little visual feedback.)

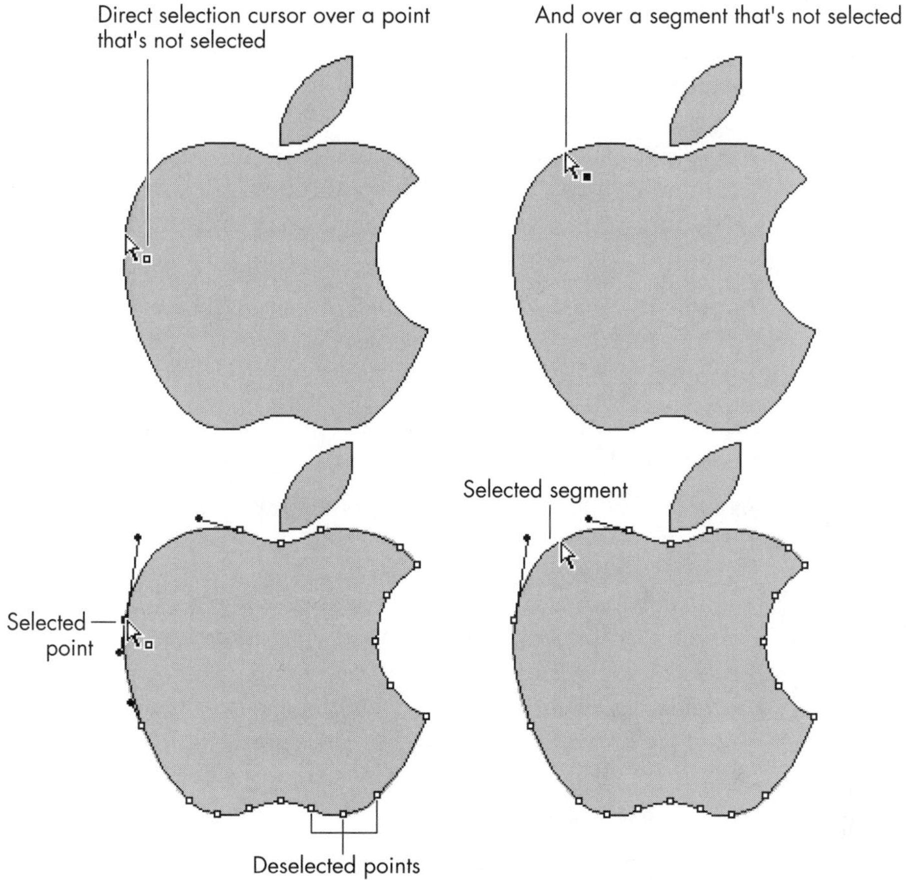

Figure 5-4: Position the direct selection tool over a point (top left) and the cursor gains a small hollow square. When over a segment (top right), the direct selection cursor gains a small black square. Select a single anchor point (bottom left) or segment (bottom right) by clicking with the direct selection tool.

You can also drag with the direct selection tool to marquee elements. All points and segments that lie inside the marquee become selected, even if they belong to different paths, as Figure 5-5 shows.

The following list summarizes these and other ways to select elements with the direct selection tool:

- If the Use Area Select check box in the General Preferences dialog box is turned on (as it is by default), you can click inside a filled shape to select the entire path. This assumes that the shape has a nontransparent fill, as addressed in Chapter 14.

- Frankly, I'm not a big fan of the Use Area Select option. If you don't click dead on a point or segment, you can easily select the entire path. Also, if a filled shape largely hides a path, it can be difficult to select that path in back. I much prefer to click on an outline when I want to select a path. This is especially true now that there are the new smart cursors for the direct selection tool. If you want to give my recommended approach a try, press ⌘-K, turn off the Use Area Select check box, and press Return.
- Shift-click on a point or segment to add it to the current selection. You can also Shift-marquee around elements. (If you Shift-click on a point or segment that's already selected, it becomes deselected. The same goes for Shift-marqueeing.)
- Option-click on a point or segment to select an entire path. This is a great way to select paths inside groups.
- Option-marquee or Shift-Option-click on paths to select multiple paths at a time.

TIP

To switch back and forth between the arrow tool and the direct selection tool, press ⌘-Tab. If you last used the direct selection tool (as opposed to the arrow tool), you can access it while any other tool is active by pressing ⌘. If you last used the arrow tool, press ⌘-Tab, then press ⌘. To switch to the direct selection tool, press the A key once or twice.

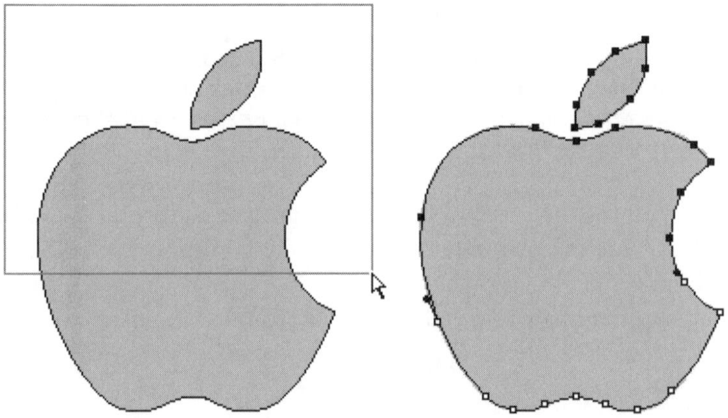

Figure 5-5: When dragging a marquee with the direct selection tool (left), all points and segments that fall inside the marquee become selected (right).

The Sad Little Group Selection Tool

Adobe added the group selection tool to Illustrator so folks who were afraid to press the Option key could select paths inside groups. In other words, you can either Option-click on a path to select it with the direct selection tool (temporarily accessing the group selection tool), or click on the path with the group selection tool. If you're not afraid of the occasional Option-click, feel free to ignore the group selection tool. I, for one, never touch it. Honestly, it's useless.

If you don't believe me, and you'd prefer to know everything about everything, you can select the group selection tool by dragging from the upper right slot in the toolbox. Then do any of the following:

- Click on a point or segment to select a whole path in a group. You can also select groups within groups by clicking multiple times on a path, but you can do this with the direct-selection tool as well so long as you hold the Option key down. I don't even know why I mentioned it. I cover all this grouping stuff in Chapter 10.
- Marquee paths with the group selection tool to select the paths, whether they fall entirely or partially inside the marquee.
- Shift-click on a path to add it to the selection. You can also Shift-marquee if you get the urge.
- Option-click on a point or segment to select it independently of its path. The Option key temporarily converts the group selection to direct selection.

See, what did I tell you? Dumb tool. Steer clear of it.

Selecting Everything

If you want to select all paths in your drawing, choose Edit » Select All or press ⌘-A. Illustrator selects every last point, segment, and other element throughout the illustration, even if it's on the pasteboard. (An exception occurs if you've either locked an element or selected a letter inside a text block, in which case Select All highlights all text in the story.)

Inversing the Selection

To select everything that's not selected and deselect what is selected, choose Edit » Select » Inverse. It's Illustrator's way of letting you reverse a selection.

Both the Select All and Inverse commands make it easier to select most of the objects in a complicated drawing. You can choose Select All and then Shift-click on the objects you don't want to select. Or start off by clicking and Shift-clicking on the stuff you don't want to select, and choose Edit » Select » Inverse. Either way works fine; it's entirely a matter of personal preference.

Hiding the Points and Handles

All those points, handles, and colored outlines that Illustrator uses to show an object is selected can occasionally get in your face. If you're aware of your selection but you want to see the selected objects unadorned, choose View » Hide Edges or press ⌘-H.

From that point on, no selection outline appears on screen, even if you select a different object. To see the selection outlines again, you have to choose View » Show Edges or press ⌘-H again.

Deselecting Stuff that You Want to Leave As Is

Selecting is your way of telling Illustrator, "This thing is messed up, and now I'm going to hurt it," or fix it, or whatever. If you don't want to hurt an object, you need to deselect it. (Folks also say "unselect," and I suppose one or two might even say "antiselect" or "get it out of the selection loop," but I think the unremarkable "deselect" sounds the least icky.)

To deselect all objects—regardless of form or gender—press ⌘-Shift-A (Edit » Deselect All) or just click with one of the selection tools on an empty portion of the drawing area.

You can make more discrete deselections using the Shift key:

- To deselect an entire path or group, Shift-click on the object with the arrow tool.
- To deselect a single point or segment, Shift-click on it with the direct selection tool.
- To deselect a single path inside a group, Shift-Option-click on it with the direct selection tool.
- You can also deselect elements and objects by Shift-marqueeing around them. Selected elements become deselected, and deselected elements become selected.

Dragging Stuff Around

Once you've selected a point or segment, you can move it around, changing its location and stretching its path. In fact, dragging with the direct selection tool is the single most common method for reshaping a path inside Illustrator. You can move selected points independently of deselected points. And you can stretch segments or move Bézier control handles to alter the curvature of a path. The next few pages explain all aspects of dragging.

Dragging Points

To move one or more points in a path:

1. Select the points you want to move with the direct selection tool.
2. Drag any one of them.
3. Squeal with delight.

When you drag a selected point, all other selected points move the same distance and direction. When you move a point while a neighboring point remains stationary, the segment between the two points shrinks or stretches in length to accommodate the change in distance, as demonstrated in Figure 5-6.

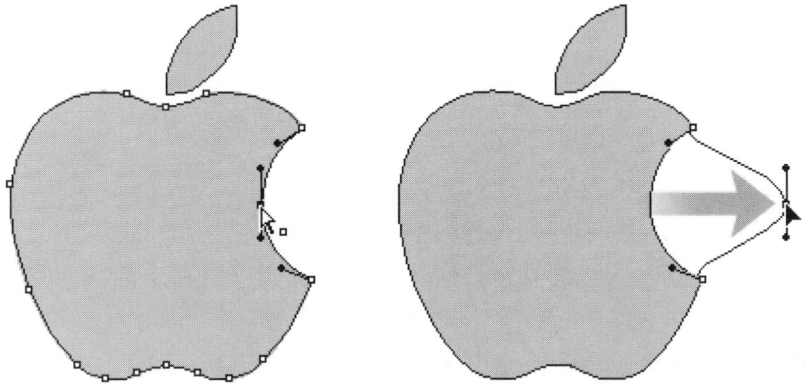

Figure 5-6: When you drag a selected point bordered by deselected points (left), Illustrator stretches the segments between the points (right).

When you move a point, any accompanying control handles move with it. As a result, the curved segments on either side of the point must not only shrink or stretch, but also bend to accommodate the movement. Meanwhile, segments located between two deselected points or two selected points remain unchanged during a move, as demonstrated in Figure 5-7. Illustrator lets you move multiple points within a single path, as in Figure 5-7, or in separate paths, as in Figure 5-8. This means you can reshape multiple paths at the same time.

Figure 5-7: When you drag more than one selected point at a time (left), the segments between the selected points remain unchanged (right).

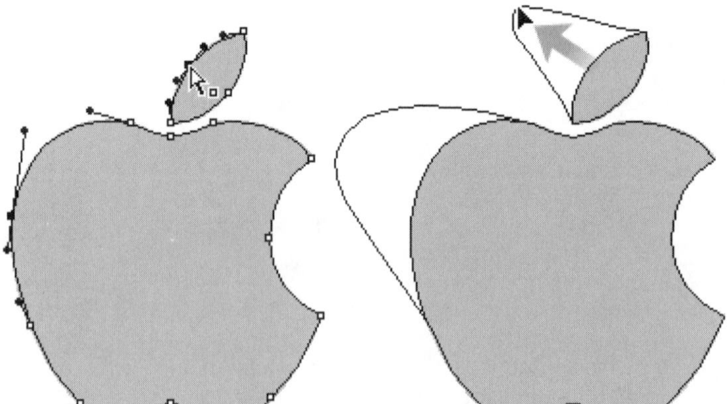

Figure 5-8: You can move multiple points even when selected points reside in different paths.

While you move a point, Illustrator displays both previous and current locations of the point and its surrounding segments. This useful feature permits you to gauge the full effect of a move as it progresses. Also worth noting: When you drag a single selected point, Illustrator displays the point, any Bézier control handles associated with the two neighboring segments, and the neighboring deselected points, as shown back in Figure 5-6. When dragging multiple points, Illustrator hides the points and handles, as in Figures 5-7 and 5-8. I, for one, wish we could see the points and handles, but Adobe thinks all that screen clutter might prove a mite confusing.

Keeping Your Movements in Line

You can constrain your cursor movements horizontally, vertically, or diagonally by pressing the Shift key. For example, if you want to move a point horizontally without moving it so much as a smidgen up or down, press the Shift key while dragging the point with the direct selection tool.

TIP

Almost every Macintosh program (and many Windows ones as well—try saying that ten times fast) assigns the Shift key to constraining cursor movements. The weird thing about Illustrator is that you press Shift after you begin dragging. (If you press Shift before you drag, you deselect the selected point on which you click, which causes Illustrator to ignore your drag.) Then you hold down the Shift key until after you release the mouse button.

You can adjust the effects of pressing Shift by changing the Constrain Angle value in the General Preferences dialog box. This rotates the constraint axes. Figure 5-9 shows what happens when you rotate the axes 15 degrees. So a horizontal (0-degree) move becomes a 15-degree move, a 45-degree move becomes a 60-degree move, and so on.

Why would you ever want to do this? You may want to move a point along an angled object without letting the point and the object drift apart. For example, the top segment along the tent object in Figure 5-10 is oriented at a 15-degree angle. To move the ball forward along the segment, I first rotate the constraint axes to 15 degrees and then drag the object while pressing Shift.

NOTE

How do I know the segment is angled to 15 degrees? You mean you can't just tell by looking at it? Then I guess it's a good thing you can measure it using the measure tool, which I discuss in Chapter 10.

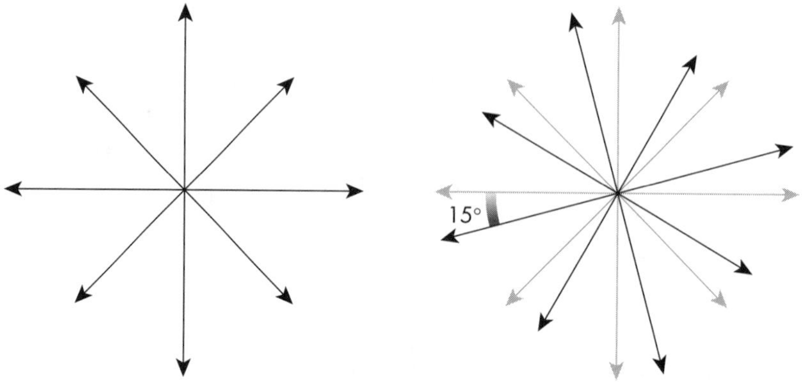

Figure 5-9: The default constraint axes (left) and the axes as they appear when rotated 15 degrees (right).

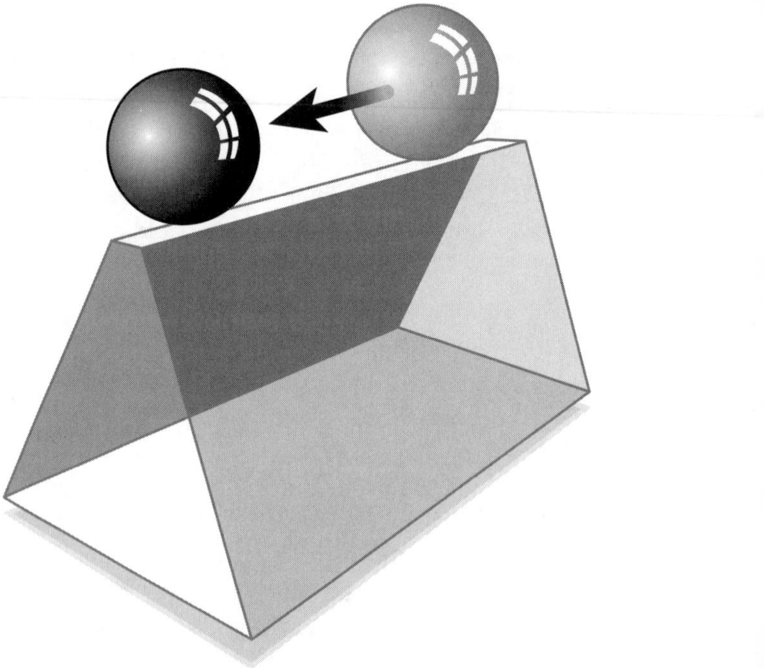

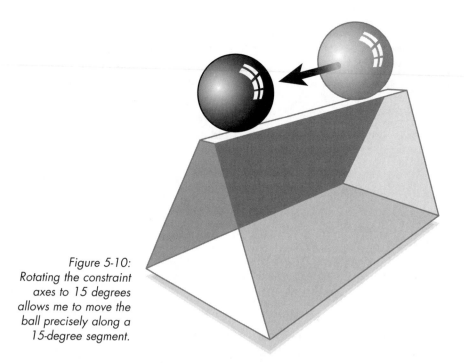

Figure 5-10: Rotating the constraint axes to 15 degrees allows me to move the ball precisely along a 15-degree segment.

Remember, the constraint axes also affect the creation of rectangles, ellipses, and text blocks. So you'll generally want to reset them to 0 degrees when you finish making your moves.

Snapping Point to Point

When dragging a point, you may find that it has a tendency to move sharply toward a stationary point in your illustration. This effect is called *snapping*, and it's Illustrator's way of ensuring that points that belong together are flush against each other to form a perfect fit.

When you drag a point within two screen pixels of any deselected point on your drawing area, your cursor snaps to the stationary point, so that both point and cursor occupy the very same spot on the page. At the moment the snap occurs, your cursor changes from a filled arrowhead to a hollow arrowhead, as shown in Figure 5-11. (This is particularly useful after a long day in the office, when your snap-perception capabilities have all but vanished.)

For example, you might drag the center point of a rectangle until it snaps to the center point of a stationary ellipse. In this way, both shapes are centered at exactly the same point.

Figure 5-11: Your cursor changes to a hollow arrowhead when snapping a point to a stationary point.

Your cursor snaps to stationary points as well as to the previous locations of points currently being moved. (This last item is more useful than it sounds. You'll see, one day it'll come in handy.) Your cursor also snaps to text blocks and to guides (covered in Chapters 6 and 10 respectively).

You can turn Illustrator's snapping feature on and off by choosing the View » Snap to Point command or by pressing ⌘-Option-plus (+).

Dragging Segments

You can also reshape a path by dragging its segments. When you drag a straight segment, its neighboring segments stretch or shrink to accommodate the change in distance, as shown in the first example in Figure 5-12. However, when you drag a curved segment, you stretch only that segment. The effect is rather like pulling on a rubber band extended between two nails, as the second example illustrates.

Figure 5-13 examines in detail what happens when you drag on a curved segment. The longer the drag, the more the segment has to bend. More important is how the segment bends. Notice the two Bézier control handles on either side of the segment. The handles automatically extend and retract as you drag. Each handle moves along an imaginary line consistent with the handle's original inclination. The angle of a control handle does not change one whit when you drag a segment, thus guaranteeing that the curved segment moves in alignment with neighboring stationary segments.

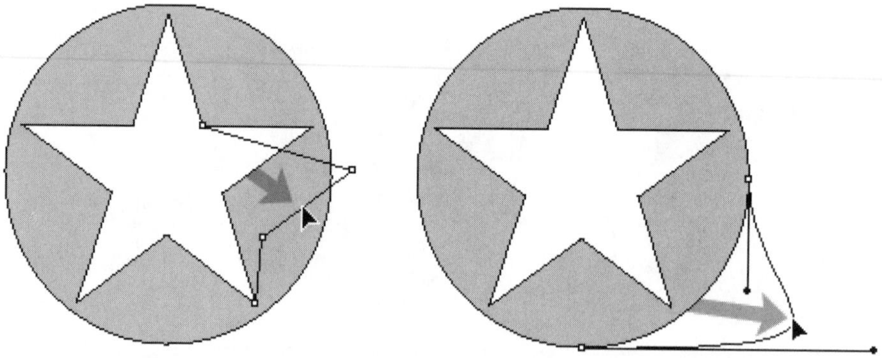

Figure 5-12: The difference between dragging a straight segment (left) and a curved segment (right).

TIP: When dragging a segment, drag on the middle of the segment, approximately equidistant from both of its points, as I have done in Figure 5-13. This provides the best leverage and keeps you from losing control over the segment. (Believe it or not, these things can spring away from you if you're not careful.)

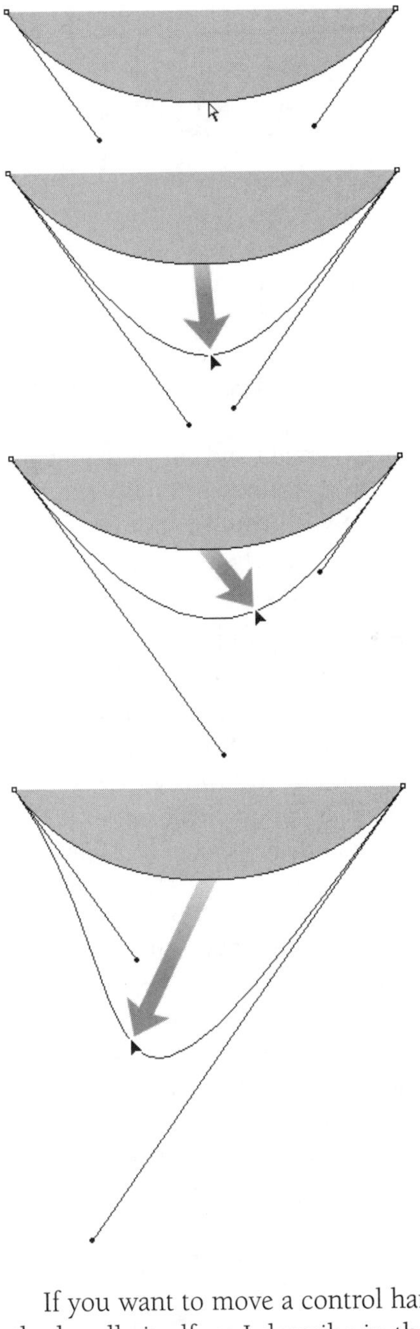

Figure 5-13:
When you drag a curved segment, each Bézier control handle moves back and forth along a constant axis.

If you want to move a control handle in a different direction, you have to drag the handle itself, as I describe in the "Dragging Control Handles" section later in this chapter.

Nudging Points and Segments

Another way to move a selected element is to press one of the four arrow keys at the bottom of your keyboard (→, ↑, ←, ↓). Not surprisingly, each of these keys nudges a selection in the direction of the arrow.

You can change the distance that a single keystroke moves a selected element by adjusting the Cursor Key value in the General Preferences dialog box. For example, setting the value to 1 point is equivalent to one screen pixel when you view the illustration at actual size. However, you can set the value anywhere from 0.01 to 1296 points—that's a whopping 18 inches. I usually keep it somewhere between 0.1 and 10 points, depending on the situation. (In fact, I'm constantly changing the value, usually setting it smaller and smaller as my illustration becomes more detailed.)

You can use arrow keys to move points as well as straight and curved segments. (Sadly, you can't move a single control handle with an arrow key; to do this, you must drag the handle with the direct selection tool.) This is very handy for stretching two segments exactly the same distance. Just click on one segment, Shift-click on the other, and whack away at the arrow keys.

The arrow keys move a selection with respect to the constraint axes. If you rotate the axes, you affect the direction in which a selected element moves. For example, if you enter 15 degrees for the Constrain Angle value in the General Preferences dialog box, pressing the right arrow key moves the selection slightly upward, pressing the up arrow moves it slightly to the left, and so on, just as I demonstrated back in Figure 5-9.

If pressing an arrow key doesn't seem to produce any noticeable result, one of two things could be wrong. First, you might have the Cursor Key value in the General Preferences dialog box set so low that you simply can't see the effect of the movement at your particular view size. Second, a palette might be active. For example, if you just got through changing the size of a font in the Character palette, Illustrator may be forwarding the arrow key signal to the palette, even if no option appears to be active. To remedy this situation, press Return, deactivating the palette. Then press the arrow keys to nudge without hindrance.

Dragging Control Handles

The only element that we've so far neglected to move is the Bézier control handle. I've saved it for last because it's the most difficult and the most powerful element you can manipulate.

After referencing control handles several times in this chapter, I suppose it's high time I defined my terminology. The *Bézier control handle* (*control handle* or *handle* or *those funky little line things* for short) is the element that defines the arc of a segment as it exits or enters an anchor point. It tugs at a segment like an invisible thread. You increase the curvature of a segment when you drag the handle away from its point, and decrease the curvature when you drag a handle toward its point.

To display a control handle, you can either select the point to which the handle belongs or select the segment it controls. You then drag the handle with the direct selection tool, just as you drag a point.

Figure 5-14 shows three paths composed of five points each. I drew the first path—the one that looks like a 2—with the pencil tool and assigned it a thick gray stroke. The second and third paths are based on the 2; the only differences are the positions of the control handles and the curvatures of the segments. The points remain unmoved from one path to the next, and yet the results are unique. The third path in particular bears little resemblance to a 2.

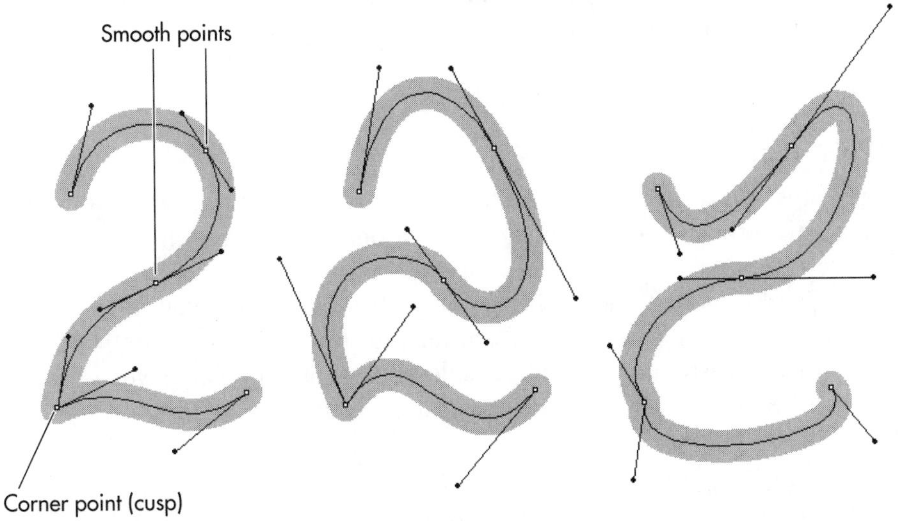

Figure 5-14: These three paths comprise five points apiece. The points remain stationary—only the control handles move.

The 2 comprises two smooth points around its loop and a special kind of corner point called a *cusp* where the loop and base meet. A cusp forms a corner between two curved segments. (We don't really care what kinds of points the endpoints are, because no segments follow them.)

The other two paths contain the same points in the same order. So not only has no point been moved, no point has been converted to a different kind of point. As a result, the bottom left point in each path remains a corner, permitting me to move the two control handles on either side of the point independently of each other. This is the very nature of a corner point.

Likewise, the points in the middle and upper right portions of the path remain smooth points. When I move one control handle, the other moves in the opposite direction, making for a sort of fulcrum effect. This ensures a continuous arc through each point. Not only is there no corner at either location, there's no hint of even the slightest crease. The path continues through the points as smoothly as a bend in the road.

TIP: Dragging a control handle can turn ugly when you're working inside a very complex illustration. If the handle rests near a point or segment from a different path, Illustrator may think you're trying to drag the point or segment rather than the handle. To bring the handle out of the fray so you can get to it more easily, drag the curved segment that the handle controls. Stretching the segment lengthens the handle; then you can drag the handle without busybody points and segments horning in.

Bézier Rules

The paths in Figure 5-14 demonstrate how control handles work, but they aren't exactly attractive. In fact, one of the reasons I assigned such heavy strokes was to cover up how very ugly these paths are.

Figure 5-14 is proof of the old Bézier adage that just because you *can* drag control handles all over the place doesn't mean you *should*. Manipulating handles is not so much a question of what is possible as of what is proper. Several handle-handling rules have developed over the years, but the best are the *All-or-Nothing rule* and the *33-Percent rule*:

- The All-or-Nothing rule states that every segment in your path should be associated with either two control handles or none at all. In other words, no segment should rely on only one control handle to determine its curvature.

- The 33-Percent rule tells us that the distance from any control handle to its point should equal approximately one third the length of the segment. So one handle covers one third of the segment, the other handle covers the opposite third, and the middle third is handle free.

The left path in Figure 5-15 violates the All-or-Nothing rule. Only one handle apiece controls each of its two curved segments, resulting in weak, shallow arcs. Such puny curves are sure to inspire snorts and guffaws from discriminating viewers.

The right example in Figure 5-15 obeys the All-or-Nothing rule. As the rule states, the straight segment has no handles and the two curved segments have two handles apiece. The result is a full-figured, properly rendered path that is a credit to any illustration.

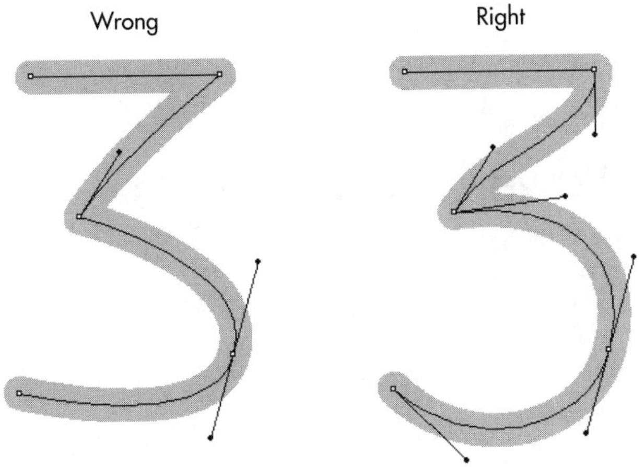

Figure 5-15: The All-or-Nothing rule says that two handles should control every curved segment, one for each of its points.

The first path in Figure 5-16 violates the 33-Percent rule. The handles are either much too short or much too long to fit their segments. The result is an ugly, misshapen mess. In the second example, each handle is about one-third of the length of its segment. The top segment is shorter than the other two, so its handles are shorter as well. This path is smooth and consistent in curvature, giving it a naturalistic appearance.

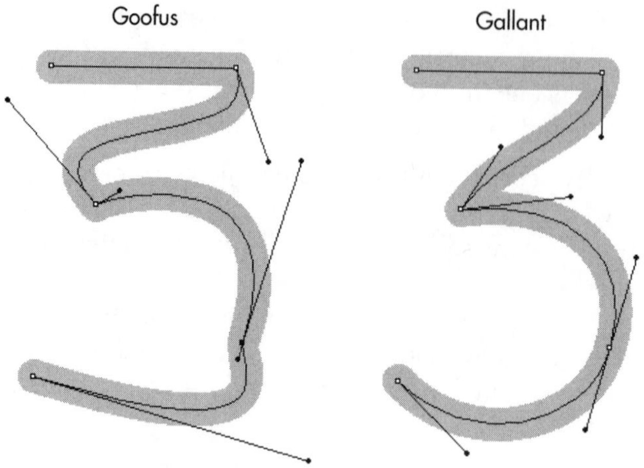

Figure 5-16: According to the 33-Percent rule, every control handle should extend about one third the length of its segment.

The Great and Powerful Pen Tool

Now that you've had a taste of Bézier theory, it's time for full immersion. The pen tool is the absolute Bézier champ, capable of creating anything from schematic newspaper charts to detailed scenes of heightened reality. For nearly a decade, Illustrator's pen tool was the reigning champ, and no other program offered anything that came close—not FreeHand, not any of the 3-D drawing programs, not even Photoshop. (However, Photoshop has cloned bits and pieces of Illustrator's pen tool over the years and, interestingly enough, the latest version of its pen even adds an innovation, the magnetic pen tool, that would make a welcome addition to Illustrator's arsenal.) Only with its fourth attempt did FreeHand finally design a tool to rival Illustrator's. Well, that's not quite true; FreeHand has finally *cloned* Illustrator's pen tool.

Pen Tool Basics

When drawing with the pen tool, you build a path by creating individual points. Illustrator automatically connects the points with *segments*. The following list summarizes how you can use the pen tool to build paths in Illustrator. I describe each of these methods in more detail later in this chapter.

- **Path building:** To build a path, create one point after another inside the drawing area until the path is the desired length and shape. You create and position a point by either clicking or dragging with the pen tool. (Clicking creates a corner, dragging creates a smooth point.) Illustrator draws a segment between each new point and its predecessor.

- **Adjusting a point:** Midway into creating a path, you can reposition points or change the curvature of segments that you've already drawn. To move a point while you are still creating it, press and hold the spacebar. You can then reposition the point on the fly. Release the spacebar and continue creating points. If you've already created a point but wish to modify it before moving on to the next point, just press the ⌘ key to access the direct-selection tool (press ⌘-Tab if the arrow tool comes up instead) and drag the points, segments, and control handles as desired. When you've finished, release ⌘ and continue adding points.

WARNING

Be sure not to ⌘-click in an empty portion of the drawing area or on a different path. Clicking off the active path deactivates it, which means you can't add any more points to it without first reactivating the path (as described in the "Extending an open path" item, coming right up).

- **Closing the path:** To create a closed shape, click or drag on the first point in the path. Every point will then have one segment coming into it and another segment exiting it.
- **Leaving the path open:** To leave a path open, so it has a specific beginning and ending, deactivate the path by pressing ⌘-Shift-A (Edit » Deselect All). Or you can press ⌘ to get the arrow or direct selection tool and click on an empty portion of the drawing area. Either way, you deactivate the path so you can move on and create a new one.
- **Extending an open path:** To reactivate an open path, click or drag on one of its endpoints. Illustrator is then ready to draw a segment between the endpoint and the next point you create.
- **Joining two open paths:** To join one open path with another open path, click or drag on an endpoint in the first path, then click or drag on an endpoint in the second. Illustrator draws a segment between the two, bringing them together in everlasting peace and brotherhood.

That's basically all there is to using the pen tool. A click here, a drag there, and you have yourself a path. But to achieve decent results, you need to know exactly what clicking and dragging do and how to use these techniques to your best advantage. If the devil is in the details, the pen tool is Illustrator's most fiendish tool. I probe the pits of the pen one level at a time in the following sections.

Defining Points and Segments

Points in a Bézier path act as little road signs. Each point steers the path by specifying how a segment enters it and how another segment exits it. You specify the identity of each little road sign by clicking or dragging, sometimes with the Option key gently but firmly pressed.

The following items explain the specific kinds of points and segments you can create in Illustrator. Look to Figure 5-17 for examples.

- **Corner point:** Click with the pen tool to create a corner point, which represents the corner between two segments in a path.
- **Straight segment:** Click at two different locations to create a straight segment between two corner points, like the first example shown in Figure 5-17.

TIP After positioning one corner point, you can Shift-click to create a perfectly horizontal, vertical, or 45-degree segment between that point and the new one. As discussed in the "Keeping Your Movements in Line" section earlier in this chapter, you can modify the angle of constraint by entering a value into the Constrain Angle option box in the General Preferences dialog box.

- **Smooth point:** Drag with the pen tool to create a smooth point with two symmetrical Bézier control handles. A smooth point ensures that one segment fuses into another to form a continuous arc.
- **Curved segment:** Drag at two different locations to create a curved segment between two smooth points, as the second example in Figure 5-17 illustrates.
- **Straight segment followed by curved:** After drawing a straight segment, drag from the corner point you just created to add a control handle. Then drag again at a different location to append a curved segment to the end of the straight segment.
- **Curved segment followed by straight:** After drawing a curved segment, click on the smooth point you just created to delete the forward control handle. This converts the smooth point to a corner point with one handle. Then click again at a different location to append a straight segment to the end of the curved segment.

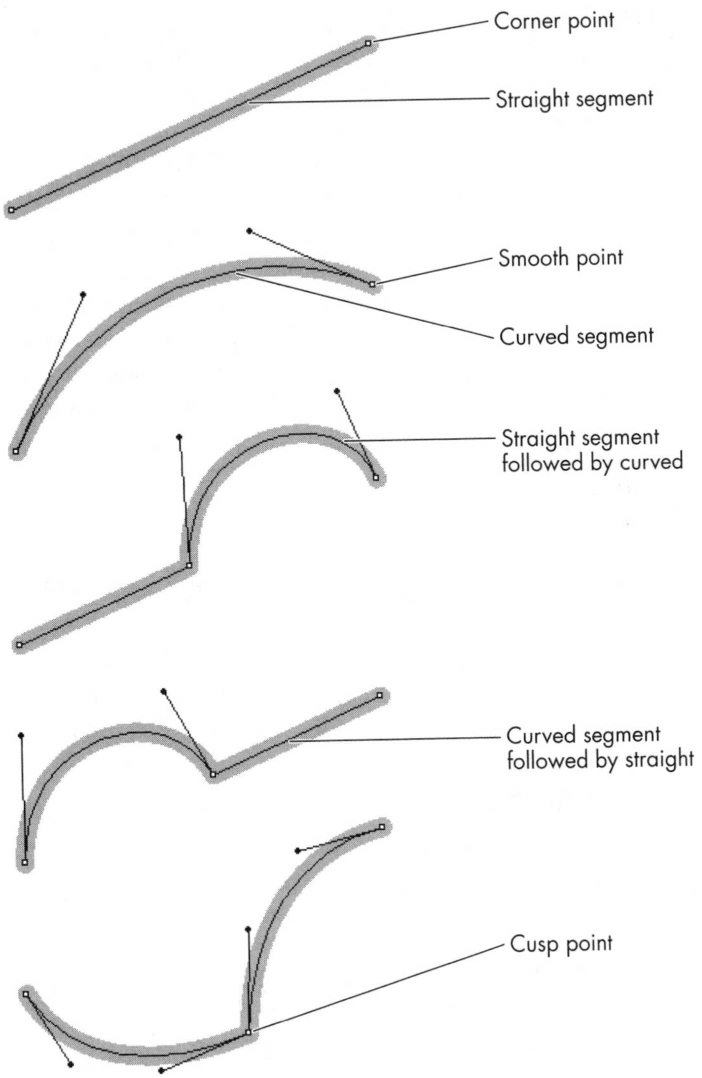

Figure 5-17: The complete annotated guide to the different kinds of points and segments you can draw with the pen tool.

- **Cusp point:** To convert a smooth point to a corner point with two independent handles (sometimes known as a *cusp point*), you have a couple of different options depending on the situation. First, after drawing a curved segment, Option-drag from the smooth point you just created to redirect the forward control handle. Then drag again at a new location to append a curved segment that sprouts off in a different direction. The last example in Figure 5-17 shows the cusp point in action.

The second method (and a great little addition to Illustrator 8) lets you modify points while they're still under construction. If you are still in the process of creating the smooth point that follows the curved segment (that is, you've clicked to set the point and dragged to form the control handles, but you haven't released the mouse button), then you can press and hold the Option key. While the Option key is depressed, you can move the forward control handle independently of the backward handle—the backward handle locks in place the moment you press the Option key. For the handles to retain their independence, you must release the mouse button before releasing the Option key. Otherwise, the handles snap back into their original rigid seesaw relationship.

Modifying the Closing Point

When you close a shape, you click, drag, and Option-drag, just as you do when creating other points. But because you modify and close in one gesture, it seems a good idea to revisit these techniques within this slightly different context:

- Click on the first point in a path to clip off any control handle that may have been threatening to affect the closing segment and you'll close the path with a corner point.
- If the first point in the path is a smooth point, drag on it to make sure it remains smooth, thus closing the path with an arc.
- If the first point is a corner point, drag to add a control handle that curves the closing segment.
- To convert a smooth point to a cusp on closing, Option-drag on the first point in the path. In this case, you must press the Option key before you start the drag. Pressing the Option key after you're into the drag has no effect.

Putting the Pen Tool to Work

Well now, that was a whole lot of information crammed into a small amount of type—perhaps too much. To make things a little clearer for those of you who are still struggling with this amazing tool, I give you the chance to try out the pen tool in the next three sections. I first show you how to use corner points, then smooth points, and finally cusps.

Drawing Free-form Polygons

Clicking with the pen tool is a wonderful way to create straight-sided polygons. Unlike the shapes you draw with the regular polygon tool, pen tool polygons may be any shape or size. These are pistol-packin' polygons of the Wild West, with no customs to guide their behavior or laws to govern their physical form. I'm talking outlaw polygons, so be sure to take cover as you click:

1. **Click to create a corner point.**

   Select the pen tool and click at some location in the drawing area to create a corner point. The little *x* next to the pen cursor disappears to show you that a path is now in progress. The new corner point appears as a filled square to show that it's selected. It is also *open-ended*, meaning that it doesn't have both a segment coming into it and a segment going out from it. In fact, this new corner point—I'll call it point A—is not associated with any segment whatsoever. It's a lone point, open-ended in two directions.

2. **Click to add another corner point.**

   Click at a new location in the illustration to create a new corner point—let's call this one point B. Illustrator automatically draws a straight segment from point A to point B, as demonstrated in Figure 5-18. Notice that point A now appears hollow rather than filled, showing that point A is the member of a selected path, but is itself deselected. Point B is selected and open-ended. Illustrator automatically selects a point immediately after you create it and deselects all other points.

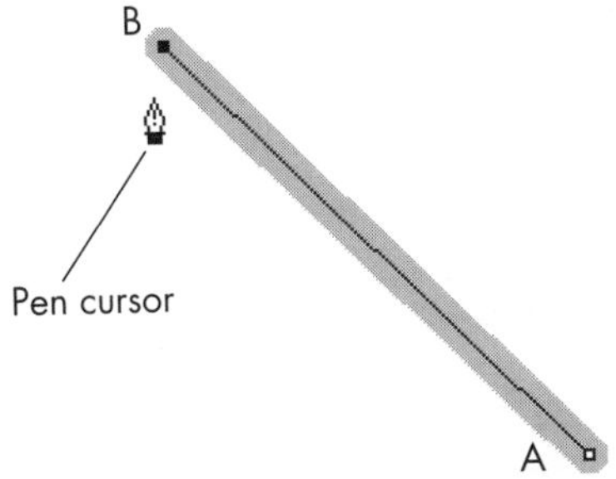

Figure 5-18: Draw a straight segment by clicking at each of two separate locations with the pen tool.

3. **Click to add yet another corner point.**

   Click a third time with the pen tool to create a third corner point—point C. Since a point may be associated with no more than two segments, point B is no longer open-ended, as Figure 5-19 verifies. Such a point is called an *interior point*.

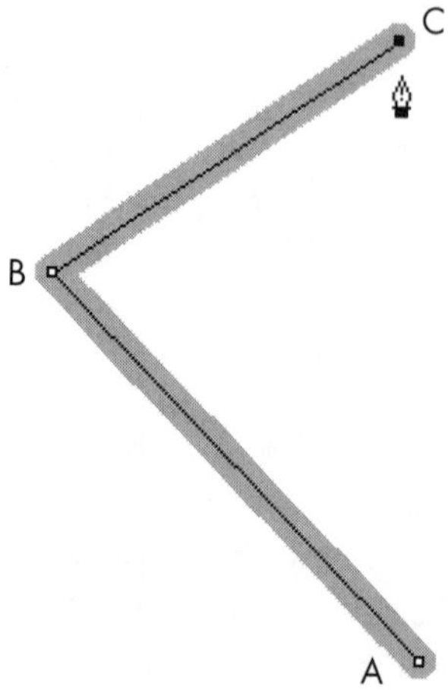

Figure 5-19:
Point B is now an interior point, incapable of receiving additional segments.

4. Click on the first point in the path.

You can keep adding points to a path one at a time for as long as you like. When you're finished, you can *close* the path by again clicking on point A, as demonstrated in Figure 5-20. Illustrator displays the close cursor to show you that it's ready to draw the last segment. If you don't see the close cursor (the pen cursor augmented with a little *o* in the bottom right), you don't have it positioned properly. (If you have the Text Label Hints option from the Smart Guides Preferences dialog box active, Illustrator will display the word *anchor*, providing you with another visual clue that you're in a position to close the path.) Since point A is open-ended, it willingly accepts the segment drawn between it and the previous point in the path.

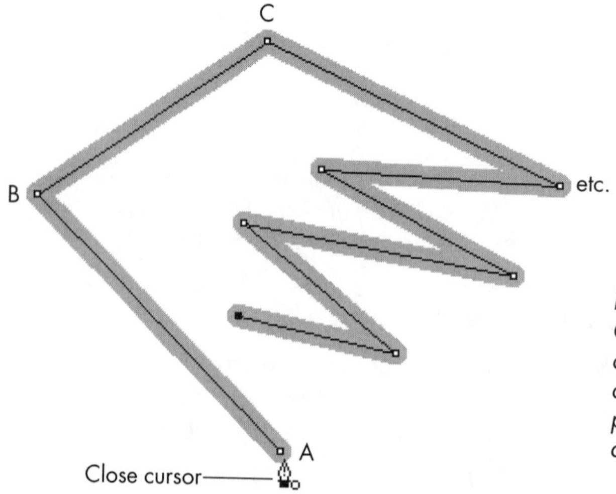

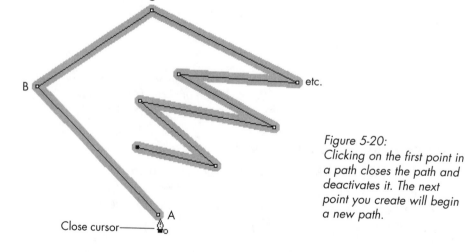

Figure 5-20:
Clicking on the first point in a path closes the path and deactivates it. The next point you create will begin a new path.

5. Click to start a new path.

All points in a closed path are interior points. Therefore, the path you just drew is no longer active. Illustrator displays the new path cursor, as in Figure 5-21, to show it will draw no segment between the next point you create and any point in the closed path. To verify this, click again with the pen tool. You create a new independent point, which is selected and open-ended in two directions, just like point A. Meanwhile, the closed path becomes deselected. The path-creation process begins anew.

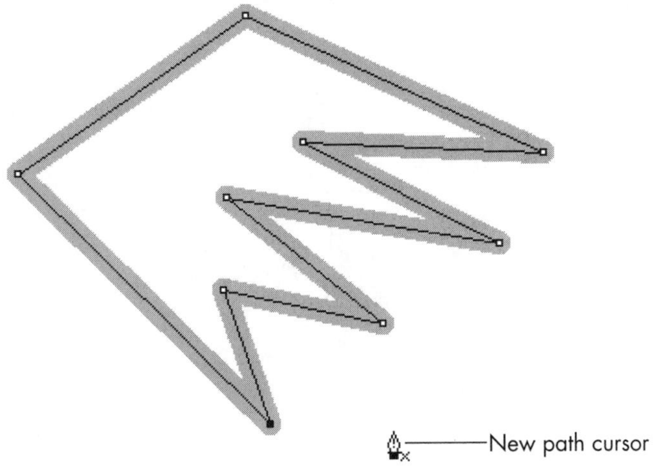

Figure 5-21: After you close a path, Illustrator adds a little x to the pen tool cursor to show that the next point you create starts a new path.

Drawing Supple Curves

Free-form polygons are great, but you can create them in any drawing program, even something old and remedial like MacDraw. The real advantage to the pen tool is that it lets you draw very precise curves.

When you drag with the pen tool to create a smooth point, you specify the location of two control handles. Each of these handles appears as a tiny circle perched at the end of a thin line that connects the handle to its point (see Figure 5-22). These handles act as levers, bending segments relative to the smooth point itself.

The point at which you begin dragging with the pen tool determines the location of the smooth point; the point at which you release becomes a control handle that affects the *next* segment you create. A second handle appears symmetrically from the first handle, on the opposite side of the smooth point. This handle determines the curvature of the most recent segment, as demonstrated in Figure 5-22. You might think of a smooth point as if it were the center of a small seesaw, with the control handles acting as opposite ends. If you push down on one handle, the opposite handle goes up, and vice versa.

Smooth points act no differently than corner points when it comes to building paths. You can easily combine smooth and corner points in the same path by alternatively clicking and dragging. However, if the first point in a path is a smooth point, you should drag rather than click on the point when closing the path. Otherwise, you run the risk of changing the point to a cusp, as discussed in the next section.

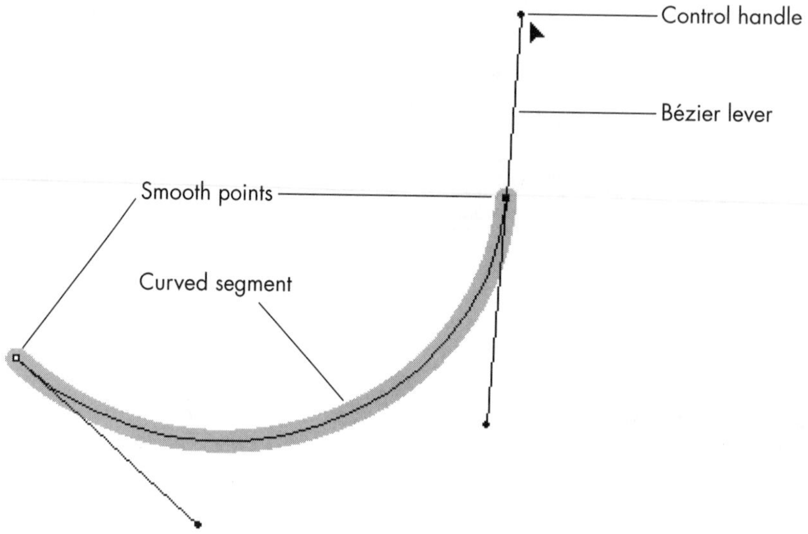

Figure 5-22: Drag with the pen tool to create a smooth point flanked by two Bézier control handles.

Creating Corners between Curves

A smooth point must *always* have two Bézier control handles, each positioned in an imaginary straight line with the point itself. A corner point, however, is much more versatile. It can have zero, one, or two handles. To create a corner point that has one or two control handles (sometimes called a cusp), you must manipulate an existing corner or smooth point while in the process of creating a path. I'll demonstrate three examples of how this technique can work.

Deleting Handles from Smooth Points

These steps explain how to add a flat edge to a path composed of smooth points:

1. **Draw some smooth points.**

   Begin by drawing the path shown in Figure 5-23. You do this by dragging three times with the pen tool: First drag downward from point A, then drag leftward from point B, and finally drag up from point C (which is selected in the figure). The result is an active path composed of three smooth points.

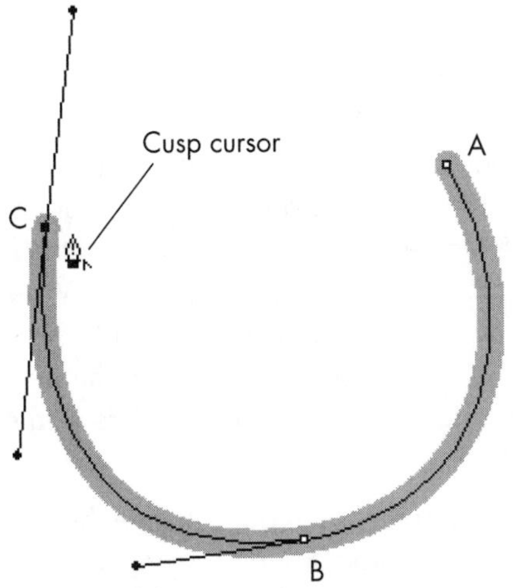

Figure 5-23:
An active semicircular path with a selected, open-ended smooth point.

2. **Click on the last point created.**

   Illustrator lets you alter the most recent point while in the process of creating a path. Suppose that you want to flatten off the top of the path to create a sort of tilted bowl, like the one in Figure 5-24. Since you can associate smooth points only with curved segments, you must convert the top two smooth points to corner points.

   To convert the most recent point—the one on the right—position the pen tool over point C so the pen changes to the cusp cursor (the normal pen cursor with an additional little carrot in the lower right corner, as in Figure 5-23). Then click to amputate the forward handle, which does not yet control a segment.

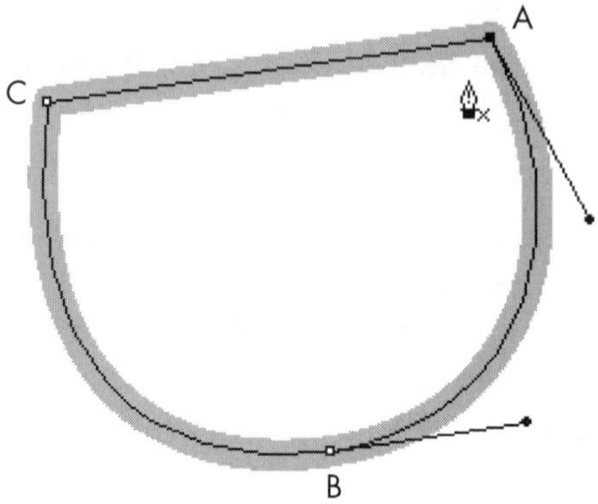

Figure 5-24:
By clicking with the pen tool on the two top points, you change the existing smooth points to corner points with one Bézier control handle apiece.

3. Click on the first point in the path.

You now have an open path composed of two smooth points (A and B) and a cusp (C). You still need to close the path and amputate a handle belonging to point A. A single operation—clicking on the first smooth point—accomplishes both maneuvers. It's that simple. With one click, you close the path and amputate the control handle that would otherwise have curved the closing segment. Hence, the new segment is straight, bordered on both sides by corner points with one handle each, as in Figure 5-24.

Illustrator now offers you another method to delete the handle from a smooth point. You construct the path as explained in step 1, except that you don't release the mouse button after dragging with the pen to form the forward control handle belonging to point C. Continue to hold down the mouse button, and press the Option key. You can now drag the forward handle independently of the backward handle. (In fact, the backward handle will not move while you have the Option key depressed.) Drag the forward handle back toward point C until the two positions coincide. Release the mouse button and then release the Option key. Proceed to step 3.

This method has the advantage of letting you modify the path while you are constructing it. The drawback is that Illustrator doesn't inform you in any way that the end of the forward handle and point C are perfectly aligned. So instead of removing the handle, you may only have reduced its length, making it too small to see at your present magnification. In this case, as you're hoping to truncate a point's forward handle, you probably should use the traditional method as the previous steps outline.

Converting Smooth Points to Cusps

These steps show you how to close the path from Figure 5-23 with a concave top, resulting in a crescent shape:

1. **Draw some smooth points.**

   Begin again by drawing the path shown in Figure 5-23 as described in the first step of the previous section.

2. **Option-drag down from the last point created.**

   All segments in a crescent are curved, but the upper and lower segments meet to form two cusps. You need to change the two top smooth points to cusps with two control handles apiece—one controlling the upper segment and one controlling the lower segment.

   To subtract a handle from a smooth point and add a new handle to the resulting corner point in one operation, press the Option key and drag from point C. The moment you begin to Option-drag, the point's identity changes from smooth to corner and a new handle emerges, as shown in Figure 5-25. This handle controls the next segment you create.

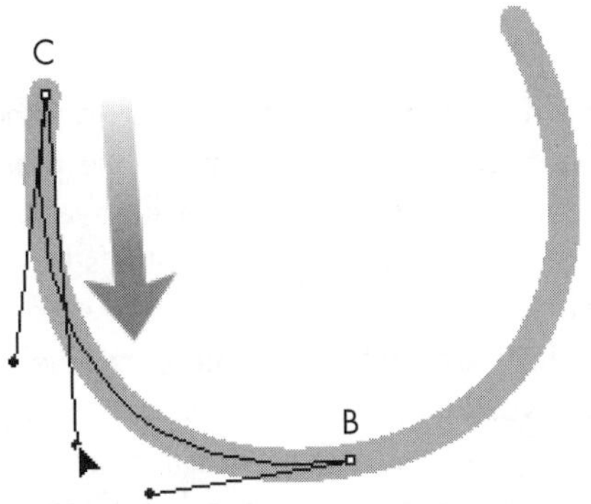

Figure 5-25:
Press the Option key and drag from the selected smooth point to convert the point to a cusp.

3. **Option-drag up from the first point in the path.**

   You close the path in a similar manner, by Option-dragging upward from point A. Notice the location of the cursor as you drag, as Figure

5-26 demonstrates. You drag in one direction, but the handle emerges in the opposite direction. This is because when dragging with the pen tool, you always drag in the direction of the forward segment—that is, the one that *exits* the current point. Illustrator positions the handle controlling the closing segment symmetrically to your drag, even if it is the only handle you're manipulating. It's kind of weird, but it's Illustrator's way.

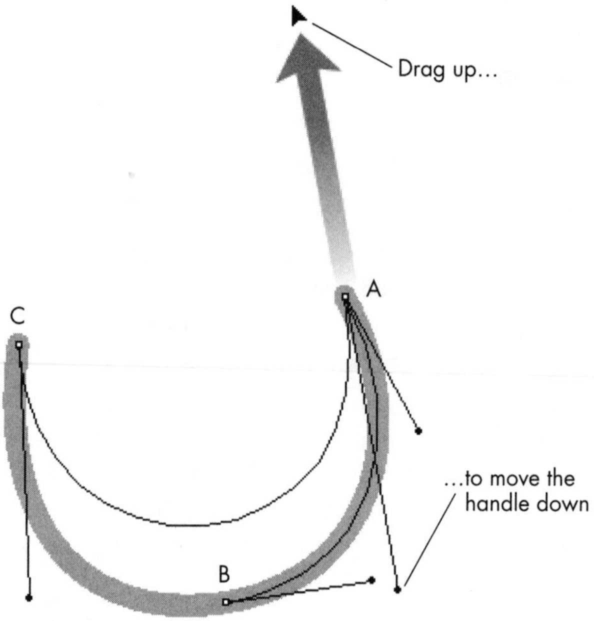

Figure 5-26: Close the path by Option-dragging up from the first point in the path.

As before, Illustrator 8's newfangled ways give you another means by which to approach for this problem. While point C is still under construction (that is, while you still have the mouse button pressed and you're dragging point C's forward control handle), press and hold the Option key. You can now reposition the forward control handle completely independent of the backward one. Drag the forward handle into place, as shown in Figure 5-25. Once it's in place, be sure to release the mouse button before you release the Option key.

Adding Handles to Corner Points

Last but not least, the next steps tell you how to add a curved segment to a path composed of straight ones:

1. **Draw some corner points.**

   Begin by creating the straight-sided path shown in Figure 5-27. Well, create something like it, anyway. Actually, it doesn't matter how many points are in the path, so long as they're all corner points.

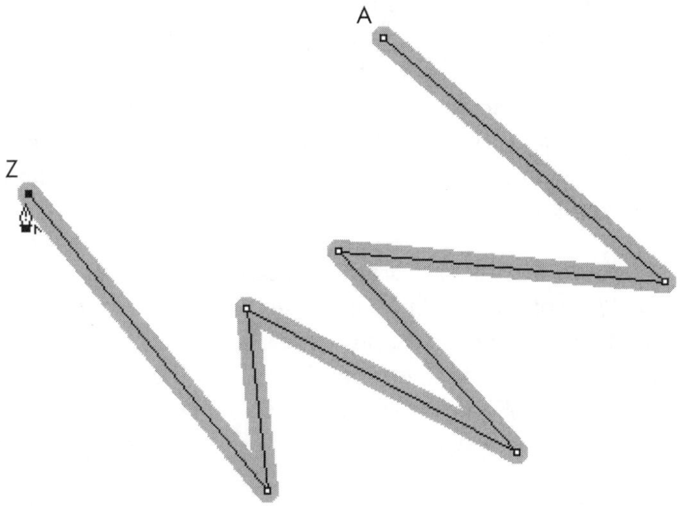

Figure 5-27: An active path composed entirely of straight segments with a selected, open-ended corner point.

2. **Drag from the last corner point created.**

   Drag from the corner point you've created most recently (point Z in the figure) to extract a single control handle, as shown in Figure 5-28.

   Note that you don't convert the corner point to a smooth point by dragging from it. The fact is, you can't change a corner point to a smooth point using the pen tool.

3. **Drag from the first point in the path.**

   To close the path, drag from the first corner point in the path, as demonstrated in Figure 5-29. Once again, you drag in the direction opposite the emerging Bézier control handle.

As you may have guessed, Illustrator now provides you with another technique for achieving these results. I should preface this explanation by saying that since this method is easy to mess up and inadvertently create a dual-handled cusp point instead of a single-handled corner point, you may prefer to follow the traditional method. Nevertheless, the new technique may come in handy, so here it is. Create the first portion of the path as you normally would, then click to position point Z, but do not release the mouse button. Without moving the mouse one iota (not even a half or a quarter of an iota), press and hold the Option key. Illustrator creates a single control handle that's ready to follow your every move. Position the handle as shown in Figure 5-28. When you're happy with its placement, release the mouse button and then the Option key. You are now ready to complete the path by closing it, as in step 3 above.

If you do accidentally drag the mouse after creating point Z, you'll create a smooth point, albeit it one with very tiny control handles. When you press the Option key, you'll drag the forward control handle around and form a cusp point akin to the one you made with the alternative method in "Converting Smooth Points to Cusps" above.

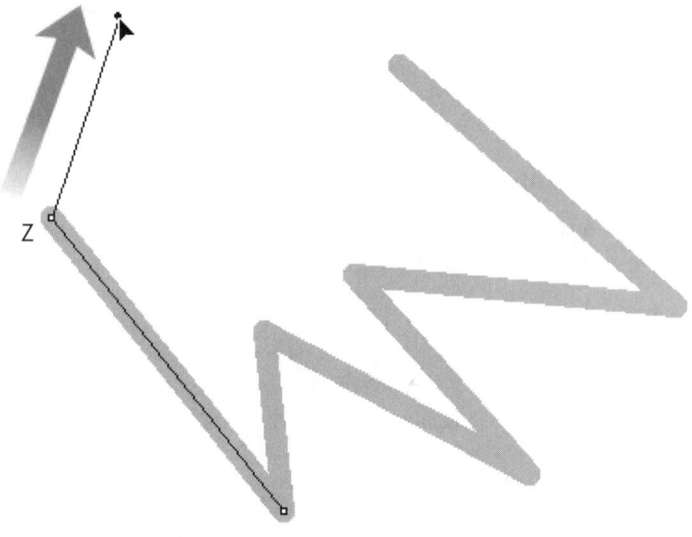

Figure 5-28: Drag from the selected corner point to add a Bézier control handle.

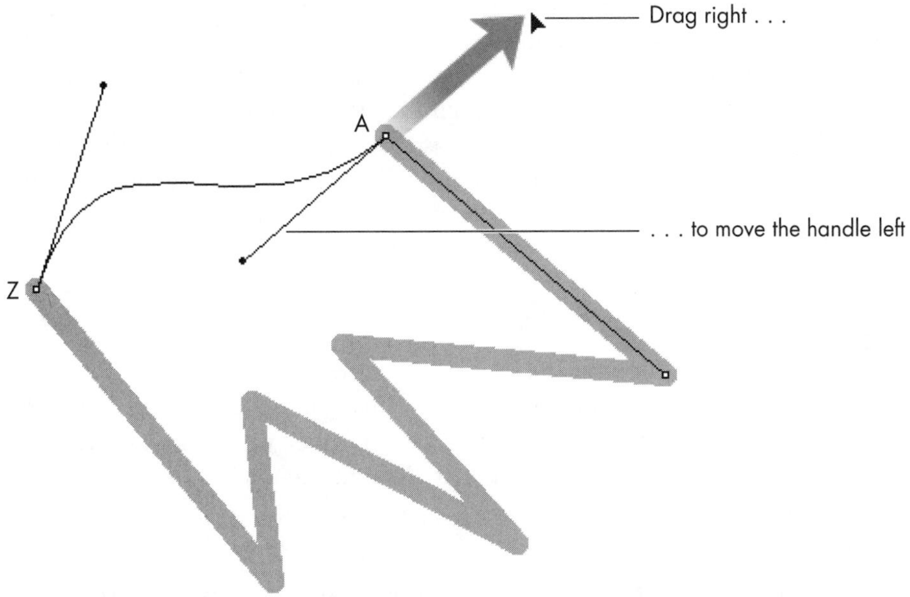

Figure 5-29: Close the path by dragging on the first corner point in the path.

Operating on Points Long after the Path Is Done

Right about now, you're probably figuring Illustrator's path-editing capabilities have completely revealed themselves to you like a lotus blossom unfurling its petals. Armed with the direct selection and pen tools, you are more or less master of all you survey.

Well, that's almost true. But there are still some unanswered questions. For example, how do you insert a point into a path? For that matter, how do you remove a point without breaking the path in half? And what do you do if you want to change a corner point in an existing path to a smooth point, or a smooth point to a corner?

Illustrator provides three tools that let you operate on existing paths, whether drawn with the pen tool or one of the tools from Chapter 4. These are the add anchor point tool, the delete anchor point tool, and the convert anchor point tool. (All those anchors weigh down my lucid prose, so I just dump them overboard, leaving the shorter tool names listed in Figure 5-30.) To select one of these tools you can drag from the pen tool slot in the toolbox and select the tool from the pop-up menu. To switch to the last used pen tool, press the P key. To select one of the others, press Shift-P to cycle through the other pen tools.

The following sections explain how to use these three tools. But you can also add points with the pen and pencil tools and delete points and segments with the direct selection tool, so I discuss these techniques as well. If it has anything to do with adding, deleting, or converting, it's covered in the next few pages.

Adding Points to a Path

A path is nothing more than an illusion your computer creates to make you think you're accomplishing something. Like an imaginary creature, it is constantly subject to revision and enhancement. It is not, in other words, in any way permanent, even if you created it years ago in a different version of Illustrator or even in a different program. What I'm trying to say here is, if a path doesn't have enough points to get the job done, don't hesitate to add some.

- **Appending a point to the end of an open path:** If an existing path is open, you can add points to either end of it. First activate one of its endpoints by clicking or dragging on it with the pen tool. When you position the pen tool over an inactive endpoint, you get the activate cursor, which looks like a pen with a little slash next to it. Drag from the point if you want to retain or add a control handle; click if you want to trim off a control handle or avoid adding one; and Option-drag if you want to change the direction of a handle. Then click and drag to add more points to the path.

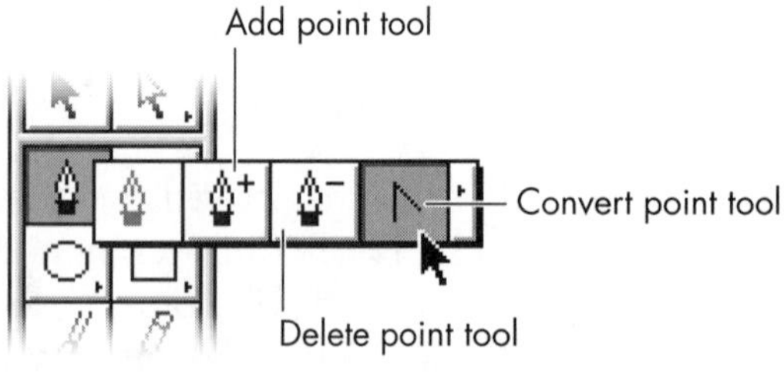

Figure 5-30: Drag from the pen icon to access three point-editing tools.

You can also lengthen an open path by dragging from one of its endpoints with the pencil tool. In the unlikely event the path touches a portion of a tracing template, you can even use the autotrace tool.

- **Closing an open path:** Once the path is active, you can close it in any of the ways discussed in the "Putting the Pen Tool to Work" section earlier in this chapter. Just click, drag, or Option-drag on the opposite endpoint with the pen tool. You can also close a path with the pencil tool by dragging from one endpoint to the other. In either case, Illustrator adds a little *o* to the cursor to show a closing is in process.
- **Insert a point into a segment:** To insert a new interior point into a path, select the add point tool and click anywhere along a segment (except on an existing point). Illustrator inserts the point and divides the segment in two. Illustrator automatically inserts a corner or smooth point depending on its reading of your path. If the point does not exactly meet your needs, you can modify it with the convert point tool, as I explain a few paragraphs from now.

The add point tool is great for filling out a path that just isn't making the grade. If a path isn't curving correctly, it may be that you're trying to make the existing points in the path do too much work. For example, the first path in Figure 5-31 obeys both the All-or-Nothing and 33-Percent rules, but it still looks overly squarish. That's because it violates a lesser rule that says handles shouldn't point wildly away from each other. To smooth things out, I clicked on the path midway between the two points with the add point tool. In this case, Illustrator inserted a smooth point, because the segment is ultimately smooth at the point where I clicked. I then used the direct selection tool to adjust the control handles and get the more rounded curve shown here.

NEW 8

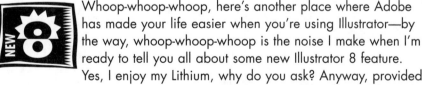

Whoop-whoop-whoop, here's another place where Adobe has made your life easier when you're using Illustrator—by the way, whoop-whoop-whoop is the noise I make when I'm ready to tell you all about some new Illustrator 8 feature. Yes, I enjoy my Lithium, why do you ask? Anyway, provided you have not opted to activate the Disable Auto Add/Delete check box inside the General Preferences dialog box, you can add a point to any active path by clicking with the pen tool, as shown on the left of Figure 5-32. Simply move the pen tool to one of the path's segments and click. The regular pen cursor gains a little plus sign (so it looks just like the add point cursor). This saves you the trouble of switching to the add point tool when you want to add a point to an active path. In Figure 5-31, I could just as easily have used the pen tool to add this point, since the path is active.

The only difference between using the add point tool and using the automated add point feature of the pen tool is that you can add points with the add point tool to any path, selected or not. To add a point with the enhanced pen tool, you must select a path first. If you don't like the pen tool's new ability, go to the General Preferences dialog box (⌘-K) and switch on the Disable Add/Delete option. The pen tool will no longer let you add points to existing segments.

With the Disable Add/Delete option turned off, you have one other option when using the pen tool: You can press the Shift key to temporarily disable the pen tool's new ability to

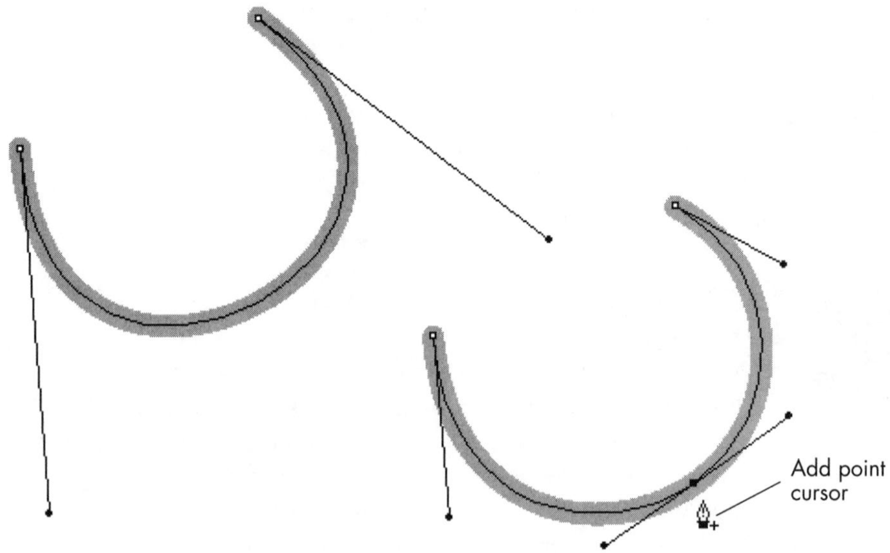

Figure 5-31: If a curve looks squarish no matter how much you monkey with the control handles (left), insert a point with the add point tool (right).

add points to existing segments. This comes in handy when you're trying to position a new point over an existing segment of that same path, as in Figure 5-32. Once the drag is under way, release the Shift key or you will constrain the construction of the point's control handles.

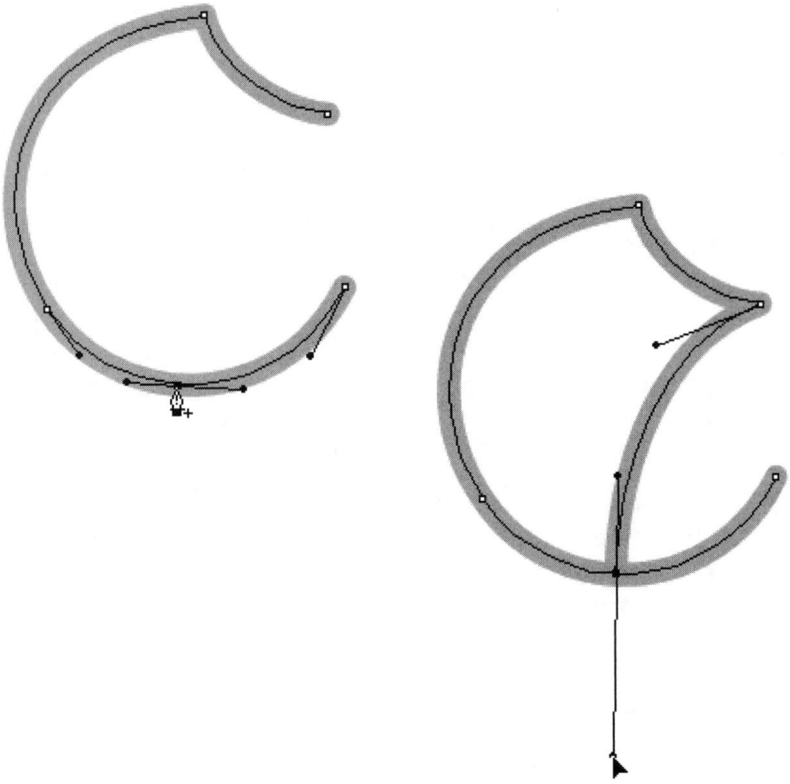

Figure 5-32: In both these examples, the Disable Auto Add/Delete check box inside the General Preferences dialog box is not selected. The example on the left shows what happens when you click on an active path with the pen tool—you add a point to the path. On the right, you see the result of Shift-clicking on an active path—the Disable Auto Add/Delete setting is ignored, and a new point that extends the original path forms over the path.

Illustrator lets you access the add point tool from the keyboard when certain tools are active:

- Press the Option key to access the add point tool temporarily when either the delete point or scissors tool is selected.
- Press Shift-P when using the pen tool and add a point; press Shift-P three more times and resume drawing with the pen tool by reactivating the point where you left off.
- Press Shift-P to cycle through the pen tools when using any tool.

Removing Points from a Path

To delete an entire path, you just select it with the arrow tool and press the Delete key. (If you're using an old keyboard, press Backspace.) If you love to use your mouse, you can choose Edit » Clear (although I must admit I've never seen anyone choose that command in my life, except one guy who constantly raved about the medicinal benefits derived from eating glue).

To delete a point or segment, try out one of the following techniques:

- **Delete a point and break the path:** To delete a point, select it with the direct selection tool and press the Delete key. When you delete an interior point, you delete both segments associated with that point, resulting in a break in the path. If you delete an endpoint from an open path, you delete the single segment associated with the point.
- **Delete a segment:** You can delete a single interior segment from a path without removing a point. To do so, click on the segment you want to delete with the direct selection tool and press Delete. Deleting a segment always creates a break in a path.
- **Delete the rest of the path:** After you delete a point or segment, Illustrator selects the remainder of the path. To delete the whole path, just press Delete a second time. This can be a handy technique if you don't want to switch to the arrow tool. Just click on some portion of the path and press Delete twice in a row to delete the whole path.
- **Remove a point without breaking the path:** If you want to get rid of a point but don't want to create a break in the path, select the delete point tool and click on the point you want to disappear. Illustrator draws a new segment between the two points neighboring the deleted point.

The flip side of the pen tool's new ability to add points to an active path is that it can also delete points just as easily—once again, provided that the Disable Auto Add/Delete check box inside the General Preferences dialog box is not selected. All you have to do is move the pen tool over one of the points of an active path and click. When the tool is in place, the regular pen cursor gains a small minus sign in the lower right corner, mimicking the appearance of the delete point tool. After you click, Illustrator redraws the path just as if you had clicked with the delete point tool, as demonstrated in the middle example of Figure 5-33.

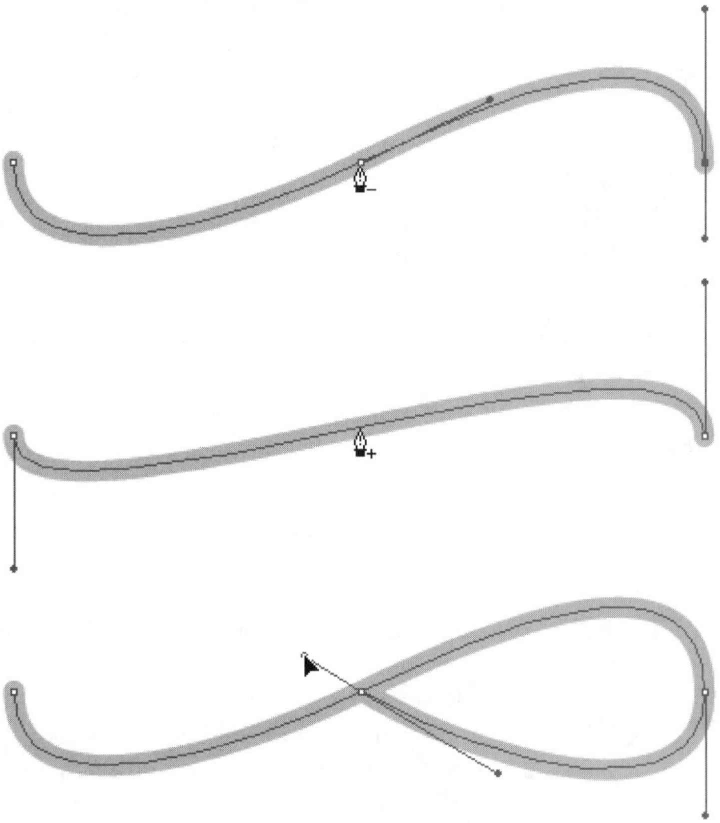

Figure 5-33: The top example shows the original curve and the placement of the pen cursor. The second example is the result of clicking on the middle point with the pen tool; the point is deleted. I Shift-dragged on the middle point in the last example. This forced Illustrator to construct a new point coinciding in position with the existing point.

The drawback here is that whereas the delete point tool allows you the freedom to delete a point from any path, selected or not, the pen tool's automated delete point feature works only on selected paths. If you find this new ability of the pen tool too intrusive, go to the General Preferences dialog box (⌘-K) and switch on the Disable Add/Delete option. The pen tool will no longer let you delete the points of existing paths.

As before, you can press the Shift key to disable temporarily the pen tool's ability to delete the points of a selected path. This comes in handy when you're trying to position a new point over an existing point of that same path, as in the bottom example of Figure 5-33. Remember to release the Shift key during the drag, unless you wish to constrain the orientation of the new point's control handles.

TIP

You can press keys to get the delete point tool when the add point, pen, or pencil tool is selected:

- Press Option to access the delete point tool when the add point tool is active. (Have you noticed that Option is a toggle between the add and delete point tools? When one is active, Option gets you the other.)
- When using the pen tool, press Shift-P twice and subtract a point; pressing Shift-P twice more switches back to the pen tool.
- When using any tool, press the P key to change to the last tool in the pen tool slot.

WARNING

Beware of deleting a point from a line that consists of only two points or a point or segment neighboring an endpoint. This will leave a single-point path, which is completely useless unless you intend to build on it immediately. Lone points clutter up the drawing area and make editing that much more confusing. (If your illustration does have lots of lone points—someone else's fault, I'm sure—choose Object » Path » Cleanup and select only the Stray Points check box.)

Converting Points between Corner and Smooth

Of the tools discussed in this chapter, I would probably rank the direct selection tool as most important, the pen tool as number two, and this next tool—the convert point tool—as number three. The convert point tool lets you change a point in the middle of a path from corner to smooth or smooth to corner. When a path is shaped wrong, this tool is absolutely essential.

You can change the identity of an interior point in any of the following ways:

- **Smooth to corner:** Using the convert point tool, click on a smooth point to convert it to a corner point with no control handle.
- **Smooth to cusp:** Drag a control handle belonging to a smooth point to move it independently of the other control handle, thus converting the smooth point to a cusp.
- **Corner or cusp to smooth:** A couple of versions ago, Adobe changed how the convert point tool behaves on cusp points. Rectifying the confusion associated with its use, the convert point tool now treats cusp points just like corner points. Drag from a corner point or cusp point to convert it to a smooth point with two symmetrical control handles.

Figure 5-34 shows a path created with the star tool. Like any star, it's made up entirely of corner points and straight segments. But with the help of the convert point tool, you can put some curve on that puppy, as the following steps show.

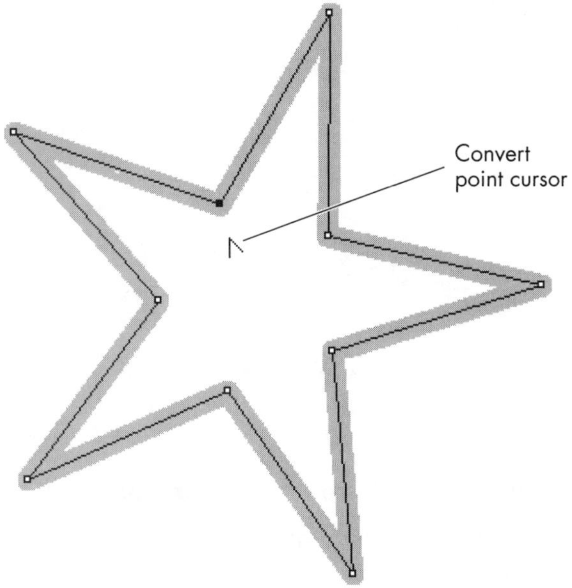

Figure 5-34:
The convert point tool, poised to add some wiggle to the star.

1. **Drag from one of the points along the inner radius.**

   Select the convert point tool and drag from one of the inner radius points, as demonstrated in Figure 5-35. The corner point changes to a smooth point with symmetrical control handles, bending both neighboring segments.

2. **Drag the inside control handle outside the star.**

   Drag the control handle that moved inside the star to a position outside the star, so that the two spikes form mirror images of each other, as demonstrated in Figure 5-36. This converts the smooth point to a cusp, permitting the control handles to move independently.

3. **Repeat Steps 1 and 2 on all the inner radius points.**

   By dragging control handles from all the points and converting them to cusp points, you can create the flower shape shown in Figure 5-37. Oh, sure, it violates the All-or-Nothing rule; each segment gets just one control handle. But after all, that's why we have rules—so we can occasionally ignore them and feel like we're getting away with something.

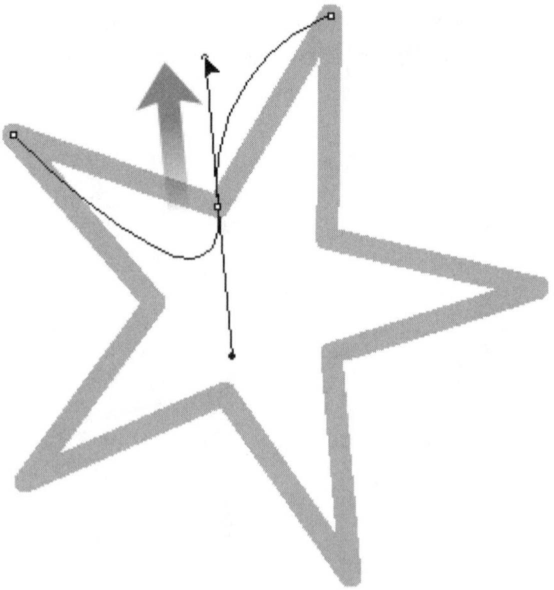

Figure 5-35: Drag from a corner point to convert it to a smooth point.

4. **Continue to adjust the handles until they're just right.**

   With the convert point tool, click and drag on any handle that doesn't suit your fancy. In prior versions of Illustrator, if you were to click on a cusp point handle with the convert point tool, you would have converted it to a smooth point. Now the convert point tool works just like the direct selection tool on handles.

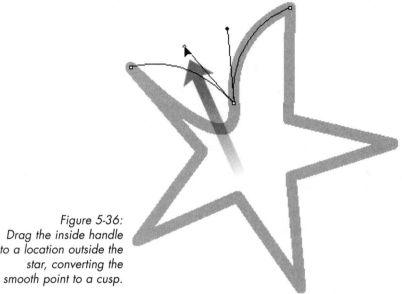

Figure 5-36: Drag the inside handle to a location outside the star, converting the smooth point to a cusp.

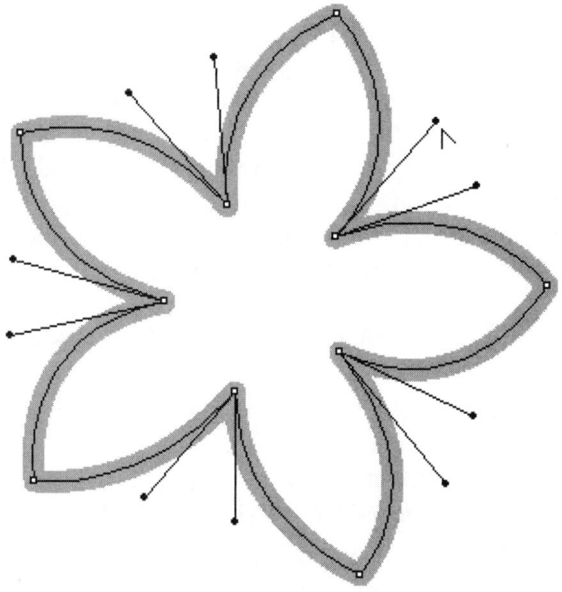

Figure 5-37: By dragging the control handles out of all the inner radius points, you get this lovely flower outline.

TIP

If you thought it was complicated to select the add point or delete point tool from the keyboard, it's nothing compared with the 90 ways to get the convert point tool. The one advantage is that you can access the convert point tool when just about any tool is selected:

- Press ⌘ and Option together to access the convert point tool temporarily when a selection tool is active.
- Press the Option key when the pen tool is selected.
- Press Shift-P three times when using the pen tool, press Shift-P three times and convert a point; press Shift-P again to continue drawing with the pen tool.
- As always, press the P key to switch your current tool to a pen tool.

The Stretch Tool

Although Adobe put it with the transformation tools—for lack of a better location, I suppose—the reshape tool (the alternate tool in the scale tool slot) is not a true transformation tool, since you are not given an origin point. The tool does not act around any one point. Instead, it stretches the selected portion of the path, anchoring it by the two points just outside that part.

Reshape is too generic a term, implying that the tool could ultimately square a circle. A better name would be the stretch tool. As you drag the selected points on a path with the reshape tool, that portion of the path stretches in or out, all the while remaining attached to the anchor points (the two points just outside the selected portion). Moderate use of the tool preserves the path's general shape. This tool comes in handy when you want to tweak the position of part of a path slightly while keeping the path's overall appearance. Moving points (and their Bézier handles) with the direct selection tool gives you control over the exact position and shape of a curve, but it can also give rather stiff and labored results if you're not careful. The reshape tool gives you a quick and easy alternative to the labor-intensive selection tools. Unfortunately, the results of the reshape tool can be somewhat unpredictable and most likely won't give you a perfect fit.

To use the reshape tool, select some of the points in an open or closed path, or select an entire open path, with one of the arrow tools. Using the reshape tool on a wholly selected closed path is the same as moving the path with the arrow tool—Illustrator doesn't know where to anchor the path for the stretch. When you use it on a fully selected open path, Illustrator assumes that the endpoints are the anchor points. Now simply drag with the reshape tool. You can start your drag on either a point or a segment of the path. If you start on a point, Illustrator stretches the path to fit your drag by changing the location of the selected points and the direction of their corresponding Bézier handles (though the handle sizes remain the same). On the other hand, if you start your drag on a segment, Illustrator adds a point to the path, and the Bézier handles of the surrounding points change size and shape accordingly.

Option-drag with the reshape tool to clone the path as you stretch it. In the top of Figure 5-38, I selected the seven rightmost points of the left flower and Option-dragged with the reshape tool to get the slightly askew flower on the right. The shape now has a bit of curve and lift, giving it more dimensionality than its flatter counterpart.

Figure 5-38: Dragging (or Option-dragging) with the reshape tool stretches the selected portion of the path slightly while leaving the rest unchanged (top). The same path, again stretched with the reshape tool, except for the superselected portion (those points with little squares), which remains rigid throughout the drag (bottom).

In general, when you drag with the reshape tool, all the selected points move with respect to each other (and with respect to all the points not selected). You can also specify whether some of the selected points keep their original positioning with respect to one another. To do so, Shift-click with the reshape tool on the points before you drag. This superselects them; they appear surrounded by a tiny square. Then, when you drag with the reshape tool, the superselected portion retains its original shape while moving with the rest of the selected portion, as shown in the lower portion of Figure 5-38. The three superselected points retain their original shapes.

Reliving the Past

Because we all make mistakes, especially when drawing and tracing complicated paths, Illustrator provides you with the ability to nullify the results of previous operations. In fact, Illustrator lets you retract several operations in a row. So when drawing anxiety sets in, remember this simple credo: *Undo*, *redo*, *relaxum*. That's Latin for "Chill; it's just a computer."

Undoing Consecutive Operations

Edit » Undo—and its universal shortcut, ⌘-Z—lets you negate the last action performed. For example, if you move a point and decide you don't like how it looks, choose Edit » Undo Move and the new point disappears. More to the point, Illustrator returns you to the exact moment before you moved the point. Better yet, you can *always* undo the last action, even if you have since clicked on the screen or performed some minor action that the command does not recognize.

> TIP
>
> Get this: You can even undo an operation performed prior to the most recent Save operation (although you cannot undo the Save command itself). For example, you can delete an element, save the illustration, then choose Undo Clear to make the element reappear. It's a real lifesaver.

Illustrator lets you undo up to 200 consecutive operations. This powerful feature takes a great deal of the worry out of using Illustrator. You can reverse even major blunders one step at a time.

To change the number of possible consecutive undos, choose the File » Preference » Units & Undos command to display the Units & Undo Preferences dialog box, then enter a new value in the Minimum Undo Levels option box. The word *Minimum* appears in the option name because Illustrator permits you to undo as many operations as it can store in its undo buffer, regardless of the option value. The value merely sets aside space in your computer's memory so Illustrator can undo at least that many operations. As a result, you may be able to undo 200 path operations even if the Minimum Undo Levels value is set to 5.

TIP To monitor how many undo levels are available at any given time, select the Number of Undos option from the status bar pop-up menu in the lower left corner of the illustration window.

After you exhaust the maximum number of undos, the Undo command appears dimmed in the Edit menu. Pressing ⌘-Z will produce no effect until you perform a new operation. And remember, Illustrator can undo operations performed in the current session only. You can't undo something you did back before the most recent time you started Illustrator.

TIP Let's say you need to make a quick 156 undos. Are you going to press ⌘-Z once for each of the offending steps? Not even. Instead, you're going to press and hold ⌘-Z. Holding these keys for a couple of seconds will let you start jumping back through the history of your drawing in units of five undos at a time. It's like watching a movie of your work coming undone.

Redoing Undo Operations

Just as you can undo as many as 200 consecutive actions, you can redo up to 200 consecutive undos by choosing Edit » Redo or pressing ⌘-Shift-Z. You can choose Redo only if the Undo command was the most recent operation performed; otherwise, Redo is dimmed. Also, if you undo a series of actions, perform a new series of actions, and then undo the new series of actions to the point where you had stopped undoing previously, you can't go back and redo the first series of undos. Instead, you can either continue to undo from where you left off or redo the later set of actions.

TIP Same as the above tip, except that now you can see your artwork come together in fast motion by holding ⌘-Shift-Z. This is especially fun to do right after you've done 200 undos.

Returning to the Last Saved File

If your modifications to an illustration are a total botch, you can revert to the last saved version of the file by choosing File » Revert or by pressing the F12 key (assuming that your keyboard comes equipped with such a key). It's like closing a file, clicking on the Don't Save button, and reopening the file in one step. You probably won't need this command very often, but keep in mind that it's there when things go terribly wrong.

If you haven't done anything to an illustration since you last saved it, or if you've never saved the drawing, File » Revert is dimmed.

CHAPTER 6

HOW TO HANDLE TYPICAL TYPE

If a picture is worth a thousand words, Illustrator must be worth a thousand Microsoft Words. (Even as I write this in Word, I'm hard pressed to think of anything that's *not* worth a thousand Words.) However powerful pictures may be, and although they admittedly bridge the boundaries of culture and language (heck, I bet extraterrestrials living in Roswell could understand them), Illustrator knows that every once in a while text comes in handy. As a result, the program has assembled some of the most flexible and uniquely capable tools for type creation and formatting you'll find in any Macintosh or Windows program.

Illustrator's type capabilities are so amazing that I'll explore them over the course of two chapters. This chapter examines the relatively basic stuff—how to create text blocks and apply formatting attributes such as typeface and style. I close out the chapter with a generous description of tabs, one of Illustrator's more recent features. Even if you know type, this chapter imparts lots of useful tips and keyboard shortcuts that you'll most assuredly want to learn.

Chapter 7 looks at type effects that are virtually unknown outside Illustrator. You can fix type to a curve, set text inside free-form text blocks, apply effects to Adobe's specialized Multiple Master fonts, convert letter outlines to fully editable paths, and even present text in the Japanese vertical style. Look for this and more in the next chapter.

Establishing Text Objects

Altogether, Illustrator provides six tools for creating text. For now, we're concerned with only one: the type tool, second down on the right side of the toolbox (the one that looks like a T). Armed with the type tool, you can create a text object—which is any object that contains type—in one of two ways:

- Click with the type tool in the drawing area and enter a few words of type for a logo or headline. This kind of text block is called *point text,* because Illustrator aligns the text to the point at which you click.
- Drag with the type tool to draw a rectangular *text block.* Then enter your text from the keyboard. Illustrator fits the text to the rectangular text block, automatically shifting text that doesn't fit on one line down to the next. Create a text block when you want to enter a full sentence or more.

I explain point text and text blocks in more detail in the following sections.

Creating Point Text

Figure 6-1 shows the three steps involved in creating point text. (Incidentally, this figure and several that follow sport default font Helvetica, 12-point text magnified to 400 percent on screen.) The three steps go something like this:

1. Select the type tool and click in some empty portion of the drawing area with the new block cursor, labeled in Figure 6-1. The new block cursor shows that you are about to create a new text object.

   After you click with the type tool, Illustrator creates an *alignment point,* which appears as an *x* in the artwork mode. (In the preview mode, you see the alignment point only if the point text is selected.) Not surprisingly, Illustrator aligns the text to this point.

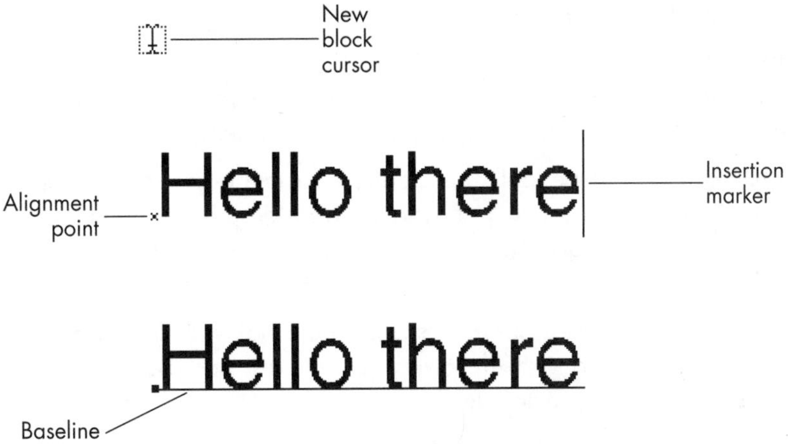

Figure 6-1: Click with the type tool (top), enter your text (middle), and select a different tool to complete the text object (bottom).

2. Enter the desired text from your keyboard. By default, the text appears to the right of the alignment point. (I explain how to change the alignment later in this chapter.) As you type, a blinking *insertion marker* flashes to the right of the last character. The insertion marker shows you where the next letter you enter will appear.

   With point text, Illustrator keeps all characters on a single line unless you tell it to do otherwise. This is why point text is better suited to a few words or less. If you want to move the insertion marker down to create a new line of type, press the Return or Enter key.

3. When you have finished entering your text, click on any tool in the toolbox except the hand, page, measure, zoom, eyedropper, or paint bucket tool. The text block appears selected, as shown in the bottom example of Figure 6-1. The alignment point now looks like a filled square, just like a selected anchor point.

You can drag the alignment point with any of the three selection tools to reposition the text in the drawing area. You can also drag point text by its *baseline,* which is the line that runs under each line of type. The baseline is the imaginary line on which letters sit. Only a few lowercase characters—*g, j, p, q,* and *y*—descend below the baseline. Lastly, you can drag point text by dragging on the text itself. The exception to this last technique is when the Type Area Select option of the Type & Auto Tracing Preferences dialog box is turned off. In this case, you can only select and drag point text by clicking and dragging on the baseline or alignment point.

Creating Text Blocks

Point text is easy to create, but because Illustrator forces all text onto a single line unless told to do otherwise, point text is not well suited to whole paragraphs and longer text. To accommodate lengthy text, you need to create a text block:

1. Drag with the type tool. This creates a rectangle, as shown in the first example in Figure 6-2, just as if you were dragging with the rectangle tool. This rectangle represents the height and width of the new text block.

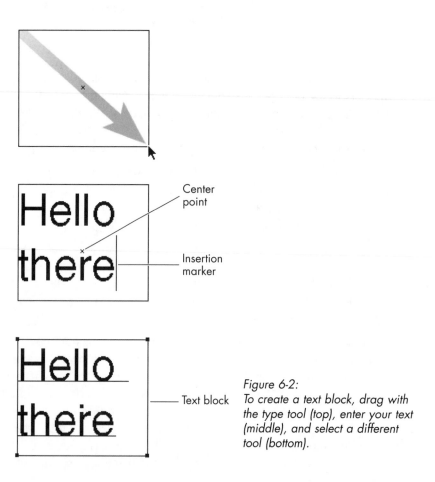

   When you release, Illustrator shows you a box with a blinking insertion marker in the top left corner. You will also see a center point, just as in a standard rectangle.

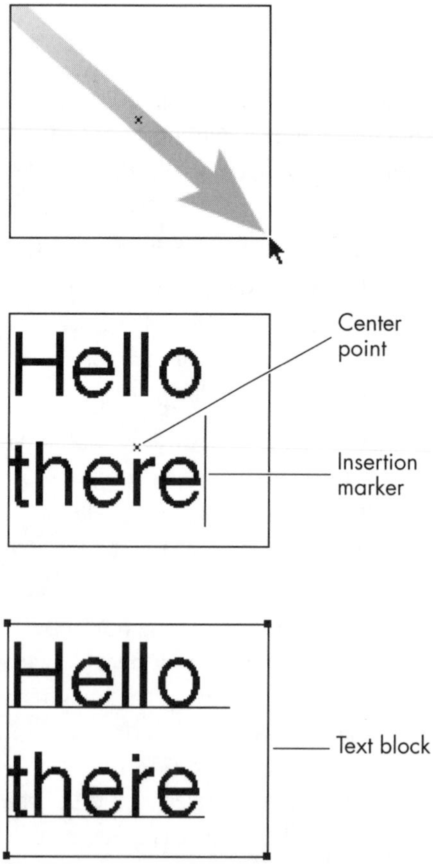

Figure 6-2:
To create a text block, drag with the type tool (top), enter your text (middle), and select a different tool (bottom).

2. Enter type from the keyboard. If a letter extends beyond the right edge of the text block, Illustrator sends the word down to start a new line of type. Known as *automatic wrapping,* this is precisely the capability that point text lacks.
3. Click on any tool (other than the hand, page, measure, zoom, eyedropper, or paint bucket tool) to stop entering text. The text block appears selected, showing off four corner points connected by straight segments and a center point hovering in the middle. Baselines underscore the type to indicate that the letters themselves are selected.

Resizing and Reshaping Text Blocks

As with point text, you can reposition a text block by dragging either the rectangular boundary or one of the baselines with the arrow tool. Additionally, you can drag directly on the text itself. Also as with point text, if you turn off the Type Area Select option inside the Type & Auto Tracing Preferences dialog box, then you will no longer be able to move or select text blocks by clicking or dragging on the text.

You can also change the size and shape of a text block with the direct selection tool. Illustrator offers a couple of new ways to resize and reshape paths—Chapter 11 discusses tugging on the bounding box and using the free transform tool—but the tried-and-true direct selection tool still provides you with an indispensable device for path modification.

For example, say that the text you entered from the keyboard doesn't entirely fit inside the text block. Or worse yet, the text block isn't wide enough to accommodate a particularly long word. Figure 6-3 illustrates both of these problems: The little square with a minus sign in it shows that Illustrator had to break the word *everybody* onto two lines. The square with a plus sign shows that there is more text that does fit inside the text block and is temporarily hidden. This text is called *overflow text.*

By resizing a text block, you can fit long words on a single line, reveal overflow text, or simply change how words wrap from one line to the next. To resize a text block, you have to use the direct-selection tool to select and modify the rectangular boundary independently of the text inside it. Here's how it works:

1. **Create your text block.**

   After creating the text block, select the direct selection tool.

2. **Deselect the text block.**

   To the consternation of many a new user, you can't resize a text block just by dragging a corner point. (On the other hand, dragging on a corner handle of the text block's bounding box does allow you to resize the block. The problem is that the bounding box doesn't afford you the same flexibility as the direct selection tool.) This is not to say that you can't reshape the block by dragging on a corner with the direct selection tool, it's just that dragging on a corner will not preserve the parallelogram nature of the block. To do so, you have to select one of the segments and drag it, just as if you were resizing a standard rectangle. And—just to make things as painful as possible—you can't select a segment until you deselect the path. So choose Edit » Deselect All or press ⌘-Shift-A to deselect the text block.

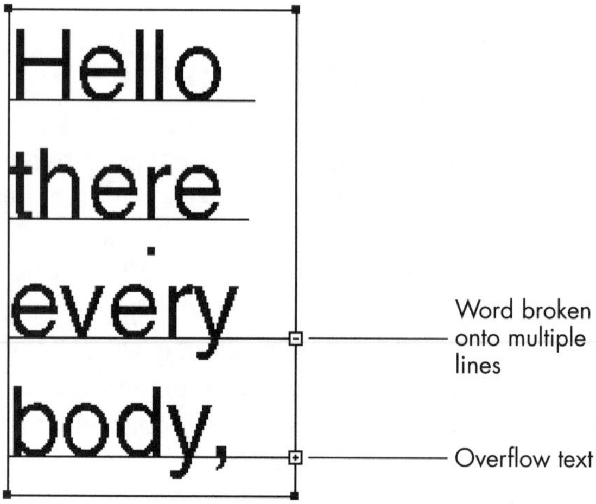

Figure 6-3: Illustrator shows you when a word doesn't fit on a line, or when text extends outside the text block.

3. Select the right or bottom edge of the text block.

If you're working in the preview mode, the text block outline disappears. This makes selecting an edge of the text block rather difficult. That's why I recommend you drag a tiny marquee around the portion of the outline you want to move. If you want to make the text block wider, drag a marquee around the right side, as in the first example of Figure 6-4. If you want to make the text block taller, marquee the bottom side. In either case, you select the desired edge. (Because it's a straight segment, you can't see that it's selected. But have faith—it is.)

Make sure you don't select a baseline. If you select a baseline, you select the entire text block, which prevents you from resizing it. So if a baseline appears, press ⌘-Shift-A and try again.

If you can't seem to get the darn segment selected, switch to the artwork mode by pressing ⌘-Y. In the artwork mode, you can see the text block outline even when it's not selected. This makes it easier to click on the segment you want to select.

4. **Shift-drag the edge.**

   To maintain the rectangular shape of the text block, Shift-drag the right segment to the right, as in Figure 6-4. Or Shift-drag the bottom segment downward. (You can also drag without pressing Shift to create diamond-shaped text blocks.)

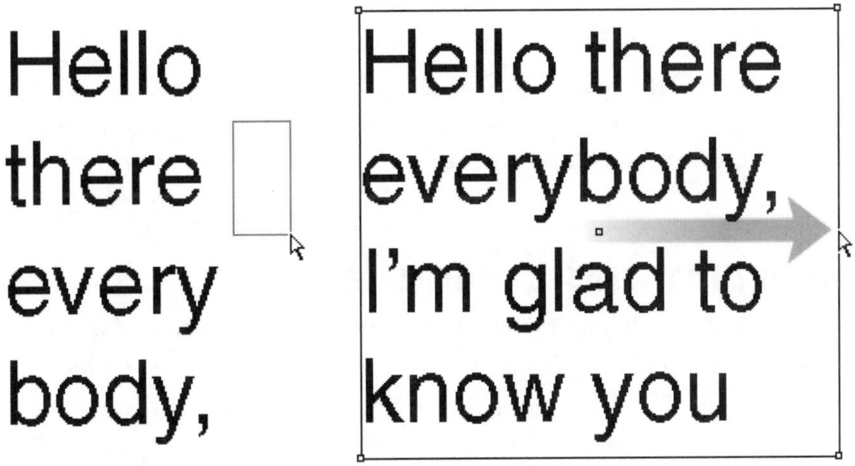

Figure 6-4: Use the direct selection tool to marquee the edge of the text block you want to expand (left), then Shift-drag the edge (right).

When you release the mouse button, Illustrator rewraps the text and displays as much overflow text as will fit. If there is still more overflow text, the little plus icon remains in the lower right corner of the text block.

To resize the height and width of a text block at the same time, select the entire block outline by Option-clicking on it with the direct selection tool. (Make sure the baselines remain invisible.) Then drag with the scale tool or the free transform tool. For more info on both of these tools, turn to Chapter 11.

You can reshape the outline of a text block using any of the techniques discussed in Chapter 5. In addition to dragging points and segments, you can do any of the following:

- Change the corner points to smooth points with the convert point tool.
- Drag the control handles to bend the segments.
- Insert or remove points with the add point and delete point tools or even with the pen tool (provided that the Disable Auto Add/Delete option inside the General Preferences dialog box isn't activated, as discussed back in Chapter 5).
- Select a segment with the direct selection tool and press Delete to open up the path.
- Extend the open path using the pen or pencil tools.

If this kind of thing interests you—and why shouldn't it?—Chapter 7 explains how to create text inside any old wacky shape, as well as how to pour overflow text from one text block into another.

Selecting and Editing Text

Before you can change a single character of type or change how text looks on the page, you have to select the type using the arrow or the type tool.

- Clicking along the baseline of a line of type with any selection tool selects all type in the object. Or, provided that the Type Area Select option inside the Type & Auto Tracing Preferences dialog box is turned off, you can click on any character to select all the text in the object. If you change the font, type size, style, or some other formatting attribute, you change all characters in the selected text object.
- With the arrow tool, click on one text object and Shift-click on another to format multiple text objects at a time. (Illustrator doesn't let you format a text block if you select just a portion of the outline with the direct selection tool.)
- If you select text with a type tool, you can edit that text by entering new text from the keyboard or format the selected text independently of other text in the object.

Selecting with the Type Tool

Though the selection tools are certainly useful, the type tool is the most common instrument for editing type in Illustrator because it affords the most control. The following items explain how to select type with the type tool:

- Drag over the characters that you want to select. Drag to the left or to the right to select characters on a single line; drag upward or downward to select characters on multiple lines. The selected text becomes highlighted—inverted colors against a black background—as shown in Figure 6-5.
- Double-click on a word to select that word. Hold down the mouse button on the second click and drag to select more words.
- Triple-click to select an entire paragraph, from one return character to the next. Triple-clicking in point text selects an entire line, since you have to press Return to go from one line to the next (a line of point text is equivalent to a paragraph). Hold down the mouse button on the third click and drag to select additional paragraphs.
- Click to set the insertion marker at one end of the text you want to select, then Shift-click at the opposite end of the desired selection. Illustrator highlights all characters between the first click and the Shift-click.

Figure 6-5: Drag across characters with the type tool to highlight them.

- Click anywhere in a text block and press ⌘-A (or choose Edit » Select All) to select all text in the object.

TIP

After you click with the type tool to set the insertion marker inside a text object, you can use the arrow keys to move the insertion marker around or select text.

- Press the left or right arrow key to move the insertion marker to the left or right one character.
- Press the up or down arrow key to move the insertion marker up or down one line.
- Press ⌘-→ to move the insertion marker one whole word to the right. Press ⌘-← to move back a word.
- Press ⌘-↑ to move the insertion marker to the beginning of the paragraph. Press ⌘-↓ to move it to the end of the paragraph.
- Press Shift along with any of these keystrokes to select text as you move the insertion marker. For example, press Shift-→ to select the character after the insertion marker. Press ⌘-Shift-↑ to select everything from the insertion marker to the beginning of the paragraph.

Replacing, Deleting, and Adding Text

After you highlight some text, you can format it (as I begin explaining in the next section) or replace it by entering new text from the keyboard.

- To delete selected text, press the Delete key.
- You can remove the selected text and send it to the Clipboard by choosing Edit » Cut (⌘-X).
- To leave the selected text intact and send a copy to the Clipboard choose Edit » Copy command (⌘-C).
- You can even replace the selected text with text that you cut or copied earlier by choosing Edit » Paste (⌘-V). The pasted text retains its original formatting.

TIP

The only way to convert a line of point text to a text block—or vice versa—is via the Clipboard. With either the arrow or the type tool, select the text you want to convert, cut or copy it, then drag with the type tool to create the text block (or click for the point text) and paste.

If you want to add text rather than replace it, just click with the type tool inside a text block to position the insertion marker. Then bang away at the keyboard and let the mouse take you where it will.

If Illustrator seems to ignore you when you enter text or press the Delete key, press the Return key. The problem is that Illustrator thinks a palette is active and is trying desperately to apply your typing to that palette; pressing Return deactivates the palette and returns control to the illustration window.

Formatting Type

Where type is concerned, *formatting* means nothing more than changing the way characters and lines of text look. Illustrator provides an exhaustive supply of formatting functions that let you modify far more than you'll ever want to. Alas, if I had owned Illustrator 8 back when I ran a service bureau, I would never have had an unfulfilled typographic desire.

You can divide formatting attributes into two categories—those that apply to individual characters of type, and those that apply to entire paragraphs.

- Character-level formatting includes options such as typeface, size, leading, kerning and tracking, baseline shift, and horizontal scaling. To change the formatting of one or more characters, you select the characters with the type tool and apply the desired options. Illustrator changes the highlighted characters and leaves surrounding characters unaltered.
- Paragraph-level formatting includes indents, alignment, paragraph spacing, letter spacing, and word spacing. To change the formatting of a single paragraph, you need only position the blinking insertion marker inside that paragraph; Illustrator changes the entire paragraph no matter how little of it you select. To change the formatting of multiple paragraphs, select at least one character in each of the paragraphs you want to modify.

TIP

If you want Illustrator to consider two different lines of type as part of the same paragraph, press the Enter key on the keypad (instead of the Return key on the main part of the keyboard) to separate them. The Enter key inserts a line break, instead of the carriage return that the Return key inserts. All paragraph formatting applied to one line becomes applicable to the other as well.

If you want to see things such as carriage returns or line breaks on-screen, choose Type » Show Hidden Characters. The carriage returns appear as paragraph symbols (Ps with vertical lines) and the line breaks appear as left-pointing arrows.

Illustrator adopts the most recently applied formatting attributes as the default settings throughout the rest of the session (or until you further modify the settings). But the next time you quit Illustrator and start it up again, the program restores the original default settings (though you can alter some defaults permanently by editing the Adobe Illustrator 7.0 Prefs file, as described in Chapter 2's "The Prefs File" section).

Character-Level Formatting

To format characters, you can either choose commands from the Type menu or avail yourself of the options in the Character palette. The latter is the more convenient.

NOTE: The one character-formatting attribute that I don't discuss in this chapter is color. To change the color of selected text, you merely change the fill color in the Color palette, as I explain in Chapter 15. You can even stroke text, as you'll learn in Chapter 16.

To display the Character palette, choose Type » Character or press ⌘-T, the universal shortcut for character-level formatting (except in Microsoft Word, but I've already mentioned what I think of that program). By default, the Character palette shows only six options, as shown in the left example of Figure 6-6. But if you choose the Show Options command from the pop-up menu (located in the upper right corner), you expand the palette to display several more options, shown on the right.

TIP: You can also hide the Character palette by pressing ⌘-T. If that doesn't work, then press ⌘-T twice, once to activate the palette and a second time to hide it.

TIP: Since the Character palette uses so many option boxes, I think that it's worthwhile to review a few useful techniques. First, when one of the option boxes is active, you can cycle through other option boxes by pressing the Tab key. To cycle backward through the option boxes, press Shift-Tab. After you have entered a value into one of the option boxes, press Return to apply your changes and deactivate the palette. If you prefer, press Shift-Return to apply a new value without deactivating the palette. This allows you to run quickly through a number of different values without having to click on the option box each time before entering new values.

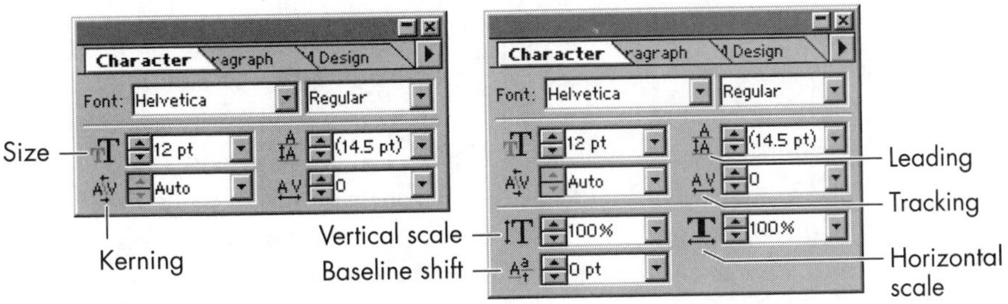

Figure 6-6: The Character palette, collapsed (left) and expanded (right).

Selecting a Typeface

The Type » Font submenu lists all typefaces installed in the Fonts folder inside the System Folder on your Mac's hard drive, or in your Fonts control panel in Windows 95.

But where most programs let you assign typeface and style separately—you might select Helvetica in one step and Bold in another—typeface and style are inseparable inside Illustrator. Illustrator lacks the ability to embellish plain typefaces with bold, italic, underline, and other fabricated styles. Instead, Illustrator relies strictly on *stylized fonts,* which provide separate design characteristics for each type style. Therefore, Helvetica Regular and Helvetica Bold are completely separate entities in Illustrator's mind, as independent as Cooper Black is from Poppl-Residenz Light. (Typefaces have notoriously odd names; it's part of the union credo.) This is much more in keeping with the historic conception of a *font,* in which characters cast from metal were housed in separate containers according to their style.

This setup is ideal for fonts with extensive collections of designer styles. The complete Helvetica font, for example, includes not only Bold and Oblique (slanted), but also Light and Black (heavier than bold). By adhering strictly to styled fonts, Illustrator simplifies the application of any font, regardless of how idiosyncratic the family may be.

You can select a font from the Type » Font submenu or from the Font pop-up menu in the Character palette. Assuming that Type Reunion is running—you have the option of installing this system extension when you install Illustrator—styles appear in submenus next to their parent typefaces. For example, to assign Times Italic, you would choose Type » Font » Times » Italic.

If you know the name of the font you want to apply, just enter the first few letters of its name into the Font option box in the Character palette. Each time you enter a character, Illustrator tries to guess which font you want. For example, if both American Typewriter and Avant Garde are available to your system, entering the letter *a* gets you American Typewriter—the first font in alphabetical order—while entering *av* gets you Avant Garde. To change the style, press the Tab key and enter the first few letters of the style, such as *b* for Bold or *i* for Italic. You can also Control-click (that's right-clicking for you Windows hep-cats) and choose a font from the Fonts submenu in the context-sensitive pop-up menu.

TrueType Incompatibilities

Sadly, Illustrator's inability to assign software styles inhibits its compatibility with TrueType fonts. If a TrueType font doesn't have a submenu of stylized fonts next to its name in the Type » Font submenu, it means that the fonts on your machine don't include the stylized versions of that font. For example, you can choose the TrueType font New York—included with all Macs—but you can't make it bold or italic in Illustrator.

Illustrator has a few other TrueType compatibility problems as well. It occasionally misinterprets TrueType font metrics (such as character width), and it has a habit of complaining when you open illustrations created with TrueType fonts. You'll likewise encounter these problems if you have both TrueType and PostScript versions of the same font installed (as QuickDraw GX requires, for example).

To help prevent these problems, the Adobe Type Manager installer (included with Illustrator 8) trashes all TrueType versions of common fonts like Helvetica and Times and replaces them with their PostScript Type 1 equivalents. It's a rather extreme solution, but most artists can get along just fine without TrueType. Let's face it, PostScript fonts offer better character outlines and are more universally compatible with commercial printers and service bureaus.

Adobe Type Manager Issues

WARNING

If the bottoms of descenders appear prematurely cut off, as in Figure 6-7, it's not a problem with your font—it's a problem with your font administrator, Adobe Type Manager (or ATM). To fix the problem, open the ATM control panel (Apple » Control Panels » ~ATM) or the Windows version (Atmfm.exe in the psfonts folder) and select the Character Shapes radio button. (This option controls how ATM deals with documents created without ATM, but since most Illustrator users have been using ATM most of their lives, Character Shapes is the more appropriate setting.) The next time you restart your computer, ATM will redraw characters in their entirety, with descenders intact.

Figure 6-7: The bottoms of descenders frequently appear cut off if you have ATM set to preserve line spacing instead of character shapes.

Note that the ATM setting doesn't affect how fonts print on PostScript printers, nor does it affect characters converted to path outlines. Regardless of which ATM option you select, these operations work just fine. However, the Character Shapes setting does affect fonts printed to non-PostScript printers, since ATM is responsible for drawing font outlines when a PostScript interpreter is not present.

TIP

Oh, and here's one more point: Recent versions of ATM let you add fonts to the Fonts folder inside the System Folder (or to the Fonts folder in the Windows folder) while Illustrator is running. The added fonts immediately become available in the Character palette and the Font menu; you don't have to quit Illustrator and restart as in the old days.

Reducing and Enlarging Type

To change the size of any selected type, choose a command from the Type » Size submenu, or enter a value into the Size option box in the Character palette. *Type size,* as it is called, is measured in points from the top of an ascender (such as a *d* or an *f*) to the bottom of a descender (such as g or *p*). You can enter any value between 0.1 (1/10 the size of the smallest character in Figure 6-8) and 1296 (four times the size of the largest character) in 0.01-point increments.

If you dramatically reduce the size of a line of type, it appears as a gray bar. Illustrator figures it's too small to be readable on screen, so why waste the time trying to draw it accurately? If you want to see text at smaller sizes, choose the File » Preferences » Type & Auto Tracing command and enter a smaller Greeking value. As long as the type appears smaller on screen than this value, Illustrator "greeks" it, replacing the type with a gray bar.

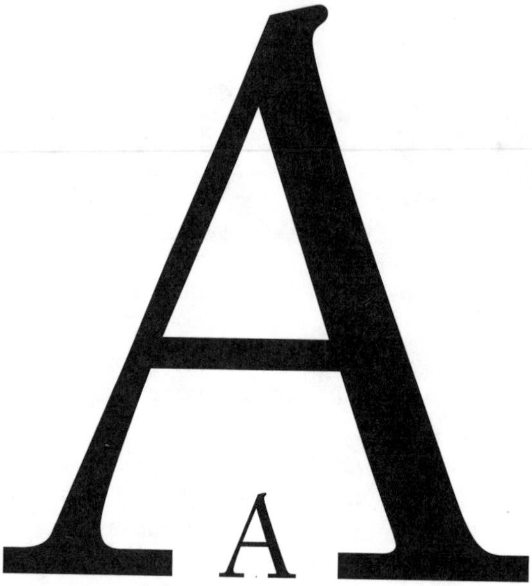

Figure 6-8:
A character set in three (yes, three) type sizes—324-point, 48-point, and 1-point. If you don't believe me, go get a large magnifying glass and take a gander. Just as a medium A is centered at the base of the giant A, a minuscule A is centered at the base of the medium A. See that speck? That's 1-point type.

TIP

To change the type size of some selected characters quickly, enter a new size value into the Size option box in the Character palette and press Return. You can also adjust the type size incrementally from the keyboard. Press ⌘-Shift-> to enlarge the characters or ⌘-Shift-< to reduce them. You can adjust the increment by changing the Size/Leading value in the Type & Auto Tracing Preferences dialog box. By default, the increment is set to 2 points. Your other option is to Control-click (known as right-clicking in Win-speak) and peruse the Size submenu for just the right size.

NEW 8

To change the type size of the selected text by five times the Size/Leading value, press ⌘-Option-Shift-> or ⌘-Option-Shift-<.

Specifying the Distance between Lines

Some programs call the distance between lines of type *line spacing*, and let you adjust line spacing by applying options such as single space and double space. These programs model themselves after the typewriter, one of the most outdated pieces of technology on the planet. Steam engines, record players, and dolls that wet themselves all offer more practical benefits for modern living than the typewriter. Though I know many typewriter-loving technophobes and hold a special place for them in my heart, typewriters are nonetheless obsolete and so are the programs that emulate them.

Illustrator derives its approach to line spacing from hot-metal typesetting, which—though it predates the typewriter by several hundred years—is more relevant to modern typographic trends. Printer operators of yore inserted thin strips of lead between lines of type, hence the term *leading* (pronounced *ledding*). Leading specifies the distance between a selected line of type and the line below it, as measured in points from one baseline to the next. Therefore, 14-point leading leaves a couple of points of extra room between two lines of 12-point type.

You can change the leading by entering a value into the Leading option box in the Character palette—Illustrator does not have a separate leading command in the Type menu. To speed things up, select some text and press Option-↓ to increase the leading or Option-↑ to decrease it. Then sit back and experience the warm glow that comes when friends and family members look over your shoulder and say, "Gosh, you're fast. I can't even insert a page into my typewriter that quickly."

Select Auto from the Leading pop-up menu in the Character palette to make the leading equal to 120 percent of the current type size (rounded off to the nearest half-point).

TIP

To set the leading to match the type size exactly—an arrangement known as *solid leading*—double-click on the A over A symbol next to the Leading option box in the Character palette. Then press the Return key to deactivate the palette and return control to the drawing area.

As with type size, you can adjust leading incrementally (according to the Size/Leading value in the Type & Auto Tracing Preferences dialog box). Press Option-↑ to reduce the leading; press Option-↓ to increase it. For more pronounced changes, press ⌘-Option-↓ to reduce the leading by five times the Size/Leading value. Press ⌘-Option-↑ to increase the leading by the same amount.

If a line of text contains characters with two different leading specifications, the larger leading prevails. If you begin a paragraph with a large capital letter, for example, you might combine a 24-point character on the same line as 12-point characters. If both the 24-point character and the 12-point character use auto leading, then the entire line will be set at 29-point leading (120 percent of the 24-point type size).

Adjusting the Space between Characters

Illustrator lets you adjust the amount of horizontal space between characters of text. When you adjust the space between a pair of characters, Illustrator calls it *kerning*. When you adjust the space between three or more characters, Illustrator calls it *tracking*.

If you're a type savant, you'll soon notice that Illustrator's idea of tracking is not the real thing. There's no automatic spacing variation between large and small type sizes, which is what proper tracking is all about. Illustrator's tracking is uniform, and should therefore be called *range kerning*.

In any case, Illustrator provides option boxes in the Character palette for both kerning and tracking—commands for these don't exist in the Type menu and appear only in the Character palette. When you click with the type tool to position the insertion marker between two characters, you will want to use the Kerning option box. When you select so much as a single character, the Tracking option box is the one for you. Don't worry if you get them confused—enter a value in the Kerning option box when you've trying to change the tracking or vice versa—because Illustrator will promptly respond by either doing nothing or flashing some annoying warning that you're mistreating it.

Normally, Illustrator accepts the dimensions of each character stored in the screen font file on disk and places the character flush against its neighbors. The screen font defines the width of the character as well as the amount of space placed before and after the character. As demonstrated in the top example of Figure 6-9, these bits of space before and after are called *side bearings*. Illustrator arrives at its normal letter spacing by adding the right side bearing of the first character to the left side bearing of the second.

However, font designers can specify that certain pairs of letters, called *kerning pairs,* be positioned more closely together than the standard letter normally allows. Whenever the two characters of a kerning pair appear next to each other, as in the case of the *W* and the *A* in Figure 6-9, Illustrator can space them according to the special kerning information contained in the font.

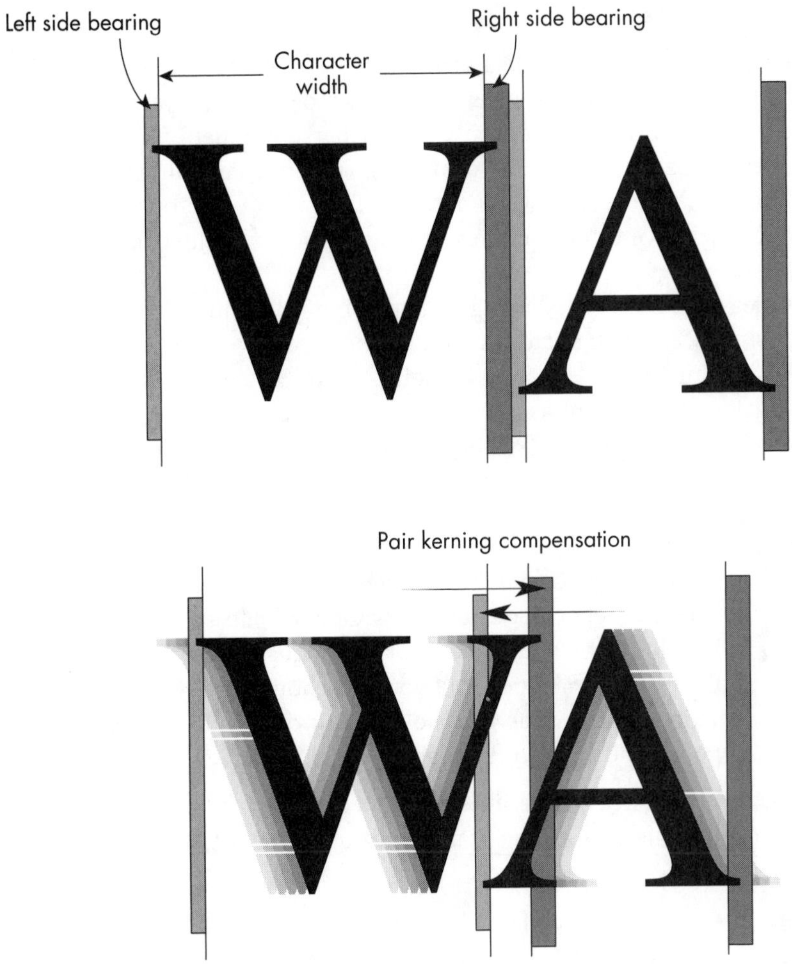

Figure 6-9: A kerning pair is a set of two letters that look weird when set shoulder to shoulder (top). Spacing them closer together (bottom) draws less attention to the letters and makes them more legible.

Illustrator always spaces kerning pairs as the font instructs. Click with the type tool to position the insertion marker between letters that you suspect to be kerning pairs. If the font does supply special instructions for those letters (and provided that you haven't changed the kerning manually), the Kerning option box displays a number in parentheses. If no parentheses appear, choose Auto from the Kerning pop-up menu and Illustrator returns the letters' placement to the factory settings.

If you aren't satisfied with the default kerning between two characters, click with the type tool to position the insertion marker between the characters and enter a value into the Kerning option box in the Character palette. If you want to change the kerning between multiple characters (tracking, in Illustrator-speak), select those characters and enter a value into the Tracking option box. Then press the Return key. A negative value squeezes letters together; a positive value spreads them apart.

Illustrator measures both the Kerning and Tracking values in 0.001 ($^{1}/_{1000}$) of an em space. An *em space* is a character as wide as the type size is tall. So if the type size is set to 12 point, an em space is 12 points wide. This ensures the kerning remains proportionally constant as you increase or decrease the type size.

A Kerning or Tracking value of 25 is roughly equivalent to a standard space character. But you can enter any value between –1,000 and 10,000 in 0.01 increments.

If you don't know what kerning value to use, you can adjust the kerning incrementally from the keyboard. Press Option-← to squeeze letters together; press Option-→ to spread them apart. By default, each keystroke changes the kerning by 0.02 ($^{20}/_{1000}$) em space, but you can change the increment by entering a new value into the Tracking option box in the Type & Auto Tracing Preferences dialog box.

For more dramatic changes, press ⌘-Option-← or ⌘-Option-→ to decrease or increase the kerning by five times the Tracking value in the Type & Auto Tracing Preferences dialog box.

To restore the Kerning value to 0, press ⌘-Shift-Q.

When kerning small type, you may not be able to see a visible difference as you add or delete space because the display is not accurate enough. In such a case, use the zoom tool to magnify the drawing area while kerning or tracking characters from the keyboard.

Changing the Height and Width of Characters

The next options in the Character palette, Vertical Scale and Horizontal Scale, modify the height and width of selected characters, respectively. You can expand or condense type anywhere from 1 to 10,000 percent (1⁄100 to 100 times its normal width) by entering a new value into either the Vertical Scale or Horizontal Scale option box and pressing Return.

Changing the height or width of a character distorts it. The Vertical Scale and Horizontal Scale options do not create the same effect as designer-condensed or -expanded fonts. For example, Figure 6-10 shows two variations on Helvetica. In the first example, I took 200-point Helvetica Bold and scaled it 45 percent horizontally. You would get the same result if you were to scale 115-point type vertically to 174 percent—go ahead and try it. Notice how the horizontal bars of the *A* and *B* are much thicker than the vertical stems. This is because Horizontal Scale affects vertical proportions and leaves horizontal proportions untouched.

While the bars and stems in a designer font may not be identical, they are proportional. The second example in Figure 6-10 shows a specially condensed font called Helvetica Compressed Ultra. The strokes vary, but there is an overall consistency that the skinny Helvetica Bold type lacks. The designer has also taken the time to square off some of the curves, making Helvetica Compressed Ultra more legible in small type sizes.

With this in mind, there are a few things to remember when using the Vertical Scale or Horizontal Scale option:

- If you *want* the type to appear distorted, go for broke. There are no hard and fast rules in page design; type that specifically calls attention to itself can be just as effective as type that doesn't, if you have a bold design and an open-minded audience.
- If slightly widening or narrowing a few lines of type will make them fit better on the page, you can get away with Horizontal Scale values between 95 and 105 percent; no one will be the wiser.
- Changing both the vertical and horizontal factors by the same amount is the same as changing the size. So if you enter 50 percent into both the Vertical Scale and Horizontal Scale option boxes, the result is the same as if you had changed the value in the Size option box to half of its original value.

TIP

To restore both the Vertical Scale and the Horizontal Scale values to 100 percent, press ⌘-Shift-X.

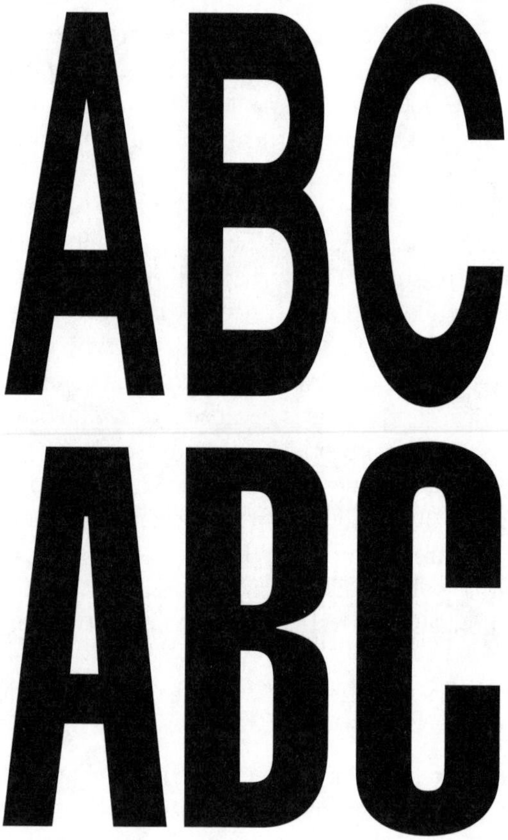

Figure 6-10:
200-point Helvetica Bold scaled horizontally 45 percent (top) compared with a specially designed font called Helvetica Compressed Ultra.

Incidentally, if you've scaled a text block disproportionately using the scale tool (as described in Chapter 11), the Font Size and Horizontal Scale values reflect the discrepancy between the current and the normal width and size of the selected type. You can reset the type to its normal width by pressing ⌘-Shift-X.

Raising and Lowering Characters

The Baseline Shift option in the lower half of the Character palette determines the distance between the selected type and its baseline. A positive value raises the characters; a negative value lowers them. The default value of 0 leaves them sitting on the baseline, where they typically belong.

You can modify the baseline shift to create superscripts and subscripts, or to adjust type along a path (as I discuss in the next chapter). To change the baseline shift, select some type and then enter any value between –1296 and 1296 points into the Baseline Shift option box.

TIP

Baseline shift is instrumental in creating fractions. First enter the fraction, using the real fraction symbol (Shift-Option-1) rather than the standard slash. Select the numerator (the top number), make it about half the current type size, and enter a baseline shift value equal to about one-third the original type size. Then select the denominator (bottom number) and match its type size to that of the numerator, but leave the Baseline Shift value set to 0. The result is a fraction like the one shown in Figure 6-11.

22/531

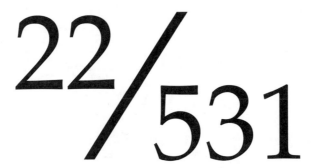

Figure 6-11: In this fraction, the type size of the slash is 160–point, while the numerator and denominator are set to 80–point. The numerator is shifted 53 points above the baseline.

TIP

You can adjust the baseline shift incrementally from the keyboard (according to the Baseline Shift value in the Type & Auto Tracing Preferences dialog box, 2 points by default). Press Shift-Option-↑ to raise the selected text above its baseline; press Shift-Option-↓ to lower the text.

To see the text really jump, press ⌘-Shift-Option-↑ or ⌘-Shift-Option-↓ to move the baseline up or down by five times the Baseline Shift value in the Type & Auto Tracing Preferences dialog box.

Paragraph-Level Formatting

Illustrator's paragraph formatting controls are found in the Paragraph palette. To display the palette, choose Type » Paragraph or press ⌘-M. By default, the Paragraph palette is collapsed, as shown in the left example of Figure 6-12. Choose the Show Options command from the Paragraph palette submenu to expand the palette and display the options shown in the right example of the figure.

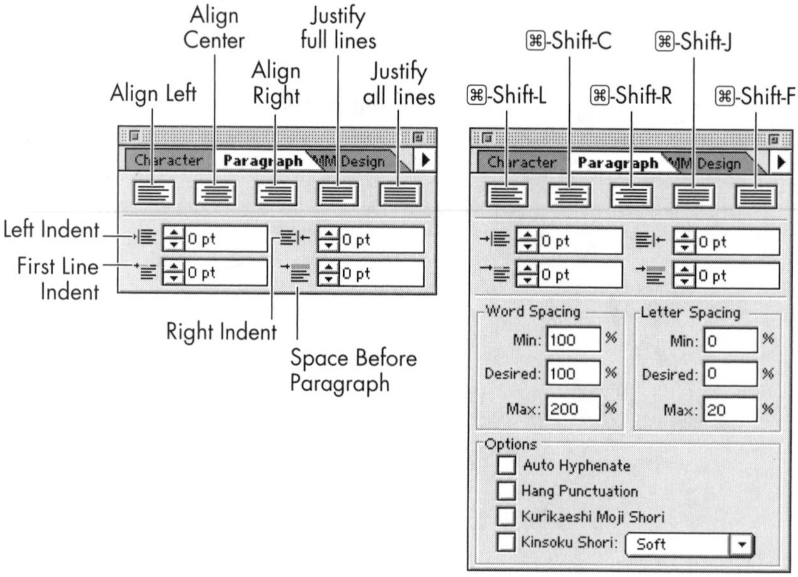

Figure 6-12: The Paragraph palette, collapsed (left) and expanded (right), with the keyboard shortcuts used to activate various options.

You can also hide the Paragraph palette by pressing ⌘-M once or twice in a row.

The Paragraph palette, like the Character palette, relies heavily on option boxes, and the same tips apply: Remember to use the Tab and Shift-Tab shortcuts to switch between the option boxes, and to press Shift-Return to apply changes without deactivating the option boxes.

Changing the Alignment

So far as I know, every computer program that lets you create type lets you change how the rows of type line up:

- To align a paragraph so that all the left edges line up (*flush left, ragged right*), press ⌘-Shift-L or select the first Alignment icon in the Paragraph palette.

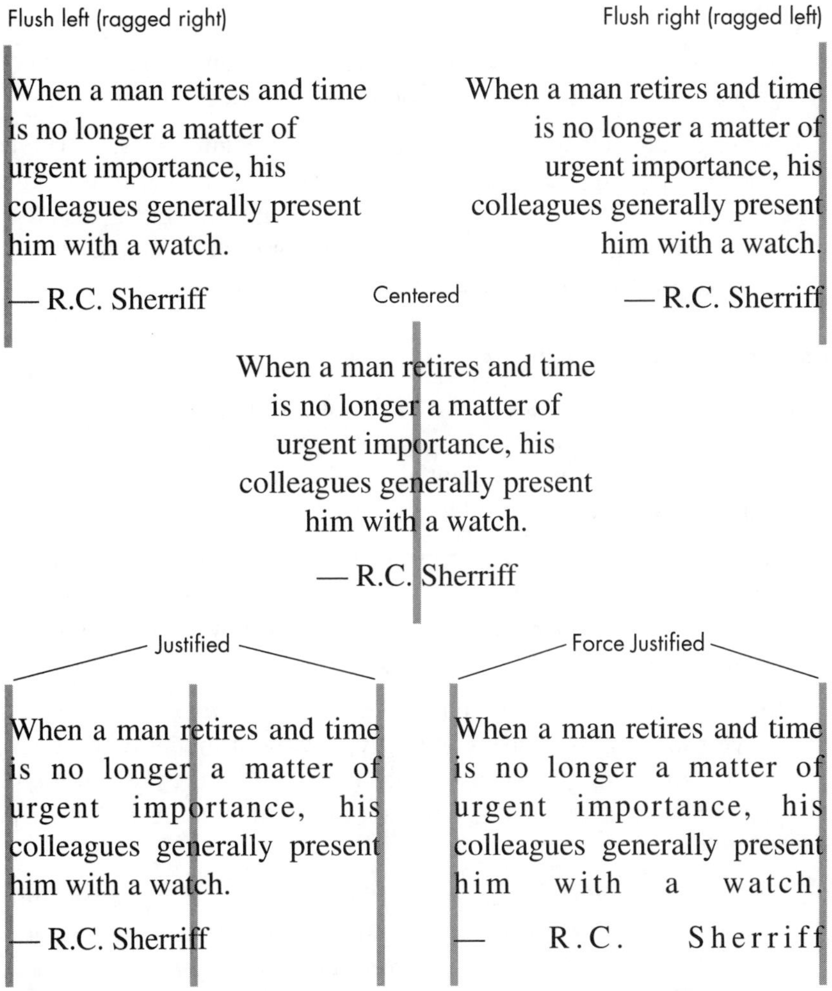

Figure 6-13: The five different alignment options available in Illustrator.

- To *center* all lines in a paragraph, press ⌘-Shift-C or select the second Alignment icon in the Paragraph palette.
- To make the right edges of a paragraph line up (*flush right, ragged left*), press ⌘-Shift-R or select the third Alignment icon.
- You can also *justify* a paragraph, which stretches all lines except the last line of a paragraph so they entirely fill the width of the text block. (The last line in a justified paragraph remains flush left.) To justify a paragraph, press ⌘-Shift-J or select the fourth Alignment icon.
- If you want to *force justify* the last line in a paragraph, press ⌘-Shift-F or click on the last Alignment icon in the Paragraph palette.

Examples of all five alignment settings appear in Figure 6-13. As you can see, I've applied all the settings to text blocks. When you align point text, Illustrator moves selected lines relative to the alignment point. Choosing the Justify and Justify Last Line options results in flush left text for each of the last lines, because each line of point text is a separate paragraph.

Indenting Paragraphs

Figure 6-14 demonstrates the two basic ways to indent a paragraph. You can indent the first line to distinguish one paragraph from another, or you can create a *hanging indent*, in which you indent all lines *but* the first line. A hanging indent is great for creating bulleted or numbered lists.

- To create a standard paragraph indent, enter a value into the First Line Indent option box in the Paragraph palette and press Return. I created the first example in Figure 6-14 with a First Line Indent value of 20 points.

  If you assign a first-line indent to a paragraph, remember that you can break a word onto the next line of type without indenting it by pressing the Enter key (Windows-ers need to use the Enter key on the keypad). Two words divided by Enter appear on different lines, but are part of the same paragraph.
- To create a hanging indent, enter a positive value into the Left Indent option box and the inverse of that value in the First Line Indent option box. For example, to create the second example in Figure 6-14, I set the Left Indent value to 20 points and the First Line Indent value to –20 points.

> You also have to set the tab so the first line lines up with the others. In the figure, I pressed the Tab key after the bullet to insert a tab character. Then I chose the Type » Tab Rulers command to display the Tabs palette and created a left tab at the 20-point mark so it lined up with the left indent. For complete information about tabs, read "The Amazing World of Tabs" near the end of this chapter.

You can enter any value between –1296 and 1296 points into any of the Indentation option boxes. The Left Indent value indents all text on the left side of a paragraph, creating a gap between the left edge of the text block and the affected paragraph. The Right Indent value indents all text on the right side of a paragraph. And First Line Indent indents the first line of a paragraph without affecting any other lines.

There's really no reason to apply Indentation values to point text (except to make it wrap around a object, as discussed in the "Adjusting the Standoff" section of Chapter 7).

Sixty years ago I knew everything; now I know nothing; education is a progressive discovery of your own ignorance.

—Will Durant

• Sixty years ago I knew everything; now I know nothing; education is a progressive discovery of your own ignorance.

— Will Durant

Figure 6-14: A paragraph with a first-line indent (top) and a hanging indent (bottom).

Adding Paragraph Leading

Enter a value into the Spacing Before Paragraph option box to insert some extra space before a selected paragraph. This so-called *paragraph leading* helps separate one paragraph from another, much like a first-line indent. Most designers use first-line indents *or* paragraph leading to distinguish paragraphs, but not both. The two together are generally considered design overkill (though I must admit I've done it and have been rather pleased with the results).

Spacing Letters and Words in a Justified Paragraph

The middle options in the Paragraph palette let you control the amount of space that Illustrator places between words and characters in a text block. As you might imagine, *word spacing* controls the amount of space between words; *letter spacing* controls the amount of space between letters.

NOTE

Now, a few of you quick-minded types are probably thinking to yourselves, "How is letter spacing, which controls the amount of space between individual characters, different from kerning, which controls the amount of space between individual characters? Call me stupid, but it sounds like the same thing to me." Well, for one, kerning applies to selected characters and letter spacing affects entire paragraphs. Also, the two are measured differently. Kerning is measured in fractions of an em space; letter spacing is measured as a percentage of the standard space character. But most important, kerning is fixed, whereas letter spacing is flexible. As we'll soon see, Illustrator can automatically vary letter spacing inside justified paragraphs between two extremes.

There are two primary reasons for manipulating spacing:

- To give a paragraph a generally tighter or looser appearance. You control this general spacing using the Desired options.
- To determine the range of spacing manipulations Illustrator can use when justifying a paragraph. Illustrator tightens up some lines and loosens others to make them fit the exact width of your text block. You specify limits using the Min. and Max. (short for minimum and maximum) options.

When spacing flush left, right, or centered paragraphs, Illustrator relies entirely on the two Desired values. In fact, the other options are dimmed. All values are measured as a percentage of a standard space, as the information contained in the current font determines. For example, a Desired Word Spacing value of 100 percent inserts the width of one space character between each pair of words in a paragraph. Reducing or enlarging this percentage makes the space between words bigger or smaller. A Desired Letter Spacing of 10 percent inserts 10 percent of the width of a space character between each pair of letters. Negative percentages squeeze letters together, and a value of 0 percent spaces letters normally.

Word: 100%, 100%, 200%

Neither can I believe that the individual survives the death of his body, although feeble souls harbor such thoughts through fear or ridiculous egotism.

—Albert Einstein

Letter: 0%, 0%, 5%

Neither can I believe that the individual survives the death of his body, although feeble souls harbor such thoughts through fear or ridiculous egotism.

—Albert Einstein

Word: 0%, 25%, 50%

Neither can I believe that the individualsurvivesthedeathof hisbody,althoughfeeblesouls harbor such thoughts through fearorridiculousegotism.

—AlbertEinstein

Letter: –15%, –10%, –5%

Neither can I believe that the individual survives the death of hisbody,althoughfeeblesouls harbor such thoughts through fear or ridiculous egotism.

—Albert Einstein

Word: 200%, 225%, 250%

Neither can I believe that the individual survives the death of his body, although feeble souls harbor such thoughts through fear or ridiculous egotism.

—Albert Einstein

Letter: 25%, 35%, 50%

Neither can I believe that the individual survives the death of his body, although feeble souls harbor such thoughts through fear or ridiculous egotism.

—Albert Einstein

Figure 6-15: Examples of several different word and letter spacing combinations. Letter spacing is constant in the left column and word spacing is constant in the right.

If you select one or more justified paragraphs, the Min. and Max. options become available. (These options appear dimmed if you have even one flush left, centered, or flush right paragraph partially selected.) These values give Illustrator some wiggle room when tightening and spreading lines of type. You're basically telling Illustrator, "I'd prefer that you use the Desired spacing, but if you can't manage that, go as low as Min. and as high as Max. But that's where I cut you off."

Word Spacing and Letter Spacing values must be within these ranges:

- The Min. Word Spacing value must be at least 0 percent; the Min. Letter Spacing must be at least –50 percent. Both must be less than their respective Desired values.
- The Max. Word Spacing value can be no higher than 1,000 percent; Max. Letter Spacing can be no more than 500 percent. Neither can be less than its respective Desired value.
- Each Desired value can be no less than its corresponding Min. value and no higher than the corresponding Max. value.

Figure 6-15 shows a justified paragraph subjected to various word spacing and letter spacing combinations. In the first column, only the word spacing changes; all letter spacing values are set to a constant 0 percent. In the second column, only the letter spacing changes; all word spacing values are set to 100 percent. Above each paragraph is a headline stating the values that have been changed. The percentages represent the Min., Desired, and Max. values respectively.

Activating Automatic Hyphenation

There are three ways to hyphenate text in Illustrator:

- If a long word wraps onto a new line, you can enter a standard hyphen character (-) to break the word onto two lines and better fill the text block. But inserting a standard hyphen can cause problems. If you edit the text later on, you may end up with stray hyphens between words that no longer break at the ends of lines.
- A better idea is to insert a *discretionary hyphen*, which disappears any time it is not needed. You can enter a discretionary hyphen by pressing ⌘-Shift-hyphen (-). If no hyphen appears when you enter this character, it simply means that the addition of the hyphen does not help Illustrator break the word. You can try inserting the character at a different location or expanding the width of the text block to permit the word to break.

- The third option is to let Illustrator do the hyphenating for you by selecting the Auto Hyphenate check box in the Paragraph palette. (This option has no effect on point text, just text blocks.)

Of all the options, I like the last one the least. It's the easiest, to be sure, but some of its suggestions are goofy—as in hyphenating *everyone* as *eve-ryone* or even as *e-ver-yone*—and Illustrator may open old illustrations and apply new hyphenation. Unless you're creating newsletters or other small documents with lots of type, it's usually safer to enter discretionary hyphens manually where needed.

Still, if you do decide automatic hyphenation is for you, here's how it works:

1. **Turn Auto Hyphenate on.**

   With the arrow tool, select the text block you want to hyphenate and turn on the Auto Hyphenate check box in the Paragraph palette. Illustrator adds hyphens where it deems necessary.

2. **Choose the Hyphenation Options.**

   If you want to limit where and how hyphenation occurs, choose the Hyphenation command from the Paragraph palette pop-up menu. The Hyphenation Options dialog box, shown in Figure 6-16, will open.

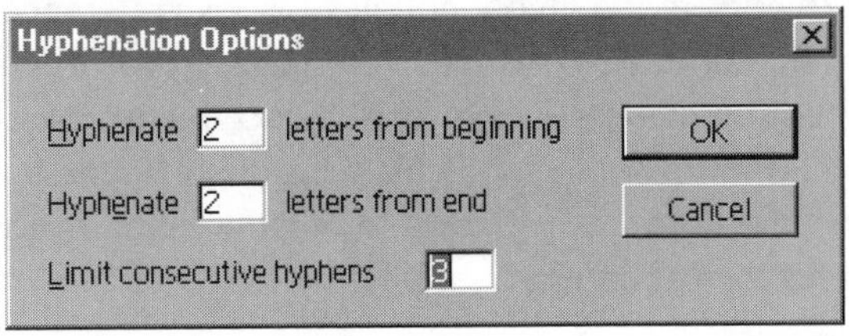

Figure 6-16: Here you can specify the limitations Illustrator will follow for automatic hyphenation.

3. **Specify how many letters must appear before and after a hyphen.**

   In the Hyphenation Options dialog box, enter a value into the first Hyphenate option box (Letters from Beginning) to specify the minimum number of letters that can come between a hyphen and the beginning of a word. Enter a value into the next option box to determine the minimum number of letters between a hyphen and the end of a word. For example, with both values set to 2, Illustrator could split the word *apple* as *ap-ple,* since both the first and last syllables are at least two letters long.

4. **Specify the possible number of consecutive hyphens.**

   If you want to limit the number of consecutive lines of type Illustrator can hyphenate, select the Limit check box and enter the maximum limit in the option box. By default, the value is set to 3, so Illustrator can hyphenate no more than three consecutive lines before it has to permit one line to go without hyphenation. But as far as I'm concerned, any more than two hyphenated lines in a row looks amateurish and interferes with legibility.

5. **Prepare to groove as Illustrator implements all your secret hyphen-related desires.**

   Click the OK button or press Return.

In addition to the hyphenation options entrusted to the Paragraph palette, you can prohibit Illustrator from hyphenating certain words by choosing File » Preferences » Hyphenation Options. Simply type the word you don't ever want to hyphenate into the New Entry option box and click on the Add button. To remove a word and permit Illustrator to hyphenate it in the future, select it from the scrolling list and click on the Delete button. Click on the OK button when you're all through.

WARNING

If you add a word in the Hyphenation Options Preferences dialog box that already exists in a text block, it won't unhyphenate without a little help from you. Select the text block, then deselect and immediately reselect the Auto Hyphenate check box in the Paragraph palette to make Illustrator reapply its automatic hyphenation.

Dangling a Quotation Mark

Select the Hang Punctuation check box to make punctuation such as quotation marks, commas, hyphens, and so on hang outside one of the edges of a text block:

- In a flush left or justified paragraph, punctuation is most likely to hang outside the left side of the text block.
- In a flush right paragraph, the punctuation hangs outside the right side.
- If the paragraph is centered, Hang Punctuation typically has no effect, since the punctuation can wiggle its way over to the left or right side.
- If you force justify the paragraph, the punctuation hangs off both sides.

I force justified the paragraph in Figure 6-17 so that all lines were both flush left and flush right. This way, Illustrator forced the quotation marks outside both sides of the text block. I also increased the type size of the quotation marks, kerned them slightly, and used a baseline shift to lower them 4 points each. You can't expect a single option like Hang Punctuation to do everything for you.

"Nothing is so ignorant as the ignorance of certainty."
—Aldous Huxley

Figure 6-17: Here I've applied the Hang Punctuation and Force Justification options to move the quote marks outside the text block.

Kurikaeshi Moji Shori and Kinsoku Shori

These final check boxes in the Paragraph palette (as well as the Kinsoku Shori options in the pop-up menu) have to do with Japanese layout rules and the Japanese type features the program includes. They work only with double-byte fonts—since there are so many characters in a Japanese font, each character requires two bytes. In other words, if you're not using a Japanese font, these options won't affect your text.

The Amazing World of Tabs

Prior to version 5.5, Illustrator didn't know a tab from a tackle box. These days, Illustrator offers some of the best tab capabilities of any program. You can create lists and tables with tremendous ease, and even throw in artistic flourishes absent from page layout programs such as PageMaker and QuarkXPress.

For those unfamiliar with the subject, tabs are little more than variable width spaces. By pressing the Tab key after entering a bullet or number, you can create hanging indents, as I showed you back in Figure 6-14. By entering tabs between items in a list, you can create columns that align precisely. Whenever you're tempted to use multiple spaces, press the Tab key instead.

There are really only two rules to using tabs:

- Never press Tab twice in a row (thus creating two tab characters).
- To specify the width of a tab character, adjust the tab stop settings in the Tabs palette.

To this day, I see more folks misuse tabs than I see use them correctly. If you never touch a tab stop and merely rely on multiple tabs or—gad!—spaces to do the work for you, you limit your formatting freedom and you make future editing more cumbersome and confusing. Whereas if you simply follow the two rules mentioned above and never, *ever* stray, you'll be fine.

Using the Tabs Palette

Choose Type » Tab Ruler (or press ⌘-Shift-T) to display the Tabs palette, shown in Figure 6-18. Known by the less formal moniker of *tab ruler,* this palette lets you position tab stops and align tabbed text.

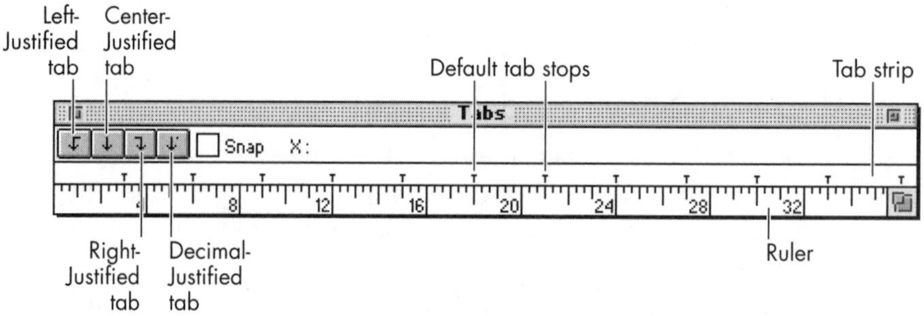

Figure 6-18: Use the tab ruler to position tab stops and align tabbed text.

Like the Paragraph palette, the tab ruler affects entire paragraphs, whether they're entirely or only partially selected. The following items explain how the tab ruler works and offer a few guidelines for using it.

- When you first bring up the Tabs palette, Illustrator automatically aligns it to the selected paragraph. To align the palette to a different paragraph, select the paragraph and click in the size box on the far right side of the title bar (or just to the left of the Windows close box).
- To create a tab stop, click in the ruler along the bottom of the palette, or click inside the tab strip just above the ruler. If you drag the tab stop,

Illustrator projects a vertical alignment guide from the Tabs palette, as labeled in Figure 6-19. The line moves with the tab stop, permitting you to predict more accurately the results of your adjustment. The Tabs palette also tracks the numerical position of the tab stop—with respect to the left edge of the text block—just below the title bar.

- When you create a new tab stop, all default tab stops (those little Ts) to the left of the new stop disappear. The default stops merely tell Illustrator to space tabbed text every half inch.
- A question mark in the tab ruler means that at least one line of selected text does *not* align to that tab stop. Just click on the tab stop to make all selected lines align.

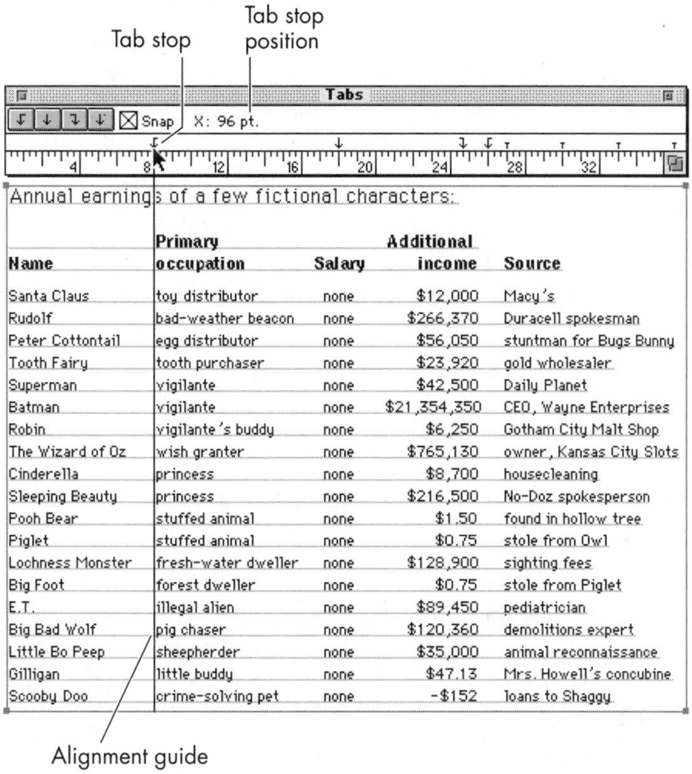

Name	Primary occupation	Salary	Additional income	Source
Santa Claus	toy distributor	none	$12,000	Macy's
Rudolf	bad-weather beacon	none	$266,370	Duracell spokesman
Peter Cottontail	egg distributor	none	$56,050	stuntman for Bugs Bunny
Tooth Fairy	tooth purchaser	none	$23,920	gold wholesaler
Superman	vigilante	none	$42,500	Daily Planet
Batman	vigilante	none	$21,354,350	CEO, Wayne Enterprises
Robin	vigilante's buddy	none	$6,250	Gotham City Malt Shop
The Wizard of Oz	wish granter	none	$765,130	owner, Kansas City Slots
Cinderella	princess	none	$8,700	housecleaning
Sleeping Beauty	princess	none	$216,500	No-Doz spokesperson
Pooh Bear	stuffed animal	none	$1.50	found in hollow tree
Piglet	stuffed animal	none	$0.75	stole from Owl
Lochness Monster	fresh-water dweller	none	$128,900	sighting fees
Big Foot	forest dweller	none	$0.75	stole from Piglet
E.T.	illegal alien	none	$89,450	pediatrician
Big Bad Wolf	pig chaser	none	$120,360	demolitions expert
Little Bo Peep	sheepherder	none	$35,000	animal reconnaissance
Gilligan	little buddy	none	$47.13	Mrs. Howell's concubine
Scooby Doo	crime-solving pet	none	-$152	loans to Shaggy

Figure 6-19: When you drag a tab stop, a vertical line drops down from the palette, showing how the adjusted text will align.

To move more than one tab stop at a time, Shift-drag a stop. All tab stops to the right of the dragged stop move in kind; tab stops to the left remain stationary.

- Select the Snap check box to align new and moved tab stops to the nearest increment on the ruler. I heartily recommend this option.

You can also snap a single tab stop on the fly when the Snap check box is turned off. To do this, press ⌘ while dragging the tab stop. You can likewise ⌘-drag to move a tab stop freely when the Snap option is active.

- To change the identity of a tab stop, select the tab stop by clicking on it, then select a different identity from the four buttons on the left side of the palette. From left to right, these buttons make tabbed text align with the left side, center, right side, or decimal point. In Figure 6-19, for example, I centered the *Salary* column by assigning a center tab stop. I aligned the *Additional income* column with a right tab stop. Decimal tab stops are ideal for aligning numbers, such as prices.

Another way to change the identity of a tab stop is to Option-click on it. Each Option-click switches the stop to the next variety, from left to center to right to decimal and back to left.

- To delete a tab stop, drag it upward, off the tab strip and out of the palette. The X: item reads **delete**. To delete all tab stops, Shift-drag upward on the leftmost tab stop in the ruler.

By default, the unit of measure in the tab ruler conforms to the unit in Illustrator's standard rulers (as set using the General Units option in the Units & Undo Preferences dialog box). But you can cycle through other units—without affecting the standard rulers—by clicking on the tab stop position indicator just to the right of the X: (which is just to the right of the Snap check box).

(Note that you must select a tab stop for this last tip to work. If you click too far to the right of the tab stop position indicator, you may end up deselecting the tab stop, which prevents you from further changing the unit of measure—until you select another tab stop, that is.)

You Mac users can also change the unit of measure in the Tab palette by pressing ⌘-Control-U, but this changes Illustrator's other dialog box and ruler measurements as well. I'm sorry to say this, but there is no Windows equivalent.

NOTE: If you want all the lines of your table to use the same tab stops automatically, be sure to press Shift-Return at the end of each line. This inserts line breaks, forcing Illustrator to recognize all the lines as part of the same paragraph, as is the case in Figure 6-19. The tab stops that you create for one line will affect other lines only within the same paragraph. If you press Return at the end of each line, you will insert carriage returns. Illustrator then treats each line as a separate paragraph, and thus the tab stops you set for one line would not impact the other lines. You would then have to set tab stops for each line independently.

Taking Tabs to a New Level

What if you don't want to align tabbed text in straightforward vertical columns? What if you want to create something a little more graphic, something worthier of your reader's attention, such as the table in Figure 6-20? Can you do this in Illustrator?

Well, of course you can. In fact, you've been able to do something like this since Illustrator 3.0. It involves wrapping the text block around several open paths, as the following steps explain:

1. **Create your text block.**

   Enter one tab—and only one tab—between each entry, just as you would normally. In the figure, for example, there is one tab between *Santa Claus* and *toy distributor*. Use line breaks (Shift-Return) to separate the lines. If you separate the lines with carriage returns (by pressing Return), Illustrator will not automatically apply paragraph-level format changes to each line.

2. **Use the direct selection tool to reshape the boundaries of the text block.**

   For example, to create the slanted block shown in Figure 6-20, I clicked on the bottom segment of the text block and dragged it to the right. You may want to work in the artwork mode, where you can see the text block outline when it's not selected.

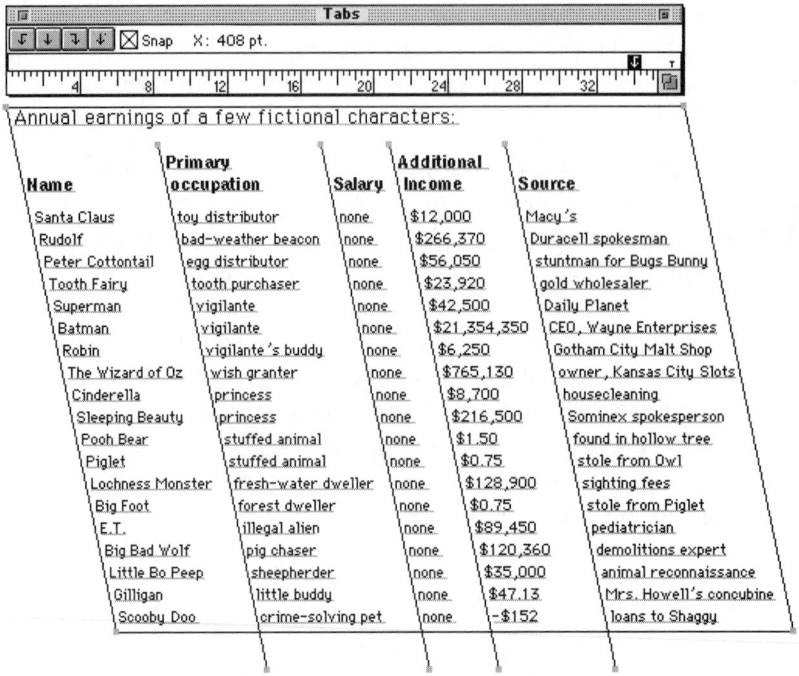

Figure 6-20: I created this slanted table—seen in the artwork mode—by wrapping tabbed text around a series of straight lines.

3. Add a tab stop to the far right side of the tab ruler.

Your text should now be a total mess, but no matter. Click in the size box in the Tabs palette to align it to the text block to your text, then create a left tab stop on the far right side of the palette. If any other tab stops exist, delete them. In Figure 6-20, for example, I positioned a single tab stop at the 34-pica mark. The purpose of this step is to eliminate all of the default tabs, thereby ensuring that each tab carries the entry following it to the next open path.

4. Draw a few open paths to serve as guides.

Ugh, your text is worse than ever. But don't try to fix it. Instead, it's time to add graphic tab stops in the form of a few open paths. In Figure 6-20, I drew a straight line with the pen tool by clicking on each of the two points on the left side of the slanted text block. This way, the angle of the line matched the angle of the block. Then I used the arrow tool to drag the line into position, just to the right of *Santa*

Claus, so it could serve as the tab stop for the *Primary occupation* column. I then cloned the line by Option-dragging it three times, thus creating three additional tab stops. (I discuss cloning in Chapter 9.)

5. **Apply the Make Wrap command.**

   To convert the lines into tab stops, select both the lines and the text block and choose Type » Wrap » Make (covered in Chapter 7). Illustrator automatically aligns each tabbed entry with the nearest line.

6. **Drag the lines into position with the direct selection tool.**

   It's unlikely the text will wrap exactly the way you hoped right off the bat. But now that the text is roughly in place, the lines act just like normal tab stops. To reposition one of these graphic tab stops, use the direct selection tool to move the line left or right.

7. **Make the lines transparent so they don't interfere with the table.**

   Once you have all the lines in place, select the lines and make their fills and strokes transparent (using the control located at the bottom of the toolbox or in the top left of the Color palette).

Graphic tabs are generally every bit as versatile as regular tabs, except for one thing: Each tab stop is the same. In other words, you can't mix left tabs and right tabs inside the same text block, and there are no decimal tabs. Rather, each entry is aligned the same way the paragraph is aligned. If the paragraph is flush left, each entry is flush left; if the paragraph is centered, each entry is centered between the graphic tabs; and so on.

Graphic tabs bridge the border between the world of sedate formatting options that every publishing program provides, and the more wild text effects Illustrator is so rightly famous for. To cross all the way over to the other side of the border, read the next chapter.

CHAPTER 7

SOME OF YOUR WACKIER TEXT EFFECTS

Creating and formatting text is all very well and good, but where Illustrator excels is in the creation of specialized—dare I say wacky?—type. You can attach text to a curve, wrap text inside an irregular outline, flow text from one text block to another, and wrap text around graphics. If you plan to use Illustrator to create pages that contain a fair amount of text, you can import text from a word processor, and then check the spelling, perform complex search and replace operations, and even export the text back out to disk. And just to prove to you that there are no limits to this wackiness, Illustrator lets you convert one or more letters to paths and then edit the character outlines, as discussed back in Chapter 5.

Illustrator is clearly one of the most proficient text-manipulation programs on the planet, superior to either QuarkXPress or PageMaker when relatively small chunks of text are concerned. In fact, only archrival FreeHand is more adept. But where FreeHand requires you to navigate through palette after palette of cryptic options—many of which are more trouble than they're worth—Illustrator provides a more hands-on approach, allowing you to drag elements around and rewarding you with immediate feedback.

Topsy-Turvy Type on a Curve

As demonstrated in Figure 7-1, Illustrator lets you bind a line of text to a free-form path. Adobe calls such a text object *path text*, but folks call it type on a curve as well.

To create type along the outline of a path, follow these simple steps:

1. **Draw a path.**

   Curved paths work better than those with sharp corners, so you'll probably want to avoid corner points and cusps and stick with smooth points. Ellipses, spirals, and softly sloping paths work best.

2. **Select the path type tool.**

   To get to the path type tool, drag from the type tool in the toolbox to display a pop-up menu. The path type tool looks like a T on a wiggly line, as labeled in Figure 7-2.

3. **Click on the path and start typing.**

   The point at which you click determines the position of the blinking insertion marker. As you enter text from the keyboard, the characters follow the contours of the path.

If your text appears on the underside of the path, or if no text appears and all you see is a plus sign inside a little box, you need to flip the text to the other side of the path. Select the arrow tool and double-click on the alignment handle, which looks like an I-beam attached to the path. Then select the type tool and click on the path to continue adding text.

You can't attach more than one line of text to a path. This means Illustrator never drops the insertion marker down to the next line, even if you press the Return or Enter key. Instead, it just inserts what looks like a space. The same goes for pressing the Tab key.

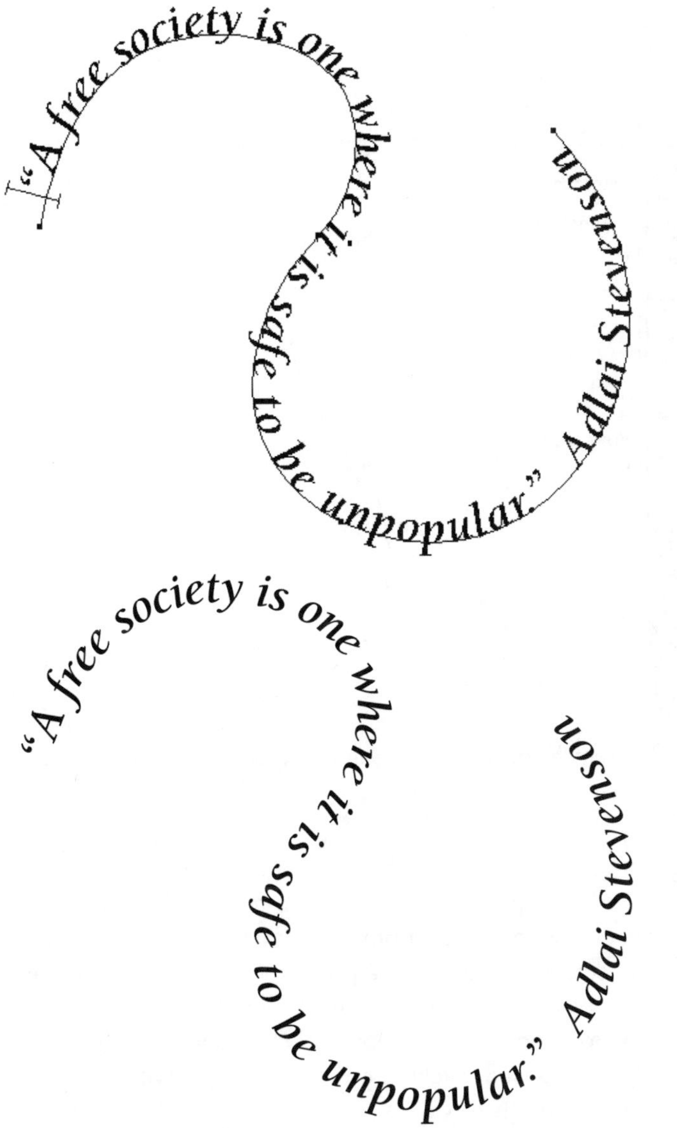

Figure 7-1: Path text as it appears when selected on screen (top) and when printed (bottom).

4. Complete the path text.

When you finish entering text, select another tool in the toolbox to finish the text object. The path text appears selected, as in the first example shown in Figure 7-1.

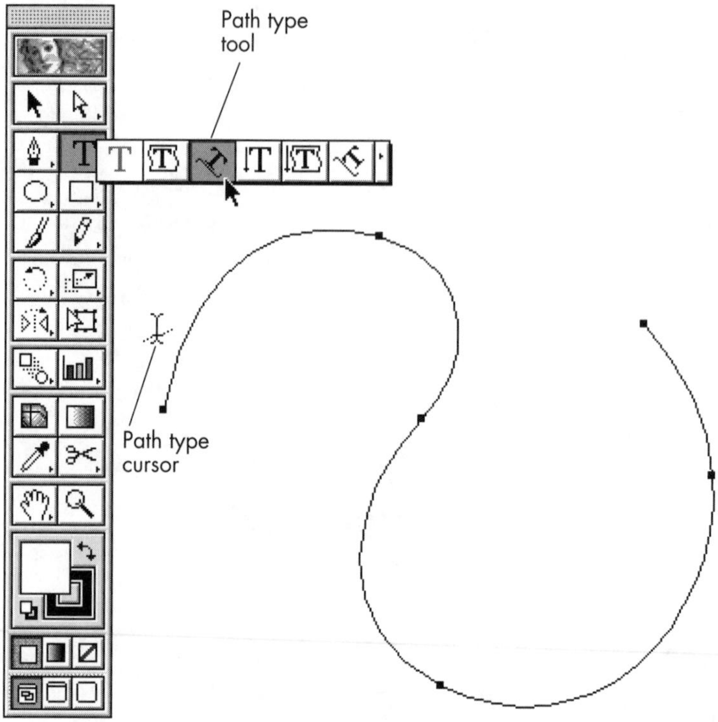

Figure 7-2: Select the path type tool, click on a path, and start typing.

TIP

You don't have to use the path type tool to create path text. In fact, it's generally easier to use the standard type tool. To attach text to an open path, just click on it with the type tool. The cursor changes to the path type cursor (as in Figure 7-2) the moment you move the cursor over the path. To attach type to a closed path, Option-click on the path. (Without Option pressed, clicking on a closed path with the type tool creates area text, which I discuss later in this chapter.)

Like point text (covered in the previous chapter), path text is ill-suited to anything longer than a sentence. When a word extends past the end of an open path, it disappears from view like a ship sailing off the edge of the world. Long text simply wraps around and around a closed path, forcing words to overlap.

Converting Point Text to Path Text

Illustrator does not provide a command for binding text to a path. To bind an existing line of point text to a path, you have to copy and paste it:

1. Select the point text with the arrow tool.
2. Press ⌘-C to copy it (or choose Edit » Copy).
3. Click an open path with the type tool, or Option-click on a closed path.
4. Press ⌘-V to paste the copied text (or choose Edit » Paste).

You can also use the contents of a text block. Just select the words inside the block with the type tool and follow Steps 2 through 4.

Moving Type Along Its Path

When you click on path text with the standard arrow tool, you select both path and type at the same time. A special *alignment handle* appears, as labeled in Figure 7-3. This handle allows you to adjust the placement of the text on the path in any of the ways shown on the next page.

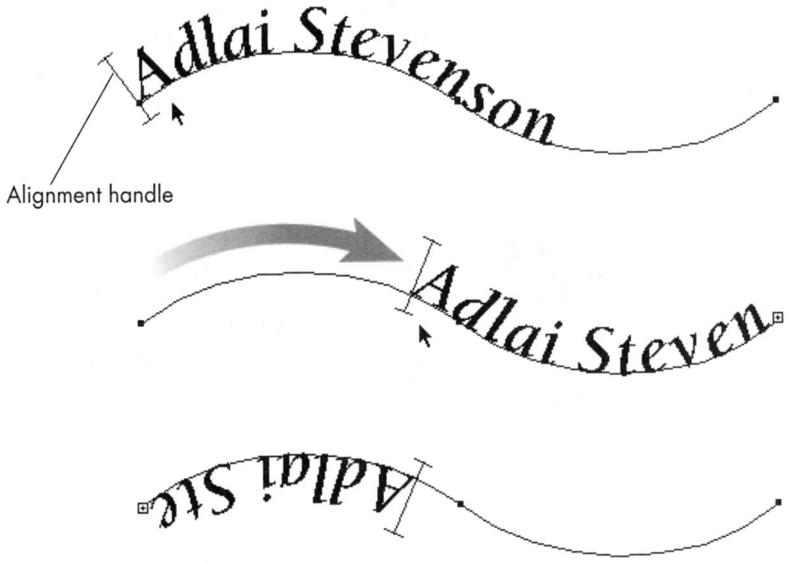

Figure 7-3: The alignment handle appears when you select both the path and the type (top). You can drag the handle to move text (middle) or double-click on it to flip the text (bottom).

- Drag the handle to slide the text back and forth along the path, as in the second example in the figure.
- Double-click on the handle to flip the text to the other side of the path, as in the third example in Figure 7-3.
- Drag the handle to the other side of the path to move the text as you flip it in the opposite direction.

TIP: In addition to clicking with the arrow tool, you can also select both path and type by Option-clicking twice on the path with the direct selection tool. Be sure to click on the path. Don't try to click at the location where you expect the handle to be; it won't do you any good. However, you can marquee around the handle if you want.

Reshaping a Path Right Under Its Text

When you create path text, you typically run into the same problems as when you enter words into a text block. If the path is too short to accommodate all of its text, for example, a plus sign appears in a small box located on the last point in the path, as shown in Figure 7-4. In path text, Illustrator makes no distinction between a single word that can't fit and a sentence. Since path type can't wrap to a second line, it either fits on the path or it doesn't.

Figure 7-4: Any amount of overflow text prompts the boxed plus sign, whether the text breaks in the middle of a word or of a sentence.

Because you can't flow path text into another text object, you have only three choices for fixing type along an inadequate path:

- Reduce the size of the type.
- Delete a few words or characters until the text fits on the path.
- Lengthen the path by reshaping it until all text is visible.

To lengthen a path with text on it, you can drag both segments and points with the direct selection tool in any way that you want. After each drag, the text refits to the path, so you can see your progress. Suppose, for example, that you want to lengthen the lower line shown in Figure 7-4. The following steps explain a few ways to do it:

1. Press ⌘-Shift-A (or choose Edit » Deselect All) to deselect the type. You must deselect the path *text* before you can select the path by itself. But before you can select one, you must deselect both.
2. Using the direct selection tool, click on the path. This selects the path without selecting the type on the path. (Notice that the alignment handle I-beam isn't visible. This shows you that the text is not selected.)
3. Drag one of the endpoints to stretch the path, as shown at the top of Figure 7-5. The type immediately refits to the path, as shown in the bottom example.

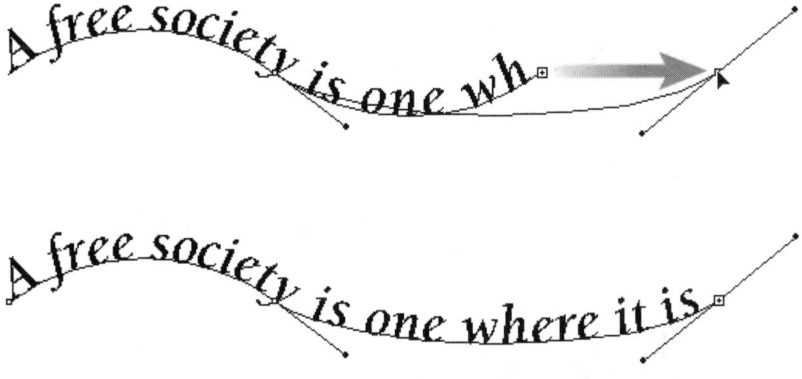

Figure 7-5: By dragging the endpoint of an open path with the direct selection tool (top), you stretch the path to accommodate more text (bottom).

4. Notice that the line no longer curves as gracefully as it used to. To correct this, you can drag down on the segment or adjust the control handles as shown in Figure 7-6.
5. If you need to lengthen your path dramatically, you might prefer to add points to the path using the pencil or pen tool. In Figure 7-7, for example, I've used the pen tool to add segments to the path. With each additional segment, more text becomes visible until eventually

no overflow text remains. When the path is long enough to accommodate its text, the boxed plus sign disappears, as Figure 7-7 shows.

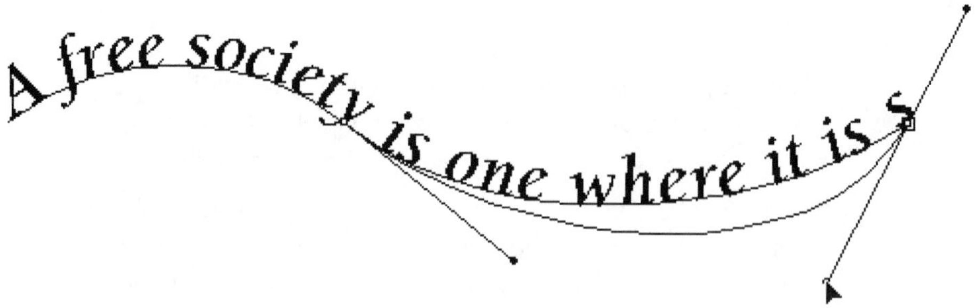

Figure 7-6: You can also move the Bézier control handles using the direct selection tool.

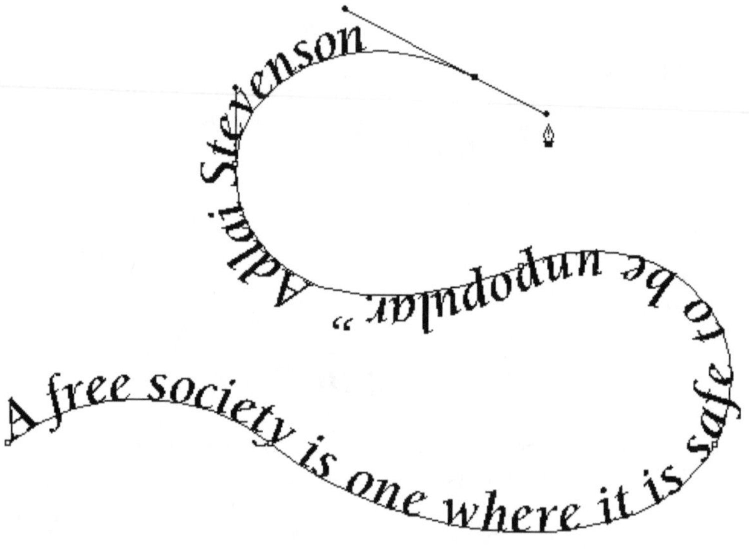

Figure 7-7: The plus sign goes away when all text is visible on the screen.

In addition to editing a path with the direct selection tool, you can use the add point, delete point, and convert point tools (as described in the "Operating on Points Long after the Path Is Done" section of Chapter 5). In fact, you can apply all of the editing techniques discussed in Chapter 5 to a path with text on it. The next section explores one way to use the add point tool.

Trimming Away Excess Path

What if instead of being too short, your path is too long? Certainly you can enlarge the type size, add words, or move points around to make the path shorter. But what if you simply want to trim a little slack off the end of the path?

You can't split it off with the scissors tool (covered in Chapter 9), because Illustrator won't let you split an open path with text on it. Instead, you can follow these steps:

1. Click with either the pen tool or the add point tool at the spot where you want the path to end, as shown in Figure 7-8. (Remember, to add a point with the pen tool, you must turn off the Disable Auto Add/Delete option in the General Preferences dialog box.)

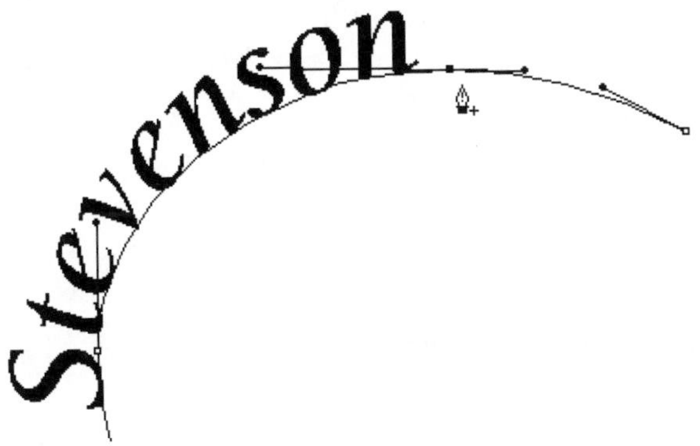

Figure 7-8: Use the add point tool to insert a point at the location where you want the path to end.

2. Select all points beyond the newly inserted point with the direct selection tool, as shown in Figure 7-9. (Don't select the new point itself.)
3. Press the Delete key. The selected points and their segments disappear, making the inserted point the new endpoint.

Normally, you don't need to worry about excess path. The path is hidden by default when you're previewing or printing an illustration. Shortening a path becomes an issue only if you want to stroke the path apart from its text—as explained in Chapter 16.

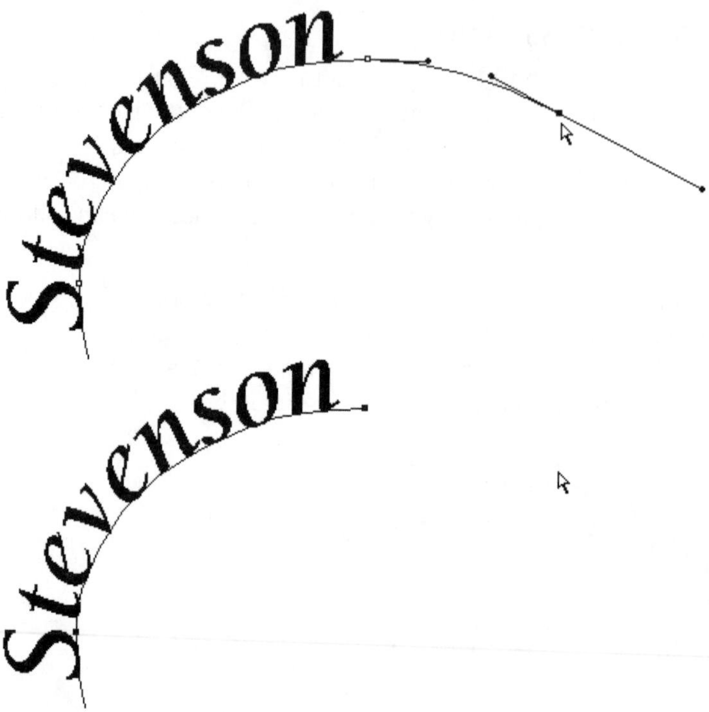

Figure 7-9: Select all points to the right of the inserted point (top) and delete them (bottom).

Shifting Type in Relation to Its Path

Illustrator lets you raise and lower type with respect to its path using baseline shift (introduced in the last chapter). The baseline of path text is the path itself, so moving type away from the baseline likewise moves it away from the path.

As you may recall from Chapter 6, you can change the baseline shift by entering a value into the Baseline Shift option box in the Character palette or by pressing Shift and Option with either the ↑ or the ↓ key. The keyboard shortcuts are generally the preferred method for shifting the baseline.

The following steps demonstrate why baseline shift is useful. They show you how to create text along the top and bottom halves of a circle—a job for baseline shift if there ever was one.

1. **Draw a circle.**

   You know, Shift-drag with the ellipse tool.

2. Option-click with the type tool at the top of the circle.

Illustrator snaps the alignment handle to the top of the shape.

3. Enter the text you want to appear along the top of the path.

I wanted to create the William Allen White quote "Peace without justice is tyranny." So I decided to enter "Peace without justice" across the top.

NOTE

Incidentally, in case you think I'm this amazingly learned guy who goes around spouting quotes from history's movers and shakers, nothing could be farther from the truth. The quotes used in the figures in this chapter and the previous one come from *Peter's Quotations* (Bantam Books). Kind of makes me seem a little more human, huh?

4. Center the text.

Press ⌘-Shift-C or click on the second icon in the Paragraph palette. Just as you can move text along a path by dragging the alignment handle, you can use Illustrator's alignment formatting functions to position text. It comes in handy when you want to get things exactly right.

5. Format the text as desired.

Press ⌘-A to highlight the text. Then format at will. I used 38-point Herculanum, an Adobe PostScript font that offers a collection of exclusively capital letters. Quite frankly, text on a circle usually looks best in all caps.

6. Clone your text.

This is the most important step and one of the trickiest to pull off. First select the path text with the arrow tool. Then drag the alignment handle around the path to the bottom of the circle. Without releasing—don't release till I tell you to—drag upward so the type flips to the other side of the path. Then drag down ever so carefully until your cursor snaps onto the bottom point in the circle. Finally, press the Option key, release the mouse button, and then release the Option key. A clone of the type moves and flips to the interior of a cloned circle, as illustrated in Figure 7-10.

7. Edit the bottom type as desired.

Click inside the cloned text with the type tool, and press ⌘-A to select it. Then enter the words that you want to appear along the bottom of the circle. I entered "is tyranny," because that's the way old Willy White would have wanted it.

Figure 7-10: Option-drag the type to the inside bottom portion of the circle. The hollow double cursor shows that you have snapped to a point and cloned both type and circle.

8. Shift the bottom text downward.

With your keen mind, you've undoubtedly noticed that the upper and lower text blocks don't align properly. You need to move the lower text outward without flipping it. While the text is still active, press ⌘-A to highlight the lower text block. Since you want to lower the type with respect to its path, press Shift-Option-↓ to move the type downward 2 points (assuming you haven't changed the Baseline Shift value in the Type & Auto Tracing Preferences dialog box). I pressed Shift-Option-↓ seven times in a row to get the effect shown in Figure 7-11.

9. Similarly lower the text along the top of the circle.

Press ⌘-Shift-A to deselect the text. Then click in the upper text block with the type tool and press ⌘-A to highlight the first words you created. Press

Shift-Option-↓ several times to lower the top text so it aligns with the bottom text. I pressed these keys eight times to arrive at Figure 7-12.

Figure 7-11: Press Shift-Option-↓ several times to lower the text along the bottom of the circle.

Figure 7-12: Highlight the upper text block and press Shift-Option-↓ several times to lower this text as well.

Just for laughs, Figure 7-13 shows the final illustration as it appears when printed. I selected both circles by marqueeing around a segment with the arrow tool. Then I cloned the circle, reduced it to 70 percent, and rotated it 30 degrees. Over and over again.

Figure 7-13: The finished text on a circle, repeated several times to create a tunnel-of-type effect.

Doing It All Again with Vertical Type

Let's pretend that the day after you become proficient with Illustrator and feel ready to take on any Illustrator-related challenges, aliens from some very boring world—and it would have to be a terribly boring world for these aliens to embark upon what I'm about to suggest—abduct you. They decide that, since you've read the definitive work on Illustrator 8 (this book) and you are undoubtedly master of all Illustrator stuff that you survey, they wish to test your skills. They whisk you away and, after they finish taking the obligatory core sampling of your brain as required of all extraterrestrials under the Alpha Centauri Convention, find you a job where your only responsibilities are to work your Illustrator magic. "No sweat," you say. "The job is in Japan," they respond. "But, I can't speak Japanese," you protest, "and I'm allergic to giant green lizard-sort-of things." But they callously reply, "You will just have to make do. Anyway, we're pretty sure that that Godzilla thingamajig is an amphibian."

Fear not, my potential-abductee friends, for Adobe has already planned for this contingency. Well, not really, but one of Adobe's aims in creating modern-day Illustrator is to design a more universal product. The hope is that the Illustrator 8 you use here in the States is the same program you would use in Japan. Aside from the fact that the Japanese version would use Japanese in the menus, dialog boxes, palettes, and anywhere else in Illustrator a person in Japan would find themselves needing to see words in Japanese, Illustrator is still Illustrator. Oh, sure, you probably wouldn't be able to read any of the commands—and thus you would undoubtedly feel rather uncomfortable trying to start up a conversation with your new coworkers—but (Adobe hopes) you would still be able to use Illustrator.

One of the functions that's meant to round out Illustrator's international savvy is the ability to add type to your illustrations that reads top-to-bottom and right-to-left, like Japanese script. Most of us will never encounter a situation in which we will need to add kanji or other Japanese characters to a drawing, but the same techniques required to add Japanese script give us additional choices for adding more familiar type.

NOTE

I'd like to take a moment to emphasize that by adding the new vertical type functions to a chapter entitled "Some of Your Wacky Text Effects," I mean no disrespect. The choice to include the description here is that it just doesn't fit in Chapter 6. I think that most readers, if they choose to use vertical type, will incorporate it as a special effect and not for its designated purpose.

Since you already know how to add horizontal type to a path, you're only a couple of minutes away from adding vertical type to your artwork. Simply draw the path (either open or closed) that you want to use as your guide for the vertical type, and then select the type tool. Position the cursor over the path. Press and hold the Option key if it is a closed path. Now press and hold the Shift key. When you press Shift, the cursor switches to the vertical path type cursor, which looks just like the path type cursor lying on its side, as shown in Figure 7-14. Click on the path and enter your text.

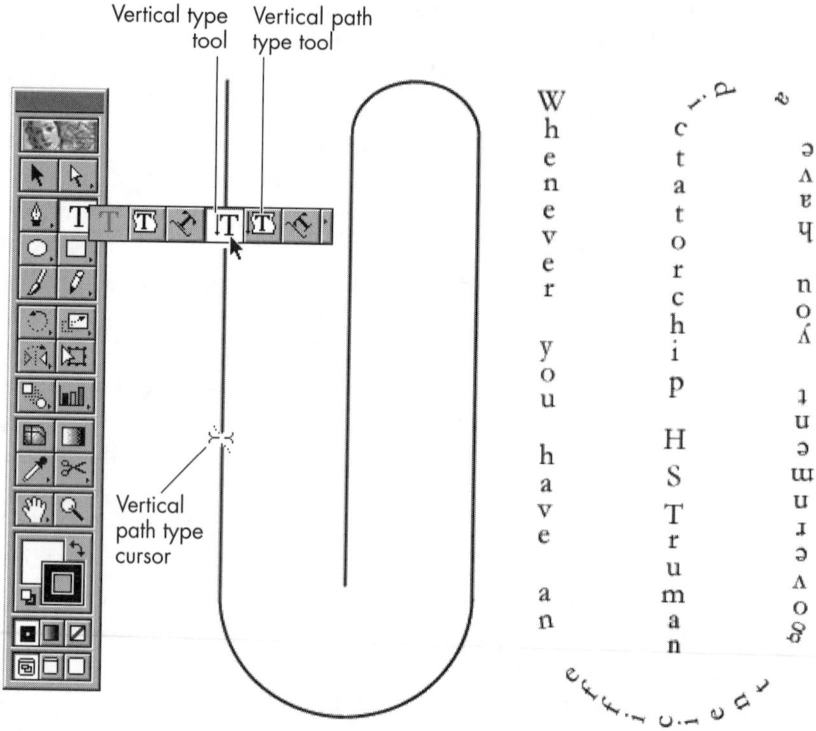

Figure 7-14: With the type tool, I Shift-clicked on the left path and entered some text (right).

TIP

Vertical type tends to be hard to read without some adjustment. In Figure 7-14, I selected each word individually—double-clicked on a word and pressed Shift-↓ to deselect the space after the word—and changed the tracking to –100 inside the Character palette. That's right, all options in the Character palette that affect the horizontal spacing of horizontally oriented type (tracking, kerning, and so on) will affect the vertical spacing of vertically oriented type. In the case of the leading and baseline shift options (options that change the vertical spacing of horizontal type), it's just the opposite for vertical type. These options will affect the horizontal spacing of vertical type.

Additionally, you can apply the Rotate or Tate Chu Yoko option to vertical path type. You'll find both of these options in the Direction pop-up menu that's part of the Character palette's Multilingual Options—displayed when you choose the Multilingual Options command from the Character palette's pop-up menu. These options change the orientation of the text. They are especially useful when you apply them to individual words.

Getting that Irritating Alignment Handle Off a Path

After you click on a path with the type tool, Illustrator thinks you want to use the path to hold text for all time. Even if you delete all text from the path at some later date, the alignment handle will hang in there, showing you that this is still path text.

Years ago, Adobe included a little plug-in that removed the alignment handle as part of Illustrator 5.5, but it was history by version 6. No matter, you don't need it. Here's how to remove the alignment handle all by yourself:

1. Select the path by Option-clicking on it with the direct selection tool. Do not use the arrow tool.
2. Press ⌘-C or choose Edit » Copy to copy the path to the Clipboard.
3. Option-click on the path again. This selects the text and displays the alignment handle.
4. Press the Delete key to destroy the path text for all time. (Don't worry, you've copied the path to the Clipboard, so it's safe.)
5. Press ⌘-F or choose Edit » Paste In Front. The path is reborn on screen with no alignment handle. Stroke the path or fill it at will.

Filling a Shape with Text

If the Adobe engineers were a typical lot, they would have added type on a curve to Illustrator, slapped it onto a features list, and sold the product. But Adobe folks are frequently (though not always) more thoughtful than that. So when they added type on a curve to version 3 back in 1991, they thought, "Gosh, if artists want text on a curve, maybe they want text inside a curve as well." And after much sagely nodding of heads, area text was born.

In area text, type exists inside a path. A standard text block is a variety of area text—text inside a rectangle. But you can create text inside polygons, stars, or free-form shapes. Heck, you can even create text inside an open path if you want.

To create type inside a path, goest thou thusly:

1. **Draw a path.**

   Unlike path text, area text works just as well with corner points as with smooth points where area text is concerned. But keep the corners obtuse—wide rather than sharp. It's very difficult, and in many cases impossible, to fill sharp corners with text.

2. **Select the area type tool.**

   Select the area type tool from the type tool pop-up menu in the toolbox. The area type tool looks like a T trapped in Jell-O, as labeled in Figure 7-15.

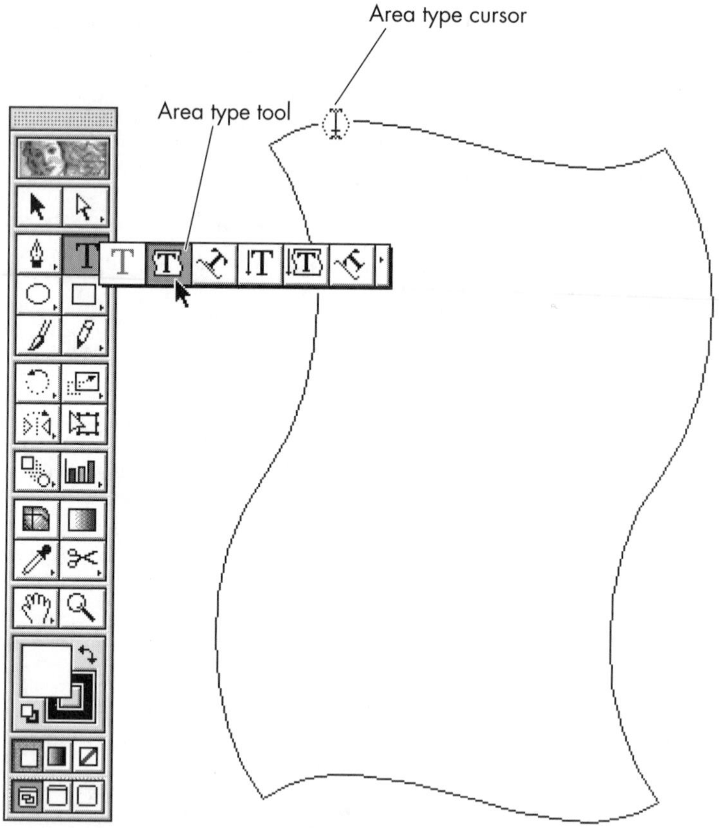

Figure 7-15: Click on the path outline with the area type tool.

3. **Click along the outline of the path and enter some text.**

   You must click on the outline of the path; you can't click inside the path to add text (even if the path is filled and the Use Area Select check box is active in the General Preferences dialog box). A blinking insertion marker appears at the top of the path. As you enter text, it fills the path. Words that would otherwise exceed the edge of the shape wrap to the next line.

4. Complete the path text.

Select the type tool, arrow tool, or some other tool to finish off the text block. You'll get something like the area text shown in Figure 7-16.

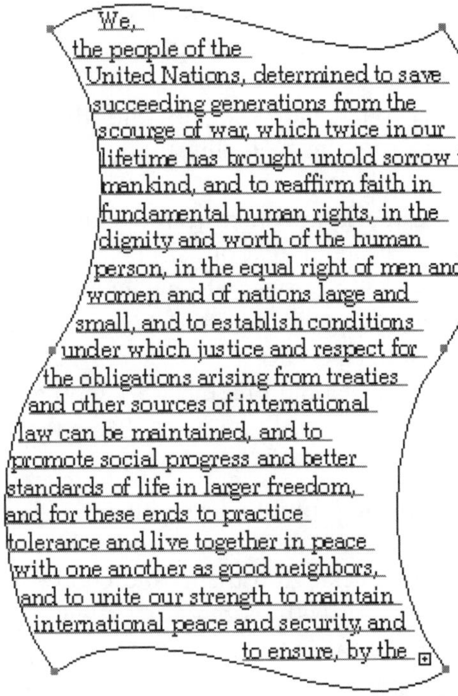
We,
the people of the
United Nations, determined to save
succeeding generations from the
scourge of war, which twice in our
lifetime has brought untold sorrow to
mankind, and to reaffirm faith in
fundamental human rights, in the
dignity and worth of the human
person, in the equal right of men and
women and of nations large and
small, and to establish conditions
under which justice and respect for
the obligations arising from treaties
and other sources of international
law can be maintained, and to
promote social progress and better
standards of life in larger freedom,
and for these ends to practice
tolerance and live together in peace
with one another as good neighbors,
and to unite our strength to maintain
international peace and security, and
to ensure, by the

Figure 7-16: Behold area text—a free-form shape filled with type.

TIP: You can also create area text with the standard type tool. Just click on a closed path to create area text, or Option-click on an open path. When the area type tool is active, press the T key five times to access the standard type tool.

One last thing about filling a shape with text: you can click on a shape with the vertical area type tool or Shift-click with the type tool to add vertical type. The only problem is that unless you are using a Japanese font designed for vertical display, the resulting text is almost impossible to read. Not only do the words fill the shape from top to bottom, but each successive line of text is placed to the left of the previous one. You may find this ideal for adding columns of symbols or even columns of the same short phrase (repeated over and over) to a shape, but if you try filling a shape with more than one-liners, I fear your audience will spend more time deciphering the text than reading it.

Flowing Text from One Shape to Another

If your text overflows the path or you simply don't like the way it wraps, you can edit the path with the direct selection tool. Press ⌘-Shift-A to deselect the text block, and then click on the path with the direct selection tool and reshape at will. (Be careful not to click on any of the baselines; that selects the entire block of area text.) As you reshape the path with the direct selection, add point, delete point, and convert point tools, Illustrator rewraps the text to fit inside the revised path outline.

You can also flow text from one area text block into another (something you can't do with point text or path text). This allows you to create multiple columns or even multiple pages of text. Figure 7-17 shows several lines of text flowed between two paths. A single collection of paragraphs flowed over many text blocks is called a *story*.

To flow text from one block to another, you need to link them. You can link text blocks in one of two ways. These techniques apply equally to area text and rectangular text blocks:

- **Use the Link Blocks command.** Select the path that contains the overflow text with the arrow tool. Then select one or more other paths (by Shift-clicking on them) and choose Type » Blocks » Link. All selected paths fill with as much overflow type as will fit, as demonstrated in Figure 7-18.

Illustrator fills the paths in the order in which they are stacked. This means if you select a path that lies behind the area text and choose Link Blocks, the beginning of the story shifts to the rear path and then continues in the forward one. If you don't like the order in which the text flows, read the section entitled "Reflowing a Story," coming up shortly in this chapter.

- **Clone the path that contains the text.** The second method for flowing text is by far the simplest. After pressing ⌘-Shift-A to deselect everything, Option-click on the text block outline with the direct selection tool. This selects the path without selecting the text inside. Next drag the path to a new location, press the Option key, and release the mouse button. When you press the Option key, you'll see the clone cursor, as shown in Figure 7-19, which indicates that Illustrator is prepared to duplicate the path. The cloned path automatically fills with the overflow type from the first path, as shown in the bottom example of Figure 7-19.

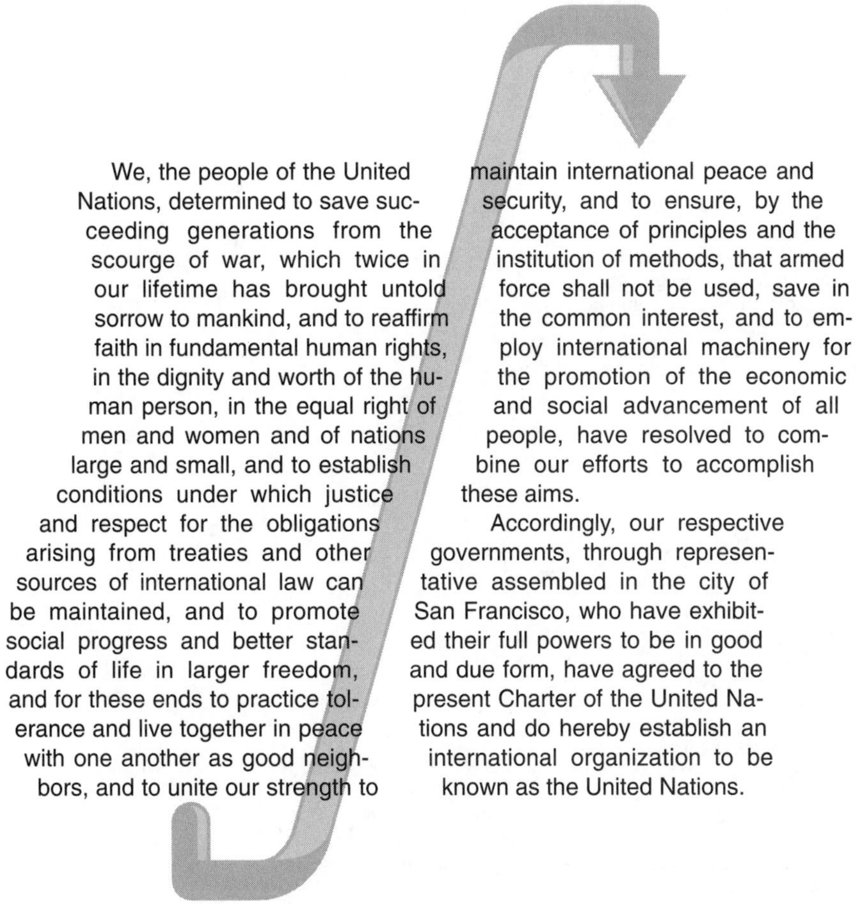
We, the people of the United Nations, determined to save succeeding generations from the scourge of war, which twice in our lifetime has brought untold sorrow to mankind, and to reaffirm faith in fundamental human rights, in the dignity and worth of the human person, in the equal right of men and women and of nations large and small, and to establish conditions under which justice and respect for the obligations arising from treaties and other sources of international law can be maintained, and to promote social progress and better standards of life in larger freedom, and for these ends to practice tolerance and live together in peace with one another as good neighbors, and to unite our strength to
maintain international peace and security, and to ensure, by the acceptance of principles and the institution of methods, that armed force shall not be used, save in the common interest, and to employ international machinery for the promotion of the economic and social advancement of all people, have resolved to combine our efforts to accomplish these aims.
Accordingly, our respective governments, through representative assembled in the city of San Francisco, who have exhibited their full powers to be in good and due form, have agreed to the present Charter of the United Nations and do hereby establish an international organization to be known as the United Nations.

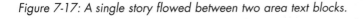

Figure 7-17: A single story flowed between two area text blocks.

TIP

If this new path also displays a boxed plus sign, more overflow text exists. Choose Object » Transform » Transform Again or press ⌘-D to create another clone automatically. Illustrator creates a third path the same distance and direction from the second path as the second path is from the first. Keep choosing this command to add more columns.

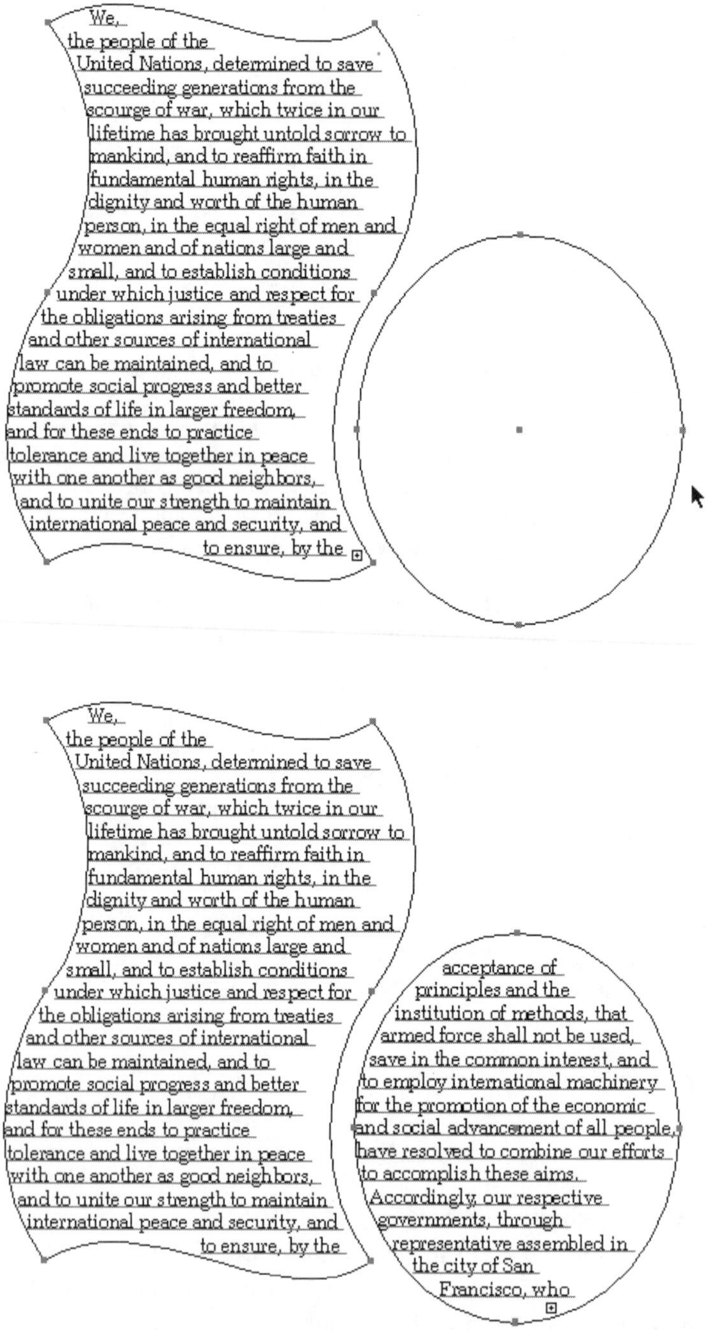
We,
the people of the
United Nations, determined to save
succeeding generations from the
scourge of war, which twice in our
lifetime has brought untold sorrow to
mankind, and to reaffirm faith in
fundamental human rights, in the
dignity and worth of the human
person, in the equal right of men and
women and of nations large and
small, and to establish conditions
under which justice and respect for
the obligations arising from treaties
and other sources of international
law can be maintained, and to
promote social progress and better
standards of life in larger freedom,
and for these ends to practice
tolerance and live together in peace
with one another as good neighbors,
and to unite our strength to maintain
international peace and security, and
to ensure, by the
We,
the people of the
United Nations, determined to save
succeeding generations from the
scourge of war, which twice in our
lifetime has brought untold sorrow to
mankind, and to reaffirm faith in
fundamental human rights, in the
dignity and worth of the human
person, in the equal right of men and
women and of nations large and
small, and to establish conditions
under which justice and respect for
the obligations arising from treaties
and other sources of international
law can be maintained, and to
promote social progress and better
standards of life in larger freedom,
and for these ends to practice
tolerance and live together in peace
with one another as good neighbors,
and to unite our strength to maintain
international peace and security, and
to ensure, by the
acceptance of
principles and the
institution of methods, that
armed force shall not be used,
save in the common interest, and
to employ international machinery
for the promotion of the economic
and social advancement of all people,
have resolved to combine our efforts
to accomplish these aims.
Accordingly, our respective
governments, through
representative assembled in
the city of San
Francisco, who

Figure 7-18: After selecting some area text and an empty path (top), choose Type » Blocks » Link to fill all selected paths with a single story (bottom).

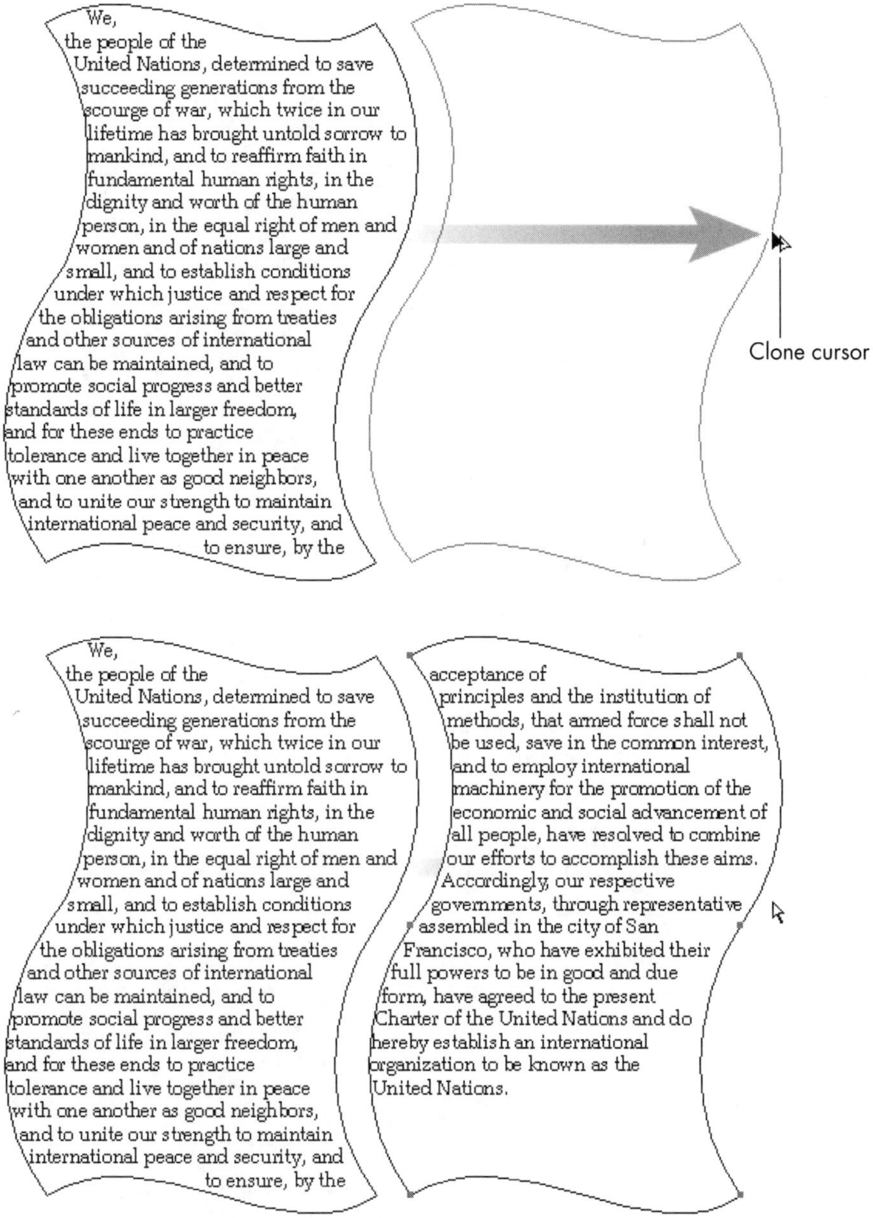
We,
the people of the
United Nations, determined to save
succeeding generations from the
scourge of war, which twice in our
lifetime has brought untold sorrow to
mankind, and to reaffirm faith in
fundamental human rights, in the
dignity and worth of the human
person, in the equal right of men and
women and of nations large and
small, and to establish conditions
under which justice and respect for
the obligations arising from treaties
and other sources of international
law can be maintained, and to
promote social progress and better
standards of life in larger freedom,
and for these ends to practice
tolerance and live together in peace
with one another as good neighbors,
and to unite our strength to maintain
international peace and security, and
to ensure, by the
Clone cursor
acceptance of
principles and the institution of
methods, that armed force shall not
be used, save in the common interest,
and to employ international
machinery for the promotion of the
economic and social advancement of
all people, have resolved to combine
our efforts to accomplish these aims.
Accordingly, our respective
governments, through representative
assembled in the city of San
Francisco, who have exhibited their
full powers to be in good and due
form, have agreed to the present
Charter of the United Nations and do
hereby establish an international
organization to be known as the
United Nations.

Figure 7-19: Option-drag a path containing text with the direct selection tool (top) to clone it and fill the clone with overflow text (bottom).

The advantage to cloning a path to flow area text is that each block of text is the same size and shape. Also, you never have to worry about text flowing in the wrong order. It always flows from the first path to the clone.

After you select a path with the direct selection tool, you have many ways to clone it. You can double-click on the arrow tool or choose Object » Transform » Move and click on the Copy button inside the Move dialog box. The Transform » Move command is also accessible through the context-sensitive pop-up menu that appears when you Control-click (pronounced right-click in the wide world of Windows). Or you can choose Edit » Copy (⌘-C) followed by Edit » Paste In Front (⌘-F) to create a duplicate directly in front of the original path; then use the direct selection tool to move the path to a new location. (I cover cloning in more detail in Chapter 9. The Move dialog box and the Object » Transform » Move and Edit » Paste In Front commands are discussed in Chapter 10.)

Selecting Linked Text Blocks

A collection of linked text blocks is a cohesive object, much like a group. You can select the entire story—all text and all paths—by merely clicking on any one of the paths with the arrow tool. But you can still access individual paths and text blocks with the direct selection tool as follows:

- Click on a path with the direct selection tool to select a point or segment. Then reshape the path as desired.
- Option-click on a path to select the entire path without selecting the text inside it. This is useful if you want to clone the path or change its stacking order (as I explain in the next section).
- Option-click on the path a second time to select the entire text block—both path and text—independently of other text blocks in the story. (Or you can click on the baseline of any line of text with the direct selection tool.) Then you can drag the text block to move it.
- Option-click on the path a third time with the direct selection tool to select the entire story, just as if you had clicked with the arrow tool.

You can also add and subtract elements from the selection by pressing the Shift key. For example, if you've selected an entire text block but you want to select only the path, Shift-click with the direct selection tool on a baseline in the text to deselect the text.

While you can select paths without the text, you cannot select text without also selecting the path. Just one of life's little inequities.

Reflowing a Story

A story flows from one text block to the next in the paths' stacking order, starting with the rearmost path and working forward. This phenomenon is known as the *linking order*. In Figure 7-20, for example, the right path is the rear path, the middle path is the front path, and the left path is in between. Therefore, the story starts in the right path, flows into the left path, and ends in the middle path, despite the fact that the story started in the left path before I chose Type » Blocks » Link.

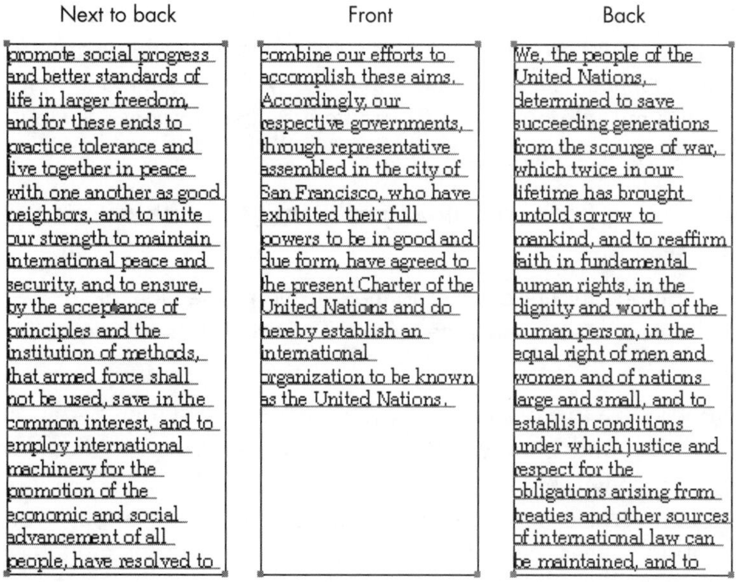

Next to back
Front
Back
promote social progress
and better standards of
life in larger freedom,
and for these ends to
practice tolerance and
live together in peace
with one another as good
neighbors, and to unite
our strength to maintain
international peace and
security, and to ensure,
by the acceptance of
principles and the
institution of methods,
that armed force shall
not be used, save in the
common interest, and to
employ international
machinery for the
promotion of the
economic and social
advancement of all
people, have resolved to
combine our efforts to
accomplish these aims.
Accordingly, our
respective governments,
through representative
assembled in the city of
San Francisco, who have
exhibited their full
powers to be in good and
due form, have agreed to
the present Charter of the
United Nations and do
hereby establish an
international
organization to be known
as the United Nations.
We, the people of the
United Nations,
determined to save
succeeding generations
from the scourge of war,
which twice in our
lifetime has brought
untold sorrow to
mankind, and to reaffirm
faith in fundamental
human rights, in the
dignity and worth of the
human person, in the
equal right of men and
women and of nations
large and small, and to
establish conditions
under which justice and
respect for the
obligations arising from
treaties and other sources
of international law can
be maintained, and to

Figure 7-20: This story flows in the stacking order, from the rear shape on the right to the front shape in the middle.

To rearrange the order in which a story flows, you can change the paths' stacking order by following these steps:

1. **Deselect the story.**

   Press ⌘-Shift-A, naturally.

2. **Send the desired starting path to the back.**

   Using the direct selection tool, select the path that's supposed to be the first text block in the story. Then choose Object » Arrange » Send To Back, or press ⌘-Shift-[(left bracket). Illustrator automatically reflows the story so that it starts in the selected path. If you prefer, Control-click (that's right-click for you Windows folks) and choose the Arrange » Send To Back command from the context-sensitive pop-up menu.

3. **Send the starting path and the next path to the back.**

   Shift-click on the path that will represent the second text block. Then choose Object » Arrange » Send To Back, or press ⌘-Shift-[(left bracket) again. This sends both selected paths to the back, with the first path the rearmost path and the second path just in front of the first.

   NOTE: In case you're wondering, "Why do I have to send that path to the back again after I already sent it to the back?"—a very reasonable question—it's because you're trying to establish a stacking sequence. Illustrator doesn't have any single command that juggles multiple paths into a specific order, so you have to do it a little bit at a time.

4. **Send the starting path, the next path, and the one after that to the back.**

   Keep adding one path after another to the selection in sequential order and choose Object » Arrange » Send To Back after selecting each path.

Obviously, you don't have to work in exactly the order I suggest above. You can select the last text block and choose Object » Arrange » Bring To Front, or ⌘-Shift-] (right bracket) if you prefer.

Illustrator has a couple of other commands that can help you simplify your stacking requirements. Whereas the Object » Arrange » Bring To Front and Object » Arrange » Send To Back commands recognize only the top and bottom of your stack, the Object » Arrange » Bring Forward (⌘-]) and the Object » Arrange » Send Backward (⌘-[) commands know about the parts in between.

These commands let you change the stacking order of a selected path by one. For example, instead of using the technique explained above, you could change the stacking order of the three paths in Figure 7-20 by first selecting only the middle path and then choosing the Object » Arrange » Send Backward (⌘-[) command. The middle path would become the "next to the back" path and the left path would move in the stacking order to become the "front" path. To achieve the same results by a slightly different method, you can select the left path and choose the Object » Arrange » Bring Forward (⌘-]) command.

These last two commands (new additions to the context-sensitive pop-up menu) work best when you know exactly where you want to move a particular path (or paths) in the stacking order. To rearrange a large number of paths, you are probably better off using the Object » Arrange » Bring To Front and the Object » Arrange » Send To Back commands, as explained above.

Here are a few other ways to reflow text inside a story:

- Reduce the size of any path to flow text out of that path and into the next path in the linking order.
- Enlarge the size of a path to flow text into that path and out of the next path in the linking order.
- To merge two stories into one, select both stories with the arrow tool and then choose Type » Blocks » Link. Illustrator combines the selected area text into one story, flowing the text between the selected paths in the stacking order of the paths.
- Delete a path in the linked object by Option-clicking on the path with the direct selection tool and then pressing the Delete key. Illustrator flows all text out of that path and into the next path.

Figure 7-21 demonstrates the effect of deleting the middle path from a story. Notice that Illustrator automatically flows the text from the middle path into the last path, while the text that used to be in the last path becomes overflow text. Therefore, deleting a path does not delete the text inside it; the text merely reflows. (This is why you can't delete a path if it's the only path in the story—there's no place for the overflow text to go.)

If you want to delete both path and text from the story, you must select both path and text before pressing Delete. As I mentioned earlier, you can select a text block independently of others in a story by Option-clicking twice on the path with the direct selection tool.

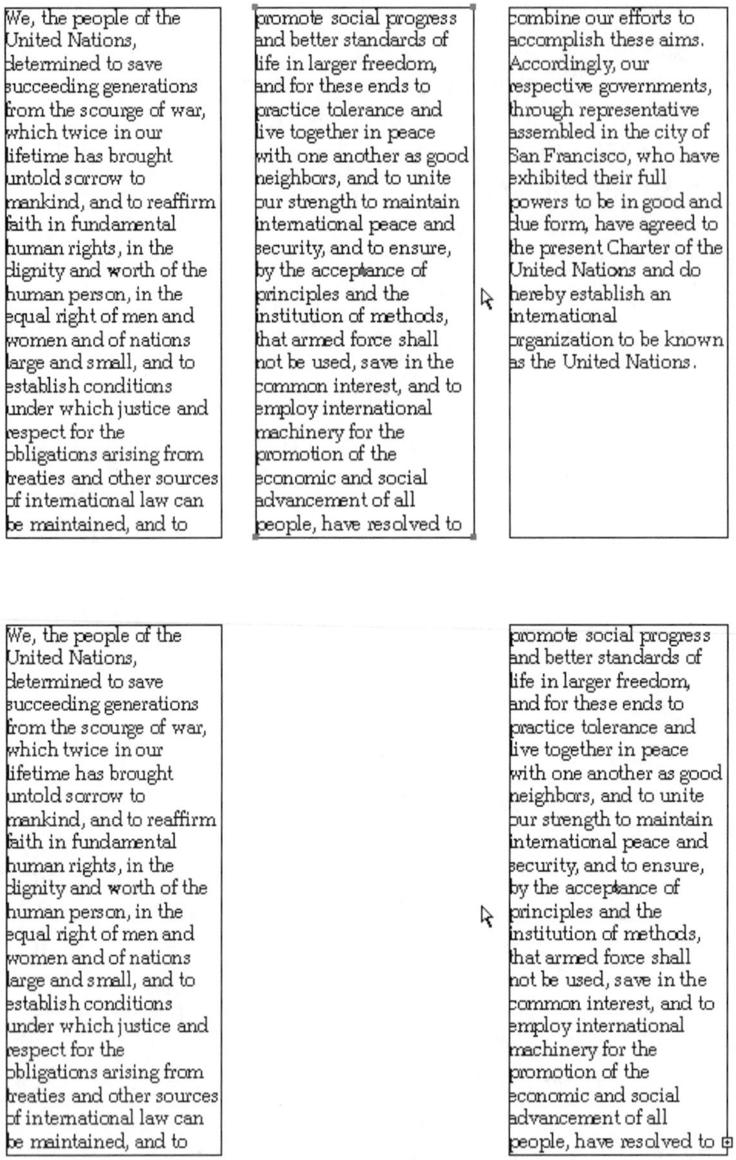
We, the people of the United Nations, determined to save succeeding generations from the scourge of war, which twice in our lifetime has brought untold sorrow to mankind, and to reaffirm faith in fundamental human rights, in the dignity and worth of the human person, in the equal right of men and women and of nations large and small, and to establish conditions under which justice and respect for the obligations arising from treaties and other sources of international law can be maintained, and to
promote social progress and better standards of life in larger freedom, and for these ends to practice tolerance and live together in peace with one another as good neighbors, and to unite our strength to maintain international peace and security, and to ensure, by the acceptance of principles and the institution of methods, that armed force shall not be used, save in the common interest, and to employ international machinery for the promotion of the economic and social advancement of all people, have resolved to
combine our efforts to accomplish these aims. Accordingly, our respective governments, through representative assembled in the city of San Francisco, who have exhibited their full powers to be in good and due form, have agreed to the present Charter of the United Nations and do hereby establish an international organization to be known as the United Nations.
We, the people of the United Nations, determined to save succeeding generations from the scourge of war, which twice in our lifetime has brought untold sorrow to mankind, and to reaffirm faith in fundamental human rights, in the dignity and worth of the human person, in the equal right of men and women and of nations large and small, and to establish conditions under which justice and respect for the obligations arising from treaties and other sources of international law can be maintained, and to
promote social progress and better standards of life in larger freedom, and for these ends to practice tolerance and live together in peace with one another as good neighbors, and to unite our strength to maintain international peace and security, and to ensure, by the acceptance of principles and the institution of methods, that armed force shall not be used, save in the common interest, and to employ international machinery for the promotion of the economic and social advancement of all people, have resolved to

Figure 7-21: Deleting the middle path (top) reflows the text into the last path (bottom).

Unlinking Text Blocks

To unlink text blocks in a linked object, choose Type » Blocks » Unlink. This command isolates the paths so that each text block is its own story. You should use the Blocks » Unlink command only when you are happy with the way text appears in each column of type and you want to prevent it from reflowing under any circumstance.

If your goal is to reflow type, do not start off by choosing Blocks » Unlink, since this busts the text apart. Simply make your changes with the direct selection tool and one of the commands from the Type » Arrange submenu, as explained in the "Reflowing a Story" section.

If you want to relink a story so that it bypasses one path and flows into another one, delete the path that you no longer need, select the new path, and then choose Type » Blocks » Link to redirect the flow. Again, do not choose the Blocks » Unlink command. (I know, I keep repeating myself, but you watch—you'll mess up and choose Blocks » Unlink one day, only to be mystified that it doesn't work the way you thought it would.)

Wrapping Type Around Graphics

For the history buffs in the audience, you should know that Illustrator was the first drawing program that allowed you to wrap text around graphics, previously the exclusive domain of page-layout programs such as PageMaker and QuarkXPress. This feature instructs Illustrator to wrap type automatically around the boundaries of one or more graphic objects, as illustrated in Figure 7-22.

Wrapping text around a graphic is a four-step process:

1. **Select the paths that you want to wrap the text around.**

   After selecting the paths with the arrow tool, choose Object » Group (⌘-G) to keep the paths together.

2. **Position the paths with respect to the text.**

   Drag the group into position, and then choose Object » Arrange » Bring To Front (⌘-Shift-]). The paths must be in front of the text block to wrap properly.

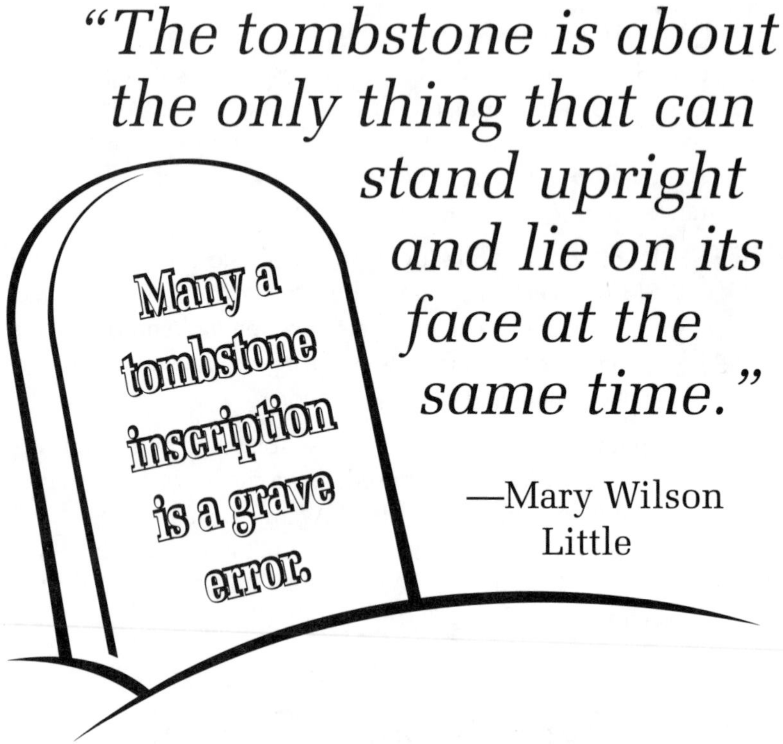
"The tombstone is about
the only thing that can
stand upright
and lie on its
face at the
same time."
—Mary Wilson
Little
Many a
tombstone
inscription
is a grave
error.

Figure 7-22: Illustrator lets you wrap type around the boundaries of graphic objects, as in the text above and to the right of the tombstone.

3. Select the text block that you want to wrap.

Shift-click on the text block with the arrow tool to add it to the selection. Illustrator can wrap text blocks and area text around graphics, but it cannot wrap point text or path text.

4. Wrap the text.

Choose the Type » Wrap » Make command, and Illustrator wraps the text around the graphics and fuses text and paths into a single wrapped object.

After this, you can select the entire wrapped object by clicking on it with the arrow tool or by Option-clicking two or three times on one of the paths with the direct selection tool (depending on whether you wrap the text around a single path or multiple grouped paths). You can also reshape the paths with the direct selection tool. Illustrator constantly rewraps the text to compensate for your edits.

You can also modify the formatting for wrapped text by clicking or dragging inside the text with the type tool—or by Option-clicking on the text blocks a few times with the direct selection tool—and adjusting the settings in the Character and Paragraph palettes. The two formatting attributes that you'll want to pay attention to are alignment and indentation:

- Select a different Alignment option from the Paragraph palette to change the way words align between the sides of the column and the boundaries of the paths. For example, the quote in Figure 7-22 is flush left, but the name is centered.
- The Indent values in the Paragraph palette determine the amount of room between the graphic and the text. The following section explores how you can use these options to their best advantage.

Adjusting the Standoff

In publishing circles, the standoff is the amount of space between a graphic and the text wrapped around it. In Illustrator, you can adjust the amount of standoff around a graphic object in two ways.

- **Increase the Indent values:** Adjust the Left and Right Indent values in the Paragraph palette. Illustrator treats the outlines of the graphic objects as additional sides to the text block. Therefore, the Left value increases the space along the right sides of the graphic objects, and the Right value adds space along the left edges. (It might sound like the opposite of how it should work, but it makes sense if you sit down and ponder it awhile. After all, the Left value moves text to the right and the Right value moves text to the left.)

  The first example of Figure 7-23 shows justified text wrapped around a circle with all Indent values set to 0. As a result, the text touches the circle, an effect that is best summed up as ugly. In the second example, I selected the text blocks by Option-clicking on them three times with the direct selection tool. Then I increased the Left value to 18 points and the Right value to 9.
- **Create a special standoff dummy:** You can also establish a standoff by creating a special path to act as a dummy for the actual graphic. If you make both the fill and stroke transparent, the standoff dummy is invisible and the text appears to wrap around thin air.

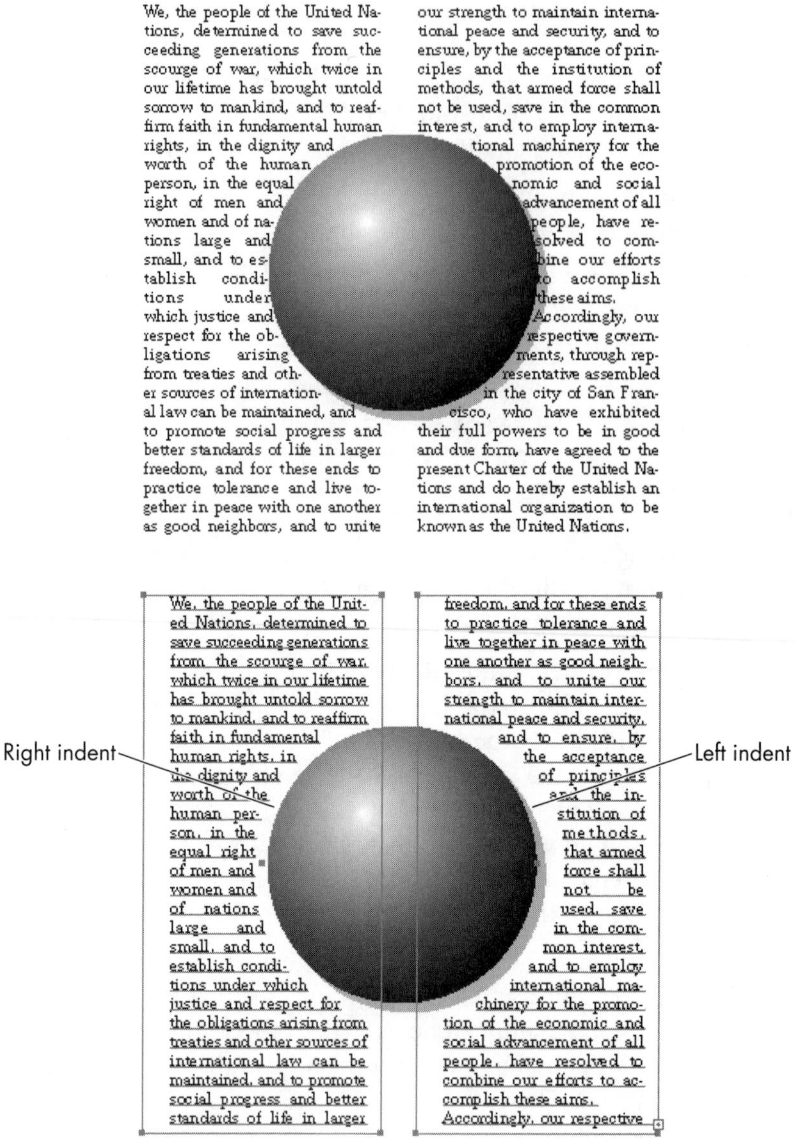
We, the people of the United Nations, determined to save succeeding generations from the scourge of war, which twice in our lifetime has brought untold sorrow to mankind, and to reaffirm faith in fundamental human rights, in the dignity and worth of the human person, in the equal right of men and women and of nations large and small, and to establish conditions under which justice and respect for the obligations arising from treaties and other sources of international law can be maintained, and to promote social progress and better standards of life in larger freedom, and for these ends to practice tolerance and live together in peace with one another as good neighbors, and to unite
our strength to maintain international peace and security, and to ensure, by the acceptance of principles and the institution of methods, that armed force shall not be used, save in the common interest, and to employ international machinery for the promotion of the economic and social advancement of all people, have resolved to combine our efforts to accomplish these aims. Accordingly, our respective governments, through representative assembled in the city of San Francisco, who have exhibited their full powers to be in good and due form, have agreed to the present Charter of the United Nations and do hereby establish an international organization to be known as the United Nations.
We, the people of the United Nations, determined to save succeeding generations from the scourge of war, which twice in our lifetime has brought untold sorrow to mankind, and to reaffirm faith in fundamental human rights, in the dignity and worth of the human person, in the equal right of men and women and of nations large and small, and to establish conditions under which justice and respect for the obligations arising from treaties and other sources of international law can be maintained, and to promote social progress and better standards of life in larger
freedom, and for these ends to practice tolerance and live together in peace with one another as good neighbors, and to unite our strength to maintain international peace and security, and to ensure, by the acceptance of principles and the institution of methods, that armed force shall not be used, save in the common interest, and to employ international machinery for the promotion of the economic and social advancement of all people, have resolved to combine our efforts to accomplish these aims. Accordingly, our respective
Right indent
Left indent

Figure 7-23: After justifying this text around a circle (top), I increased the Left and Right Indent values to 18 and 9 points respectively (bottom).

The following steps explain how to create your very own standoff dummy. These steps assume that you've already wrapped text around a few graphics and that you aren't altogether pleased with its appearance.

1. **Draw the dummy path.**

   I drew the path shown in Figure 7-24 with the regular polygon tool. I was able to position the polygon exactly by occasionally pressing the spacebar while drawing the shape. (As you may recall, the spacebar lets you move the shape while you're in the process of drawing it.)

2. **Make the fill and stroke transparent.**

   In the bottom portion of the toolbox, click on the Fill icon to bring it in front of the Stroke icon, and then select the None icon or press the forward slash (/) key. If necessary, you can also click on the Stroke icon (or press the X key) and select the None icon. (Part IV covers the Paint Style controls of the toolbox in extreme depth.)

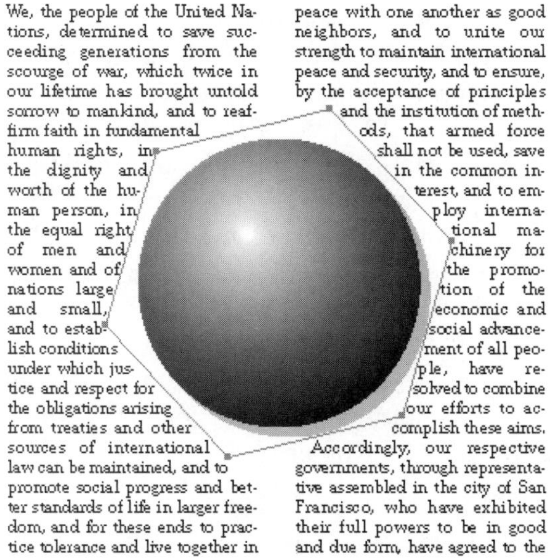
We, the people of the United Nations, determined to save succeeding generations from the scourge of war, which twice in our lifetime has brought untold sorrow to mankind, and to reaffirm faith in fundamental human rights, in the dignity and worth of the human person, in the equal rights of men and women and of nations large and small, and to establish conditions under which justice and respect for the obligations arising from treaties and other sources of international law can be maintained, and to promote social progress and better standards of life in larger freedom, and for these ends to practice tolerance and live together in
peace with one another as good neighbors, and to unite our strength to maintain international peace and security, and to ensure, by the acceptance of principles and the institution of methods, that armed force shall not be used, save in the common interest, and to employ international machinery for the promotion of the economic and social advancement of all peoples, have resolved to combine our efforts to accomplish these aims. Accordingly, our respective governments, through representatives assembled in the city of San Francisco, who have exhibited their full powers to be in good and due form, have agreed to the

Figure 7-24: This unfilled, unstroked polygon serves as a dummy path, creating a standoff that is not only larger than the circle but is differently shaped as well.

3. **Cut the path to the Clipboard.**

   Choose Edit » Cut or press ⌘-X.

4. **Select one of the graphic objects.**

   Option-click on a path inside the wrapped object with the direct selection tool.

5. **Choose Edit » Paste In Back.**

   Or press ⌘-B. Because you used the direct selection tool to select the graphic object in Step 4, Illustrator pastes the dummy path between the object and the text block, making the dummy path part of the wrapped object.

6. **Press the ↑ key, and then press the ↓ key.**

   Illustrator is a little slow to recognize the new dummy path, so you need to give it a little nudge to get the program's attention. When you press the ↑ key, Illustrator suddenly wraps the text around the dummy path. Pressing the ↓ key just puts the path back where it was.

I followed these steps to create the standoff shown in Figure 7-24. The polygon is selected in the figure. If it were not selected, it would be invisible. (To see the dummy path, switch to the artwork mode by pressing ⌘-Y.)

Using Tabs with Wrapped Objects

Here's a weird little function that's left over from the old days, back when Illustrator didn't really support tabs. It still comes in handy once in a blue moon. You can force text in a wrapped object to jump to the other side of a path by clicking with the type tool just to the left of the appropriate word. After you've positioned the insertion marker, press the Tab key. If Illustrator only nudges the word when you press the Tab key, try pressing Tab a few more times. Eventually, the word will move to the other side of the graphic. (I know, I know, I told you not to press the Tab key more than once in a row in the last chapter. But what can you do? Wacky situations call for wacky measures.)

The function won't work unless the graphic object is located entirely inside the text block so that the text inside the block flanks both sides of the graphic. (This is not the case in Figure 7-24, for example, in which the graphic is situated to the right of one text block and to the left of the other.)

If the graphic is situated to one side or the other of the text, you can force a word onto the next line by positioning the insertion marker to the left of the word and pressing Shift-Return. As you may recall from Chapter 6, pressing Shift-Return inserts a line break character but keeps all lines in the same paragraph.

Importing and Exporting Text

I would guess that you'll prefer to enter text while working in Illustrator most of the time. But with its free-flowing text, multiple pages, and excellent drawing tools at your disposal, keep in mind that Illustrator is quite the program for creating graphic-rich layouts.

That's why Illustrator lets you import text documents that were created with major word processing programs. After all, word processing programs are faster for text entry, and they permit luxuries such as style sheets, thesauruses, and glossary and revision capabilities. Despite Illustrator's crack text capabilities, you should find it easier to use a word processing program to edit text and apply formatting attributes.

You can also export text from Illustrator into these same word processing file formats. Doing so allows you to recover and work with text that has been laid out in an Illustrator document and even lets you transfer it to a mightier layout program such as QuarkXPress.

Preparing Your Text for Import

When importing a text file, Illustrator reads the file from disk and copies it to the illustration window. As this copy is being made, the text file passes through a filter that converts the file's formatting commands into formatting commands recognized by Illustrator.

NOTE: To import text, you must have installed the so-called Claris XTND System, a translation utility that lives in your System Folder inside a folder called Claris. (You can install Claris XTND at any time by running the Illustrator installer program.) Illustrator's text filters reside inside the Claris Translators folder in a file called XTND for Illustrator. The great thing about the Claris XTND System is that multiple programs can use it at the same time. (Claris, incidentally, is Apple's software publishing subsidiary.)

Assuming that everything is installed correctly, Illustrator 8 lets you import text in the following formats:

- Microsoft Word for the Mac, MS-DOS, and Windows
- RTF (Rich Text Format), Microsoft's coded file format
- MacWrite, versions 4.5 and 5.0
- MacWrite II, versions 1.0 and 1.1
- MacWrite Pro, version 1.0
- WriteNow 3.0
- WordPerfect for the Mac, versions 2.0, 2.1, 3.0, and 3.5
- WordPerfect for the PC, versions 5.0 and 5.1

- Plain text with no formatting whatsoever, also known as ASCII (pronounced ask-ee)

For those few but proud WordPerfect 3 users in the audience, be sure to save your files in the WordPerfect 2.1 format. Almost no one uses MacWrite or WriteNow anymore, but if you do, be sure that you save your text document in one of the formats listed above. And finally, if you're that rarest of all living creatures, the Nisus user, I recommend the Word 5 or RTF format.

PageMaker and QuarkXPress also let you export text in many of the formats listed above. Again, Word 5 or RTF are your best bets. (These are the most common formats and ones Illustrator is likely to support most consistently.)

The absolute last alternative is the plain text format, which sacrifices all formatting and leaves you with nothing but a string of characters, spaces, tabs, and carriage returns. You'll have to reformat the text in Illustrator.

Import filters may not be able to convert all formatting attributes correctly from a word processor file. The following list describes how Illustrator handles a few prevailing formatting attributes and offers a few suggestions for preparing each:

- **Typeface:** Illustrator is supposed to use the typeface specified in the word processor, but sometimes it gets mixed up. If Illustrator can't find the typeface in your system—if the document was created on another machine, for example—it substitutes Helvetica. But even when the typeface is available, Illustrator may flip out and substitute Chicago.
- **Type style:** Illustrator does not apply styles the way word processors do. As I dutifully explained in the previous chapter, Illustrator requires that you specify typeface and style together by selecting a stylized font. As a result, bold and italic styles convert successfully, but most others do not. If Illustrator comes across a style for which a stylized font does not exist—underline, outline, strikethrough, small caps, and so on—the program simply ignores the style. The happy exceptions are superscript and subscript styles, which transfer intact thanks to Illustrator's baseline shift function.
- **Type size and leading:** All text retains the same size and leading specified in the word processor. If you assign automatic leading or "single spacing" inside the word processor, Illustrator substitutes its own automatic leading, which is 120 percent of the type size.
- **Alignment:** Illustrator recognizes paragraphs that are aligned left, center, and right, as well as justified text.
- **Carriage returns:** Illustrator successfully reads carriage return characters (which you create by pressing the Return key); each carriage return

indicates the end of a paragraph. Some word processors also offer line-break characters, which knock words to the next line without adding paragraph spacing. Although Illustrator offers a line-break character of its own, the program converts line breaks from imported text into carriage returns. Therefore, you're well advised to steer clear of line breaks and use carriage returns only to distinguish the ends of paragraphs (not the ends of lines).

- **Indents:** All paragraph indents, including first-line, left, and right indents remain intact. (Hanging indents won't look quite right, since Illustrator doesn't import tab stops.) Adjusting the margins in your word processor may also affect indentation in Illustrator. To clear the indents, just click on the individual Indent option names in Illustrator's Paragraph palette.
- **Paragraph spacing:** Some word processors divide paragraph spacing into two categories: "before spacing," which precedes the paragraph, and "after spacing," which follows the paragraph. Illustrator combines them into the Leading before ¶ value in the Paragraph palette, essentially retaining the same effect. (Separate before and after paragraph spacing are useful only when a program offers style sheets, which Illustrator does not.)
- **Tabs, tab stops, and tab leaders:** Illustrator imports tab characters successfully. But it ignores the placement of tab stops, and tab leaders (such as dots and dashes) are a complete mystery to the program. Use the Tabs palette (⌘-Shift-T) to reset the tab stops as desired.
- **Special characters:** Many word processors provide access to special characters that are not part of the standard character set. These include em spaces, nonbreaking hyphens, automatic page numbers, date and time stamps, and so on. Of these, only the discretionary hyphen character (⌘-Shift-hyphen in Illustrator) transfers successfully.
- **Page markings:** Illustrator ignores page breaks in imported text as well as headers, footers, and footnotes.

If you can't find a formatting option in this list, chances are Illustrator simply ignores it.

Importing Text into Columns

You can import text into any kind of text object. But because point text and path text are so badly suited to long stories—path text doesn't even support carriage returns or tabs—you'll most likely want to import stories into area text blocks.

To import a story into a bunch of text blocks, grab your partner and follow these steps:

1. **Create your first text block.**

   Select the type tool and click on the outline of a closed path. Or drag with the type tool to create a new text block. If you want to append an imported story inside a text block that you've already started, click at the point inside the text where you want to insert the story.

2. **Choose File » Place.**

   This displays the Place dialog box, which looks just like a standard Open dialog box.

3. **Locate the text file on disk and open it.**

   If you can't find the file, but you know it's there, select All Available from the Show pop-up menu in the lower left corner of the dialog box. This shows you all formats that Illustrator supports. If that doesn't work, Illustrator doesn't recognize the file; go back to your word processor and try saving it in a different format.

   After you locate your file in the scrolling list, double-click on it or select the file name and press Return. After a few moments, Illustrator displays the imported text inside the text block.

4. **Flow the text into additional paths.**

   Unless your text file contains less than a paragraph of text, Illustrator probably won't be able to fit all the text into a single block. You can enlarge the path by reshaping it with the direct selection tool. But more likely, you'll want to flow the text into additional paths as explained in the previous "Flowing Text from One Shape to Another" section.

Exporting Text to a Text File

Illustrator's Export plug-in allows you to export text from Illustrator to disk using one of the common word processing formats that I mentioned earlier. Keep in mind that when you export text from Illustrator, you save only the type and its formatting attributes. No path information is included.

For example, if you export a line of path type that surrounds a circle and then open the text file in a word processor, the type looks like any other line of type, oriented from left to right along a straight line. You won't see so much as a trace of a circle. Therefore, one of the purposes of File » Export is to save text that you want to arrange differently in another program.

TIP

To export fancy type including paths and everything, export the illustration in the EPS format, as described in the "Saving an EPS Illustration" section of Chapter 3. You won't be able to edit the type, but it will look great.

Here's how to export text from Illustrator:

1. **Select the text you want to export.**

   Use the type tool to select one or more characters from any kind of text object. You must use the type tool to select; you can't select the text with the arrow tool. You can export a single letter or an entire story. (To select the entire story—even if you can't see all of it on screen—click inside the block with the type tool and press ⌘-A.)

2. **Choose File » Export.**

   This displays the Export dialog box, which looks just like the standard Save dialog box.

3. **Select a file format from the File pop-up menu.**

   You can select from any of the formats that Illustrator imports. Use the format that your word processor supports best.

4. **Name the file and specify a destination on disk.**

   This is just like saving an illustration. Press Return when everything's ready to go. Illustrator exports the selected text to disk as instructed.

Checking Your Spelling

Imagine what it must be like to be a kid today. (Unless you are a kid, in which case, you must already have a fair grasp on the topic.) Ah, to have grown up in a time of calculators and spell checkers. These two devices automate almost everything that we learned back in grade school, with the possible exceptions of social studies and P.E. Here I am in my 30s, and already I feel like saying, "Back in my day, we had to add numbers by hand—with pencils!—and we had to know how to spell *squirrel* and stuff! And, by thunder, we liked it! Kids nowadays can add and spell any daggum way they please and let the machines clean up after them! It's a disgrace, I tell you, a complete disgrace!")

Spell checkers are so prevalent, in fact, that even Illustrator offers one. Without the help of an outside application, Illustrator can transform the sentence, "Teh couw rann awai wyth theh sponn," to something that English-speaking humans might find recognizable.

1. Choose Type » Check Spelling.

Because Illustrator automatically checks the spelling of all text, hidden or visible, in your drawing, you don't have to select any text.

Illustrator sets about revealing your mistakes. (No need to click on any Start button, as in some programs.) If Illustrator doesn't locate any words missing from its dictionary, it displays an ego-stroking message about your excellent spelling. If the program finds mistakes—the more likely scenario—it lists all mistakes throughout the entire document in the Misspelled Words list at the top of the Check Spelling dialog box, as in Figure 7-25.

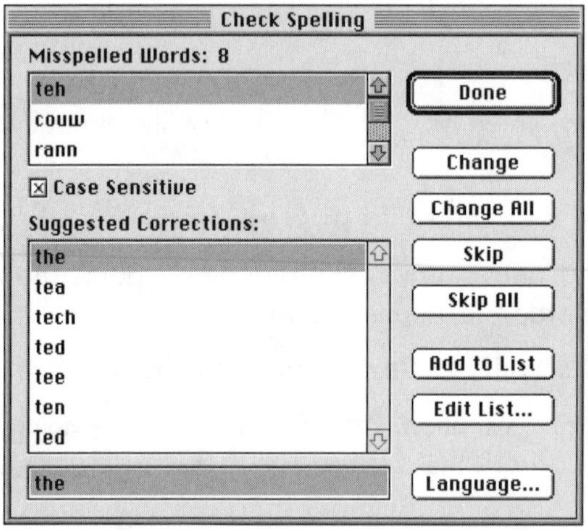

Figure 7-25: Illustrator finds all spelling mistakes in one pass so that you can examine and correct them in any order you please.

2. Select all words that are spelled properly.

Scroll through the Misspelled Words list to see which words are truly misspelled and which words Illustrator is simply too inexperienced in the ways of the world to know. If a word is spelled to your satisfaction, you can either add it to Illustrator's dictionary or simply skip the word for the time being.

TIP: To select all the words that are spelled correctly, Shift-click on a first and then last word in a group of words to select all of them; or ⌘-click on each word to add one word at a time to the selection. You can also ⌘-click to deselect a word.

3. **Click on the Add to List button.**

   This adds the selected words to Illustrator's auxiliary dictionary, so that the program will never again bug you about the spelling. (Don't worry if you add a word that you didn't intend to; you can always delete it later by clicking on the Edit List button.)

   If you'd rather ignore the words for the time being, click on the Skip button. Click on Skip All to tell Illustrator to ignore all occurrences of these particular words.

4. **Select a word that's misspelled.**

   To correct a word that is indeed misspelled, select it from the Misspelled Words list. (You can correct only one misspelling at a time.) In the illustration windows, Illustrator highlights the first occurrence of the word in the story and displays a few alternative spellings in the Suggested Corrections list.

5. **Select the proper spelling.**

   If one of the alternative spellings in the Suggested Corrections list is correct, click on it. If none of the spellings are correct, enter the new spelling in the option box below the list.

6. **Click on the Change button.**

   Or you can press the Return key or double-click on the proper spelling in the Suggested Corrections list. If you know that many words are misspelled in the same way, click on the Change All button to correct all misspellings at once. Illustrator corrects the spelling of the words in the illustration window and moves on to the next misspelled word.

7. **End the spell checking.**

   After you tell Illustrator to either add, skip, or change every word in the Misspelled Words list, an alert box tells you it's finished. If you want to cut things off early, click on the Done button, press the Escape key, or press ⌘-. (period).

After you enter a proper spelling in the option box below the Suggested Corrections list, you may wonder how you can add the new spelling to Illustrator's auxiliary dictionary. If you click on the Add to List button, Illustrator adds the word from the Misspelled Words list, not the correctly spelled word you entered in the option box. To add a new spelling to the dictionary, you must first apply the new spelling to the illustration window, then close the Check Spelling dialog box, and again choose Type » Check Spelling.

To edit the auxiliary dictionary—whether during this or some other session—you choose Type » Check Spelling and click on the Edit List button. Illustrator displays the Learned Words dialog box shown in Figure 7-26. Here you can select a word and delete it by clicking on the Remove button; change the spelling of the word by replacing a few characters and clicking on Change; or create a variation on a spelling by clicking on Add. Note that Illustrator is smart enough to know that an 's on the end of a word doesn't constitute a misspelling, something Microsoft didn't figure out until Word 6. So you don't have to create variations like Eeyore's and Tigger's to cover your bases. However, if you want to prepare for plurals, such as Kangas or Roos, you have to add those.

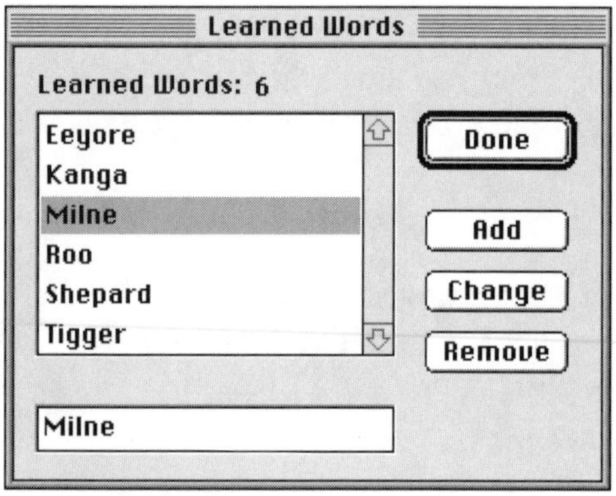

Figure 7-26: You can review the words that you've added to the dictionary from the Learned Words dialog box.

TIP

Illustrator saves the auxiliary dictionary to disk as USEnglish Dictionary in the Plug-Ins folder inside a folder called Text. (Windows users will find the analogous file, USEnglish.dct, inside the Text Filters directory, which resides inside the Plug-ins directory.) This means you can take the dictionary from one machine and copy it to another to maintain a consistent auxiliary dictionary. Although you can open the dictionary in SimpleText or Notepad—the mini word processors that come with all Macs or Windows machines respectively—don't do it. Illustrator uses a bunch of special characters in the file; mess them up, and you can damage your dictionary for good.

Let's see, what have I missed in the Check Spelling dialog box? Oh yeah:

- The Case Sensitive check box lets you correct words depending on whether they're capitalized or not. For example, you might want to change wol to owl, but add Wol to the dictionary (since that's the owl's proper name).

- The Language button lets you add a dictionary for a different language, such as U.K. English. You must open the appropriate dictionary from disk. Look for the files in the Text folder inside the Plug-Ins folder.

The Check Spelling command is a wonderful feature. Even if your illustration doesn't contain much text, you'd be surprised how often you will find a misspelled word. Choosing Type » Check Spelling only takes a moment and is always worth your time.

Searching and Replacing Stuff

Another of Illustrator's amazing features is its ability to automatically search for bits of text and replace them with other bits of text. For example, you can search and replace characters, words, fonts, and even special design characters. The following features are absolute gems. Don't forget they're here; they can save you a lot of time.

Replacing Words and Phrases

The Find/Change command lets you locate all occurrences of a particular collection of characters and replace each with a different collection of characters. You can search for as many characters as you like, including spaces.

1. **Click with the type tool on the location where you want to begin the search.**

   You don't have to perform this step. If you have selected the arrow tool, for example, Illustrator searches all stories throughout the entire drawing, from beginning to end. But if you want to limit your search to a specific area of a story, click in the story with the type tool. By default, Illustrator searches forward from the insertion marker; it does not search the text before the insertion marker. (You can reverse the direction of the search by selecting the Search Backward check box, as we'll soon see.)

2. **Choose Type » Find/Change.**

   Illustrator brings up the Find/Change dialog box, pictured in glorious Technicolor in Figure 7-27.

3. **Enter the text you want to find and the text you want to replace it with.**

   Enter the search text in the Find What option box, press Tab, and then enter the replacement text in the Change To option box. If you don't want to replace the text—you're just trying to find it—don't enter anything in the Change To option box.

4. **Click on the Find Next button.**

   Or press Return. Illustrator highlights the first occurrence of the word in the illustration window.

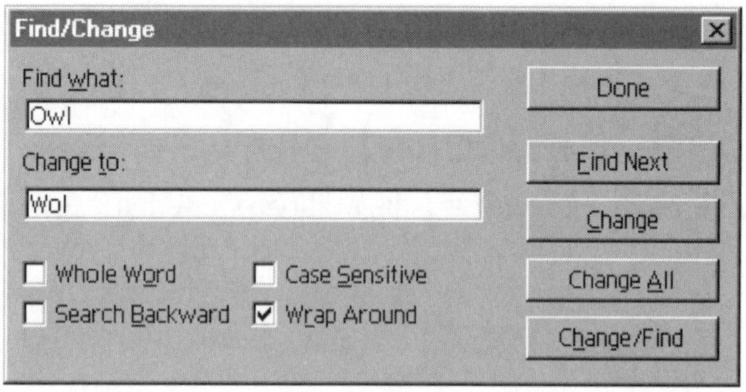

Figure 7-27: Use the Find/Change dialog box to search for some text and replace that text with some other text.

5. **Replace the word and move on.**

   Click on the Change button to replace the selected text. Or click on the Change/Find button to replace the text and then look for the next occurrence of the Find What text. (If it finds no more occurrences of the Find What text, Illustrator callously beeps at you.) Or click on Change All to replace all Find What text with the contents of the Change To option box.

6. **When you're finished, click on the Done button.**

   Or press ⌘-. (period) or Esc.

You can modify your search by turning on and off the check boxes in the middle of the dialog box:

- **Whole Word:** When you check this option, you limit the search to whole words that exactly match the Find What text. With this option unchecked, for example, searching for *owl* would cause Illustrator to find the characters inside gr*owl* and c*owl*ick. With Whole Word checked, the word *owl* must appear by itself.
- **Case Sensitive:** Select this check box to search for characters that exactly match the uppercase and lowercase characters in the Find What

text. Searching for *Owl* would find neither *owl* nor *OWL* when this option is selected.

- **Search Backward:** This option begins the search at the insertion marker and proceeds backward toward the beginning of the story.
- **Wrap Around:** To search the entire illustration, no matter where the insertion marker is currently located, select Wrap Around. This option begins the search at the insertion marker and proceeds to the end of the story, starts over at the next story, starts again at the beginning of the first story, and winds up back at the insertion marker.

Neither Search Backward nor Wrap Around is of any use when the arrow tool is selected, since Illustrator automatically searches all text in the illustration.

WARNING

Type » Find/Change can be used to search and replace text inside locked and even hidden text blocks. So if you click on the Find Next button, only to be greeted by neither a beep nor any highlighted text inside the illustration window, the text block is probably hidden. When this occurs, click on Done to close the Find/Change dialog box, and then choose Object » Show All (⌘-Option-3) to reveal the hidden text.

Replacing One Font with Another

You can press the Type » Find Font key combination to launch another of Illustrator's amazing search functions. This time, instead of replacing words, Illustrator lets you search for one font and replace it with another.

Why would you want to do that? Imagine, for example, that an associate created an illustration a couple of years back using the font Geneva. You think Geneva is pretty smelly, so far as fonts go, so you want to replace all occurrences of this font with a different one that you like better. Here's how you'd proceed:

1. **Choose Type » Find Font.**

   In response, the Find Font dialog box bounds into view, as shown in Figure 7-28.

2. **Select the font that you want to remove from the Fonts in Document list.**

   Illustrator highlights each occurrence of the font in the illustration window.

3. Select the substitute font from the Replace Font From list.

Initially, this list contains only the names of those fonts that are used in the current illustration. If you want to choose from a wider variety of fonts, select the System command from the Replace Font From pop-up menu, which instructs Illustrator to list every font loaded on your system—a potentially time-consuming task.

TIP

You can pause the font listing by clicking anywhere on an empty portion of the dialog box. To start the listing again, turn on and off one of the check boxes at the bottom of the dialog, or switch between the pop-up menu commands.

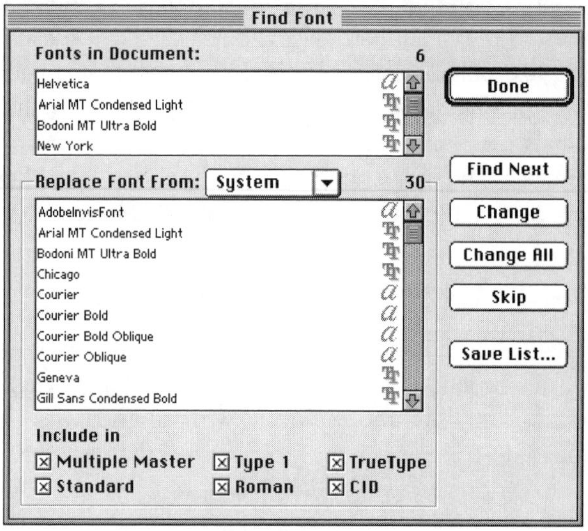

Figure 7-28: You can replace one or more occurrences of a font with a different font from the Find Font dialog box.

4. Click on Change or one of the other buttons.

The Change button replaces the first occurrence of the bad font and searches for the next. To change all occurrences of the font simultaneously, click on the Change All button. If you're feeling a little more selective, you can opt not to change the found font and click on the Find Next button (or just select the font name again) to ignore that occurrence of a font and move on to the next. The Skip button performs the exact same function as the Find Next button. Sloppy sloppy.

5. **Click on the Done button when you're finished.**

   Or press Return, Escape, or ⌘-. (period).

Use the check boxes to select which kinds of fonts you want to be displayed in the two lists. Click on the Save List button to save a list of the fonts used in your document to a text file. This font list is handy for a service bureau or a commercial printer when you want them to output or print your work. (If this kind of thing interests you, check out the description of File » Document Info in Chapter 18.)

Automatic Character Changes

If you still aren't convinced that Illustrator's gone totally nuts in the desktop-publishing department, here are two more commands that prove it beyond a shadow of a doubt: Change Case and Smart Punctuation, both located on the Type menu (where else?).

Type » Change Case lets you change lowercase text to initial caps or all caps, change all caps to lowercase or initial caps, or make some other variation.

1. Select the text you want to change. For example, perhaps you want to change some text you entered after accidentally pressing the Caps Lock key.
2. Choose Type » Change Case.
3. Select the desired option. In this case, select the Lower Case radio button (which really ought to be one word.)
4. Press Return or click on OK.

The Change Case command is so simple, a sightless tree frog could use it. Type » Smart Punctuation is a slightly more complicated command. This command searches for all "dumb" punctuation in your document—straight quotes, double hyphens, double spaces after periods—and replaces them with their more acceptable and better looking "smart" equivalents—curly quotes, en dashes, and single spaces after periods.

Select the characters you want to change with the type tool, and then choose Type » Smart Punctuation to display the Smart Punctuation dialog box shown in Figure 7-29. Select the check boxes representing the kinds of punctuation you want to change, and press the Return key or click on OK.

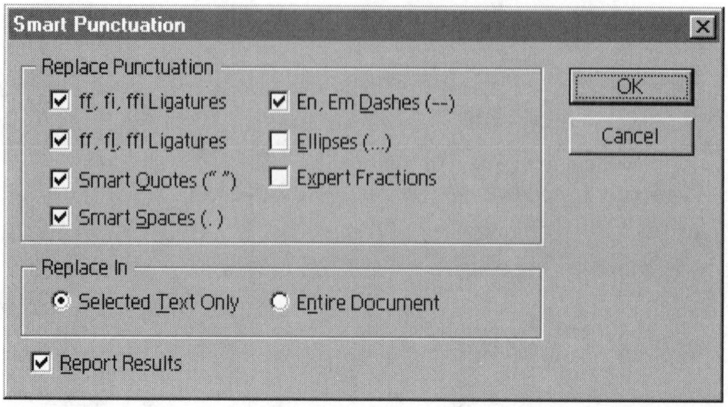

Figure 7-29: Use the options in the Smart Punctuation dialog box to convert various characters in your illustration to more design-acceptable characters.

NOTE: Unfortunately, the check boxes are a little convoluted. Three of them—ff, fi, ffi Ligatures; ff, fl, ffl Ligatures; and Expert Fractions—require that a so-called Expert Collection font be on hand. The Expert Collection is an Adobe typeface that contains a second alphabet of special typographic symbols, including small caps, ligatures (two characters joined into one), and fractions. Additionally, the Expert Collection must correspond to the base font. For example, to take advantage of the Utopia Expert Collection, the text that you want to change must be in the font Utopia. Text set in Univers, for example, will not be changed. Lots of great Expert Collection fonts exist—including variations for Bembo, Bodoni, and Caslon, among others—but they are definitely in the minority.

Very quickly, let's look at each option:

- **ff, fi, ffi Ligatures:** If a font comes with an Expert Collection, this option replaces ff, fi, and ffi with their respective ligatures. In Figure 7-30, for example, I've set several words in Adobe Caslon. I also loaded the Adobe Caslon Expert Collection into my system. When I selected this check box and clicked on OK, Illustrator replaced the black letters in *affable*, *fickle*, and *difficult* with their equivalent, single-character ligatures from the Expert Collection. If I had used a standard font, Illustrator would have replaced the *fi* in *fickle* and *difficult* with the common *fi* ligature (which is also available by pressing Shift-Option-5 [Mac only]), but that's the only ligature change.

affable, fickle,
difficult,
flowery, afflicted

affable, fickle,
difficult,
flowery, afflicted

Figure 7-30: After entering a few words in Adobe Caslon (top), I applied the Smart Punctuation command to convert the ligatures (in black) to the single-character equivalents from the Expert Collection font (bottom).

- **ff, fl, ffl Ligatures:** Tell me what's wrong here. That's right, the ff ligature is repeated unnecessarily in this option. But whatever the name of the option, it was responsible for replacing the black letters in *flowery* and *afflicted* in Figure 7-30. (It would have also taken care of the *ff* in *affable*, but the previous option got to it first.) If no Expert Collection font is available, Illustrator replaces the *fl* in *flowery* and *afflicted* with the *fl* ligature (Shift-Option-6 [Mac only]), available to most fonts.
- **Smart Quotes:** This option turns straight quotes (") into curly ones (“ and ”) and straight apostrophes (') into curly ones (’). Of course, you don’t need this option, since you already enter your quotes correctly in the first place using Option-[(left bracket), Shift-Option-[(left bracket), and Shift-Option-] (right bracket), right?
- **Smart Spaces:** If you learned to type on a typewriter, someone somewhere may have taught you to enter two spaces after a period. This is a cardinal sin in typesetting. In typesetting, you enter only one space after a period. Why? Because using two spaces makes a big gap in the text and looks awful; take my word for it. Spaces on a computer can be of any width that the program chooses, particularly in justified text. If Illustrator has to stretch one space to justify a line, it has to stretch two spaces twice as far, which interrupts the readability of the paragraph. Bad typewriter habits must die!

- **En, Em Dashes:** This option is a little off. It replaces two hyphens in a row with an en dash (–, which you can access by pressing Option-hyphen [Mac only]) and three hyphens with an em dash (—, Shift-Option-hyphen [Mac only]). The problem is, most folks who don't use real em dashes in the first place use double-hyphens as a substitute. I've never heard of anyone using triple hyphens. Furthermore, en dashes are equivalent to minus signs, so few folks think to use them at all. My suggestion is to ignore this option and learn the proper keyboard equivalents, Option-hyphen and Shift-Option-hyphen.
- **Ellipses:** This option replaces three periods with the special ellipsis symbol, accessed by pressing Option-; (semicolon) [Mac only]. The only reason to use this character is to prevent the periods from breaking to the next line.
- **Expert Fractions:** Every Adobe typeface includes three fraction characters, ¼, ½, and ¾. But thanks to the way Apple structured the extended character set, none of these characters is available when using the Mac. No way, no how. You can access them easily in Microsoft Windows (by pressing [with NumLock on] Alt-0188, Alt-0189, and Alt-0190), but not on the Mac. Forget it. So Adobe smartly built fractions into the Expert Collections, which include fractions in ⅛ increments. Figure 7-31 shows three fractions created with the standard slash symbol and set in the font Apollo, and the single-character versions from the Apollo Expert Collection. If you don't have access to an Expert Collection font, build your own fractions as explained in the "Raising and Lowering Characters" section of Chapter 6.

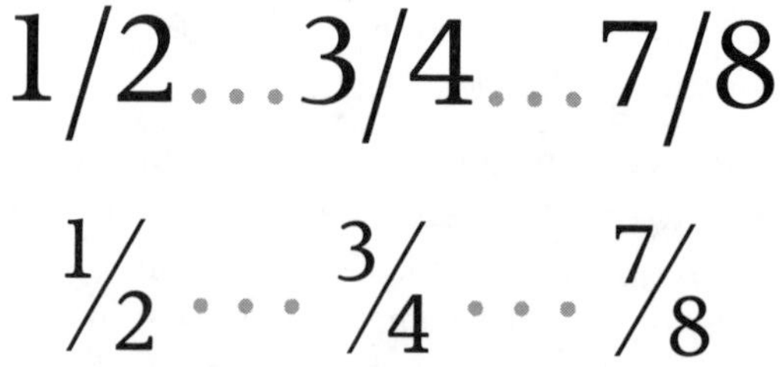

Figure 7-31: I created three fractions using the standard slash symbol (top) and then used the Smart Punctuation command to replace them with designer fractions from the Expert Collection font (bottom).

Select the Report Results check box if you want Illustrator to present you with an alert box after it's smartened up your document. The alert box lists the variety and quantity of each dumb punctuation that has been replaced.

Select the Entire Document radio button to search and replace characters throughout the illustration, whether selected with the type tool or not. I prefer to keep this option set to Selected Text Only—which requires you to select text with the type tool—since this way, I know exactly what Illustrator is up to.

Dividing Tables into Rows and Columns

Back in Chapter 6, I explained how to set up tables using the Tabs palette. Although tabs offer many advantages, they have one irritating limitation—they can't accommodate multiple lines of type per entry. If you want to wrap a heading or table entry onto two lines, you must wrap and tab the text manually.

For example, Figure 7-32 shows a detail from Figure 6-19. To create the two-line headings Primary occupation and Additional income, I had to enter the text on two separate lines and tab the text into position—as in Tab, *Primary*, Tab, Tab, *Additional*, Return, *Name*, Tab, *occupation*, and so on.

Figure 7-32: As shown in this detail from Figure 6-19, you can create two-line headings in tables manually using tabs.

The Rows & Columns Command

Thank golly, you can create complex tables that permit multiple lines per entry by using the Rows & Columns command. After selecting a text block or other area text with the arrow tool—not with the type tool—you choose Type » Rows & Columns. This displays the Rows & Columns dialog box shown in Figure 7-33.

Here you can specify the number of columns and rows you want in the text block, the width and height of each column and row, the amount of space (called the gutter) between each pair of columns and rows, and the width and height of the entire text block. (In case you get confused, columns are vertical and rows are horizontal.)

You can click on the arrow icons to incrementally change the values in the option boxes. Because changing any value affects at least one other value, the arrows come in quite handy. Whenever possible, Illustrator tries to maintain consistent values in the Number (of Columns), Number (of Rows), Total (Width), and Total (Height) option boxes. This means if you make a change to the Column Width value, Illustrator adjusts the Column Gutter value—rather than the Number (of Columns) or Total (Width) value—to compensate. Bigger column width, smaller gutter, and vice versa.

Click on the Text Flow option to change the order in which text flows through the columns and rows—that is, from left-to-right and then top-to-bottom, or from top-to-bottom and then left-to-right. Illustrator offers two more flow designs; from right-to-left and then top-to-bottom, or from top-to-bottom and then right-to-left. The Add Guides check box creates horizontal and vertical lines that are the entire width and height of your page—useful for establishing grids. (For more on this topic, check out Chapter 10.)

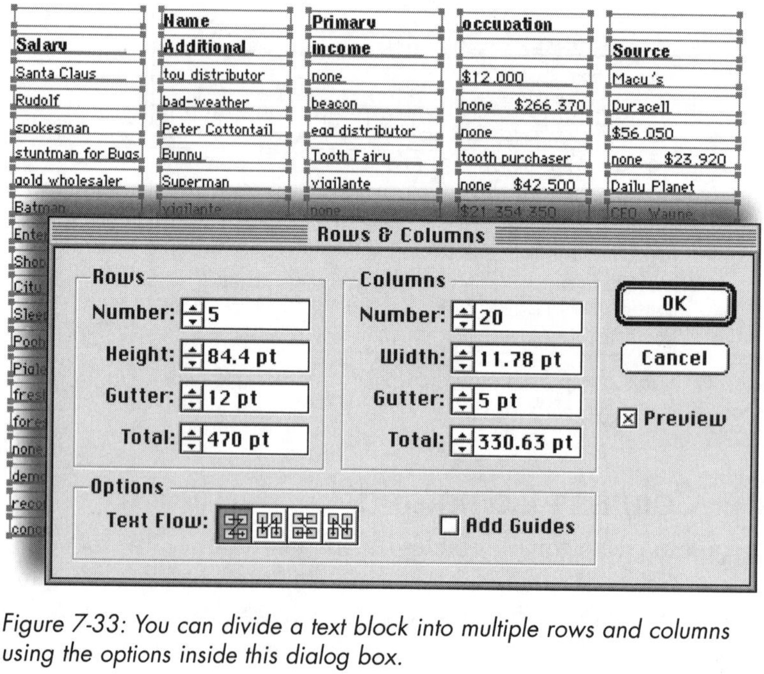

Figure 7-33: You can divide a text block into multiple rows and columns using the options inside this dialog box.

As long as the Preview option is checked, Illustrator continually updates the selected text block as you make changes. Unfortunately, this goes a long way toward slowing down the program, particularly on older machines. I prefer to deselect the Preview check box when making changes and then reselect it when I want to view the results.

NOTE: Just so you know that times do get better, here's a bit of historical trivia from Illustrators gone by. Back in version 5.5, the Preview check box actually applied your changes to the selected text block. Clicking on the Cancel button, therefore, did not cancel the operation but instead left the most recent preview in effect. This problem was eliminated in Illustrator 6. The Cancel button cancels, just as it should.

Modifying Rows and Columns Manually

After you create the desired number of rows and columns, you may have to edit the rows and columns a bit by hand to get the perfect fit and look, and you'll certainly have to edit the text to fit. Notice that all this filter does is break a text block into multiple text blocks that are linked together. Therefore, you can resize the text blocks any way you like.

For example, in Figure 7-34, I used the direct selection tool to select the top segments in the first row, then I dragged the segments upward to allow room for both lines of text in the table heads. I also adjusted the width of the rows to better fit the text.

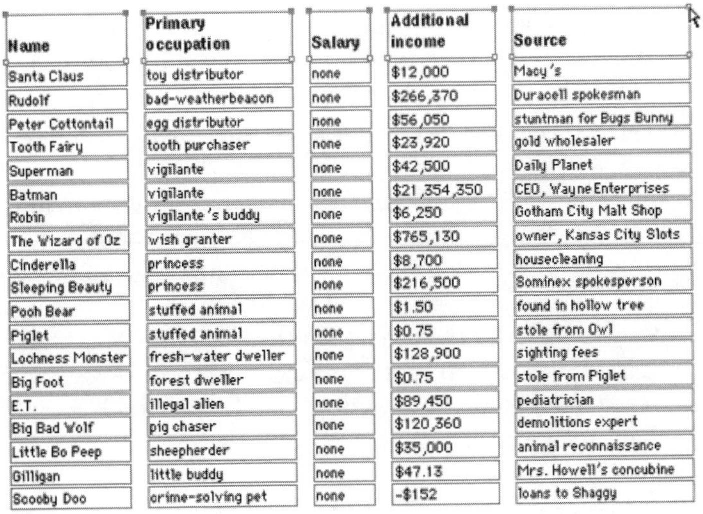

Name	Primary occupation	Salary	Additional income	Source
Santa Claus	toy distributor	none	$12,000	Macy's
Rudolf	bad-weatherbeacon	none	$266,370	Duracell spokesman
Peter Cottontail	egg distributor	none	$56,050	stuntman for Bugs Bunny
Tooth Fairy	tooth purchaser	none	$23,920	gold wholesaler
Superman	vigilante	none	$42,500	Daily Planet
Batman	vigilante	none	$21,354,350	CEO, Wayne Enterprises
Robin	vigilante's buddy	none	$6,250	Gotham City Malt Shop
The Wizard of Oz	wish granter	none	$765,130	owner, Kansas City Slots
Cinderella	princess	none	$8,700	housecleaning
Sleeping Beauty	princess	none	$216,500	Sominex spokesperson
Pooh Bear	stuffed animal	none	$1.50	found in hollow tree
Piglet	stuffed animal	none	$0.75	stole from Owl
Lochness Monster	fresh-water dweller	none	$128,900	sighting fees
Big Foot	forest dweller	none	$0.75	stole from Piglet
E.T.	illegal alien	none	$89,450	pediatrician
Big Bad Wolf	pig chaser	none	$120,360	demolitions expert
Little Bo Peep	sheepherder	none	$35,000	animal reconnaissance
Gilligan	little buddy	none	$47.13	Mrs. Howell's concubine
Scooby Doo	crime-solving pet	none	-$152	loans to Shaggy

Figure 7-34: You can edit the divided text blocks independently by using the direct selection tool.

To force a word into the next text block—whether to the right or down from the current block—enter a carriage return by pressing the Return key. (Don't use the tab key, since the width of each tab may vary depending on the location of the tab stops in the Tabs palette.) To set up the table head, therefore, I entered Return, *Name*, Return, *Primary occupation*, Return, Return, *Salary*, Return, *Additional income*, and so on. Adding the Return before *Name* and the double Return before *Salary* ensure that each of these entries appears on the second line. This method may sound as cumbersome as entering all those tabs back in Figure 7-32, but it has one important advantage—you can enter words in order, rather than having to cut and paste them into different positions to make them line up properly.

If you want to later go back and add more rows and columns, just select all of your text and rechoose Type » Rows & Columns. Keep in mind, however, that Illustrator resizes and respaces the selected text blocks to make them absolutely identical, which may necessitate some additional reshaping on your part.

Fitting Multiple Master Fonts on the Fly

Only two more commands left in the Type menu—Fit Headline and Create Outlines. The first shrinks or stretches a line of type to fit the width of a column, and the second converts character outlines to paths, as I discuss in the next section.

The Fit Headline command modifies a line of text to make it fill the entire width of a text block. The command takes an entire paragraph, from one carriage return to the next, and puts it all on one line. Therefore, you'll want to apply it to headlines of no more than a few words in length, such as "Monkey Brains" in Figure 7-35.

To use this command, click in the paragraph you want to shrink or stretch with the type tool and choose Type » Fit Headline. You can apply the command only after selecting the text with the type tool—clicking inside the paragraph will do this—and the paragraph must be set inside a text block or area text.

The top two examples in Figure 7-35 show what happens when you apply the Fit Headline command to a line of type. In the first example, the single word Monkey is too narrow to fit the width of the column. When I chose Type » Fit Headline, Illustrator added sufficient kerning to the letters to stretch them across the text block. In the second example, the two-word paragraph is too wide to fit. Fit Headline reduced the kerning of these characters to make them fit.

But let's be honest. You could have kerned the text yourself by pressing Option-← or Option-→. And you wouldn't have kerned Monkey Brains to the point that the characters overlapped, as they do in the second example in the figure. That's just plain ugly.

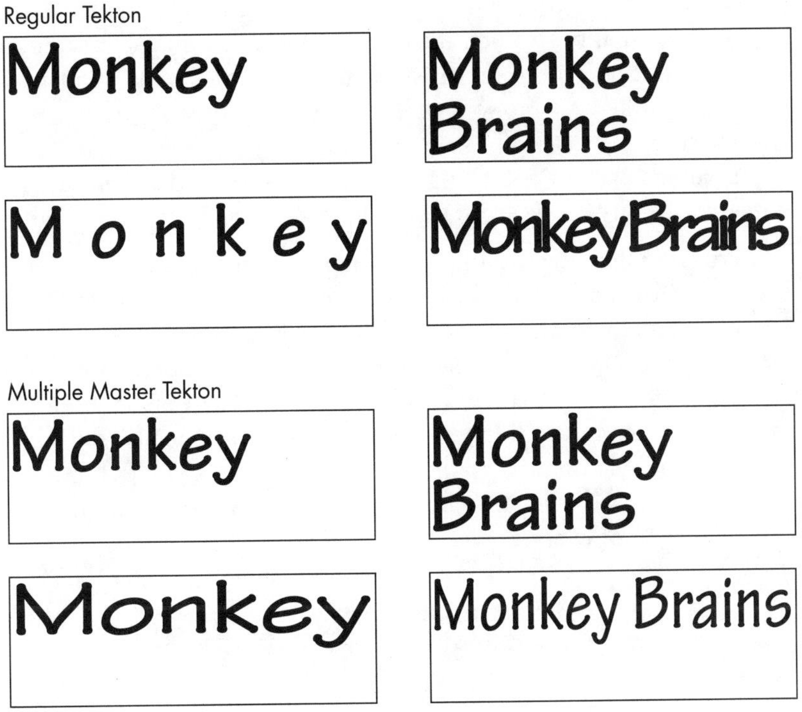

Figure 7-35: The results of applying the Fit Headline command to lines of type that are too narrow (left) and too wide (right) for their text blocks.

In fact, Fit Headline is actually designed to work with Multiple Master fonts, which are special PostScript fonts designed by Adobe. Unlike the Expert Collection fonts, which are just extra sets of characters, Multiple Master fonts are entirely different creatures. These fonts permit an application to consult pairs of opposing master designs, each of which represent extremes in formatting attributes. For example, one master design might be very bold, while its opposite is very light. Or one might include fat characters, while its opposite includes thin ones. The program then blends the two master designs to arrive at unique variations, called instances. Each Multiple Master typeface permits literally thousands of variations in weight, width, size, and slant. Although it's been rather slow to catch on with designers, Multiple Master technology is absolutely amazing stuff.

If a paragraph is formatted with a Multiple Master font, you can press Type » Fit Headline to adjust the weight and width of the font on the fly to fit the text across the length of the text block. The lower two examples of Figure 7-35 feature a Multiple Master version of the font Tekton. Notice how Illustrator stretches the word Monkey to fit the line, exaggerating the weight and expanding the width of each character. None of the distortion that you get with either the Vertical Scale or Horizontal Scale option appears here; the proportions of the characters appear uniform and even, and the kerning remains unchanged as well. The condensed Monkey Brains text is likewise proportional. Though significantly reduced in weight and width, it is just as legible and unremarkable as the original text. Illustrator adjusts all characters according to designer-approved specifications, which is the inherent beauty of Multiple Master fonts.

Provided that you are using a Multiple Master typeface in your drawing and it's selected, you can use the MM Design palette to generate stylistic variations. Click on the MM Design tab in the Character palette to bring the panel to the front, as shown in Figure 7-36. Adjust the slider bars to modify the weight, width, and other attributes. (The specific sliders available depend on the selected font.) After you get an effect you like, click OK. Illustrator adds the variation to the font menu of every application you run from now on.

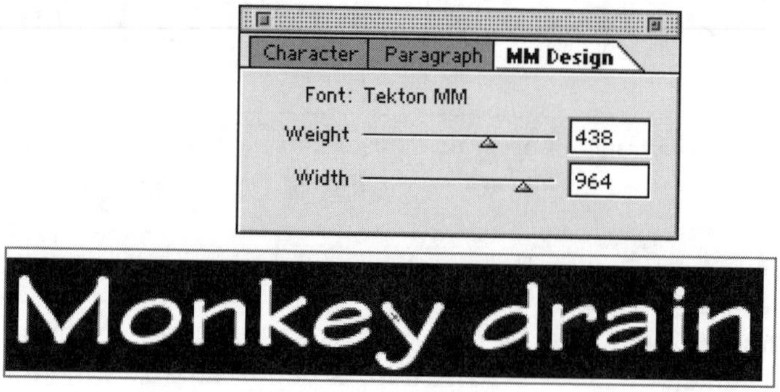

Figure 7-36: You can vary a Multiple Master font in Illustrator using the MM Design palette.

Converting Character Outlines to Paths

The outlining ability in Illustrator is both its most essential and straightforward feature. By choosing Type » Create Outlines (⌘-Shift-O [not zero]), you can convert any selected text block into a collection of editable paths, composed of points and sections (see Figure 7-37). The only catch is that the type must be selected with the arrow tool—you can't highlight it with the type tool. You may also Control-click and choose Create Outline, but this works only if the type was selected with the arrow tool. This will seem but a small inconvenience when you see how quickly and powerfully the command performs.

The top example in Figure 7-37 shows a three-character text block selected using the arrow tool. The bottom example shows the characters after choosing the Create Outlines command. The characters are now standard paths, composed of points and segments, just like those created with the pencil or pen tool.

Of the three characters in the figure, notice that Illustrator has converted the T and G into a single path apiece, while it converted the ampersand into three paths. To make interior paths transparent, like those in the ampersand, Illustrator converts each character into a compound path. In this way, it lets you see through the holes in the character to the objects behind it (as discussed in Chapter 9).

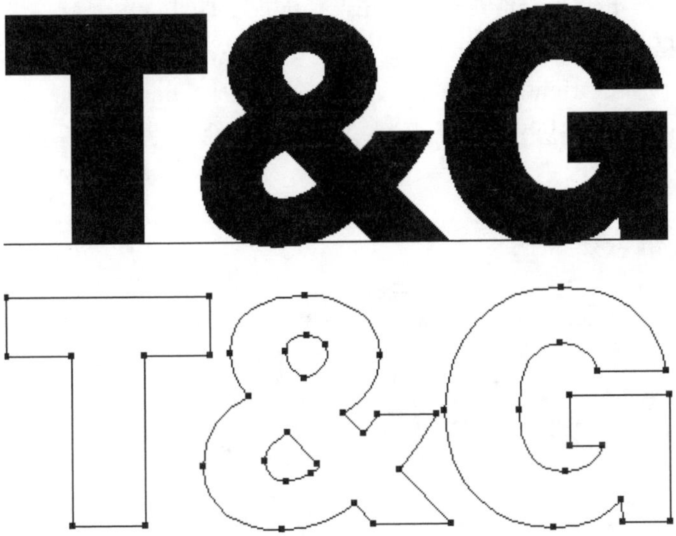

Figure 7-37: Select a text block (top) and choose Type » Create Outlines to produce a collection of fully editable points and segments (bottom).

Compound paths are all very well and good, but they can also get in your way. If you later try to join part of a path in the ampersand to another path, for example, Illustrator will refuse to participate, whining that the two paths have to be part of the same group. If you encounter something along these lines, select the character with the arrow tool and choose Object » Compound Paths » Release (⌘-Option-8). The transparent areas will fill with color, but you'll be able to edit the paths with absolute freedom.

After you choose the Create Outlines and Release commands, you can reshape, transform, duplicate, and otherwise manipulate converted type in any manner, as demonstrated by the fantastic example in Figure 7-38. It may not be art, but by golly, it's possible.

TIP

It's frequently a good idea to convert logos and headline text to paths, even if you don't plan on editing them. By doing so, you'll eliminate the chance that the text will shift or the font won't print correctly. For example, I don't know if the designers I'm working with have Tekton loaded on their machines—I assume they don't—so I converted the characters back in Figure 7-35 (and half a billion other figures in this book) to paths to ensure that they print correctly. It increases the size of the file on disk significantly, but insurance has its price.

If you want to reserve the right to edit the text from the keyboard, save one copy of the illustration prior to choosing Type » Create Outlines, and save another copy afterward.

Figure 7-38: And to think, this was once Helvetica.

CHAPTER 8

THIS IS YOUR BRAIN ON GRAPHS

This seems to me as good a time as any to take a moment out of our busy Illustrator learning schedules and look back on the knowledge we've amassed so far. Just since Chapter 4, we've learned how to create about every kind of graphic and text object on the planet, including geometric shapes, free-form paths, text blocks, path text, and hundreds of infinitesimal variations too tedious to mention.

That leaves just one more item that you can create in Illustrator—a combination of paths and text known as the graph. Yes, few folks know it (and even fewer folks seem to care), but Illustrator lets you create a graph from an everyday average spreadsheet of numbers. And it does a very good job of it.

"Illustrator for graphs?" I hear you arguing. "Surely there are better products for this purpose." Granted—I argue back (tastefully sidestepping the obvious "stop calling me Shirley" joke)—Microsoft Excel provides better number-crunching capabilities, PowerPoint and Persuasion let you build presentations around graphs, and no program competes with DeltaGraph Professional when it comes to scientific and highfalutin' business graphs guaranteed to please longhairs and think tankers in roughly equal portions. But if you're looking to create simple graphs with designer appeal—like those picture charts that are forever popping up in *USA Today*—using a program like Illustrator is your best bet.

But before I go any further, let me answer some important questions:

- What is the difference between a graph and a chart?
- Are these two terms interchangeable?
- Will snooty power graphers look down their noses at me if I say "chart" when I mean "graph," or vice versa?

The answers are: Nada, yes, and who gives a flying fish? The term "chart" is a little more inclusive than "graph." Television weather reporters use charts (not graphs) to show cold fronts, and navigators use charts (not graphs) to make sure your plane doesn't plow into a mountainside, but basically anything that can be called a graph can also be called a chart. So for the purposes of this chapter, they are one and the same.

What I personally rail against is the use of the term "graphic" to mean graph in Harvard Graphics and Freelance Graphics, two PC charting programs that are altogether useless for drawing. A graphic is a brilliant illustration that sparks the interest, enthusiasm, and imagination of the viewer; a graph is a bunch of lines and rectangles that bores folks silly.

In Illustrator, a graph can be a graphic.

Creating a Graph

Though you wouldn't know it to look at it, Illustrator offers a lot of graphing options. In fact, you can easily get mired down by these options—with so many options, each making such a tiny difference in the outcome of your graph, and each just plain hard to use. To help you out, I've provided the following handy-dandy chart-making steps. Illustrator's many minute graphing variations are likely to make more sense after you've had a chance to create a few graphs of your own.

1. **Decide what kind of graph you want to create.**

   Illustrator provides nine graph tools that correspond to its nine kinds of graphs—four kinds of bar graphs (of both the horizontal and vertical flavors), as well as a line graph, an area graph (filled lines), a scatter graph (a line graph variation), a pie graph (usually called a pie chart), and a radar graph (a circular style popular in Japan). Never fear, I explore each of these graphs in excruciating detail later in this chapter.

   To specify the kind of graph you want to create, drag your cursor to the right from the graph tool slot on the toolbox, as shown in Figure 8-1, and choose your tool.

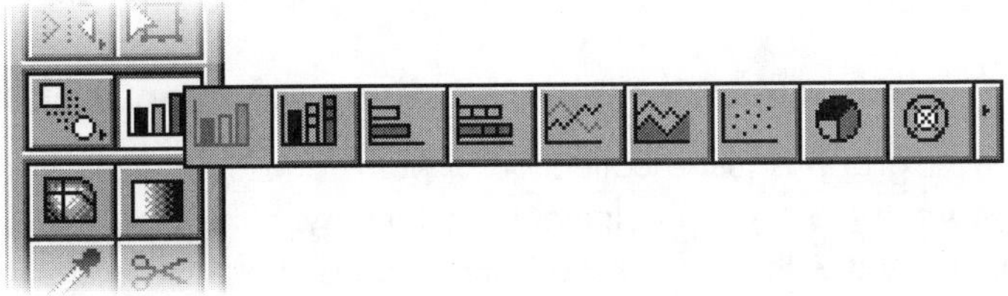

Figure 8-1: Choose one of the nine graph tools offered by Illustrator.

2. **Drag with the graph tool.**

   The dimensions of your drag determines the size of the graph. After you release the mouse button, Illustrator displays the Graph Data window, where you enter the numbers you want to graph.

3. **Enter or import your data.**

   You can either enter numbers directly into the Graph Data window or import them from a spreadsheet program. If you hate math, make a coworker give you the numbers. You're an artist, darn it, not an accountant!

4. **Press the keypad Enter key.**

   Illustrator closes the Graph Data window and generates a chart from your numbers. You can just sit there and admire the wonderful world of automation.

5. **Change the Graph Type attributes.**

   With the graph selected, double-click on the graph tool icon in the toolbox, and then choose the Object » Graph » Type command—or Control-click and choose the Type command from the context-sensitive pop-up menu to display the Graph Type dialog box. You can monkey around with a bunch of weird options until Illustrator creates a graph more or less to your liking. You can even change the kind of graph if you want.

TIP

This is one place in which Control-clicking (right-clicking in Windows) comes in handy. With a graph selected, Control-click to display a context-sensitive pop-up menu that contains all the commands in the Object » Graph submenu. This is probably the fastest way to access any of these commands. Although this tip is a bit more helpful for Win-folk (since it requires only a twitch of a finger on the right mouse button), I will refer to this technique as Control-clicking throughout this chapter.

6. **Edit the graph manually with the direct selection tool.**

   Ultimately, a graph is just a collection of paths and point text. This means you can move graph elements and text with the direct selection tool, edit the text with the type tool, and fill and stroke the paths with different colors.

You can revisit Steps 3 through 6 as many times as you want to modify the graph again and again. To modify the data for a selected chart, for example, choose Object » Graphs » Data and edit the numbers in the spreadsheet. You can even import an entirely new set of numbers.

You should keep in mind two important points:

- Applying options from the Graph Type dialog box or Graph Data window may negate manual changes that you've made with the direct selection and type tools. Illustrator tries to retain your manual changes when possible, but you should be prepared to reapply your modifications. Or better yet, try to get the automated stuff in Steps 3 through 5 out of the way before you make manual changes in Step 6.
- In Illustrator, a graph is a special kind of grouped object. Some path operations—particularly the Join and Pathfinder commands that I discuss in Chapter 9—won't work on paths inside a group. You also can't convert type to outlines inside a graph. If you need access to these functions, you must first ungroup the graph by choosing Object » Ungroup (or by pressing ⌘-Shift-G).

WARNING

While the Ungroup command expands your range of creative adjustments, it also terminates the graph, eliminating any link between the one-time chart and its data. After you press ⌘-Shift-G, you forfeit your ability to apply options from either the Graph Type dialog box or the Graph Data window. So don't ungroup until you are absolutely 100 percent satisfied with the numerical data represented in the graph.

You can of course backstep an operation by pressing ⌘-Z (or by choosing Edit » Undo). If you apply a few options in the Graph Type dialog box and upset a manual adjustment, or if you ungroup the graph and think better of it, the Undo command is always at the ready to bring things back to their previous state.

Defining the Graph Size with the Graph Tool

Any graphing tool's main purpose is to determine the rectangular dimensions of a chart. You draw with a graphing tool just as if you were drawing with the rectangle tool. In other words, you can avail yourself of any of these techniques:

- Drag to draw the chart boundary from corner to corner.
- Option-drag to draw the boundary from center to corner.
- Shift-drag or Shift-Option-drag to draw a square boundary.
- Click to display the tiny Graph dialog box, which contains Width and Height option boxes. Enter the horizontal and vertical dimensions of the desired chart and press Return. The click point becomes the upper left corner of the chart boundary.
- Option-click with the graph tool and enter the numeric dimensions if you want the click point to serve as the center of the graph.

Regardless of how you define the boundary of the graph, this area encloses only the graphic elements of the chart. The labels and the legend extend outside the boundary. In Figure 8-2, for example, the dotted outline shows the dimensions of the drag with the graph tool. The gray area represents portions of the graph that lie outside the boundary. You can change the size of the labels and you can move the legend if you need to, but they do take up space.

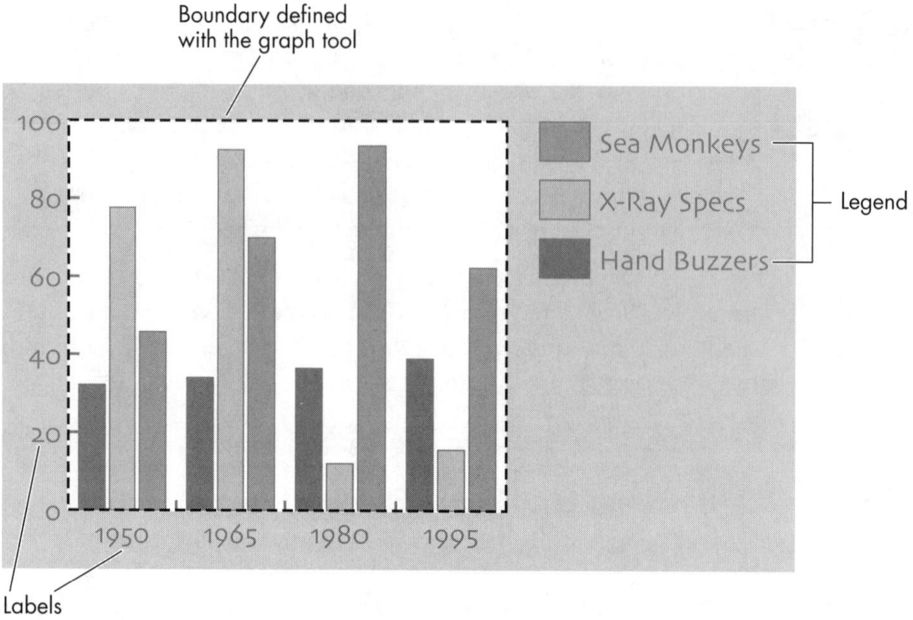

Figure 8-2: You can specify the graph's boundary (represented by the dotted outline) by dragging or clicking with the graph tool.

Don't worry too much if you don't know exactly how large or small you want the graph to be when you first create it. You can always enlarge or reduce it with the scale tool later. (The scale tool is a prominent topic of Chapter 11.) However, if you resize the graph disproportionately, you'll likewise disproportionately stretch text and other elements.

Figure 8-3 demonstrates what happens when you scale two kinds of graphs—column and pie—disproportionately. I created the top two examples by clicking with the graph tool and entering *14p* and *12p* (14 and 12 picas) into the Width and Height options. To create the bottom two examples, I entered *8p* and *10p* for the Width and Height values, resulting in graphs that were taller than they were wide. I then enlarged the bottom graphs disproportionately with the scale tool.

The scaled column graph generally looks fine; only the text appears stretched. The pie graph, however, does not fare as well. Because each pie is a perfect circle, the shapes suffer when you scale them disproportionately. So my advice is to go ahead and scale column, bar, line, and area graphs however you want; but be careful to scale scatter graphs (which have square points in them), pie graphs, and radar graphs (which rely on circles) by the same percentage vertically and horizontally.

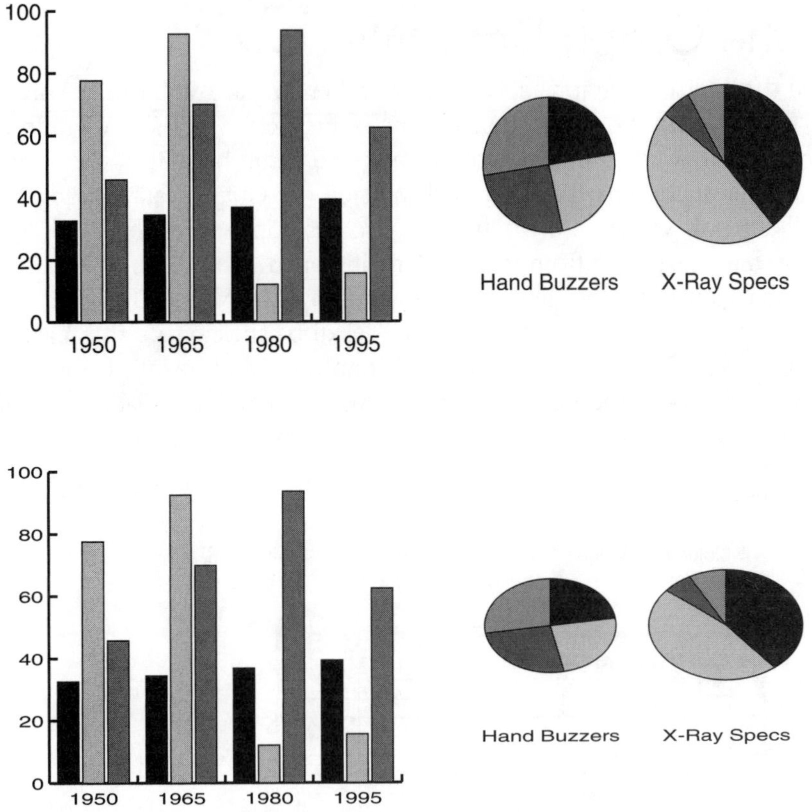

Figure 8-3: While I created the top two graphs at the sizes shown here, I drew the bottom graphs at smaller sizes and enlarged them disproportionately.

TIP

Scaling is a necessary part of the graphing process. But that's no excuse for stretched or squished text. After you scale, return your text to the proper proportions using the Horizontal Scale option in the Character palette. While the graph is still selected, click on the Horizontal Scale pop-up menu and choose the 100 percent option. Illustrator restores the type to normal scaling.

If this makes the text to small or too large for the graph, enter a new Size value or increase the Vertical Scale number.

Using the Graph Data Window

After you drag with the graph tool (or click and enter the graph dimensions), the Graph Data window pops up on screen, as in Figure 8-4. This is a window, not a dialog box, that contains its own size box and scroll bars. It is also more functional than a dialog box. You can click outside the Graph Data window to bring the illustration window to the front of the desktop. Although the Graph Data window may disappear from view, it remains open behind the illustration window, so that you don't lose any changes you may have made. To bring the Graph Data window back to the front of the desktop, click on its title bar or choose the Object » Graphs » Data command from the Graph menu. Better yet, Control-click and choose the Data command. (Alas, while Graph Data is for all intents and purposes an open window, Illustrator does not list it as an option on the Window menu.)

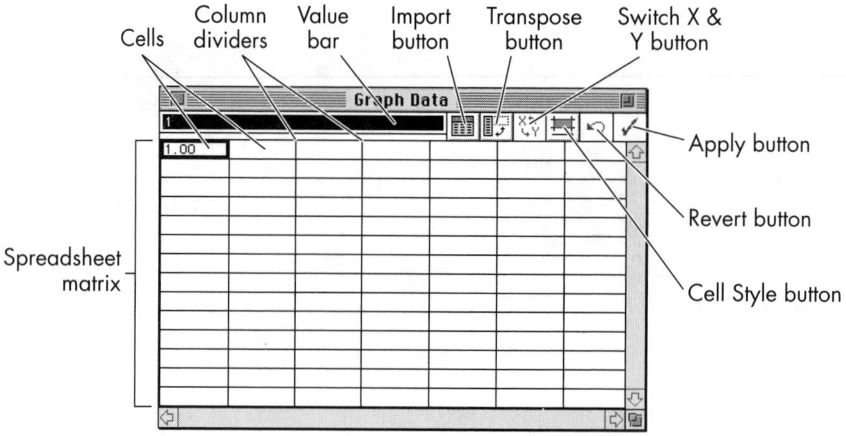

Figure 8-4: You enter data into a spreadsheet made up of rows and columns of cells in the Graph Data window.

The spreadsheet matrix that occupies most of the Graph Data window is similar to the matrix provided in a standard spreadsheet program like Excel. The spreadsheet contains rows and columns of individual containers, called *cells*. Numbers entered into the cells can represent dollars, times, dates, or percentages (though you should avoid symbols, such as $, %, among others). You can even enter words for labels and legends.

Unlike a true spreadsheet, however, you cannot enter formulas in the spreadsheet matrix because Illustrator lacks a calculation feature. (You can't even take advantage of Illustrator's adding function, which works in many palettes and dialog boxes, including the little dialog box that opens when you click with the graph tool.)

Data entered from the keyboard appears in the value bar at the top of the spreadsheet (labeled in Figure 8-4). Press Return (the Enter key on a Windows system), the arrow keys, or Tab to transfer the data from the value bar into the current cell and advance to another cell.

As you type, most keys insert the standard characters that appear on the key. Some keys and characters, however, perform special functions:

- **Tab or right arrow:** Accepts the data in the value bar and moves one cell right (to the next cell in the row).
- **Left arrow:** Accepts the data in the value bar and moves one cell left.
- **Return or down arrow:** Accepts the data in the value bar and moves one cell down (to the next cell in the column).
- **Up arrow:** Accepts the data in the value bar and moves one cell up.
- **Quotation marks ("):** Enter straight quotation marks around numeric data to use a number as a label, such as a product number or year. If a cell consists entirely of numbers without quote marks, Illustrator interprets the data as a value and graphs it.

  If you want Illustrator to display the quotation marks in the graph, use the curly opening and closing marks, “ and ” (Option-left bracket and Shift-Option-left bracket), rather than the straight quotation marks.
- **Vertical line character (|):** If you want a label to contain multiple lines of text, enter the vertical line (Shift-\) to represent a line-break character.
- **Keypad Enter key:** Accepts the data in the value bar and selects the OK button, exiting the Graph Data window.

For most kinds of charts, you can enter legend text into the top row and labels into the left-hand column of cells. To create such graph text, delete the data from the very first cell (at the intersection of the first row and column) and leave it empty. All other cells in the top row and left column should contain at least one non-numeric character or quotation marks around the numbers, as shown in Figure 8-5.

TIP

If you don't want Illustrator to create a legend, enter a label or a value into the first cell and fill the top row of cells with values. If I deleted the first line of items from the matrix in Figure 8-5, for example, and scooted up the other rows, I would get labels but no legend.

	Hand Buzzers	X-Ray Specs	Sea Monkeys	
"1950"	32.57	77.60	45.70	
"1965"	34.44	92.50	69.90	
"1980"	36.84	12.04	93.60	
"1995"	39.34	15.55	62.34	

Figure 8-5: As long as the first cell is empty, you can use the top row and the left column to hold labels.

If after entering a label or legend text, you can't see the full text inside the cell, it isn't because the text is lost; the cell is just too narrow to display it. You can widen the cell by dragging a column divider (labeled in Figure 8-4) as described in the "Changing the Way Cells Look" section later in this chapter.

Importing Data from Disk

Because the Graph Data window provides no calculation capabilities and its cell-editing functions are limited—you can't insert, delete, or sort cells—you may prefer to import values created in another program. You can create your data in any spreadsheet program capable of saving a tab-delineated file, which is a plain text file with tabs between values and carriage returns between rows. Virtually every spreadsheet program supports this format, including Microsoft Excel, Claris Resolve, the age-old MacCalc, and Lotus 1-2-3. The file can originate on a PC just as easily as on a Mac.

You can even create your data in a word processor such as Microsoft Word or WordPerfect. When entering the data, insert tabs between values and insert carriage returns between rows of values. Then save the finished file as a plain text document.

To import data from disk, open the Graph Data window and click on the cell where you want the imported data to start. Click on the Import button to display the Import Graph Data dialog box, which behaves like the Open dialog box. Locate the file you want to import and double-click on its name in the scrolling list, or select the file and press Return. The imported data appears in the spreadsheet in rows and columns starting in the selected cell.

If any of the cells below or to the right of the selected cell already contain data, Illustrator replaces the old data with the new.

Subscribing to Published Data on a Macintosh

If you create graphs with any degree of regularity, you'll appreciate the Graph Data window's support for your Mac system software's publish and subscribe function—a feature not found on Windows. (Although Illustrator does provide limited support for Microsoft's OLE, that is Object Linking and Embedding, it does not support linking—Illustrator will not automatically update an illustration that relies on data from another file when that file is modified in the original application.) In a nutshell, you can use Excel, Word, or some other program to publish a spreadsheet to disk, and then you can subscribe to it inside Illustrator. From this point on, whenever you modify the published spreadsheet from Excel or Word, the graph in Illustrator will automatically update.

TIP

This little-known technique (discovered, I must confess, not by myself, but by Thunder Lizard cofounder and crack trainer Steve Broback) involves a tiny bit more work than simply importing a spreadsheet from disk. But it's one of those classic situations for which a little effort expended now ensures far less effort in the future.

Here's what you do:

1. **In Excel or Word, select the numbers that you want to graph in Illustrator.**

   Just drag over the numbers with the cursor to highlight them.

2. **Choose Edit » Publishing » Create Publisher.**

   This command takes the data and publishes it inside something called an edition file. (Don't you just love all this newspaper lingo? You publish a late-breaking edition from one program, and another program scurries to subscribe to it.) The Create Publisher command brings up a modified Save dialog box.

3. **Enter a name for the edition and press Return.**

   That's it. You don't have to select any special options when you're working in either Excel or Word. (The same holds true for most other applications, although I can't vouch for all of them.)

4. **Switch to Illustrator.**

   If the sacred program is not running, by all means, fire it up.

5. **Create a new graph with the graph tool.**

   Or select an existing graph with the arrow tool and choose Object » Graphs » Data—feel free to Control-click. You can just as easily apply published data to a graph you created eons ago as to a new one.

6. **Click on the cell where you want the published data to start.**

   Any cells to the right and down will be overwritten.

7. **Choose Edit » Publishing » Subscribe To.**

   You can access this command from the Graph Data window.

8. **Locate the edition file, select it, and press Return.**

   Illustrator loads the published numbers into the Graph Data spreadsheet. A heavy border surrounds the published data, as shown in Figure 8-6. Although you can select cells inside this heavy outline, you cannot modify their contents.

   The border always appears when you click inside a subscribed cell. If you don't want to see the border when some other cell is selected, choose Edit » Publishing » Hide Border.

	Hand Buzzers	X-Ray Specs	Sea Monkeys
"1950"	32.57	77.60	45.70
"1965"	34.44	92.50	69.90
"1980"	36.84	12.04	93.60
"1995"	39.34	15.55	62.34

Figure 8-6: The heavy border shows that the data inside comes from an edition file on disk.

9. **Press the Enter key.**

   Illustrator closes the Graph Data window and updates the graph in the illustration window.

That's it for establishing a link between data saved to disk and a graph created in Illustrator. To update the graph in the future, all you have to do is update the data in the original Excel or Word document—you never open the edition file—then save the modified document as you normally would by pressing ⌘-S. Excel or Word automatically saves both the original document and the published data at once.

When you switch back to Illustrator, the program automatically updates the graph, whether or not the Graph Data window is open, entirely without any help or encouragement from you.

NOTE

If the graph doesn't appear to have changed, the default publish and subscribe setting may be messed up. In Excel, choose Edit » Links and make sure the Automatic radio button is selected. In Word, choose Edit » Publishing » Publisher

Options and make sure the On Save radio button is selected. And last but clearly not least, open up the Graph Data window in Illustrator, click on the subscribed data, choose Edit » Publishing » Subscriber Options, and select Automatic from the Get Editions radio buttons.

If you ever want to break the link between the Illustrator graph and the edition file on disk, choose Edit » Publishing » Subscriber Options from the Graph Data window, and then click on the Cancel Subscriber button. Then click on the Yes button in the meddlesome alert box.

Selecting and Modifying Cells

You select cells in the spreadsheet by dragging across them. Or you can press the Shift key while pressing one of the arrow keys to add to a range of selected cells or delete from them. All selected cells become highlighted—white against black—except the cell that you're entering data into, which has a big, fat border around it.

Although you can't perform fancy tricks like inserting or deleting cells inside the Graph Data window, you can move data around within cells using one of the following techniques:

- Cut or copy data from one location and paste it into another. You can either use the keyboard shortcuts ⌘-X, ⌘-C, or ⌘-V; choose commands from the Edit menu; or access the commands from the context-sensitive pop-up menu that appears when you Control-click.

TIP: For example, to nudge all cells upward one row (the effect achieved by deleting a row in Excel), select the cells, press ⌘-X, click on the first cell in the row you want to replace, and press ⌘-V.

- Click on the Transpose button to swap rows and columns of data in the spreadsheet matrix. The data in the top row goes to the first column, and vice versa. This button affects all data in the spreadsheet, regardless of which cells, if any, are selected.
- Click on the Switch XY button to swap columns of data in a scatter chart. The data in the first column moves to the second, the data in the second column moves to the first, the data in the third column moves to the fourth, and so on. This button is dimmed when you're creating or editing any kind of chart except a scatter chart, and it applies to all data in the spreadsheet.

- You can delete the contents of multiple selected cells by choosing Edit » Clear or by pressing the Clear key. (Pressing the Delete key deletes the contents of the active cell only.)
- Press ⌘-Z or choose Edit » Undo to undo the last operation—also easily accessed by Control-clicking. If you just finished changing a cell value, for example, ⌘-Z restores the previous data in the value bar. As in the rest of Illustrator, you have multiple undos inside the Graph Data window, so edit with impunity. You can even undo large operations such as importing, transposing, or pasting data.

Copying Data from a Different Graph

The fact that the Graph Data window stays up on screen makes it easy to copy data from one graph and paste it into another. For example, suppose that you just dragged with the graph tool to start a new graph, and Illustrator has displayed the Graph Data window. Suddenly, you remember that you wanted to create this new chart based on a chart you created a few days ago. But you don't even have that old chart open right now. No problem. You can access the data without even closing the Graph Data window:

1. Click in the illustration window to bring it to front. This gives you access to Illustrator's standard menu commands.
2. Press ⌘-O and open the illustration that contains the chart that you want to copy.
3. Select the chart with the arrow tool.
4. If you can see a smidgen of the Graph Data window, click on its title bar to bring it to front. Otherwise, choose Object » Graphs » Data or Graphs » Data from the context-sensitive pop-up menu. The Graph Data window shows the data for the selected graph.
5. Drag over the data that you want to copy from the previous chart and press ⌘-C (or choose Edit » Copy).
6. Click on the title bar for the illustration window that contains the new chart in progress. If necessary, select the chart with the arrow tool.
7. Click on the Graph Data window again. When you bring the Graph Data window to front, it automatically shows the data for the selected chart.
8. Click the first cell and press ⌘-V (or choose Edit » Paste). There's your data. Now you can edit it in any manner you deem appropriate.

You can copy as much data or as little data as you wish. To highlight the cells you want to copy, just drag over them. And click on a cell before pressing ⌘-V to decide where you want the pasted data to start.

TIP

Illustrator lets you paste any type into the Graph Data window. You can copy words or paragraphs from a block of text in the illustration window and paste them into a graph. You can also copy data from the spreadsheet and paste it into a text block.

Changing the Way Cells Look

The final adjustment that you can make to cells in the Graph Data window is purely cosmetic. The Cell Style button allows you to adjust both the width of the columns in the spreadsheet and the number of digits that follow a decimal point. These controls affect only the appearance of data in the spreadsheet; they do not affect the appearance of the chart in the illustration window.

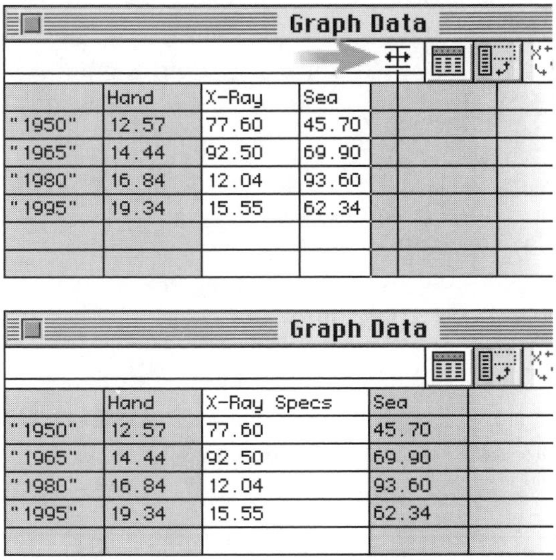
Graph Data
Hand
X-Ray
Sea
"1950" 12.57 77.60 45.70
"1965" 14.44 92.50 69.90
"1980" 16.84 12.04 93.60
"1995" 19.34 15.55 62.34
Graph Data
Hand
X-Ray Specs
Sea
"1950" 12.57 77.60 45.70
"1965" 14.44 92.50 69.90
"1980" 16.84 12.04 93.60
"1995" 19.34 15.55 62.34

Figure 8-7: Drag a column divider (top) to change the width of a column of cells (bottom).

Click on the Cell Style button to display a dialog box that contains the following two option boxes:

- **Number of Decimals:** Enter any value between 0 and 10 into the Number of Decimals option box. This option determines the number of significant digits—that is, the number of characters that can appear after a decimal point in a cell.

- **Column Width:** This value controls the default width of each cell in the Graph Data window, measured in digits. Enter any value between 1 and 20.

TIP: To adjust the width of a single column of cells, drag the corresponding column divider, as demonstrated in Figure 8-7. The column is widened or narrowed by the nearest whole-digit increment.

Transforming Your Data into a Graph

So far, I've instructed you to press the Enter key to update the graph in the illustration window. But this isn't the only way to go. The Graph Data window provides many ways for you to update the graph; or you can exit the window without updating.

The following is a brief explanation of the update, exit, and reversion elements in the Graph Data window:

- **The Apply button (Option-keypad Enter):** Click on the Apply button or press Option-Enter to update the graph in the illustration window without leaving the Graph Data window. If you can't see the graph because the Graph Data window is in the way, drag the Graph Data title bar to move the window partially off the screen. By keeping the Graph Data window up on the screen, you can quickly make changes if the data doesn't graph the way you hoped it would.

- **The Revert button:** Click on Revert to restore the data that was in force the last time you clicked on the OK or Apply button.

- **Close box:** If you want to exit the Graph Data window without implementing your changes, click in the close box in the upper left corner of the window, and then click on the Don't Save button in the alert box (or press the D key).

TIP: You can also cancel your modifications to a graph by simply selecting a different object in the illustration window or in a different drawing altogether. Illustrator displays an alert box asking you if you want to save your changes to the last graph. Press D if you don't want to, or press Return if you do.

You can undo the creation or alteration of a chart after clicking on the OK or Apply button by pressing ⌘-Z.

Organizing Your Data for Different Kinds of Graphs

You might hope that you could enter your data in any old way and have Illustrator graph it in the precise manner you've envisioned in your head, but Illustrator isn't quite so gifted at reading your mind. Therefore, you have to organize your data in a manner that Illustrator—mildly dictatorial program that it is—deems appropriate.

Just to keep you on your toes, Illustrator requires you to organize your data differently for different kinds of graphs. The following sections explore each of the nine kinds of graphs and tell you how to set up your data for each.

Column Chart Data

When creating a plain old everyday column graph—also called a grouped column chart for reasons that will become apparent as our graphing journey progresses—Illustrator expects you to organize your data in what I will henceforth call "standard form." But before I tell you what that standard form is, a word or two about this classic kind of chart.

Column charts are most commonly used to demonstrate a change in data over a period of time. The horizontal axis (X-axis) may be divided into categories such as units of time (i.e., days, months, or years). The vertical axis (Y-axis) tracks values, which may be measured in units sold, dollars or other currency, or whatever your favorite commodity may be.

As shown in Figure 8-8, columns rise up from the X-axis to a height equivalent to a value on the Y-axis. The taller the column, the greater the value it represents.

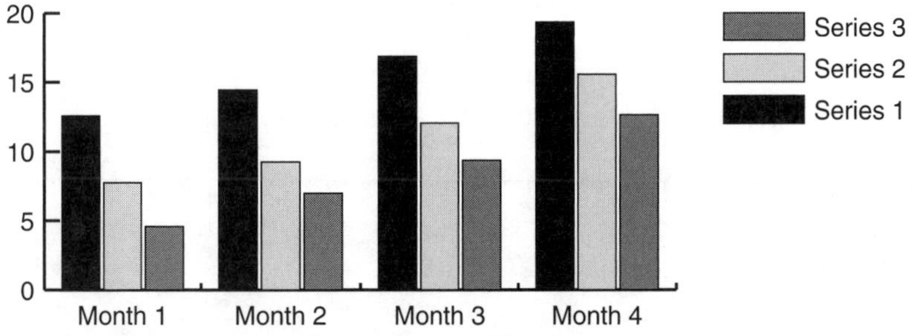

Figure 8-8: An example of a standard column chart, in which series of vertical columns are clustered together to show change in multiple items over time.

You can graph multiple collections of data in the chart. Each collection is called a series. Back in Figure 8-2, for example, Sea Monkeys, X-ray Specs, and Hand Buzzers are each separate series. Corresponding columns from each series are clustered together for the sake of visual comparison. Hence, this type of chart is known in some circles as a cluster column chart.

By default, columns from different series are filled with different gray values (although you can apply your own colors using the direct selection tool, as I explain later in the chapter). The colors representing the series are defined in the legend, which appears in the upper right portion of Figure 8-8.

To create a column chart, arrange your data as shown in Figure 8-9. Here are a few details to keep in mind:

- Delete the contents of the first cell, and leave it empty.
- Enter series labels in the top row of cells. This text will appear in the legend.
- Enter X-axis labels in the left column. They will appear underneath the chart along the horizontal axis.

	Series 1	Series 2	Series 3	
Month 1	12.57	77.60	45.70	
Month 2	14.44	92.50	69.90	
Month 3	16.84	12.04	93.60	
Month 4	19.34	15.55	12.63	

Figure 8-9: Organize column chart data into columns under series labels. This data corresponds to the column chart shown in Figure 8-3.

- Organize each series of data into a column under the appropriate series label. Do not enter any characters other than numbers. If you use a currency symbol, such as $, £, or ´, Illustrator won't graph the value.
- Illustrator generates the Y-axis labels automatically, in accordance with the data. You can customize the Y-axis labels using options in the Graph Type dialog box, which I naturally explain later.

Stacked Column Chart Data

Stacked column charts are much like column charts, except that columns from each series are stacked on top of one another rather than positioned side by side. A stacked column chart shows the sums of all series.

You can create a percentage chart similar to the one shown in Figure 8-10 by organizing your data so that all values for each series add up to 100. Percentage charts demonstrate relative performance. If Department A is trouncing Department B, you can broadcast the news with a percentage chart.

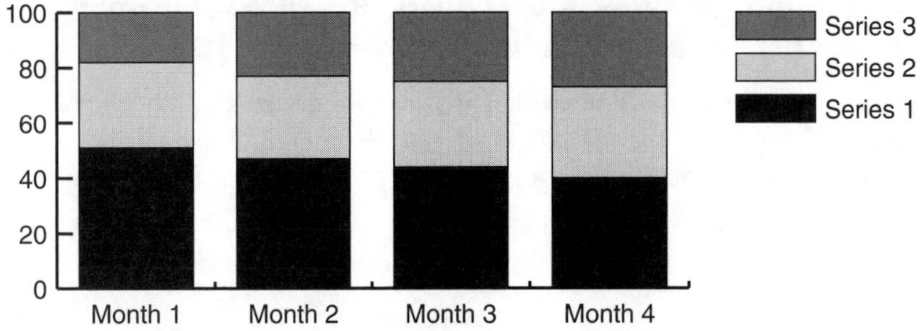

Figure 8-10: This percentage chart is a variety of the stacked column chart, in which each column of series values adds up to 100.

You arrange data for a stacked column chart in the standard form, with series labels in the top row and X-axis labels in the left column, as shown in Figure 8-11. Organize series of data into columns under the series labels. Whatever you do, don't enter a percentage symbol or any other non-numeric characters. If you do, Illustrator won't graph the value.

	Series 1	Series 2	Series 3	
Month 1	51.00	31.00	18.00	
Month 2	47.00	30.00	23.00	
Month 3	44.00	31.00	25.00	
Month 4	40.00	33.00	27.00	

Figure 8-11: This data corresponds to the percentage chart shown in Figure 8-10. Notice that the values along each row add up to 100.

TIP

Illustrator can't automatically convert sales values to percentages, so you can either enter the percentages manually or make a program like Excel do the work.

To make Excel convert values to percentages, follow these steps:

1. **Enter the sales values in Excel in the standard form.**

   Don't even think about percentages. Just enter normal values.

2. **Select each row of values one at a time, and click on the AutoSum button.**

   Labeled in Figure 8-12, the AutoSum button looks like a sigma (Σ) in the ribbon bar. Excel creates a sum total for each row in the column after the selection (the bold items in the figure).

3. **Create a new cell in which you divide the first sales number by the first sum and multiply the result by 100.**

   Make sure that you fix the column letter using the dollar sign character. For example, if the first cell were B2 and the sum cell were E2—as they are in Figure 8-12—you'd enter *B2/$E2*100* (where / is the division symbol and * is multiply).

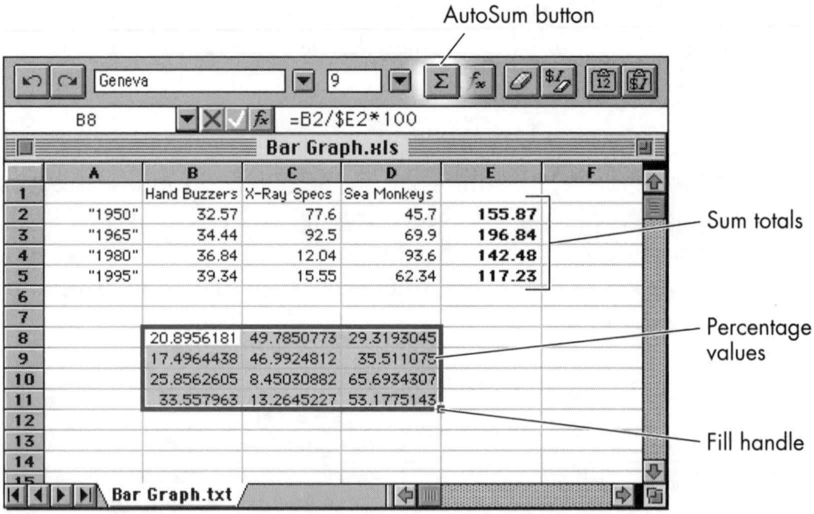

Figure 8-12: A collection of percentage values created in Excel 5 and ready to publish for use in Illustrator.

NOTE

I know, you're thinking, "But, Deke, how is it you know so much about creating formulas in Excel?" The truth is, while my first major in college was art, my second was math. The one thing I never studied was writing (which I demonstrate daily in my peculiar abuse of the English language).

4. **Duplicate the formulas to the right and then down by dragging the fill handle.**

   The fill handle is that little square in the lower right corner of the selected cell (labeled in Figure 8-12). You drag it to the right and then drag down in two separate movements. This creates a matrix of new percentage values. They may not look like percentages—just a bunch of long numbers like the selected cells in Figure 8-12. But they'll work fine. And don't change the number formatting—remember, Illustrator can't read percent signs.

5. **Select the new percentage values and publish them.**

   Follow the same steps I outlined back in the "Subscribing to Published Data" section earlier in this chapter. If you prefer not to (or can't) use the publish function, select the new data and copy it (⌘-C).

6. **Switch to Illustrator and subscribe to the data.**

   Create a new stacked column chart, enter your own labels in the top row and left column, and subscribe to the Excel data starting in the second-to-top, second-to-left cell. If you copied the new data from Excel, paste (⌘-V) after entering the labels.

7. **Press the keypad Enter key.**

   You now have a percentage chart.

Provided you've used the publish function, you can update the chart in the future by just editing your sales values in Excel. The program will automatically calculate the totals and percentage numbers and ship them off to Illustrator every time you press ⌘-S.

Bar Chart Data

Bar charts are the horizontal equivalents of column charts. Whereas columns move up to indicate increasing value, bars move to the right, as shown in Figure 8-13. You enter data into the Graph Data dialog box in the exact same manner that you do for a column chart. Illustrator automatically switches the category and value (i.e., X and Y) axis for you.

In previous versions of Illustrator, you could achieve a similar effect by rotating a column graph 90 degrees, but you then would have to add the labels and legend as separate text blocks. Now you can simply choose to display your data in this more leisurely form.

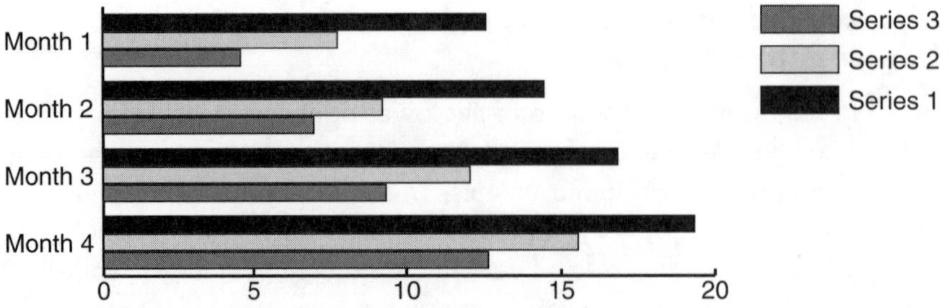

Figure 8-13: The bar chart is the lazy sibling of the column chart.

You might think that you could convert a column chart into a bar chart by clicking on the Transpose button in the Graph Data dialog box. But this will not result in a bar chart. Instead, you will have a column chart in which the labels and legend are located in the wrong places.

Stacked Bar Chart Data

What's to say when it comes to stacked bar charts? If you've seen a bar chart and a stacked column chart you can surmise the structure of a stacked bar chart. The picture you have in mind probably looks much like Figure 8-14. You can apply the same technique, explained above in the stacked column chart discussion, to your bar chart data.

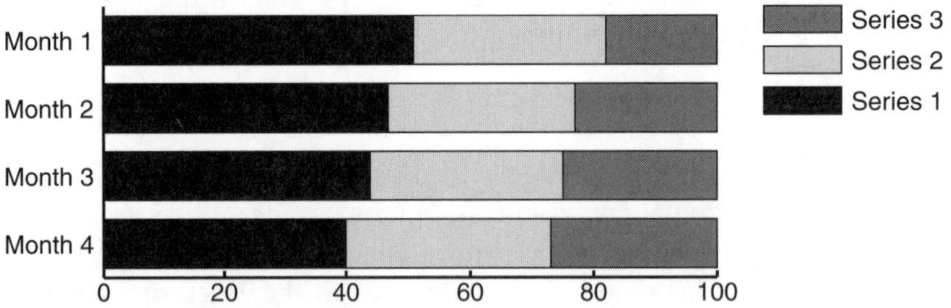

Figure 8-14: As seen here or in your mind's eye, a stacked bar chart fulfills all your horizontal bar stacking needs.

Line Chart Data

Like column charts, line charts are generally used to show changes in items over a period of time. Straight segments connect points representing values, as shown in Figure 8-15. Several straight segments combine to form a line, which represents a complete series. The inclination of a segment clearly demonstrates the performance of a series from one point in time to the next. Because large changes result in steep inclinations, line charts clearly show dramatic fluctuations.

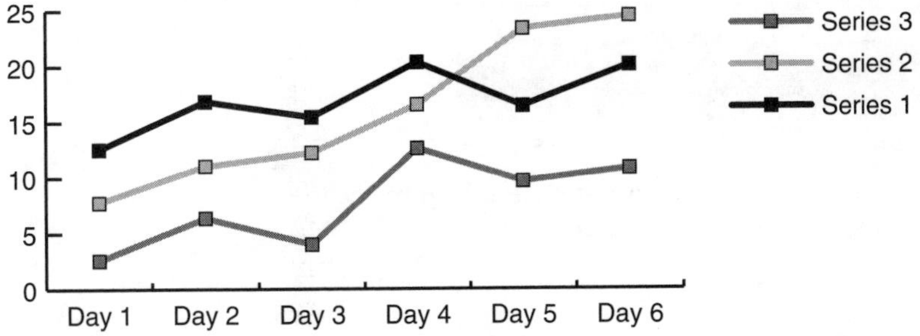

Figure 8-15: A line chart comprises straight segments connecting square value points.

Figure 8-16 shows the data used to create Figure 8-15. As with column charts, you organize the data into the standard form, with series labels at top, X-axis labels on the left, and columns of series data.

	Series 1	Series 2	Series 3	
Day 1	12.57	7.76	2.57	
Day 2	16.84	11.04	6.36	
Day 3	15.44	12.25	3.99	
Day 4	20.34	16.55	12.63	
Day 5	16.42	23.35	9.65	
Day 6	20.08	24.49	10.82	

Figure 8-16: Here's the data for the line chart in Figure 8-15. Each column of numbers results in a single line.

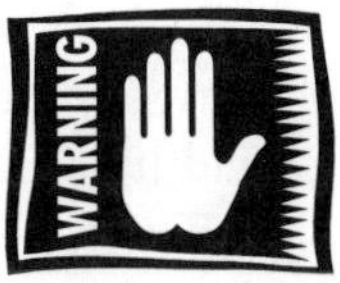

Although line chart data may fluctuate dramatically, you don't want series to cross each other more than one or twice in the entire chart. If the series cross too often, the result is what snooty graphing pros derisively call a "spaghetti chart," which is difficult to read and can prove more confusing than instructive.

Area Chart Data

An area chart is little more than a filled-in line chart. However, the series of an area chart are stacked one on top of another—just as in a stacked column chart—to display the sum of all series, as shown in Figure 8-17.

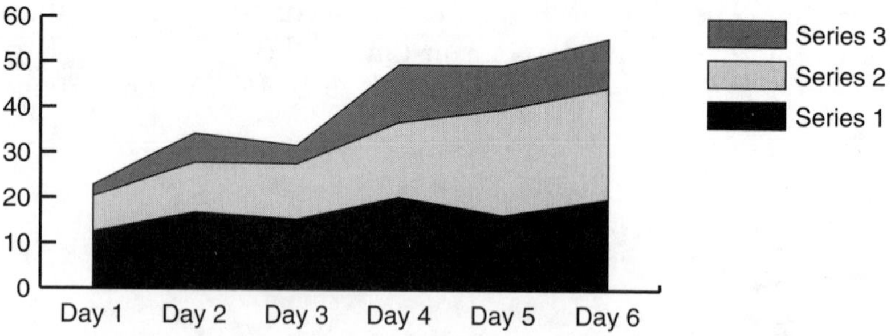

Figure 8-17: In an area chart, series are stacked on top of each other and filled in with colors or gray values.

When you create an area chart, arrange your data in the standard form. In fact, Figure 8-17 uses the same data as the line chart from Figure 8-15. The data appears in Figure 8-16.

If you encounter the spaghetti effect (overlapping lines) when creating a line chart, the easiest solution is to convert the line chart into an area chart.

Scatter Chart Data

Like a line chart, a scatter chart plots points on the horizontal and vertical axes and connects these points with straight segments. However, rather than merely aligning series of values along a set of X-axis labels, the scatter graph pairs up columns of values. The first column of data represents Y-axis (series) coordinates; the second column represents X-axis coordinates. This setup permits you to map scientific data or to graph multiple series that occur over different time patterns.

For example, in Figure 8-18, the black line (Series 1) connects 13 points, while the gray line (Series 2) connects 10. And yet both lines run the entire width of the graph. You tell Illustrator which X-axis and Y-axis coordinates to plot; Illustrator just connects them with segments. This is the most versatile kind of graph you can create.

Figure 8-19 shows the data for the scatter chart in Figure 8-18. The data is arranged into pairs of columns, each pair representing a separate series.

- Enter series labels into the top row of cells, one label for each odd column (first, third, fifth, and so on). Leave even-numbered cells empty. As with line charts, the series labels appear in the legend.

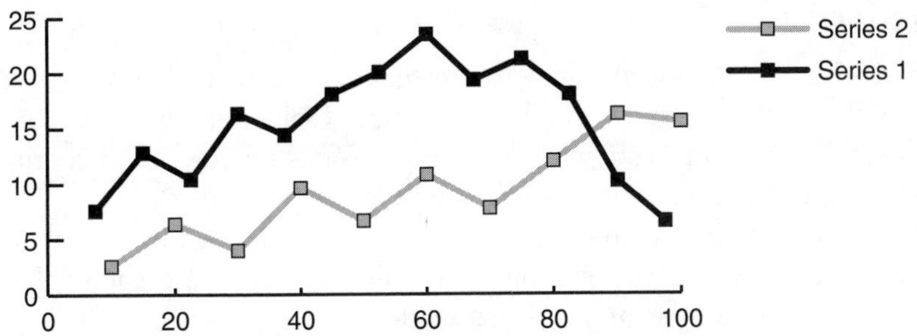

Figure 8-18: Illustrator plots points in a scatter graph at specific X,Y coordinates and connects the points with straight segments.

- Enter Y-axis (series) data in the odd-numbered columns.
- Enter X-axis data in the even-numbered columns. Illustrator plots side-by-side columns of data as paired points. In other words, each pair of values in the first and second columns is plotted as a point in the first series, each pair in the third and fourth columns is plotted as a point in the second series, and so on.
- Illustrator automatically generates Y-axis and X-axis labels that correspond to the data.

Series 1		Series 2		
7.57	7.50	2.57	10.00	
12.84	15.00	6.36	20.00	
10.44	22.50	3.99	30.00	
16.34	30.00	9.63	40.00	
14.42	37.50	6.65	50.00	
18.08	45.00	10.82	60.00	
20.06	52.50	7.76	70.00	
23.49	60.00	12.04	80.00	
19.35	67.50	16.25	90.00	
21.26	75.00	15.55	100.00	
18.05	82.50			
10.24	90.00			
6.56	97.50			

Figure 8-19: Each series of scatter chart data takes up two columns, with the Y-axis values first and the X-axis values second.

Pie Chart Data

A pie chart is the easiest kind of chart to create. However, pie charts are not nearly as versatile as the column and line varieties. Only one series can be expressed per pie. If you want to show more than one series for comparative purposes, each series gets a pie of its own, as shown in Figure 8-20.

The advantage of a pie chart is that it always displays a series of values in relation to the whole. The entire series inhabits a 360-degree circle, and each value within the series occupies a percentage of that circle.

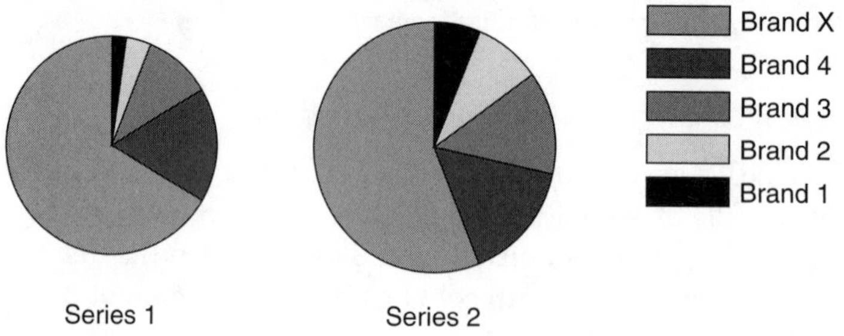

Figure 8-20: Two pie charts, each representing a single series. The first pie is smaller than the second because the second series includes larger values.

Figure 8-21 shows the data for the pies in Figure 8-20. You organize data for a pie chart in virtually the opposite way that you organize it for a column or line chart, with the series running across the rows instead of down the columns. Here are a few guidelines:

- Delete the contents of the first cell and leave it empty, just like always.
- Enter value labels in the top row of cells. These labels appear in the legend.
- Enter series labels in the left column. These labels appear as titles below the pies, as in Figure 8-20. (If you plan on graphing more than two series, I recommend you use a different kind of chart.)

	Brand 1	Brand 2	Brand 3	Brand 4	Brand X	
Series 1	0.98	1.56	4.07	6.76	26.57	
Series 2	3.24	4.67	6.99	8.25	29.34	

Figure 8-21: Organize pie chart data into rows. Each row represents a different pie.

- Organize each series of data into a row to the right of the series label.

TIP: If you want to take a couple of series from a column chart and represent them inside pie charts, copy them from the spreadsheet for the column chart, paste them into the pie chart spreadsheet, and click on the Transpose button to switch the rows and columns.

Radar Chart Data

Though big in Japan, a radar chart isn't as well recognized in the U.S. It resembles a spoked wheel with string running between the spokes. Though it may look more like a design than a functional graph, a radar chart, shown in Figure 8-22, is essentially a line chart rolled-up.

Since radar charts are closely related to line charts, I used the data from the line chart in Figure 8-15 to create the radar chart in Figure 8-22.

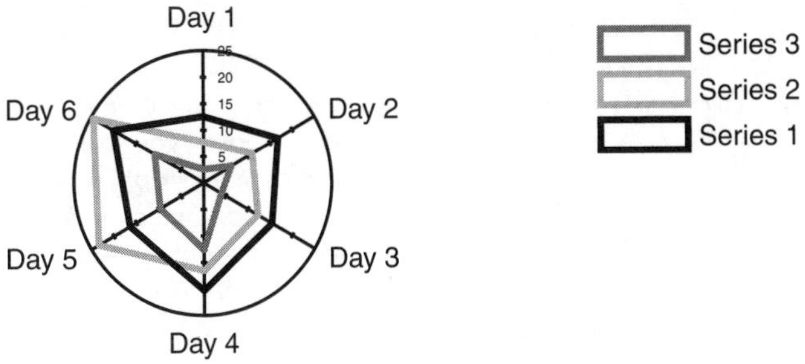

Figure 8-22: A non-Euclidean approach to line graphing.

Applying Automated Changes to a Graph

Remember the six basic steps required to create a graph in Illustrator? (If not, you can refresh your memory by peeking at the "Creating a Graph" section at the beginning of this chapter.) So far, we've exhausted the first four. Step 5 encouraged you to apply automated changes using the Graph Type dialog box. That's what these next sections are all about.

To access these options, select the graph you want to edit and double-click on the graph tool icon in the toolbox, or choose Object » Graphs » Type, or Control-click and choose Type. Illustrator displays the Graph Type dialog box, shown in

Figure 8-23. This dialog box is quite complicated and provides access to a bunch of options that you don't see on first perusal, including two other dialog boxes.

You can apply options from the Graph Type dialog box to an entire graph selected with the arrow tool or to a partial graph selected with the direct selection tool. For example, if you Option-click three times on a straight segment in a previously deselected line graph with the direct selection tool, you select the entire series, including the color swatch in the legend. You can then modify that one segment independently of the others inside the Graph Type dialog box.

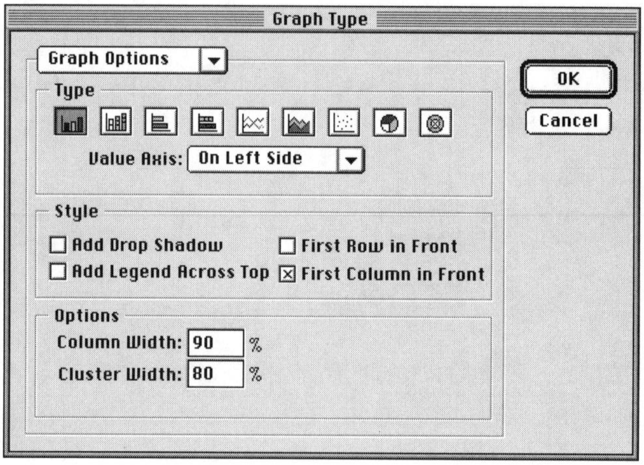

Figure 8-23: You can Control-click and choose Type to display the Graph Type dialog box, which lets you apply automated adjustments to a selected graph.

Converting and Tweaking a Graph

You can convert a selected graph from one variety to another—say, from a column chart to a line chart—by clicking on an icon from among the nine buttons along the top portion of the dialog box. Just click on a button, press Return, and, whamo, the chart is changed.

Most likely, you could've figured out that little bit of information without my help. I mention it by way of introduction to an additional set of options in the bottom portion of the Graph Type dialog box. These specialized options change depending on which kind of graph you've selected.

The following list explains the options associated with each type of chart:

- **Column:** When you click on the column button, two options appear in the Options area at the bottom of the Graph Type dialog box, as pictured in Figure 8-24. The Column Width value controls the width of each column in the chart. A value of 100 percent causes columns to touch each other, rubbing shoulders, as it were. The default value of 90 percent allows slight gutters between columns, and values greater than 100 percent cause columns to overlap.

The second option, Cluster Width, controls the width of each cluster of columns, again measured as a percentage value. The last column from Series 1 touches the first column of series 2 at 100 percent. The default value of 80 percent allows a gutter between clusters. (I don't recommend using values greater than 100 percent because they cause clusters not only to overlap each other but to overlap the vertical axis as well. Frankly, it can be mighty ugly.)

- **Stacked Column:** The Options area contains the same options listed above, whether you select a grouped or stacked column chart (see Figure 8-24).

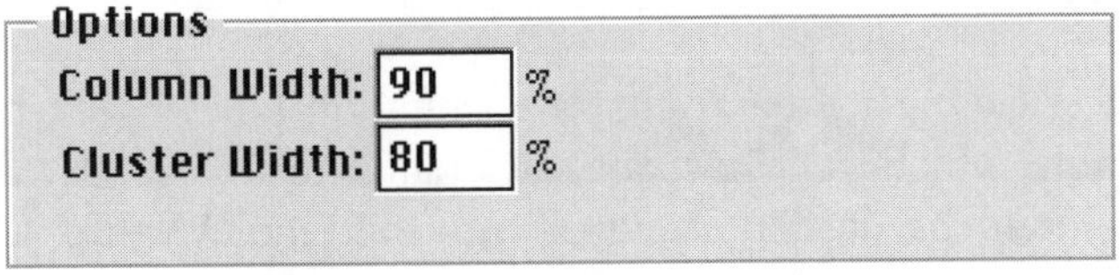

Figure 8-24: Use these options to control the width of columns and clusters of columns in a chart.

- **Bar:** Click on this button and the Options area changes slightly, as shown in Figure 8-25. The Bar Width option allows you to control how wide the bars should be, just as the Column Width option did for columns. The Cluster Width option works the same way as above.

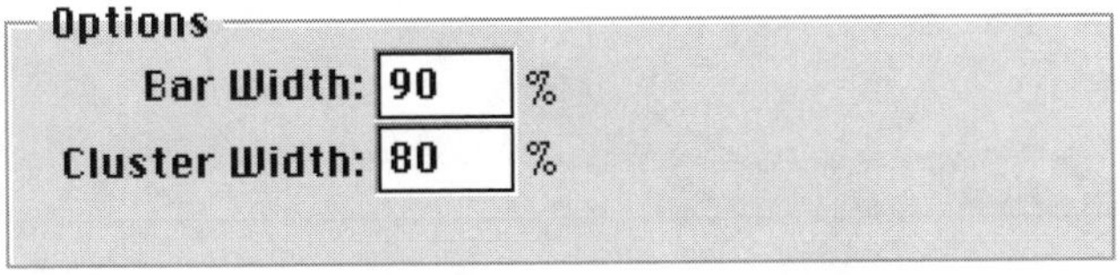

Figure 8-25: Use these options to change the width of bars and clusters of bars in a bar chart.

- **Stacked Bar:** These options look and work the same as those for the bar chart (see Figure 8-25).

- **Line:** When you click the Line chart button, four check boxes appear in the Options area, as shown in Figure 8-26. Select the Mark Data Points check box to create square markers at the data points in each line. Turn off the check box to make the square markers disappear. Select the Connect Data Points check box and Illustrator will draw straight segments between points. Deselect this option and stray markers appear without lines. (Turn off both check boxes to make the series disappear entirely.)

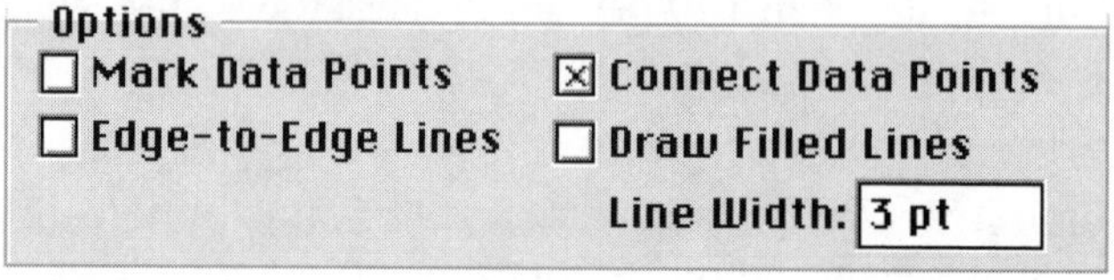

Figure 8-26: Use these options to change the square points and straight segments associated with line graphs (and scatter charts).

When you select Connect Data Points, the Draw Fill Lines check box becomes available, which lets you create thick paths filled with gray values or colors. Enter the desired thickness into the Line Width option box. Figure 8-27 shows a line graph with paths 12 points thick. Generally, you don't need data points when using fat paths, so you can turn off the Mark Data Points check box.

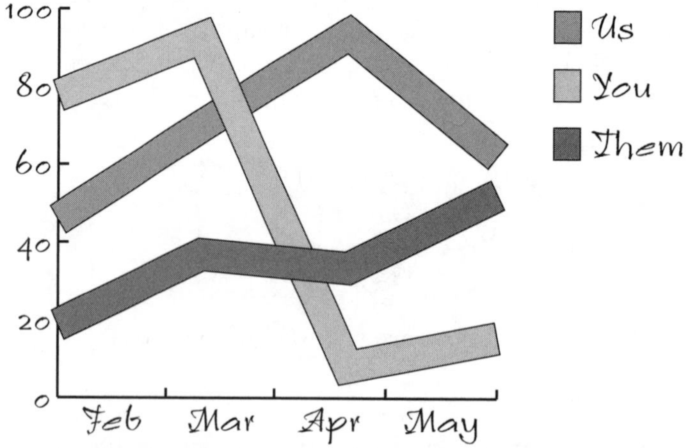

Figure 8-27: A line graph with the Fill Lines check box selected, the Width value set to 12 points, Mark Data Points unselected, and the Edge-To-Edge Lines selected.

Select Edge-to-Edge Lines to draw lines that extend the entire width of the chart, starting at the Y-axis and continuing to the end of the X-axis. This option is turned on in Figure 8-27. (By default, it is off.)

- **Area:** I don't know why, but there are no special options associated with an area chart. I wish Illustrator provided at least the Edge-to-Edge check box to eliminate the gaps between the data lines and the Y-axis; but alas, no such option exists.
- **Scatter:** When you click on the Scatter Graph Type button, three check boxes appear in the Options area. These are the same options that appear for a line graph, as shown in Figure 8-26, except the Edge-to-Edge check box does not appear here.
- **Pie:** When you click this button, the Options area grants you three pop-up menus for editing a pie chart. Pictured in Figure 8-28, these commands let you change the placement of the pie labels (using the Legend pop-up commands), the size of the graphs (using the Position pop-up commands), and the method by which each chart is sorted (using the Sort pop-up commands). By default, the Standard Legend command is selected in the Legend Options pop-up menu, which results in a typical legend that identifies the gray values and colors in the graph. If you instead choose the Legends in Wedges command, Illustrator omits the legend and labels the pie slices directly, as in Figure 8-29. (You'll have to modify the colors of the slices to see the labels, as I have in the figure—the first slice is black by default.) Choose No Legends to trash the legend altogether.

Figure 8-28: You can change the way slices are labeled when editing a pie chart.

The Position Options pop-up menu is oddly named since it offers three commands that have more to do with the size of the pie chart that its position. The Ratio command, the default, causes multiple pies to display according to each pie's total value, as shown in the top left of Figure 8-30. Choose the Even command to make all pies the same size, as shown in the bottom left of Figure 8-30. Finally, you can choose the

Stacked command to display your pies concentrically as a single pie-a-licious chart, shown at the right in Figure 8-30. All three variations in the figure below use the same graph data.

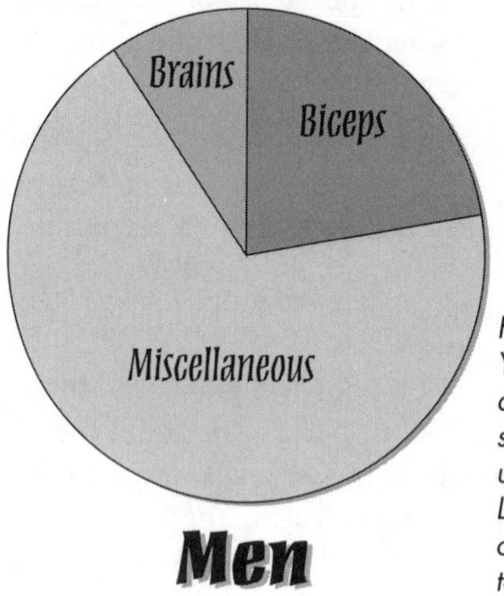

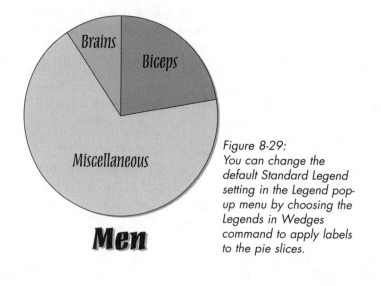

Figure 8-29: You can change the default Standard Legend setting in the Legend pop-up menu by choosing the Legends in Wedges command to apply labels to the pie slices.

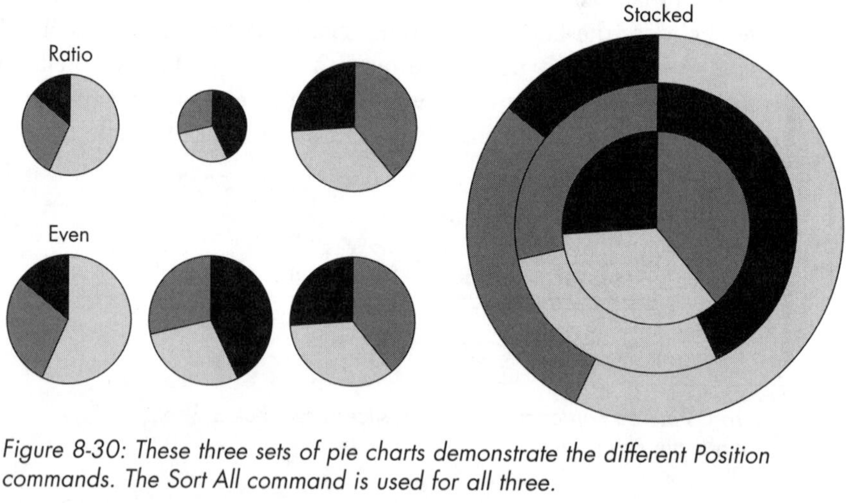

Figure 8-30: These three sets of pie charts demonstrate the different Position commands. The Sort All command is used for all three.

By choosing a command from the Sort Options menu, you can orient the pie chart. Think of the individual pies as "clocks" and the dividing lines between the categories as marking off the time. No matter how you choose to sort a pie chart, one of the dividing lines will point at the 12:00 position, as you can see in Figure 8-31. The piece that extends clockwise from this dividing line is determined by the Sort Options commands. The top-row pie charts result when you choose the Sort All command. The largest piece in each individual pie is the first slice; thus, each pie chart could have a different first piece. The middle-row charts result from you choosing the Sort First command—"Sort by Largest" would be a more appropriate name. When you choose this command, the first piece for all the pies is determined by the category with the largest total value. If you create a pie graph that consists of only one piece, the Sort All and Sort First commands render the same results. The bottom-row charts reflect the usage of the Sort None command—another poorly named command. Here all the pies lead off with the piece that represents the value of the first category (i.e., the first column in the Graph Data window). Once again, all three graphs share the same graph data.

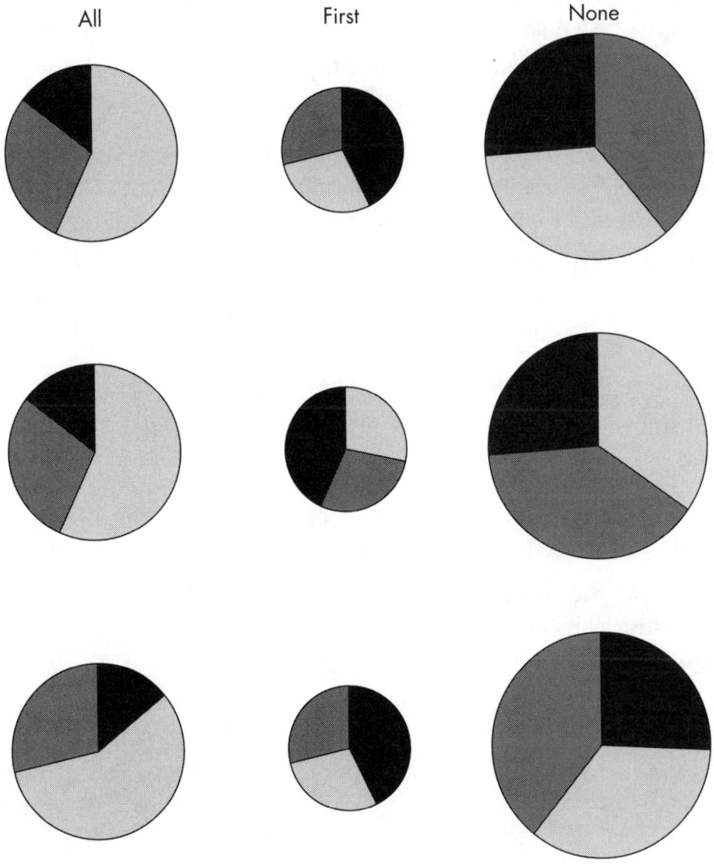

Figure 8-31: Illustrator relies on the Sort Options command to determine which category takes first position in a particular pie chart.

- **Radar:** Click on the Radar button to use all the same options that you'd have with a line chart. Feel free to re-gander Figure 8-26.

Adjusting Axes and Labels

You use the Value Axis pop-up menu located below the buttons in the Graph Type dialog box to control the appearance and positions of the vertical and horizontal axes in a selected chart. This command is dimmed when you're working on a pie chart, since pie charts have no axes, and only one command exists when editing a radar chart. The same basic collection of commands is available for all other charts.

Use the following commands to control the placement of the vertical Y-axis for the column, stacked column, bar, stacked bar, and scatter graphs:

- **On Left Side:** Select this command to make the Y-axis appear on the left side of the chart, as it does by default. You can then modify the axis by choosing the Value Axis command from the main pop-up menu at the top of the Graph Type dialog box.
- **On Right Side:** Select this command to send the Y-axis to the right side of the chart. Again, modify the axis by choosing the Value Axis command. The On Right Side command is not available for scatter graphs.
- **On Both Sides:** Select this command to make the Y-axis appear on both sides of the chart. You can't create a chart with two different Y-axes, as you can in more sophisticated graphing programs.

The bar and stacked bar charts offer two slightly different commands:

- **On Top Side:** Choose this command to make the value axis stretch across the top of the selected graph.
- **On Bottom Side:** Choose this command, the default setting for bar and stacked bar graphs, to extend the value axis along the bottom.

After you have set the position of the value axis, you'll want to explore the other options Illustrator has for your value-axis-modifying pleasures. Choose the Value Axis command from the main pop-up menu at the top of the Graph Type dialog box. One of the Graph Type dialog box's alter egos will display, as shown in Figure 8-32. Here You can specify the location of tick marks and labels on the value axis. The options in the Add Labels and Tick Values areas affect the labels for the value axis, while the options in the Tick Marks area control the size of tick marks, those little lines that indicate numbers along the axes.

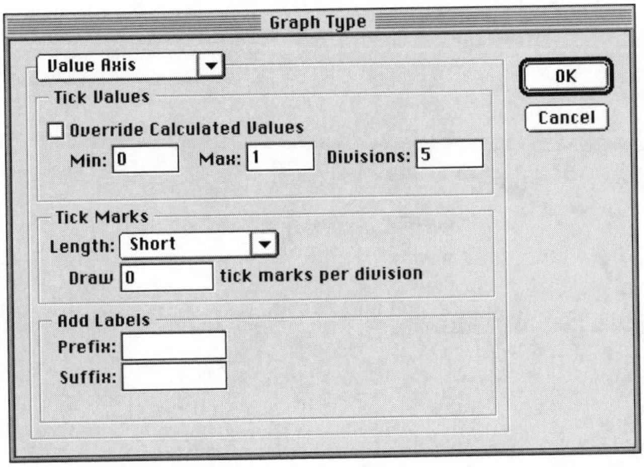

Figure 8-32: Choosing the Value Axis command shuttles you this version of the Graph Type dialog box, in which you can modify labels and tick marks on the value axis.

We first encounter some nutty options related to the occurrence of tick marks:

- **Override Calculated Values:** By default, this check box is selected. Illustrator automatically determines the number of tick marks and labels that appear on the axis without worrying your pretty head about it.
- **Min, Max, and Divisions:** If you want to specify a range of labels in an axis to enhance the appearance of a chart, deselect the Override Calculated Values check box and enter values into the three option boxes. The Min value determines the lowest number on the axis, the Max value determines the highest number, and the Divisions value determines the increment between labels.

  In Figure 8-33, I've raised the Min value to 50 and changed the Divisions value to 10. Illustrator now graphs any data values under 50 below the X-axis. This way, I can track poor performance. For example, this chart tells me I can take Them off probation, but I'm afraid I'm going to have to fire You.

TIP: To turn a chart upside down, so that the highest number is at the bottom of the axis and the lowest number is at the top (as in Figure 8-34), enter a negative value in the Divisions option box. To create an axis without labels, enter 0 in this option box.

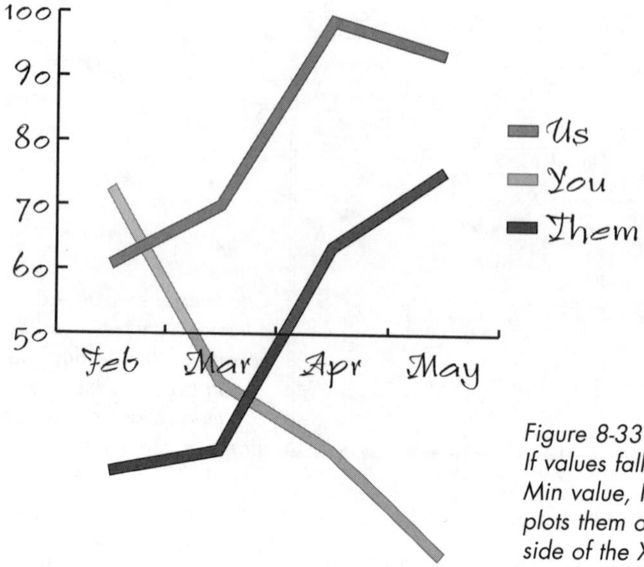

Figure 8-33: If values fall below the Min value, Illustrator plots them on the south side of the X-axis.

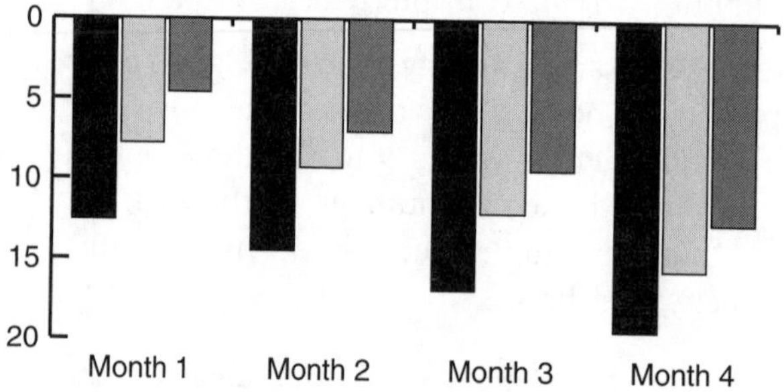

Figure 8-34: Flip a chart upside down by entering a negative value in the Divisions option box.

You use this set of commands to change the tick marks' appearance:

- **Length:** You can choose a length of None, Short, and Full Width for your tick marks from this pop-up menu. Choose None to display no tick marks on the current axis. This command does not affect the placement or appearance of labels. Choose Short to display short tick marks that extend from the axis toward the chart, as by default. Choose Full Width to create tick marks that extend the full width or height of the chart. Figure 8-35 show the result of choosing the Full Width command.
- **Draw __ Tick Marks per Division:** This option should read "Tick Marks per Label," because it allows you to control the number of tick

marks per labeled increment. In Figure 8-36, I've applied a value of 4 to the vertical axis, which creates four tick marks per label.

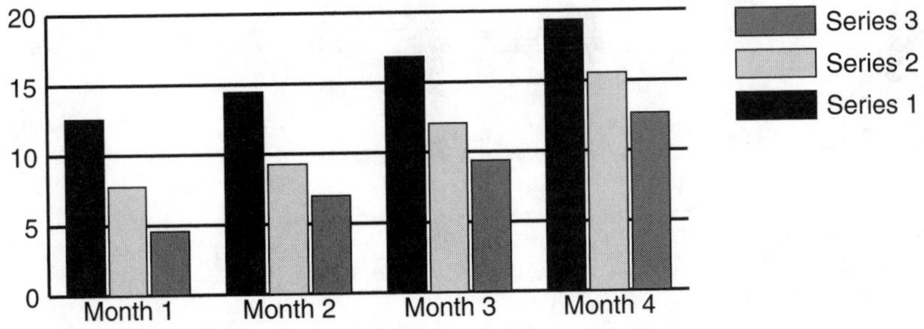

Figure 8-35: Select the Full Width command to extend the tick marks across the entire chart.

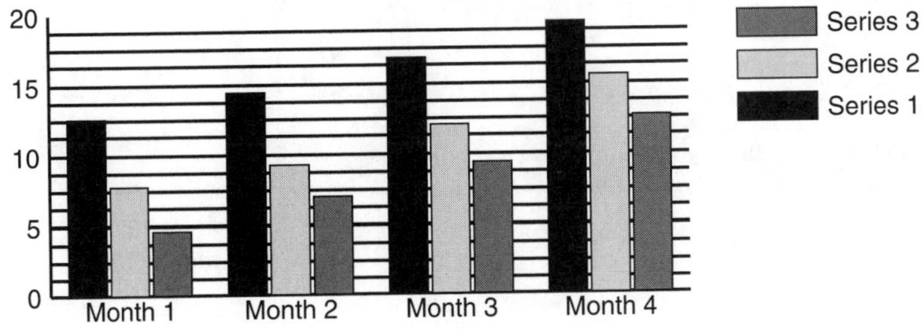

Figure 8-36: The same chart after entering a value of 4 into the Draw __ Tick Marks per Division option box.

You use these options to add labels to a chart:

- **Add Labels Prefix/Suffix:** These option boxes let you enter symbols or words up to nine characters long to precede or follow each label in a chart. For example, enter $ in the Prefix option box to precede every label with a dollar sign, as shown in Figure 8-37. Enter the letter g in the Suffix option box to indicate that each value is in thousands of dollars.

Now that you've perfected your value axis, choose the Category Axis command from the main pop-up menu at the top of the Graph Type dialog box and display the other version of this dialog box, as shown in Figure 8-38. Choose this command, that is, provided you aren't editing a radar chart or a scatter graph. With a radar graph, you're limited to the Value Axis options (as discussed above) and with a scatter chart, you get the Bottom Axis command that takes you to a dialog box with the exact options list above.

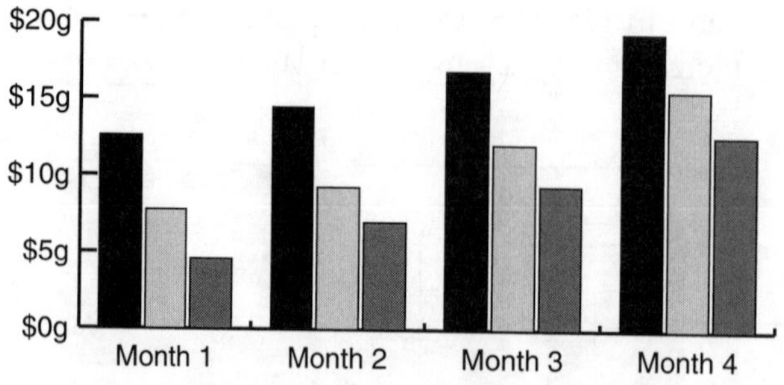

Figure 8-37: Enter characters to precede and follow the labels, such as the $ and g shown here, using the Prefix and Suffix option boxes.

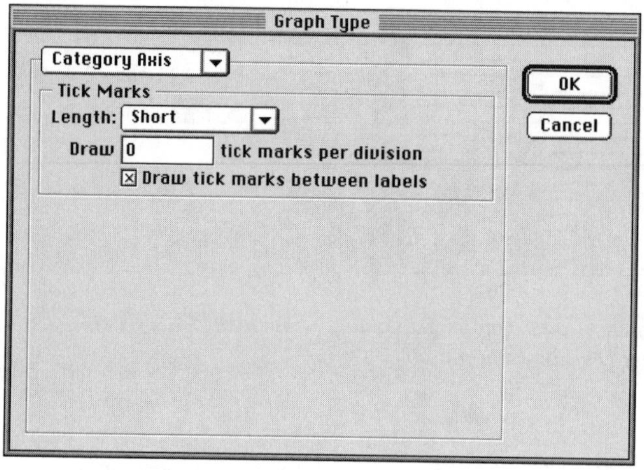

Figure 8-38: Choose the Category Axis command to open this mostly empty version of the Graph Type dialog box, where you can change the tick marks on the category axis.

The Tick Marks Length and the Draw __ Tick Marks per Division options that you see here are the same as the ones first shown back in Figure 8-32. You'll find one new option here:

- **Draw Tick Marks Between Labels:** When this check box is selected—as it is by default—tick marks appear centered between labels, as demonstrated by the vertical lines in the leftmost example of Figure 8-39. If you turn off the option, each tick mark is centered above its label, as shown in the rightmost example of Figure 8-39.

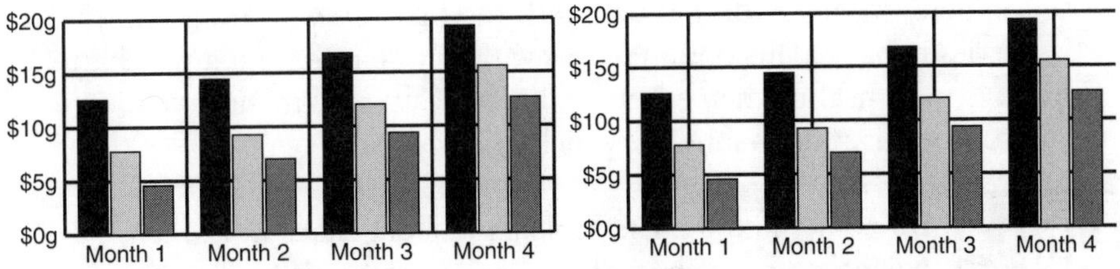

Figure 8-39: When working on a column, bar, line, or area chart, deselect the Draw Tick Lines Between Labels check box to create tick marks directly above the labels along the horizontal axis, as seen in the example on the right.

Other Weird Graph Style Options

Now that we've polished off the Value Axis and the Category Axis versions of the Graph Type dialog box, let's return to the plain and tall Graph Type dialog box (shown in Figure 8-23) to explore four remaining options, all of which are more or less useless. I speak, of course, of the Style check boxes in the middle portion of the dialog box—Add Drop Shadow, Add Legend Across Top, First Row in Front, and First Column in Front. These dorky options work as follows:

- **Add Drop Shadow:** Select this check box to create drop shadows behind the columns, bars, lines, pie slices, or areas in a chart. This option is easily one of the dopiest in all of Illustrator. The drop shadow is always black, and you can't modify the distance between the shadow and the graph elements. You can more easily create your own drop shadow by selecting a few elements, copying them (⌘-C), pasting them in back (⌘-B), nudging them into the desired position with the arrow keys, and applying a fill color.
- **Add Legend across Top:** This option moves the legend from the right side of the chart to the top of the chart. The text is listed horizontally instead of vertically. Unfortunately, Illustrator has a nasty habit of overlapping text when you select this option, particularly when more than three series are involved. You're better off moving the legend manually.
- **First Row in Front:** Select this check box to layer elements representing rows of data in the selected chart in descending order, with the first row in front and the last row in back. This option is useful only when modifying a column or bar chart in which the Cluster Width is set to greater than 100 percent. Because each row of data equates to a cluster, you can modify which cluster appears in front and which appears in back.
- **First Column in Front:** Finally, a halfway useful option! Select this option to layer elements representing columns of data (we're talking

series, here) in descending order, with the first series in front and the last series in back. This option works with any chart except a pie chart. But it is most useful when editing a line or scatter chart, since it allows you to prioritize the manner in which lines overlap.

Do not turn off the First Column in Front check box when editing an area chart. If you do, the last series will completely cover all other series in the chart.

Manually Customizing a Graph

If you've been reading this chapter sequentially, your brain is undoubtedly a little numb by now. Either that, or you've been reading the book in bed in lieu of a sedative. I mean, let's face it, taking in Illustrator's half million graphing options is a daunting—not to mention boring—task.

That's why it may come as a welcome shock that one tool—the direct selection tool—is more capable than every option in all the Graph Type dialog boxes combined. Armed with the direct selector, you can move elements around, apply different colors, edit the size of text and legend swatches, and just plain customize the heck out of your graph.

Selecting Elements Inside Graphs

To get anywhere with the direct selection tool, you need to understand how to select elements inside a graph. A graph is actually an extensive collection of grouped objects inside grouped objects, inside other grouped objects, which are—needless to say—grouped. This means a lot of Option-clicking with the direct selection tool.

The following list demonstrates a few of the different kinds of selections you can make with the direct selection tool:

- Click on a point or segment in the graph to select that specific element. You can then move the point or segment. However, you cannot delete it by pressing the Delete key, since this would leave a gap in the path, and Illustrator does not permit gaps in graphs.
- Click on a text object to select it. All text in a graph is point text, so be sure to click along the baseline of the text (not on one of the letters).

You can then change the font, type size, alignment, and half a dozen other formatting attributes without affecting any deselected text in the graph.

- Option-click to select a whole object in the chart, such as an axis or a column.
- Option-click a second time to select an entire axis, including tick marks and labels, or to select an entire series. If you Option-click a second time on some text, you select all text belonging to that subgroup in the graph. For example, Option-clicking twice on some legend text selects all legend text.
- Option-click a third time on a column to select an entire series as well as its color swatch in the legend. Now you can apply a different color from the Paint Style palette to modify the fill or stroke of the series.
- Option-click a fourth time to select all series and legend swatches in the chart.
- Option-click a fifth time to select the entire chart.

This is a rather imprecise science, and different kinds of charts require a different number of Option-clicks, depending on how many series are involved and other factors. For example, you may find you need to Option-click only twice to select a series and its legend swatch in a line chart, while you had to Option-click three times in a column chart. Keep an eye on the screen as you Option-click to monitor your progress.

Selecting Multiple Series Inside a Graph

Another handy key to keep in mind when selecting graph elements is Shift. As you know, you can press this key to select multiple objects, but pressing it just as easily deselects objects. Therefore, you have to be deliberate in your actions, particularly when the Option key is involved.

For example, suppose you want to select two series of columns in a column chart, including their swatches in the legend. Here's how you'd do it:

1. **Using the direct selection tool, Option-click on a column in the chart.**

   This selects the column.

2. **Option-click on the column again.**

   This second click selects all other columns in the series.

3. **Option-click on the column a third time.**

   Now the legend swatch becomes selected.

4. **Shift-Option-click on a column in a different series.**

   Illustrator adds this new column to the growing collection of selected objects.

5. **Option-click on that same column again.**

   This is the important step, the one that baffles thousands of users on a daily basis. If you Shift-Option-click again, you deselect the column; but without the Shift key, you can't add to the selection, right?

   Wrong. So long as the item on which you Option-click is selected, Illustrator broadens the selection to include the next group up. Therefore, this Option-click selects the other columns in this series.

6. **Option-click a third time on this column.**

   This selects the swatch for the series in the legend. You now have two entire series of columns selected independently of any other series in the graph.

It's operations like this that make users of other programs, including FreeHand, roll their eyes and utter nasty comments. Not that FreeHand has a better method for dealing with this situation—FreeHand doesn't even offer a graphing function—it's just that Illustrator's methods seem so complicated.

But the truth is, this operation makes absolute sense once you understand the order of the Illustrator universe. These steps may be cumbersome, but they are impeccably logical. Come to terms with these steps and you'll never have problems selecting objects inside Illustrator again. The good news is, it simply doesn't get more complicated than this.

TIP

What good is selecting a couple of series in a chart? I'll tell you. You can switch selected series to a different chart type, as in Figure 8-40. This chart started off as a column chart, but I wanted to highlight my client's product, hand buzzers. Therefore, I decided to convert the sea monkeys and x-ray specs series to line graphs. I first selected both series, as outlined in the previous steps, and double-clicked on the graph tool to display the Graph Type dialog box. I then selected the Line button from the Type options, modified the Line Graph Options, and pressed Return.

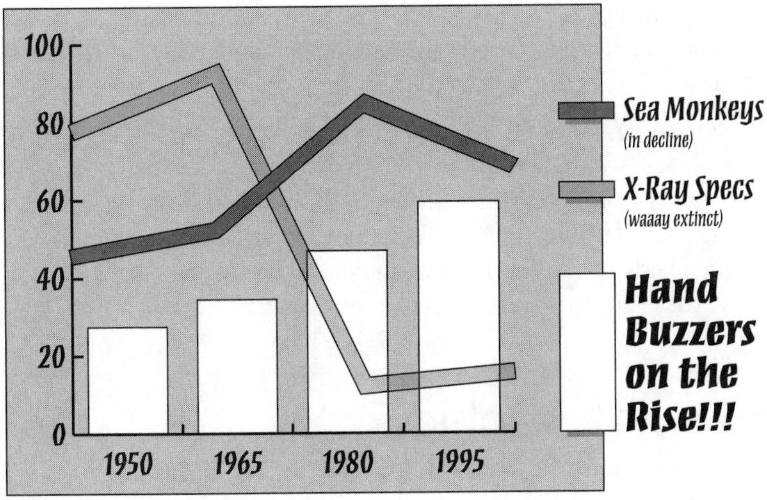

Figure 8-40: Starting from a column chart, I converted two of the series to line graphs.

Obviously, I didn't stop there. In fact, I ended up ungrouping the graph to achieve some of the effects. To create the faded intersection between the x-ray specs line and the hand buzzer columns, I cloned the shapes and combined them using Filter » Pathfinder » Intersect, as explained in Chapter 9. I also added drop shadows behind the legend swatches, another technique covered in Chapter 9. Like any other kind of art you can create in Illustrator, graphs are limited only by your creativity, ingenuity, and patience.

More Custom Modification Options

Once you figure out how to select items in graphs with some degree of predictability, you'll discover hundreds of methods for altering them. Rather than wasting reams of paper stepping you through every possible variation, I offer a few parting tidbits of wisdom to whisk you on your way:

- One of the first things I edit after creating a graph is the legend. I hate where Illustrator puts this thing, and I hate how big it is. The text and swatches in the legend are parts of several different subgroups, but because they are physically separated from other graph elements, you can easily select them by marqueeing them with the direct selection tool. Then you can drag them anywhere you want or use the scale tool to reduce their size.

- You can edit text inside a graph with the type tool, as I did in Figure 8-40. But be careful; if you have to go back later and edit the data, Illustrator restores the text entered into the Graph Data window. (Unfortunately, Illustrator is not smart enough to implement your text changes into the spreadsheet automatically.)
- You can edit paths inside a graph with the add point, delete point, and convert point tools without first ungrouping the path. Again, changes that you made inside the Graph Data window or Graph Type dialog box may override these adjustments.

Graphing with Graphics

What kind of illustration program would Illustrator be if it didn't allow you to create graphs with pictures? In a valiant effort to satisfy you, the customer, Illustrator lets you create pictographs, which are graphs in which series are represented by graphic objects. The graphics can form columns in a column chart, like the cent symbols in Figure 8-41, or they can appear as markers in a line or scatter chart. The following sections describe how pictographs work.

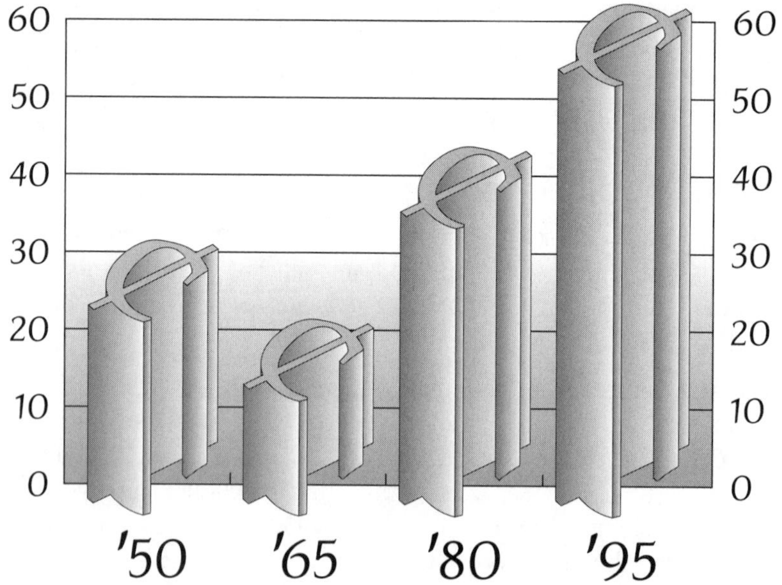

Figure 8-41: Using Illustrator's pictograph feature, you can create graph designs and apply them to column, bar, line, and scatter graphs.

Creating a Graph Design

You create pictographs by establishing graph designs—collections of graphic objects that can be applied to a chart. The following steps describe how to transform a few common, everyday objects into a graph design in Illustrator:

1. **Draw the objects and fill them as desired.**

   Figure 8-42 shows how I constructed the objects in the cent chart. Many of the tools and commands I used are covered in later chapters.

   I started with a large Palatino character (Option-4 for ¢) and converted it to paths (example 1 in the figure). Then I rotated and slanted it with the rotate and shear tools (2). Next I selected several points and segments along the outline of the shape by clicking and Shift-clicking at the spots indicated by the arrowheads in the figure (3). I copied the selected elements to the Clipboard (⌘-C), pressed ⌘-Shift-A to deselect the elements, and chose Edit » Paste in Front (⌘-F).

   I dragged the selected items down to a point at which I could more easily work on them. Then I Shift-Option-dragged them downward to clone them (4). These open paths represent the tops and bottoms of the sides coming down from the cent sign back in Figure 8-41; all I had to do was connect them with straight segments. To do this, I used the direct selection tool to select the endpoints of corresponding paths (like the selected points in example 4 in the figure) and chose Object » Path » Join (⌘-J). Then I Option-clicked on the newly joined path with the direct selection tool to select the whole path and pressed ⌘-J again. I repeated this for each pair of paths.

   Finally, I selected all the paths (except the cent itself) and filled them with gradations from the Gradient palette (5). I also had to fill the interior of the cent sign with a gradation, but because the path was serving as a hole in the cent sign, I had to make a duplicate. I selected it, copied it (⌘-C), pressed ⌘-Shift-A to deselect everything, and pasted the path in front (⌘-F). Then I filled it with the same gradation as the other paths. To finish it off, I dragged the sides up to the cent outline so sides and cent snapped into alignment.

2. **Draw a straight, horizontal line across the middle of the portion of the graph you want Illustrator to elongate when applying the design to a column chart.**

   If you're designing a marker for a line graph, you don't need to add this horizontal line, and you can skip to Step 4.

Use the pen tool to draw a horizontal line slightly wider than the graph design by clicking at one point and Shift-clicking at another. Then position the line along the spot where any stretching should occur. For example, I created the line in about the middle of the sides of the cent symbol, as indicated by the dotted line in Figure 8-43. Doing this tells Illustrator to stretch the sides, not the cent symbol itself.

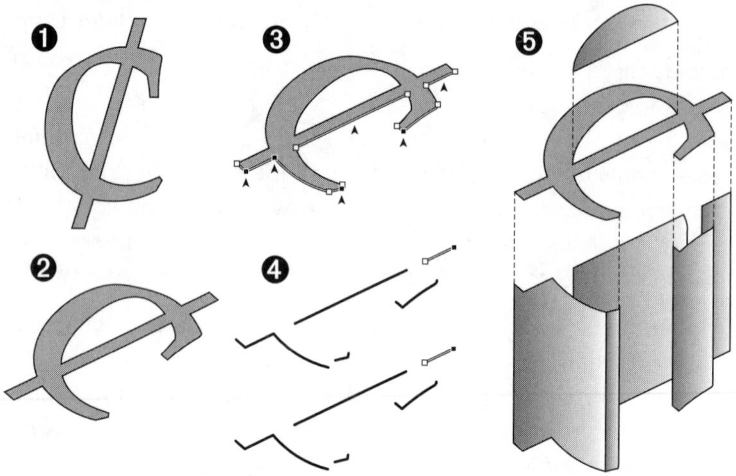

Figure 8-42: The steps involved in creating a cent symbol with mock 3-D sides.

3. **Select the horizontal line and choose View » Make Guides.**

   Or press the memorable shortcut ⌘-5. (That's, I say, that's sarcasm, my boy.) The line becomes dotted (or solid, depending on the settings in your Guides & Grids Preferences dialog box), as pictured in Figure 8-43. Also, make sure View » Lock Guides is turned off. If the Lock command has a check mark next to it, choose the command to unlock the guide. Illustrator requires that you convert the line to a guide for the stretching function to work. (For more about guides, turn to Chapter 10.)

4. **Draw a rectangle to specify the boundaries of the graph design.**

   Where graphs are concerned, Illustrator thinks largely in terms of rectangles. Columns are rectangles, for example, and line graph markers are squares. When creating a graph design, you have to tell Illustrator how the design fits onto the standard rectangle.

Use the rectangle tool to draw a boundary around the graph design as I have done in Figure 8-43. If the rectangle doesn't completely enclose the design, the design may overlap graph elements. For example, my design extends below the rectangle; therefore it will overlap the X-axis, as it does back in Figure 8-41. The design also extends over the top of the rectangle, so it will rise slightly higher than the data value. (If you're feeling very strict about your data, make sure the top of the rectangle exactly touches the top of the graph design.) The fact that the rectangle is wider than the design, however, keeps the design slightly slimmer than a standard column.

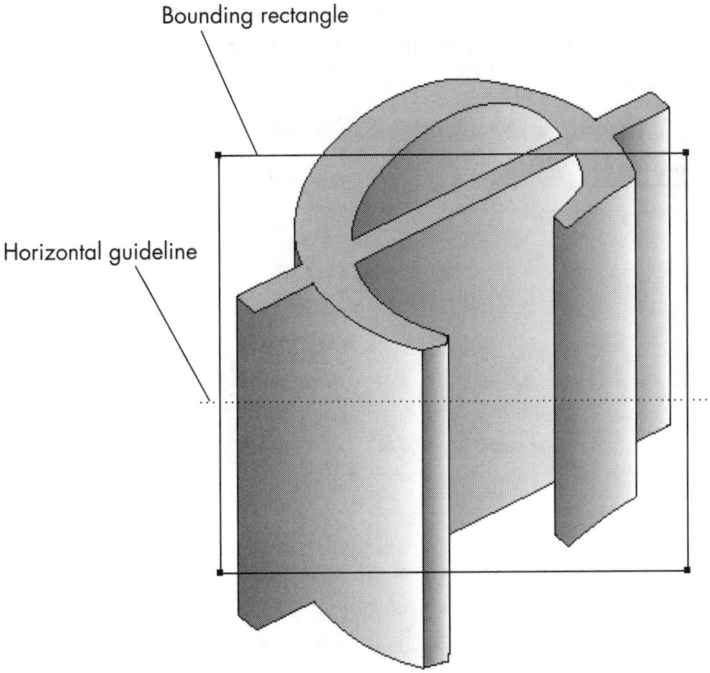

Figure 8-43: Draw a horizontal guideline across the stretchy portion of the graph design, and then create a rectangle to demonstrate the design's boundaries.

5. Send the rectangle to the back of the illustration.

Choose Object » Arrange » Send To Back, or press ⌘-Shift-[(left bracket). This may sound like an inconsequential step, but it's very important. Illustrator insists on the boundary rectangle being in back.

6. Make the fill and stroke transparent.

Select the None icon in the toolbox.

7. Select all graph objects and choose Object » Graphs » Design.

Select the graph design, horizontal guide, and rectangle. (If these are the only objects in the illustration, press ⌘-A.) Then choose Object » Graphs » Design to display the Graph Design dialog box shown in Figure 8-44.

8. Click on the New Design button.

Illustrator shows you a preview of the graph design cropped inside your bounding rectangle, as in Figure 8-44. (Don't worry, the actual graph design is not cropped.) The program also adds an item to the scrolling list called New Design, followed by a number.

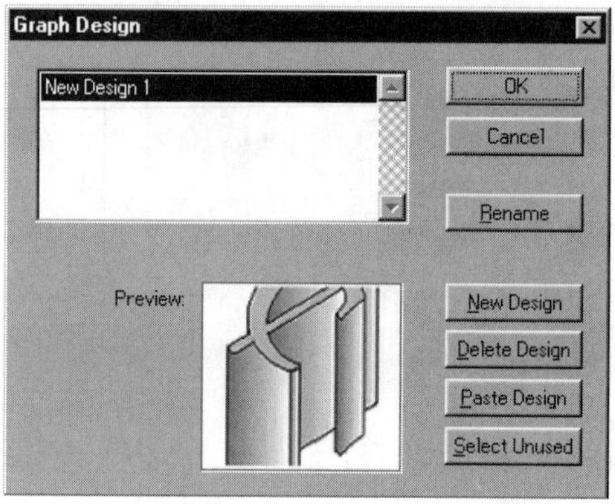

Figure 8-44: Illustrator crops the preview in the Graph Design dialog box to reflect the top and bottom edges of the bounding rectangle.

If Illustrator complains when you click on New Design, it's because the rectangle is not the backmost object you've selected. It may be because you didn't properly follow Step 5, or it may be that you accidentally selected other objects farther back yet. In any case, press Escape to close the dialog box, press ⌘-Shift-A to deselect everything, select the rectangle, cut it (⌘-X), make sure the arrow tool is active, and paste the rectangle in back (⌘-B). Now try Steps 7 and 8 again.

9. Enter a name for the design and press Return.

The graph design is now ready to apply to any column, bar, line, or scatter graph.

TIP

Your new graph design is available to all other open illustrations. But if you close the illustration in which you created the graph design before applying it to a chart, the design is no longer available. If you want to make a graph design available to all future illustrations whether this particular document is open or not, open the Adobe Illustrator Startup file in the Plug-ins folder. Then choose Object » Graphs » Design to display the Graph Design dialog box, and click on the Paste Design button. This creates a copy of the design inside the Startup file. Press Return to leave the dialog box, move the design to a suitable spot in the illustration window (but don't delete it!), and save the Startup file to disk.

Organizing Graph Designs

In addition to allowing you to create new graph designs, the Graph Design dialog box provides the following options for organizing and editing existing graph designs:

- **Delete Design:** Click on this button to delete a selected design from the scrolling list. Illustrator removes the design from all open illustrations! Therefore, don't delete a design when a graph using the design is open.

TIP

If you delete a design and you didn't mean to, press Escape or click on the Cancel button to cancel the operation. If you realize your mistake only after pressing Return or clicking on the OK button, you can still restore the graph design by pressing ⌘-Z.

- **Paste Design:** Even if you throw away the original copy of your graph design, it may not be lost for good. So long as the design has been applied to a graph, you can retrieve the original objects. Inside the Graph Design dialog box, select the design name from the list and click on the Paste Design button. Illustrator pastes the original objects into the illustration window. Then press Return to close the dialog box and edit the objects as desired. (If you leave the dialog box by pressing the Escape key, Illustrator cancels the paste operation.)
- **Select Unused:** Click on this button to select all designs that are not applied to graphs in any open illustration. Then you can click on the Delete Design button to get rid of them.

TIP

After you edit the pasted objects, you can redefine the graph design and all open graphs that use the design. Select the objects and choose Object » Graphs » Design. Then select the design name from the list and press Return or click on the OK button. (That's it; no special buttons to press.) Illustrator displays an alert box asking if you want to redraw all graphs or just redefine the graph design for future graphs. Press Return to do both.

You can rename a pattern by clicking on the Rename button. In the Rename dialog box, enter a new name and click on OK or hit Return.

Applying a Design to a Column Chart

To apply a design to a column chart or a stacked column chart, select the column chart with the arrow tool or select the single series that you want to convert to a pictograph with the direct selection tool. Then choose Object » Graphs » Column to display the Graph Column dialog box shown in Figure 8-45.

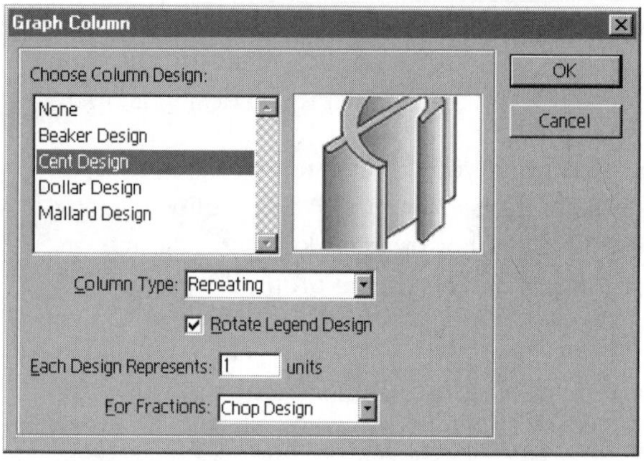

Figure 8-45: Use the Graph Column dialog box to apply a graph design to a column chart.

Select a graph design from the scrolling Choose Column Design list (select None only when you want to remove a graph design from the selected series), choose a command from the Column Type pop-up menu, and press the Return key. Illustrator applies the design to all selected series.

The Column Type pop-up menu allows you to change the way Illustrator stretches or repeats the graph design from one column to the next. Figure 8-46 demonstrates the effect of the four options in the order they appear in the dialog box. Here's how each option works:

- **Vertically Scaled:** Choose this command to stretch the graph design vertically to represent different values, as demonstrated at the top of Figure 8-46. Notice that in the case of the cent symbol, Illustrator stretches both the sides and the cent outline itself. This is sometimes useful, though it's not the best match for my cent design.

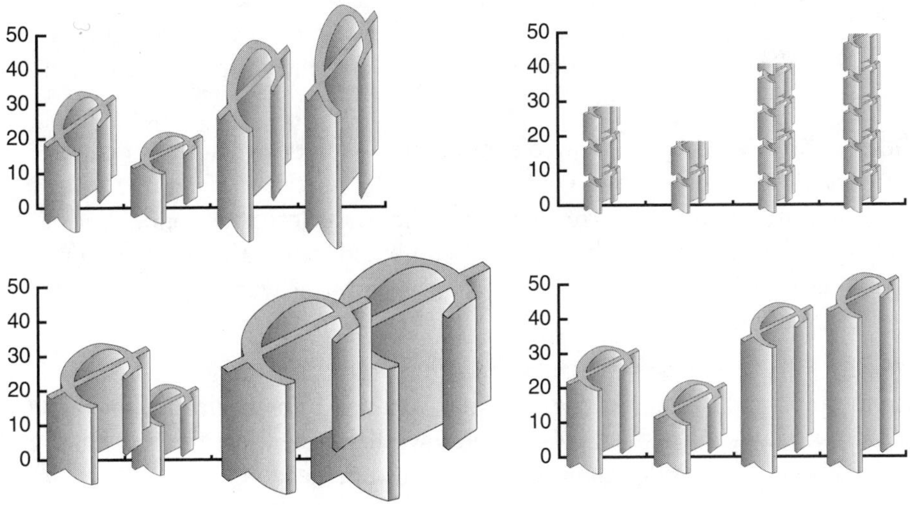

Figure 8-46: The Vertically Scaled (top left), Uniformly Scaled (bottom left), Repeating (top right), and Sliding (bottom right) options change the way Illustrator applies a graph design to a column chart.

- **Uniformly Scaled:** Select this command to scale the graph design proportionally according to the size of the data, as shown in the second example on the left in Figure 8-46. Large values have a tendency to take over the graph; this option is useful primarily when your data has little variation.

- **Repeating:** If you want to repeat the graph design over and over again, choose this command. Illustrator creates stacks of the object, as in the example at the upper right in Figure 8-46. This style of pictograph is very popular—you can stack coins, dollar bills, cars, footballs, computer monitors, little disembodied Newt Gingrich heads...in short, anything you want.

  When the Repeating command is selected, the otherwise-dimmed For Fractions pop-up menu becomes available. Enter a value in the Each Design Represents option box to determine the data increment represented by each repetition of the graph design. For example, if a value in the selected series is 49, and you enter 10 for the Each Design Represents value, the design repeats four full times and a fifth partial time, just like the last column in the figure.

The two For Fractions commands determine how Illustrator slices or scales the last graph design to accommodate remaining data that doesn't divide evenly into the Each Design Represents value. Select the Chop Design command to lop off the extraneous top design, as in Figure 8-46; select the Scale Design command to vertically scale the top design to fit its fractional value.

- **Sliding:** Select this option to elongate the graph design at the spot indicated by the horizontal guideline, as in the final example at the lower right in Figure 8-46. This is usually the most desirable option, and it certainly looks the best when combined with the cent design. Illustrator stretches the sides of the design but leaves the cent symbol itself unmolested.

Select the Rotate Legend Design check box to display the graph design on its side in the legend. (I omitted the legend in Figure 8-46 by neglecting to enter any column headings in the Graph Data window.) If you deselect the Rotate Legend Design check box, the design appears upright in the legend.

Applying a Design to a Line Chart

To apply a design to a line or scatter chart, select the graph with the arrow tool or select the specific markers you want to change with the direct selection tool. (Do not select the line segments.) Then choose Object » Graphs » Marker, which brings to life the Graph Marker dialog box shown in Figure 8-47.

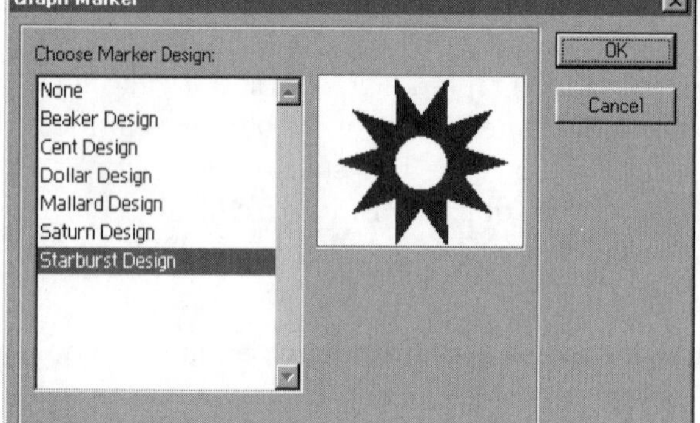

Figure 8-47: Use the Graph Marker dialog box to apply a graph design to the markers in a line or scatter chart.

Select a graph design from the scrolling Marker Design list and press Return. Illustrator applies the graph design to the individual markers in the chart.

To create Figure 8-48, I Option-clicked twice on one set of markers with the direct selection tool to select all the markers in one series, and then I applied the starburst graph design. I then Option-clicked twice on the other set of markers and applied the Saturn design.

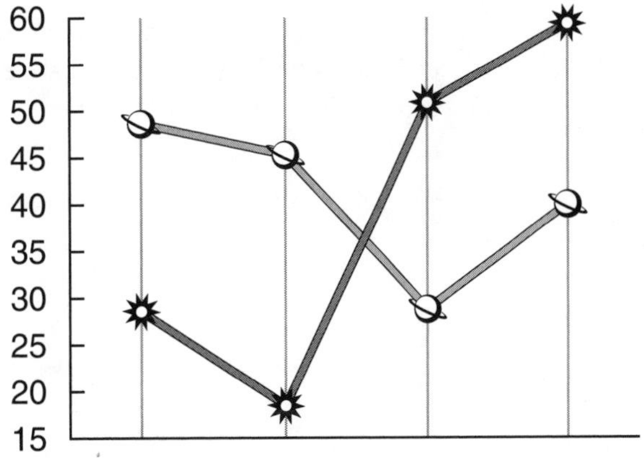

Figure 8-48: I applied two different sets of graph designs to the markers of a line graph.

Illustrator determines the size of a graph design based on the size of the bounding rectangle that you drew when defining the original graph design. The bounding rectangle is reduced to match the size of the square marker that normally appears in a line or scatter chart. Therefore, to create a design that scales to a reasonable size, draw a relatively small bounding rectangle. Figure 8-49 shows the bounding rectangles as dotted outlines for the starburst and Saturn patterns.

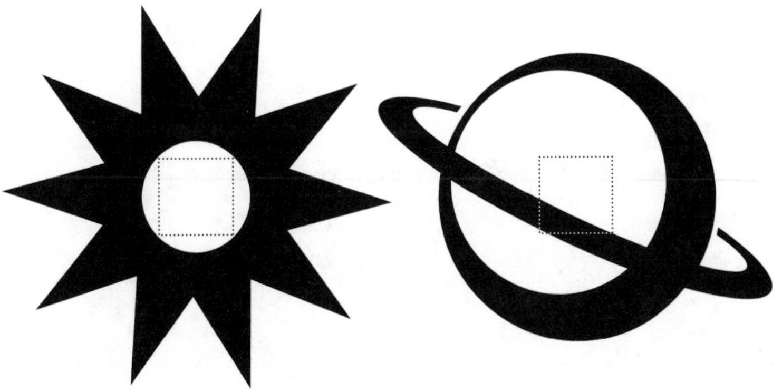

Figure 8-49: I created small bounding rectangles to make the graph designs appear large in the line graph in Figure 8-48.

If you don't like how large Illustrator draws the markers and you don't feel like going back and messing around with the original graph designs, you can scale them on the fly by choosing Object » Transform » Transform Each. Option-click on one of the markers three times to select the entire series—or four times to select all markers—and choose Object » Transform » Transform Each. Then enter values larger than 100 percent into the Horizontal and Vertical option boxes and press Return. (To scale the markers proportionally, make sure the Horizontal and Vertical values are identical.)

PART THREE
CHANGING

CHAPTER 9

MODIFYING AND COMBINING PATHS

Now that you've had the opportunity to create every kind of object available to Illustrator, it's time to talk in earnest about messing these objects up. This chapter specifically discusses how to edit paths created with the drawing tools covered in Chapters 4 and 5. You can clone paths to create copies, join paths together and hack them apart, and carve transparent holes in otherwise filled paths.

As the pièce de résistance, you can combine simple paths into highly intricate ones using an assortment of so-called Pathfinder filters. Though indisputably some of Illustrator's most enigmatic capabilities—many artists I've talked to are only vaguely aware that they exist—the Pathfinder filters can easily cut your drawing time in half if you'll only invest the time to learn them.

With the exception of cloning, you can't apply the operations covered in this chapter to text unless you first convert the characters to paths using Type » Create Outlines (⌘-Shift-O). And you can edit elements inside graphs only if you first ungroup the graphs by pressing ⌘-Shift-G or by choosing Object » Ungroup.

NOTE: In fact, you'll have to ungroup portions of the graph more than once to break apart the nested groups. To be sure, press ⌘-Shift-G four times to ungroup every single object in the graph. Or you can simply wait and see if Illustrator complains when you try to perform an operation; if it does, press ⌘-Shift-G and try again.

One Million Ways to Replicate

While creating a pencil sketch on paper, you have to draw each pencil stroke from scratch. Then you have to trace pen strokes, add colors, and otherwise embellish the artwork—again, one stroke at a time—to convert the sketch into a usable illustration. Not so in Illustrator. Certainly, you have to draw many paths from scratch, but you can also duplicate paths and reshape or combine them to create different lines and shapes. It's like having an artistic replicator within easy reach. Each path that you create or reshape becomes fresh grist for the mill.

Adobe understands the benefits of duplicating paths, which is why it has blessed Illustrator with so many techniques for cloning and copying. Each of these is useful in different situations, as I explain in the following sections. If you aren't already familiar with these techniques, study these sections carefully and commit the techniques to memory. Those poor souls who don't understand duplication miss out on one of the keys factors that gives Illustrator the edge over the common household pencil.

If you think you know pretty much everything about duplication already, at least skim the next few sections. I'm confident that you'll pick up a handful of techniques that you never heard of, had forgotten, or hadn't considered in quite this context. I'm equally confident you'll find a way to put these new techniques to work in the very near future. Simply put, duplication is one of those areas with which you can't be too familiar.

Plain Old Copying and Pasting

Most folks are familiar with the Clipboard, which is a portion of memory set aside to hold objects that you want to duplicate or transfer to another program. It's kind of like the Memory button on a calculator. You store something one minute and retrieve it the next.

I've discussed a few Clipboard techniques in previous chapters, and I'll continue to sprinkle in more later on. But now's a good time for an overview of the three most fundamental Clipboard commands: Cut, Copy, and Paste.

- You can copy selected objects to the Clipboard by pressing ⌘-C (or choosing Edit » Copy). To remove the selected objects from the illustration and send them to the Clipboard, press ⌘-X (Edit » Cut).
- Press ⌘-V (Edit » Paste) to retrieve the objects from the Clipboard. Illustrator pastes the objects in the center of the illustration window and selects them so that you can immediately set about manipulating them.
- After pasting, the objects remain in the Clipboard until the next time you press ⌘-C or ⌘-X. Both commands shove out the old contents of the Clipboard and bring in the new.

You might be thinking, "I understand ⌘-C for Copy, but why ⌘-X for Cut and ⌘-V for Paste?" You've no doubt heard colleagues speculate that the X looks like a pair of scissors or that the V stands for vomit, but these suggestions lack the ring of truth. It's very simple, really. The first few commands in the Edit menu are assigned the first few keys along the bottom row of the keyboard. ⌘-Z, X, C, and V activate Undo, Cut, Copy, and Paste, respectively. It's like this for all Mac applications and most Windows programs.

NOTE

Illustrator also adds neighboring keys D, F, and B to the duplication family—⌘-D for Transform Again, ⌘-F for Paste In Front, and ⌘-B for Paste In Back, as in Figure 9-1. I explain these commands in an upcoming section, but for now, just keep in mind that the lower left corner of the keyboard is where the duplication action is.

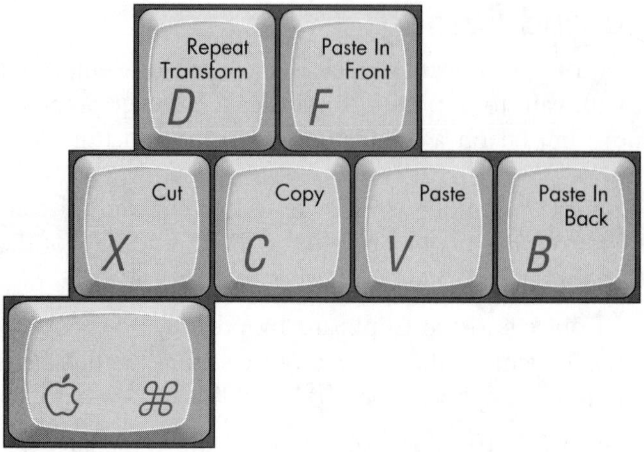

Figure 9-1: Ever notice that all of Illustrator's duplication shortcut keys are clustered in one corner of the keyboard? Coincidence or alien intervention? You decide.

Pasting Paths into Other Programs

You can also use the Clipboard to hold objects that you want to transport to another program. For example, you can copy paths from Illustrator and place them inside, say, a PageMaker document using the standard Copy and Paste commands.

Illustrator always adds a PostScript description of its paths to the Clipboard. (This is why you may get the message "Converting Clipboard to EPS (AICB) format" when you switch out of Illustrator.) Adobe calls this feature PostScript on the Clipboard, and most of Adobe's other products support it, including the most recent versions of Photoshop, PageMaker, and PageMill (the World Wide Web page-layout utility).

If a program does not support PostScript on the Clipboard (older versions of Microsoft Word, for example, are completely ignorant on this and many other subjects), pasting an Illustrator graphic produces the placeholder shown in Figure 9-2. The graphic may print correctly to a PostScript printer—though I wouldn't place money on it—but it sure as heck won't look right on screen.

Figure 9-2: If you see this after pasting paths inside another program, you'll know that the program you're using doesn't fully support PostScript on the Clipboard.

TIP

On the Mac, you can transfer Illustrator objects to a PostScript-stupid program by pressing the Option key when choosing Edit » Copy inside Illustrator (or press ⌘-Option-C). This instructs Illustrator to copy PICT versions of the paths to the Clipboard. Then you can paste them in Word or any other program that supports PICT by pressing ⌘-V as usual. (You can also press ⌘-Option-C to avoid Clipboard errors when transferring paths between Illustrator and Photoshop, as I discuss in Chapter 13.)

Creating Clones

The Clipboard isn't the only means for copying paths and segments in Illustrator. In fact, you can completely bypass the Clipboard—and leave the contents of the Clipboard intact—by dragging a path and pressing the Option key. This technique is called cloning.

To clone a path, select it with the arrow or direct selection tool, drag the path, press and hold the Option key in mid drag, release the mouse button, and release Option. It's very important to press the Option key after you start to drag, since Option-clicking with the direct selection tool selects whole paths and groups. And you have to keep Option pressed until after you release the mouse button to create the clone. So again: drag, press Option, release the mouse button, and release Option.

Illustrator positions the clone just in front of the original path. If you clone multiple shapes, Illustrator positions the clones in front of the foremost original. If the original paths lie behind other paths—which were not cloned—the clones lie in back of these paths as well. No big deal, of course; these are merely nuances of cloning that I think you should be aware of.

NOTE

You can also use the Option key with the scale, rotate, reflect, and shear tools to clone a path while transforming it. Chapter 11 tells all there is to know on the subject.

Nudge and Clone

You might think that you could nudge and clone a path by pressing Option with an arrow key. And, provided you do not have any text or text block selected, this is exactly what you can do.

Before version 8, if you wanted to nudge and clone, you had to press ⌘, Shift, and Option, plus one of the arrow keys. But, thankfully, them annoying days are gone. Now you simply select the path and press Option-arrow key. This clones the path and moves it in the direction indicated by the amount specified in the Cursor Key option box of the General Preferences fame. This is a useful way to create clones that are evenly spaced from their originals.

If a text block is selected or if any of the selected paths contain text, you can press Option-arrow key to change the text's leading or tracking as reflected in the Character palette. If you wish to nudge and clone the path of a text block without affecting the text, select the path by Option-clicking it with the direct selection tool and then press Option-arrow key. Keep in mind that if the path you are cloning contains text within its borders, the new path is linked to the original path and will automatically fill with any text that does not fit inside the original. You may recall that this work just like the techniques discussed in the "Flowing Text from One Shape to Another" section of Chapter 7. On the other hand, if the path you are cloning includes text that flows around the perimeter, the new path is completely independent of the original path.

To nudge and clone the path a considerably further distance from the original, press Option-Shift-arrow key. This moves a path ten times the amount entered in the Cursor Key option box.

Cloning Partial Paths

If you Option-drag or Option-arrow key a path in which all points are selected, Illustrator clones the entire path. But you also can clone individual points and segments that you've selected with the direct selection tool. In fact, Illustrator was the first drawing program for the Mac that let you duplicate bits and pieces of a path. This precise control over partial paths is one of the primary ingredients that distinguishes a professional-level program like Illustrator from the greater midrange morass.

Figure 9-3 shows what happens when you clone a single segment independent of the rest of the path. If you Option-drag a straight segment (or press Option-arrow key when the segment is selected), you clone the segment at a new location, as demonstrated in the two left-hand examples in the figure. If you clone a curved segment, you stretch the segment and leave its points at their original positions, as in the right-hand examples.

Figure 9-3: Option-drag a straight segment (top left) to move and clone the segment (bottom left). Option-drag a curved segment (top right) to stretch and clone the segment (bottom right).

Figure 9-4: Option-drag selected points (top examples) to clone all segments connected to those points (bottom).

When dragging or nudging one or more selected points, you clone the points as well as any segments connected to those points. Whether straight or curved, each segment between a selected point and a deselected point stretches to keep up with the drag, as Figure 9-4 illustrates.

Copying in Place

The problem with Option-dragging partial paths, therefore, is that doing so almost always results in distortions. You can Option-drag a straight segment without changing it, but you stretch segments when you clone curved segments or selected points.

This is why so many experienced Illustrator artists duplicate partial paths using the Copy and Paste In Front commands. By simply pressing ⌘-C followed by ⌘-F (Edit » Paste In Front), you can copy one or more selected points and segments to the Clipboard and then paste them directly in front of their originals. No stretching, no distortion; Illustrator pastes the paths just as they were copied.

Also worth noting, the Paste In Front command positions the pasted paths at the same spot where they were copied. (By contrast, Edit » Paste positions the paths in the middle of the illustration window, regardless of the placement of the originals.) Therefore, ⌘-C, ⌘-F creates a copy in place.

NOTE

Edit » Paste In Back (⌘-B) works just like the Paste In Front command, except that it pastes the copied paths in back of the selected elements. Unless you specifically want to change the stacking order of objects (as explained in Chapter 10), Paste In Front is usually preferable, since it permits you to easily select and edit paths after you paste them. With Paste In Back, some path or other undoubtedly covers the pasted paths, making them difficult to access.

Cloning in Place

TIP

You can also create a quick duplicate directly on top of the original by pressing Option-↑ followed by the ↓ key. This creates a clone and then nudges it back into place.

Perhaps this wonderful technique strikes a few of you as odd, even dopey. I've demonstrated it at several conferences lately, only to be met with puzzled stares and not a few derisive guffaws. "Surely you aren't suggesting we devote both hands to this bizarre keyboard medley," mock the boldest hooligans in the front rows, "when we can just press ⌘-C, ⌘-F?"

But, of course, this is precisely what I'm suggesting, and I'll tell you why. ⌘-C, ⌘-F replaces the contents of the Clipboard; Option-↑, ↓ does not. If you don't mind replacing the Clipboard, ⌘-C, ⌘-F is great. If you'd rather leave the sleeping Clipboard in peace, Option-↑, ↓ is just the ticket.

Naturally, you can exploit or ignore this clever trick as you see fit. I mention a few specific reasons for cloning in place in later chapters, but it's ultimately up to you to decide its merit. If you do choose to add Option-↑, ↓ to your regular repertoire, remember this: When used with partial paths, it results in the same distortion as Option-dragging. Option-↑ distorts the path and clones it, and because Illustrator selects the entire clone, pressing the ↓ key moves all points and leaves the distortion intact.

However, you can anticipate the distortion and fix it as follows:

1. With the direct selection tool, select the points that you want to clone.
2. Press Option-↑. This clones the points and surrounding segments and selects the cloned path in its entirety.
3. Shift-click on two endpoints in the cloned path to deselect them. These points weren't selected when you cloned the path, so they shouldn't be selected now.
4. Press the ↓ key. The distortion goes away, making all segments in the clone identical to their counterparts in the original path.

Needless to say, these steps imply an additional level of effort that may prompt clone-in-place obstructionists to roll their eyes even more emphatically. But I maintain that all good things have their price. More importantly, if you want to avoid the Clipboard, there is no better method to duplicate in place.

Creating a Series of Clones

After Option-dragging or Option-arrowing, you can repeat the distance and direction that a clone has moved by choosing Object » Transform » Transform Again or pressing ⌘-D. This command creates series of clones, as shown in Figure 9-5.

If you clone an entire path, the Transform Again command duplicates the path over and over again, as shown at the top of Figure 9-5. This is a standard series duplication—hence the keyboard shortcut ⌘-D—dating back to the first MacDraw more than a decade ago.

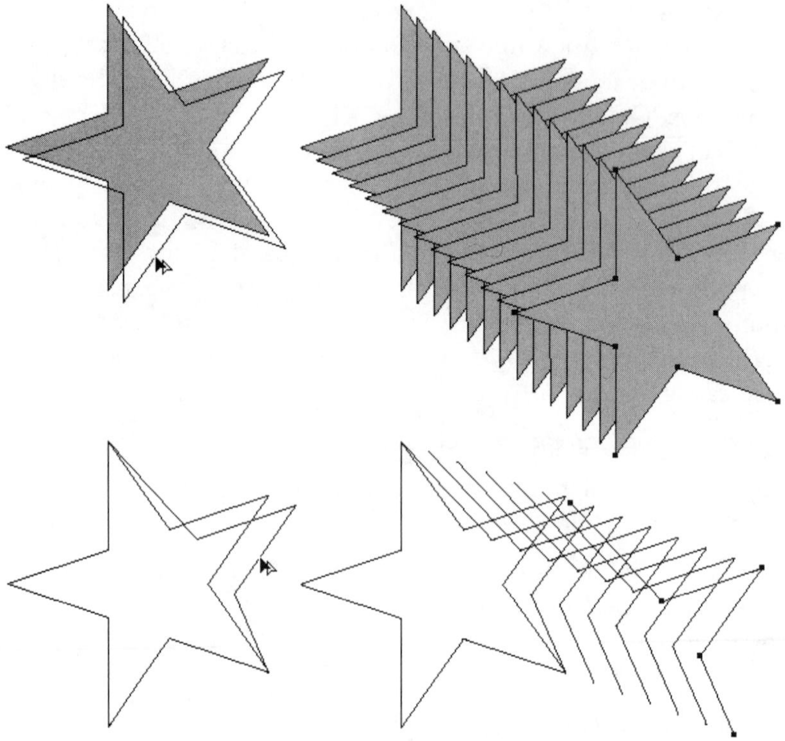

Figure 9-5: After cloning a path (top left), press ⌘-D to create a string of equally spaced clones (top right). If you create a series of partial clones (bottom), Illustrator applies the same movement to all points.

You can also apply Object » Transform » Transform Again to a partially cloned path. But rather than further distorting the path each time it's repeated, Illustrator moves all selected points the same distance and direction, as the bottom examples in Figure 9-5 show.

In addition to creating a linear series of paths, you can use the Transform Again command in one of the following ways:

- After dragging one path, you can move another path the same distance and direction by selecting the path and pressing ⌘-D. No cloning occurs. This is why Illustrator calls the command Transform Again; it's frequently more useful for repeating a simple movement or another transformation than for cloning.
- You can also repeat a resizing, rotation, or another transformation, whether or not the transformation involves cloning. For more on this topic, check out Chapter 11.

Expanding the Clone

A little-known command for cloning paths is Offset Path. This command clones a selected path and expands the outline of the clone an equal distance in all directions.

Select a path and choose Object » Path » Offset Path. The dialog box shown in Figure 9-6 appears. Enter the numeric distance of the expansion into the Offset option box. If you want to create a slimmer, smaller path, enter a negative value. Then press Return.

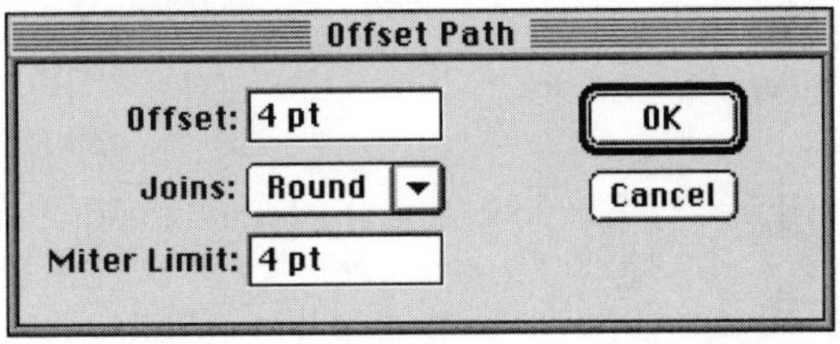

Figure 9-6: Enter a value into the Offset option box to specify how far Illustrator should expand a selected path.

In the first example of Figure 9-7, I applied an Offset value of 4 points to a letter set in the Linotype font Notre Dame and converted to paths. The original letter appears as white; I filled the cloned path with light gray. I want you to notice four things about the clone in the figure, all of which are indicative of the Offset clone command:

- Offset Path is the one cloning operation that positions clones in back of their originals, so that all paths are plainly visible.
- You can enter negative values into the Offset option box. In this case, Illustrator places the diminutive clone in front of the original.
- The outline of the clone has lots of overlapping folds at the corners of the shape. To remove these, press the Unite button inside the Pathfinder palette, as I did to create the second example in Figure 9-7.
- Expanding a path is not the same as scaling it. Object » Path » Offset Path dilates the path inward and outward, as the light gray shape shows. By contrast, the scale tool enlarges the interior areas so that they no longer align with the original.

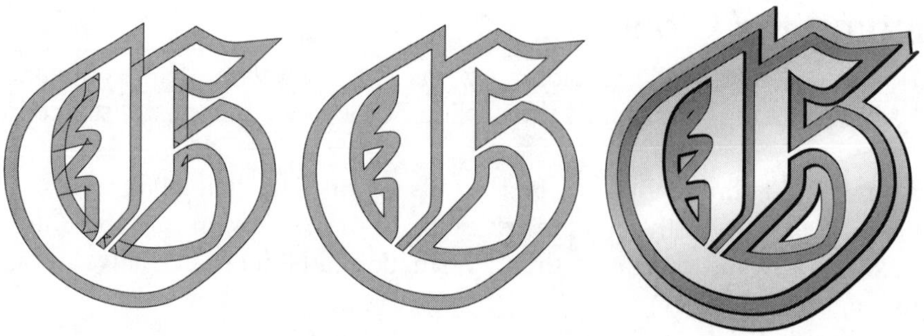

Figure 9-7: The results of applying an Offset value of 4 points (left), removing the corner folds with the Unite command (middle), and repeating the Offset Path and Unite commands (right).

To create the final example in Figure 9-7, I reapplied the Object » Path » Offset Path command to the first clone, and then clicked the Unite button to remove the corner folds. I then copied each path (⌘-C)—one at a time—pasted the copy behind the original (⌘-B), and nudged the copy a few fractions of a point down and to the right. I also added a thicker stroke to each copy, creating the impression of depth (a technique I explore in Chapter 16). To top things off, I filled the three front paths with gradations.

In addition to the Offset option box, the Offset Path dialog box (Figure 9-6) offers the Joins and Miter Limit options, both of which affect how Illustrator draws the corners of the cloned paths. The default Joins setting, Miter, creates pointed corners, but you can also round off the corners (Round) or cut them short (Bevel). The Miter Limit value chops the corner short if the path threatens to grow too long. For more information on these basic stroking concepts, consult Chapter 16.

In Illustrator 8, the behavior of the Offset Path command has changed slightly and, as far as I'm concerned, for the worse. It treats closed paths as explained above, just as it did in past versions of Illustrator. With open paths, on the other hand, Instead of creating a new open path that's set to the side of the original—much as the term offset would suggest, Illustrator now creates a closed path that outlines the original path.

The problem with the new version's Offset Path command is that a useful feature has been lost and no new functionality has been gained. The closed path that Illustrator creates when you use the Offset Path command on an open path is the exact same closed path that you can create using the Outline Path command—the command directly above the Offset Path command. All you need to do is set the open path's stroke weight to twice the Offset value from the Offset Path dialog box and then apply the Outline Path command.

If you want to a more useful result from the Offset Path command, you will need to delete part of the new closed path. The easiest thing to do is to cut the path apart with the scissors (as explained in just a few sections) and delete the undesired portion.

Dragging and Dropping

The one remaining method for duplicating objects allows you to drag an object from one illustration window and drop it into another. Naturally, you have to be able to see at least a little bit of the illustration window you're dragging from and the one that you're dragging into on your computer screen at the same time. Then, armed with the arrow tool or direct selection tool, simply drag one or more selected objects out of one window and into a background window. As illustrated in Figure 9-8, a dotted outline shows the position of the dragged objects, and a hollow arrow cursor with a plus sign in a box appears inside of the background window to show that this window is poised to receive. As soon as this cursor appears, you can release the mouse button to drop the selection.

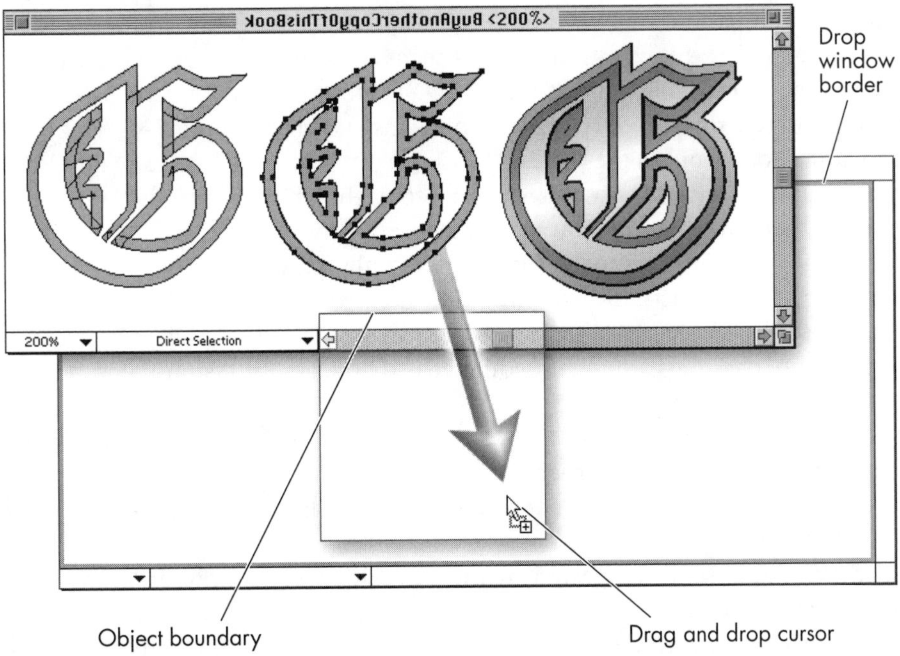

Figure 9-8: Drag selected objects from one window and drop them into another to clone objects between illustrations.

There's no need to press the Option key when dragging and dropping. Illustrator automatically clones the object, leaving the original in one window and adding a duplicate to the second. (As with other cloning techniques, the Clipboard contents remain unchanged.) After your drop, Illustrator brings the receiving window to front, so that you can position the object and edit it if need be.

Once the object is inside the other application window, you can modify the item on the fly. To do this, double-click the object that now resides in the other program and Illustrator will launch (unless, of course, it is currently running). Illustrator will display the object in a new window. You can make all the necessary changes (just as you can to any open drawing) and then simply click the window's close box. The corresponding object in the other program will automatically update to reflect the changes you made.

You can also drag and drop objects from Illustrator into other applications. I discuss how to drag and drop paths into Photoshop, for example, in Chapter 13.

Dragging Scraps and Clips

If you've been using the Mac for any period of time, you undoubtedly know about the Scrapbook. After choosing the Scrapbook command from the Apple menu, you can paste items into the Scrapbook window to create a sort of Rolodex of Clipboard stuff. Later, when you need to use an item, you just copy it from the Scrapbook and paste it into your favorite program.

What you didn't know—what nobody seems to know—is that you don't have to copy objects from Illustrator to paste them into the Scrapbook. You can drag and drop objects directly into the Scrapbook, as shown in Figure 9-9. Again, the Clipboard is totally out of the picture. Illustrator creates both PostScript and PICT representations on the fly, so that you can copy the objects from the Scrapbook and paste them into Word if you fancy that.

You can also create small files consisting of only the selected element by dragging objects from Illustrator and dropping them onto the desktop. On a Mac, these are so-called picture clippings, while on a Windows system, the word is Scrap. Picture clippings are little holding cells that keep objects until you need to use them later. When you drag and drop objects onto the desktop, Illustrator works with the system software to create a picture clipping file, which looks like a frayed page with a bent corner. You can double-click on the file icon at the Finder level to view its contents, as in Figure 9-10. (Illustrator doesn't have to be running for you to view the picture.)

The Windows' scrap is created in the same manner (simply drag and drop selected items onto the desktop), but unfortunately, you cannot view its contents as you can on a Mac. Instead, double-clicking on a scrap launches Illustrator (that is, if Illustrator is not already running) and opens the scrap as an independent window.

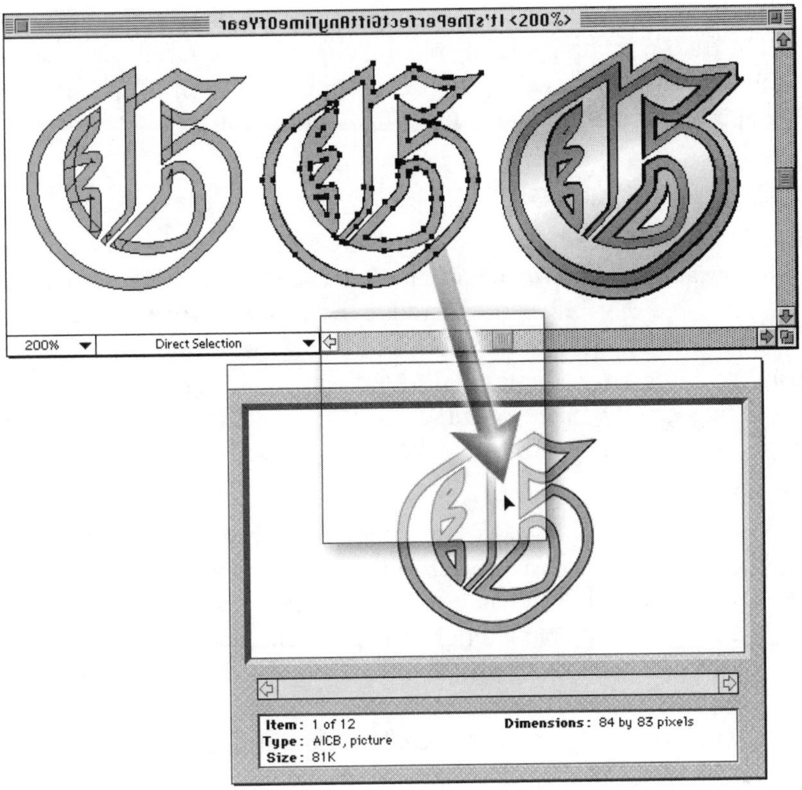

Figure 9-9: Don't copy and paste to transfer objects to the Scrapbook; just drag and drop!

Figure 9-10: Double-click on a picture clipping file icon (left) to view its contents (right).

Any time in the future, you can add the objects from a picture clipping or a scrap into an illustration by dragging the picture clipping or scrap file and dropping it. You can likewise drop the file into the Scrapbook (on a Mac), Photoshop, or some other application that supports the Illustrator format.

What about Auto-Scrolling?

Since Illustrator 6 introduced drag and drop, it's easy to drag objects out of the illustration window accidentally when you simply meant to invoke the auto-scroll function. See, in the old days, Illustrator scrolled the window when you dragged an object outside the window. This way, you could make big movements without zooming away from the page. Typically, the farther you dragged, the faster it scrolled. But no more. Any time you drag outside the illustration window in Illustrator 8, the program tries to do a drag and drop, even if there's no receiving window in the background.

TIP These days, to make Illustrator automatically scroll the window as you drag an object, you need to hover your cursor over a scroll bar or title bar. For example, after you grab an object, drag it onto the right scroll bar and hold it there; Illustrator scrolls to the right. If you drag the object onto the title bar, Illustrator scrolls upward. But what if you want to scroll to the left, where no scroll or title bar appear? In this case, drag the object to the left edge of the window. It's tricky, but it works. When you've scrolled far enough, drag the object back into the window and drop it into place.

Joining Points and Paths

Enough duplicating already. It's time to do something different with all these paths we're making, starting with joining. Illustrator's Join command lets you join two open paths to create one longer open path. Or you can connect two endpoints in a single open path to form a closed path.

Here's the scoop on using Object » Path » Join:

- Drag one endpoint onto another with the direct-selection tool so that it snaps into alignment. Then select the two endpoints (by marqueeing around them with the direct selection tool) and choose Object » Path » Join, or press ⌘-J. This fuses the two endpoints into a single interior point. Illustrator displays the Join dialog box, which lets you select whether you want to fuse the points into a corner point or a smooth point. Make your selection and press Return.

WARNING If you don't see the Join dialog box after pressing ⌘-J, your points aren't coincident—that is, one point isn't exactly, precisely snapped into alignment with the other. Press ⌘-Z to undo the join, and then try again to drag one point into alignment with the other, or just press ⌘-Option-Shift-J. The latter averages and fuses the points, as I explain shortly.

If so much as 0.001 point stands between two selected points, Object » Path » Join bypasses the Join dialog box and simply connects the points with a straight segment. (To put things in perspective, 0.001 point is roughly 0.3 micron, the size of one of your tinier bacteria—no joke—hence the insightful Figure 9-11.) Though one might argue Illustrator is a little too ready to join points in this way, it's a terrific method for quickly closing off a shape. So if you need a straight segment in a hurry, select two endpoints and press ⌘-J.

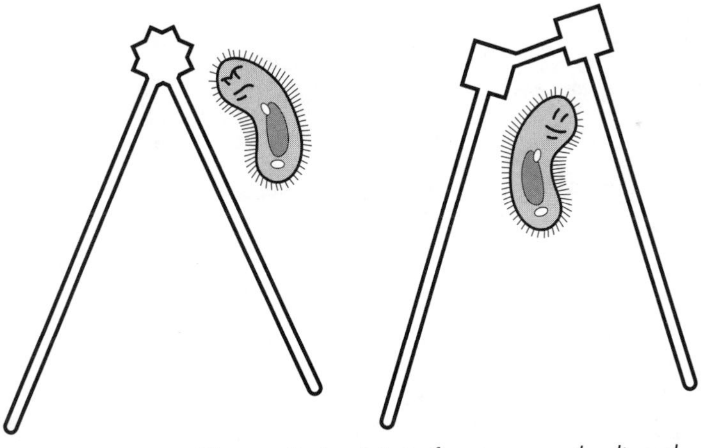

Figure 9-11: Press Object » Path » Join to fuse two exactly aligned points into a single point (left). But if a bacterium can fit between the points (right), Illustrator connects the points with a straight segment.

TIP If you aren't particularly concerned with the placement of your points, and you want to join the points into one, press ⌘-Option-Shift-J. This brings the points together by averaging their locations and then fuses them into a corner point.

To undo the effects of ⌘-Option-Shift-J, you must press ⌘-Z twice in a row—once to undo the joining and again to undo the averaging. Weird but true.

To close an open path, you can select the entire path with the arrow tool and press ⌘-J. If the endpoints are coincident, a dialog box comes up, asking you how you want to fuse the points. Otherwise, Illustrator connects the points with a straight segment.

WARNING

Whatever you do, don't press ⌘-Option-Shift-J when an entire path is selected. Illustrator averages all points in the path into a single location, creating a very ugly effect. If you mess up and do what I told you not to do, press ⌘-Z to make it better.

The Join command is a great way to join similarly shaped open paths to create a shape that looks like a variable-width line. Figure 9-12 shows a plethora of spirals created by joining two spiral paths. Here's how I created each variation:

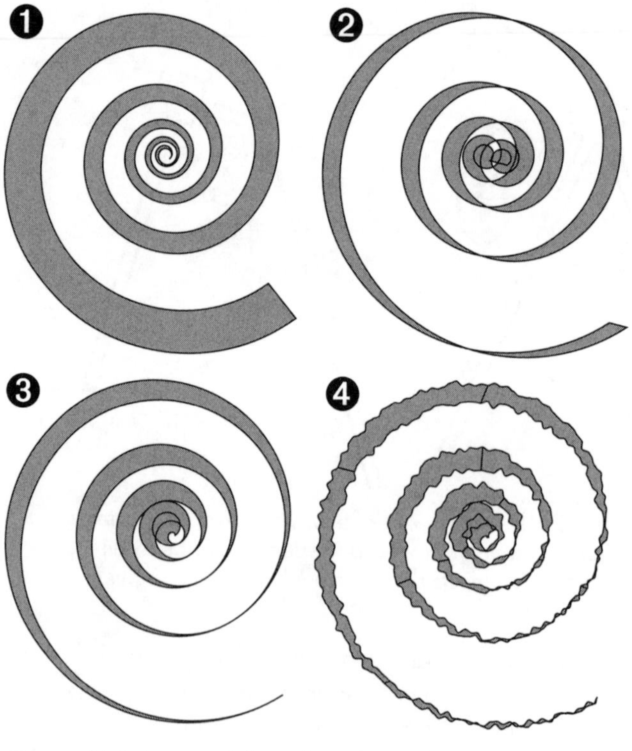

Figure 9-12: I created these four shapes by joining two open spiral paths.

- To create the first spiral (labeled 1 in Figure 9-12), I drew two paths of different sizes with the spiral tool. Both paths had the same decay and an equal number of segments. I then dragged one path by its inner endpoint so it snapped onto the inner endpoint of the other path. I marqueed these inner points with the direct selection tool and pressed ⌘-J to fuse them. Next, I Option-clicked on the path with the direct selection tool to select the entire thing and pressed ⌘-J again to connect the outer endpoints with a straight segment.

- To create the second shape (2) in the figure, I drew a spiral and cloned it to create two identical paths. I moved the two spirals a few points away from each other and joined the corresponding endpoints in either path with straight segments.

- The bottom left shape (3) is the result of cloning a spiral with Object » Path » Offset Path. Since Illustrator now exclusively creates a closed path when executing the Offset Path command, I deleted the inner portion of the new path by selecting it with the direct selected tool and hitting the Delete key. I then selected the remainder of the clone, dragged it by its inner endpoint so it snapped into alignment with the original, and fused the inner endpoints into one. Finally, I selected the two outer endpoints with the direct selection tool and pressed ⌘-Option-Shift-J to average and fuse them.

- The last shape (4) is a bit of a cheat, but it shows you where joining can ultimately take you. All I did was take the third path (3) and apply Filter » Distort » Roughen. Inside the Roughen dialog box, I set the Size value to 1 and the Detail value to 30, and I selected the Smooth radio button. See Chapter 12 for more info on Roughen and other automated special effects filters.

NOTE

Those little lines across the last spiral are the points at which I had to split the sucker because it was too complicated to print. I clicked with the scissors tool where I wanted to assign breaks and connected opposite sides with straight segments using the Join command. (The scissors tool is the topic of the very next section.)

Splitting Paths into Pieces

The opposite of joining is splitting, and Illustrator provides three basic ways to split paths apart. I touched on the first method in Chapter 5: You can select a segment or an interior point with the direct selection tool and press the Delete key. This deletes one or two segments and leaves a gaping rift in the path. You either split an open path into two paths or open a closed path.

But what if you want to break apart a path without creating a rift? Or what if you want to break a path in the middle of a segment? The answer to either question is to use the scissors tool, knife tool, or Object » Path » Slice. The scissors tool creates a break at a specific point, the knife tool creates a free-form slice, and the Slice command uses a selected path to slice through all other paths that it comes in contact with. The only things lacking are a nail file and a toothpick. (Er, that was a pocket knife joke, in case you missed it.)

Snipping with the Scissors

The scissors tool is one of Illustrator's earliest tools, predating just about every path-editing tool but the arrow tool. Its operation hasn't changed that much since the old days. You click anywhere along the outline of a path to snip the path at that point. The path need not even be selected. As Figure 9-13 shows, you can click on either a segment or a point.

Whenever you click with the scissors tool, Illustrator inserts two endpoints. As the second example in Figure 9-13 illustrates, you can drag one endpoint away from the other with the direct selection tool. The problem is, one endpoint is necessarily in front of the other. Why a problem? Every so often, you'll want to drag the point that's in back, and you won't be able to get to it because the front point is in the way.

Naturally, you can drag the front point out of the way, and then drag the rear point. But that means moving both points.

TIP

What if you want the front point to stay exactly where it is and just move the rear one? The solution is to select both points, deselect the top one, and nudge the bottom point clear with the arrow keys. To select both points, marquee around them with the direct selection tool. Then Shift-click on the point to deselect the top point. Now just the bottom point is selected. Press an arrow key three or four times to nudge the bottom point so you can easily select it, and then drag it to the desired location.

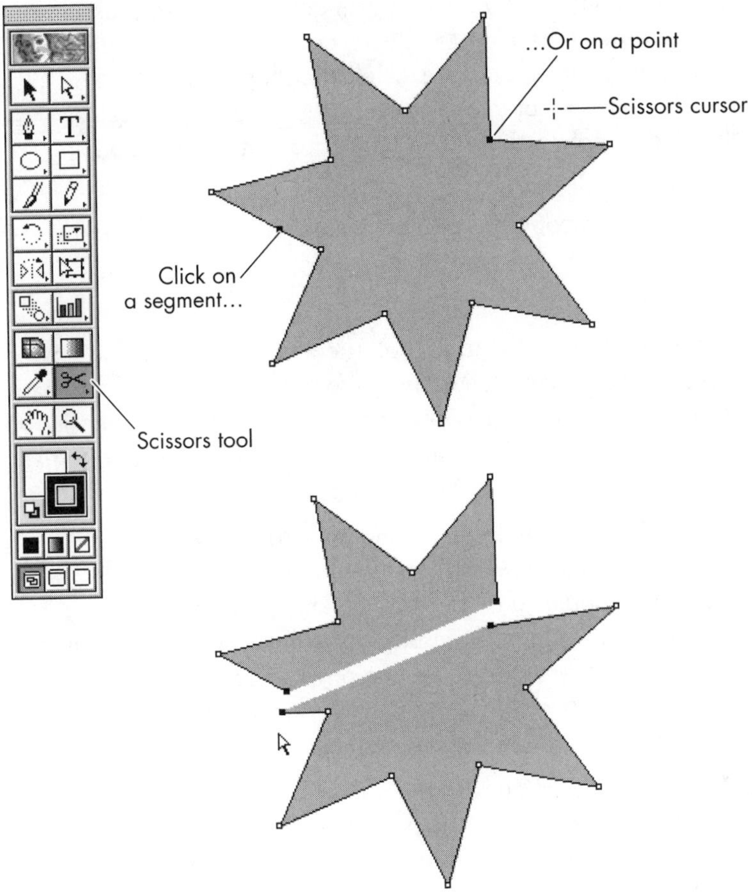

Figure 9-13: Snip a break in a path by clicking on the outline of a path with the scissors tool.

Inserting a Point with the Scissors Tool

Incidentally, Illustrator didn't offer an add point tool (discussed in Chapter 5) until version 3, and yet, you always had this capability with the scissors tool. Just Option-click. Clicking with the scissors tool inserts two endpoints; Option-clicking inserts a single interior point. Makes sense, right?

TIP

Which brings me to an interesting tip. As Chapter 5 explained, the add point tool automatically determines the identity of a new point—corner or smooth—based on the shape of the segment on which you click. But what if you don't like the point that Illustrator creates? What if it creates a corner point when you want a smooth point? Well, just undo the point insertion (⌘-Z), select the scissors tool, and click at that same point. Next, select both points with the direct selection tool and then press ⌘-J to join them. Select the kind of point you want to create from the Join dialog box, and press Return.

Illustrator always gives you control; you just need to know how to find it.

Wielding the Knife

The other path-splitting tool is the knife tool; the alternate tool in the scissors tool slot. It looks like a little X-acto blade. The knife tool can slice multiple paths at a time. First assemble the objects that you want to cut through. The knife tool splits paths only and it doesn't affect text, unless the text is first converted to paths with Type » Create Outlines.

NEW 8

Used to be that you could use the knife tool to slice apart any nontext objects whose path was crossed. Nowadays, if one or more paths are selected, the knife tool will sever those paths but leave all unselected paths unchanged (assuming that the knife tool crosses one or more selected paths). On the other hand, if nothing in your document is selected, the knife happily dices up any path that gets in its way.

To operate the knife tool, just drag with it, much as you would with the pencil tool. (Illustrator tracks your knife gestures a little differently than the pencil tool—with a more accurate solid line that adjusts slightly as you drag—but this is a minor point. You probably don't care. Sorry to bother you.) As demonstrated in Figure 9-14, Illustrator's knife tool slices through all closed paths and all open filled paths that it comes into contact with. (I changed the fills of the left and right halves of the slashed objects to better demonstrate the effects of the knife.) To be on the safe side, I selected all the paths that I wanted the knife to recognize.

NOTE

Although the knife tool has come a long way and can now even be considered a worthwhile tool, it still has a couple of small quirks. The first one is that it doesn't affect unfilled open paths. Second, it automatically closes filled open paths after it splits them into pieces. Why it does this is beyond me, but since both of these problems are easy to work around, I simply thank the Adobe folks for fixing this once wretched tool.

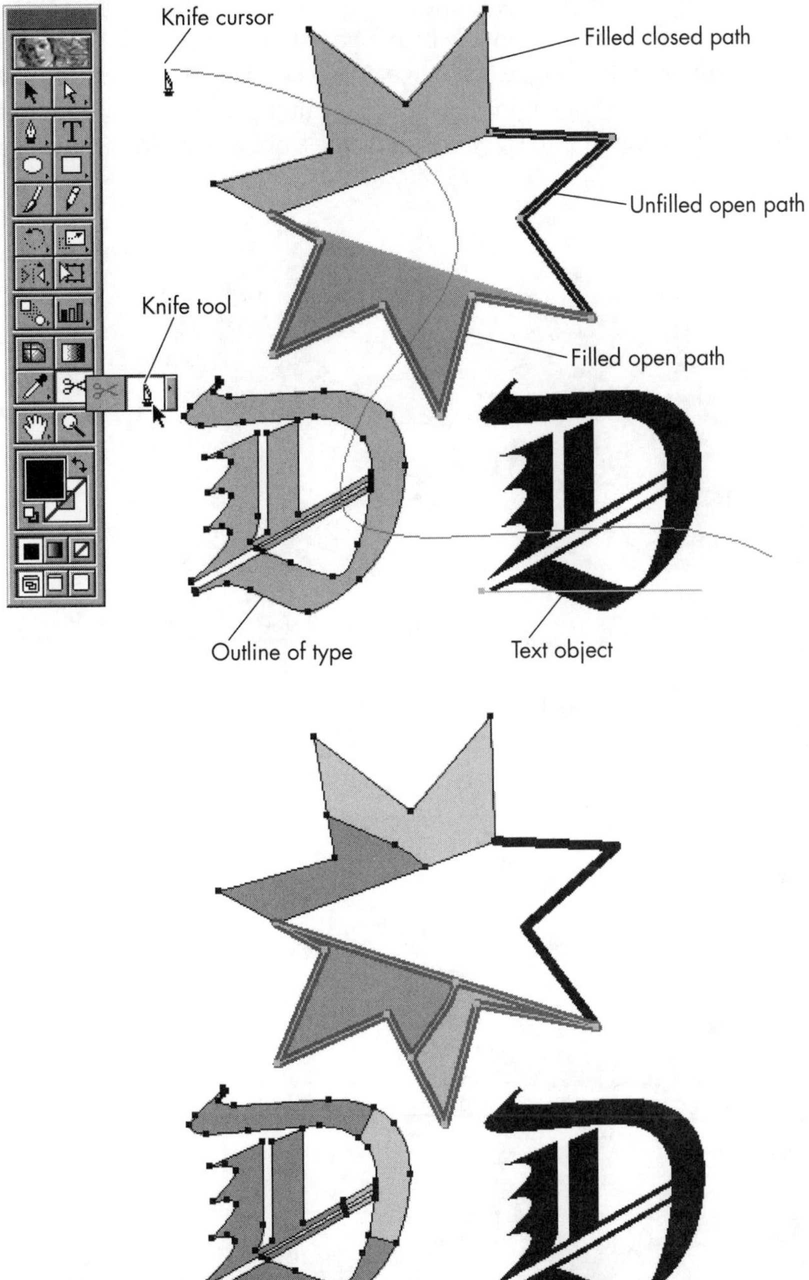

Figure 9-14: Drag with the knife tool (top) to cut through paths (bottom). Open paths with transparent fills and text are not affected.

To make nice straight cuts, use the Option key while you're dragging with the knife tool. Be sure to press the Option key before you start your drag. If you press it after you're already into the drag, it will have no effect. Press and hold both the Option and the Shift key to constrain the slices to a multiple of 45 degrees (plus whatever value you've entered into the Constrain Angle option box in the General Preference dialog box).

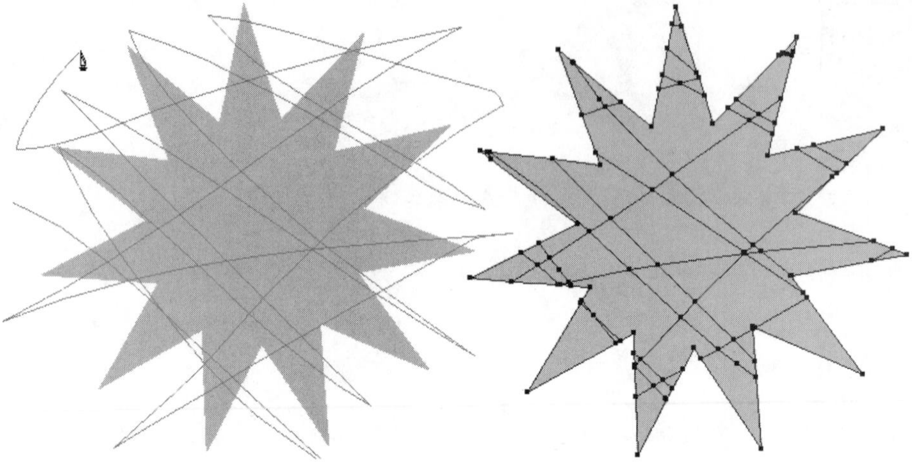

Figure 9-15: Drag willy-nilly with the knife tool (left) to hack a path into a bunch of shards (right).

Figure 9-16: This lovely star is the product of haphazard knife handling and meticulously filling the paths with radial gradations.

One of my favorite uses for the knife tool is indiscriminate slashing. (What better way to use a knife tool?) For example, in Figure 9-15, I started with a star and then scribbled back and forth over it with the knife tool. This busted up the path into 50 or so pieces, as shown on the right side of the figure. I then filled each shard with one of three different gradations to create a sort of stained glass effect, as shown in Figure 9-16

Slicing with a Path

The bad news about the knife tool is that it doesn't offer much control. You can't carefully position points and control handles to specify the exact directions of your slice, and you can't edit the slice after drawing it.

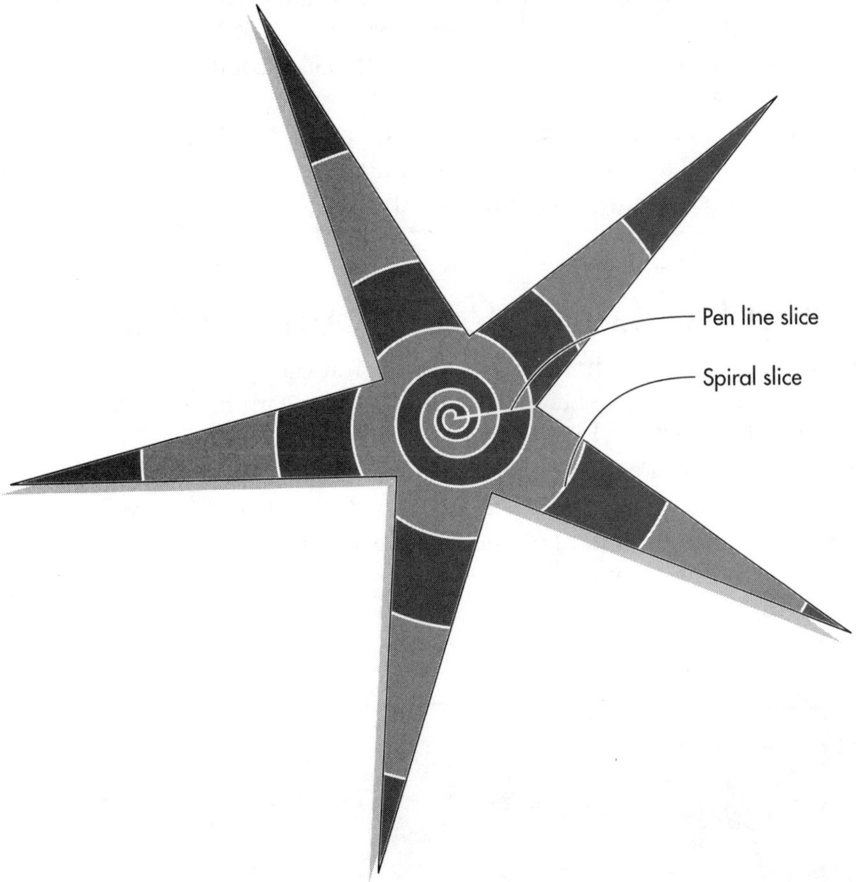

Figure 9-17: Using Object » Path » Slice, I twice sliced into a star, first with a spiral tool and then with a small straight line created with the pen tool.

That's why Illustrator provides the Slice command. After drawing a path with any of Illustrator's precision drawing tools, you can use the path to cut through filled objects in your drawing. Here's how it works:

1. Assemble the filled objects that you want to hack to pieces.
2. Draw the path that you want to use to slice the objects. You can use the pen tool, star tool, spiral tool, or any other drawing tool.
3. Position the path over the objects. Then choose Object » Path » Slice. Illustrator slices through all objects that the selected path overlaps.

In Figure 9-17, I used a spiral to slice through a star. After cutting with the spiral, I drew a short straight line into the center of the shape with the pen tool (as noted in the figure) and chose the Slice command again. That permitted me to fill different loops of the spiral with different colors. Note that I had to apply these two slices in two different passes. You can't use the Slice command on more than one cutting path at a time.

Like the knife tool, the Slice command has a habit of deleting unfilled, open paths. To cut the paths instead of deleting them, make sure that the slicing object doesn't overlap an unfilled, open path more than once.

Carving Holes into Compound Paths

Illustrator lets you carve holes inside a path. You can see through these holes to objects and colors that lie behind the path. A path with holes in it is called a compound path, which is what this section is about.

The most common kind of compound path is converted text. Consider the baroque character in Figure 9-18. This character is actually the combination of three paths—the serrated ruffles on the left side, the main body of the B, and the hole inside the B (filled with white in the figure). Illustrator automatically combined these three paths into a single compound path when I chose Type » Create Outlines.

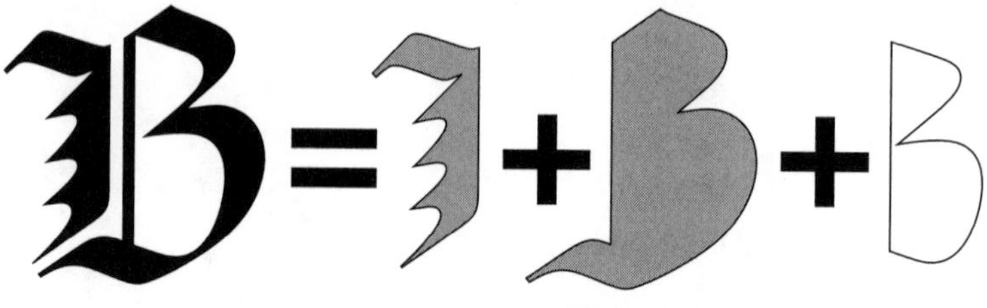

Figure 9-18: This character of type comprises three paths all combined into a single compound path.

At this point you might ask, "Why do you need a path with a hole in it? Why not just stick the smaller path in front of the bigger path and fill the smaller path with the background color?" Two reasons:

- First, the background may contain lots of different colors, as in Figure 9-19. To create the first B in the figure, I filled the interior shape with light gray in an attempt to vaguely match the background, but it doesn't look right at all. The second B is a proper compound path, allowing us to see through the B to anything behind it.
- Second, working with opaque paths limits your flexibility. Even if you can get away with filling an interior path with a flat color, you'll have to change that color any time you change the background or move the objects against a new background. But with a compound path, you can move the object against any background without changing a thing. You can even add elements like drop shadows without modifying the compound path one iota. It's flexibility at its finest.

Figure 9-19: Three filled paths set in front of a multi-colored background (left) compared with a compound path with a transparent hole carved into it (right).

Creating a Compound Path

Now as I said, Illustrator automatically turns letters into compound paths. But you may want to create additional compound paths of your own. Doughnuts, eyeglasses, windows, ski masks, and guys shot full of bullet holes are just a few of the many real-world items that lend themselves to compound paths.

To make a compound path, do the following:

1. **Draw two shapes.**

   Make one smaller than the other. You can use any tool to draw either shape. The paths can be open or closed, though you'll probably want to stick with closed paths to ensure even curves and continuous strokes. (You can use open paths, but the fills get flattened off at the open edge.)

2. **Select both shapes and choose Object » Compound Paths » Make.**

   Or press the keyboard equivalent ⌘-8. Where the two shapes overlap, the compound path is transparent; where the shapes don't overlap, the path is filled.

   For example, I've combined a circle and a star in Figure 9-20. The center of the compound path is transparent, because that's where the two shapes overlap. The outer areas are opaque because the shapes don't overlap. Couldn't be simpler.

If you combined shapes without getting any holes at all, you must have drawn the shapes in different directions. The solution is to select one of the shapes with the direct selection tool, click on the Attributes palette, and click the Reverse Path Direction button that is not active. For a detailed explanation of this weird phenomenon, read the "Reversing Subpath Direction" section a few short pages from now.

3. **Edit the individual shapes in the compound path with the direct selection tool.**

   After you combine two or more shapes into a compound path, select the entire path by clicking on it with the arrow tool. If you want to select a point or segment belonging to one of the subpaths—that's the official name for the shapes inside a compound path—press ⌘-Shift-A to deselect the path and click on an element with the direct selection tool. You can then manipulate points, segments, and control handles as usual.

Option-click with the direct selection tool to select an entire subpath. The second example of Figure 9-20 finds me dragging the circle independently of the star. Notice how Illustrator automatically alters the opaque and transparent areas to account for this movement. You can actually move a hole with respect to the rest of the object. (Wouldn't it be great if you could do that in real life? Think how many favorite old shirts and socks you could recover.)

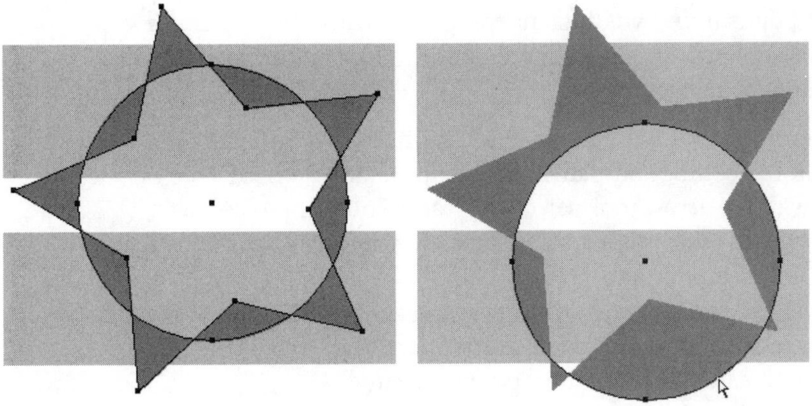

Figure 9-20: After combining a circle and a star into a compound path (left), I can move the circle independently of the star to shift the transparent area (right).

With the direct selection tool, Option-click a second time on a subpath to select the entire compound path. If you decide later to restore the compound path to its original independent parts, select the entire path and choose Object » Compound Paths » Release, or press ⌘-Option-8.

Working with Compound Paths

Compound paths are very special and wonderful things that you can screw up very easily. If you know what you're doing, you can juggle tens or hundreds of subpaths and even add holes to existing compound paths. But by the same token, you can accidentally add a hole when you don't mean to, or you may encounter a perplexing error message when editing a subpath in a manner that Illustrator doesn't allow.

The following tidbits of information are designed to help eliminate as much confusion as possible:

- You can edit subpaths with the direct selection tool, and even use the add point, delete point, and convert point tools. You can even apply the scissors and knife tools to a compound paths.
- You can't connect a subpath from one compound path with a subpath from a different compound path or a different group, whether with the Join command or the pen or pencil tool. This may sound like something you'll never want to do, but believe me, one day, you'll try to connect points from two different compound paths or groups and you'll go absolutely nuts trying to figure out why Illustrator won't let you do it. It happens to everybody.

  When (not if) it happens to you, you have two options. Give it up, or break the compound paths and groups apart. If you decide on the latter, with the arrow tool, select two paths you want to connect. This also selects all other subpaths associated with these paths. Then press ⌘-Option-8 once and press ⌘-Shift-G about four times in a row. This is overkill, but it's preferable to wasting a lot of time with trial and error. Who knows how many nested groups are involved? Then join the paths and re-create the compound path as desired.
- Another wonderful constraint is that you can't combine shapes from different groups or compound paths into a single compound path. If, when you press ⌘-8, Illustrator complains that the selected objects are from different groups, press ⌘-Option-8 and ⌘-Shift-G a few times to free the chains that bind the objects, and then try pressing ⌘-8 again.
- You can combine as many shapes inside a compound path as you like. You can likewise add subpaths without releasing the compound path. There are two ways to do this. One way is to select the compound path with the arrow tool, Shift-click on the shapes you want to add, and press ⌘-8 again. That's what I did to add the smaller circle to the mix in Figure 9-21. (This doesn't create a compound path inside a compound path or anything weird like that. It just adds the new shapes as a subpaths.)

TIP Alternatively, you can select the shapes that you want to add to the compound path and cut them by pressing ⌘-X. Then select any subpath in the compound path with the direct selection tool—not the arrow tool!—and press either ⌘-F or ⌘-B to paste the cut shapes in front or in back of the selection. This automatically makes the pasted shapes part of the compound path.

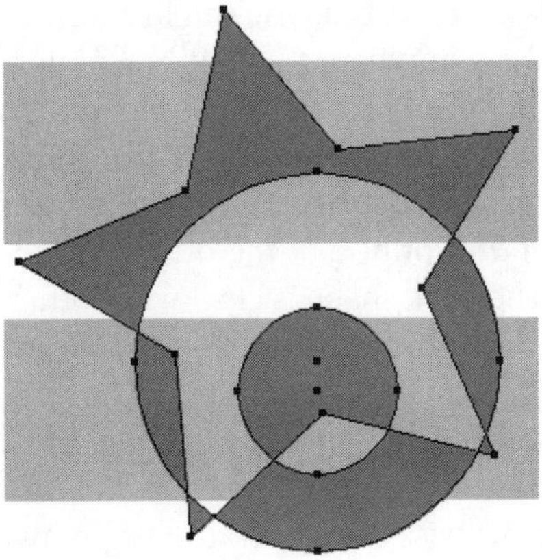

Figure 9-21: I added the smaller circle to the existing compound path by selecting all paths and again pressing ⌘-8.

Because you can paste a shape into a compound path, you may find yourself doing it accidentally when you don't want to. To avoid pasting inside a compound path, select the entire compound path with the arrow tool and press ⌘-F or ⌘-B. Or deselect all objects in the illustration (⌘-Shift-A) and paste away. In either case, Illustrator understands that the pasted path and compound path are to be treated as two separate entities.

So far as Illustrator is concerned, a compound path is a single path. Therefore, changing the fill or stroke of one subpath in the compound path changes all other subpaths as well. So if you ever change the color of one shape, and another shape changes as well, you can rest assured both shapes are part of the same compound path.

Reversing Subpath Direction

By this time, you've probably created a compound path or added a new subpath, only to find that you're not getting any holes. You think you did something wrong, or perhaps I failed to convey a step or two. Neither is the case. It's just that Illustrator needs a little kick in the rear end to make it shape up and fly right.

See, Illustrator calculates opaque and transparent areas in a compound path based on the directions in which the subpaths flow. This may be news to you, but each segment in a path actually goes from one point to another point. This implies a clockwise or counterclockwise flow.

For one subpath to create a hole in another, the two paths have to flow in opposite directions. Alternately clockwise and counterclockwise paths do the trick.

At this point you might think, "Oh, great, now I have to pay attention to how I draw my shapes." Luckily, you don't. When you combine two or more shapes into a compound path, Illustrator automatically changes the backmost shape to a clockwise flow and all others to counterclockwise. It does this regardless of how you drew the shapes! I emphasize this because I have heard experts expound on stage and in print that the original draw directions matter, and this simply is not true. The back shape is clockwise, others are counterclockwise—it's that cut and dry.

Illustrator's default approach works swell when the rear shape in the selection is also the largest shape. The first example in Figure 9-22 shows precisely this setup. The large backmost circle flows clockwise, and the two smaller squares flow counterclockwise. Therefore, the counterclockwise squares cut holes in the clockwise circle. But things go awry in the second example, in which one of the squares is in back. The circle and square do not cut holes into the rear square, which leaves the forward square opaque.

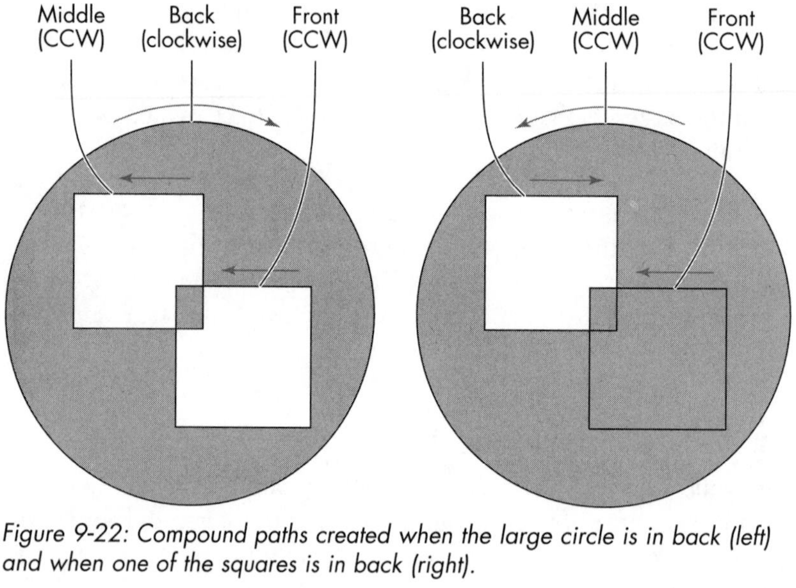

Figure 9-22: Compound paths created when the large circle is in back (left) and when one of the squares is in back (right).

But Illustrator wouldn't be Illustrator if it didn't give you the power to correct the situation. You can change the direction of any path by selecting it with the direct selection tool and modifying the setting in the Attributes palette. Here's how to correct a problem like the second example in Figure 9-22:

1. Press ⌘-Shift-A to deselect everything.

2. Select one of the subpaths that doesn't seem to be behaving correctly with the direct selection tool.
3. Click on the Attributes tab to bring the Attributes palette into focus. The Attributes palette is shown in Figure 9-23.

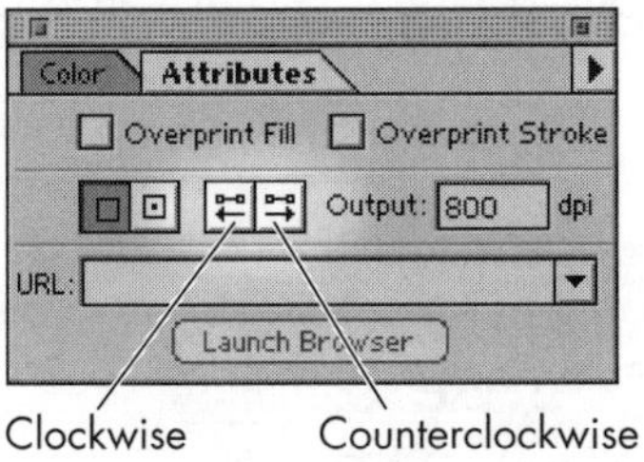

Figure 9-23: Use the Reverse Path Direction On and Off buttons to change the selected subpath direction.

4. Click on the Reverse Path Direction button that is not active. This changes the flow of the path from counterclockwise to clockwise or vice versa depending on which direction the path originally went.
5. Now select one of the other misguided subpaths (if there are any others) and, again in the Attributes palette, click on the nonactive Reverse Path Direction button to switch the flow of the subpath to the other direction.

Keep selecting paths and fiddling with the Reverse Path Direction buttons as much as you want until you get things the way you want them. Keep in mind that you can achieve transparency only in areas where an even number of subpaths overlap. If an odd number of subpaths overlap, the area is always opaque. For example, back in Figure 9-22, the small center space where the circle and both squares overlap is filled with gray regardless of the directions of the subpaths.

NOTE Oh, and one last bit of explanation about the Reverse Path Direction buttons: You might think these buttons would change the direction of the path from the way you drew it to the opposite direction. But no. This option is actually a very simple toggle. When the Reverse Path Direction On button is active, the subpath flows in a clockwise direction; and when the other one is active, the subpath flows counterclockwise.

The Reverse Path Direction buttons are dimmed unless a subpath inside a compound path is selected. You cannot change the direction of standard paths for the simple reason that there's no point in doing so.

Use a Path to Clip a Path

The last items on my list of things to discuss—and then I'll let you poor people go home to your families—are the Pathfinder filters. Illustrator provides a total of 13 buttons in the Pathfinder palette, as shown in Figure 9-24. Each of these buttons applies a different Pathfinder filter, all of which permit you to combine simple paths into more complex ones. You can merge paths together, subtract one path from another, break paths into bits, and perform other path operations.

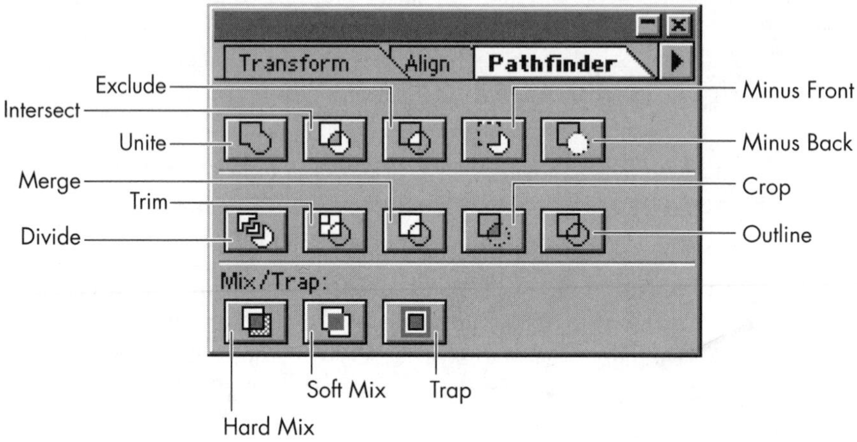

Figure 9-24: The new Pathfinder palette with all 13 filters labeled.

For you experienced users, just to put your minds at ease, the buttons in the Pathfinder palette are the same as the commands that you found on the Object » Pathfinder submenu in Illustrator 7. I guess that Adobe felt that it's more convenient to have these filters in a palette so that you can get to them easily when you want them and hide them away when you don't.

As you become more adept at using the Pathfinder filters, you'll find them very helpful for assembling primitive shapes—such as rectangles, ovals, polygons, and stars—into more elaborate paths, rather than drawing the elaborate paths from scratch with the pen tool. You can also use the filters to generate translucent color overlays and drop shadows.

In the following sections, I explain every one of the Pathfinder filters except Trap. The Trap filter lets you generates so-called "traps" to eliminate gaps in color printing. I cover this particular filter with the other printing functions in Chapter 18.

Rather than merely discussing the filters in the order they appear in the Pathfinder palette, I examine them in logical order to help you make sense of the filters and determine when and if they might prove beneficial. I also step you through a few specific techniques so you can get a feel for using the filters.

I don't know anyone who uses all 13 of the Pathfinder filters. So don't feel too frustrated if you walk away from this chapter thinking, "I'll be hog-tied if I know what to do with this Outline filter," because that's the exact same thing the experts think. Some filters are great, and some are fairly lame. The next few sections will make it clear which—according to at least one artist—are which.

Adding Shapes Together

The Unite filter combines all selected shapes into a single path. Illustrator removes all the overlapping stuff and turns the selected paths into a single, amalgamated object. It fills and strokes this new object with the fill and stroke from the foremost of the selected paths.

In the top left of Figure 9-25, for example, I selected the star, circle, and stripes at top and clicked the Unite button in the Pathfinder palette. The result is the single combined path in the middle of the figure.

You can use the Unite filter to combine simple objects to create more complex ones. You can also use the filter to create drop shadows, as shown in the bottom left example of Figure 9-25. Here's what you do:

1. Select the objects that you want to cast a shadow.
2. Copy the objects (⌘-C) and paste them in back of the selection (⌘-B). Because the Unite filter replaces the selected objects with the united path, if you want to keep your objects, you need to duplicate them first.
3. Click the Unite button. Illustrator combines the selected paths into one.
4. Use the arrow keys to nudge the united path down and to the left or right a little. In the bottom left of Figure 9-25, I nudged the path down 4 points and right 3 points.
5. Use the controls in the toolbox to delete the stroke, and use the Color palette to change the fill as desired.

By duplicating and uniting the selected objects, you can create a drop shadow behind multiple objects at one time. Of course, this technique is designed to work with a flat background. On the left of Figure 9-25, for example, I've created a gray shadow against solid white. How do you cast a multicolor shadow against a multicolor background? Well, I still have a few a Pathfinder filters left to discuss, and when I do, you can be sure that this technique will be among them.

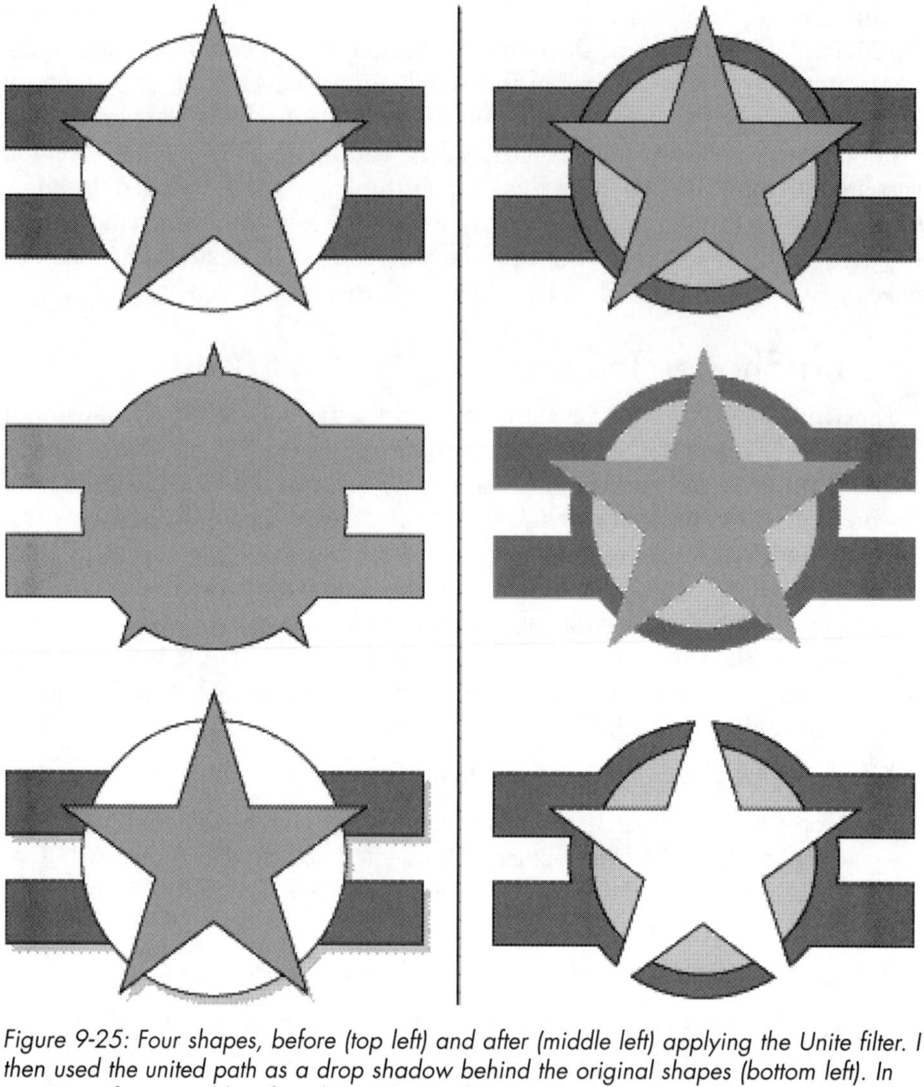

Figure 9-25: Four shapes, before (top left) and after (middle left) applying the Unite filter. I then used the united path as a drop shadow behind the original shapes (bottom left). In contrast, after assembling five shapes (top right), I applied the Merge filter (middle right) and deleted the central star shape (bottom right).

Illustrator provides another filter for combining paths, the Merge filter. This filter unites paths with the same fill color. It also clips surrounding shapes to prevent overlaps, and (for reasons I can't imagine) it deletes the stroke.

In the rightmost examples of Figure 9-25, I start out with an additional compound path that serves as a dark gray border around the star that matches the dark gray of the stripes. When I select all five shapes and click the Merge button, Illustrator combines the dark gray paths into one, as shown in the middle example of the figure. Because the Merge filter also removes overlaps, I was able to delete the star path to create a "negative space" effect, in which the surrounding objects maintain the shape of the star. I also assigned new strokes to create the last item on the right of Figure 9-25.

Subtracting Shapes from Each Other

Illustrator provides three Pathfinder filters—Exclude, Minus Front, and Minus Back—that subtract shapes from each other:

- The Exclude filter is a kind of poor man's compound path function. It removes all overlapping sections of the selected shapes. As shown at the top of Figure 9-26, this leaves a series of holes, much like those in a compound path. The difference is that each filled area is actually a separate shape. In the figure, the Exclude filter has converted my four original paths into 16 new shapes filled with gray.

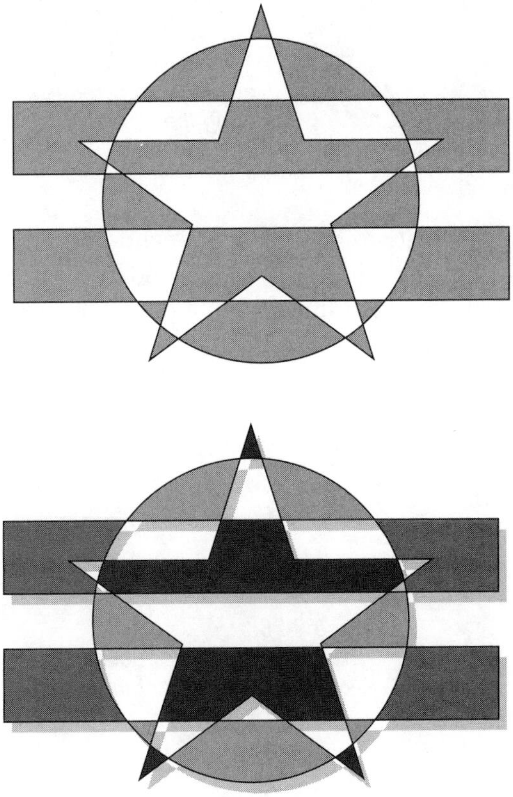

Figure 9-26: After applying the Exclude filter to the star, circle, and stripes (top), I filled the paths with different shades of gray and added a drop shadow (bottom).

The downside of using the Exclude filter is that you can't transform one of the original paths to reposition a hole, as you can inside a compound path. The advantage of using the filter is that you can fill the individual excluded paths with different colors, as I have done in the bottom example of Figure 9-26.

An exception occurs if one of the selected shapes falls entirely inside another when you apply the Exclude filter. In this case, Illustrator has no choice but to convert the shapes into a compound path.

- The Minus Front filter clips all selected paths out of the rear path in the selection. In Figure 9-27, for example, I selected the star and the circle and clicked the Minus Front button. The result is a circle with a star cut out of it.

Figure 9-27:
The result of clipping the star out of the circle with the Minus Front filter. Again, I added a drop shadow using the Unite filter.

- Minus Back is exactly the opposite of Minus Front; it clips all selected paths out of the front path in the selection. In Figure 9-28, I selected the circle and stripes and clicked the Minus Back button. This left the circle with a two stripes cut out of it.

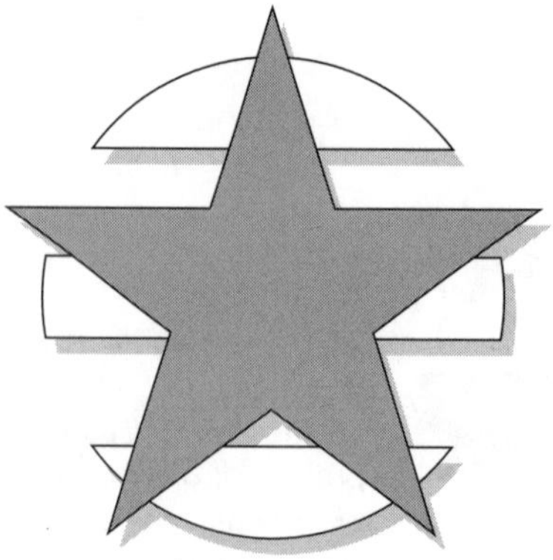

Figure 9-28:
Here I used the Minus Back filter to clip the stripes out of the circle.

Both Minus Front and Minus Back filters are capable of clipping multiple paths out of a single path. In Figure 9-28, for example, I cut two stripes out of one circle. But what if I want to do it the other way around? What if I want to cut the circle out of the two stripes? If I merely select all three paths and clicked the Minus Front button, Illustrator clips both the circle and one of the stripes out of the backmost stripe. No matter how I rearrange the shapes, I get scraps from one stripe or the other, but not both. The solution is to bring our old friend the compound path into the picture.

TIP: When you combine shapes into a compound path, Illustrator is fooled into thinking that they're all part of one path. In Figure 9-29, I selected the two stripes and pressed ⌘-8 to combine them together. They don't overlap, so there aren't any holes, but they're all one path so far as Illustrator is concerned. Then I selected the circle and chose the Minus Front filter. Illustrator clipped the circle from the compound stripes, resulting in what you see in the figure.

Figure 9-29: After combining the stripes into a compound path, I selected stripes and the circle and applied the Minus Front filter.

Finding Overlap and Intersection

The rest of the Pathfinder filters are devoted to the task of finding and separating the intersecting portions of selected shapes. Foremost among these is the Intersect filter, which merely retains the overlapping sections of a bunch of selected shapes and throws away the areas where the shapes don't overlap. Illustrator fills and strokes the resulting shapes with the colors from the frontmost shape in the selection.

WARNING: If every one of the selected paths does not overlap at some location, the Intersect command delivers an error message telling you that the filter would delete everything if Illustrator were dumb enough to let it finish.

The following steps explain how I used the Intersect filter to create the sequence of objects shown in Figure 9-30:

1. I selected the familiar star and circle shapes and copied them to the Clipboard (⌘-C).
2. Next I clicked the Intersect button to retain the overlapping portions of the selected star and circle. This resulted in the rounded-off star shown at the top of the figure.

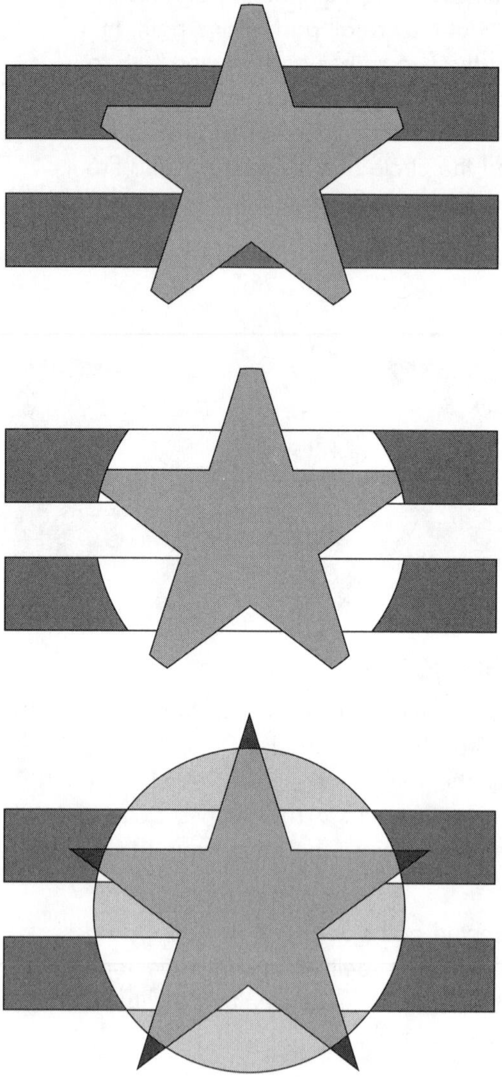

Figure 9-30: The results of applying the Intersect filter to the star and circle (top) and to the circle and compound stripes (middle). Then I restored the original star and circle and changed their fills (bottom).

3. I pasted the star and circle behind the rounded star (⌘-B). Then I deleted the pasted pointy star for the moment, because, frankly, it was in my face. (It wasn't gone forever, as you'll see when I retrieve it in Step 7.)

4. I next selected the dark stripes and combined them into a single compound path by pressing ⌘-8.

5. I pressed Option-↑, ↓ to create a quick clone of the stripes. Why didn't I simply copy them? Had I done that, I would have replaced the star and circle in the Clipboard, which I needed later (in Step 7). See, I told you that clone-in-place trick would come in handy.

6. I Shift-clicked on the circle to add it to the selection and chose the Intersect command again. (I could have alternatively pressed ⌘-4, since Intersect was the last filter applied, as I explain at the end of this chapter.)

TIP

Because the stripes were a single compound path, Illustrator found the intersection of each stripe and the circle, as verified by the rounded white stripes in the middle example in Figure 9-30. Had I neglected to combine the stripes in Step 4, Illustrator would have given me an error message, since the stripes don't overlap each other. All paths have to overlap to produce an intersection, but Illustrator gives the subpaths in a compound path special dispensation.

7. Finally, with the newly intersected shapes selected, I pressed ⌘-B to paste the original star and circle in back of the rounded stripes. I then filled the circle with light gray and the star with dark gray to get the effect shown at the bottom of Figure 9-30.

In addition to Intersect, Illustrator provides six Pathfinder filters that split paths into pieces based on the way the paths overlap. All of these commands group the resulting paths together, and all except Outline remove the strokes from the paths. So be prepared to ungroup paths or edit them with the direct selection tool. And you'll have to reapply the strokes, as I've done throughout the figures.

Here's how the six remaining filters work:

- **Crop:** The Crop filter uses the front selected path to crop all other paths in the selection. In Figure 9-31, I selected the circle and stripes, copied them to the Clipboard, and clicked the Crop filter. The results were the two rounded dark gray stripes. Then I pasted the original circle and stripes behind the cropped shapes and changed the stripes to black.

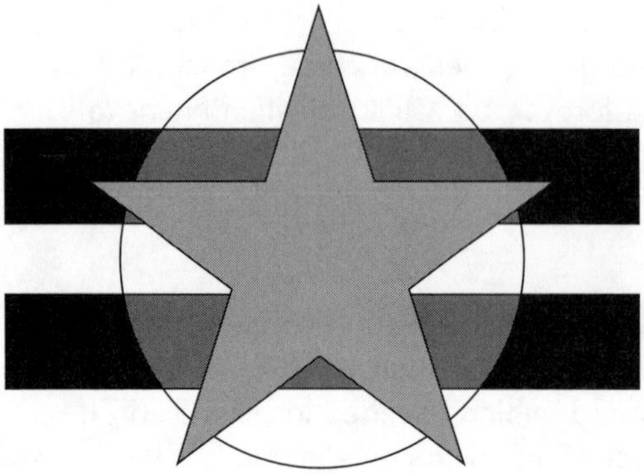

Figure 9-31:
The result of cropping a copy of the stripes inside a copy of the circle and changing the original stripes to black.

- **Divide:** This filter subdivides all paths according to how they overlap. As shown in the top example of Figure 9-32, the paths don't look much different after you apply the filter, but they are in fact separated into many more shapes than before. In the second example, I've nudged the shapes apart, so you can see how the filter has divvied up the paths and deleted hidden areas.

TIP

Divide is a wonderful filter for creating shadows against a multicolor background. The top example in Figure 9-33 shows the united path (created back in Figure 9-25) positioned against three differently colored shapes. I selected all shapes and applied the Divide filter. Then I adjusted the colors of the shadow shapes to get the subtle darkening effect shown in the second example in Figure 9-33. Finally, I pasted the original star, circle, and stripes in front of the shadow to create completed artwork at the bottom of the figure. (To see a similar technique applied to gradient shadows, check out Chapter 15.)

- **Trim:** This filter works just like Divide, except that it only clips rear shapes, while leaving front shapes intact. Or if you prefer, it's just like Merge, except that it doesn't unite shapes that have the same fill. If you find that Divide breaks up your shapes too much, try Trim instead. I must say, however, that I've never used it in my life and am absolutely bereft of ideas for your using it.

- **Hard and Soft:** The Hard and Soft filters break up objects just like the Divide filter. But they also change the fills of the new paths to represent a mix of the colors in the overlapping objects. The Hard filter mixes the colors in the objects at their highest percentages—that is, the highest amounts of cyan, magenta, yellow, and black ink from all overlapping objects. The Soft filter lets you specify what percentage of the inks you want to blend, thus resulting in lighter colors than the Hard command.

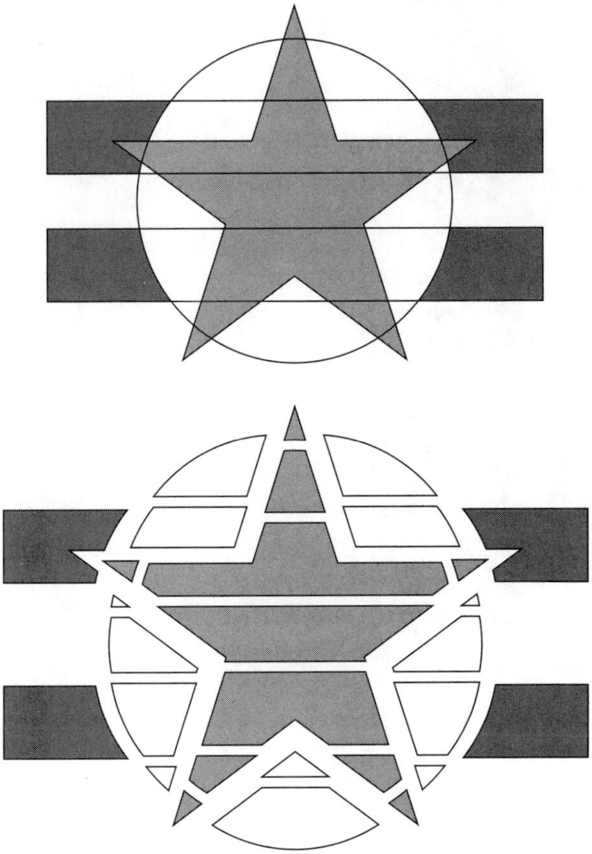

Figure 9-32: The result of applying the Divide filter to all shapes (top) and then nudging them apart (bottom).

As Figure 9-34 illustrates, both filters are wonderful for blending colors from different shapes. Unfortunately, Figure 9-34 doesn't quite do them justice. See, both Hard and Soft are meant to be used with color illustrations, and here I am faking the effect in grayscale. In fact, if you try to mix two gray shapes with Hard, you'll always get the darkest of the gray values, not a darker blend as shown in the figure. Still, the figure gives you a rough idea of what you can expect.

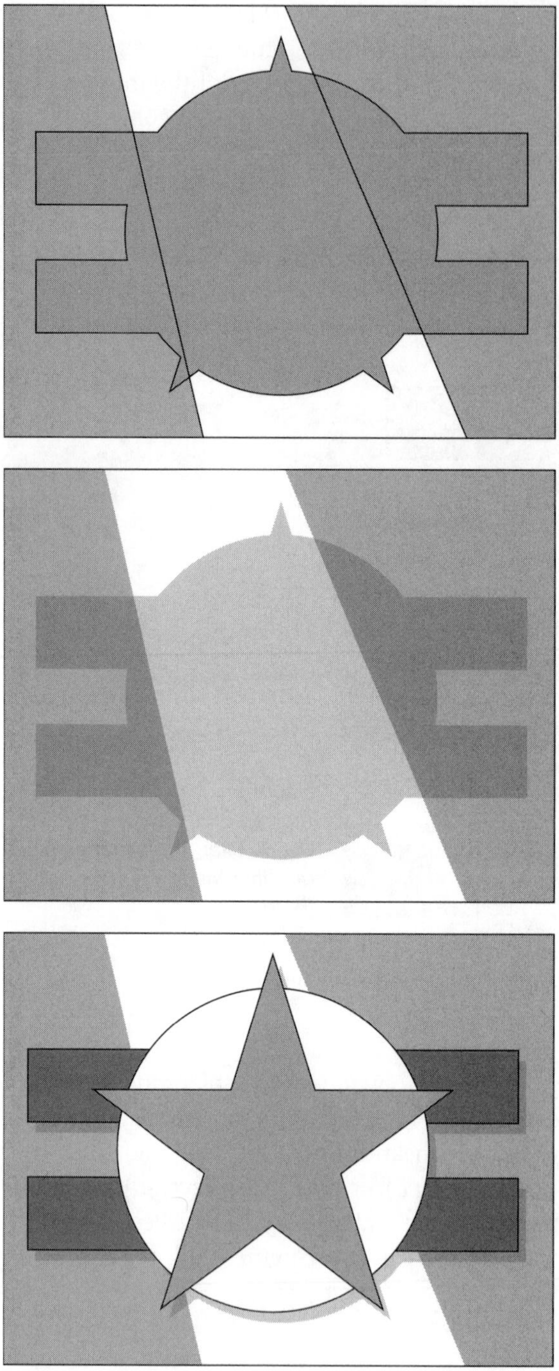

Figure 9-33:
Starting with the united shadow shape, I divide the shadow against three differently colored shapes (top), adjust the gray values (middle), and paste in the objects casting the shadow (bottom).

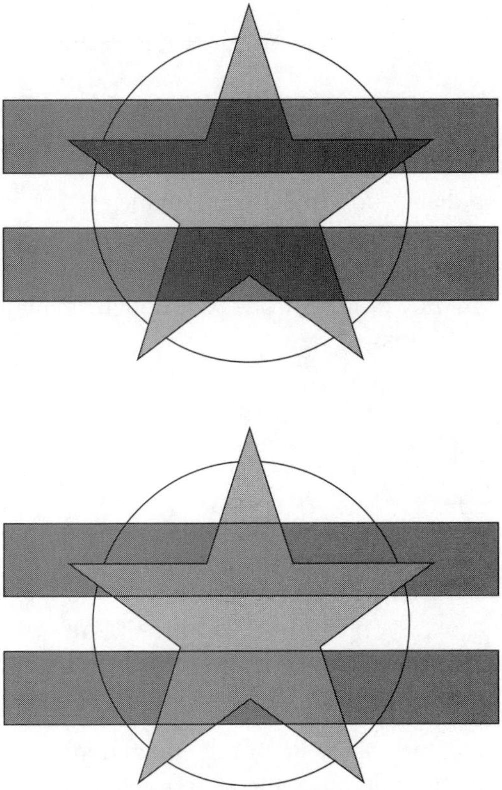

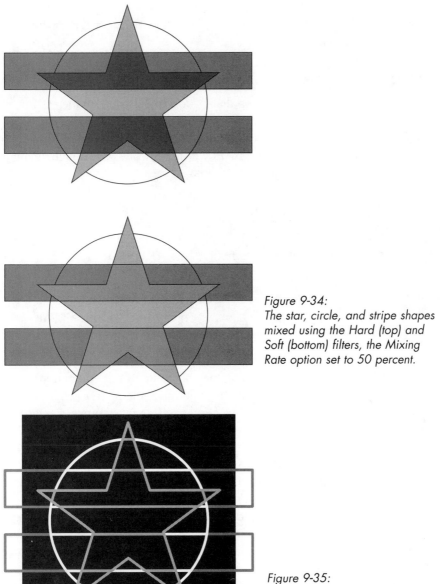

Figure 9-34:
The star, circle, and stripe shapes mixed using the Hard (top) and Soft (bottom) filters, the Mixing Rate option set to 50 percent.

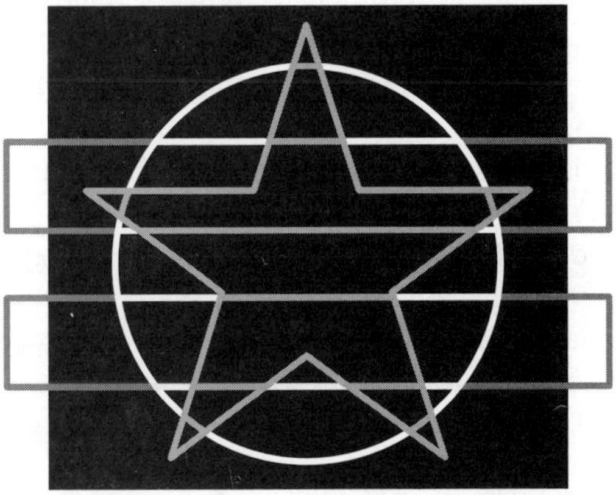

Figure 9-35:
The results of applying the Outline filter to our familiar cast of shapes.

- **Outline:** Outline draws open paths around overlapping areas of selected shapes and strokes these paths with the old fill colors. Figure 9-35 shows this filter applied to the star, circle, and stripes. I've thickened up the strokes (the filter applies 0-point strokes, which is utterly stupid) and added a black rectangle in back so you can see the white outlines around the circle.

Pathfinder Options

You can use the Pathfinder Options dialog box to set the parameters for all Pathfinder operations, and does so in an incredibly complicated way. When you choose the Pathfinder Options command from the Pathfinder palette's pop-up menu, Illustrator displays the dialog box shown in Figure 9-36. Though small, it will melt your brain if you look at it for too long.

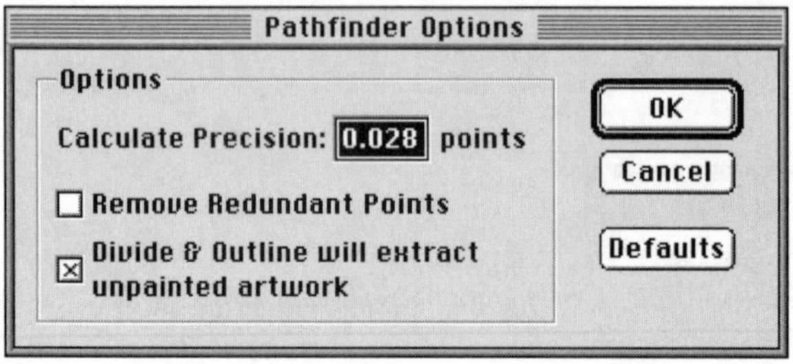

Figure 9-36: My guess is that whoever designed this dialog box has since moved on to a successful career at Microsoft.

The first option lets you control the accuracy of the Pathfinder operations. This value has to be larger than 0.001 point (0.3 micron, remember?), which means that no path will stray farther than one bacterium off its true course. Larger values are less accurate, but they also speed up the performance of the filters. The maximum value is 100 points, but you probably don't want to go much higher than 4 or 5. I don't recommend changing this value, except for adjusting the Trap filter, as I discuss in Chapter 18. And then be sure to change it back when you're done.

The two check boxes in the Pathfinder Options dialog box delete points that overlap each other and objects created by the Divide and Outline commands that have transparent fills and strokes. I recommend you select both these options and leave them selected, unless you have some special reason for retaining overlapping points and invisible objects.

Reapplying a Pathfinder Filter

Oh, and one more thing: You can reapply the last Pathfinder command you used by either choosing the second command in the Pathfinder palette's pop-up menu, Repeat Pathfinder, or by pressing ⌘-4.

CHAPTER 10

DEVELOPING A FLAIR FOR THE SCHEMATIC

Every so often, I run into artists who tell me that they use FreeHand because it offers better precision drawing controls—rulers, guides, grids, and so on. Others tell me they use Illustrator because they don't need all those precision controls. The irony is that Illustrator offers all the standard schematic tools and even some that you won't find anywhere else—frequently outperforming FreeHand, and pretty thoroughly making mincemeat of CorelDraw and other illustration programs.

Illustrator has even improved on the control it offers you. You can use automated grids in your drawing, which help to keep basic illustration elements in alignment. (Strangely, Illustrator 4.1 for Windows provided a grid, but such an option was absent from Illustrator through version 6. Were we to assume Windows users liked grids more than Mac folks, or that grids were easier to pull off on the Windows side? No matter, for we now all have grids. This is just another way that Adobe has succeeded in bringing us all a bit closer together.) Additionally, Illustrator provides smart guides, a system of pop-up alignment guides that help you position and create objects at precise locations.

Illustrator provides a more flexible system of guidelines, a superior measuring function, and center points for all shapes. (FreeHand aligns objects only.) With the advent of smart guides, I would go so far as to say that Illustrator is better than FreeHand in the precision department.

So if you're the type who values a structured drawing environment, keep your chin up and continue reading. This chapters explain everything, from distance to distribution, groups to grids and guidelines, and locks to layers. If it helps you toe the line, it's front and center in the following pages.

Measuring and Positioning with Microscopic Precision

One of my favorite things about using Illustrator is that you can measure dimensions and distances right inside the program. There's no need to print the illustration and measure the output, which is dreadfully inconvenient. And you sure as heck wouldn't want to take a pica pole to the screen, which is horribly inaccurate. Fortunately, Illustrator's built-in capabilities are both more convenient and more accurate than either of those alternatives. Where else can you click on screen to measure discrepancies as slight as 0.0001 point, roughly the length of bacteria razor stubble?

NOTE

Okay, bacteria don't actually shave—they'd get caught in the blades. But if an average-sized bacterium had eyes, its pupils would be about 0.0001 point across. Infectious diseases have a hard time measuring distances as small as 0.0001 point, and at your relatively gargantuan height of 4,000 to 5,000 points tall, you can't get anything close to that kind of accuracy without a powerful microscope.

Illustrator provides three sets of measuring and positioning devices:

- The horizontal and vertical rulers are handy for tracking the cursor. They're about as accurate as real-life rulers, which means that they're good enough for simple alignment but you can't quite measure bacteria with them.
- The measure tool records scrupulously precise dimensions and distances into the Info palette. When the palette is up on screen, you can measure an object just by selecting it. You can even record values with the measure tool, and then turn around and move an object that precise distance and direction.
- The Transform palette lets you position objects according to numeric coordinates. You can move objects or clone them by merely entering a value and pressing Return or Option-Return. The palette has its disadvantages, but it can be useful for quick adjustments.

The following sections explain these items, as well as Object » Arrange » Move, which captures all the pertinent statistics recorded with the measure tool. Together, the rulers, measure tool, Info palette, Move command, and Transform palette form a powerful collection of measuring and positioning gadgets. I doubt you'll find their equal in any program this side of a Cray supercomputer.

Adding Rulers to the Illustration Window

Illustrator gives you two rulers—one vertical and one horizontal—that track the movement of your cursor. To bring them up on screen, press ⌘-R or choose View » Show Rulers. If nothing is selected, you can even Control-click (right-click on the Windows side) and choose the Show Rulers command from the context-sensitive pop-up menu. The horizontal ruler appears along the top of the illustration window, and the vertical ruler appears on the left side, as in Figure 10-1.

TIP You control the unit of measure used by both rulers by choosing the File » Preferences » Units & Undos command and selecting an option from the General Units pop-up menu. Alternatively, if you're working on a Mac, you can cycle through the units—from picas to inches to millimeters and back to picas—by pressing ⌘-Control-U. U know, U for units.

Windows users can now right-click on the rulers to display a pop-up menu that contains all five unit options.

As on traditional rulers, whole picas, inches, and centimeters are indicated by long tick marks; individual points and millimeters appear as short tick marks. If you magnify the view size, the units on the rulers become more detailed; as you zoom out, some of the tick marks drop away.

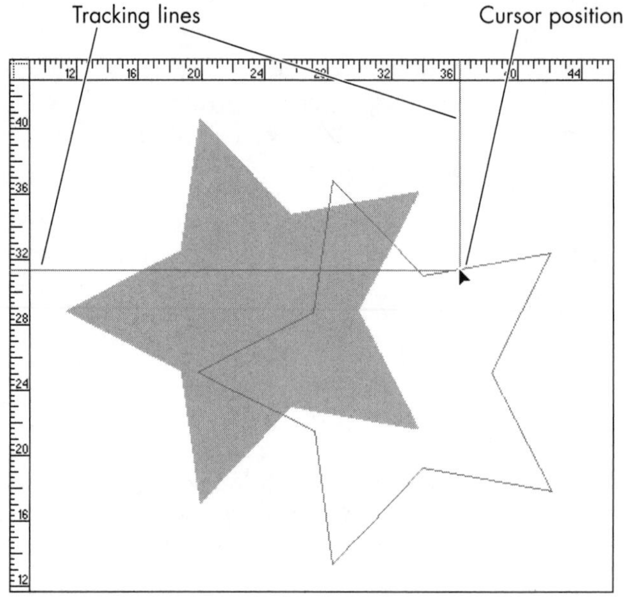

Figure 10-1: The horizontal and vertical rulers track the cursor position.

The rulers constantly track the position of the cursor, so long as the cursor is inside the illustration window. Figure 10-1 labels the dotted tracking line in each ruler. As you can see, the rulers track the tip of the cursor, known as the hot spot. In the figure, the hot spot measures 31 picas, 6 points above and 36 picas, 3 points to the right of the absolute zero point where the rulers begin (as explained in the next section).

Illustrator displays rulers independently for each open drawing, so you can have one illustration window with the rulers visible and another with the rulers hidden. Illustrator saves the ruler status along with the illustration file; if the rulers are up when you save the file, they'll be up again next time you open it.

TIP

To make the rulers come up for all new illustrations, open the Adobe Illustrator Startup file in the Plug-ins folder, press ⌘-R to display the rulers, draw a rectangle (or something simple) and then delete it to get the Save command's attention, and press ⌘-S. From now on, each new illustration window will come with rulers.

To get the rulers the heck out of the way, press ⌘-R or choose View » Hide Rulers. If nothing is selected, Control-click and choose Hide Rules. Oh sure, you already knew that, but we don't leave any stone unturned around here.

Setting the Point Where All Things Are Zero

The point at which both rulers show 0 is called the zero point or ruler origin. By default, the ruler origin is located at the bottom left corner of the artboard. If you change the size of the artboard or the location of the page boundary, the ruler origin may get jostled around a bit.

You can relocate the ruler origin at any time by dragging from the ruler origin box, which is that little square where the rulers intersect. In Figure 10-2, I've dragged the ruler origin onto a point in the star, allowing me to measure all distances from that point. The ruler values update after you release the mouse button. The new ruler origin affects not only the rulers but also the coordinate positioning values in the Info and Transform palettes.

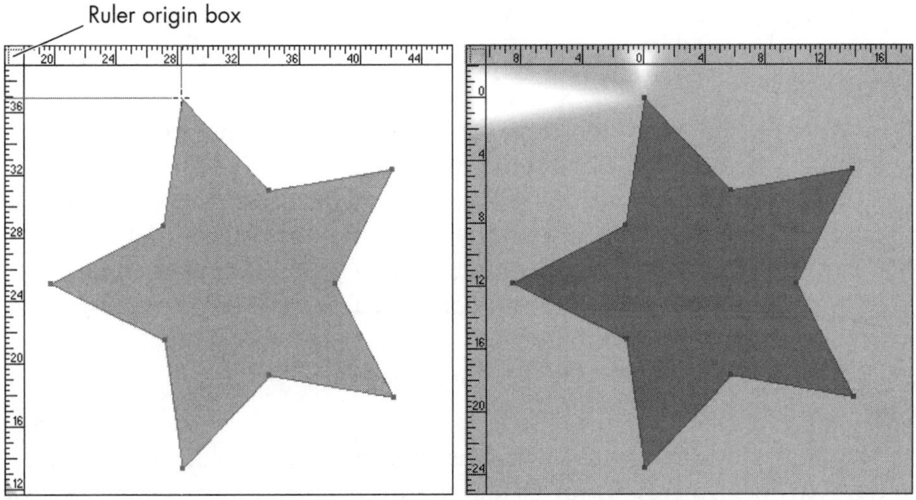

Figure 10-2: Drag from the ruler origin box (left) to reposition the zero point (right).

TIP: If you ever want to reset the ruler origin to default position in the bottom left corner of the artboard, simply double-click the ruler origin box.

TIP: You can save a revised ruler origin with the Adobe Illustrator Startup file. For example, you might prefer to have the zero point in the lower right corner of the illustration. Your change will affect all future illustrations.

Measuring the Minutia

The measure tool and its sidekick, the Info palette, are Illustrator's dynamic duo of precision positioning features. You can use both items to measure distances and objects in three ways:

- Select the measure tool, the second alternate tool in the hand tool slot. In the illustration window, drag from one location to another. The Info palette will automatically open and come into focus. Here Illustrator lists the distance and direction between the beginning and end of your drag. If you click with the measure tool, the Info palette lists the distance and angle between the new click point and the previous one.
- If the Info palette is not open, choose Window » Show Info or press F8. Then use the arrow tool to select the object that you want to measure. The width and height of the segment appear automatically in the palette.
- With the Info palette on screen, drag with any of the shape tools to see information about the size of the path you're creating. When you move the pen tool cursor, the Info palette tells you the distance and direction of the cursor from the last point. When you drag an object with the arrow tool, the palette tells you the distance and direction of the drag. When using the scale or rotate tool, the palette lists the percentage of the scaling or the angle of rotation. The Info palette is constantly trying to tell you something when you create and edit objects.

Assuming that the Snap to Point toggle command in the View menu is switched on, the measure tool snaps to an anchor point when you click within 2 screen pixels of it. In Figure 10-3, for example, I dragged from one anchor point to another to measure the precise distance between the two. Sadly, when you're using the measure tool, Illustrator doesn't give you any snap cursors to show that you've hit the points, but you can see the cursor snap into place if you watch carefully. Just trust The Force, Luke.

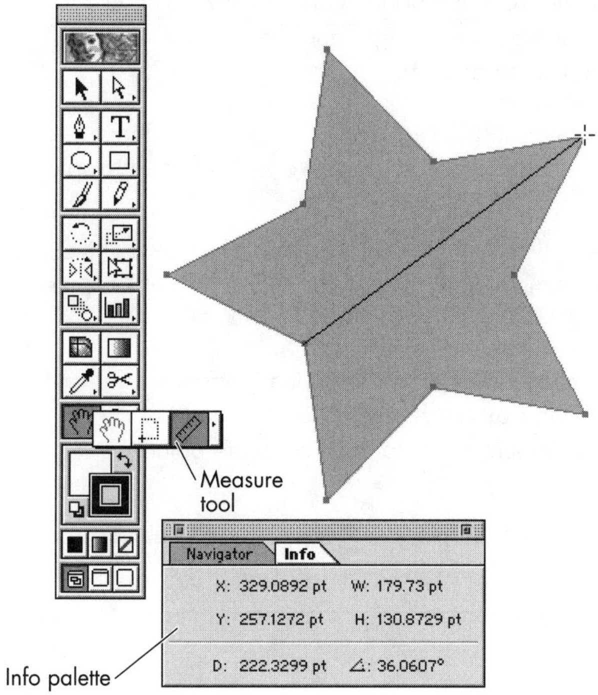

Figure 10-3: Drag with the measure tool and the Info palette will display the distance and direction between two points.

The Info palette can include as many as six numeric values. Here's what they mean:

- **X, Y:** When using a drawing tool, the X and Y values in the Info palette represent the coordinate position of your cursor, as measured from the ruler origin.

  When you use the measure tool, the values tell the last place you clicked with the tool (or released when dragging). This way, you know at what point Illustrator is measuring from the next time you click—providing that you are proficient at reading coordinates.

  If the direct selection or arrow tool is active, the X and Y values indicate the top left corner of the selection.

If you want Illustrator to take the stroke weight of the selected object into consideration, check the Add Stroke Weight in the General Preferences dialog box. Since the X and Y values are measured from the top left corner, the X value will decrease by half the stroke weight and the Y value will increase by that same amount.

And when you use a transformation tool, the X and Y values represent the center of the scaling, rotation, reflection, or skew. More on this topic in Chapter 11.

- **W, H:** The W and H values list the width and height of a selected object. They also tell you the dimensions of a rectangle, ellipse, text block, or graph as you draw it.

With the Add Stroke Weight option in the General Preferences dialog box active, the W and H values will increase by an amount equal to the size of the object's stroke weight.

When you move an object or drag with the measure, pen, convert point, or gradient vector tool, the W and H values tell you the horizontal and vertical components of your drag, as demonstrated by the W and H values in Figure 10-4.

- **D:** This item tells the direct distance between one point and another, as the crow flies. When you drag with the pen or convert point tool, this value indicates the length of the Bézier lever, which is the distance between the anchor point and the control handle. When you're using other tools, the D value simply tells you the distance of your drag.
- **Angle:** The ∠ item indicates the angle of your drag, as measured from the mean horizontal. Figure 10-4 shows how Illustrator measures counterclockwise starting at 3 o'clock; 90 degrees is a quarter circle, 360 degrees is a full circle.

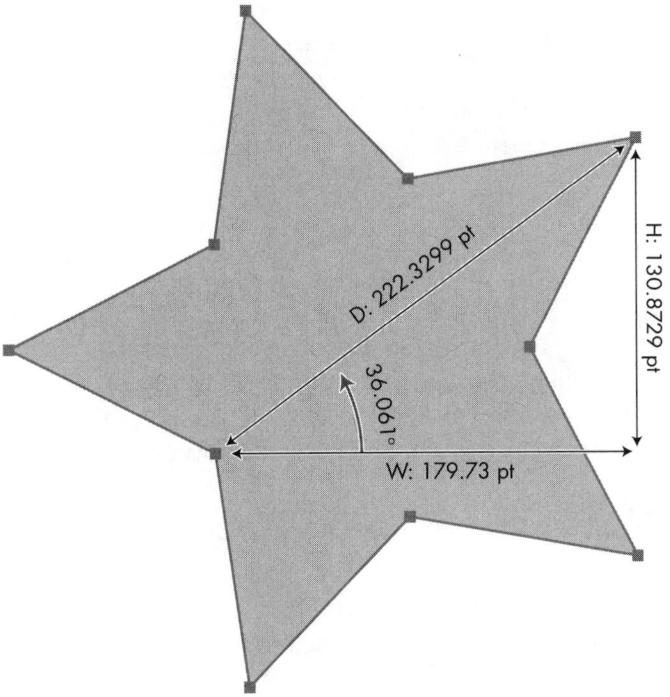

Figure 10-4: The values from the Info palette in Figure 10-3 diagrammed onto the star shape.

TIP

If you want to exactly match the angle of a measured line, you can write down the angle value in the Info palette and then enter it into the Constrain Angle option box in the General Preferences dialog box. This rotates the constraint axes, permitting you to Shift-drag objects relative to the angled line, as I discussed back in the "Keeping Your Movements in Line" section of Chapter 5.

WARNING

Keep in mind that rotating the constraint axes also affects the angle value in the Info palette. For example, if the Constrain Angle value in the General Preferences dialog box is set to 40 degrees and you measure a horizontal line, the Info palette tells you the line is set to –40 degrees. In other words, don't trust the angle value in the Info palette except when the Constrain Angle value is set to 0 degrees.

When you use the rotate tool, the angle value tells you the angle of rotation. The reflect tool uses the angle value to impart the angle of the reflection axis. When you use the shear tool, you get two angle values, one for the axis, and the other for the skew. I cover all these wacky terms in Chapter 11 when I explore transformations in earnest.

- **W%, H%:** These values appear when you scale an object. They tell you the change's width and height, measured as percentages of the object's original dimensions.

When you use the zoom tool, the Info palette tells you the current view size (which is redundant, since Illustrator tells you this in the Size bar as well as in the title bar). When you're editing text, the Info palette lists the type size, font, and tracking information. When you're kerning, the second item lists the general tracking values minus the kerning value to give you an overall kerning total.

Translating Measurement to Movement

After you measure a distance with the move tool, Illustrator automatically stores those W, H, D, and angle values in a tiny buffer in memory. Use the tool again, and the previous measurements are tossed by the wayside to make room for the new ones. Illustrator also uses this buffer to track movements you make by dragging with the arrow or direct selection tool, or by nudging with the arrow keys. Again, the measurements of the most recent action replaces the previous contents of the buffer.

You can translate these buffered measurements into movements by selecting an object or two and choosing Object » Transform » Move. Or try one of the following shortcuts:

- Control-click, or right-click as the case may be, and choose the Transform » Move command from the context-sensitive pop-up menu.
- Double-clicking on the arrow tool icon in the toolbox also works. This is a weird way to go, admittedly, but it stems from an old Illustrator shortcut, Option-clicking on the arrow tool icon. Since a lot of Illustrator folks used the old shortcut by pure force of habit, Adobe felt that they should keep it (or at least, its updated cousin) around. The shortcut is a leftover from Illustrator 1.0, when Option-clicking on the arrow tool was the only way to access the Move feature. (Sigh.) Those were the days—back when Illustrator didn't support color and you had to ungroup a circle to edit it. Makes me kind of misty just thinking about it.

Whatever method you use, you get the Move dialog box shown in Figure 10-5. As you can see, the option boxes contain the same values I recorded in the Info palette back in Figure 10-3. The Move dialog box always supplies you with the buffered distance and angle values, which permit you to quickly move objects a measured distance or to repeat a move made by dragging with the arrow tool. You can likewise negate a move by changing positive values to negative and vice versa. Or you can retain just the horizontal portion of a move by changing the Horizontal value to 0 and inverting the Vertical value. Then again...well, you get the idea. There are all kinds of ways to rehash old measurement and movement information.

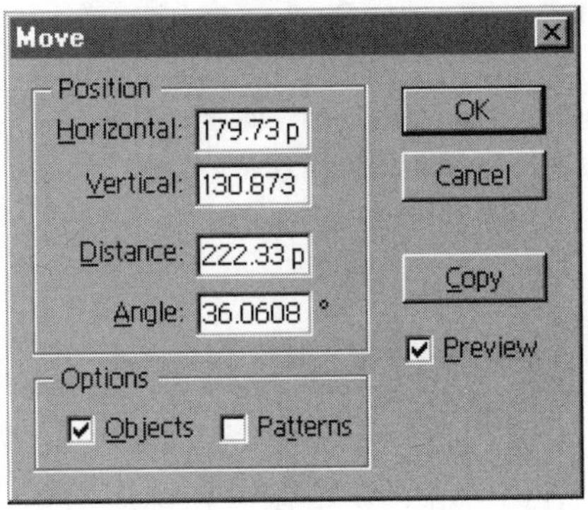

Figure 10-5: The Move dialog box always presents you with the results of your last measurement or movement.

If you feel the urge, you can even enter totally new values into the various option boxes. You can express your move by entering values into the Horizontal and Vertical option boxes or the Distance or Angle option boxes. Since these are two different ways to express the same information, changing one set of values automatically changes the other.

You can also do math inside the option boxes. Simple arithmetic, but math nonetheless. Enter + to add, – to subtract, * to multiply, and / to divide. For example, if you know you want to move a select object 3 points farther than your last measurement, you can enter +3 after the value in the Distance option box. Then press Tab and watch Illustrator do the math for you. This technique works inside other palettes and dialog boxes as well, including the Transform palette.

Use the bottom two check boxes, Objects and Patterns, to select what is to be affected by the move. Check the final check box, Preview, to see what your changes will look like before they occur. You must specify what you want to preview. If you want to preview a move, make sure that both the Preview and Objects check boxes are selected. To see a preview of the object moving with its tile pattern intact, click on the Patterns check box as well. For the lowdown on these options, consult the authoritative Chapter 15.

TIP: You can move the selected objects the specified distance and direction by pressing the Return key. To clone the objects before moving them, click on the Copy button or press Option-Return.

NOTE: One regrettable difference between the Move dialog box and the Info palette is that the former is slightly less accurate. The Move dialog box accepts no more than three digits after the decimal point, so measured values get rounded off. For example, the H: 130.8729 value from Figure 10-3 becomes a Vertical value of 130.873 in Figure 10-5. And D: 222.3299 loses two digits on its way to a Distance value of 222.33. In most cases, such a small increment won't make a lick of difference in your printed output. But if it does matter, you may want to resort to Illustrator's automatic alignment options, which I discuss later in this chapter.

Coordinate Positioning

The last item on the precision position parade is the Transform palette—formally known as the Control palette, and it's the subject of Figure 10-6. After you select the objects you want to change, you open the Transform palette by choosing Window » Show Transform Palette, or you can press F8 and click on the Transform tab. You can then enter values into any one of the six option boxes and press Return to apply them to one or more selected objects.

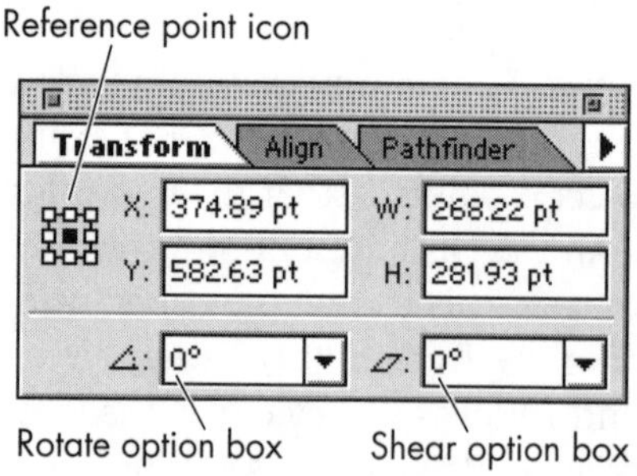

Figure 10-6: The Transform palette, courtesy of the Transform Elves and Wood Nymphs Association.

The first item in the Transform palette is the reference point icon. You can use this icon to specify whether the coordinates in the X and Y option boxes represent the upper left corner of the selection, the middle of the selection, or one of seven other locations. Click on one of the little points in the icon to relocate the reference point. Illustrator updates the X and Y values automatically.

Illustrator positions the reference points around an object with respect to its imaginary bounding box, as illustrated in Figure 10-7. Therefore, the center indicated by the reference point icon in the Transform palette is almost never the true center of the object (except with very simple shapes like rectangles and ellipses). In Figure 10-7, I've marked the real center of the star with a gray X, which lies several points to the right of the bounding box center. In fact, *anytime* Illustrator calculates the center of an object—a theme I will revisit several times in this chapter and in the next—it uses the bounding box center. It's something to keep in mind as you use Illustrator's automated tools.

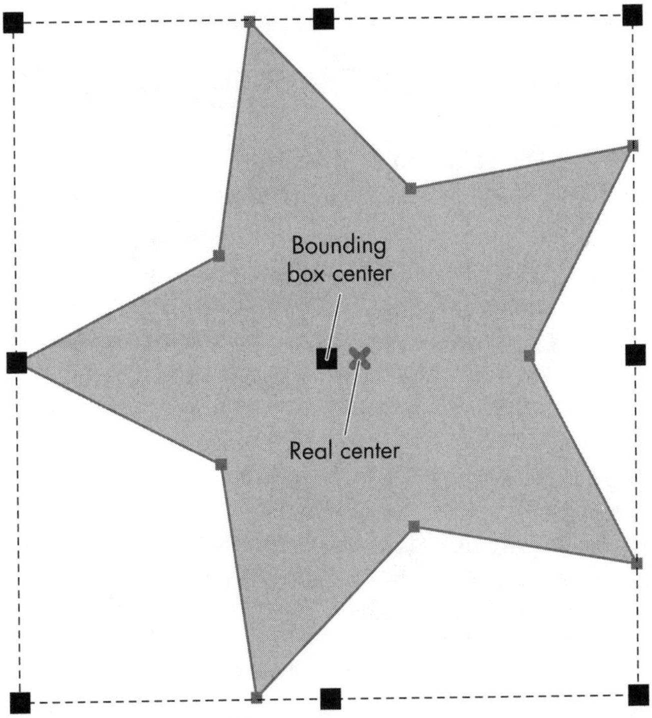

Figure 10-7: The center of the bounding box is rarely equivalent to the true center of an object.

You can enter new values into the X and Y option boxes to change the location of the object on the artboard. You can also adjust the W and H values to change the width and height of the bounding box, which in turn stretches or shrinks the selected object. The shear and rotate options on the right side of the palette let you reshape and rotate selections. Chapter 11 covers these transformations in depth.

As in the Move dialog box, you can perform arithmetic calculations in the X, Y, W, and H options using the standard +, –, *, and / operators. You can even do math inside the shear or rotate option boxes.

TIP: Amazing as it may seem, you can clone objects directly from the Transform palette. Just enter a value into one of the option boxes and press Option-Return if you want to clone the selection and exit the Transform palette. Or press Option-Tab—that's right, Option-Tab—to clone and tab to the next option box. Very cool implementation, I must say.

Aligning and Distributing Objects

To display the Align palette, choose Window » Show Align, or press F8 and click on the Align tab. Shown in Figure 10-8, this dainty little palette contains six Align Objects icons and six Distribute Objects icons. Three icons in each row let you align or distribute horizontally; three allow you to do the same vertically. Select the objects that you want to align or distribute, and then click on an icon. Illustrator adjusts the objects immediately. For example, click on the first icon in the top row to align the selected objects along their left edges, click on the second icon to center the objects, and click on the third icon to align the right edges.

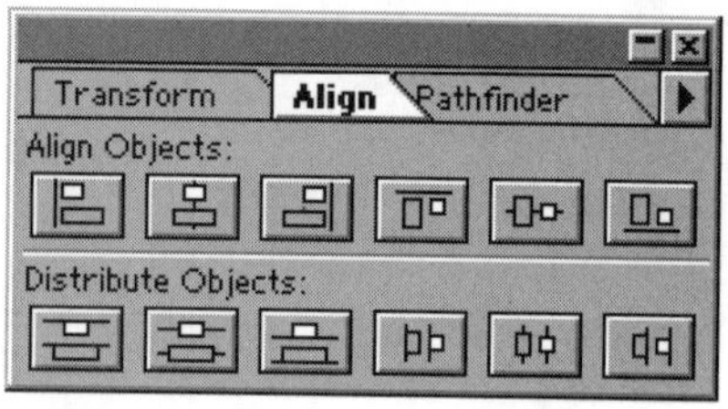

Figure 10-8:
Select the objects that you want to align or distribute and click on an icon in the Align palette.

When aligning objects, Illustrator aligns to the most extreme object in the group. For example, if you align selected objects along their left sides, the leftmost object remains stationary and the other objects line up with it.

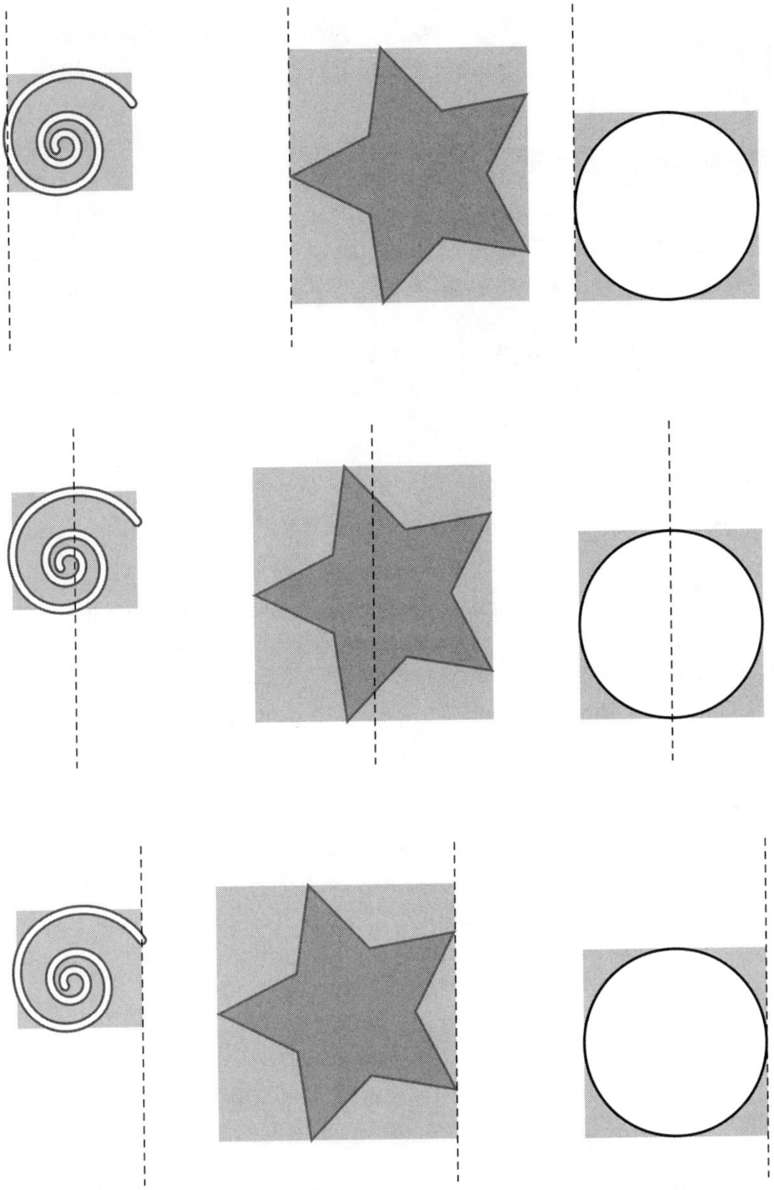

Figure 10-9: Select some objects and click one of the buttons in the Distribute Objects row. The gray rectangles represent bounding boxes; the dotted lines show which portions of the bounding boxes get distributed.

As with the Transform palette, the options in the Align palette work from the bounding boxes of selected objects. This means that centered objects in particular may not look properly centered. If you encounter this problem, try the workaround I suggest in the upcoming "Adding a Center Point" section.

You must select three or more objects to use one of Illustrator's Distribute Objects options. This is because Illustrator compares the space among objects when distributing them; you have to select three objects to have two spaces to compare.

Rather than evening out the amount of space between objects—which is what you might expect—the Distribute Objects options even out the space between the edges or centers of the bounding boxes. Figure 10-9 shows the effects of clicking the last three buttons in the Distribute Objects row on three objects. The figure depicts the bounding box for each object as a gray rectangle; I've also used dotted lines to show which portion of the object is distributed. As you can see, it's the dotted lines—not the objects themselves—that are evenly spaced.

To align or distribute multiple objects together, first group the objects by choosing Object » Group (⌘-G). For example, I grouped each of the simple paths with its bounding box before I applied settings from the Align palette.

Aligning Individual Points

The options in the Align palette affect whole objects at a time. But Illustrator also lets you align selected points independently of their objects by choosing Object » Path » Average (⌘-Option-J). You can arrange two or more points into horizontal or vertical alignment, or you can snap the points together to make them coincident. In each case, Illustrator averages the locations of the points, so all points move.

First select the points you want to align with the direct selection tool. Then press ⌘-Option-J, or even easier, Control-click and, from the context-sensitive pop-up menu, choose the Average command. Either way, the Average dialog box will display, providing you with three radio buttons. You can either make all points coincident (Both), arrange them in a horizontal line (Horizontal), or arrange them vertically (Vertical).

In the top example of Figure 10-10, I selected the bottom three points in each of two star shapes. Then I applied the Average command and selected the Horizontal radio button. Illustrator responded by flattening off the bottoms of both stars, as shown in the bottom example. Kinda makes it look like they're comin' out of the earth, don't it?

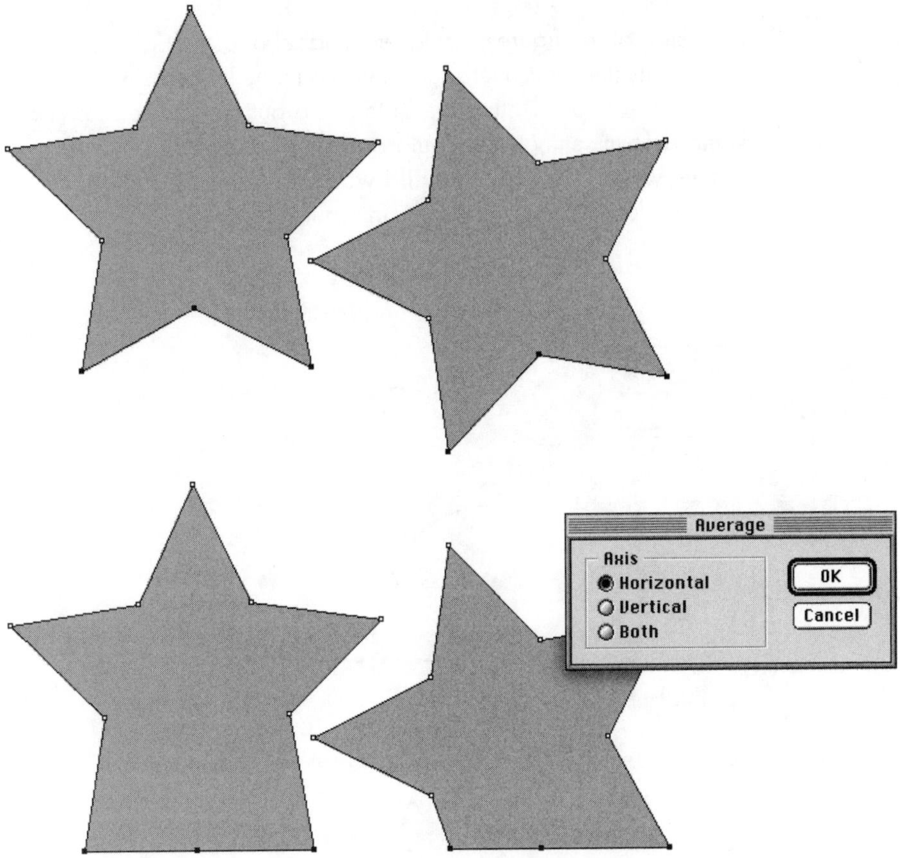

Figure 10-10: After selecting a few points in a couple of shapes with the direct selection tool (top), I aligned the points into horizontal formation (bottom).

Lots of folks use the Average command to move two points together before fusing them with Object » Path » Join. If that's all you want to do, just press ⌘-Option-Shift-J and have done with it (as I advised in Chapter 9). You're better off using the Average command when you want to align points in formation or bring points together from different shapes *without* joining them.

You can even average the alignment points in point text, which is a great way to arrange bits of point text into columns or to align labels with callout lines. The hyper-realistic medical illustrations in Figures 10-11 and 10-12 show what I mean.

After creating the series of labels and callout lines along the right side of the figures, I selected a label and the rightmost point in its line and averaged their locations by pressing ⌘-Option-J and selecting the Both radio button. (This option is the default setting, so I could press ⌘-Option-J and immediately whack the Return key if I wanted to.) I repeated this for each label to get the results in Figure 10-11.

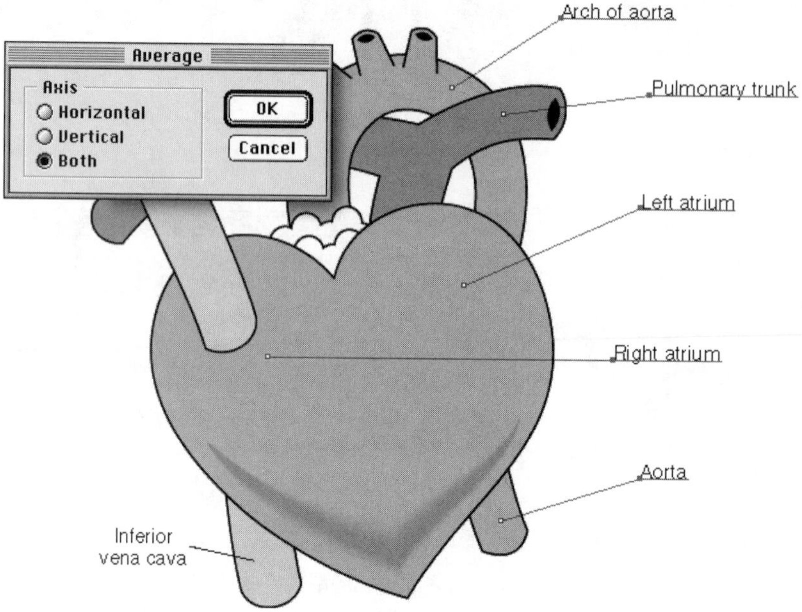

Figure 10-11: One by one, I selected each piece of point text and the right point in its callout line and averaged their locations.

Then I selected all labels and the right points in their callout lines and pressed ⌘-Option-J again, this time selecting the Vertical radio button. Illustrator arranged the labels into one column, as in Figure 10-12.

Labels don't look so hot stuck to their callout lines, so I would next select the point text and nudge it to the right and down a few points with the arrow keys. And finally, I would ship the illustration to Johns Hopkins where it would be used to train the surgeons of tomorrow.

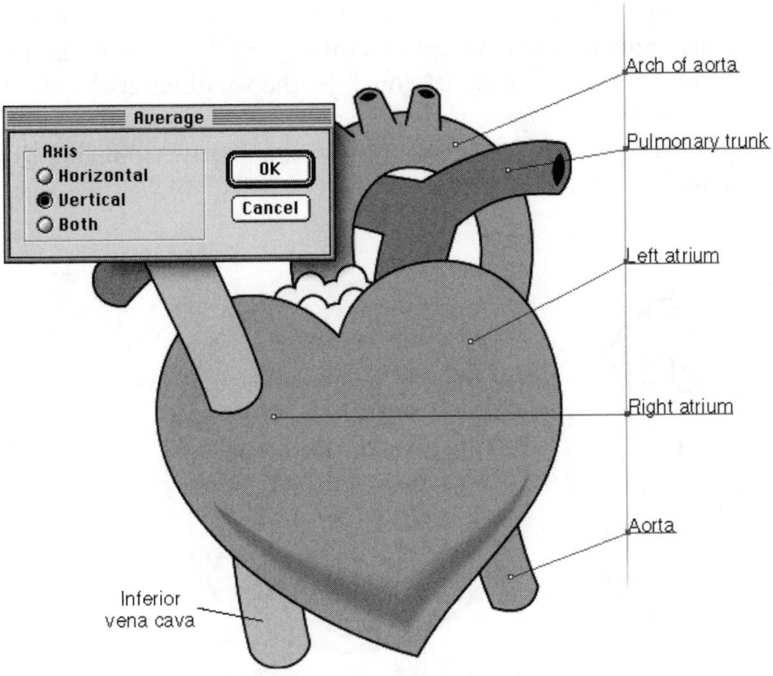

Figure 10-12: Then I selected all point text and right points in all callout lines and arranged them into a vertical column.

Adding a Center Point

Illustrator lets you assign a center point to any object by selecting the object and clicking on the Show Center button in the Attributes palette. This center point acts just like the ones Illustrator automatically includes with rectangles and ellipses. You can view the center point in the artwork mode or when the object is selected in the preview mode. You can also drag the object by its center point.

This should be a great feature. For example, you should be able to drag the center point from one point onto the center point from another shape and have Illustrator align the points exactly. Unfortunately, just like the Transform and Align palettes, Illustrator positions the center point with respect to the bounding box, which is rarely the true center of the shape except in the case of rectangles (which are the same shape as their bounding boxes) and ellipses (which are uniformly round).

For example, suppose that you wanted to center a star inside a circle. If you first drew the circle, and then drew the star from the circle's center point, you'd end up with two precisely aligned shapes, as demonstrated in Figure 10-13. This is because Illustrator knows where the real center of a star is when you're drawing it. But if you add a center point to the star, and then drag the center point until it snaps onto the center point in the circle, you'll get the weird effect shown in Figure 10-14. (The same thing happens if you select the two shapes and click on the fifth icon in the top row of the Align palette.) Illustrator hasn't centered the shapes; it has centered the bounding boxes.

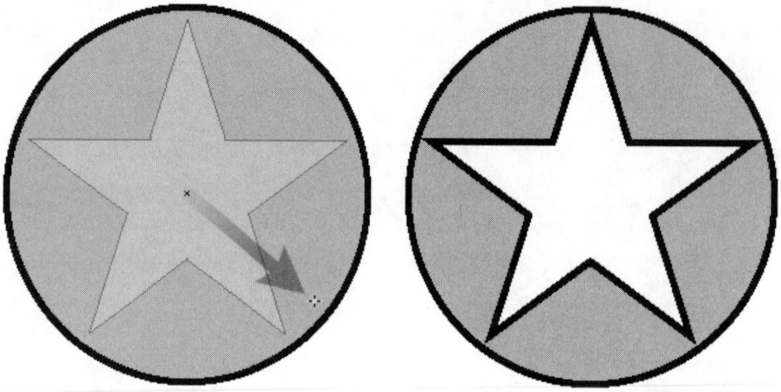

Figure 10-13: When I drag from the center point of a circle with the star tool (left), Illustrator precisely aligns both star and circle by their true centers (right).

Figure 10-14: If I add a center point to the star and then drag the star by the point until it snaps to the circle's center point, the shapes align like this.

TIP

Luckily, there's a workaround that's as old as the first version of Illustrator. To create your own accurate center point, follow these steps:

1. **Delete any center point you've already added with the Attributes palette.**

   Select an object and click on the Don't Show Center button in the Attributes palette.

2. **Duplicate the shape in place.**

   Press ⌘-C, ⌘-F to go the copy-in-place route. Or press Option-↑, ↓ to clone.

3. **Choose Object » Path » Add Anchor Points.**

   This technique accounts for the locations of points only, which means that curved segments can throw it off. If the shape includes any curved segments, apply the Add Anchor Points command to double the number of anchor points in the shape. If it has lots of curved segments, choose the command a couple more times to reapply it.

4. **Average all points in the shape.**

   Press ⌘-Option-J or Control-click and choose Average to bring up the Average dialog box. Immediately press Return to accept the default Both setting. This causes Illustrator to average all points in the path. If the path is composed entirely of straight segments—as with a star—you'll see what looks like a single point in the middle of the shape. If the path included curved segments, you'll see a point with a bunch of squiggles coming out of it. In both cases, you're actually seeing a bunch of points clustered into a single location.

5. **Shift-click on the point with the direct selection tool and press Delete.**

   Now you have a gob of points, but you want to keep just one of them. Shift-click on the selected center point with the direct selection tool to deselect the single foremost point. The point turns hollow to show that it's still part of a selected path. Then press Delete to clear all points except the one you just deselected. This leaves one true center point.

6. **Change the fill and stroke to transparent.**

   Some printers will try to print the fill or stroke of a single, disconnected point. To avoid this, it's a good precaution to make the point transparent.

7. **Group the center point with the shape.**

   Shift-click on the path with the arrow tool (or Shift-Option-click with the direct selection tool) and press ⌘-G to group the selection.

Now if you drag the center point with the arrow tool, you can snap it to the center point of another path to precisely align the two.

WARNING: This procedure has one downside, however: Unlike automatic center points, custom center points don't automatically reposition themselves when you reshape a path. That is to say, the custom centers remain on target when you move or transform the entire grouped shape, but if you alter individual points and segments, the center becomes inaccurate.

Creating and Using Custom Guides

Another way to align objects is to establish a system of guidelines (or just plain guides). These are special kinds of paths that appear as dotted or solid lines on screen but never print. You can choose the form and color that your guides take in the Guides & Grid Preferences dialog box. Assuming the Snap to Point option is turned on in the General Preferences dialog box, your cursor aligns to the guideline any time you drag within two pixels of it. Unlike standard paths, your cursor snaps to any position along the outline of a guide, regardless of the placement of anchor points.

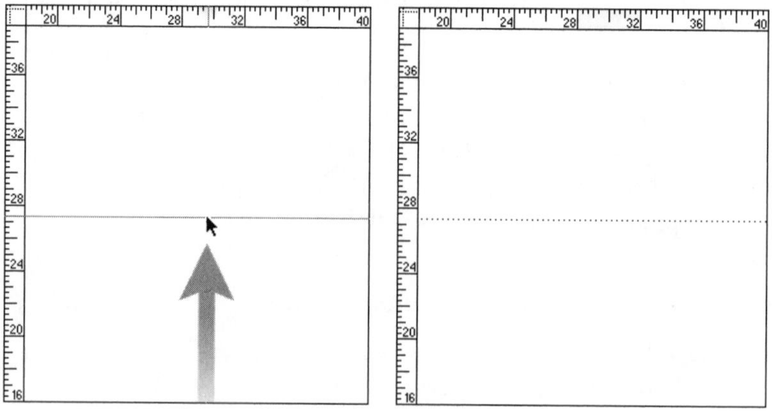

Figure 10-15: Dragging from the top ruler (left) creates a horizontal guideline that stretches the entire width of the pasteboard (right).

You can create a guide in one of the following ways:

- Drag from one of the rulers to create a perpendicular guide that runs the entire width or height of the pasteboard In Figure 10-15, for example, I dragged from the horizontal ruler to create a horizontal guide. The guideline appears in the illustration window as a dotted line, clearly distinguishing it from printing objects.

TIP: If you change your mind while dragging a guide from one of the rulers, press the Option key to rotate it 90 degrees. Option-dragging from the horizontal ruler creates a vertical guide. The guide remains rotated only so long as the Option key is down.

- To create a custom guideline in the shape of a circle, star, or even a character of type, select a path that you've drawn in the illustration window and choose View » Make Guides. You can also use the shortcut ⌘-5 or Control-click and choose Make Guides.

Figure 10-16: Press ⌘-5 to convert selected paths—including converted text and compound paths (top)—to custom snap-to guidelines (bottom).

You can convert all varieties of paths to guidelines, including compound paths. You can even convert groups, selections inside groups, and the bars or lines inside graphs. The one thing you can't turn into a guide is text (unless you first convert the text to paths with Type » Create Outlines, like the big R in Figure 10-16). So if you get an error message when pressing ⌘-5, you can be sure your selection includes some text. Deselect the text and try again.

To create a guideline without sacrificing the original path, copy the path (⌘-C), paste it in back (⌘-B), and then choose View » Make Guides (⌘-5) to convert the duplicate to a guideline.

TIP If you convert a single path within a group to a guideline, without converting other paths in the group, the guideline remains a member of that group. Drag the group with the arrow tool, and the guide moves as well. It's a very handy way to keep certain guides and objects together.

Unlocking and Editing Guides

By default, Illustrator locks guides so they don't get too tangled up with your printed paths. You can't select a locked guide by simply clicking on it, which prevents you from messing it up. To unlock all guides in an illustration, choose View » Lock Guides, or press ⌘-Option-; (semicolon). If you like, you can Control-click and use the Lock Guides command provided in the context-sensitive pop-up menu. For this command to appear in this somewhat erratic menu, you must have either a guide selected or nothing at all selected. After you click it, the check mark in front of the Lock Guides command disappears, showing that the lock is now off.

Once the guides are unlocked, you can select and manipulate them as you can any other graphic object. When you click on a guide with the arrow or direct selection tool, Illustrator shows you the guide's anchor points to let you know it's selected. Use the direct selection tool to reshape the guide. Shift-click or marquee to select multiple guides at a time. Press the Delete key to delete a selected guide. You can also move guides or transform them. You can even use the add point, delete point, and convert point tools on a guideline.

Once you've gotten the guides the way that you want them, press ⌘-Option-semicolon again to relock them. This locks all guides, not just those that were selected.

Manipulating Locked Guides

TIP

As fortune would have it, it's not absolutely necessary to unlock a guide in order to select it. To select a locked guide, ⌘-Shift-drag on it with the arrow or direct selection tool. The guide will remain selected throughout your drag and return to its locked status after you release the mouse button.

The following items describe ways to manipulate a locked guide:

- To move a locked guide with the arrow or direct selection tool, ⌘-Shift-drag it to a new location. After beginning the drag, release the keys to move the guide without constraint.
- Press Option along with the other keys to clone a locked guide. Be sure to keep the Option key pressed until after you release the mouse button.

You can't reshape a locked guide, since you can't select a point or segment independently of any others. And you can't select or manipulate multiple locked guides at the same time unless they are members of the same group or compound path.

TIP

Want to hear a weird one? If a guide is part of a group or a compound path, it and its pals remain selected after you ⌘-Shift-drag them. This is true even if the other paths in the group or compound path are also guides. This means that after you move the guides, you can then scale or rotate them from the Transform palette, even though they're still locked. To take advantage of this peculiarity, I group each and every path—by itself—before I make it a guide. This way, I have a wider range of editing options when the guides are locked.

Converting Guides to Objects

If your eyes grow tired from editing guidelines, or if you simply want to turn a guide into a printing object, you can convert a guide back to a path. To do so, unlock the guide by pressing ⌘-Option-; (semicolon), select it, and then choose View » Release Guides (or press ⌘-Option-5). Just to be consistent, you may also Control-click and choose Release Guides from the resulting menu. Illustrator converts custom guides back to paths, even remembering their original fill and stroke colors. Ruler guides convert into lines—these lines will have no fill and zero stroke weight, mmm, handy—which extend the entire width or length of the pasteboard.

TIP

To convert a locked guide back into a path, ⌘-Shift-double-click on the guide.

It's Grid for You and Me

Another of Illustrator's handy positioning features is the optional grid system. By simply choosing View » Show Grid or by pressing ⌘-quote ("),a network of equally spaced horizontal and vertical lines stripe your pasteboard. If you feel so inclined, Control-click and activate the grid from your friendly context-sensitive pop-up menu. This is one of those times when nothing must be selected for the command to appear in the menu. You can choose the color and style of the lines that make up a grid, just as you can for your guides, in the Guides & Grid Preferences dialog box (shown back in Chapter 2). There you also specify the spacing of the grid lines and the number of divisions per grid line. Choose a grid line spacing of 72 points with 5 subdivisions, and you get a lattice of lines spaced 12 points apart (72 divided by 5). Select the Lines command from the Style pop-up menu to see grid lines and divisions; select Dots to see the grid lines sans the divisions.

On first glance, you may think that this is a case of guide overkill. It might seem that you could achieve the same results using guides, and guides don't take over your entire drawing area. Moreover, the grid-related commands are rather limited. In addition to commands for showing and hiding grids, as mentioned above, the only other command is View » Snap To Grid (⌘-Shift-quote), and it beats me why on earth you would want a grid and not have things automatically snapping to it.

But friends, I'm here to tell you that beneath the grid's mild mannered appearance beats the heart of a powerful ally. The grid function offers you these handy features:

- Provided that the Grids In Back check box inside the Guides & Grid Preferences dialog box is active, grids let you easily distinguish between unfilled objects and objects filled with white. The unfilled objects are transparent and allow you to see the grid lines behind them, and the filled objects block your view of the grid. Guides always appear on top.
- A grid gives you a quick-and-easy way to produce guides that are equally spaced. You could do the same thing with guides, but it's just faster to choose View » Show Grid and set the structure in the Guides & Grid Preferences dialog box.

- You can set up your grid line spacing in different units than the general units. In the Guides & Grid Preferences dialog box, enter a value into the Gridline every option box followed by the type of units you want. You can then have your rulers set to, say, centimeters and your grids marking off inches.
- Since a grid is subject to the value set in the Constraint Angle option box (in the General Preferences dialog box), you can have an angled grid. Guides, on the other hand, are limited to the standard up-and-down or side-to-side format.

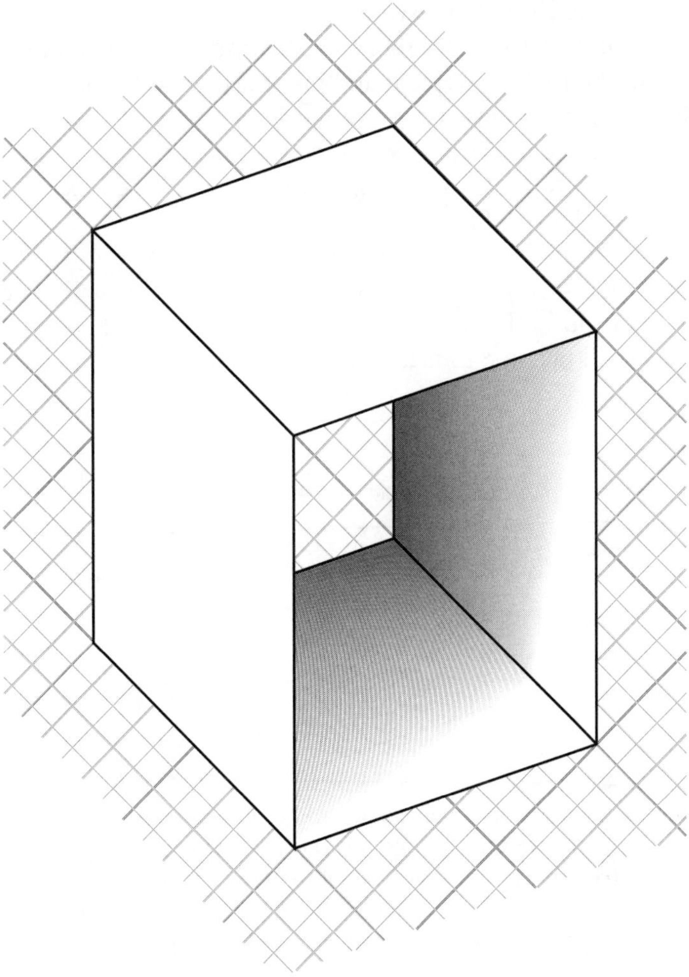

Figure 10-17: With a Constrain Angle value of 45 degrees, I turned on the grid and quickly drew one of them freaky perspective boxes.

An angled grid allows you to create perspective drawings quickly and easily. I drew the box in Figure 10-17 with the aid of an angled grid. I chose View » Show Grid and entered 45 into the Constrain Angle option in the General Preferences dialog box. With four quick clicks of the pen tool, I created the top of the box and filled it with white—that's why you can't see the grid behind it. After selecting the rectangle, I Option-dragged it down to form the bottom of the box. With four more clicks, I created the left side of the box and duplicated it by Option-dragging up and to the right with the arrow tool. I then pressed ⌘-Shift-[(left bracket) to send the right side to the back of the stack. The whole process took less than five minutes.

I could have also constructed this figure with customized guides. I'd simply draw a rectangle and slant it with the shear tool (as explained in Chapter 11) to form the front of the box. Then I'd duplicate it and move it up and to the left to form the back. Using the Make Guides command (⌘-5), I'd convert these two parallelograms to guides and use the pen tool to connect the corners with four separate objects that would serve as the sides, top, and bottom of the box. This process would take only a bit longer than it did using a grid.

The real power of a grid is its flexibility. With the same grid shown in Figure 10-17, I constructed the box in Figure 10-18. Once again, I could have used guides to draw it, but I made both the boxes shown in these two figures in roughly half the time it would take me to make them using guides.

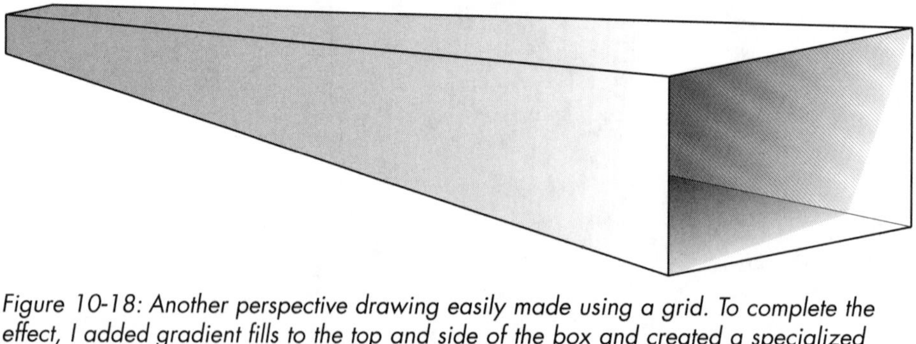

Figure 10-18: Another perspective drawing easily made using a grid. To complete the effect, I added gradient fills to the top and side of the box and created a specialized blend for the interior shadow. Blends are the major topic of Chapter 17.

Smart Guides

Illustrator 8 introduces a system of automated guides that might just make the old-fashioned guides and grids obsolete for all your precision drawing and positioning needs. Smart guides consist of *alignment guides, path labels,* and *path highlights*. The alignment guides are temporary guidelines that pop in and out of existence as you drag the cursor around the screen. Path labels consist of a number of little text hints that display to inform you where your cursor is within the document. Path highlights ring the outline of a path to tell you that the cursor is positioned over a path. Smart guides are completely independent of traditional guides, with the exception that their color matches that of traditional guides and is determined in the Guides and Grids Preference dialog box.

Perfect Position

Alignment guides (also known as construction guides), the driving force behind smart guides, resemble traditional ruler guides in that they extend the entire length of the pasteboard, but, unlike ruler guides, they display only as long as you need them. To see alignment guides, first turn them on with the View » Smart Guides toggle command (⌘-U). Then, from the Smart Guides Preferences dialog box (pictured back in Chapter 2), make sure that the Construction Guides option is active.

Alignment guides will appear to help you position the points of a path as you create or manipulate it. The guides inform you that you're aligned with respect to the origin point of your drag. By default, the guides align at multiples of 45 degrees. Secondary alignment guides will appear to tell you that you are also aligned to other points of interest (not to be confused with Teddy Roosevelt's upper left bicuspid forever preserved at Mt. Rushmore). You determine these secondary alignment points by dragging over them with your active tool. At first glance, this is a bit confusing so I'll give a quick demonstration of how alignment guides can assist you in drawing a right triangle with two equal sides.

1. **Click with the pen tool to set the triangle's first point.**

   Be sure that the Smart Guides command is active. For clarity, I've turned off the other smart guide options in the Smart Guides Preferences dialog box, namely the Text Label Hints and Object Highlighting options.

2. Move the pen tool to the right.

As you move the pen directly horizontally from this first point, an alignment guide displays, as shown in Figure 10-19. This shows that you are aligned with respect to that first point.

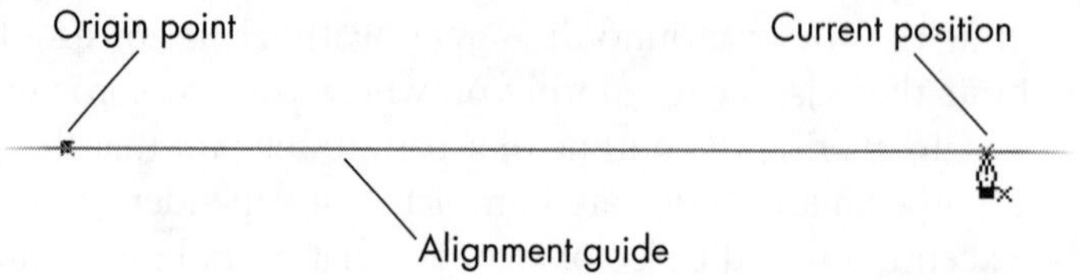

Figure 10-19: Click to set the triangle's first corner point and move the cursor directly to the right. An alignment guide will show that you're on track.

3. Click to set the triangle's second corner point.

The second point will be directly to the right of the first point.

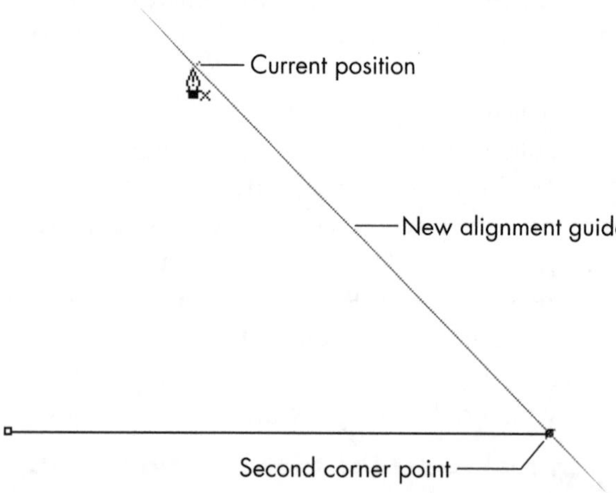

Figure 10-20: A new alignment guide shows that the present cursor position makes a 45 degree angle with the horizontal and is aligned with respect to the second corner point.

4. **Move the cursor up and to the left.**

   When you aligned with the second corner point, a new alignment guide will appear as shown in Figure 10-20. If this guide doesn't display, choose the 90º and 45º Angles command from the Angles pop-up menu in the Smart Guides Preferences dialog box.

5. **Move the cursor over the first point and then move the cursor straight up.**

   This seemingly arbitrary positioning is of the utmost importance. By moving the cursor over the first corner point you're telling Illustrator that you want to use this as a secondary alignment point. As you move the cursor upwards, a secondary alignment guide will display, as shown Figure 10-21.

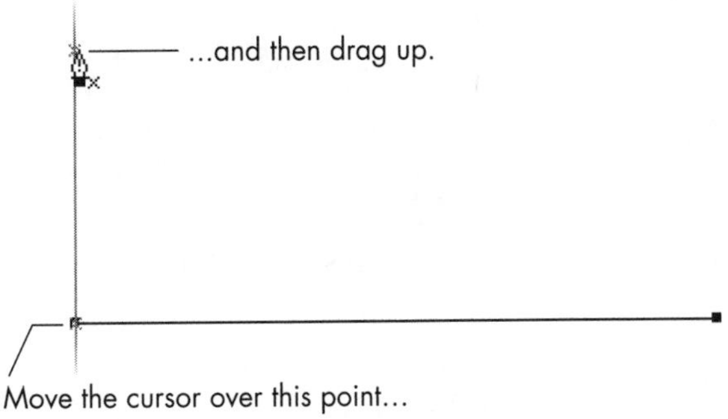
...and then drag up.
Move the cursor over this point...

Figure 10-21: First move the cursor over the point you want to use as a secondary alignment point and drag straight up to see a secondary alignment guide.

6. **Continue until both guides display.**

   As you continue to move the cursor up, all the while aligned with the first corner point so that the secondary alignment guide remains visible, you will eventually cross the point where the first alignment guide again displays, as shown in Figure 10-22. This point is in perfect alignment with the triangle's other two corner points, directly above the first and at a 45 degree angle up and to the left of the second.

7. **Click to set the third corner.**

   Position a point with perfect precision.

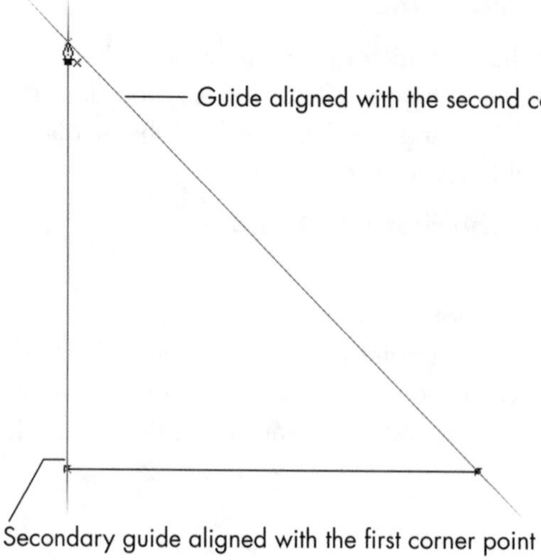

Figure 10-22: Moving the cursor directly upwards will eventually display the intersection of the two alignment guides.

8. Click again at the original point.

This closes the path, completing your perfect right triangle with two equal sides.

The display of alignment is not limited to when you're simply moving the cursor around the screen. The guides will also appear when you are dragging to create paths or dragging paths around to position them. You can also define as many secondary alignment points as you wish. Just be sure to move the cursor over the other points with which you want Illustrator to align. Although you many have a number of active alignment points, Illustrator will only display two alignments at a time (either an alignment guide and a secondary alignment guide, or two alignment guides).

Precise Transforming

If you want Illustrator to display alignment guides while you're manipulating a path with one of the transformation tools, then activate the Transformation Tools option in the Smart Guides Preferences dialog box. The primary alignment guide will display with reference to the point from which you started your drag, not the transformation's origin point. You may define secondary alignment points by dragging the cursor over points of the various other paths that comprise your artwork. Unfortunately, you cannot set the transformation's origin point as a secondary alignment point, since this is not a "physical" point in the world of Illustrator.

TIP

If you know that you're going to want to use the transformation origin as a secondary alignment point, simply construct a point at that location with the pen tool before you start the transformation. Then select the object you want to transform and click on the point you just made with the transformation tool. After you've begun dragging the cursor, be sure to move it over the point, indicating to Illustrator that you want it to use the point as a secondary alignment point.

Alignment Angles

By default, an alignment guide will pop in when the angle formed between your cursor's current and original positions and the horizontal is some multiple of 45 degrees. But, as you probable have guessed, Illustrator doesn't limit you with such mundane options. In the Smart Guides Preferences dialog box you can choose from seven predefined angular alignment options (all of which appear in the Angles pop-up menu) or enter up to six custom angles. If you choose to rebel geometrically, simply enter the angle with which you want the alignment guides to conform in the six option boxes below the Angles pop-up menu. Illustrator will reflect your choices in the little alignment guide display box located to the right of the Angles pop-up menu.

The angle of the various alignment guides also depends on the value in the Constrain Angle option box of the General Preferences dialog box. For example, if the General Preferences' Constrain Angle is set to 0 degrees and the Smart Guides Preferences' Angles is on the 90° and 45° Angles setting, then the angle of an alignment guide could be 0, 45, or 90 degrees. If the Constrain Angle is changed to 15 degrees, the resulting alignment guide's angles could be 15, 60, or 105 degrees. Just think of the Constrain Angle value as a starting point for the angles of the alignment guides.

Sticking to Smart Guides

Unlike with traditional guides and grids, your cursor has no option but to snap to any smart guide. If an alignment guide is visible, then Illustrator will snap the path or point you're dragging to the guide once you release the mouse button. Anytime you're within a certain distance of the position of a smart guide, the smart guide appears and Illustrator is ready to snap you to it. This distance is the snapping tolerance. By default, the snapping tolerance is set to 4 screen pixels. In the Snapping Tolerance option box in the Smart Guides Preferences dialog box you can choose any value from 0 to 10 pixels inclusively. The higher the value, the more readily Illustrator displays the smart guides.

Your Position Spelled Out

Another feature of smart guides are path labels. When the Text Label Hints option in the Smart Guides Preferences dialog box is checked and the Smart Guides command is in effect, Illustrator will show you little labels to inform you as to the position of the cursor with respect to various parts of your document. Figure 10-23 shows a collage I've constructed to show you a few of them.

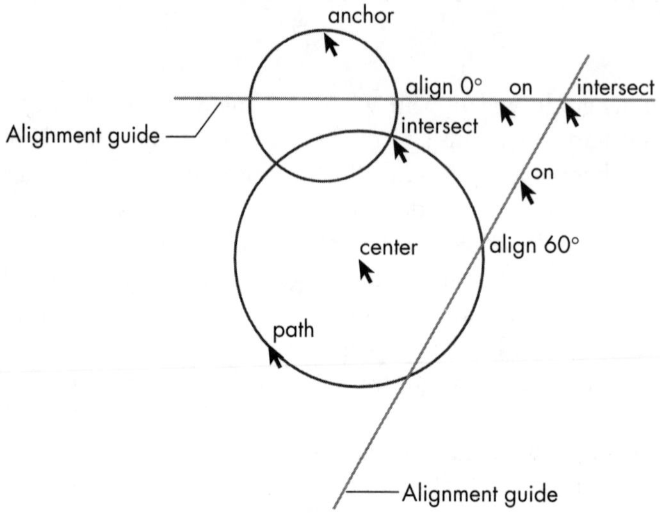

Figure 10-23: With the Text Label Hints option active, Illustrator will display various labels to inform you of the cursor's position.

Path Highlights

Smart guides have one other feature: path highlighting. With the Object Highlighting option in the Smart Guides Preferences dialog box checked and the Smart Guides command set to the on position, Illustrator will temporarily highlight the outline of any path that your cursor crosses. This allows you to easily see paths that are partially (or even entirely) obscured by other paths. Illustrator even highlights paths that have no fill or stroke. Although Illustrator will highlight locked paths, it will not acknowledge hidden paths.

Assembling Paths into Groups

Most of the time, you'll apply transformations to whole paths rather than to individual points or segments. You may even want to transform multiple objects at a time. So imagine that instead of working with paths and objects, you could manipulate whole pieces of artwork. A boy here, a dog there, a great white shark preparing to eat the both of them a few meters away. This is the beauty of grouping, which allows you to assemble throngs of elements into a single object.

Suppose, for example, that you've created a graphic made up of several paths. You want to rotate the graphic, but you're afraid of upsetting the fragile relationship between the paths during the transformation. To safeguard the basic appearance of the graphic, select the objects and choose Object » Group. Or press the common-as-dirt keyboard equivalent, ⌘-G.

Illustrator always groups entire objects. Even if you select a single point in one object and a segment in another, the two objects join the group in their entirety. There's no way to group a couple of points or segments independently of others in a path.

You can group paths, compound paths, text objects, imported images, or any other kind of artwork. You can even group other groups. Illustrator permits infinite hierarchies of groups, so that one group may contain two groups that each contain six others, and so on. It's like a giant family tree of object protection.

Selecting Objects Within Groups

Paths and text blocks inside groups remain autonomous objects. You can apply different fills and strokes, reshape the paths, move and transform them, and do most of the same things that you can do to ungrouped paths and text blocks. As for its few limitations, Illustrator does a good job of beeping at you and telling you where you've gone wrong if you step over the line.

To edit objects inside groups, you have to first select them:

- Click any object in a group with the arrow tool to select the entire group.
- To edit text inside a group, drag across the characters as you normally would with the type tool.
- If you use the direct selection tool to click on a point or segment inside a group, you select that one element independently of all other points and segments in the group. You can also Shift-click and marquee elements with the direct selection tool, just as when working with non-groups.
- Option-click on a path twice in a row—it's not necessary to double-click—to select the entire path and the group that contains that path.
- Option-click a third time to select the group that contains the selected group. Each successive Option-click selects the next group up.

TIP: There's no limit to the number of ways you can select paths inside extensive, multi-story groups. To select two groups inside a larger group, for example, Option-click twice on one group, then Shift-Option-click on a path in the other group and Option-click a second time on that same path.

- If Option-clicking with the direct selection tool is too confusing, you can use the group selection tool—that hollow arrow with the plus sign in the direct selection tool slot. It works just like the direct selection tool with the Option key down, but some folks find it easier to work with.

If you clone an object within a group by Option-dragging it, the clone becomes part of the group as well. Or you can copy a path inside a group and paste it in front or in back to make it part of the group. Illustrator also lets you use the Clipboard to transfer outside objects into a group. To do this, select the object you want to insert into the group, cut it (⌘-X), select any path inside the group with the direct selection tool, and choose Paste In Front or Paste In Back (⌘-F or ⌘-B).

TIP: If you want to duplicate an object separately of its group, be sure to deselect the group before pasting it. That is, select the object with the direct selection tool, copy it (⌘-C), press ⌘-Shift-A to deselect the group, and choose one of the Paste commands (⌘-V, ⌘-F, or ⌘-B). I know, it sounds like a lot of nit-picky mumbo jumbo, but once you try it out a few times, you'll quickly get the hang of it.

Ungrouping

You can ungroup any group by choosing Object » Ungroup, pressing ⌘-Shift-G, or choosing the Ungroup command after you Control-click. You have to ungroup each group one level at a time. So if a group contains three other groups, for example, you'd have to press ⌘-Shift-G four times in a row to disassociate all of them.

Ungrouping is occasionally an essential part of the reshaping process. Most notably, you can't combine two paths from different groups, whether by joining their endpoints or by making them into a compound path. So if you want to join two open paths from different groups into a single longer path, for example, you have to first ungroup the paths and then apply the Join command.

Distinguishing Groups from Non-Groups

What if ungrouping a path doesn't produce the desired effect? It may be that the object wasn't grouped in the first place. Illustrator permits you to create various kinds of collective objects, including compound paths, linked text blocks, and wrapped objects. You can determine exactly what kind of object you've selected by displaying the commands in the menu. If Object » Ungroup is black, you have a group on your hands; if the command is dimmed, the selection is not a group. The same goes for Object » Compound Paths » Release, Type » Blocks » Unlike, and Type » Wrap » Release. Find a black command and you've found your culprit.

When Grouping Isn't Protection Enough

Grouping helps to protect the relative placement of objects, but it doesn't get objects out of your way when you're trying to edit a complex illustration. Nor does it protect your artwork from the unpredictable motor skills of less adept artists who may come after you.

For those of us who have learned a little something about what we're doing, Illustrator provides a laundry list of protection alternatives. You can lock objects, preventing you or anyone else from accidentally selecting and altering them. You can temporarily hide an object if it impairs your view of other objects. And you can relegate entire collections of objects to independent layers, which you can in turn lock and hide as you choose.

I explain locking and hiding in the next few pages. Because layers are a more involved topic, I discuss them toward the end of the chapter, after a smidgen of transitional information.

Putting an Object under Lock and Key

Locking an object prevents you from selecting it. This means you won't be able to delete the object, edit it in any manner, or change its fill or stroke. Once an object is locked, it immediately becomes deselected. If you attempt to click on a locked object with a selection tool, you will instead select some nearby unlocked object or select no object at all. Likewise, neither marqueeing nor choosing the Select All command selects a locked object. Until you unlock the object, it remains off limits.

You lock objects by selecting them and choosing Object » Lock command (or by pressing ⌘-2). You can't lock a single point or segment independently of other elements in a path. If you specifically select one point in a path and choose the Lock command, Illustrator locks the entire path.

You can, however, lock a single path inside a group or other collective object (graph, compound path, etc.). Unfortunately, this doesn't afford much protection, since Illustrator allows you to continue editing that path so long as you click on some other object in the group.

TIP: When working on a very specific detail in an illustration, you may find it helpful to lock every object *not* included in the detail. With potentially hundreds of objects, it could be difficult and time consuming to select every one of them. So instead, you can simply select the objects that you *don't* want to lock and press the Option key while choosing Object » Lock command. If keyboard equivalent is more to your liking, you can press ⌘-Option-Shift-2.

NOTE: Here's another weird one that you might find helpful if you remember it long enough to put it to use. When the guides are unlocked (View » Lock Guides is off), you can lock individual guides by selecting them and choosing Object » Lock. In other words, View » Lock Guides and Object » Lock work completely independently of each other. They can even be in force at the same time.

Locking is saved when you save an illustration. Therefore, when you open a file, all objects that were locked during the previous session are still locked. This is a great way to protect special objects so that mischievous hands don't mess them up. Of course, there's always the risk a clever user will find and choose Object » Unlock All; but you're not trying to protect the file from clever users, are you?

Unlocking Everything that Was Ever Locked

Because you can't select a locked object, there's no way to indicate which objects you'd like to unlock and which you'd like to leave locked. So you have to unlock all locked objects at the same time.

To do so, choose Object » Unlock All (⌘-Option-2). Illustrator unlocks all locked objects and selects them, so that you can see which objects were locked clearly and manipulate them if necessary. You can now Shift-click with the arrow tool on the few objects you want to leave unlocked and press ⌘-2 to relock the others.

Sending Objects into Temporary Hiding

If an object is really in your way, you can do more than just lock it; you can totally hide it from view. You can't see a hidden object in any display mode, nor does it appear when the illustration is printed. Since a hidden object is always invisible, you can't select or manipulate it.

You hide objects by selecting them and choosing Object » Hide Selection (⌘-3). You can't hide a single point or segment; Illustrator always hides entire paths at a time. But you can hide objects inside groups, compound paths, and other collective objects. The path disappears, but it still moves and otherwise keeps up with the group when you select the entire group with the arrow tool.

TIP

To hide all objects that are not selected and leave the selected ones visible, Option-choose Object » Hide Selection or press ⌘-Option-Shift-3.

Unlike locking, hiding is not saved with the illustration. Adobe's afraid that you'll forget the hidden objects were ever there. Therefore, when you open an illustration, all objects in the file are in full view.

Hiding Unpainted Objects

Illustrator 3 provided a command that hid only transparent objects. Since you couldn't work in the preview mode, the idea was that you might want to see only those objects that are stroked and filled in the artwork mode. Of course, nowadays, you can work in the preview mode, where such objects are automatically invisible. But if you prefer to work in the artwork mode, you can still hide just the unpainted objects by selecting one of them, choosing Edit » Select » Same Paint Style, and then pressing ⌘-3. For more on selecting shapes by their colors, see Chapter 14.

Revealing Everything that Was Hidden

You can't select a hidden object any better than a locked one, so there's no way to show a specific object. Instead, you have to display all hidden objects at the same time by choosing Object » Show All or by pressing ⌘-Option-3. Illustrator shows all previously hidden objects and selects them. This way, the objects are called to your attention, allowing you to easily send them back into hiding if you want.

The Celebrated Stacking Order

When you preview or print an illustration, Illustrator describes it one object at a time, starting with the first object in the illustration window and working up to the last. The order in which the objects are described is called the stacking order.

The first object described lies behind all other objects in the illustration window. The last object sits in front of its cohorts. All other objects exist on some unique tier between the first object and the last.

Left to its own devices, stacking order would be a function of the order in which you draw. The oldest object would be in back; the most recent object would be in front. But Illustrator provides a number of commands that allow you to adjust the stacking order of existing paths and text blocks.

All the Way Forward or Back

Two commands in the Object » Arrange submenu let you send objects to the absolute front or back of an illustration. If you select an object and choose Object » Arrange » Bring To Front, Illustrator moves the object to the front of the stack. The object is treated exactly as if it were the most recently created path in the illustration and will therefore be described last when previewing or printing.

By selecting an object and choosing Object » Arrange » Send To Back, Illustrator treats a selected object as if it were the first path in the layer and describes it first when previewing or printing.

Lots of programs provide Bring To Front and Send To Back commands. But Illustrator offers some weird keyboard equivalents. Rather than ⌘-F and ⌘-B, which was used in everything from the first MacDraw onward, Illustrator uses ⌘-Shift-] (right bracket) for Bring To Front and ⌘-Shift-[(left bracket) for Send To Back. And provided you have something selected, these two commands also appear on the context-sensitive pop-up menu that springs to life when you Control-click.

You can apply both commands to whole objects only. If a path is only partially selected when you choose either command, the entire path is moved to the front or back of the illustration. If you select more than one object when choosing Bring to Front or Send to Back, the relative stacking of each selected object is retained. For example, if you select two objects and press ⌘-Shift-] (right bracket), the forward of the two objects becomes the frontmost object and the rearward of the two objects becomes the second-to-frontmost object.

Relative Stacking

When creating complicated illustrations, it's not enough to be able to send objects to the absolute front or back of an illustration. Even a simple drawing can contain more than a hundred objects. Adjusting the layering of a single object from, say, 14th-to-front back to 46th-to-front would take days using Bring To Front and Send To Back.

Fortunately, Illustrator allows you to send one object in front of or behind another using Clipboard commands. To change the stacking order of an object, select it and press ⌘-X to jettison it to the Clipboard. Then select the path or text block that the cut object should go behind, and press ⌘-B (Edit » Paste In Back). Or, if you'd rather place the cut object in front of the selection, press ⌘-F (Edit » Paste In Front). In either case, Illustrator restores the object to the exact location from which it was cut. Only the stacking order is changed.

If multiple objects are selected when you press ⌘-B, Illustrator places the contents of the Clipboard in back of the rearmost selected object. Not surprisingly, ⌘-F pastes the cut object in front of the frontmost selected object. If no object is selected, ⌘-B sends the object to the back of the illustration; ⌘-F sends it to the front of the illustration.

Illustrator provides two commands specifically designed to change the selected item or items rank in the stack by one. Choose Object » Arrange » Bring Forward or press ⌘-] (right bracket) to advance the selected object one step closer to the front of the stack; choose Object » Arrange » Send Backward or press ⌘-[(left bracket) to shove it one closer to the back. Although you would probably never feel inclined to use these commands to move the 46th-to-front up to 14th-to-front or vice versa, they are great to use when you want to nudge a path a couple of steps forward or three steps backward in the stacking order.

The Effect of Grouping and Combining on Stacking

Combining objects into groups also affects the stacking order of the objects in the illustration. All paths in a group must be stacked consecutively. To accomplish this, Illustrator uses the frontmost selected object as a marker when you choose the Group command. All other selected objects are stacked in order behind the frontmost one.

The same holds true for compound paths, linked text blocks, wrapped objects, joined paths, and paths combined with the Pathfinder filters. Ungrouping or otherwise breaking apart objects does not restore their original stacking order.

You can select an object inside a group with the direct selection tool and change its stacking order using the Bring To Front and Send To Back commands. But Illustrator keeps the selected objects inside its group. So rather than sending an object to the front of the illustration when you press ⌘-Shift-] (right bracket), Illustrator just sends it to the front of the group, while leaving the stacking order of the overall group unchanged.

You can also cut an object from a group and then paste it inside or outside of the group using the Paste In Front and Paste In Back commands. Since Illustrator automatically deselects everything when you cut an object—because the selection has disappeared—pressing ⌘-B or ⌘-F sends the cut object to the absolute back or front of the illustration.

Working with Independent Drawing Layers

In addition to the stacking functions, Illustrator offers self-contained drawing layers (or simply layers), an almost essential capability for creating complex illustrations. Illustrator was late to join the layering game—version 5 was the first to offer layers, years behind drawing rivals FreeHand and Canvas—but its layers are quite possibly the best of any drawing program.

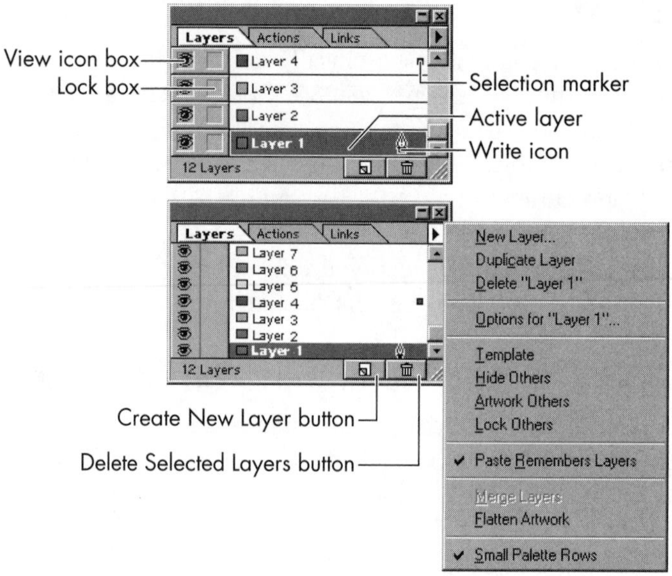

Figure 10-24: Click on the right-pointing arrowhead (top) to display the Layers palette menu (bottom).

Layers act like transparent pieces of acetate. You can draw an object on any layer and see clearly through all layers in front of it, down to all layers in back of it. An illustration can contain any number of layers, each layer can contain any number of objects, and you can name layers and alter their order as you see fit. You can even hide layers, lock them, and change their display mode independently of each other.

To display the Layers palette, choose Window » Show Layers (or press F7). All existing drawing layers in the illustration are listed as options in a scrolling list inside the Layers palette. The top of Figure 10-24 shows the default display mode. If you are working with a number of layers or simply prefer to see more layers in the same amount of space, choose Small Palette Rows from the pop-up menu. You display the pop-up menu by clicking the right-pointing arrowhead in the upper right corner of the palette. The smaller rows display and the menu appears unfurled at the bottom of Figure 10-24.

Adding Layers to an Illustration

Illustrator automatically creates flat illustrations with only one layer apiece. To add a drawing layer to the illustration, choose the New Layer command from the Layers palette menu or click on the Create New Layer button. The position of the new layer depends on which layer is presently active.

The first thing that you'll probably notice is that Illustrator has presumptuously named the new layer and assigned it a color. If you find this impertinence to your disliking, either choose the Options command from the pop-up menu or double-click on the layer in the Layers palette. The Layer Options dialog box displays, as shown in Figure 10-25. Enter a layer name of up to 31 characters long into the Name option box and choose a color from the Color pop-up menu.

As I said, you can specify the color that Illustrator assigns to selection outlines by selecting an option from the Color pop-up menu. If you're new to layers, you may think that Illustrator always shows selected points, segments, and control handles in blue, but this isn't necessarily the case. The program uses different colors to show you what layer you're working on. If you always accept Illustrator's default colors, points on the first layer are blue, those on the second layer are red, followed by bright green, a darker blue, yellow, magenta, cyan, gray, and black. But you can also select from orange, teal, brown, and lots of other colors, or you can define a custom color by selecting the Other option.

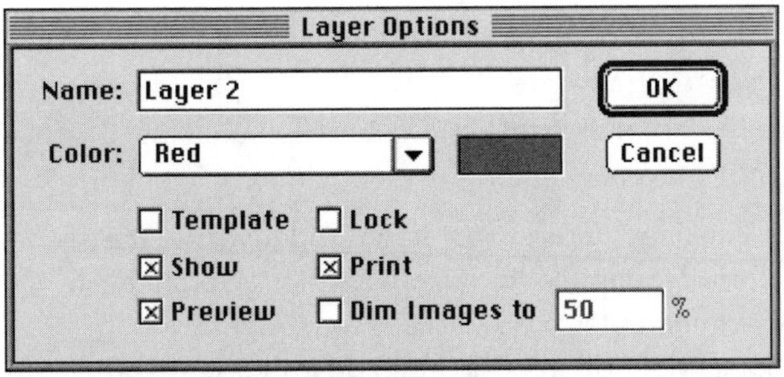

Figure 10-25: Illustrator lets you name layers, specify the color of selections, and modify display and locking options.

Note that Illustrator does *not* allow you to replace an existing drawing layer by creating a new layer with the same name. You can have as many layers with the same name as you like and they can even use the same color (though you probably want to avoid this since it makes for a mighty confusing illustration).

Although you probably will be concerned only with the name and color of a new layer and won't want to change any of the check boxes at first, I'll go ahead and run over the other options in this dialog box since we're here. These options are generally more useful after you've added a few objects to the layer and you've had a little time to consider how you want the layer to interact with the rest of your illustration. They allow you such choices as these:

- Turn on the Template check box to create a locked, nonprinting layer that is intended to show dimmed images. This is ideal for images that you wish to trace.
- To hide all objects on the layer, turn off the Show check box.
- To view the objects on the new layer in the artwork mode, turn off the Preview check box.
- Select the Print check box and all objects on the layer will print. Deselect it and all the objects won't print.
- Select the Lock check box to lock objects on the layer so they can't be accidentally altered.
- Select Dim Images to diffuse imported images so that you can easily distinguish them from graphic objects and text blocks created in Illustrator, as you may recall from Chapter 4. The default setting is 50 percent, but feel free to set any value from 0 to 100 percent.

After you press Return, the layer's new name and color (if you changed either) appears just above the last active layer.

In case your thinking, "Gosh, I bet I can add layers to the Adobe Illustrator Startup file to make Illustrator give me multiple layers when it creates a new illustration," permit me to dash your hopes right off the bat. You can't. Nor can you drag and drop entire layers between illustrations, the way you can in Photoshop. What a shame.

The Layers palette also includes a New Layer button. It's the button located in the bottom right corner with the page icon on it. You can simply click on this button or click on it in conjunction with some keys to add a new layer:

- Click the New Layer button to create a layer just above the last active layer.
- Option-click on the New Layer button to first display the Layer Options dialog box before creating a layer just above the last active layer.
- ⌘-Option-click on the New Layer button to create a layer just below the active layer in the layers list.
- ⌘-click on the New Layer button to create a layer at the top of the layers list.

Moving Objects Between Layers

When you select an object in the illustration window, the corresponding drawing layer becomes highlighted in the scrolling list. You'll also see a tiny colored selection marker along the right edge of the Layers palette. This marker represents the selected objects. If you select multiple objects on different layers, Illustrator shows multiple selection markers, one for each layer on which the objects sit.

To move the selected objects from one layer to another, drag the colored selection marker up or down the scrolling list. You can drag the marker to any layer that is neither hidden nor locked. You can drag only one marker at a time; so if you have objects selected on two layers, for example, and you want to move them all to a third layer, you have to drag one selection marker to the third layer and then drag the other.

As you drag the marker, the cursor changes to a finger to indicate that you are moving objects between layers, as in Figure 10-26. Upon releasing the mouse button, Illustrator transfers the selected objects from one layer to the other. The points and segments in the objects appear in the new layer's color to show that the move is complete, as in the second example in Figure 10-26.

TIP

To clone selected objects between layers, Option-drag the selection marker inside the Layers palette. The cursor changes to a finger with a plus sign. After you release the mouse, the selected objects exist independently in both layers, just as though you had copied them from one layer and pasted them into another. You can also clone all objects on one layer to a brand-spanking-new layer by dragging the layer you want to duplicate onto the New Layer button. The cloned layer appears just above the original layer.

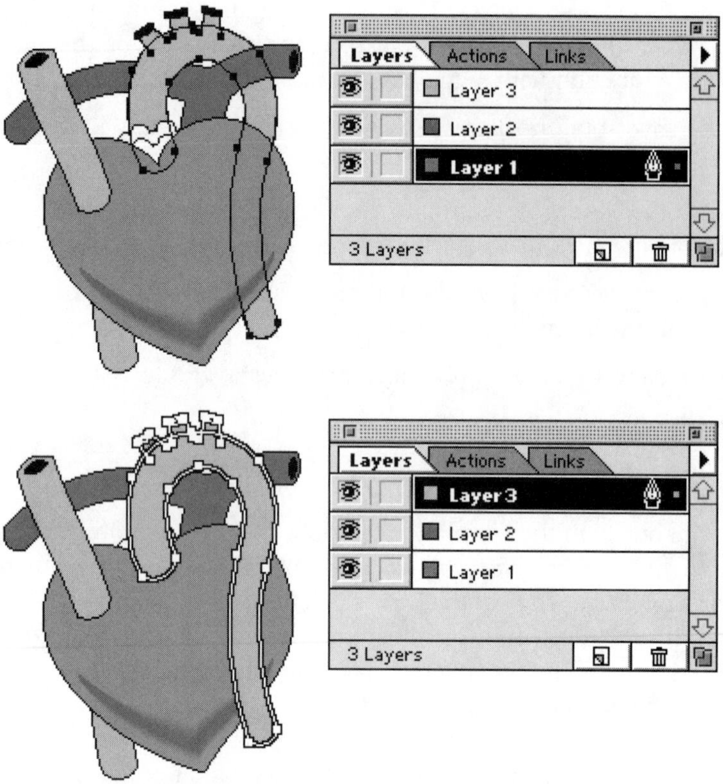

Figure 10-26: Drag a selection marker (top) to move the marker and all selected objects to different layers (bottom).

Creating, Combining, and Stacking Objects on Layers

The highlighted name in the Layers palette represents the active drawing layer, on which future objects will be created. To change the active drawing layer, click on a layer name in the scrolling list. Then start drawing to create objects on that layer.

A group, compound path, or other collective object must exist on a single layer. So if you group or otherwise combine objects from different layers, Illustrator sends all objects in the group to the layer belonging to the frontmost object. You'll notice this happen right away, because the points and outlines of the selected objects will all change to the same color.

You can change the stacking order of objects within a layer using the Send To Back and Bring To Front commands. For example, if you apply the Bring To Front command to an object on Layer 1, Illustrator brings it to the front of that layer only, not all the way to the front of the illustration.

If you want to also be able to change the stacking order inside layers with the Paste In Front and Paste In Back commands, choose the Paste Remembers Layers option in the Layers palette to turn it on. (Or you can select the Paste Remembers Layers check box in the General Preferences dialog box.) When turned on, this option instructs Illustrator to remember which layer an object came from when you send it to the Clipboard. Illustrator then pastes the object back onto that same layer, regardless of which layer is active. If cut or copied objects come from multiple layers, Illustrator pastes them back onto multiple layers.

TIP

When the Paste Remembers Layers option is turned on, copying and pasting an object from one illustration into another pastes both the objects and the layer. Therefore, to copy an entire layer from one illustration to another, first turn on the Paste Remembers Layers option. Then click on the layer name you want to copy and choose Lock Others from the palette menu (or click on the pencil icon) to lock the other layers so you can't select them. Press ⌘-A and ⌘-C to copy all the objects on the unlocked layer. Then switch to the other illustration and press ⌘-V. Illustrator pastes the objects on a new layer and adds the copied layer name to the Layers palette.

By default, however, the Paste Remembers Layers option is turned off. This allows you to cut and copy objects from various layers and paste them onto the single active layer in the illustration. I'm not crazy about this default setting, since you can already clone objects between layers by Option-dragging the selection marker. Also, the default prevents you from using ⌘-B and ⌘-F for interlayer stacking. But you can easily switch between turning the option on and off, and whatever setting you select will be saved from one session to the next with the other preference settings.

Modifying Your Layers

After you've created a few layers and added some objects to those layers, you can change the way the layers look, protect layers, change their order, and generally monkey around with them. In fact, one of the primary purposes of layers is to permit you to change huge clumps of objects at a time. Illustrator lets you modify layers—and all the objects on those layers—in the ways shown on the following page.

- To change the order of layers in the illustration, simply drag a layer name up or down in the Layers palette. The top layer is in front, and the bottom layer is in back. Illustrator likewise shuffles the objects assigned to that layer behind or in front of objects in other layers.
- To change the name of a layer, double-click on it to display the Layer Options dialog box (shown in Figure 10-26). Enter a new name and press Return.
- If you wish to switch a layer to a template, choose Template from the pop-up menu. The layer becomes a locked, nonprinting, dimmed layer meant for graphics that you intend to trace.
- The first column of check boxes in the Layers palette lets you change the display mode for each layer. A solid or hollow eyeball icon in front of a layer name indicates that all objects on that layer appear on screen. A solid eyeball icon means that the layer shows up in both the artwork and preview modes, while a hollow eyeball icon means that the layer displays in the artwork mode at all times.

TIP: ⌘-click on the eyeball icon to toggle the layer between the preview mode and perpetual artwork mode. ⌘-Option-click on the eyeball icon to display all layers except the active layer in the artwork mode. These techniques will speed up screen redraw if Illustrator is chugging along a tad too slowly.

- Click on an eyeball icon to hide it and, by so doing, to hide all objects on that layer in the drawing area. Option-click on the eyeball icon to hide all objects on all the other layers. Unlike Object » Hide Selection, Illustrator saves the state of a hidden layer. It's a wonderful way to hide sensitive drawings from future users. To display objects on a hidden layer, click in front of the layer name in the first column.
- If you want to protect layers without losing sight of their contents, you need to lock the layer by clicking in the check boxes of the second column of the Layers palette. By default, a layer's lock check box is empty, indicating that the layer is unlocked and that you can manipulate the objects on that layer. Click on the check box to display a pencil with a red slash in front and lock all objects on that layer. This allows you to work in another layer without risking accidentally manipulating or deleting an object in the locked layer.

You can protect the contents on all other layers by Option-clicking on one of the layer's lock check box. Then click in front of specific layer's lock check box to indicate the additional layers you want to unlock.

If you select a locked layer, your cursor becomes a little pencil with a line through it. This shows you that you can't write to this layer unless you first unlock it.

To prevent a layer from printing, double-click on it and turn off the Print check box in the Layer Options dialog box. But remember what you've done! Illustrator doesn't give you any warnings when printing that some layers are turned off. Many an artist has lost his hair trying to figure out why certain objects aren't printing from his illustration while others are printing just fine.

- You can select more than one layer at once. Shift-click on a layer other than the active one to select all layers from the active layer to the layer you clicked on, inclusively. ⌘-click on another layer to select that layer as well. All layers between will remain unselected.
- Choose Merge Layers from the pop-up menu to place all objects belonging to all of the selected layers on the bottommost selected layer. Illustrator will remove the other selected layers from the Layers palette.
- To smoosh together all non-hidden layers into a single layer, choose Flatten Artwork from the pop-up menu. All of the objects from the discarded layers will appear on the topmost layer. If any hidden layers are present, Illustrator will give you the option to move the layers' contents along with all the other artwork or to discard them.
- You can delete a layer—even if it's chock-full of text and paths—by clicking on the layer name and choosing Delete from the Layers palette menu or clicking on the Delete button—the one with a trash can icon. If the layer contains any objects, an alert box appears, warning you that you are about to delete a layer that contains artwork. To delete a layer without Illustrator's cautioning, Option-click on the Delete button.

  If you delete a layer by mistake, you can press ⌘-Z to immediately restore it and its objects.

Vacuuming Your Illustration

I've made a lot of noise in this chapter about protecting your illustration from clumsy coworkers, clients, and (gasp!) freelancers who may get your accounts in the future. But what if it's the other way around? What if an incredibly gifted person like you has to muck about inside cruddy pieces of artwork created by some imbecile from your company's dim past?

Back when I worked in a service bureau, I used to have this problem all the time. We were constantly getting files from folks who didn't quite know what they were doing. As a result, they tended to leave remnants of their previous efforts behind. Stray points, transparent shapes, and empty text blocks littered the virtual landscape like roaches laid waste with a bug bomb.

That's why Illustrator includes the Cleanup filter. You won't need it very often, but when you do, it's great. Just choose Objects » Path » Cleanup to display the dialog box in Figure 10-27. You can opt to delete single points that have no segments, paths that have no fill or stroke, and text blocks that have no text. All the refugees from the Island of Misfit Objects get whisked clean away.

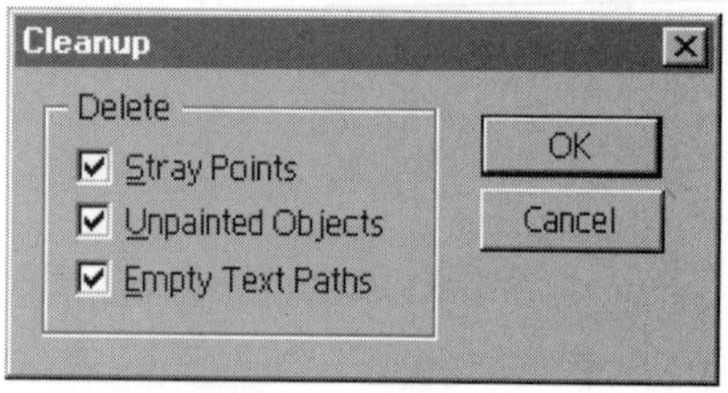

Figure 10-27: Illustrator lets you scrub away random rubbish from old illustrations.

WARNING

Watch out for the Delete Stray Points check box. If you've added your own custom center points (as discussed earlier in the "Adding a Center Point" section of this chapter), turn off the Delete Stray Points option! Otherwise, Illustrator will delete your center points faster than you can say, "Aaugh, wait, I didn't mean to do that!" Naturally, you can press ⌘-Z to reverse the procedure. But the change is so subtle, you may not notice the loss of your center points for a few minutes, or even longer. And by then, you may be stuck with it.

TIP

If you want to delete just stray points, you can skip this dialog box by choosing Edit » Select » Stray Points. This selects all the stray points in your document. Then just punch the Delete key and away they go.

CHAPTER 11

TRADITIONAL HOMESPUN TRANSFORMATIONS

Back when Illustrator first came out in 1987, we couldn't believe our luck. Right there in the toolbox were four splendid transformation tools. They allowed us to scale, rotate, flip, and slant absolutely any object you could create in Illustrator, whether path or text. Heck, you could even transform individual points and segments. Wow!

Ah, how easily amused we were back then. To think that we actually put up with a mere four transformation tools when now, we have…well, the very same four transformation tools. Only now you can,uh, scale, rotate, flip, and slant objects. Oh, and you can also transform partial paths.

If all this sounds familiar, it is. Adobe hasn't done much to Illustrator's transformation tools since the program's inception. The way you use the tools changed slightly a few versions back, and Illustrator 6 incorporated the scale and rotate options into the Transform palette, as well as rolling the old Move, Scale, and Rotate Each filters into Object » Transform » Transform Each. But the basic transformations themselves are identical to earlier versions.

Illustrators 5 and 6 added a series of special effects filters, many of which are very useful (as I explain in the next chapter). There's even one filter, Twirl, that you can apply using a tool. Unfortunately, it falls short of being a true transformation tool, since you can't modify the appearance of gradients, tile patterns, and other fill effects with a filter; and you can't press the Option key or ⌘-D to duplicate the effects of any filter.

With version 7, Adobe finally got around to implementing one transform-related feature that you would have thought it would have included originally with the tool: you can see your origin while transforming. You can even drag the origin around if you wish. I guess that Adobe was trying to get back to its roots—you know, its origin. Hee, hee.

Illustrator 8 makes a considerably better stab at stirring up the stagnant transformation pond. Adobe has promoted one of the filters to the more powerful category of fully functioning transformation tool. The free transform tool, with its roots in the Free Distort filter of Illustrator past, lets you both distort and transform selected paths in terms of a bounding box. With this single tool you can perform any transformation (or series of transformations) that the traditional transformation tools allow you. And, as with the standard four, you can use the ⌘-D shortcut to limit the tool's actions to partial paths and even repeat any modifications. The only drawback to this marvy tool is that while you're applying the modifications you also duplicate them. This shortcoming should really disqualify the tool from rising to the ranks of true transformation tool but, I have faith that Adobe should soon correct this oversight, so I've decided to include the free transform tool's description in this chapter.

So in essence, if you're familiar with previous versions of Illustrator, you'll have little problem adjusting to the transformation functions in version 8. But even for you world-weary oldtimers (and faithful readers of previous editions), this chapter is still worth reading. I've added lots of specific techniques for using the tools designed to help new and experienced users alike, which I hope will spark your imagination and send you off in bold, new directions of your own.

Making Objects Bigger and Smaller

Let's start things off with a bang by talking about scaling. In case you're unclear, scaling means enlarging or reducing something, or making it thinner or fatter or taller or shorter. Put a fellow on the rack, and you're scaling him. See how it works?

The Scale Tool and the Origin Point

After selecting one or more objects—paths, text, or imported images (it matters not)—drag with the scale tool in the drawing area. Illustrator enlarges or reduces the selection with respect to its center. If you drag away from the center of the selection, as in Figure 11-1, you enlarge the objects. If you drag toward the center, you reduce them. It's so simple, a child could do it. (And no doubt many have.)

NOTE

The scale tool calculates the center of a selection the same way every other function in Illustrator does, based on a rectangular bounding box. Therefore, it may not always suit your needs, especially if you're trying to keep objects aligned as you resize them.

Good thing you don't have to accept the default center. You can scale a selection with respect to any point in the illustration window. This origin point (also called a reference point or scale origin) represents the center of the transformation. To demonstrate how an origin point works, I have enlarged a star several times over with respect to a single origin in Figure 11-2. All of the white arrows in the figure emanate from the origin, showing how the points move outward uniformly from this one point.

Figure 11-2 shows a proportional enlargement. In non-proportional resizings (as in Figure 11-1), you don't get such clean lines from the origin point. But one fact remains: The portions of the selection that are closest to the origin change the least. This is not to say that objects closer to the origin point resize less dramatically than objects farther away. All selected objects scale by the same percentages. But as Figure 11-3 illustrates, objects located farther away from the origin move more dramatically.

In Figure 11-3, the white circles represent the original objects, the dark ovals represent the scaled objects, and the origin point is that thing at the top. While the top oval close to the origin point barely moved at all, the bottom oval moved quite a distance. When the origin lies outside the object, the scale tool scales the distance between the selected object and the origin point as well as the object itself. If this sounds strange, give it a try and see.

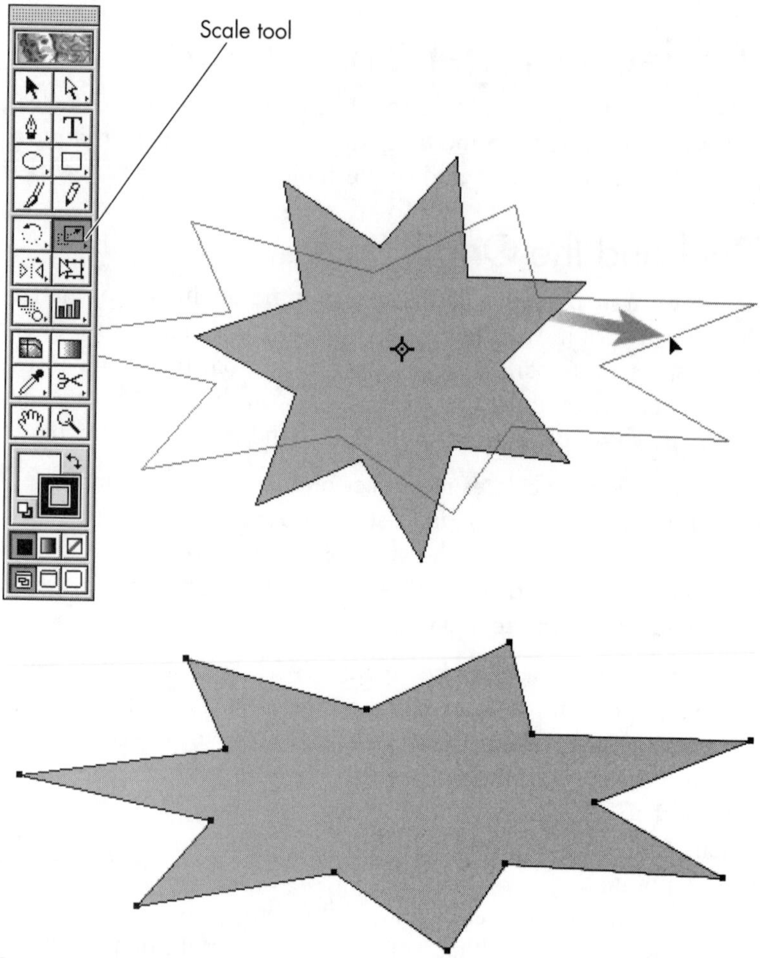

Figure 11-1: Using the scale tool, drag away from the center of a selection (top) to enlarge it (bottom).

Therefore, the origin point affects the positioning of objects, while the distance you drag with the scale tool determines the extent of the resizing. The following steps explain how to set the origin point and scale from it:

1. Select the objects you want to scale.
2. Click with the scale tool where you want to position the origin. Provided the View »Snap to Point command is active and you click within 2 points of an anchor point or guideline, Illustrator snaps the origin to that point.

Figure 11-2: A star scaled repeatedly with respect to a single origin point.

3. Drag with the scale tool. Illustrator resizes the objects with respect to the origin. If you drag away from the origin, you enlarge the selection. If you drag toward the origin, the selected objects shrink.

TIP

After clicking to set the origin point, begin dragging about an inch or two away from the origin. This gives you room to move inward and provides you with more control. If you ignore my advice and start the drag too close to the origin, you have too little room to maneuver, making it difficult to reduce the selection and magnifying the effects of your cursor movements. Likewise, if you don't click to set the origin (and instead accept the default center origin), be sure to start dragging an inch or two away from the center.

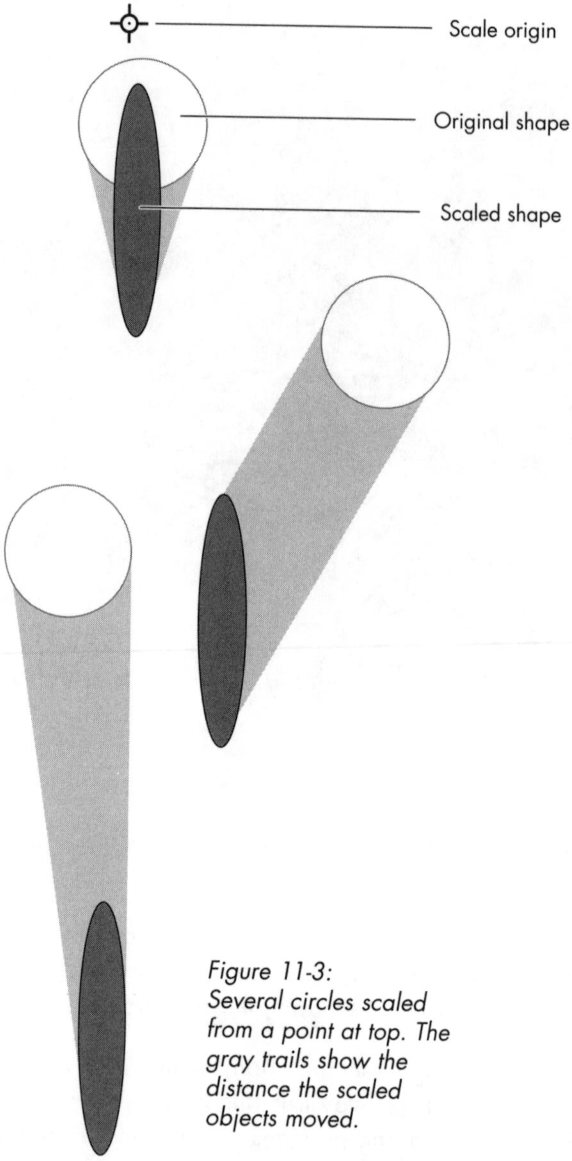

Figure 11-3: Several circles scaled from a point at top. The gray trails show the distance the scaled objects moved.

TIP

If you drag from one side of the origin point to the other, you flip the selection. Although Illustrator also provides a separate reflect tool, the scale tool is the only one that lets you flip and resize at the same time. (By contrast, the reflect tool lets you flip and rotate simultaneously.)

Scaling with the Shift Key

As you do when drawing and reshaping paths, you can use the Shift key to constrain a transformation. However, Illustrator goes well beyond the constraints provided in most drawing and layout programs:

- You can Shift-drag to scale a selection proportionally, so the height and width of a selected object are equally affected. Or you can scale the selection exclusively horizontally or vertically while pressing Shift.

  For example, if you Shift-drag up and to the right, you scale the selection proportionally, as in the top example of Figure 11-4. But if you Shift-drag to the right—while keeping the up and down movement to a minimum—you scale the width of the selection without changing its height, as in the bottom example.

NOTE

If the shape seems to jump around a lot while you press the Shift key, it's because you began your drag in a bad place. Release and press ⌘-Z to put things back where they were. Then click to set the origin, and start your drag in a diagonal direction from the origin. For example, you can start the drag up and to the right or down and to the left of the origin. But when you start the drag in a horizontal or vertical alignment with the origin, you run into problems. This is particularly limiting when you want to perform a proportional scaling.

- In truth, my advice so far assumes that you haven't rotated the constraint axes from their default 0-degree setting. If you have changed the constraint axes, you can still scale proportionally using the Shift key but you can no longer scale the selection exactly horizontally or vertically. Instead, you scale in line with the constraint axes angles.

As it turns out, rotating the constraint axes is an essential first step when scaling rotated shapes. For example, suppose you want to lengthen the rotated paths in Figure 11-5. Here's what you'd do:

1. First determine the angle of rotation by dragging across a flat segment with the measure tool. I dragged across the bottom segment in Figure 11-5 to produce the angle value of 16.534 degrees in the Info palette.

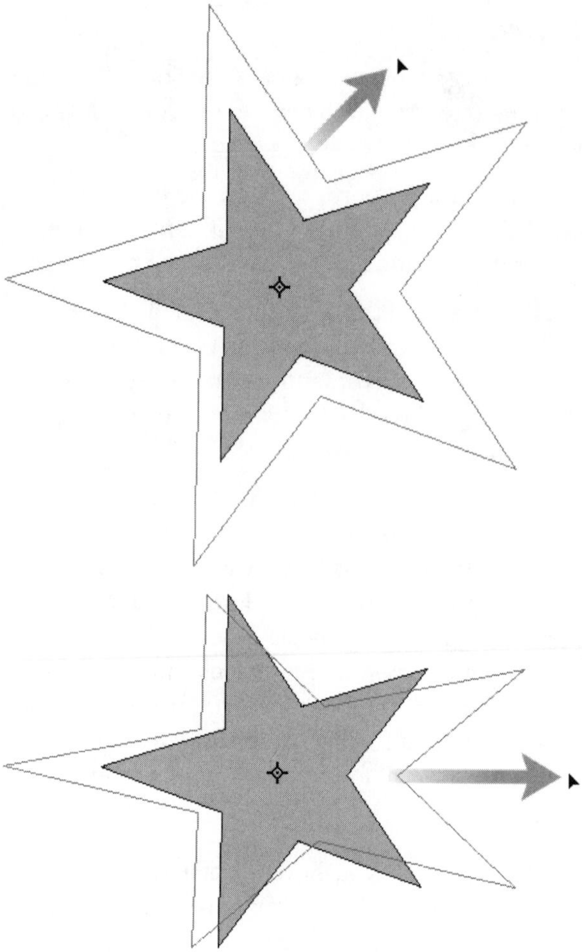

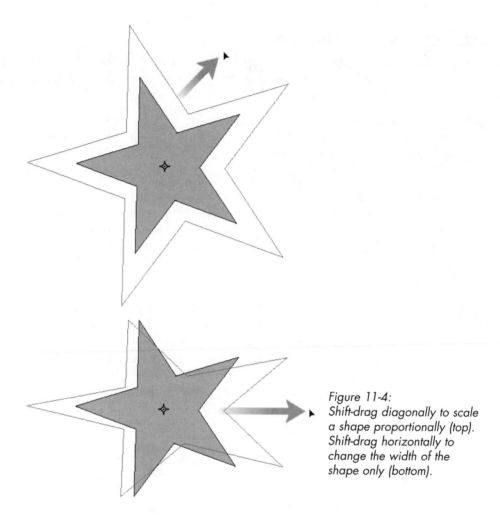

Figure 11-4:
Shift-drag diagonally to scale a shape proportionally (top). Shift-drag horizontally to change the width of the shape only (bottom).

2. Press ⌘-K to display the General Preferences dialog box and enter the angle value from the Info palette into the Constrain Angle option box. Naturally, I entered 16.534. Press Return to apply the rotation.

3. Click with the scale tool to set the origin (or don't click to accept the bounding box center as the origin). Then Shift-drag with the scale tool to change the height or width of the selection.

In Figure 11-6, I Shift-dragged downward to lengthen the selection. Notice how Illustrator exactly stretches the height of the objects without affecting the width in the slightest.

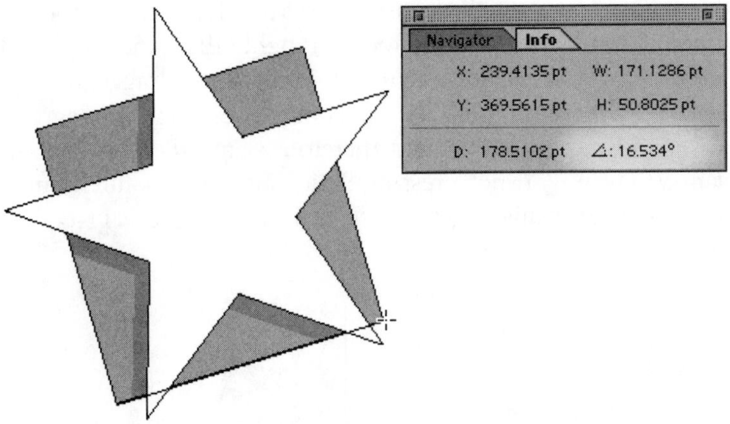

Figure 11-5: Drag across a straight segment in a group of rotated paths to discover the angle by which you should rotate the constraint axes.

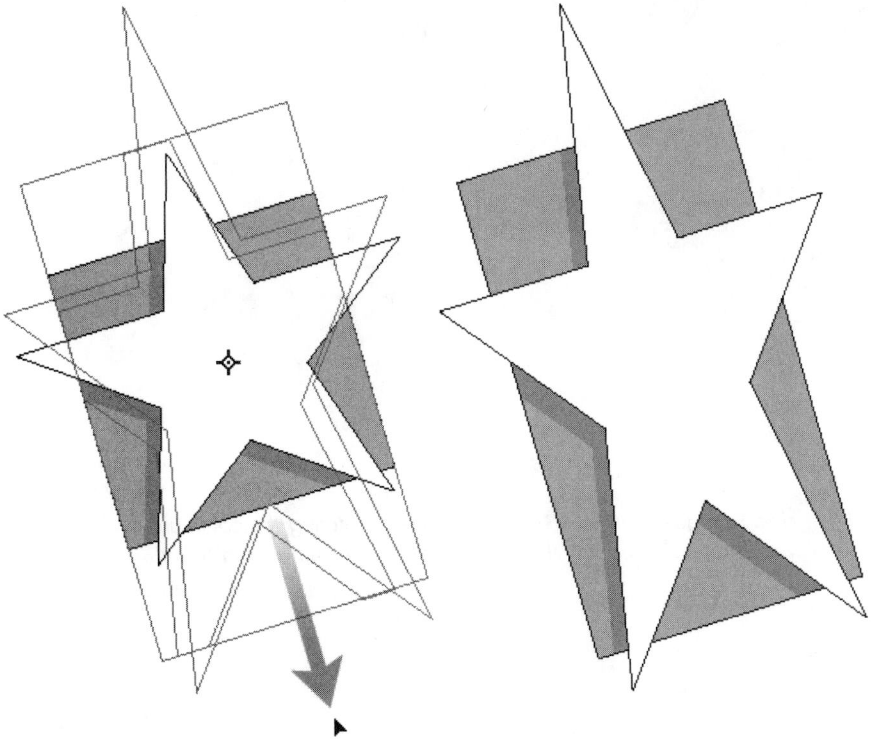

Figure 11-6: After rotating the constraint axes 16.534 degrees, I Shift-dragged with the scale tool (left) to make the shapes taller but not wider (right).

Is it absolutely necessary to rotate the constraint axes before scaling rotated shapes? Couldn't you just drag with the scale tool at roughly the same angle and produce the same results? Absolutely not! Figure 11-7 shows me dragging at the very same angle as in Figure 11-6, with the constraint axes set to 0 degrees. Illustrator scales along the standard axes and therefore slants the shapes as it scales them. You can get away with not pressing Shift, but you absolutely must rotate the constraint axes if you want to get the effect shown in Figure 11-6.

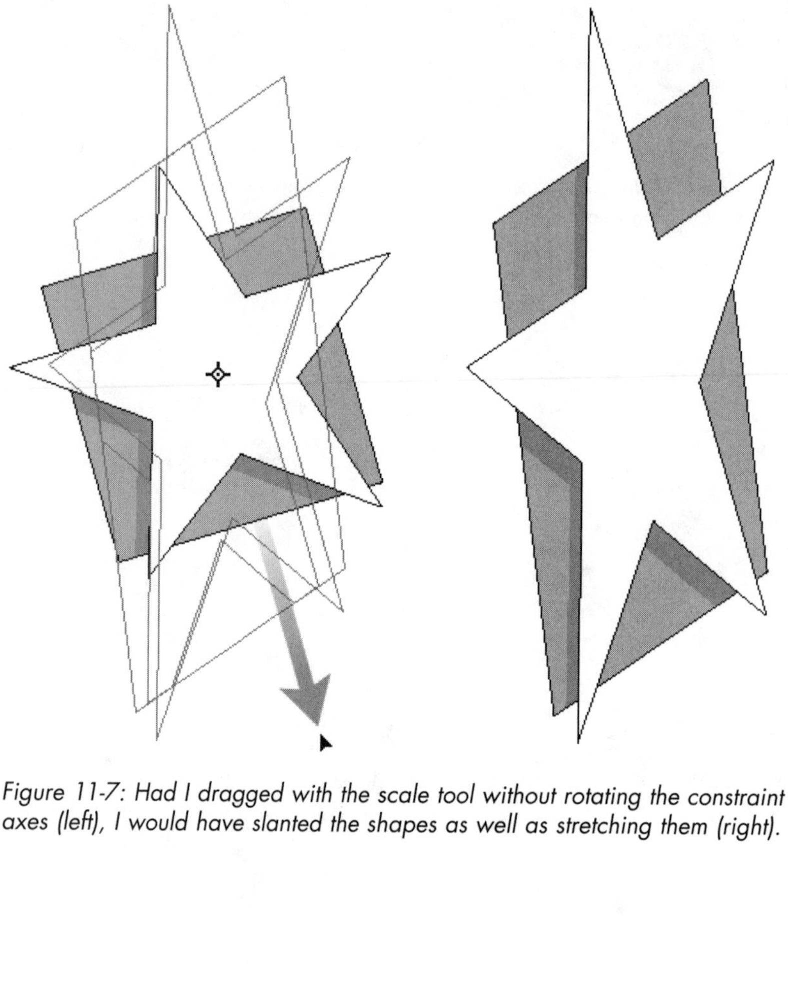

Figure 11-7: Had I dragged with the scale tool without rotating the constraint axes (left), I would have slanted the shapes as well as stretching them (right).

Duplicating Objects as You Scale Them

The scale tool also lets you clone objects as you scale them. To scale a clone and leave the original unchanged, press the Option key in mid-drag and keep the key pressed until after you release the mouse button. If you enlarge the selection, you may cover up the original with the clone, but the original will be there, lurking in the background. (If you're at all concerned, press ⌘-Shift-[(left bracket) to send the clone in back of the original so you can see all the shapes.)

After you scale a clone, you can create a series of scaled clones by pressing ⌘-D or choosing Object » Transform » Transform Again. This is a particularly useful technique for creating perspective effects. By reducing a series of clones toward a far off origin, you create the effect of shapes slowly receding into the distance.

For example, I began with three white stars and a 25 percent rectangle, as shown in Figure 11-8. (I slanted the two outside stars slightly with the shear tool, which I'll explain later in this chapter.) I selected the three stars and pressed ⌘-8 to form a compound path, which is necessary for the upcoming Intersect filter step. To create the shadow behind the shapes, I selected the rectangle and the three-star compound path; clicked with the scale tool at the origin point, as shown in the figure; and Shift-Option-dragged to proportionally reduce the objects (very slightly) and clone them. I sent the shape to the back (⌘-Shift-[) copied the clone (⌘-C) for later, clicked on the Pathfinder palette's Unite button to combine them into a single shape, and filled the shape with black. This formed the dark portion of the drop shadow. To form the lighter portion, I pasted the copy of the clone just in front of the original rectangle (⌘-F). I then deselected all and deleted the rectangle (and only the rectangle) that I just pasted. (I'll explain the method behind this madness in just a moment.) With the smaller rectangle out of the way, I selected the original rectangle and cloned it by copying it and pasting it in front (⌘-C and ⌘-F). With the clone still selected, I additionally selected the most recently pasted three-star compound path. Next I clicked on the Pathfinder palette's Intersect button and set both the fill and stroke of the resulting three shapes to 40 percent gray.

Figure 11-8: Using the origin point shown, I cloned and scaled the rectangle and stars to create the black drop shadow.

I couldn't simply apply the Intersect filter to the copy of the clone—the copy of the clone of the scaled three-star compound path and rectangle—because if I had, the resulting three shapes would not have spanned the height of the original rectangle and thus the shadows of the front three-star compound path would have been too short.

To create the perspective effect, I selected all the shapes—including the drop shadow—and grouped them (⌘-G). (The grouping was merely a precaution to facilitate future editing.) I clicked again at the origin point with the scale tool and again Shift-Option-dragged toward the origin to create a proportional clone. The clone was in front of the original, so I pressed ⌘-Shift-[(left bracket) to send it to the back. Then I pressed ⌘-D to create another reduced clone and ⌘-Shift-[(left bracket) to send it to the back. I kept pressing ⌘-D and ⌘-Shift-[(left bracket)—a total of 18 times in a row, in fact—until I arrived at the effect in Figure 11-9.

For a more interesting effect, don't press the Shift key while creating the clones. Thus the clones are not limited to proportional duplicates of the original. In Figure 11-10, I used the first set of stars, bars, and shadows from Figure 11-9 and clicked at the same origin point with the scale tool. I then Option-dragged the paths making sure to drag slightly more inward than downward and sent the result to the back of the stack. Again, I pressed ⌘-D and ⌘-Shift-[(left Bracket) 18 times and ended up with a series of paths that give a slightly more realistic effect.

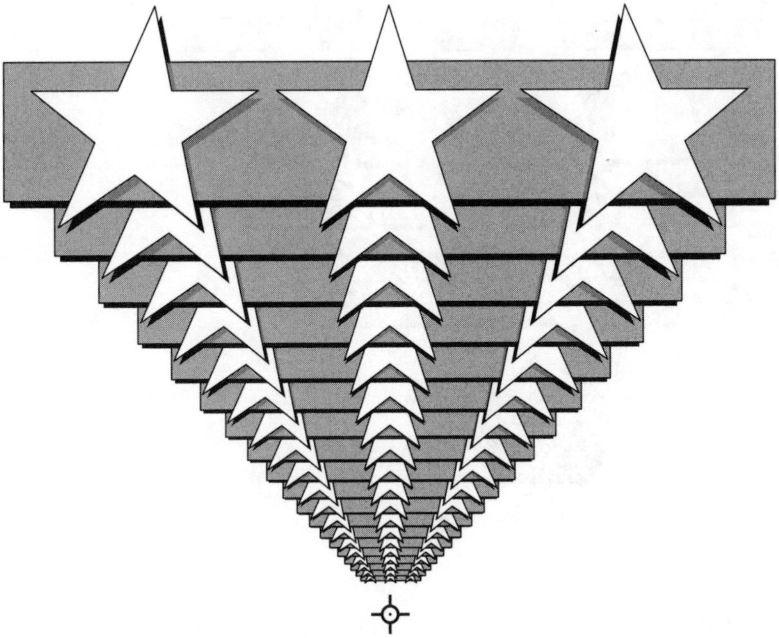

Figure 11-9: I scaled and cloned all shapes, sent them to the back, and duplicated the action several times in a row.

Finally, as a real time waster, I decided that Figure 11-10 needed some color variation. To do this, I selected the path furthest back and darkened all the grays by an additional 25 percent each. Since its black shadow couldn't go any darker, I then lightened the top path's black shadow by 25 points. Now, since all the paths of the top group had different color from their counterparts in the bottom group, I could effectively use the Filter » Colors » Blend Front to Back command—I don't discuss this filter until the end of Chapter 14, but this is just such a perfect application. Unfortunately, to achieve the proper effect, I couldn't simply select all the paths and apply the filter. Instead, I had to ungroup all the paths (by pressing ⌘-Shift-G three times in a row) and individually blend the like sets of paths separately. I had to blend the 19 rectangles separately from the 19 left stars, the 19 middle stars, the 19 right stars, the 19 star shadows, and the 19 main shadows. It was a pain, and I had to take my time in selection the various sets of paths—to make it easier on myself, I was always sure to lock sets of paths after I had blended them—but I fee that the final result (Figure 11-11) was worth it.

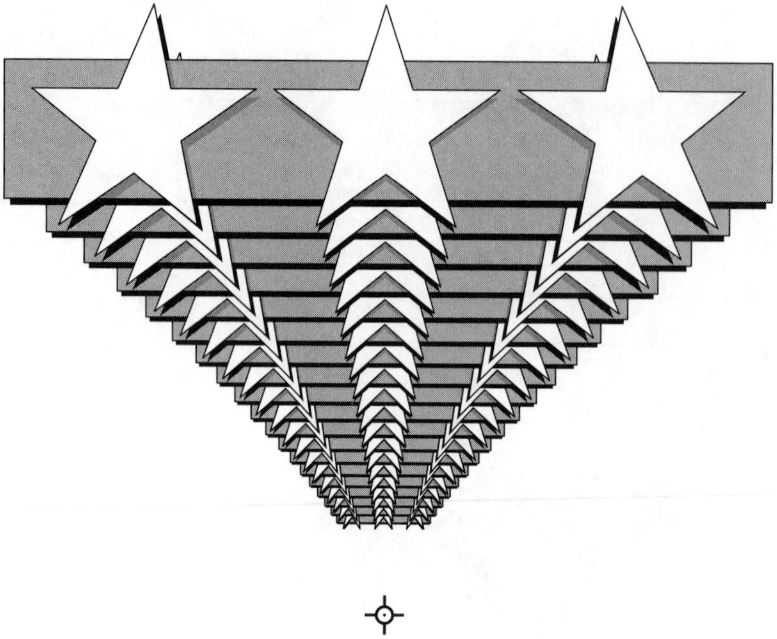

Figure 11-10: I repeated the same process that resulted in Figure 11-9, except that I didn't restrict myself to proportional scaling. This gives a slightly more realistic effect.

Perspective duplication is an extremely easy effect to perform, and it looks great when applied to simple shapes and large letters converted to paths. Figure 11-12 is an example of perspective text. Starting with some converted black text, I reduced a cloned version of the text (using the origin as shown) and filled the clone with white. Then I selected the black text again and cloned and reduced it very slightly. I repeated the reduced clone by pressing ⌘-D about 12 times in a row to get a perspective effect similar to what you see in the figure.

I could have stopped there, but since all these paths mean a lot of work for the printer, I thought I'd simplify things by selecting all the black paths and clicking on the Pathfinder palette's Unite button. Depending on the complexity of the paths, this command can take several minutes to complete. After it was done, I stroked the path with a 6-point outline to get the end result shown in Figure 11-12.

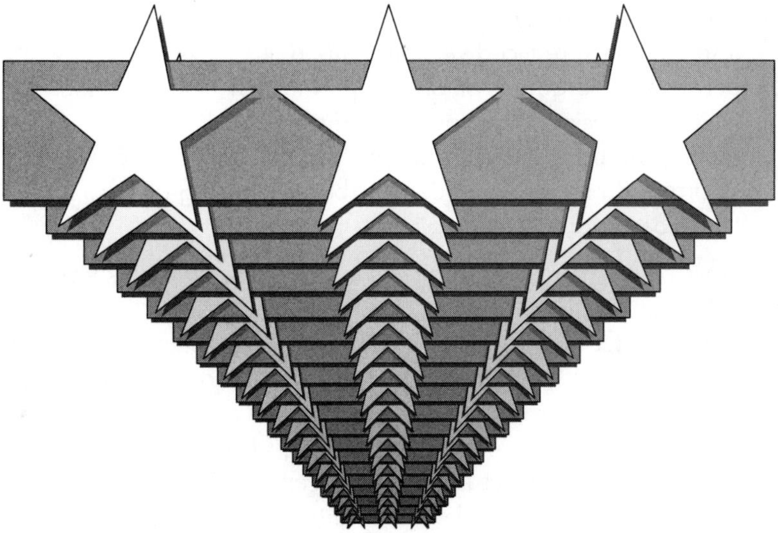

Figure 11-11: Starting with the paths from Figure 11-10, I darkened the colors of the bottom group and then used the Filter » Colors » Blend Front to Back command on each set of like paths.

Figure 11-12: I created this effect by scaling and duplicating a series of black letters behind the white ones.

A few of you brainy types are thinking, "But, Deke, can't you just create one reduced version of the paths and blends between the large and small group of letters?" No. No that is, if you're using Illustrator 7. But since you, oh lucky reader, are using Illustrator 8, you can indeed. You see, Illustrator 8 provides considerably better blending abilities than does its predecessors.

To give Illustrator's blending abilities a try, let's start once again with some converted black text. Be sure to group the text first with the Object » Group command (⌘-G). Clone and reduce the black text twice—once slightly and once more dramatically. Fill the slightly reduced clone with white and force it to the top of the stack by pressing ⌘-Shift-] (right bracket). Select the two black lines of text, apply a hardy stroke weight (6 or so), and choose Object » Blends » Make (or ⌘-Option-B). Illustrator will construct a blend between the two paths. If this is the first time you've used the Make Blend command (or if it's the first time you've used the command since your most recent launching of Illustrator), the blend will consist of only three steps: the two original paths and just one blending path. This is undoubtedly less than what you had hoped. With the blend still selected, choose Object » Blends » Blend Options and then choose Specific Steps from the Spacing pull-down menu. Enter a suitable value, one that will sufficiently fill your blend. You may have to try a few different values, so be sure to make use of the Preview check box. To prevent the blend from becoming more complicated than necessary, use the smallest value that just meets your needs.

For those of you who've never heard of the blend tool—and wish I would quit making little inside references to the more experienced half of the class—you can learn all about this feature in Chapter 17.

Scaling with the Bounding Box

For the past 11 years, Illustrator was just about the only application on the planet that supported scaling but didn't let you scale by dragging on a selected object's corner handle. Well, that's simply no longer the case.

Illustrator 8 provides a quick and dirty scaling method in the form of a standard eight-handled bounding box.

To use the new bounding box, first activate the aptly named Use Bounding Box option inside the General Preferences dialog box. Once done, any and all paths that you select with the arrow tool (and only the arrow tool) or one of the selection commands will automatically gain an eight-handled box that encloses all the selected paths—in other words, partially selected paths will not display with a bounding box.

The orientation of this bounding box is initially up to Illustrator and is based on the path or paths selected. For example, the bounding box of the top left star in Figure 11-13 is aligned to match the angle at which I drew the star. If you don't like the default orientation of a bounding box, you can either choose Object » Transform » Reset Bounding Box or Control-click and choose Transform » Reset Bounding Box from the context-sensitive pop-up menu, which is what I did to realign the bounding box of the top right star in Figure 11-13. When you select more than one path, the bounding box that Illustrator constructs will usually align in such a way that it is square with the page, as shown at the bottom of Figure 11-13. If this is not the case and you want the bounding box to square with the page, you can, once again, choose one of the Reset Bounding Box commands.

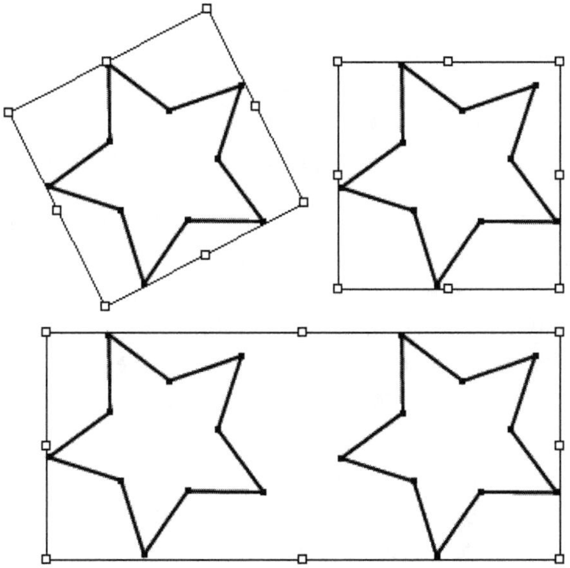

Figure 11-13:
When the Use Bounding Box check box is activated, each wholly selected path will display an eight-handled bounding box that encloses just the path.

The real power of the bounding box is in its use:

- Drag on a corner handle to scale the selected objects. Shift-drag a corner handle to scale proportionally. In either case, the opposite corner serves as the scale origin.
- Option-drag on a corner handle to scale the object around its center. Option-Shift-drag a corner handle to scale proportionally around the object's center.

- Drag on one of the bounding box's side handles (including the top and bottom handles) to limit the scaling to either horizontal or vertical changes. The opposite side's handle serves as the scale origin.
- Shift-drag a side handle to once again scale proportionally, except that in this case the opposite side's handle serves as the scale origin.
- Option-drag a side handle to horizontally or vertically scale the object from the center.

Resizing by the Numbers

The scale tool is one of my favorite tools, but it's not the only way to resize objects in Illustrator. You can also enlarge and reduce object sizes by entering precise numeric values into two different dialog boxes and one palette.

Scaling from the Transform Palette

Let's start with the least capable (but most convenient) of the three scaling options, the Transform palette. The Transform palette (the present-day name for the Illustrator 6 Control palette) includes a Shear option box (discussed in the upcoming "Slanting Objects the Weird Way" section) and, instead of a single Scale option box, you enter values in the W (for width) and H (for height) option boxes to scale objects. After you select an object, you enter a percentage into either the W or H option box, as spotlighted in Figure 11-14. The number you enter must be followed by the % symbol—if you leave off the % symbol, Illustrator will change the dimension numerically. Values below 100% shrink the selection; values above 100% enlarge it. All resizings are proportional and accurate to 0.01 percent.

TIP: Don't forget that Illustrator is now capable of doing the math for you in any option box. So instead of entering 200% into the W or H option box to double a dimension, you can simply punch in *2 after the current value in the box—*2 tells Illustrator to multiply the current value by 2, the same as 200% of the value. Illustrator doubles the value when you press Return or Tab and changes the dimensions accordingly.

To scale uniformly, you can enter the same percentage value into both the W and H option boxes. To scale non-uniformly, enter different values into these boxes. In either case, after you enter values, press Return to apply the changes and deactivate the palette; press Tab to apply the scaling and highlight the rotate option box; or press Shift-Return to apply the changes yet leave the focus on that last used option box inside the Transform palette. You can even repeat the operation by pressing ⌘-D.

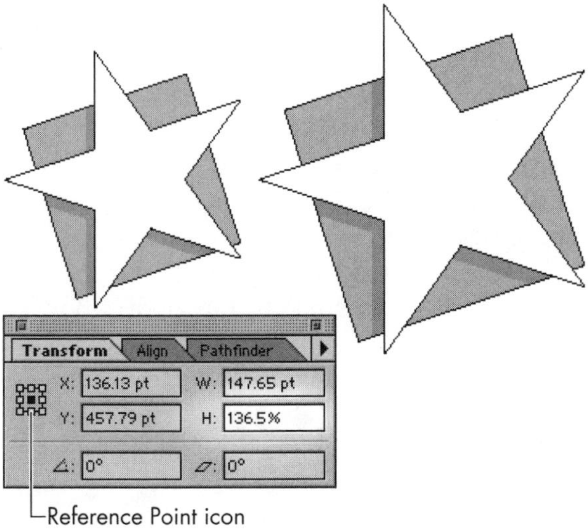

Figure 11-14: Enter a percentage (i.e., a number explicitly followed by a % sign) into either the W or H option box and press ⌘-Return to scale a selected object uniformly.

TIP

If you're scaling uniformly, you needn't enter the same information twice. Instead, punch in a number followed by the % sign into either the W or H option box and press ⌘-Return. Illustrator will copy the percentage to the other box and scale the selected object uniformly. To remain focused on the Transform palette, press ⌘-Tab. Press ⌘-Option-Return and ⌘-Option-Tab to copy the value and scale a clone.

But the fun doesn't end there:

- Press ⌘-Shift-Return to scale uniformly and leave the focus on the last used option box.
- Press Option-Return to apply the scaling to a clone of the path. Press Option-Shift-Return to scale a clone and leave the focus on the last used option box.
- Press ⌘-Option-Return to uniformly scale a clone. Press ⌘-Option-Shift-Return to uniformly scale a clone and leave the focus on the last used option box.

You can also use the Transform palette to choose from nine predefined origin points. To reposition the origin point, click on one of the nine squares in the Reference Point icon—that little square made of squares located on the left side of the Transform palette and labeled in Figure 11-14. All points are measured with respect to the selection's rectangular bounding box.

Using the Scale Dialog Box

After selecting a few objects on your Things To Scale list, double-click on the scale tool icon in the toolbox or Control-click and choose the Scale command from the Transform submenu. This brings up the Scale dialog box captured in all its radiant glory in Figure 11-15. Illustrator automatically positions the origin point in the center of the selection (according to the big, bad, bounding box).

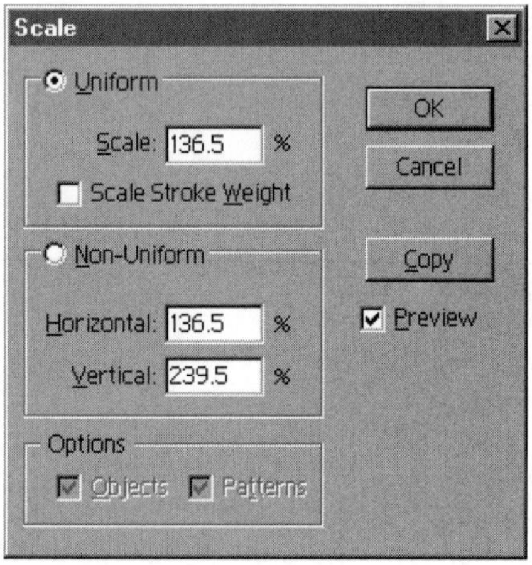

Figure 11-15: In the Scale dialog box, you can specify the exact percentage by which a selection is enlarged or reduced.

If you want to position the origin point yourself, Option-click in the illustration window with the scale tool. (When you press the Option key, Illustrator gives you a lot of hints that something's about to happen. You'll see a tiny ellipsis next to the scale tool cursor, and if the status bar in the lower left corner of the illustration window is set to Current Tool, it reads Scale: click to choose origin. What a communicative program.) Option-clicking with any transformation tool simultaneously positions the origin point and displays the appropriate dialog box.

To proportionally scale the width and height of the selection, enter a value into the Uniform option box. This value is accurate to 0.001 percent, 10 times more accurate than the scale value in the Transform palette.

When the Uniform radio button is selected, you can have Illustrator likewise scale the line weights of all selected objects. When the Scale Line Weight check box is activated, Illustrator scales the line weight by the Uniform value. A 4-point stroke subject to a 125 percent scaling changes to 5 points thick. If the check box is off, the stroke is unaffected.

WARNING

Illustrator remembers this Scale Line Weight setting the next time you Shift-drag with the scale tool. (The option affects proportional scalings only.) So if you find that your line weights are getting thicker and thinner as you scale them, you know the culprit. Double-click on the scale tool icon and turn off the Scale Line Weight check box. (You can also modify this setting in the General Preferences dialog box.)

To independently scale the width and height of an object, enter values into the Horizontal and Vertical option boxes. A Horizontal value less than 100 percent makes the selection thinner; a value greater than 100 percent makes it wider. The values in the Vertical option box translate to taller and shorter. If you enter negative values, Illustrator flips the selection.

The Objects and Patterns check boxes are used strictly to modify objects with tiled fills. If you want to learn about these options—for all four transformation dialog boxes—read the stirring account in the "Transforming Tiles inside Object" section of Chapter 15.

If you're ever in doubt of your changes, use the Preview check box to see the possible yet currently unrealized future. Click it on and off to see your changes appear and disappear, ad nauseam.

To scale the selection, press Return or click on the OK button. Click the Copy button to clone the selection and scale it.

NOTE

Oh, and one more thing. All of Illustrator's transformation dialog boxes act as recording devices, keeping track of the last transformation applied, whether you used a tool or the dialog box itself. Sadly, the Scale dialog box ignores the results of the Transform palette, and it doesn't pay attention to the next command, Transform Each. But it knows what the scale tool is up to.

Scaling from Multiple Origins

Illustrator 5 introduced filters that allowed you to scale from a different origin point for each and every selected object. Illustrator 6 combined these filters into a single more functional command known as Object » Transform » Transform Each. Illustrator 7 did nothing to improve upon this, and version 8 carries on this fine tradition.

When you choose the Transform Each command from either the Object » Transform submenu or from the Transform submenu in the context-sensitive pop-up menu (you know, Control-click), Illustrator displays the dialog box shown in Figure 11-16. You enter the amounts by which you want to resize the width and height of the selected objects into the first two option boxes. To perform a proportional resizing, enter the same value for both Horizontal and Vertical. Then press Return to apply the changes, or click on the Copy button to clone and scale. (For the present time, Option-Return doesn't work inside this dialog box.)

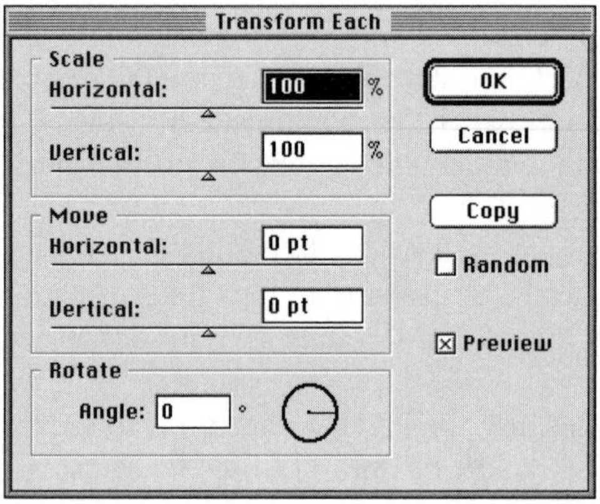

Figure 11-16: Use the Transform Each dialog box to scale each selected object from its center.

When you apply the Transform Each command, Illustrator scales each selected object with respect to its own center. In the first example of Figure 11-17, for example, I added festive bobbles to the spikes on the star. But after a few moments of intense scrutiny, I decide the bobbles are uniformly too small. Back in the old days, I would've had two options—scale each bobble one at a time to prevent them from shifting around or redraw the darn things. But in present day Illustrator, I can simply apply Object » Transform » Transform Each. By entering 150 percent into both the Horizontal and Vertical option boxes, I achieved the larger bobbles in the second example of Figure 11-17. (I also darkened the circles to make them stand out.)

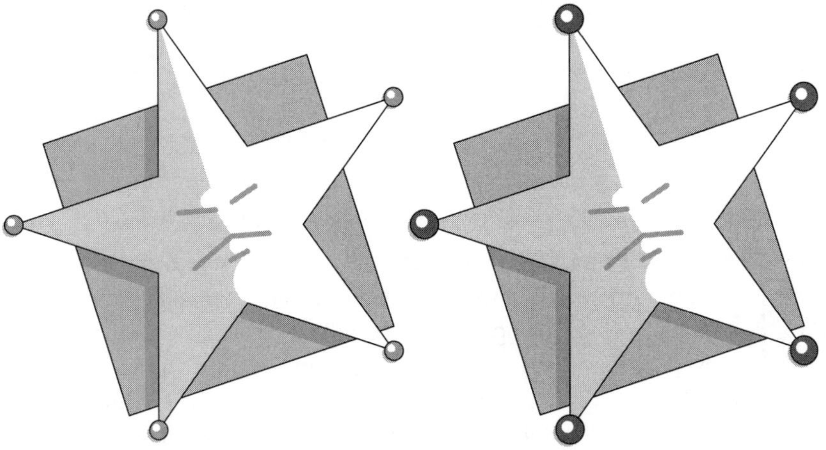

Figure 11-17: After selecting the small bobbles on the star's spikes (left), I enlarge every one of them using the Transform Each command (right).

Why not just use the scale tool, Transform palette, or Scale dialog box? Because all of these functions work from a single origin point, which can shift the objects in different directions. Figure 11-18 shows what happens when I double-click on the scale tool icon, enter a value of 150 percent, and press Return. The bobbles actually move away from their shared center. By contrast, the Transform Each command ensures that the objects scale in place.

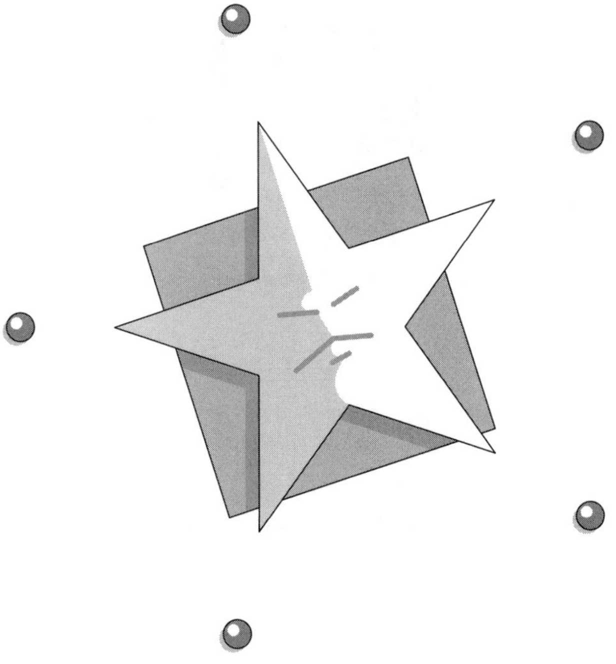

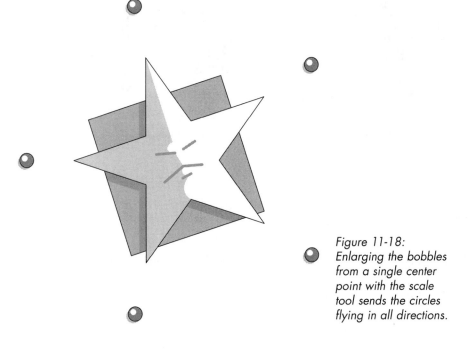

Figure 11-18: Enlarging the bobbles from a single center point with the scale tool sends the circles flying in all directions.

Select the Random check box to apply random resizings to individual selected objects. Illustrator scales each selected path to a different percentage, ranging from 100 percent to the values you enter into the Horizontal and Vertical option boxes. In Figure 11-19, I randomly scaled and nudged the converted letters in the word "wacky." I entered 150 for Horizontal and 300 for Vertical. I also entered 20 points into the Move Vertical option box. Illustrator randomly scaled and moved the letters within the specified ranges, as shown in the second example in the figure.

TIP: Always turn on the Preview check box when you use the Random option. This way, you can see Illustrator's random effect before applying it. If you don't like what you see, turn Preview off and then turn it back on again. This forces Illustrator to generate a new random effect. Keep clicking on the Preview check box until you get what you want. Then press Return.

Figure 11-19: Here I used Transform Each to randomly scale and nudge a few letters created in the wonderfully wacky font Sho.

Scaling Partial Objects

Whether you select just a few points or a whole path, both the Transform palette and the Object » Transform » Transform Each command affect entire paths at a time. But you can use the scale tool or Scale dialog box to scale partially selected paths and text objects.

For example, you can use the scale tool to enlarge a text block without changing the size of the text inside it. Option-click on the rectangular text container with the direct selection tool, and then click with the scale tool to set the origin point and drag away. So long as you haven't selected any text—you don't see any baselines, do you?—Illustrator enlarges or reduces the containers and rewraps the text inside.

You can also scale selected points and segments in a path. The primary advantage of this technique is that you can move points symmetrically. See, Illustrator doesn't provide any specific means for moving points away from or toward an origin point. Moving is the one transformation that has nothing to do with origins (which is why I don't discuss it in this chapter). The closest thing to an origin-based move function is the scale tool.

Consider the sinister Figure 11-20. In the first example, I've selected four points in the star that makes up the outer shape. (I've added halos around the selected points to make them easier to locate.) After setting the origin point at the bottom of the shape I dragged up and inward on the upper right point. This caused all selected points to move up and in toward the center, based on their proximity to the origin point. Because the two upper points were far away from the origin, they moved up dramatically, forming sharp bat ears. The lower points were closer to the origin, so they moved only slightly to form the chin, as the example on the right shows.

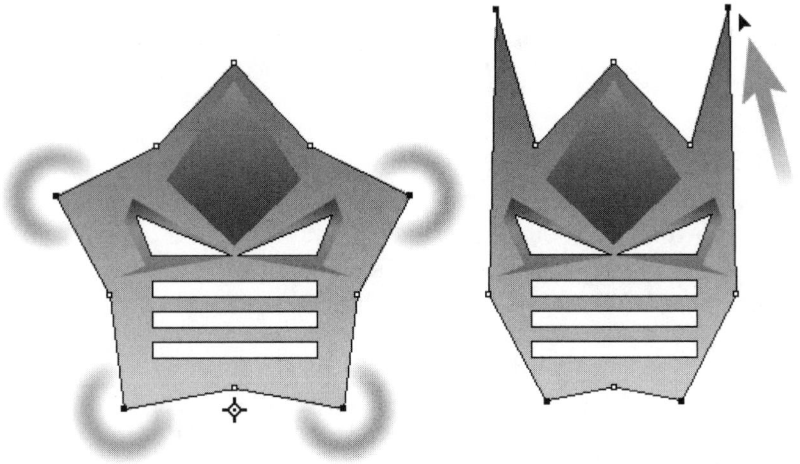

Figure 11-20: After selecting four points (surrounded by halos on left), I dragged with the scale tool to move the points according to their proximity to the origin.

Whenever you apply the scale tool to a selected point, you stretch the neighboring segments, just as you do when dragging points with the direct selection tool. You can also apply the scale tool to selected curved segments. In Figure 11-21, I took an everyday, average circle and selected each of its segments with the direct selection tool, without selecting any of the points. (I marqueed the bottom two segments and then Shift-marqueed the top two.) Then I dragged with the scale tool to enlarge the selection from the center, as the figure shows. Illustrator stretches the segments an equal distance in four directions.

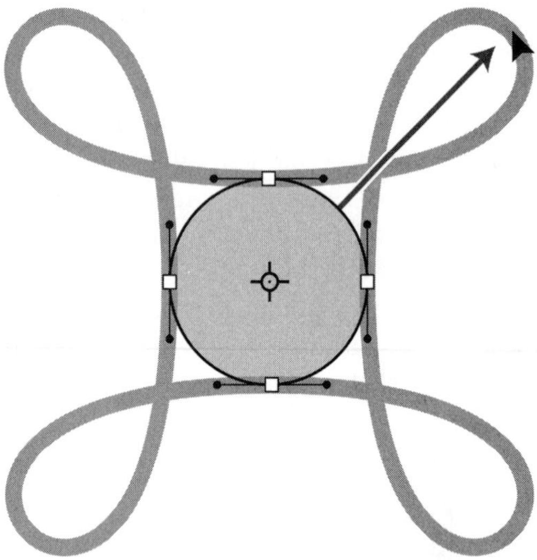

Figure 11-21:
By dragging the selected segments in a circle with the scale tool, I stretched the segments in perpendicular directions.

So in addition to its normal resizing functions, the scale tool does double duty as a symmetrical move tool. It's little surprise, if you think about it. All the scale tool is doing is moving and stretching segments away from and toward a fixed point. Once you understand its geometry, the scale tool becomes a never-ending source of inspiration. (And I'm not just saying that to be poetic.)

Rotating Objects Around the Origin

After you know how to use one transformation tool, the other three standard transformations become putty in your capable grasp. The rotate, reflect, and shear tools share many common characteristics with their scale sibling. So rather than laboriously examining every single detail of each tool as if this is the first word of Chapter 11 you've ever read, I'll make quick work of the familiar stuff and stick in as many tool-specific tips and techniques as these humble pages will permit.

For example, here's a summary of the basic workings of the rotate tool—the left-hand neighbor of the scale tool—with occasional figures:

- Drag with the rotate tool to rotate a selection around its bounding-box center. Or click to set the origin point and then drag to rotate, as shown in the second example of Figure 11-22. Because rotation is a strictly circular movement—in fact, you always rotate in perfect circles—the origin point acts as a true center, as the arrows in the figure demonstrate.

TIP It doesn't matter where you start dragging when using the rotate tool. At any time, you can gain more precise control over a rotation by moving the cursor farther away from the origin. Slight movements close to the origin can send your objects into exaggerated spins that are difficult to control.

- Press the Shift key when dragging to rotate in 45-degree (⅛ turn) increments. (The constraint axes have no influence over Shift-dragging with the rotate tool.)
- Press the Option key after you begin dragging and hold it until the drag is finished to rotate a clone of the selection. Then you can repeat a series of rotated clones by pressing ⌘-D or choosing Object » Transform » Transform Again.

  In the top example of Figure 11-23, I started with two simple paths: a spiral (black) and a two-point curve (gray). I rotated a clone of the spiral 45 degrees by clicking with the rotate tool and Shift-Option-dragging the spiral. Then I duplicated the spiral clone six more times by mercilessly beating ⌘-D. I needed to create only three duplicates of the two-point curve since I wanted to connect every other spiral. So I Shift-Option-dragged the curve 90 degrees and pressed ⌘-D twice.

  After joining the spirals and curves at their endpoints, I embellished these basic paths with layered stroking effects (as I explore in typically systematic fashion in Chapter 16). Then I added some text and skewed it with the shear tool. The result is a lovely frilly pattern that I plan to market as Deke's Designer Embroidery Coasters. Put in your order today.
- Select an origin from the reference point icon on the left side of the Transform palette. Then enter a value into the palette's rotate option box (bottom right) and press Return or Tab to rotate the selection. Press Option-Return or Option-Tab to clone and rotate.

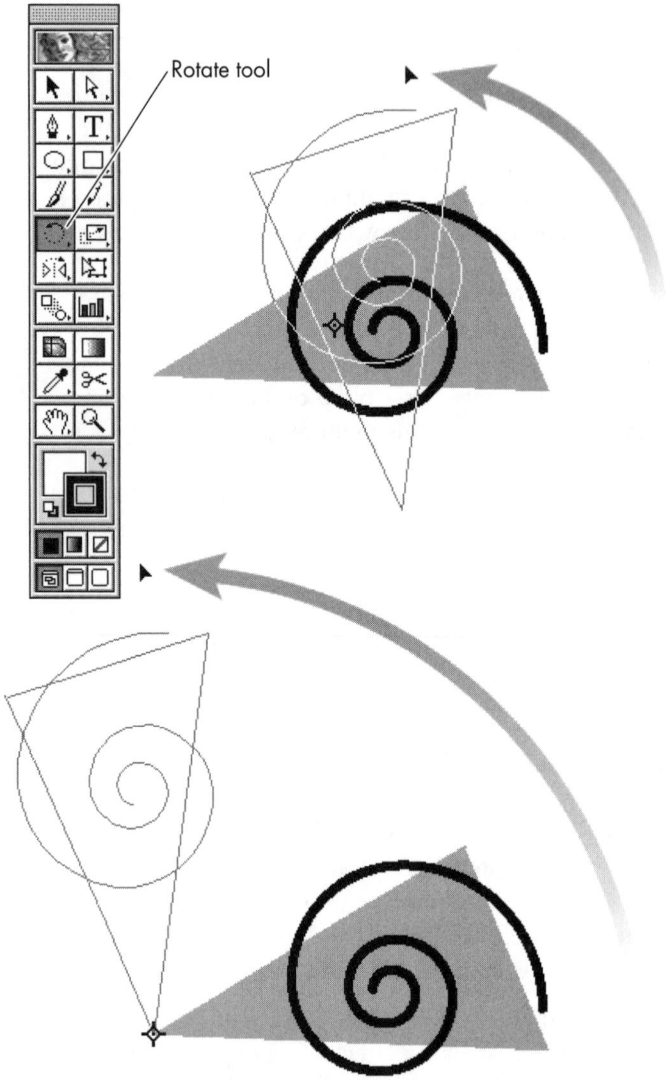

Figure 11-22: The difference between merely dragging with the rotate tool (top) and first clicking at the tip (origin point) of the triangle and then dragging (bottom).

Illustrator interprets rotations in degrees. A full circle is 360 degrees, so a 360-degree rotation would return the selection to its starting position; while a 180-degree rotation would turn it upside down. Positive values rotate counterclockwise; negative values rotate clockwise.

Figure 11-23: After repeatedly rotating and cloning a spiral and a curved segment (top), I joined a pair of spirals with each curve and duplicated the paths using progressively heavier strokes (bottom).

- Double-click on the rotate tool icon in the toolbox or Control-click and choose Rotate from the Transform menu to display the Rotate dialog box. Enter a value into the Angle option box and press Return to rotate the selection, or click Copy to rotate and clone. Illustrator rotates the selection around its center.

  If you want to position the origin point, Option-click with the rotate tool to bring up the Rotate dialog box. The point at which you click becomes the origin.

- Choose Object » Transform » Transform Each and enter a value into the Rotate option box (or drag the bar inside the circle pictured to the right of the option box) to rotate multiple objects around their individual centers. To demonstrate the principle of individual rotation, I've appended little stars to the big star's spikes in the left example of Figure 11-24. In retrospect, I decided I wanted to have the little stars rotated at the same angle as the larger one. I first used the measure tool to find the angle of the top side of one of the large star's arms. (I dragged from left to right, as labeled in the figure.) This same side is horizontal in each of the little stars, so the measurement tells me the precise amount I need to rotate.

  Then I chose Object » Transform » Transform Each and entered the measured value—18.214 degrees—into the Rotate option box. Illustrator rotated each selected shape around its center to produce the darkened stars on the right side of the figure.

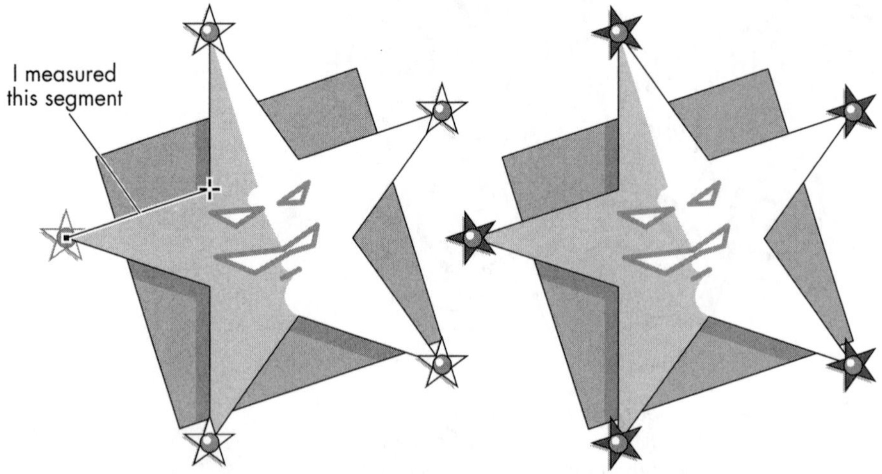

Figure 11-24: After measuring the angle of the large star (left), I used the Transform Each command to rotate the little stars 18.214 degrees (right).

Had I used the Rotate dialog box or the Transform palette to rotate the little stars, I would have caused the shapes to pivot away from their points, as in Figure 11-25. As when scaling, the Transform Each command rotates selected objects in place.

Figure 11-25: Using any of the other rotate functions moves the little stars around in a partial circle.

- Select the Random option inside the Transform Each dialog box to rotate selected objects randomly within the range specified in the Rotate option box. For example, if I enter a Rotate value of 30 degrees, Illustrator rotates each object anywhere from 0 to 30 degrees.
- You can use the rotate tool and the Rotate dialog box to move selected points around in a circle. In Figure 11-26, for example, I added points to a star by choosing Object » Path » Add Anchor Points. Then I selected the new points only (which appear inside the circular highlight in the figure). I clicked with the rotate tool at the star's exact center—which I determined using the Object » Path » Average technique (outlined in "Adding a Center Point" in Chapter 10)—and dragged to move the selected points around in a circle. This allowed me to edit the shape while maintaining radial symmetry—meaning that each spike looks the same as the other spikes.

Stars are wonderful transformation primitives because they have straight sides that jut in and out and they are born with radial symmetry. In other words, you can have a lot of fun rotating and scaling partial stars. The central shape in Figure 11-27 began life as a five-pointed star. I added points over and over again with Object » Path » Add Anchor Points. Then I carefully selected corresponding points on each spike and alternatively scaled and rotated them. That's it; I never drew a line.

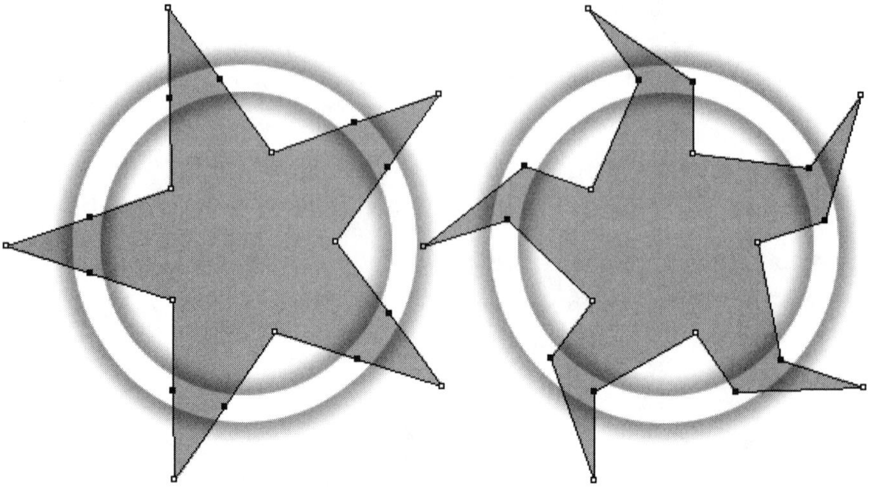

Figure 11-26: After adding points to the star, I selected the new points (left) and rotated them around the shape's center (right).

Figure 11-27: This figure's central shape was a five-pointed star before I attacked it with the Add Points command and the scale and rotate tools.

Flipping Objects Back and Forth

Most drawing programs provide Flip Horizontal and Flip Vertical commands so that you can quickly reflect selected objects. But not Illustrator. So far as Illustrator is concerned, those commands might be easy to use but they don't provide enough control. So in typical Illustrator fashion, the reflect tool is hardly convenient for quick flips but just the thing when accuracy is paramount.

The following is everything you need to know about flipping in Illustrator:

- The reflect tool works a little different than its fellow transformation tools. When you drag with the reflect tool, you change the angle of the reflection axis. As demonstrated in Figure 11-28, the reflection axis is like the mirror that the selection is reflected into. The portions of the object that lie on one side of the axis flip to the other. Because you can tilt the mirror, the reflect tool flips and rotates objects at the same time.
- If you immediately start in dragging with the tool, the reflection axis hinges on the center of the selection. But if you first click to set the origin point and then drag with the reflect tool, the axis pivots on the origin. In the top example of Figure 11-28, for instance, I clicked below and to the left of the selection. I then began dragging in a direct line above the selection, which resulted in a vertical axis. As I dragged down and to the right, the axis inclined into the position shown in the second example in the figure.
- Shift-drag with the reflect tool to constrain the axis to a 45-degree angle. When the axis is upright, the selection flips horizontally. When the axis is horizontal, the selection flips vertically.
- Press the Option key when dragging to flip a clone. You can repeat a flipped clone by pressing ⌘-D, but why would you want to? You would only end up creating a clone of the original positioned directly in front of it.
- Most of the time, it's easier to flip using the Reflect dialog box. To bring up the dialog box, double-click on the reflect tool icon in the toolbox or Control-click and choose Reflect from the Transform menu. Or you can Option-click with the reflect tool in the illustration window to set the origin point.

  The Reflect dialog box contains three options for specifying the angle of the reflection axis around which the flip occurs. Select the Horizontal option to flip the selection vertically, just as a gymnast swinging on a horizontal bar flips vertically. Select the Vertical option to flip the selection horizontally, like a flag flopping back and forth on a vertical flagpole. You can also enter a value into the Axis Angle option box to specify the exact angle of the axis. A value of 0 indicates a horizontal axis; 90 indicates a vertical axis..

Press Return to flip the selection. Click Copy to clone and flip.

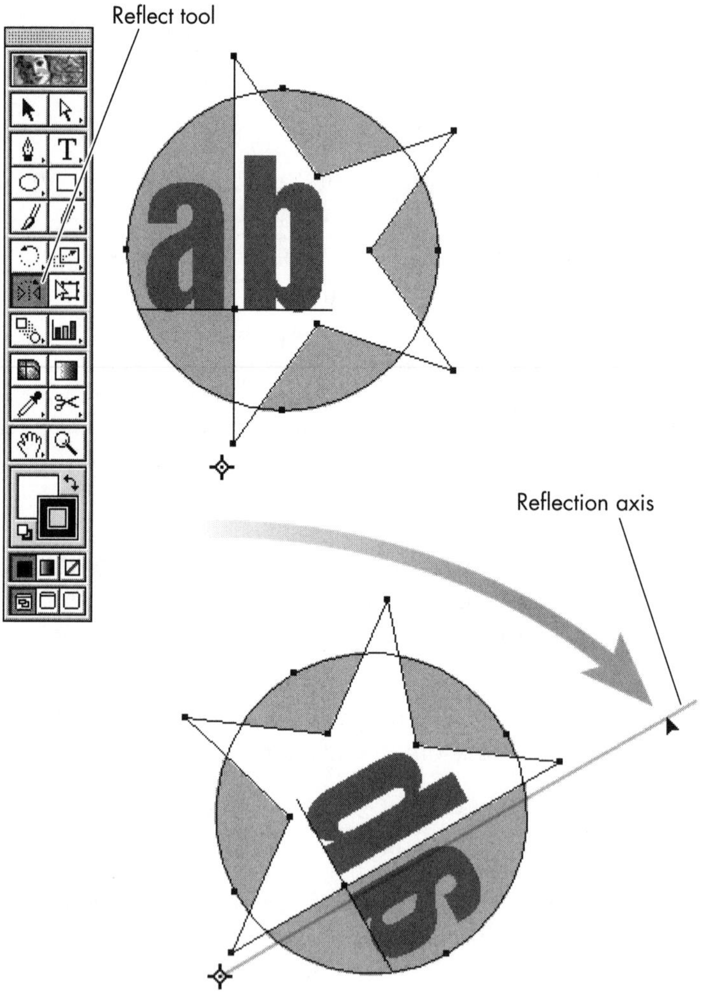

Figure 11-28: Click with the reflect tool to set the origin point (top); then drag to flip and rotate the selection around the reflection axis.

Compared to the scale and rotate tools, the reflect tool is very dull. You can't perform special effects with it. And although you can flip partial paths, there's rarely a reason to do it. Still, it's a very practical tool, and Illustrator would be the worse without it. When you gotta flip, you gotta flip.

Slanting Objects the Weird Way

The final transformation tool is the oddly named shear tool—the alternate tool in the reflect tool slot. Rather than removing wool from sheep—as the tool's name implies—the shear tool slants selected objects.

NOTE

Now, does "shear" suggest slanting to you? It doesn't to me either. Let's see, hmmm...nope, Webster's doesn't say anything about slanting when defining the verb "shear"—just cutting and cropping. Granted, the noun "shear" can be a force that causes something to slide against itself relative to a parallel plane of contact. But 1) most folks don't know what the heck that means; 2) it's not the same thing as slanting, now, is it? And 3) why name one tool after a noun when the rest are verbs? Here I've been making fun of the name of this tool since the first edition of my book, and Adobe refuses to budge! Doesn't the company even care about new users?! FreeHand calls its tool the skew tool, which is a little obscure but, you know, it ultimately makes sense. But shear! What kind of word is shear? Why not sheer? Or how about Cher?! I mean, those makes about as much sense as shear!! I know, let's just give it a little symbol, like the artist formerly known as . . . blaaugh! (Crash.) Oops, sorry. I got so excited I fell out of my chair.

Despite its dopey name, this is an important tool. It slants objects horizontally, vertically, or in any other direction. So don't be put off by the name. This tool deserves to be part of your daily transformation regimen.

Because the shear tool is a little more demanding than the other transformation tools, I devote the entire following section to explaining its basic operation. After that, I cover the Shear dialog box.

Using the Shear Tool

As with the other transformation tools, you can start right in dragging with the shear tool. But I recommend that you don't. Of all the transformation tools, this is the most difficult to control. So you're best off specifying an origin point to keep things as predictable as possible.

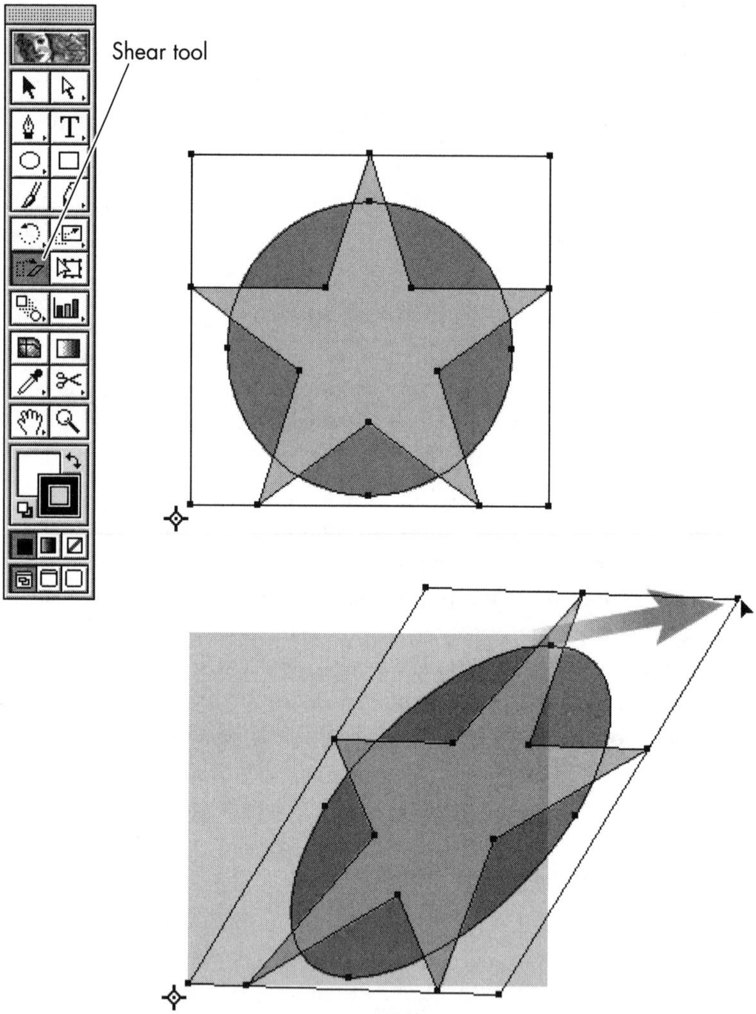

Figure 11-29: Click in a corner with the shear tool (top), and then drag from the opposite corner to slant the selection (bottom).

Click to set the origin point. I find if helpful to set the origin in the lower left corner of the selection. Then I move the cursor to the opposite corner of the selection—upper right—and begin dragging. Illustrator slants the selection in the direction of your drag, as demonstrated in Figure 11-29.

Illustrator figures two ingredients into slanting an object—the amount of slant applied and the axis along which the slant occurs. The distance of the drag determines the amount of slanting; the angle of the drag determines the angle of the axis.

Notice that although I dragged up and to the right in Figure 11-29, the selected objects slanted slightly downward. I dragged up about 10 degrees, so the axis is angled at 10 degrees. The weird thing is, when dragging with the shear tool, all axis angles clockwise from 45 degrees around to –135 degrees (about 1:30 to 7:30 on a clock face) slant objects downward. Axis values from –135 to 45 degrees (7:30 to 1:30) slant objects upward. Mathematically, it doesn't have to be this way, but so it is when you're using the shear tool.

WARNING: Meanwhile, if you drag in a 45-degree or –135-degree direction, Illustrator stretches the selected objects all the way to Tierra del Fuego. If you notice your objects going haywire, just move your mouse up or down a little to restore the selection to a recognizable state.

Slant Sensibly with Shift

TIP: Because of the odd way Illustrator calculates the effect of dragging with the shear tool, I almost always keep the Shift key down while I'm dragging. Shift-dragging with the shear tool constrains the axis to multiples of 45 degrees. As I've told you, two of these multiples—45 and –135—turn the axis into a force of absolute evil. But if you Shift-drag in a roughly horizontal or vertical direction, you'll achieve very predictable results.

The shear tool is especially useful for slanting type and adding shadows. I've accomplished both of these tasks in Figure 11-30. To create the first shadow at the top of the figure, I clicked with the scale tool along the baseline of the letters, then I Option-dragged from the top of the letters down past the baseline to flip and scale a clone. I then filled the clone with gray. In the second example, I clicked with the shear tool along the baseline of the letters and Shift-dragged from left to right to slant the shadow horizontally. Finally, I selected all letters, clicked at the base of the first T with the shear tool, and Shift-dragged up on the M. This slanted the letters vertically, as in the last example in the figure.

Figure 11-30: After flipping a clone of the letters with the scale tool (top), I slanted the clone horizontally with the shear tool (middle). I then selected all letters and slanted them vertically (bottom).

Defining the Slant and the Axis

Illustrator lets you slant and clone by pressing the Option key while dragging with the shear tool. You can also display a Shear dialog box by double-clicking on the shear tool icon in the toolbox, by Option-clicking with the tool in the illustration window, or even by doing the infamous Control-click.

As shown in Figure 11-31, the Shear dialog box offers a Shear Angle option box for specifying the angle that you want your objects to slant and three Axis options for specifying the axis along which the slant should occur.

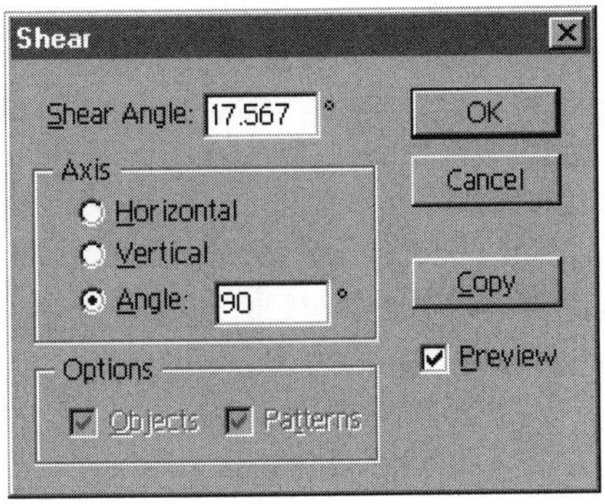

Figure 11-31: You can set the shear angle and the axis along which the slant should occur in the Shear dialog box.

Specify the angle of the shear axis exactly as you would the angle of the reflection axis inside the Reflect dialog box. Select the Horizontal option to slant the selected objects to the left or right; select the Vertical option to slant up or down. You can also angle the axis by entering a value into the Angle option box in the Axis section of the Shear dialog box. Because the axis extends to either side of the origin point, values greater than 180 degrees are repetitious. (Values of 45 or –135 degrees don't cause problems in the Shear dialog box; they just mess things up when you're trying to drag with the shear tool.)

Regardless of the selected Axis options, you'll want to enter a value for the Shear Angle option at the top of the dialog box. Here's where things get tricky. Illustrator interprets just about every other value that's measured in degrees in a counterclockwise direction. (It's the standard geometry model that you undoubtedly learned or neglected in an ancient math course.) This is true for rotations, angled axes (including the shear axis), and directional movements. The only exceptions to the rotation direction are the Shear Angle option box at the top of the Shear dialog box and the Angle option box in the Twirl dialog box (see Chapter 12), which Illustrator applies in a clockwise direction. Therefore:

- When the Horizontal radio button is selected, a positive Shear value slants the selection forward and a negative value slants it backward. Seems sensible.
- But when the Vertical radio button is selected, a positive Shear value slants the selection up on the left side of the origin and down on the right, so it looks like it's pointing downward. A negative value slants the selection upward. That's just plain weird.

A Shear value of 30 degrees creates a pretty significant slant. Anything beyond 90 to –90 degrees is repetitive. And you definitely don't want to enter anything from about 80 to 90 degrees (positive or negative) because it pretty well lays the selected objects flat.

Slanting is easily the least predictable of the transformations. I considered including a huge chart showing what happens to an object when you apply all kinds of different Shear Angle and Axis Angle values, but take my word for it, you would've been more confused after looking at the thing than you probably were before. That's why I recommend sticking with horizontal and vertical slants when possible. If you need to slant objects a little up and a little over, do it in two separate steps. It'll save wear and tear on your brain.

Free Transform for All

NEW 8

Until now, Illustrator was missing one basic kind of transformation that's standard in just about every drawing program, from the ancient MacDraw to the midrange Windows's wünderkind CorelDraw. Even image editor Photoshop offers it. I speak, of course, of eight-point distortion, which allows you to yank on the handles of a selected object to stretch it. Eight-point distortion is useful for simulating perspective or for simply fitting an object into a new space.

In Illustrator 8, you select a path (or paths) with the arrow tool and then choose the free transform tool from the toolbox. Illustrator will display the standard eight-handled bounding box that just surrounds the paths. As with the bounding box that appears when you select the Use Bounding Box option (from within the General Preferences dialog box), the orientation of the bounding box depends on the original paths. If you don't like the orientation Illustrator assigns the box, either choose Object » Transform » Reset Bounding Box or Control-click and choose Transform » Reset Bounding Box. Illustrator will slap the bounding box into shape, aligning it such that it squares with the artboard and its pages.

When you move the free transform tool around a selected object, Illustrator displays a number of different cursors depending on the tool's location in terms of the object's bounding box. As shown in Figure 11-32, seven different cursors are associated with the free transform tool when it's in use. Four of these cursors (the ones flanked with two arrows) appear automatically, depending only on the location of the tool in terms of the bounding box. The other three cursors (the plain or augmented grayed arrowheads) appear only after you press ⌘ after you start dragging one of the bounding box's handles.

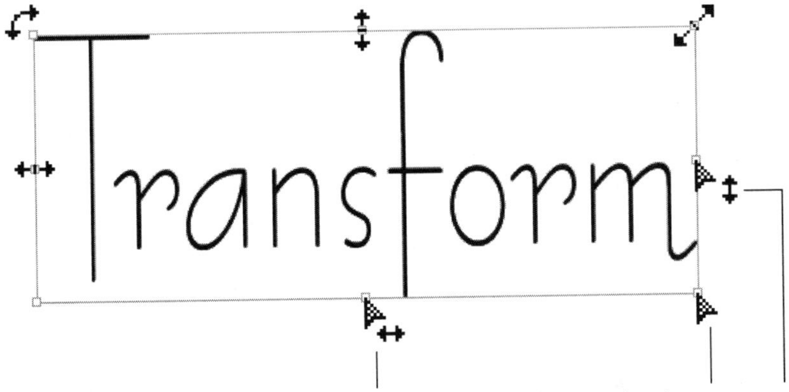
Transform
These three cursors appear only when you press the ⌘ key after you've started to drag one of the handles.

Figure 11-32: The free transform tool uses seven different cursors to indicate the modification that the tool's ready to perform.

WARNING

Illustrator provides one other cursor for the free transform tool. If you switch to the free transform tool when nothing is selected, the tool's cursor looks just like the arrow tool. In this form, it is absolutely useless. A number of times, I found myself trying to select a path with the free transform tool because of this redundant use of the arrow cursor. So if you're trying to use the arrow cursor but find that you can't select paths, make sure that you aren't using the free transform tool.

Here's the skinny on what you can do when you're using the free transform tool on selected paths:

- Drag a corner handle to scale the selected objects. Shift-drag a corner handle to scale proportionally. In either case, the opposite corner serves as the scale origin.
- Option-drag a corner handle to scale the object around its center. Option-Shift-drag a corner handle to scale proportionally around the object's center.
- Drag one of the bounding box's side handles (including the top and bottom ones) to limit the scaling to either horizontal or vertical changes. The opposite side's handle serves as the scale origin.

- Option-drag a side handle to horizontally or vertically scale the object from the center.
- Drag from any location outside the free transform bounding box—the cursor changes to its curved two-headed form—to rotate the object around the center.
- Shift-drag from outside the bounding box to constrain the rotations to multiples of 45 degrees (plus whatever value you've entered into the Constrain Angle option box in the General Preferences dialog box). These 45-degree multiples are measured relative to the orientation of the bounding box and not to the orientation of the page. Thus, if your bounding box is not initially square with the page, it is not possible to Shift-rotate with the free transform tool to make your object square to the page.

NEW 8

Rotating with the free transform tool can result in a bounding box that is not square with your page. If you prefer your world to be square, either choose Object » Transform » Reset Bounding Box or Control-click(and choose Transform » Reset Bounding Box any time your bounding box becomes crooked.

- Press the ⌘ key after you've started dragging a corner handle to move that corner independent of the other three corners. This allows you to freely distort the object. For you seasoned users, this works exactly the same as the now defunct Illustrator 7 Free Distort filter.

NOTE

Even though you can transform text with the free transform tool, it does have some limitations in this regard. The last technique and the following three—the ones that include pressing the ⌘ key while you're dragging a corner handle—do not work with normal text. To perform these transformations, you must first convert the text to paths via the Type » Create Outlines command (⌘-Shift-O).

- Press ⌘-Shift while dragging a corner handle to limit the direction of your drag to follow along one of the sides of the bounding box. For example, in the top portion of Figure 11-33, the bounding boxes were initially square with the page. I pressed ⌘-Shift while dragging the corner handles and my drags were constrained to vertical and horizontal only. In the bottom portion of Figure 11-33, the bounding boxes were initially set at roughly 24.5 degrees. When I pressed ⌘-Shift while dragging the corner handles, my drags were limited to angles that matched those of the bounding box—roughly 24.5 and 114.5 (90 + 24.5) degrees.

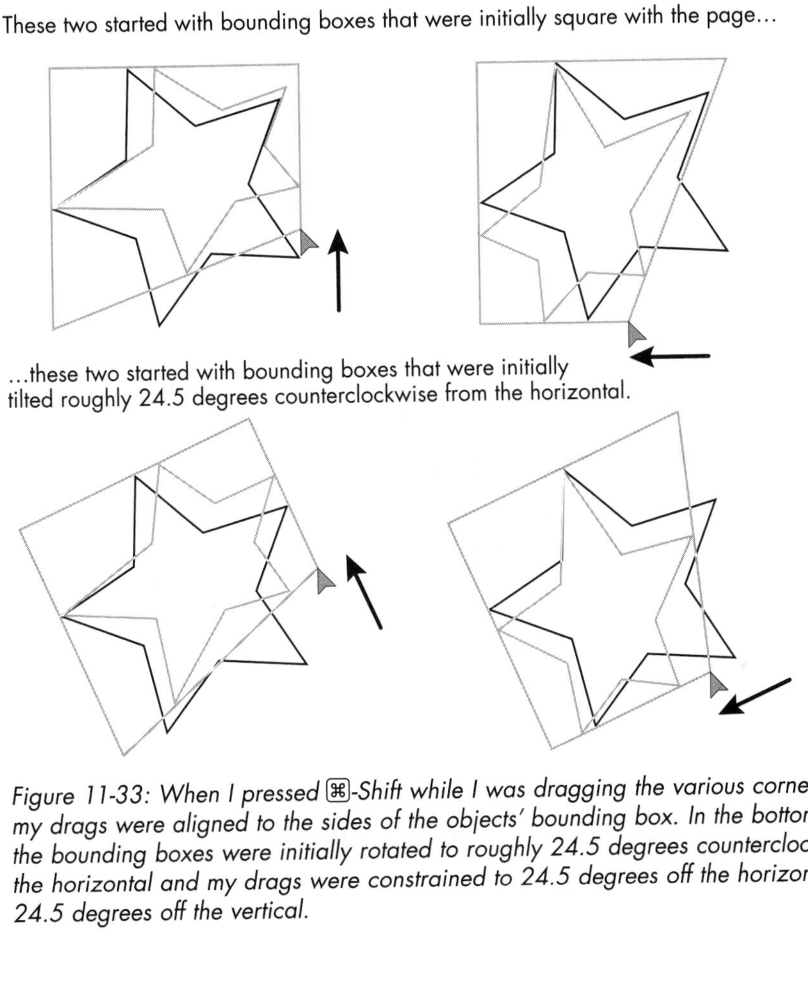

Figure 11-33: When I pressed ⌘-Shift while I was dragging the various corner handles, my drags were aligned to the sides of the objects' bounding box. In the bottom examples, the bounding boxes were initially rotated to roughly 24.5 degrees counterclockwise from the horizontal and my drags were constrained to 24.5 degrees off the horizontal and 24.5 degrees off the vertical.

- Press ⌘-Option while you drag a corner handle to force the opposite corner to mimic your every move, except in the opposite direction. As you can see in the top example of Figure 11-34, as I ⌘-Option-dragged the bottom right corner down and to the right, the top left corner moved up and to the left. Depending on the direction of your drag, you can press ⌘-Option to rotate, scale and even flip the object. In the bottom portion of Figure 11-34, by pressing ⌘-Option while I substantially dragged the bottom right corner, I was able to rotate and flip the original object. Additionally, I scaled the paths, resulting in a slightly taller and thinner version of the original.

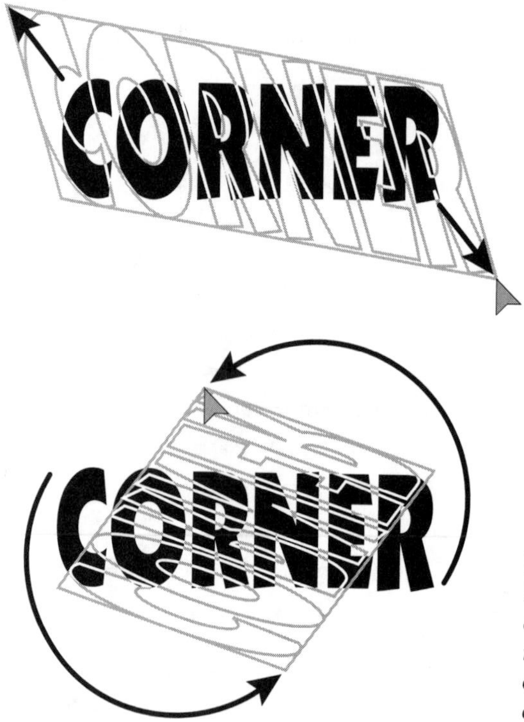

Figure 11-34: Press ⌘-Option while dragging a corner handle to cause the opposite corner to move in the opposite direction.

- Press all three keys (⌘-Option-Shift) to force one of the adjacent corner handles to mimic your moves, except in the opposite direction. Also, all movement will be constrained in such a way that they align with one of the bounding box's sides. (This is true for both bounding boxes that are square with the page and those that are not, but since it's easier to explain this in terms of horizontal and vertical movements, I'll use objects in which the bounding boxes start off square with the page.) The top example of Figure 11-35 shows how the top right corner shot upward as I ⌘-Option-Shift-dragged the bottom right corner. This is a result of dragging more vertically than horizontally. Conversely, had I dragged more horizontally than vertically, the appropriate corner handle would have moved just as far in the other direction. The bottom example of Figure 11-35 illustrates the bottom left corner moving left to counter my rightward ⌘-Option-Shift-drag of the bottom right corner.

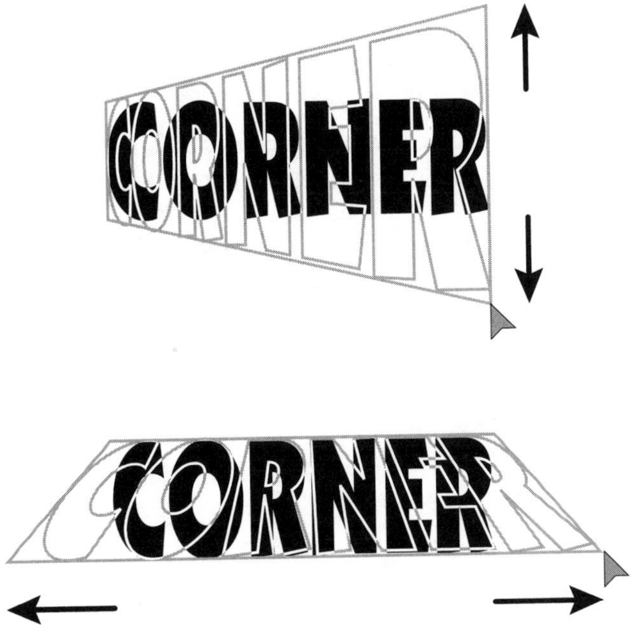

Figure 11-35: I pressed ⌘-Option-Shift while I dragged a corner handle to constrain the movements of both that corner and one of its adjacent corners to either horizontal or vertical. These directions are functions of the bounding box's original orientation.

- While dragging one of the handles positioned along the sides of the free transform tool's bounding box (including the top and bottom sides) press the ⌘ key to unhinge the bounding box from its rigid rectilinear confines. You can then reshape the bounding box as a parallelogram in which the opposite sides of the box remain parallel but adjacent sides do not have to remain perpendicular to one another. In this case, three of the four sides will move with your drag; only the opposite side remains immobile.
- Press ⌘-Shift while you drag one of the side handles to manipulate the bounding box as a parallelogram in which the side you drag remains aligned with its original position. If your bounding box is originally squared with the page, you'll be able to drag vertically or horizontally (depending on whether the side you drag is one of the vertical sides or the horizontal sides of the bounding box). All the while, the side handle will remain a constant distance from the opposite side.

- If, while dragging a side handle, you press ⌘-Option, you can manipulate the bounding box as a parallelogram that pivots around the box's center instead of around the opposite side.
- Press all three of these special keys while doing that side handle drag to reshape the bounding box as a parallelogram that pivots around the box's center, while the opposite sides of the box remain a constant distance away from one another. This way, you change only the corners' angular sizes.

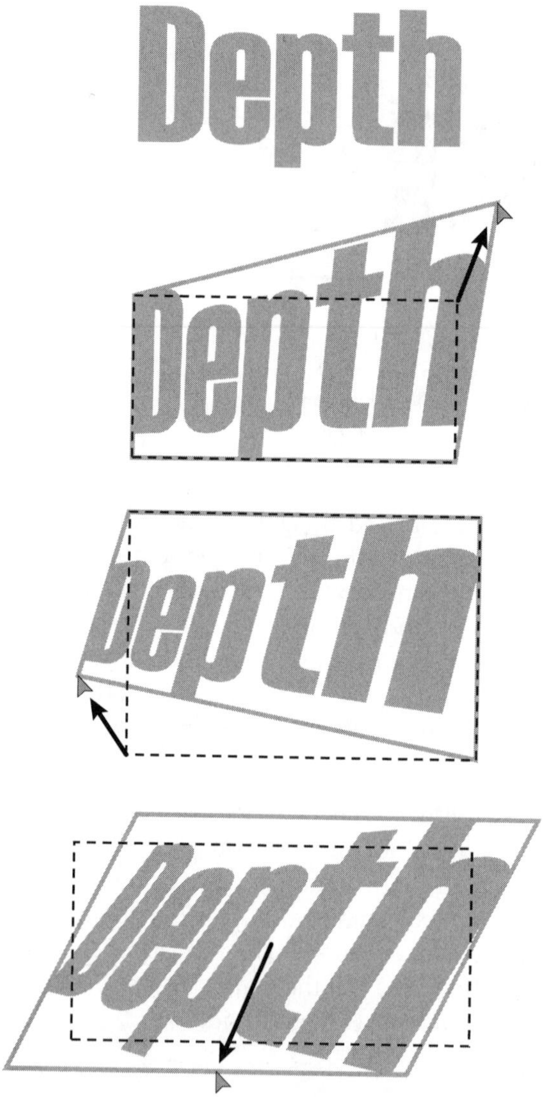

Figure 11-36:
You can achieve great perspective effects like this by using a variety of free transform tool techniques.

Although the free transform tool's many uses mean you have a heap to remember, the tool affords you some of the best and (once mastered) easiest transformation and distortion abilities in this and any other drawing program. By mixing and matching the techniques mentioned above, you can create complicated and sophisticated perspective effects. In fact, with the help of a few other filters, you can create stuff that looks like it came out of a 3-D program.

For example, in Figure 11-36, I started with some point text that I converted to paths with the Type » Create Outline command (⌘-Shift-O). I then transformed it three times. Twice I pressed the ⌘ key while I dragged corner handles (first on the top right handle and then on the bottom left handle). Once I pressed both the ⌘ and Option keys while I dragged the bottom handle. In three quick drags, I transformed the text into a word that practically jumps off the page.

To complete the effect, I've taken my distorted text from the example in Figure 11-36 and chose Object » Path » Offset Path to clone and expand the individual characters. I sent the expanded clone to the bottom of the stack and then nudged the offset path down and to the right a few points, so that they aligned as shown in Figure 11-37. Finally, I filled both sets of paths with different gradations (as I will explain in Chapter 15). The result is a surprisingly realistic beveled effect.

Figure 11-37: After cloning and expanding the distorted text (with the Offset Path filter), I nudged it over a bit and then filled both sets of paths with gradients.

Even though it has a lot going for it, the free transform tool does possess one glaring flaw; you can't clone a path when you're transforming it with the free transform tool. This is a real shame, especially since there's still another available key that's common to every keyboard I've ever seen—the spacebar—which could be used for a cloning option. Sure, using four keys may be less than appealing to some, but having the option of cloning while transforming with the free transform tool, simply by pressing an additional key, is better than no option at all.

TIP

If you want to transform a clone of a path with the free transform tool, be sure to clone the path first—with the Copy and Paste in Front commands (⌘-C and ⌘-F)—and then use the free transform tool on the cloned path.

CHAPTER 12

HOG-WILD SPECIAL EFFECTS

Every so often, someone informs me that he or she prefers Photoshop to Illustrator because "I'm just not a vector person." It's not that Illustrator isn't a fine product that permits you to create terrific artwork; it's a matter of feeling comfortable and creative inside the program. In Photoshop, inspiration comes in the form of scanned images, which you can enhance or distort using a mouth-watering collection of special effects filters. But in Illustrator, you have no choice but to draw everything from scratch. Right?

Not exactly. Clearly, Bézier curves are more labor intensive than pixels. (I think anyone who isn't trying to sell you something would admit that.) But you don't have to painstakingly draw each and every curve by hand. You can rough out primitive compositions with ellipses, stars, text characters, and the like, and then embellish these objects using Illustrator's automated functions.

If you read Chapters 9 and 11, you already have a sense of the marvels you can accomplish by combining and transforming shapes. But that's only the proverbial tip of the iceberg. In this chapter, I show you how to apply a wide range of bona fide special effects—functions so radical that they can mutate common shapes into extraordinary forms that would take you minutes or even hours to draw by hand. In Figure 12-1, for example, I started with nothing more than a line of type and a five-pointed star. A quick distortion and two filters later, I arrived at the unqualified masterpiece that you see before you. As you can see, Illustrator lets you run roughshod over objects in the same way that Photoshop lets you use and abuse images. Both programs are equal parts finely tuned graphics applications and platforms for fortuitous experimentation.

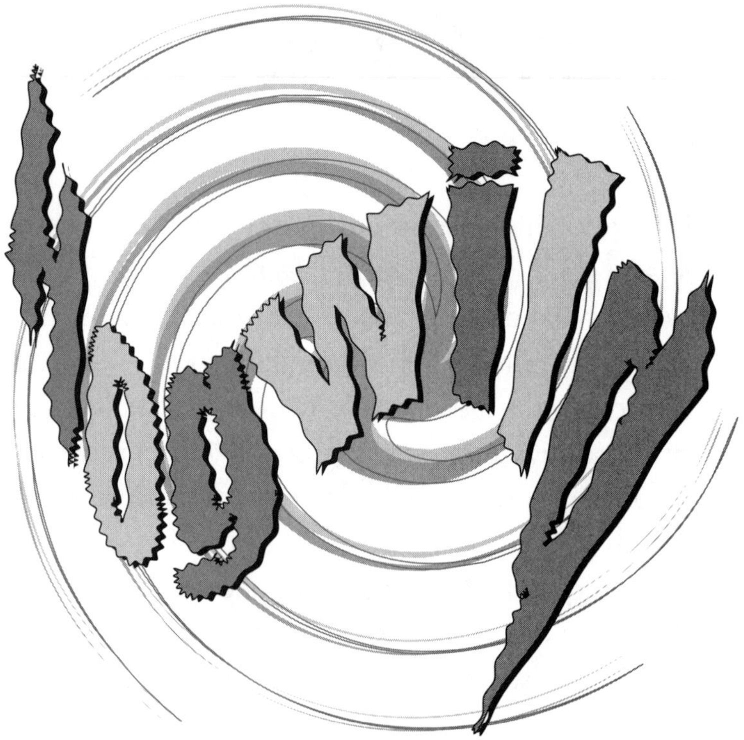

Figure 12-1: Thanks to the Twirl and Zig Zag filters, I was able to convert a humble star and collection of converted type into some very strange and complicated paths.

Throughout the following pages, I look at the special effects functions of Illustrator and explain a little bit about how they work and why they're better than they were in Illustrator 5. Why am I comparing Illustrator 8 to Illustrator 5 and not to Illustrator 7? Because nothing covered in this chapter has really changed since the improvements made back in Illustrator 5. (The only notable exception is that the old Free Distort filter has disappeared to make room for the free transform tool that I described in Chapter 11.) I also include some information and opinion about add-on filters from companies like MetaCreations, Extensis, and Hot Door. Although you have to fork over more cash to purchase these packages—in the $130 range—they can significantly enhance your ability to create and obliterate objects in Illustrator.

Freelance Features

Most of Illustrator's capabilities are built into the main application. But many tools and commands come from little subprograms called plug-ins. By default, all plug-ins reside in the Plug-ins folder inside the same folder that contains the Illustrator application. (You can change this using File » Preferences » Plug-ins, as described in Chapter 2, but few folks ever do.) When you launch Illustrator, the program loads all the plug-ins into memory and makes them available as tools, commands, and palettes in the program.

NOTE

You can get information about any plug-in by choosing the About Plug-ins command from the Apple menu (or from the Help menu in the Windows version). Then select a filter from the scrolling list and click on the About button to see who wrote it. Okay, so this isn't the sort of revelation that you circle with a highlighter. (Only a couple of you will scurry to your diaries and scribble, "Illustrator suddenly made sense today when I learned how to use the About Plug-in command!") But it's an organizational tool I thought you should know about.

You can add plug-ins from other companies by copying the files into Illustrator's Plug-ins folder or into one of several subfolders; or you can create a new folder. Illustrator loads the plug-in during startup as long as it is located somewhere inside the Plug-ins folder.

Some plug-ins manifest themselves as tools and palettes, and a few appear as commands under the Edit, Object, and Type menus. But most show up as commands in the overflowing Filter menu. Because the commands in the Filter menu vary dramatically in purpose and approach, I discuss them in context throughout this book. But just so we're all on the same wavelength, here is a complete list of the commands in the Filter menu, with brief snippets about what they do and where to turn for more information:

- **Filter » Colors (Chapter 14):** Illustrator lets you modify the colors of many objects simultaneously using the commands in the Filter » Colors submenu. But, of course, you'll need some color theory under your belt to understand these commands, which is why Chapter 14 exists.
- **Filter » Create » Object Mosaic (Chapter 13):** Illustrator offers some weird filters, but this one may be the weirdest. It traces a bunch of colored squares around an imported image to convert the image to an object-oriented mosaic. Now there's something we can all integrate into our artwork!
- **Filter » Create » Trim Marks (Chapter 18):** Apply this filter to create eight small lines that serve as guides when you trim your printed illustration. The eight lines mark the corners of the selected objects' bounding box (see Chapter 10). Trim marks are like crop marks, but they are considerably more versatile.
- **Filter » Distort (Chapter 12):** These special effects filters are discussed in this very chapter. They muck up objects but good!
- **Filter » Pen and Ink (Chapter 17):** My nomination for the most difficult commands to use in all of Illustrator appears in this submenu. But, they're powerful. You can design custom fill patterns, including dots, crosshatches, and squiggles. If you've ever envied FreeHand's PostScript fills patterns, the Pen and Ink commands may be Illustrator's answer.
- **Filter » Stylize » Add Arrowheads (Chapter 16):** This command adds an arrowhead to the end of a line. Illustrator bases the size of the arrowhead on the thickness of the stroke, which is why I discuss the filter in Chapter 16.
- **Filter » Stylize » Drop Shadow:** Okay, everyone repeat after me: "The Drop Shadow filter is absolutely worthless, devoid of merit, and incapable of producing anything resembling remotely acceptable results." It clones selected paths, sends them to back, and colors them so they don't look anything like drop shadows. I explain more satisfactory shadow techniques in Chapters 9, 11, and 17.
- **Filter » Stylize » Round Corners:** This last filter rounds off the corners in a selected path. You enter a Radius value—as you do when specifying the rounded corner of a rectangle—and Illustrator does the rest.

In fact, you can use this filter to round off the corners of a rectangle long after you draw the shape. You can also apply it to stars, characters of text, and other shapes that have lots of corners. In Figure 12-2, I've applied a Radius value of 12 points to a star, a rectangle, and some type converted to paths.

> **NOTE** The filters that appear in the third portion of the Filter menu are used for placed images. These commands are dimmed unless you've selected an image in your artwork. For a solid rundown of these filters, jump ahead to Chapter 13.

After you choose a command from the Filter menu, it appears at the top of the menu (even if you later undo the command). This allows you to quickly reapply the filter by choosing the first command in the menu or by pressing the keyboard equivalent, ⌘-E. To reapply the filter with different settings, choose the second command in the Filter menu or press ⌘-Option-E.

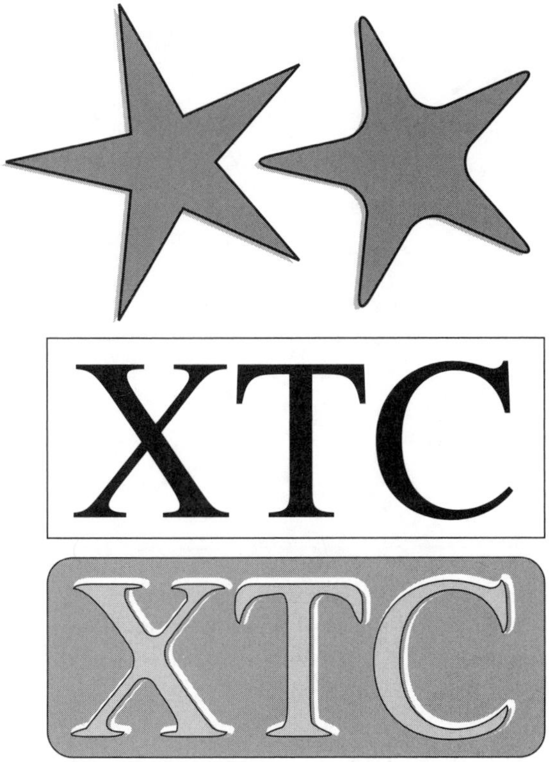

Figure 12-2: Here I've applied the Round Corners filter to a star, a rectangle, and some Times Roman text.

The Twirl Filter and Tool

Illustrator provides two variations on the Twirl filter. One is the command Filter » Distort » Twirl and the other is the twirl tool, the alternate tool in the rotate tool slot. Both twist selected objects around a central point, like spaghetti twirling around a fork.

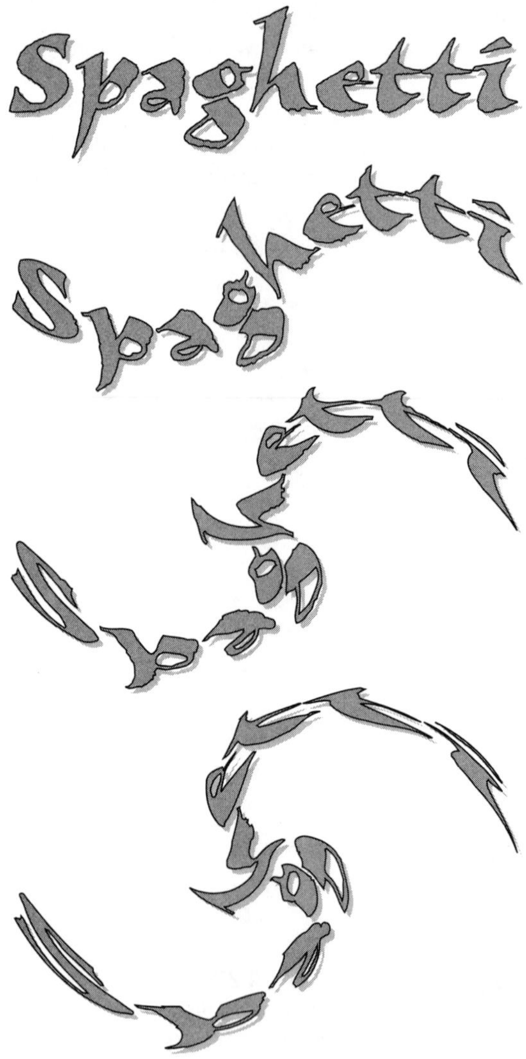

Figure 12-3: The results of twirling a line of converted Visigoth type 0, –60, –120, and –180 degrees.

Having problems visualizing this? Well, imagine for a moment that you're in Little Italy, admiring a strand of tacky spaghetti that's slightly stuck to your plate. A man in a striped shirt plays an accordion as you begin to twirl the noodle, coaxing it gingerly from the dish. Maybe it's the music, maybe it's the wine, but you can't help but notice that the part of the noodle that's closest to the fork rotates most dramatically, while the faraway portions stretch to keep up, not yet willing to release their grip on the plate. Now imagine that you can twirl your fork up to 32,768 degrees—more than 91 complete rotations—and you have Illustrator's Twirl filter.

In case you're simply not in the mood for pasty pasta analogies, Figure 12-3 shows the effect of the twirl filter on some virtual spaghetti converted to paths. Each line of type is twirled 60 degrees more than the line above it.

Twirling in Illustrator

To twirl a selection, choose Filter » Distort » Twirl and enter the amount of twirl you want to apply in degrees. A positive value twirls clockwise, a negative value twirls counterclockwise. Figure 12-3 demonstrates the effects of three negative twirls (–60, –120, and –180 degrees).

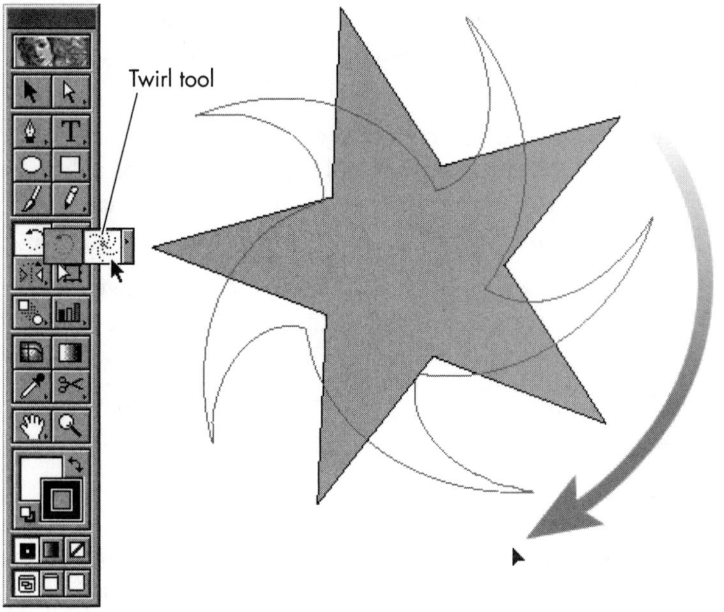

Figure 12-4: Use the twirl tool to drag around a selected shape to twist it by some arbitrary amount.

If you prefer the tangible, real-time feedback of a tool, select the twirl tool and click to mark the object's origin point. Then drag in the illustration window to twirl all selected objects. In Figure 12-4, I've dragged the selection about a quarter turn clockwise. You can drag up to 91 times around a selection to increase the magnitude of the twirl. But more than two revolutions tends to result in a lot of straight edges.

TIP

You can also Option-click with the twirl tool to bring up a dialog box and enter a numeric Twirl value. This is the same dialog box that appears when you choose Filter » Distort » Twirl. But what the heck, Option-clicking with a tool is sometimes more convenient than choosing a command.

One thing still missing from the twirl experience is a visible origin point. You click to set it and then hope that it's where you want it as you drag. Illustrator 8 provides a visible origin for the four transformation tools, but Adobe seems to have overlooked implementing it for the twirl tool and filter. Well there's always Illustrator 11.

Here's a list of other things that don't work now but ought to one day:

- If this were a typical transformation tool, you'd be able to press the Option key before releasing with the twirl tool to clone the selection. But sadly, this function is absent from the twirl tool.
- When you display the Twirl dialog box, it should tell you the degree that you last spun an object with the twirl tool. But although this value changes every time you use the tool, there seems to be no correlation. Heck, it'll show you a negative value after a positive twirl.
- The Shift key has no effect on your drag, you can't repeat a twirl by pressing ⌘-D, and you can't twirl partial paths (just whole paths at a time).

Now you know why I didn't discuss the twirl tool with the transformation tools in Chapter 11. Even the modest reflect tool could wipe the floor with this thing.

All Hail Curve Fitting

While still not as sophisticated as it should be, present-day Illustrator's twirl functions are significantly better than the old Twirl command back in Illustrator 5. In that version, the Twirl filter merely shuffled selected points around; it had no effect over control handles or the curvature of segments, nor was it able to introduce anchor points of its own. To get halfway decent results, you had to triple or quadruple the number of points in a path using the Add Anchor Points filter.

So what? "Why should we concern ourselves with ancient history?" you may ask. It's because Illustrator 6 included a little thing called curve fitting, and Illustrator 8 continues the tradition. Curve fitting makes all the difference in the world. This permits Illustrator to accurately calculate complex distortions when applied to straight and curved segments alike.

Figure 12-5 tells the whole story. I started with the two semicircles shown in the background of the figure. Then I twirled the shapes 300 degrees in both versions 5 and 8 to produce the foreground shapes.

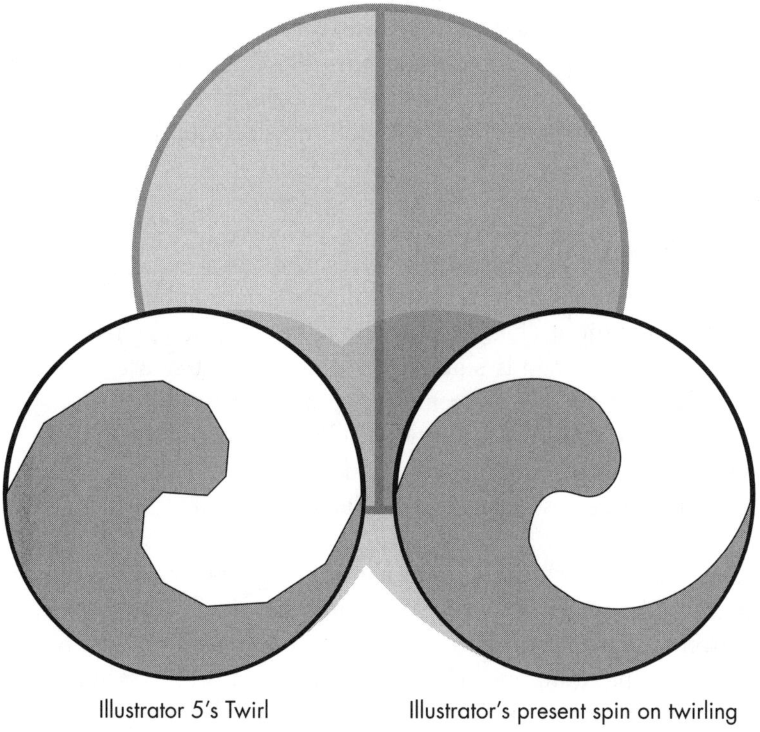

Figure 12-5: The results of twirling two semicircles (background) using Illustrator versions 5 and 8.

- In Illustrator 5, I had to choose Add Anchor Points four times in a row to get a halfway decent effect. And even then, the Twirl filter merely moved the points to different position, resulting in a jagged effect composed entirely of straight segments.
- Using the Illustrator we all love today, I didn't have to add a single point. Thanks to the new curve fitting, the Twirl filter was able to add

its own points and control handles where needed to create curved segments. The effect isn't perfect—the curve still looks a little flat in places —but it's a huge improvement.

Illustrator now makes curve fitting available to all plug-ins. This means MetaCreations, Extensis, and other companies can also take advantage of it when they design their filters. It may seem like a small thing—and, I might argue, one that Adobe should have introduced in Illustrator 5—but it will undoubtedly have a big effect on the way that we work inside drawing programs in the next few years. Thanks to curve fitting and the improved special effects filters that go with it, we'll be able to spend less time fastidiously constructing paths and more time exploring areas of personal style and object composition. When Adobe and other vendors make good on the promise of curve fitting, Twirl and other filters will seem less like special effects and more like common transformation tools.

The Scary Path Wigglers

You can use the other four commands in the Filter » Distort submenu to mess up the outline of a path without changing the direction or general shape of the path. In other words, the commands shake up a path without steering it completely off course. That's why I call these filters "path wigglers." Of course, you don't have to call them that. In fact, if you said, "Golly, you should see what I can do with a path wiggler!" in public, I'd be surprised if someone didn't slap you. (I wouldn't be surprised if Congress makes it a misdemeanor to say "path wigglers" on the Internet.)

Figure 12-6 demonstrates each of the path wigglers applied to lines of boring old Helvetica Inserat. The word "ghosts" is the product of the Roughen filter, "zombies" comes from Zig Zag, "monsters" was scrambled by Scribble and Tweak, and "vampires" received the blunt end of Punk and Bloat. (I used the free transform tool and the Twirl filter to abuse "Halloween.") Also worth noting, the frayed outline was a standard rectangle before I subjected it to the Roughen filter.

Figure 12-7 shows the dialog boxes associated with the four path wigglers. I show them all together because they share a few common elements. Depending on the filter, you can adjust the amount of wiggling, the quantity of wiggles, and just what it is that gets wiggled. You can also view the results of your settings in the illustration window by selecting the Preview check box. Each time you press the Tab key, Illustrator updates your paths on screen.

TIP

Two of the filters—Roughen, and Scribble and Tweak—produce random results within a specified range. You can force Illustrator to generate new results without changing the range by turning the Preview check box off and back on.

Figure 12-6: The path wiggler filters can turn common, dreary typefaces into something very frightening.

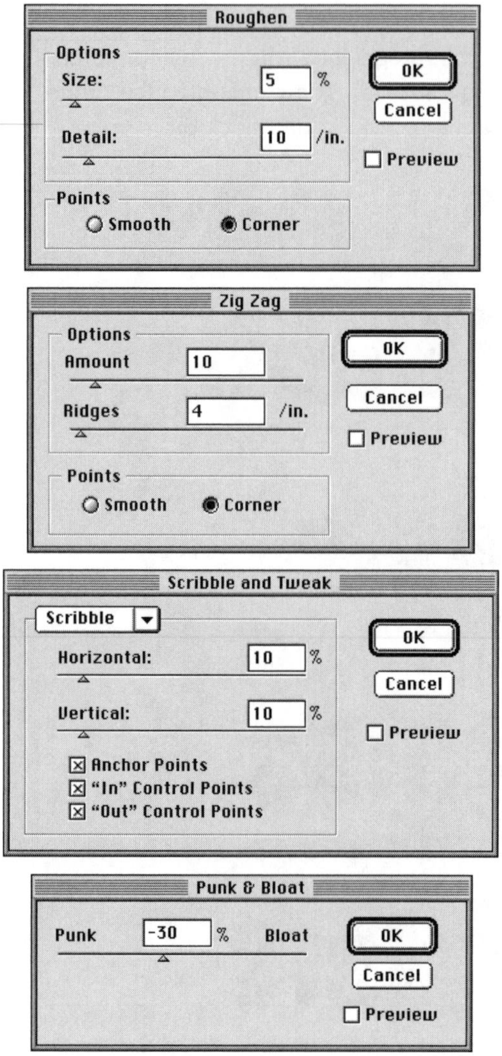

Figure 12-7: Each of the path wiggler dialog boxes offers a Preview check box so you can see the results of your settings before pressing Return.

The following paragraphs explain how each of the path wiggler filters work, in the order their dialog boxes appear in Figure 12-7. I include a figure with each description to give you an idea of how different settings affect a few typical paths.

- **Roughen:** The Roughen filter adds points to selected objects and then moves the points in random directions, giving your paths a serrated, spiky look. The Size value indicates the distance that each point can move, expressed as a percentage of the longest segment in the path. The

Detail value determines the number of points that Illustrator adds to each inch of segment. Select the Smooth radio button to convert all points in the paths to smooth points; select Corner to make them all corner points.

Figure 12-8 shows the results of various Size and Detail values applied to some converted text. In fact, the letters themselves tell the settings. For example, S2D4 means a Size value of 2 percent and a Detail value of 4 points per inch. The shape in the background started off as an eight-pointed star. The Smooth radio button was selected in every case.

Figure 12-8: Various Size and Detail values were applied to converted text with the Roughen filter.

- **Zig Zag:** Zig Zag gives your paths an electric jolt by adding a series of zigzags. The Amount value controls the distance that each point can move, which in turn determines the size of the wiggles. Use the Ridges value to specify how many zigzags Illustrator adds per segment—the dialog box claims that the filter will add ridges as a function of inches, but instead the filter adds ridges per segment. As you can see in Figure 12-9, long segments—like the sides of the As—get long wobbly ridges, while the ridges along short segments—as on the bottoms of the characters—are more tightly packed.

Figure 12-9: A few sample Amount and Ridges values applied to character outlines with the Zig Zag filter.

- **Scribble and Tweak:** Unlike Roughen or Zig Zag, the Scribble and Tweak filter does not add points to selected objects. Rather, it moves existing points and control handles in random distances and directions. The pull-down menu at the top of the dialog box offers two choices: Scribble and Tweak. Ultimately, they both do the same thing; the only difference is that Scribble moves points and control handles a percentage of the longest segment (just like the Roughen filter), while Tweak measures movements in points. For some reason percent symbols appear in both the Scribble and the Tweak variety of the dialog box, but rest assured, Tweak does indeed measure movements in terms of pixels.

Use the Horizontal and Vertical values to specify the maximum distance that points and control handles can move. Use the check boxes to decide which elements move. If you want to move the points but not the handles, turn off the two Control Points options. (The "In" option controls handles associated with segments entering points; the "Out" option controls handles for outgoing segments.) If you want to make the points stationary and move just the handles, turn off the Anchor Points check box and turn on the other two.

Figure 12-10: With the Scribble and Tweak filter set to Scribble, I adjusted the locations of anchor points (left) and control handles (right).

Figure 12-10 shows the results of moving elements with both the Horizontal and Vertical values set to one of three percentage values. I moved just the points in the left column and just the handles in the second column.

Figure 12-11: A sampling of values applied with the Punk and Bloat filter.

- **Punk and Bloat:** The Punk and Bloat dialog box is the simplest of the bunch, featuring a single slider bar and related option box. Negative values (which tend toward Punk) move points outward from the center of a path and twist segments inward. This creates an angular, almost Gothic, look. Positive values (on the Bloat side) move segments inward and curve segments outward, turning them into puffballs. The left column of Figure 12-11 demonstrates a few Punk values, while the right column shows off Bloat. Which kind of path would you rather be?

The So-Called Third-Party Solutions

Folks in the computer biz are forever going on about "third parties." These aren't the sort of drunken revelries that start after midnight, after you've polished off hors d'oeuvres at the Johnsons and Twister at the Greens. It's more in the spirit of legal parties—you know, like when the party of the first part wants to take the party of the second part for every penny the party's worth.

As it just so happens, you're the first party. I'll bet you didn't even know that you were actually involved in all this, but you're number one. And in this particular case, Adobe is the second party, since Adobe created Illustrator. If some other company comes along to enhance the functions inside Illustrator, that company becomes the eagerly awaited third party.

Presently, several third parties provide plug-ins for Illustrator. In the next few pages, I'll introduce you to three such parties—MetaCreations, maker of KPT Vector Effects; Extensis, the folks who sell VectorTool; and Hot Door, the company that brings you Transparency and CADTools. These aren't the only companies working to bolster Illustrator's core features. But where special effects are concerned, these three happen to offer the most interesting plug-ins around.

TIP

Oh, and because FreeHand 5, 7, and 8 support Illustrator filters, you can use any third-party filter collection with FreeHand as well. And you don't even have to copy the filters to two different folders. Just create an alias of the folder that contains the filters inside Illustrator's plug-ins folder (using File » Make Alias, at the Finder desktop). Then place the alias inside the Xtras folder, which is inside the Macromedia folder inside your System Folder. On the Windows side, create a shortcut of the folder (right-click on the folder and choose the Make Shortcut command). Place the folder shortcut in the Xtras folder inside the English folder. You'll find the English folder inside the main folder in which you installed FreeHand.

KPT Vector Effects

The filter package that I find myself using most often is KPT Vector Effects ($130) from MetaCreations (800/472-9025 or http://www.metacreations.com)—a Mac only product. Furthermore, it appears that MetaCreations has decided to discontinue Vector Effects and the product will remain available only while supplies last. This means that there's no way to guarantee that the product will fully support future versions of Illustrator. Though the interface is a tad prominent for some folks' tastes, Vector Effects is a truly inspired collection of filters that enhances Illustrator's capabilities.

NOTE: KPT stands for Kai's Power Tools, named after MetaCreations' popular and affable evangelist. The strange thing is that Vector Effects was created and programmed by a fellow named Sree Kotay, who had originally called the package Sree's Cool Tools. But when one licenses one's product, one learns servility.

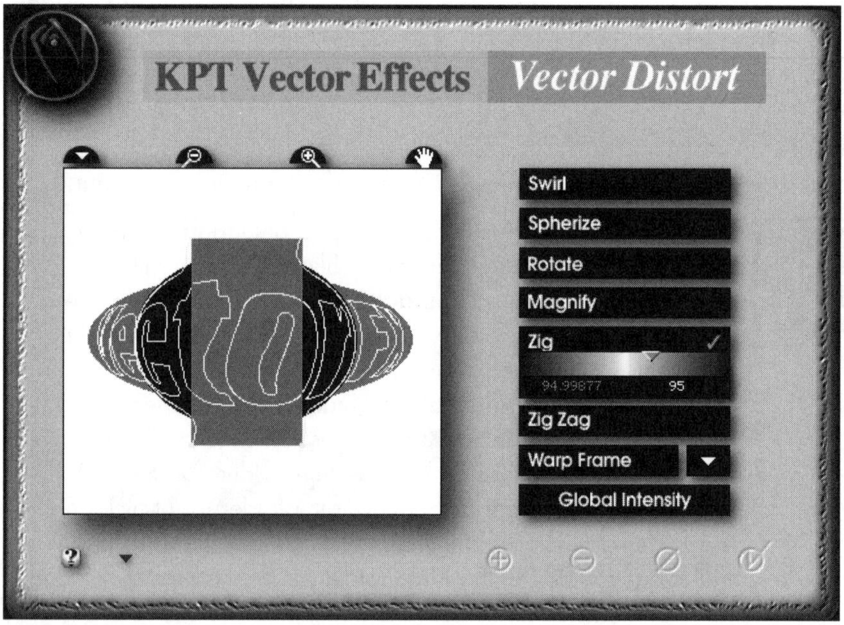

Figure 12-12: Dialog boxes in Vector Effects are like separate programs unto themselves.

Though Vector Effects works its magic from inside dialog boxes, it provides excellent previewing capabilities and lets you apply several effects at once. In the

Vector Distort dialog box, for example, you can view your selection inside a preview window, as shown in Figure 12-12. You can magnify the preview, scroll it with a hand tool, and so on. You then add "influences," which are areas of distortion. In Figure 12-12, I've created three influences, two of which bend the selection outward as though it's projected onto a sphere, while the other warps the selection. (The three influences appear as different regions of gray inside the preview area.) Though it takes a little getting used to, Vector Effects provides a very flexible working environment. You can even save your settings for later use or select from an array of preset distortions.

Altogether, Vector Effects includes 13 filters, which allow you to precisely position points, adjust the colors of selected objects, and apply special effects. Figure 12-13 demonstrates three of the effects. The 3D Transform filter rotates and extrudes objects in three-dimensional space, as in the first example in the figure. The Warp Frame filter lets you distort a selection by bending its bounding box. The middle example is one possible result. And the ShatterBox filter subdivides objects and nudges them in random directions, as in the last example.

Figure 12-13: Effects created using the 3D Transform (top), Warp Frame (middle), and ShatterBox (bottom) filters included with KPT Vector Effects.

VectorTools

Extensis (800/796-9798 or http://www.extensis.com) is a Portland, Oregon-based company that's quickly making a name for itself in the plug-in business. Extensis creates extensions for PageMaker, QuarkXPress, and Photoshop, not to mention VectorTools ($130, or $50 when upgrading from DrawTools, the old name for VectorTools) for Illustrator. Unfortunately, the product is available only for the Mac. Though not quite as versatile as Vector Effects, VectorTools provides many of the same distortion effects without the huge, screen-gobbling interface.

Figure 12-14 shows the VectorShape palette that contains all of VectorTool's special effects. Here I've clicked on the Free Projection button. A preview box displays the result of the Free Projection, which works very much like Vector Effects' Warp Frame. The dialog box is less distracting, but the preview doesn't allow you to zoom in and out. On the plus side, you can clone the selection as you distort it by clicking on the Save button, and you can select from a menu of presets as in Vector Effects. Click on the Apply button to see your changes applied to the selected items, as I've done in Figure 12-14.

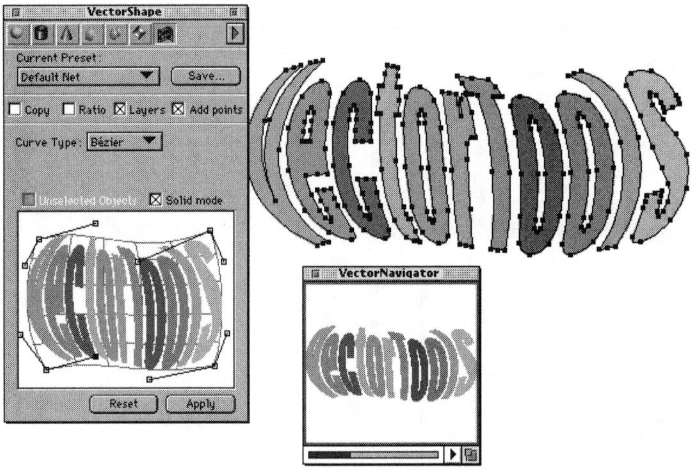

Figure 12-14: With VectorTools you can bend the bounding box around a selection to distort the shapes inside. The updated shapes appear in the background. Also pictured, the new VectorNavigator palette that shows you all objects currently visible on the pasteboard.

The obligatory Figure 12-15 shows a few of the tricks you can pull off with VectorTools. To create the gray sphere in the background, I applied the Sphere Shape effect to the word "VectorTools" in Helvetica Inserat. The filter wrapped the text around a sphere, distorting it almost beyond recognition. I then added the wavy text by applying the Free Projection Shape effect to that very same collection of converted Helvetica Inserat characters. It looks like a line of path text, except that all the letters are positioned upright. Finally, I create the base of the sphere using the Cone Shape effect, which naturally wraps the selection around a cone. All of these effects are represented by buttons that appear along the top of the VectorShape palette.

Figure 12-15: I modified a line of converted text using the Sphere (background), Free Projection (wavy text), and Cone (bottom) effects. Also worth noting, I originally created this figure for my book on Illustrator 6, and back then, VectorTools was called DrawTools. Instead of updating this figure to reflect the new name, I've decided it would be best for everyone if I just took a nap. Nighty-night.

VectorTools includes previews throughout its dialog boxes, but some of the options are still a teeny bit technical. But it provides many of the same distortion effects that Vector Effects does as well as a few unique tricks of its own, and Extensis plans to keep VectorTools in production. The latest upgrade was specifically designed to be compatible with both Illustrator 8 and FreeHand 8. VectorTools also includes a few filters for mixing and replacing colors and a sophisticated magic wand tool—you can select objects with the same fill color, the same stroke color, the same stroke weight, and even the same area. Also included are a number of palettes: the Navigator palette, that's similar to Illustrator's palette by the same name (shown in Figure 12-14); a Library palette that functions as a clipboard containing a number of copied objects for on-the-fly pasting; and a Styles palette that records text styles as well as object styles (fill and stroke attributes). You can also adjust the stacking order of objects by switching two selected objects, for example, or simply by nudging them a level forward or back.

Transparency

Adobe and Macromedia (the makers of FreeHand) are in a continuous battle to see who can put together the most useful drawing program, the one that offers its users the most practical tools and filters. Although Adobe has added some remarkably valuable features to Illustrator with the most recent version, I've got to hand it to Macromedia for its latest star attraction in FreeHand 8: transparencies. A transparency is a special fill that, while adding color to an object, lets you see dimmed versions of any artwork that may lie behind the transparency. It's as though you're looking at a portion of your document through a piece of colored glass. For those of you who have given up wearing your rose-colored glasses, with transparencies, you can at least make sure that your vector-based creations don't.

Figure 12-16: With the Hot Door Transparency plug-in, the sunglasses can show a tinted view of the background, just like their real-world counterparts.

Unfortunately, nothing of the sort exists in Illustrator. Nothing, that is, if you don't have the Hot Door Transparency plug-in. Hot Door (888/236-9540 or http://www.Hot Door.com), a recent upstart out of Grass Valley, California, writes plug-ins for both Photoshop and Illustrator. Its $39 Transparency plug-in (available for both the Mac and Windows platforms) adds a new palette to Illustrator 8. After you add a fill to an object, you simply need to click on the Transparency palette's Make button and decide how opaque you want the fill to be.

In Figure 12-16, the lenses of the sunglasses use transparent fills. The parts where the lenses overlap empty portions of the document show the true color of the fills. Where they overlap the background objects, the lenses give a slightly dimmed view of the distorted squares that lie below them. If this were a color plate, you'd see that these background objects take on a tint of the lenses' original color. If you want, you can choose to have the transparent fills remain live, constantly updating to reflect changes you make to the fill's color and the background object's form.

CADTools

Another offering from Hot Door, the CADTools plug-in, gives you 34 new tools, all designed to aid you in precision drawing or adding dimensional tags to your artwork. In addition to a precision rectangle tool, CADTools offers a wall tool. This lets you draw rectangles of any length in which the width is fixed. With its arc tool, you can draw as little or as much of a circle as you want. Its fillet tool allows you to round sharp corners.

You need merely to drag with one of the dimension tools to measure and tag the size of both straight and curved paths. You can measure the curvature of circular arcs and even Bézier curves. You control both the units and the scaling of the tags. (In fact, CADTools offers a few units not included in Illustrator.) In addition to the 18 standard scaling ratios that it provides, CADTools lets you choose your own custom scaling ratio with a precision up to 1/32 of whatever unit you're using. CADTools also provides a CADTracker palette, an enhanced version of Illustrator's Info palette. The CADTracker palette gives you dimensional and angular feedback automatically as you draw or measure with one of the tools. This information that it provides is presented in terms of your chosen scaling ratio.

As shown in Figure 12-17, all the dimension lines (including arrowheads) and numerical tags were added using the CADTools plug-in. To set the scaling of the tags, I measured a convenient reference point of the drawing in Illustrator and divided this value into the numerical size I wanted it to be. For example, measured in Illustrator, the bottom of the legs were 2.5 inches apart. I wanted this distance to measure 24 7/8 inches, so I divided 24 7/8 by 2.5 to get 9.95. This means that I used a 1:9.95 scaling ratio to arrive at the values you see in the figure. From there on out, all the other measurements I tagged automatically conformed to this scaling.

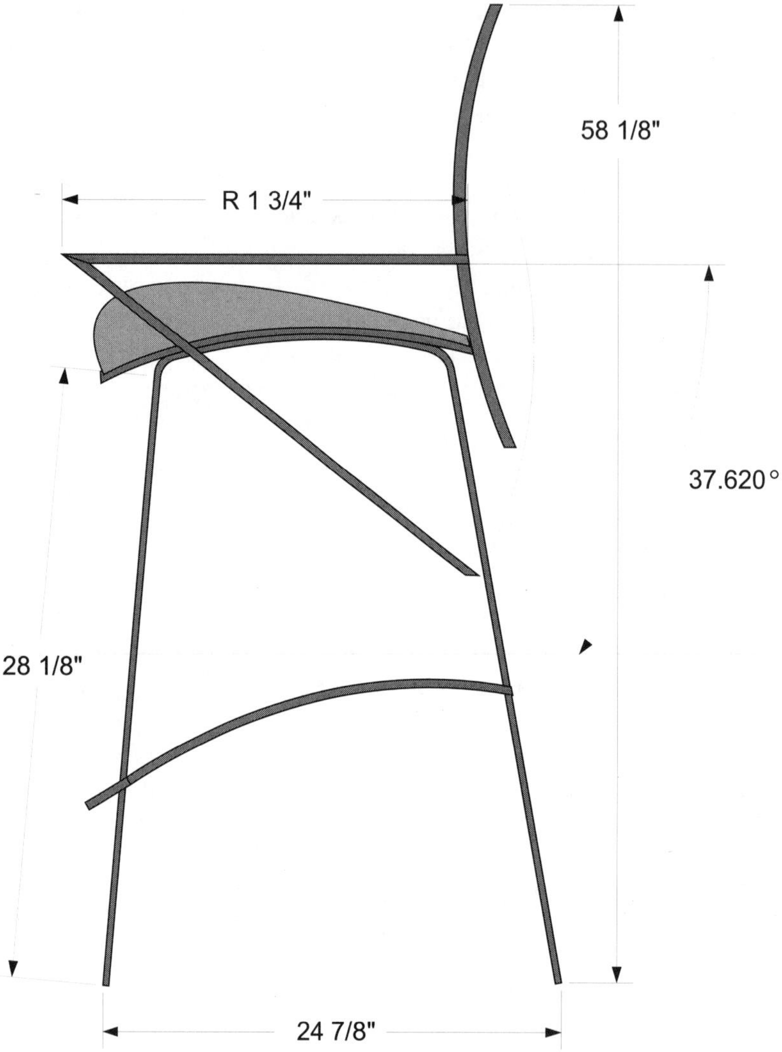

Figure 12-17: Along with the lovely chair that Illustrator lets you draw, you can quickly add its dimensions with CADTools from Hot Door.

Probing the Third Dimension

If you're more comfortable using Adobe products, you have another option: Adobe Dimensions. It's more expensive ($199 new, $69 when upgrading) than some of the other parties' products, but it works seamlessly with Illustrator since it's from Adobe (800/685-3505 or http://www.adobe.com). Dimensions is essentially a 3-D plug-in for Illustrator that runs as a separate application. It lets you do many of the same things that you can do with either Vector Effects or VectorTools, but it require you to put a bit more effort into learning how to use it.

The fact that Dimensions is a 3-D drawing program means that you have to spend a fair amount of time navigating 3-D space on your 2-D screen. If you're unfamiliar with drawing in 3-D, you'll undoubtedly find it confusing, bewildering, and nerve-wracking, just as all artists do. But if you're willing to invest a little effort, it makes a nice addition to Illustrator.

I wish I could show you how Dimensions works from start to finish. But that would take a few hundred pages that are better spent on Illustrator's core features. So, instead, I'll walk you through a simple exercise that integrates both Dimensions and Illustrator. If the exercise piques your interest, read the documentation included with your copy of Illustrator. (As we all know, no one reads the documentation—and if they did, I'd be out of a job—but go ahead and do it this one time.)

Figure 12-18: A line of type created in the font Mezz in Illustrator (top) and the same text extruded in Dimensions (bottom).

One of the things Dimensions excels at is creating three-dimensional type. Figure 12-18 shows a line of type created in the Adobe font Mezz, followed by the same text embellished using Dimensions. The following steps show you how you can create your own 3-D type:

1. **Create some text in Illustrator, and make it big.**

   You can create the text in Dimensions, but Illustrator is faster and it provides better controls. In fact, it's almost always a good idea to create your base objects in Illustrator and then port them over to Dimensions.

2. Copy the text to the Clipboard.

You don't have to convert the text to paths. Dimensions does this automatically. Just select the text in Illustrator and press ⌘-C. Or you can drag-and-drop from Illustrator to Dimensions.

3. Launch the Dimensions application.

If this is the first time you've launched the program, you'll be asked for a serial number. I'd love to give you my number, but if I did that, Adobe would hire thugs to rough me up. And none of us want that, do we?

If you have a lot of fonts loaded into your system, Dimensions takes approximately three years to boot up. Just wait it out.

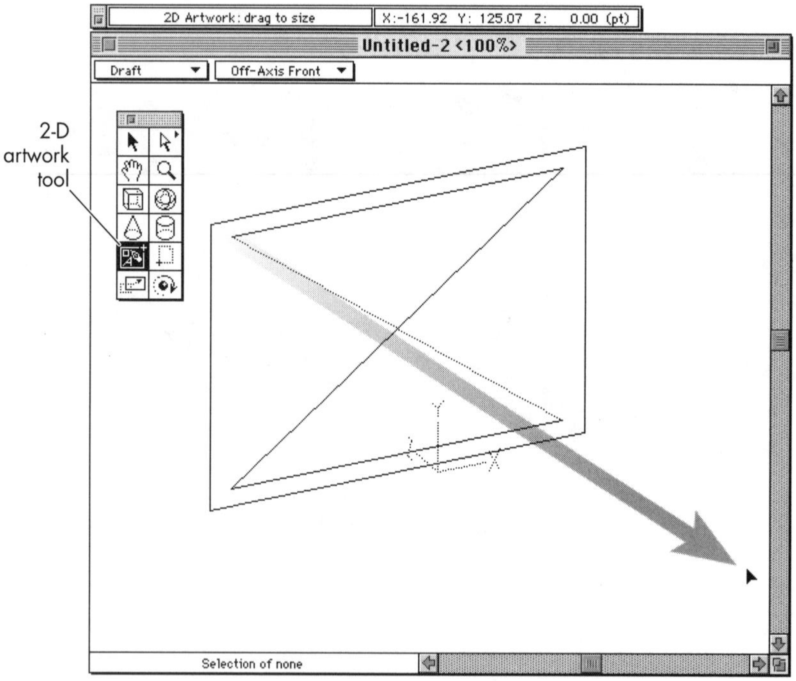

Figure 12-19: Drag with the 2-D artwork tool to add text to your new Dimensions document.

4. Drag inside the Dimensions document window with the 2-D artwork tool.

After Dimensions starts up, it displays an empty document window, just like Illustrator. To add free-form objects to the document—as opposed to cubes, spheres, and other primitive shapes—you have to create a two-dimensional canvas. You do this by dragging with the 2-D artwork tool, labeled in Figure 12-19. Drag to create as big a canvas as you can, but don't knock yourself out. Size isn't important. (At least, that's what I keep telling myself.)

When you release the mouse button, Dimensions displays a 2-D drawing window. The tools in the toolbox also change, as you can see in Figure 12-20. The 2-D drawing window has much in common with Illustrator's illustration window, including many of the same tools and many of the same keyboard equivalents.

5. **Paste the text from the Clipboard.**

   When you press ⌘-V, Dimensions adds the text to the 2-D drawing window, as shown in Figure 12-20. Then click on the close button in the upper left corner of the window. The program asks you if you want to apply your changes. Press Return to answer in the affirmative.

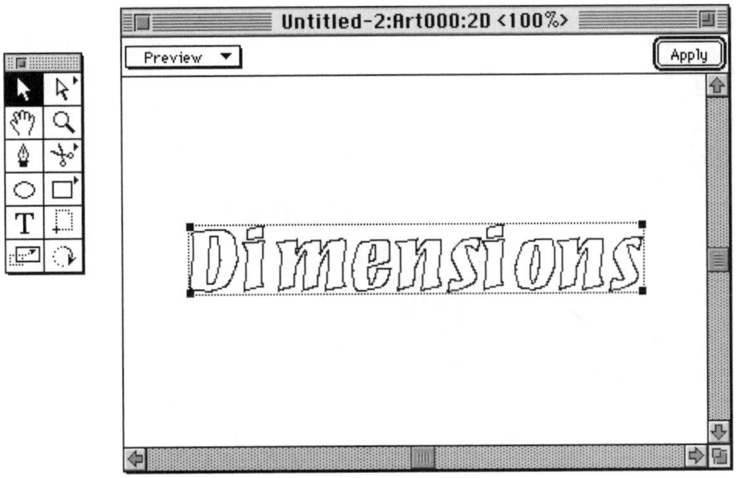

Figure 12-20: Paste the text copied from Illustrator into Dimensions' 2-D drawing window.

6. **Switch to Wireframe mode and Choose Operations » Extrude.**

   Choose Wireframe from the mode pop-up menu in the top left corner of the screen. To activate the extrude command, you press ⌘-E.

Dimensions displays the Extrude palette pictured in Figure 12-21. To extrude an object, you pop it off the screen into the world of three dimensions. Extruding a shape adds sides to it, giving the object depth. The letters back in Figure 12-18 were extruded, as were those way back in Figure 12-13.

The Extrude palette lets you specify the depth of the extrusion. You can also bevel the edges to give the corners a sculpted look.

7. Enter a value into the Depth option box.

I entered 20 points, but you can enter anything you want. To get an idea what the extrusion looks like, click on the Apply button in the palette. It may be hard to make out what's going on with all the anchor points, but you should be able to get a rough idea.

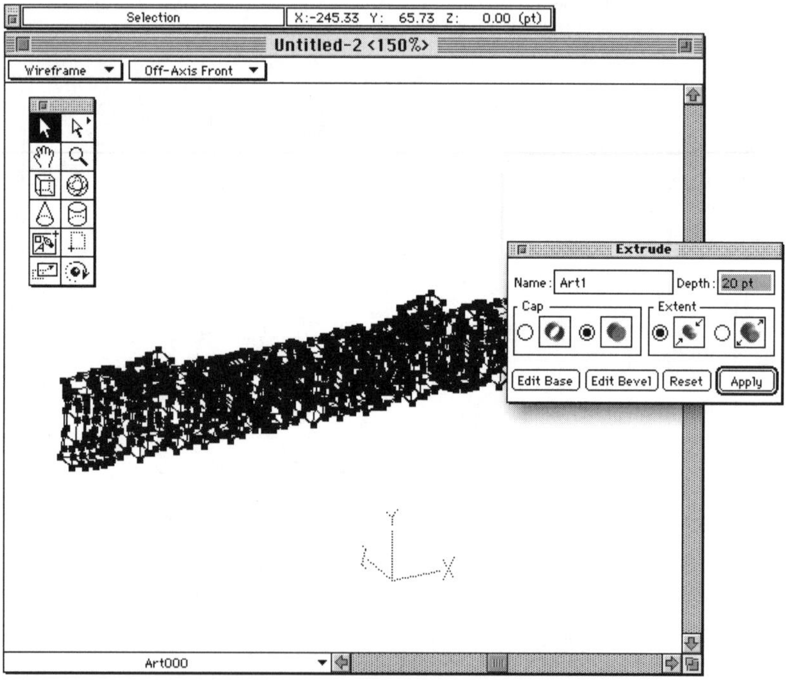

Figure 12-21: Use the options in the Extrude palette to give the letters depth and carve a bevel into the corners.

8. Click on the New Bevel button at the bottom of the Extrude palette.

This option allows you to add a beveled edge to the text. (This button appears as Edit Bevel in Figure 12-21 because I've already added a bevel.) A dialog box comes up, asking you to find a bevel on disk. Locate the Bevel Library folder inside the same folder that contains the Dimensions application, and open it. Then open any bevel that sounds fun.

9. Close the bevel dialog box, and click on the Apply button in the palette.

Dimensions wants you to see what your bevel looks like so that you can edit it, but you don't have to leave it up on screen. The bevel is now loaded, so you can close the window to get it out of your way. Select a different Extent option if you want to—the bottom option adds a bevel around the edges of the shapes; the top option carves into the shapes. Then click on the Apply button to add the bevel to the selected text.

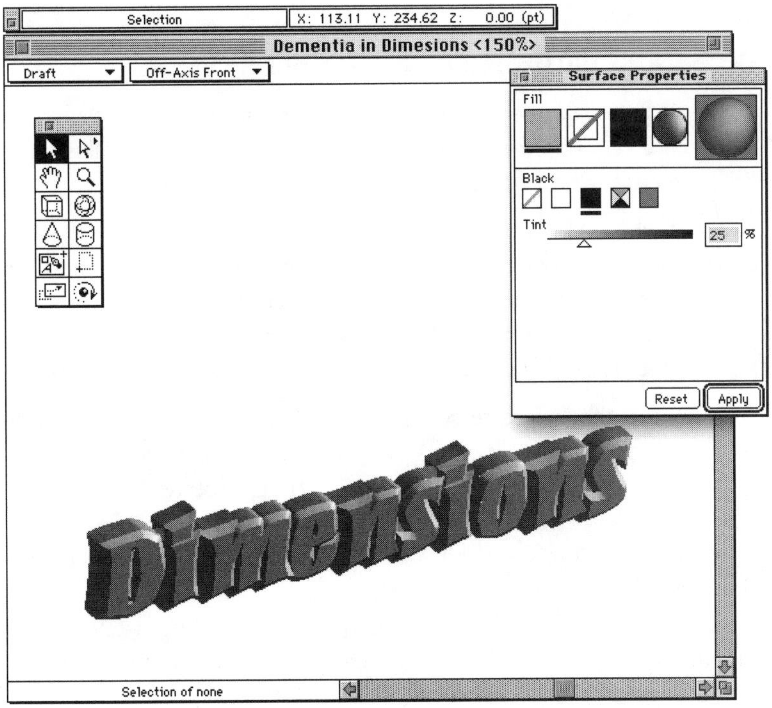

Figure 12-22: Lighten the color of your text so that Dimensions has sufficient color range to create shadows and highlights.

10. Fill your text with the color of your choice.

Right now the text is probably black. You can change the color by choosing Window » Show Surface Properties or by pressing ⌘-I.

As shown in Figure 12-22, the Surface Properties palette permits you to fill selected shapes with gray values or colors. In the figure, I merely changed the Tint slider to 25 percent to select a light gray. But you can make the color whatever you want.

11. **Choose Draft from the mode pop-up menu.**

    This produces a shaded preview of the letters on screen. It may take a minute or more depending on the speed of your computer, but go ahead and let 'er rip. After the command is finished Dimensions beeps at you. If you're having problems seeing the text for all the anchor points, just click on an empty portion of the screen to deselect everything. That's what I did to look at my text in Figure 12-22.

12. **Select the text and copy it.**

    Click on the letters to select them. Then press ⌘-C to send the text to the Clipboard.

13. **Go back to Illustrator and paste the 3-D text.**

    Dimensions creates its 3-D objects and shading as a series of filled paths. You can edit these paths in any way you see fit in Illustrator. But take care—the pasted text is actually one big group.

    To create the 3-D text shown in Figure 12-18, I selected all the letters by alternately Option-clicking and Shift-Option-clicking with the direct selection tool. Then I filled the letters with light gray and stroked them with thin black outlines. I also pressed ⌘-Shift-[(left bracket) to send them to the front of the group, so that the strokes showed clearly.

Believe it or not, that exercise covered about 10 percent of Dimensions' capabilities. You can create basic objects like cubes, spheres, cones, and cylinders using the drawing tools in the toolbox. You can also rotate objects in 3-D space with the trackball tool (in the lower right corner of the toolbox).

Dimensions is not what I'd call a powerful program. And it isn't nearly as convenient for extruding type as Vector Effects' 3D Transform filter. But it shares much of the same "look and feel" as Illustrator—including a few identical keyboard equivalents. If you're willing to at least give it half a chance, you may discover that it's a handy little tool.

CHAPTER 13

BECOMING MASTER OF THE RASTER

Illustrator 6 was the first version of the esteemed illustration program to recognize pixels in all of their splendor. In the other previous versions, you could import EPS images. But the program merely tagged the file on disk for printing purposes and displayed a low-resolution preview of the image on screen. Present-day Illustrator supports a wide range of file formats and allows you to either tag or integrate most of them. This means you can view individual pixels on screen, edit pixels using Photoshop filters, convert paths and text objects to pixels, and even trade images with cousin Photoshop.

But this pixel awareness comes at a price. Images take up lots of room in memory and equally large amounts of room on disk. For example, if you import a high-resolution Photo CD image into Illustrator, the illustration file takes up about 35MB on disk. That's right, 35MB, big enough to fill 25 floppy disks or more than a third of a zip!

Why so big? After all, a Photo CD file takes up 5MB on a CD-ROM. Understand, though, that Illustrator expresses each and every illustration file in PostScript code. This is why Illustrator is so good at printing to PostScript printers—it already has the code ready and waiting. Illustrator likewise converts an imported Photo CD image into PostScript, which is an extremely inefficient image-handling format. Also important, Photo CD images are compressed on disk to make them as small as possible, whereas Illustrator offers no image compression whatsoever. So the image grows inside Illustrator's decompressed PostScript tummy from 5MB to seven times that size.

NOTE: How does Illustrator handle such enormous files? In the old days, Illustrator kept the illustration in memory at all times, even when saving the file to disk. (In fact, saving is merely the duplication of data from RAM to your hard drive.) But if you have, say, 12MB of RAM assigned to Illustrator, there's no way it can keep a 35MB image in memory. So Illustrator saves a portion of the illustration to a temporary file on disk called a *scratch file*. Scratch files slow down Illustrator tremendously because it takes the program much longer to access data from a disk—which is mechanical—than from RAM circuitry—which is exclusively electronic.

The moral, therefore, is to import small images into Illustrator. This can mean a full-page image containing 72 pixels per inch (ppi) or a quarter-page image at twice that resolution. (Resolution is measured linearly—both tall and wide—so doubling the resolution quadruples the number of pixels.) The important thing is to keep the pixels to a minimum.

If you want to work with a high-resolution image that fills a big portion of the page, first save the image in a convenient format. Then import it into Illustrator using File » Place, as directed in Chapter 3. Make sure that the Link check box is checked in the Place dialog box. This way, Illustrator merely tags the file on disk and imports the small preview image, just as in the old days.

For more on the differences between the file format, read the following section. If you think you already have this confusing bit of theory figured out, skip ahead a couple of pages to the next section, in which I begin imparting some actual techniques.

Linked or Embedded

In Illustrator, a linked image is a unique kind of object. If you import an image and select the Link check box, Illustrator creates a link to the image file on disk. The image consumes very little room in the illustration—100K tops—regardless of how much space the original image takes up on disk.

TIP: To find a linked file on disk, you double-click on the file's link in the Link palette. The Link Information dialog box will appear. Here you'll see the hierarchy of folders that contain the image, in which you can find the original file on disk.

If you deselect the Link option in the Place dialog box, Illustrator will import all the pixels into the illustration and convert the pixels into PostScript code, an operation known as embedding (or as parsing in the olden days). Because Illustrator saves all the pixels to disk, the illustration may take up 1MB or more of disk space. But embedding also lets you take advantage of a whole bunch of special effects options. Here are a few of the things you can do to so-called embedded images that you can't do to linked images:

- Use Object » Rasterize to convert a color image to grayscale. You can also convert a color image to black and white or change the number of pixels in an image.
- Apply Photoshop-compatible plug-ins, such as the Gallery Effects filters included with Illustrator 8.
- Choose Filter » Create » Object Mosaic to convert a embedded image to a bunch of colored squares that resemble a mosaic pattern. You can then edit those squares using any of Illustrator's tools or commands, just as if you had drawn them with the rectangle tool.
- Convert an image to black and white via the Object » Rasterize command, and you can colorize the image from the Color palette.
- Colorize grayscale images using Filter » Colors » Adjust Colors, as explained in the "Adjusting Values" section of Chapter 14.
- Use the Link Information dialog box and the File » Selection Info command to find out all kinds of information about a embedded image that it refuses to share when a linked image is selected. This information is especially useful if you've stretched or shrunk the image with the scale tool.

- Magnify a embedded image to see more detail (depending on the resolution of the image). Magnifying a linked image merely causes the pixels to appear larger.

If you want to modify a linked image by any of the above methods, you simply need to first embed the image. To do so, select the image and choose Embed Image from the Links palette's pop-up menu. If you intend to rasterize an image, you need not embed a linked image first. The Rasterize command automatically embeds an image when it converts the image to pixels.

Illustrator doesn't completely ignore linked images. Whether an image is linked or embedded, Illustrator lets you move, scale, rotate, flip, or slant it. You can view black-and-white versions of any image in the artwork mode (if the Show Images In Artwork check box is turned on in the Document Setup dialog box).

If all this sounds confusing, you're not alone. Frankly, Illustrator's image management scheme is much more convoluted than it ought to be. But while strange, the distinction between linked and embedded images is very important for you to understand. My advice is to read the rest of this chapter to get a feel for how images work in Illustrator. By the end of the chapter, you should understand all of your options, and you'll be equipped to determine whether the benefits of embedded images are truly worth the price.

Hoist that Raster and Rake those Pixels

You know you've finally reached the enviable status of Hopeless Computer Dweeb when you know the meaning of the word "rasterize." In regular human terms, it means to convert objects to pixels. You probably aren't aware of it—you're so busy paying attention to things that actually matter—but your computer is constantly rasterizing things. Every time you edit an object, Illustrator and your system software rasterize paths to display them as pixels on screen. With the help of Adobe Type Manager, Illustrator rasterizes characters of type to screen pixels. And when you print your artwork, your printer rasterizes the mathematical path definitions as teeny printer pixels. Rasterizing is as integral to your computer's existence as generating red blood cells is to yours.

Legend has it that the word "rasterize" was coined during the early days of monitor development. Your monitor displays stuff on screen by projecting pixels in horizontal rows. (It happens so fast—about 60 to 75 times a second—that your gullible eyes interpret the screen image as both continual and stationary.) It's almost as if the monitor were raking pixels across the screen, which is where the word *raster*—Latin for *rake*—comes in. Nowadays, rasterize is used for any kind of pixel creation, whether on screen, inside a printer, or inside a program like Illustrator.

Object » Rasterize is merely Illustrator's way of saying, "Here I am making all these pixels. Maybe you'd like to play around with them for a while." Here are some things you need to keep in mind when you use the command.

- When applied to paths or text objects, the Rasterize command converts the objects to pixels. The pixels appear inside a rectangular image boundary, just as if you had imported an image from disk.
- When applied to a placed image, the Rasterize command lets you change the number of colors in the image or increase or decrease the number of pixels.

The Rasterizing Options

When you choose Object » Rasterize, Illustrator greets you with the dialog box shown in Figure 13-1. The dialog box offers the following options:

- **Color Model:** Use this pop-up menu to specify whether you want to create a color image, a grayscale image, or a black-and-white image. Two options, RGB and CMYK, result in color images. Choosing the RGB option results in an image that takes up less room on disk but may not print exactly as it appears on screen. A CMYK image takes up more space on disk but prints more accurately. For more information about the amazing world of RGB and CMYK color theory, read Chapter 14.

  To convert a selection to a grayscale image, select the Grayscale option. Select Bitmap if you want the image to contain black pixels only. All other pixels inside the image boundary will be transparent.

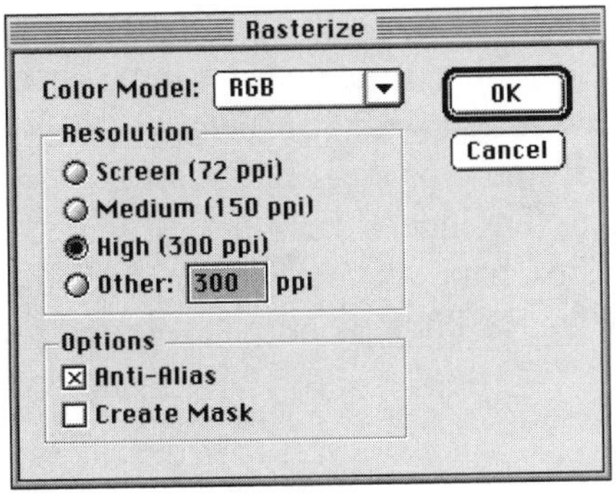

Figure 13-1: Use the Rasterize dialog box to convert selected objects into an image. Or you can change the number of colors and pixels inside an image.

- **Resolution:** Select one of the first three radio buttons or enter a value into the Other option box to specify the number of pixels in the image. Select Screen for 72 ppi, Medium for 150 ppi, and High for 300 ppi. Figure 13-2 demonstrates the effect of converting the sea lion from Chapter 1 to an image using the Screen and Medium settings. An image rasterized at the High setting is virtually indistinguishable from the original objects, even when printed from an imagesetter or another high-resolution device.

  As you can see in the figure, a high-resolution image looks smoother than a low-resolution one, but it also takes up more space on disk. As a general rule of thumb, an image with twice the resolution takes up four times as much space on disk. In Figure 13-2, for example, the image at left consumes about 100K, while the image at right consumes about 400K.

WARNING

After you enter a high-resolution value and press Return, you may experience a long initial delay before Illustrator displays a progress bar. The delay can be so long, in fact, that you may think Illustrator has crashed. Before you give up and restart your computer, though, allow Illustrator a solid couple of minutes to show some sign of life.

- **Anti-Alias:** If you want to soften the transitions between neighboring pixels of different colors, select this option. Anti-aliasing (pronounced anti-alias-ing) is an oddly named blurring technique that eliminates jagged edges while only slightly reducing the focus of an image. (The story behind its name is more convoluted than the origin of "rasterize.") If you prefer that Illustrator convert objects to pixels without any blurring, turn the check box off.

  Figure 13-3 compares an image created with and without anti-aliasing. The difference is slight at this medium resolution (150 ppi), but you can still make out subtle differences. The bottom image is more sharply focused, but the edges are sometimes jagged, particularly along the black outline. Anti-aliasing is much more pronounced at lower resolutions, but you may want to turn it off at higher resolutions to speed up the rasterizing time. This check box has no effect whatsoever on file size, and the option is dimmed when the Bitmap option is selected from the Color Model pop-up menu.

NOTE

If the Anti-aliased Artwork option in the General Preferences dialog box is active when you rasterize a path, the final image will automatically have softened edges whether or not you've selected the Anti-Alias option in the Rasterize dialog box. In fact you get a slightly better anti-aliasing effect if you rasterize paths with the General Preferences' Anti-aliased Artwork option on and the Rasterize's Anti-Alias option off. To get twice the usual amount of anti-aliasing, turn on both the options. If you want your final image sans the anti-aliased edges, be sure to turn off the anti-alias related options in both the General Preferences and the Rasterize dialog boxes.

- **Create Mask:** Choose this option to mask transparent portions of the original objects to keep them transparent. It is useful only when rasterizing objects, not when converting placed images. Understanding this option requires a bit of background explanation, which I do at length in the following section.

Screen, 72 ppi

Medium, 150 ppi

Figure 13-2: The sea lion illustration from Chapter 1 rasterized at 72 (left) and 150 (right) ppi.

Figure 13-3:
An image rasterized at 150 ppi with the Anti-Alias check box turned on (top) and off (bottom).

Maintaining Transparency

All pixels inside an image, except for those in black-and-white images, are opaque. In other words, there is no such thing as a transparent pixel inside a grayscale or color image. So the transparent areas in selected objects become white pixels when rasterized. In Figure 13-4, for example, I've rasterized a line of type at 20 ppi. (To soften the edges of the text, I checked the Anti-Alias option. This is why the pixilated text consists of a myriad of grays.) As the second example shows, the areas between letters become white.

To make these areas transparent, you have to "mask" them away by selecting the Create Mask check box. Illustrator uses the original character outlines to determine which portions of the image are opaque and which are transparent, as in the third example in Figure 13-4. (I added the black outlines around the letters to make the mask more obvious.) The image's low resolution combined with the smooth outlines of the mask produces the unusual appearance of tiled letters.

Though indisputably useful, the Create Mask check box can cause problems. As I discuss in Chapters 17 and 18, masks slow down printing time considerably and may even prevent an illustration from printing altogether. And there is no more precarious item you can mask than an image.

Figure 13-4:
If I select some type (top) and rasterize it without creating a mask, the transparent areas between letters turn white (middle). A mask ensures that the transparent areas remain transparent (bottom).

Consider Figure 13-4. Character outlines constitute an extremely complex mask because Illustrator has to combine them into a single, elaborate compound path. Only by lowering the rasterizing resolution to 20 ppi was I able to get the illustration to print. (Prior to that, my LaserWriter kept pooping out.) If you want to use a higher resolution image, make sure your original objects are fairly simple. Or just leave the Create Mask check box turned off and live with the white pixels.

Putting Object » Rasterize to Good Use

The Rasterize command is one of Illustrator's slyest features. On the surface, it looks rather simple and limited. I mean, how often are you really going to want to convert objects to pixels? But if you're willing to invest a little time and imagination, the Rasterize command turns out to be a robust feature with a fair number of practical uses.

The following are a handful of techniques designed to expand your raster awareness. Every one of them was impossible prior to version 6 of Illustrator:

- Object » Rasterize is one of only two commands in Illustrator that's capable of automatically converting a color illustration to grayscale. If you're curious how a color illustration looks in grayscale, select and clone all objects in the illustration, and then rasterize the objects as a low-resolution grayscale image with Anti-Alias turned off. Because your original objects are still intact, you can then use the grayscale image as an approximate visual model for how you should manually recolor the objects in your illustration.

- You can also select an object and choose Filter » Colors » Convert To Grayscale. This filter lets you convert color illustrations to grayscale without resorting to pixels but will convert only solid fills and strokes. Gradients and pattern will not convert; you will need to use Object » Rasterize. (Check out Chapter 14 for the whole story.)

TIP

When you rasterize objects to a black-and-white image using the Bitmap option, the white pixels become transparent. You can then select a Fill color in the Color palette to specify the color of the black pixels. Add the fact that those black-and-white images take up relatively little room on disk, and you have a great means for creating quick texture patterns.

In Figure 13-5, for example, I started out with a compound path in which converted characters of text cut "holes" into a black rectangle. (This way, I can see through the text in the last example in the figure.) I next drew a rectangle in front of the compound path and filled it with a gradation. To arrive at the third example, I rasterized the gradation using the Bitmap option and a resolution of 72 ppi; then I clicked on the Black icon in the Color palette and changed the Tint value to 50 percent to fill the rasterized image with gray. In the final example, I sent the bitmapped image to back, cloned and nudged it ever so slightly, and filled the clone with white. This way, the white bitmap partially covered the gray one, creating an embossed texture.

Figure 13-5: After combining text with a rectangle (top), I drew a gradient rectangle (second), converted that rectangle to a bitmap, and filled it with gray (third). Then I sent the bitmap to back, cloned and nudged it, and filled the clone with white (bottom).

I know FreeHand artists who go absolutely nuts with bitmap texture effects. Since Illustrator supports black-and-white images, you can, too.

WARNING: You *must* assign a color to the black pixels in a black-and-white image. If you want the pixels to stay black, then click on the Black icon in the Color palette. Otherwise, the fill for the image is set to None. Although the pixels appear black on screen, they print as transparent.

- You can confirm the resolution of a selected image, whether rasterized inside Illustrator or imported via File » Place, by choosing File » Selection Info. Inside the Selection Info dialog box, choose the Embedded Images option. Illustrator shares with you several tidbits of information about the image, including a Resolution item, spotlighted in Figure 13-6. (In Illustrator, you can disproportionately resize an image—just like any other object—with the scale tool. This squishes or stretches the pixels, which is why the Selection Info dialog box lists two Resolution values—one horizontal and the other vertical. If you haven't scaled the image, the two values are identical.) When you finish noting the Resolution value, press Return or click on the Done button to close the dialog box.

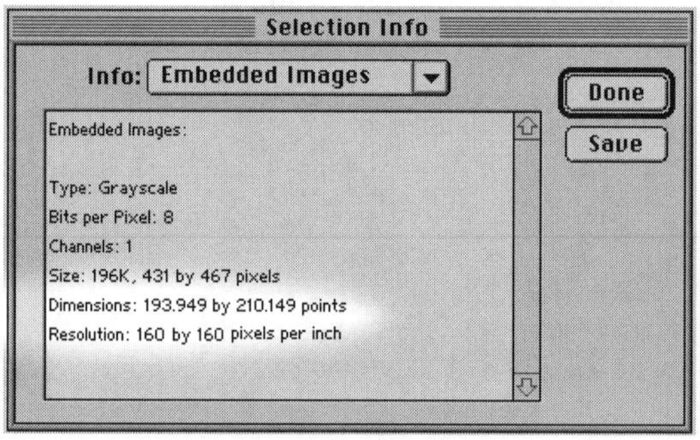

Figure 13-6: Choose File » Selection Info and select the Embedded Images option to discover the resolution of a selected image.

- If you import a black-and-white image, Illustrator (depending on the image's format) may treat the white pixels as opaque and not as transparent. You can make the white pixels transparent by using the Rasterize command.

TIP

To make white pixels transparent, check the resolution of the image using File » Selection Info, as directed in the previous item. (This is very important, since the Rasterize command has no inkling of the resolution of a selected image.) Then choose Object » Rasterize, select the Bitmap option, and enter the Resolution value that you noted inside the Selection Info dialog box. This ensures that you don't mess up the image while fixing it. After you press Return, Illustrator makes the white pixels transparent and lets you assign a color to the black pixels.

- Rasterizing can also be a problem—although it is rather rare—when importing grayscale images or dragging and dropping a grayscale image from Photoshop. If Illustrator complains that an image is RGB during the printing cycle, when you know darn well the image is grayscale, convert it to grayscale using Object » Rasterize, taking care to maintain the resolution as directed above.

- If an image is taking up too much room on disk or in memory, you can lower its resolution by selecting a different Resolution option in the Rasterize dialog box. Make sure to keep the Anti-Alias check box turned on to ensure the best transitions. Changing the number of pixels in this way is called resampling, because Illustrator has to generate new pixels by averaging the old ones. In technospeak, this averaging is called interpolating.

NOTE

If you're an experienced Photoshop user, you may be wondering what kind of interpolation Illustrator uses when resampling images. When Anti-Alias is turned on, Illustrator uses *bilinear* interpolation, which means the program averages five pixels at a time. (Photoshop's more sophisticated *bicubic* interpolation factors in nine pixels.) When Anti-Alias is off, Illustrator doesn't average pixels at all; it just throws away the pixels that it deems inappropriate. (This is the same as Photoshop's "nearest neighbor" interpolation.)

- Raising the Resolution value is never a good idea; Illustrator isn't smart enough to generate detail out of thin air, so doing this just increases the number of pixels without providing any benefit.

TIP

You can convert a black-and-white bitmap to a credible grayscale image by lowering the resolution by about half and selecting the Grayscale option. Make sure Anti-Alias is turned on. Illustrator automatically generates five or six levels of gray.

Fusing Objects and Images

TIP

I have one last tip up my sleeve before I move on to bigger and better things, and this one is my favorite: You can fuse objects and imported images into a single image using Object » Rasterize. This allows you to use Illustrator as an object-oriented image editor—kind of like a poor man's Live Picture.

Figure 13-7: Starting with a Digital Stock image (top), I drew an ellipse around it (middle) and rasterized the circle into the image (bottom).

For example, I imported the top image in Figure 13-7 from a Digital Stock Professional CD. But I wasn't happy with the circular strip of neon surrounding the Deli sign. It was too dark; it needed some punching up. So I traced around the outline of the neon with the oval tool and assigned it a thick white stroke and no fill. I had to slant the oval with the shear tool to make it match the image, as in the second example of the figure.

I checked the resolution of the image using File » Selection Info; it turned out to be 160 ppi. Then I selected both image and ellipse and chose Object » Rasterize. I selected the Grayscale option, entered 160 into the Other option box, and turned on Anti-Alias to soften the edges of the oval. When I pressed Return, Illustrator set about rasterizing the ellipse into the image, as you can see in the last example in Figure 13-7.

Although Photoshop offers its own object-oriented tools—including the pen tool and a few others—Illustrator provides a much wider range of drawing options. So if you find that you can't accomplish a certain effect in Photoshop, try turning the job over to Illustrator. After adding objects and rasterizing them into the image, you can save the final effect as a PSD file (as explained back in Chapter 3) and then open it up again in Photoshop.

Trading Artwork with Photoshop

Illustrator and Photoshop have been able to trade paths and pixels back and forth for a few years now. But Illustrator 8 and Photoshop 5 have become closer trading partners than ever before. You can drag and drop artwork or transfer it via the Clipboard. The results vary depending on which direction you drag—from Illustrator into Photoshop or vice versa—and what kind of objects you have selected. The following sections tell all.

Dragging Objects into Photoshop

Just as you can drag selected objects from an illustration window and drop them into the Scrapbook (as I explained in Chapter 9), you can drag objects from Illustrator into Photoshop. Since Photoshop can't accommodate objects—except as selection paths—the program converts the objects into pixels, much like choosing Object » Rasterize does.

Because Photoshop is a faster and more efficient image handler than Illustrator, you may find that dragging and dropping from Illustrator into Photoshop is frequently a preferable alternative to using the Rasterize command. But you should keep the following tidbits of information in mind.

- You must be using Photoshop 3.0.5 or later. Earlier versions don't support drag-and-drop.
- You must have enough RAM to run Illustrator and Photoshop at the same time. I can barely get the two programs to play ball on my 32MB PowerBook—and even then, drag-and-drop works sporadically—so I'm recommending that you have at least 48MB of RAM.
- Make sure that an image window is open in Photoshop so you have a place to drop the objects from Illustrator.
- You can drag any path or text object from Illustrator into Photoshop.

You can now drag any placed images from Illustrator to Photoshop 5. Photoshop will automatically convert the image to the EPS format. If you are using Photoshop 3 or 4, you will need to export the image from Illustrator in EPS, PSD, or one of the other image formats and then open the file in Photoshop.

- After you drop the objects into the image window, Photoshop sets about rasterizing them in the background. You remain inside Illustrator; the system does not automatically switch you to Photoshop. If you want to see the objects rasterize, you must switch to Photoshop manually by clicking on the image window. A progress bar keeps you apprised as Photoshop churns away.
- The rasterized objects appear in Photoshop as an independent layer. This permits you to move the objects into place before applying them to the underlying image.
- When using the Rasterize command, you specify the number of colors and resolution manually. But Photoshop decides these things automatically, according to the color mode and resolution of the image window. The higher the resolution, the more pixels Photoshop assigns to the rasterized objects.

  Figure 13-8 shows the difference between a line of type before and after it was dragged from Illustrator to Photoshop when the image resolution is set to different values, specifically 72 ppi and 180 ppi. In both cases, the text was formatted at 100-point type in Illustrator, but when I raised the resolution in Photoshop, the letters grew in pixels.

  Therefore, in dragging from Illustrator to Photoshop, the image resolution directly affects the size of rasterized objects. If the objects appear too small, delete them, increase the resolution of the Photoshop image using Image » Image Size, and drag the objects from Illustrator again.

Figure 13-8: A line of 100-point text dragged from Illustrator into Photoshop when the image resolution was set to 72 ppi and 180 ppi.

Photoshop likes to generate error messages when rasterizing Illustrator objects. If Photoshop complains that it can't find a font or some other gibberish and it offers you a Continue button, click on that button or press Return. About 50 percent of the time, the program will come through just fine, despite its whining.

NOTE

If you don't quite know your way around Photoshop, and you've found this book helpful, I encourage you to check out my *Macworld Photoshop Bible* from IDG Books. Not only is it the best-selling guide to Photoshop, but it was at last report the number one book on *any* desktop publishing topic. (Thanks to my vast fortunes, I've paid off my K-Mart credit card and instructed my comptroller to redirect my purchasing power to Sam's Membership Warehouse.) *Macworld Photoshop Bible* makes a great gift, so buy several copies. And be sure to ask about the case discount. My wife and cat thank you.

Dragging Images into Illustrator

You can also drag images from Photoshop and drop them into Illustrator. You can either select the image you want to drag with one of the selection tools and then drag it over or drag an entire image or layer with Photoshop's move tool. (If you drag a layer, the previously transparent pixels turn white inside Illustrator.) Illustrator imports the image as an embedded image. If you're dragging from Photoshop 5, the image drops into Illustrator at its original resolution. To change the resolution, choose Photoshop's Image » Image Size command and enter the preferred value into the Resolution option box. To preserve the image's original size, be sure to check the Resample Image option in the Image Size dialog box.

WARNING

When dragging from an older version of Photoshop into Illustrator, it's important to remember that the image comes over at 72 ppi. When you drag, Photoshop 3 and 4 exports the selection to an external clipboard in PICT format. The PICT format is set to 72 ppi. No matter what the original resolution of the selection, the resolution of the dragged image in Illustrator is 72ppi. To make sure you don't lose (or gain) any pixels in the transition, set the image resolution to 72 ppi in Photoshop using Image » Image Size before you start the drag. Then drag and drop the image into Illustrator and resize the image as desired using the scale tool.

TIP

After dragging an image from an older version of Photoshop, what if you want to set the image to a very specific resolution? For those of you who dread math, I have bad news. You have to use division, and on a calculator, no less. Divide 72 by the desired resolution. Then multiply that number by 100. Select the image, double-click on the scale tool icon in the toolbox, and enter the resulting value into the Uniform option box.

For example, say you drag-and-dropped an image into Illustrator and you want to set it to 160 ppi. You would divide 72 by 160 to get 0.45. Then multiply 0.45 by 100 to get 45 percent. Double-click on the scale tool, enter 45, and press Return. Illustrator shrinks the image down to size. Because the number of pixels remains constant, Illustrator has to squish the pixels into a smaller space, thereby upping the image's resolution. To confirm that you've got it right, choose File » Selection Info and take a look at the Resolution value. It should be right on.

Copying and Pasting Paths

Provided that you are using Photoshop 5, you can now drag and drop paths from Photoshop to Illustrator. Why would you want to? Well, say that you've traced a path around an image inside Photoshop and you want to use that path as a mask inside Illustrator (as I explain in Chapter 17). You need to transfer that mask as an object, not as an image. Man, life just keeps getting better.

If you prefer (or if you are not using the latest version of Photoshop), you can use the Clipboard to transfer a path from Photoshop to Illustrator. Copy the path in Photoshop (⌘-C), switch to Illustrator, and then paste (⌘-V).

No matter how you get the path into Illustrator, it appears selected inside the program, but with neither fill nor stroke. Be sure to assign a fill or stroke from the Color palette to keep track of the path in the preview mode.

You can likewise use the Clipboard to transfer paths from Illustrator into Photoshop without converting them into pixels. When you paste Illustrator objects into Photoshop, a little dialog box asks if you'd like to paste the objects as pixels or as paths, as shown in Figure 13-9. Select the second radio button—Paste As Paths—if you want to use the objects as selection outlines or clipping paths. You can then edit the paths with the five path editing tools in Photoshop's toolbox, all of which work like their counterparts in Illustrator.

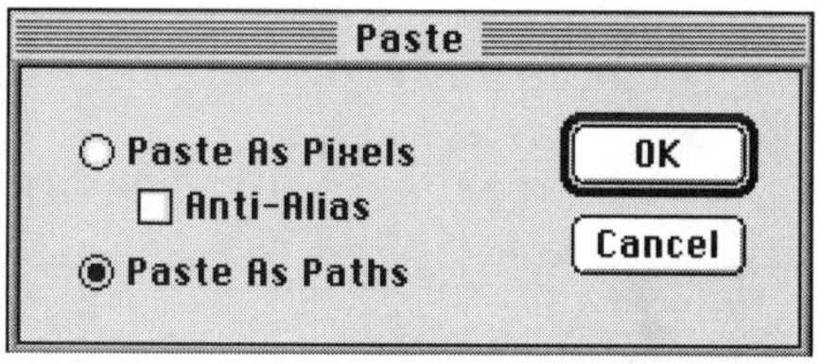

Figure 13-9: This dialog box allows you to transfer paths intact from Illustrator into Photoshop.

If the Paste command doesn't seem to work inside Photoshop, display the Edit menu to see if the Paste command is dimmed. If it is, Illustrator didn't transfer the Clipboard properly, a common problem. Go back to Illustrator and press ⌘-Option-C to copy a PICT version of the selected objects. Then return to Photoshop and try pasting again to get the Paste dialog box in Figure 13-9.

The Better Autotracing Tool

Remember how enthusiastically I berated Illustrator's wretched autotrace tool in Chapter 4? (If not, you can go back and read the "Tracing Templates no Longer a Black-and-White Issue" section for my thoroughly indignant appraisal.) To sum up: you can trace only one path at a time, you can't scan images directly into Illustrator, and the tracing feature is badly implemented. It's inconvenient, inadequate, and altogether inept.

Illustrator's tracing capabilities are so bad, in fact, that they are outclassed by Photoshop's capabilities. That's right, Photoshop is a better tracing tool than Illustrator. You can trace multiple paths at a time, you can trace grayscale and black-and-white images alike, and you don't have to monkey around with a template. It couldn't be more convenient.

The following steps explain how to trace a scan inside Photoshop and transport the paths into Illustrator:

1. **Open the scanned image in Photoshop and edit it as desired.**

   Line drawings and text will trace most successfully. Even Photoshop's tracing function doesn't accommodate photographs and other continuous-tone artwork.

   If you don't have a scan, you can create something directly inside Photoshop. In Figure 13-10, I started off with a simple line of text formatted in the font American Typewriter. Then I modified it with the Ripple and Spherize distortion filters, two effects that are not available inside Illustrator.

Figure 13-10: I used Photoshop to embellish some text with a couple of special effects that are beyond Illustrator's capabilities.

2. Covert the artwork to grayscale.

If your artwork is in color, convert it to grayscale by choosing Mode » Grayscale. You don't absolutely have to perform this step, but you'll get the most predictable results if you do.

3. Convert the image into a selection.

You need to convert the image into a selection in order to take advantage of Photoshop's tracing function. And by far the easiest way to do this is to switch to the Channels palette (by choosing Window » Show Channels) and ⌘-click on the word Black. Or just press ⌘-Option-1. This automatically selects all the light areas and deselects the dark areas.

4. Choose Select » Inverse to inverse the selection.

You want to trace the dark areas, not the light ones, so you need to inverse the selection.

5. Choose the Make Path command.

Switch to the Paths palette (Window » Show Paths) and choose the Make Work Path command from the palette menu, as shown in Figure 13-11. Photoshop displays a dialog box that requests a Tolerance value. This option works exactly like the Curve Fitting Tolerance option in Illustrator's General Preferences dialog box (discussed in Chapter 4). For the best results, enter a value of 1 or 2 and press Return.

TIP: To bypass the dialog box, you can click on the Make Work Path button—the button with the icon showing the two points complete with Bézier handles—along the bottom of the Paths palette.

In either case, Photoshop converts the selection to a series of paths. Unlike Illustrator's autotrace tool, Photoshop generates multiple paths simultaneously, so you don't have to waste a lot of time clicking.

6. Option-drag with the arrow tool to select the paths.

You can select the arrow tool by dragging on the pen tool slot (seventh tool icon on the left side of the toolbox), or just press the A key. Then hold down the Option key and click the paths to select them. (The arrow tool works like the direct selection tool in Illustrator, so pressing Option ensures that you select entire paths.)

Figure 13-11: Choose the Make Work Path option to convert the selection to paths. The paths appear by themselves in the bottom example.

7. Copy the paths, switch to Illustrator, paste the paths, and fill them with black.

Or, if you're using Photoshop 5, simply drag and drop the paths from Photoshop into Illustrator.

When you paste (or drop) the paths into Illustrator, they appear without stroke or fill. You'll do well to fill them with black so you can see them in the preview mode.

8. Restore any compound paths.

Photoshop doesn't know a compound path from a pile of compost, so it's little surprise that the holes in the *a* and *e* in the word *Granite* show up opaque in Illustrator. To create holes, press ⌘-8 (Object » Compound Path » Make) while everything's still selected. You'll probably have to redirect some of the paths by fiddling with the direction buttons in the Attributes palette.

For example, to create the top example in Figure 13-12, I used the direct selection tool to select all paths except the ones along the insides of the *a* and *e*. Then I clicked on the Reverse Path Direction button that was not active. Next I selected the paths inside the *a* and *e* and clicked on the other Reverse Path Direction button.

You can then edit the traced paths as you would any other kinds of objects inside Illustrator. To create the second effect in Figure 13-12, I applied Object » Path » Offset Path with a value of 3 points, and followed by selecting the Unite filter from the Pathfinder palette. Then I selected the original paths and repeated the process with an Offset value of 1.5. I filled the back compound path with black, the next with gray, and the front path with white. Then I nudged the white and gray paths with the arrow keys. To create the drop shadow, I again cloned the black path, sent it to back (⌘-minus), filled it with light gray, and nudged it into position.

Figure 13-12: After pasting the paths into Illustrator, I combined them into a compound path (top) and used the Offset command along with a few Pathfinder filters to create a series of depth effects (second through last).

To create the third example in Figure 13-12, I went a few steps farther. I selected the white path, chose the Offset Path filter yet again, and entered a value of –1.5, which traced along the insides of the letters. I brought this new path to front (⌘-= [equal sign]) and filled it with gray. To cut away the overlapping salvage generated by the Offset Path command, I clicked the Divide button in the Pathfinder palette. Then I carefully Shift-clicked with the direct selection tool on each letter to deselect the main characters of text and pressed Delete to get rid of the salvage. I pressed ⌘-Shift-G and ⌘-8 to ungroup the selection and restore the compound path (necessary to counteract the consequences of the Divide filter). And I filled the shapes with gray.

I next copied the new compound path (⌘-C), pasted it in front (⌘-F), and nudged it slightly down and to the right. I Shift-clicked on the first compound path with the arrow tool to select it as well and clicked on the Pathfinder palette's Intersect button. By finding the intersection of the two compound paths, I was able to create the inset carved shapes. I filled these with light gray, as in the bottom example in Figure 13-12. Then I pasted the original compound path in back (⌘-B) to complete the effect.

Obviously, I did most of the work on these letters after bringing them into Illustrator. But the original shapes came directly from Photoshop. The fact is, Photoshop is a terrific tool for tracing grayscale line drawings and text effects. Simply stated, if you have Photoshop, you never need use Illustrator's sickly autotrace tool again.

Applying Image Filters

You can apply two kinds of filters to embedded images in Illustrator. The first is the entire category of Photoshop-compatible filters and the second is the Object Mosaic filter (Filter » Create » Object Mosaic). The irony is that the single Object Mosaic filter offers more potential than all the Photoshop-compatible filters put together.

Both FreeHand 8 and Illustrator 8 support Photoshop-compatible filters. But by the admission of folks at both Macromedia and Adobe, this is more of a sales feature than a practical tool. Think about it. If you're like 90 percent of Illustrator users, you already own Photoshop, which is far better at handling Photoshop-compatible filters than any drawing program.

So why in the world would you apply filters in Illustrator?

- If you don't have enough RAM to run Photoshop and Illustrator at the same time, there is a certain convenience factor to applying filters in Illustrator. You might prefer to use Photoshop filters inside Illustrator rather than quit Illustrator, launch Photoshop, apply a few filters, quit

Photoshop, and return to Illustrator. To put it mildly, quitting and restarting programs over and over makes your tushy hurt.

- You can apply Photoshop filters to test effects on small or low-resolution images in Illustrator. Then you can return to Photoshop and apply the filters to a larger, high-resolution image.

So that's it. Kind of makes you want to rush out and experiment with those Photoshop-compatible filters as soon as possible, huh? Meanwhile, the Object Mosaic filter converts pixels into object-oriented squares. You can then edit these squares in Illustrator like any other paths. Suddenly, you have pixel-for-pixel control over an image, directly in Illustrator. It's not the kind of thing you need to do on a daily or even weekly basis, but it can be helpful once in awhile.

Photoshop-Compatible Filters

Ever heard of the Gallery Effects filters? These were the first commercially sold filters for Photoshop. Well, whether you've heard of them or not, you might want to know a thing or two about them if you plan to use Illustrator and Photoshop.

Gallery Effects was originally created by some folks at a company called Silicon Beach, the same people who created SuperPaint and who now sell SmartSketch (the latter being a wonderful program, by the way). But before Silicon Beach could get the filters to market, Aldus—the creator of PageMaker—bought the company. A few years later, Adobe bought Aldus and got Gallery Effects in the bargain.

Personally, I'm not a big fan of the Gallery Effects collection. These filters invoke a bunch of "gee-whiz" effects, many of which you can already apply using Photoshop's native filters (with a heck of a lot more flexibility). Granted, many of the Gallery Effects filters are intriguing, but most are too peculiar to be useful on a regular basis.

Now I don't know what the folks at Adobe think, but their opinion of Gallery Effects can't be too terrifically high. After all, rather than selling the three collections of filters independently for $100 to $200 apiece—as Aldus did—Adobe tosses the whole kit and caboodle in for free along with Illustrator. So, at least from a marketing perspective, these filters have been reduced to a means of promoting one of Illustrator's capabilities.

When you install Illustrator, you may install 50-some image filters into the subfolders inside the Plug-ins folder. Just so you know what you've got, Figure 13-13 shows examples of 12 standard filters applied to a single image. I don't know about you, but just looking at this figure makes me hungry.

If you decide that I'm nuts and the Gallery Effects filters are great—it's been known to happen—you can find the larger collection on the CD-ROM that comes with Illustrator. Just look in the Adobe Products folder. Copy the filters into the

Plug-ins folder on your hard drive. They'll be available inside the Filter menu the next time you start Illustrator.

Figure 13-13: Twelve of the Gallery Effects filters that are installed along with Illustrator applied with their default settings.

Better yet, if you have Photoshop 4 or later, trash the image filters in Illustrator's Plug-ins folder (i.e., the two Photoshop Effects folders and the Photoshop Filters folder). In Photoshop, which installs with all these filters, you can make partial selections, mix filter images with the underlying original, and perform all kinds of other tricks that are beyond Illustrator's capabilities.

Converting an Image into Squares

Select an image and choose Filter » Create » Object Mosaic to convert the image into a series of colored rectangles. The rectangles imitate pixels—and each rectangle takes up the same amount of room on disk and in memory as a similarly-sized pixel would—but you can edit the rectangles just as if you had drawn them with the rectangle tool.

When you choose Filter » Create » Object Mosaic, Illustrator displays the dialog box shown in Figure 13-14. It contains a lot of options, but they're fairly easy to use:

- **Current Size, New Size:** The Current Size area shows the dimensions of the image in points. You can adjust the size of the mosaic picture by entering new values in the New Size option boxes.
- **Tile Spacing:** Enter the amount of space you want Illustrator to insert between rectangles in the Tile Spacing option boxes. To make the rectangles fit snugly together—usually my preference—leave the values set to 0.

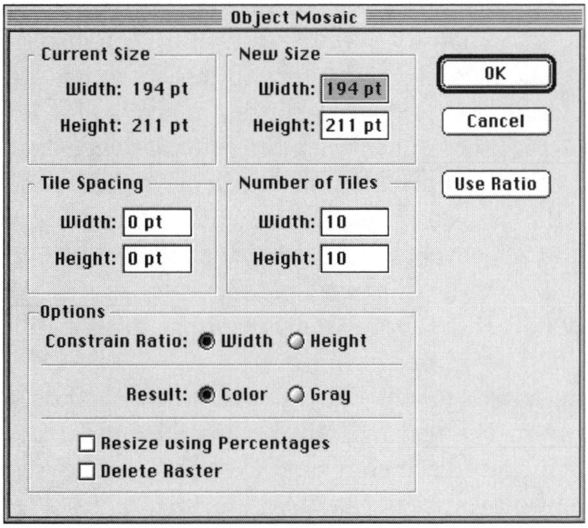

Figure 13-14: Use this dialog box to convert a embedded image into a series of object-oriented rectangles.

- **Number of Tiles:** Enter the number of rectangles that Illustrator should draw horizontally and vertically into the Number of Tiles option boxes. If you enter a Width value of 40, for example, Illustrator draws 40 rectangles across the width of the image.
- **Use Ratio:** If you want the New Size and the Number of Tiles values to conform to the ratio of the original image, you can enter the desired values into either the two Width or the two Height option boxes and then click on the Use Ratio button. For example, let's say you want the

mosaic to be 300 points wide with 30 tiles across. First, enter each value into the appropriate Width option box. Then select the Constrain Ratio Width radio button to tell Illustrator to change the Height values and leave the Width values intact. And finally, click on the Use Ratio button to automatically adjust the Height values so that you'll get a proportional mosaic made up of perfect squares.

- **Color/Grayscale:** If you want Illustrator to fill the tiles with CMYK colors, select the Color radio button. Select the Gray option to fill the rectangles with shades of black.
- **Resize Using Percentages:** If you want to use percentages to determine the change in width and height instead of specifying the exact dimensions in the New Size option boxes, select this option.
- **Delete Raster:** Select this option to delete the image after converting it to a mosaic. To retain the original image, turn off the check box.

After you apply the Object Mosaic command, Illustrator draws the rectangular tiles and combines them into a single group to facilitate editing. One of my favorite ways to edit tiles is to choose Object » Transform » Transform Each, because it permits you to scale or rotate each tile with respect to its center. You can also introduce some randomness to the tiles so they appear a little less rigid.

Take a look at Figure 13-15. I start out with a mosaic 40 tiles wide and 21 tiles tall. I've stroked each tile with a thin black outline. To achieve the second example in the figure, I chose the Transform Each command, selected the Random check box, and adjusted the Scale values. I set the Horizontal value to 200 percent and the Vertical value to 150. The third example shows the results of random movements (2 and 3 points), and the fourth shows random rotations (up to 90 degrees).

If you want the mosaic rectangles to look like true mosaic tiles, you need to add highlights, like those shown in Figure 13-16. In the first example, I cloned the mosaic. Then I used the Transform Each command to shrink the tiles to 80 percent horizontally and 20 percent vertically. (Random was turned off.) After nudging the tiles into position, I deleted their strokes and filled them with white.

To create the second example in Figure 13-16, I again cloned the mosaic. Then I used Object » Transform » Transform Each to reduce each tile to 60 percent horizontally and vertically. To lighten the tiles, I chose Filter » Colors » Saturate (a command I discuss in the next chapter) and entered a value of –30 percent. And I deleted the strokes. That's it; I didn't even have to move the tiles.

For the final effect, I selected the original mosaic from the previous example and used the Transform Each command to rotate the tiles 30 degrees. This gave the tiles a slightly 3-D effect, as though each tile were a square bead.

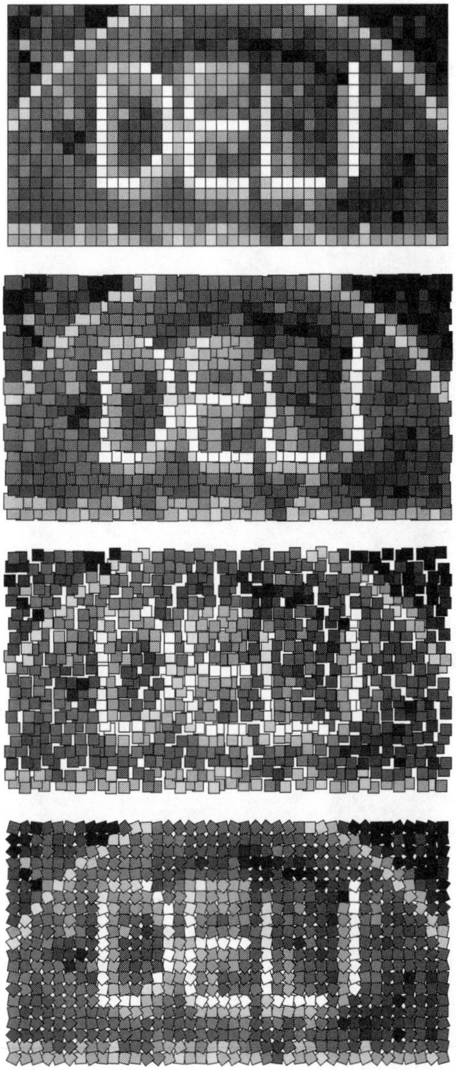

Figure 13-15:
An image converted to a mosaic 40 tiles wide and 21 tiles tall (top) followed by the effects of random scaling (second), movements (third), and rotations (bottom) applied with the Transform Each command.

Mosaics can slow down Illustrator's redraw speed dramatically, and they can take a very long time to print. If you're not sure what kind of effect you want to apply, try it out on a small mosaic pattern with 10 tiles or fewer. Then after you have the effect figured out, apply it to a larger mosaic. This will save you a considerable amount of time and help to prevent general exasperation.

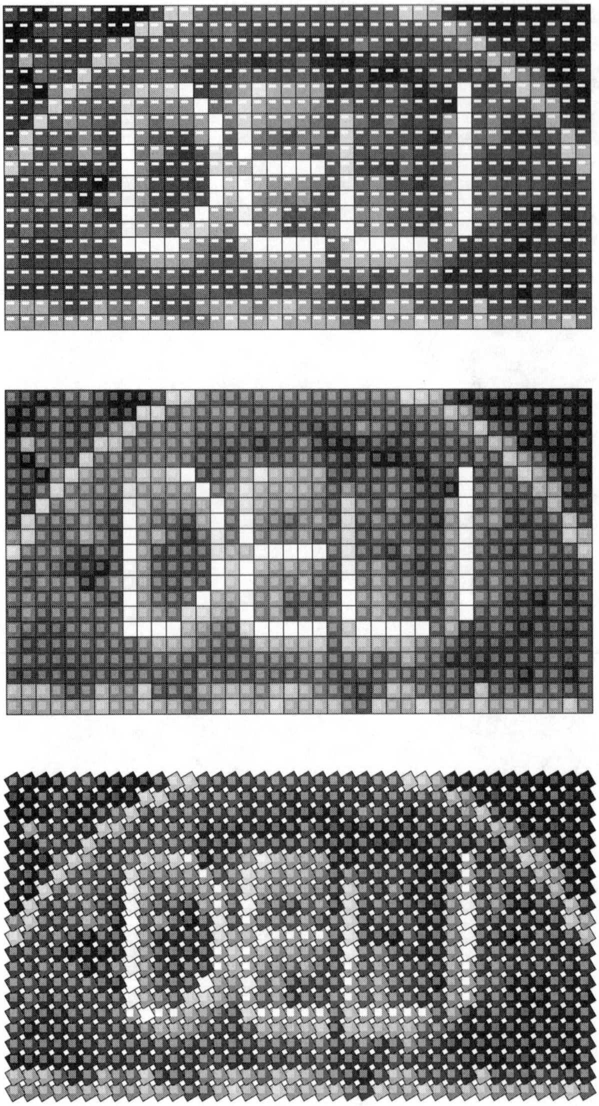

Figure 13-16: Three variations on highlighted tiles, all created by cloning the tiles and scaling or rotating them with Transform Each.

Hatching a Sketch

With the new Photo Crosshatch filter, Illustrator will transform an embedded graphic into a vector object by approximating the graphic with a number of little lines or hatches. Illustrator first converts the graphic to grayscale and then applies hatches to those gray values that fall within a certain range. Figure 13-17 shows the result of hatching the same graphic with an increasing number of layers. Each layer will cover a different range of grayscale values from 0 or white to 255 or black.

The first set of hatches in Figure 13-17 consists of one layer. The hatches represent the gray values that fall between 0 and roughly 64. The Gray Values slider bar inside the Photo Crosshatch dialog box, discussed in detail below, determines this range. Unfortunately, the slider bar only allows you to choose an approximate range by positioning the triangles along its length and doesn't give you any numerical feedback. The second set of hatches in Figure 13-17 (top right) has two layers. The first layer covers the 0 to 64 range and the second covers the grays that fall into the 0 to 128 range. In addition to covering a different range of gray values, the hatches of the different layers are drawn at different angles.

Figure 13-17: I took the same graphic and applied the Photo Crosshatch filter four times. I used the same settings in each application except that I varied the number of layers from one (top left) to four (bottom right).

Each and every time you choose the Filter » Photo Crosshatch command you're presented with the Photo Crosshatch dialog box, shown in Figure 13-18. The different settings let you take the static, uniform hatches that comprise each layer and subtly adjust them as a whole to give the final effect a more realistic appearance.

The settings work as follows:

- **Density:** This setting dictates the distance between the lines that form the crosshatch. Use the slider bar to choose a value from 0.5 to 10 pixels.
- **Dispersion Noise:** This option affects the Density setting. For example, with the Dispersion Noise set to 50 percent and the Density at 3 pt, the distance between the hatches can range from a maximum of 7.5 pixels all the way down to 0 pixels. Well, not quite zero. In fact, the minimum distance is dictated by the Thickness setting. A Thickness of 1 point means that the minimum distance will be 1 point. Enter a non-zero value in the Dispersion Noise option box to give the result a more realistic look.

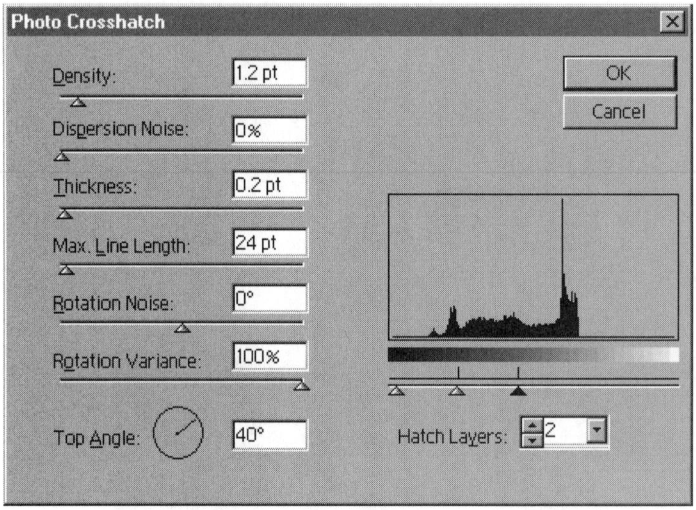

Figure 13-18: The values in the Photo Crosshatch dialog box let you decide on the appearance of the hatches that make-up each layer.

- **Thickness:** Choose a stroke weight for all the hatches anywhere between 0.1 and 10 points.
- **Max. Line Length:** This value determines the longest length of any hatch.
- **Rotation Noise:** To vary the amount that each hatch is rotated from the default, enter a value into the Rotation Noise option box. For example,

with a value of 20 degrees and a Top Angle of 50 degrees, the hatches on the top layer could vary anywhere between 30 and 70 degrees.

- **Rotation Variance:** If you have more than one hatch layer, then with this setting you can choose the amount of the angular difference between the different layers.
- **Top Angle:** No matter how many hatch layers you have, the hatches on the topmost layer will appear at this angle (plus or minus the value in the Rotation Noise option box).
- **Hatch Layers:** You can choose to have from one to eight hatch layers. Each of these layers can cover a different range of grayscale values.

Adding a Border Around an Image

Before I close the chapter, I want to pass along one last bit of wisdom that'll make you slap yourself on the head. (But don't do it too hard; I don't want some kind of lawsuit over this thing.)

TIP

Every once in a while, I hear someone complain that Illustrator can't automatically draw borders around images the way QuarkXPress and other programs do. If you share this concern, follow these amazingly straightforward steps:

1. **Select the image.**

   Select any old placed image that appears in you document.

2. **Bring up the Info palette.**

   Press F8.

3. **Note the W and H values.**

   If they're really long—with four digits after the decimal point—write the values on a Post-it note and stick the note on the wall next to your favorite Dilbert cartoon.

4. **Click on the top left corner of the image with the rectangle tool.**

   Up comes your pal, the Rectangle dialog box.

5. **Enter the values you wrote on the Post-it note.**

   Look for the Dilbert cartoon.

6. **Press Return.**

   Illustrator creates a rectangle the exact size of your image.

7. **Assign a stroke to the rectangle and make the fill transparent.**

   Ooh, get a load of that lovely border.

8. **Select image and border and group them.**

   Press ⌘-G, naturally. Now the border can't get away so easy.

"Cool," I can hear you say, "Now if only Illustrator provided a cropping tool." In fact, Illustrator arguably provides the best cropping capabilities of any program on earth. But it's a big topic that's equally applicable to objects and images, so I don't discuss it in this chapter. Turn to Chapter 17, and keep an eye out for the many appearances of the word "mask."

PART FOUR
COLORING

CHAPTER 14

THE SLIPPERY SCIENCE OF COLOR

Back before I immersed myself in computer graphics, I could never understand how companies managed to own colors. In a world where colors are as free and abundant as dirt, color technologies like Technicolor and the Pantone Matching System represent multimillion-dollar businesses. Even children's Crayola colors are trademarked. Is no tint of grassy green or hue of rosy red safe from these marauding color pirates?

The fact is, the colors we see in nature are ours to enjoy, free from corporate intrusion. But it takes technology and science to represent colors in film, in photographs, on the printed page, and on your computer screen. For example, to represent a sprig of evergreen on a piece of paper, you can't take the sprig and mush it into the paper fibers. You have to find natural and synthetic colors that blend together to create a reasonable facsimile. This imitation of the real world is what the slippery science of color is all about.

In this chapter, I explain a little bit about color theory and a whole lot about how color works in Illustrator. I show you how to select colors from predefined, trademarked libraries or how to define your own colors using combinations of primary printing pigments. I also introduce the Color palette, the Swatches palette, the eyedropper and paint bucket tools, the Color filters, and all the other major points of interest along Illustrator's Great Color Way.

The Great White Light and the Breakaway Color Republics

I hate theory, you hate theory—I don't think I've ever met anyone who just loves a good dose of theory. But I'm afraid I have to share a few basic color observations before moving on to the more exciting and practical discussions of how you use color in Illustrator. See, color is a highly misunderstood topic, particularly among the folks who work with it every day. Whether you're a graphics novice or a publishing professional, it pays to arm yourself with as much basic color knowledge as possible. Just as it helps to know a little something about motors when you take your car in for repair, it helps to know the fundamentals of color when you enter a print shop.

The most common misconception is that color exists in the real world. Plants, rocks, and most animals are completely unaware of color as we know it. This is because similarly colored objects share no common chemical or physical properties. And a single chemical—like copper—may change in color dramatically under slightly different conditions.

Color is all in your head. It's based on so-called white light from the sun or some other light source filtering through or bouncing off a surface. The light then passes into your eye and mutates into nerve impulses that shoot into your brain. Color is a fantastic illusion that humans (and other primates) perceive differently than any other life form, and you and I may even perceive somewhat differently than each other. If you were visited by a being from another planet, chances are very good that you and that person would have no common color vernacular whatsoever. You can't hear, feel, smell, or taste color because color is an inherent ingredient in sight. In fact, you don't see color; your brain makes it up as a means of interpreting the light waves registered by your eye.

The World According to Your Eye

So let's talk about your eye. Inside this amazing orb are a bunch of light-sensitive cells called rods and cones. Rods pick up dim light and are good for detecting brightness and motion. Cones are responsible for color—they react best to strong light. Cones hang out in the central portion of the retina, and rods populate the outer regions. Therefore, you can judge colors most accurately by examining them in daylight and looking directly at them.

Cones come in three types. Generally speaking, each type is sensitive to red, green, or blue light. If all cones are stimulated, you see white. If both the red and green cones get excited but the blue cones shut down, you see yellow. What's important here is that the light coming into your eye may bounce off a yellow object, pass through a yellow filter, or come from a combination of red and green lights shining together. Your eye doesn't know the difference.

Computer screens and televisions fool your eye by speaking directly to your cones. The inside of the monitor is coated with red, green, and blue phosphors that emit light. So a yellow pixel is really a combination of red light shining for the benefit of the red cones and green light going to the green cones. If there's no blue light coming from the pixel, the corresponding blue cones take a nap.

RGB Light

Therefore, red, green, and blue are the primary colors of light. In theory, all visible colors can be expressed using a combination of these three basic ingredients. Intense lights, or multiple lights projected together, produce lighter colors. That's why red and green mix to form yellow, which is lighter than either red or green. Similarly, red and blue mix to form a hot pink called magenta, and blue and green make a bright turquoise called cyan. Full intensities of all three primaries form white; equal amounts of each color in lesser quantities make gray; and the absence of red, green, or blue light is black.

This is called the RGB color model. You may also hear someone refer to it as the additive color model, since increasing the amount of a primary color increases the brightness. Electronic scanners read photographs by shining red, green, and blue lights on them, which is why the RGB color model is a favorite of Photoshop. It is also useful for illustrations for the Web, CD-ROMs, and any Illustrator creation that you expressly intend for people to see on screen. You'll want to use the CMYK color model (mentioned in just a few paragraphs) for illustrations you intend to print. You can also import RGB images into Illustrator or rasterize objects using the RGB color model.

HSB Schemings

Another way to look at the colors that you see is to start with a set of base colors and then vary the intensity of the colors. That's what you get with the HSB color model.

HSB stands for hue, saturation, and brightness. Hue is the pure color, your own personal rainbow. Saturation dictates the amount of the hue you see. The greater the saturation, the more intense the color. Brightness determines the amount of black added.

HSB is more of a variation of RGB than a separate color model. It's ideal for when you want to find a different shade of an RGB color. Take an RGB color, switch it to its HSB equivalent with the HSB command in the Color palette's pop-up menu, adjust the saturation and brightness, and switch it back to RGB when you're satisfied.

CMYK Pigments

Unfortunately, paper is not capable of shining light in your face the way a monitor is. Instead, light reflects off the surface of the page. So it's a lucky thing that white light—whether from the sun or from an artificial light source—contains the entire visible spectrum. Just as red, green, and blue light mix to form white, white contains red, green, and blue, as well as all other combinations of those colors. Every single color you and I can see is trapped in a ray of sunlight.

When you draw across a piece of white paper with a highlighter, the ink filters out sunlight. A pink highlighter, for example, filters out all nonpink light and reflects pink. This is the exact same way that professional printing colors work. There are three primary inks—cyan, magenta, and yellow—all of which are translucent pigments that filter out different kinds of light:

- Cyan acts as a red light filter. When white light hits a white page, it passes through the cyan ink and reflects all light that is not red—i.e., green and blue.
- Likewise, magenta ink filters out green light.
- And yellow ink filters out blue light.

So an area that appears red on screen prints in magenta and yellow on paper. The magenta and yellow ink filter out the green and blue light and leave only red to bounce back off the page. Cyan and magenta mix to form blue; cyan and yellow make green. All three inks together ought to make black. (I'll tell you why they don't in a minute.) And a complete absence of ink reveals the white page. Because less ink leads to lighter colors, this is called the subtractive color model.

In a perfect world, CMY would be the exact opposites of RGB. But colored inks are not nearly as reliable as colored lights. It's a simple trick to split white light into its pure primary components. You've probably seen it done with prisms. But generating pure inks—such as a cyan that filters all red and no green or blue whatsoever—is practically impossible. Throw in the bleached piece of wood pulp that passes for an absolute white backdrop and you can see how ink purity might prove a real problem. Cyan, magenta, and yellow simply can't manage on their own.

To compensate, color printing throws in one additional ink: black. Black is the key color—the one that helps the other inks out—which makes black the K in the CMYK color model. Black ensures deep shadows, neutral grays, and—of course—nice, even blacks.

Cyan, magenta, yellow, and black ink are the four printing primaries. Some folks call them process colors, which is why CMYK printing is sometimes called four-color process printing. (The word process is an old printing term, simply meaning that the colors are automatically generated to imitate a wider range of colors.)

Process inks are measured in percentages. The maximum intensity of any ink is 100 percent, and the minimum is naturally 0 percent. For example, 100 percent black is pitch black, while 75 percent black is dark gray and 50 percent black is medium gray. Here are some more recipes to keep in mind:

- 50 percent cyan plus 50 percent magenta is a light violet. Increase the cyan to make the color more blue; increase the magenta to make it purple.
- 50 percent magenta plus 50 percent yellow is a medium scarlet. Increase the magenta to make the color more red; increase the yellow to make it more orange. 100 percent yellow by itself is a lemon yellow. To get a cornflower yellow, add about 15 percent magenta to 100 percent yellow.
- 50 percent yellow plus 50 percent cyan is grass green. Add more yellow to get a bright chartreuse; add more cyan to tend toward teal. To get a sea blue, combine 100 percent cyan and 20 percent yellow.
- You can add the complementary ink (the odd CMY ink out) to deepen a color. For example, if you have 50 percent cyan plus 50 percent magenta, adding the complementary ink—yellow—creates mauve. Add the complementary ink instead of black when you want to darken a color without dulling it.
- Adding black both darkens a color and makes it duller. Just a hint of black—10 percent to 25 percent—is great for creating drab colors like olive, steel blue, beige, and brick red.

- Brown is an amalgam of everything, with the emphasis on magenta and yellow. For example, 20 percent cyan and black with 60 percent magenta and yellow is a rich sienna.

NOTE: All these color combinations assume that you're printing to white paper. Because all inks except black are translucent, any paper color except white will blend in with the colors and change how they look, usually for the worse. When you're new to publishing, it's tempting to experiment with different colored papers; after all, white is so boring. But about 90 percent of all professional work is printed to white paper because white permits the widest range of colors. Unless you have a specific reason for doing otherwise, stick with white paper.

But even though you can create a wealth of colors with CMYK, it simply can't measure up to RGB. The CMYK model has a smaller gamut—or color range—than its RGB cousin. Vivid colors in particular—including bright reds and oranges, brilliant greens and blues, and eye-popping purples—fall outside the CMYK gamut. That's why spot colors exist.

Spot Colors

Spot colors (also known as solid colors) are separate inks that you can add to the four basic process colors or that you can use instead of the process colors. For example, you might print a two-color newsletter using black and a spot color. Or, if you can't match a client's logo using process colors, you can add the proper spot color to your four-color printing job.

Pantone is probably the best known vendor of spot colors, offering a library of several hundred premixed inks that are supported by just about every major commercial print house in the United States. Like many other desktop publishing programs, Illustrator provides complete support for the Pantone Color Matching System (or PMS for short).

The problem with adding spot colors is that they increase the cost of your print job. For every spot color that you add, you have to pay for the ink and the printing plate, as well as the time and labor required to feed the paper through another run. (Each color has to be printed in a separate pass.) Even companies with deep pockets rarely print more than six colors per page (CMYK plus two spots). This is also the reason that the Pantone Color Formula Guide 1000—which contains every spot color in the company's library—costs close to $100.

Getting the Right Color

The number one problem with color printing is that what you see on screen may not match what you get back from the printer. As discussed in the "Color Matching" section of Chapter 2, you can use Illustrator's built-in color management to correct the colors on your monitor. But while this is important when printing imported images (as I discuss in Chapter 18), it isn't particularly adept at making on-screen colors more accurate. You can also experiment with an automated color management tool such as Apple's ColorSync. But ColorSync and other programs are best suited to correcting color images created in Photoshop, and few color management programs provide specific support for Illustrator.

The tried-and-true system is to arm yourself with swatch books from Trumatch (212/302-9100) and Pantone (201/935-5500). With a swatch book in hand, you don't have to rely exclusively on the colors you see on screen; you can refer to the book to see how the colors look when printed. Trumatch's $85 Colorfinder shows a huge range of process color combinations. Pantone's Color Formula Guide 1000 is the first and foremost reference for spot colors. Both are pictured in gorgeous black-and-white in Figure 14-1.

Figure 14-1: If you're serious about color printing, the Pantone Color Formula Guide and Trumatch Colorfinder swatch books are a must.

Pantone also provides a $75 CMYK color book called the Process Color System Guide. It contains more colors than its Trumatch equivalent, and it lists the ingredients in CMYK order (as opposed to Trumatch's initially confusing YMCK). But the Trumatch numbering system is more logical, and the Colorfinder book has one major advantage. It was created on a Macintosh computer.

Unfortunately, no color swatch book is 100 percent reliable. The colors age over time, so that your book may look slightly different than your printer's book. But if you store the book in a sensible location—put it in a drawer, don't leave it sitting on a windowsill—it should remain accurate for a full year or more.

TIP

If you have any concerns about a color, take your swatch book in with you and tell the guy at the desk that you expect him to nail Color X on the nose. If the guy says, "Now, lady, much as I'd like to, it's very difficult guarantee an *exact* match," while picking his teeth with some card stock, take your business elsewhere or expect a big savings. If he shows you his swatch book and you find that your colors are a bit different, chances are that you can arrange an equitable compromise. Many printers will provide swatch books that they print themselves if you're a regular client.

The fact is, predictable color is achievable. But the methods for getting good color haven't changed much since the old days.

- Don't believe everything you see on screen.
- Refer to a swatch book when in doubt, and be willing to change your swatch book every year or two.
- Find a good print house. Printers are like car mechanics—some are excellent, and others exploit their customers' inexperience. If you ever for a minute think that you're being fed a line, get a second opinion. Consider it a bad sign if your printer knocks Illustrator's output capabilities. Illustrator is by no means perfect, but when it comes to color printing, there's no better piece of software. This is one case of a bad carpenter blaming his tools.
- Develop a close working relationship with your print house. Where color is concerned, you're at the printer's mercy. But most professional printers are willing to help you out and make you happy.

After a full decade of electronic publishing, I manage to get the colors I want—or a reasonable facsimile—about 80 percent of the time. And nearly all of the 20 percent of color problems that I have are image printing inaccuracies that I have to rectify in Photoshop. With a little bit of effort, you can get Illustrator to perform very reliably.

Finding Your Colors in Illustrator

You define all new process colors in the Color palette by adjusting the different slider bars. Depending on which color model you are using (all of which are accessed through the Color palette's pop-up menu), the slider bars will vary the CMYK, RGB, or HSB amounts. All spot colors are found in the Swatches palette or are imported from third-party swatch libraries.

- Once you've created colors in the Color palette, you can either use the color right away or you can save it for later. If you want to save a color so that you can use it over and over again, choose the New Swatch command from the Swatches palette's pop-up menu or simply drag the color onto the Swatches palette. You will then have the option of naming the color as well as deciding whether you wish to convert it to a spot color.
- You can also use one of the predefined colors in the Swatches palette. Or you can load entire libraries of spot colors from the Window » Swatch Libraries submenu.

I discuss all of these options—and more—in the next sections.

Editing Colors in Illustrator

Prior to version 7, Illustrator's Paint Style palette was its primary color control center. From there you could choose the paint style for all the fills and strokes in your illustration. It was the second most essential palette in Illustrator, second only to the toolbox. Now all the options and controls that you used to find in that one palette have been relegated to a portion of the toolbox and two other separate palettes, the Color palette and the Swatches palette. Figure 14-2 shows a montage of the locations of all your color-related controls.

In the Color palette, you can choose the color model that will best mix your favorite shade of "tickle-me" pink. The Swatches palette stores a number of predefined solid colors (as well as predefined gradients and patterns, both discussed in upcoming chapters). The icons in the Color palette and in the bottom portion of the toolbox lets you switch your focus between fill and stroke and between paint styles.

TIP

Remember, to quickly switch the focus from the Fill icon to the Stroke icon and vice-versa in the Color palette and in the bottom portion of the toolbox, press the X key. To trade the color between the icons, press Shift-X.

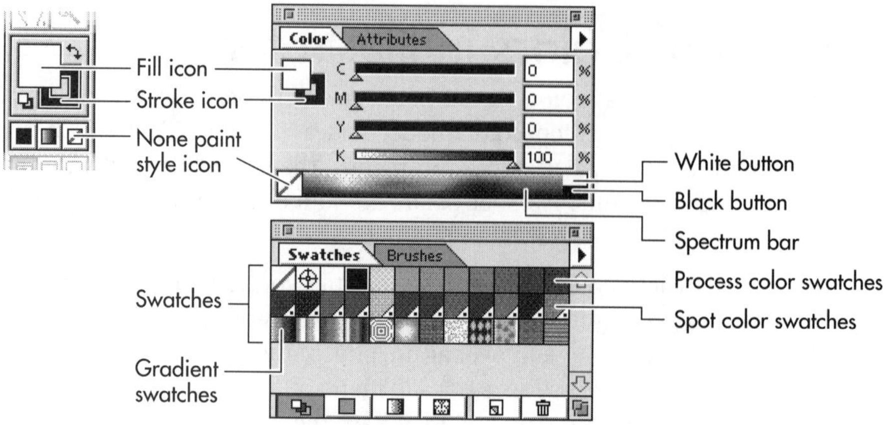

Figure 14-2: The toolbox and the Color and Swatches palettes provide for all your needs when you're creating and editing colors.

To display the Color palette, press F6 or choose Window » Show Color. The Swatches palette responds to your pressing F5 or choosing the Window » Show Swatches command. Choose Window » Show Tools to make the toolbox appear.

All three of these palettes contribute to the Illustrator color experience, and I will refer to all of them throughout this chapter. I cover fill and stroke in greater detail in Chapters 15 and 16. But for now, I will say this: You decide whether you want to modify the fill or stroke of a selection by clicking on the Fill or Stroke icon in the Color palette or the toolbox (or just press the X key). Then you can apply a color using one of the following techniques:

- To create your own process color, choose the color model from the Color palette's pop-up menu. Click on the spectrum bar along the bottom of the Color palette to approximate the color of your dreams. Then modify the slider bars that appear by dragging on the little triangle that accompanies each bar, or change the values in the option boxes to the right of each bar.

To cycle through the different color models, Shift-click on the spectrum bar at the bottom of the Color palette. To move from the RGB model to the HSB model and then to the CMYK model, simply Shift-click on the spectrum bar twice. Be sure to hold down the Shift key while clicking on the spectrum bar or you will change your color and not your color model.

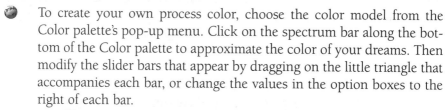

- The Color palette's pop-up menu contains two commands that systematically change the values of the current color: Invert and Complement. Invert changes the color to its opposite. For example, a color (in terms of its RGB components) made up of 100 red, 150 blue, and 200 green inverts to 155 red, 105 blue, and 55 green. The original value and the inverted value for each component must add up to 255. Invert will not change the color's model (a CMYK color remains CMYK and a RGB stays the course) but the math makes sense only in terms of the RGB color space.
- Complement alters colors in a similar manner (although the result is quite contrary to what you might expect based on any color theory with which I'm familiar). Whereas the Invert command bases its changes on 255, the Complement command uses the sum of the lowest and highest RGB values. Say we start with a battleship blue that breaks down into 55 red, 95 green, and 120 blue. Complement would add the lowest and highest values (55 and 120, yielding 175) and then subtract each value from this total. The resulting components would be 120 red (175–55), 80 green (175–95), and 55 blue (175–55). Again, Illustrator doesn't change the color space of the original, it's just that the math only works in terms of RGB.
- If you are working in either RGB or HSB and a little yellow warning symbol pops up directly under the Fill and Stroke icons while you're adjusting the slider bars inside the Color palette, Illustrator is telling you that the color you've created will not directly translate into the CMYK color model. Since Illustrator is first and foremost a printing program, the assumption is that all of the colors you see on screen are going to directly correlate to the colors you see when your document is printed.

  If you have no intention of printing your illustration, you can confidently ignore this warning and happily go about using your color with reckless disregard of any CMYK ramifications. On the other hand, if you want to bring you color within the bounds of the CMYK gamut, either readjust the slider bars until the warning disappears or click the color box that lies just to the right of the warning symbol. Illustrator will change your color to a closely matching color that lies within the CMYK spectrum. If the color that Illustrator chooses is not to your liking, use the slider bars to tweak the color to met your needs.
- Select a color that looks good from the color swatches in the Swatches palette. By default, the first two rows of swatches are process and spot colors. If you switched the order of the swatches, choose Sort By Kind

from the pop-up menu to resort all the swatches. If you click on a process color, the Color palette will display the color along with its tint slider bar (as discussed shortly). You may switch to one of the other color models by choosing it from the pop-up menu in the Color palette.

- If you choose a spot color from the Swatches palette—a swatch with a small dot in the lower right corner, the Color palette displays the color and a single bar. You can use the bar to choose the particular tint of the spot color you want to use.
- To use white, just click on the White box at the right end of the spectrum bar in the Color palette. If you're working in grayscale, you can also move the K slider triangle all the way to the left or enter 0 into the option box.
- To color an object black, click on the Black box (just below the White box) on the spectrum bar. In grayscale, you have the option of either moving the K slider triangle to the far right or entering 100 into the option box.

You can easily vary the amount of black ink in a fill or stroke without adding color in both the CMYK and HSB models. In CMYK, you simply adjust the K slider bar. In HSB, adjust the S or B slider bar. In the RGB model it's a bit more difficult. Your best bet is to drag vertically in the spectrum bar at the location of your color. Exclusively black tints are known as gray values, because they print to black-and-white printers as well as color ones.

NOTE: A common misconception is that gray values aren't colors because they don't include CMY. But black ink is just as much of a color pigment as CMY or any spot color. The only non-color is white, because white prevents all inks from printing and reveals the paper color (which may or may not be white).

Applying Colors

Illustrator automatically updates the colors of selected objects every time you drag a slider triangle or press the Return or Tab key after entering a value in option box value of the Color Palette. Click on a color in the Swatches palette to compel Illustrator to affect the fill or stroke of the selected objects.

TIP: Clicking in the Color or Swatches palette changes the color of selected objects, but only the color of their fill or stroke, depending on which icon is active in the Color palette and the toolbox. The attribute icon (Fill or Stroke) that overlaps the other is the active icon. Illustrator offers a few ways for you to change the color of the attribute (fill or stroke) that is not active.

- You can drag a color swatch (from the Swatches palette) and drop it onto the Fill or Stroke icon. It doesn't matter which icon is active. You need to be careful to drop the swatch squarely on the icon of the attribute that you want to change.
- While dragging a color (from either the Color or the Swatches palette), press and hold down the Shift key. Drop the swatch on any object, whether it's selected or not—yep, that's right, you can affect unselected objects. This will change the color of the attribute that is not active. For example, say you have a rectangle with a green fill and a red stroke. In the Swatches palette, you find an ideal blue that you want to use as the rectangle's new fill color. With the Stroke icon active (inside the Color palette and the toolbox), you can either bring the Fill icon into focus and drag the swatch onto the rectangle or Shift-drag the swatch onto the rectangle.
- Another way to change the color of the icon that's not currently active is to Option-click on the spectrum bar at the bottom of the Color palette. The active icon will remain unchanged but the other icon will adopt the color on which you just clicked.

The power of these techniques is that they allow you to edit the fill and stroke of an object without first activating the Fill and Stroke icons.

Playing with the Color Swatches

By default, Illustrator offers a number of predefined process colors in the Swatches palette. (You'll also find a few gradations and pattern swatches.) However, you can add and delete colors and values to your heart's content:

- To append a gray value or a process color that you've created in the Color palette to the scrolling list of color swatches, click on the New Swatch button at the bottom of the Swatches palette—it's the one with the page icon. You can also choose New Swatch from the pop-up menu in the Swatches palette. The new color will appear at the end of the list of swatches, so you may need to scroll down the field to see it.
- Drag the color from the Color palette to the scrolling field in the Swatches palette. This gives you control over the exact placement of the new addition among the other swatches in the list. The top of Figure

14-3 shows how the Swatches palette responds when you add a new color to the list.

- You can also drag the color from the Fill or Stroke icon and drop it into the list of swatches.
- If you don't like a color swatch, you can replace it with a new color by Option-dragging a color from the Color palette onto that particular swatch. The bottom example of Figure 14-3 shows the reaction of the Swatches palette to this swatch replacement operation.

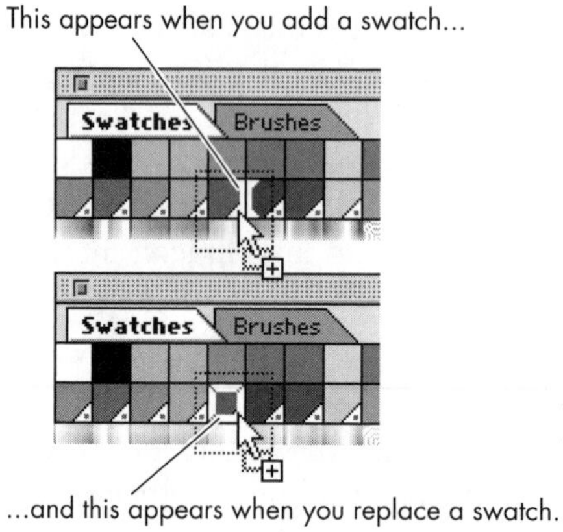
This appears when you add a swatch...
Swatches
Brushes
Swatches
Brushes
...and this appears when you replace a swatch.

Figure 14-3:
The Swatches palette tells you when you're about to add a swatch (top) and when you're about to replace a swatch.

- Option-drag a swatch onto another swatch. The swatch that you drag will move to the new position and the swatch that was there will disappear, leaving you with one less swatch in your list.
- To duplicate a swatch, drag the swatch onto the New Swatch button in the Swatches palette. You can also click on a swatch and choose Duplicate Swatch from the pop-up menu.
- To delete a swatch, drag it onto the Delete button in the Swatches palette—the one with the trash can icon. No warning or whining from Illustrator, just a simple extraction.
- You can also delete a swatch by clicking on the swatch and then clicking on the Delete button or selecting the Delete Swatch command from the pop-up menu in the Swatches palette. In this case, Illustrator will display an alert box to make sure you want to delete the color. This is not all that helpful since you can simply choose Undo to retrieve the swatch if you want to. To avoid this warning, you can Option-click on

the Delete button. When you press the Option key, no warning appears; the color just up and disappears.

TIP: To delete several colors at a time, first select a number of swatches with either the Shift or the ⌘ key. Click on one swatch and then Shift-click on another swatch to select those swatches and all swatches between the two. You can ⌘-click on any other swatch to add it to the selection. Now click on the Delete button (Option-click to circumvent the warning). This is a useful way to clean out an entire section of swatches and start over on them.

TIP: The color swatches are saved with the illustration. They do not translate from one illustration to the next. If you want to save a set of color swatches that you intend to use again and again, open the Adobe Illustrator Startup file that resides in the Plug-ins folder. Then edit the color swatches inside that illustration and save them to disk. From that point on, all new illustrations will use those same color swatches.

TIP: If you have a problem getting Illustrator to use the color swatches from the Adobe Illustrator Startup file in a new illustration, try this: Close the new illustration and open the Adobe Illustrator Startup file. Then press ⌘-N to create another new illustration and close the Startup file. The color swatches should now look hunky-dory.

Using the Slider Bars

You wouldn't think something like slider bars would deserve their own section, but Adobe has built a bunch of little convenience features into the slider bars in the Color palette:

- Notice how the slider bars appear in different colors? This shows you what colors you'll get if you drag the slider triangle to that position. Each time you drag a slider triangle (or enter a value into an option box and press the Tab key), Illustrator updates the colors in the slider bars. This way, you're constantly aware of the effect that modifying a primary pigment will produce.
- If you like a color along the length of a slider bar, just click on it. The slider triangle for that ink will immediately jump to the clicked position.

TIP: To create a lighter or darker tint of a process color, Shift-drag the slider triangle. As you drag, all the slider bars change to demonstrate the tint. To gain the most control, Shift-drag the triangle associated with the highest intensity color. (Any ink set to 0 percent does not move, since adding the ink would change the color rather than the tint.)

- You can also Shift-click on a spot along a slider bar to adjust the tint by leaps and bounds. All inks (not set to 0 percent) change to maintain a constant hue. If the point at which you click is too high to maintain a consistent tint, only that one ink will change. To make certain you change the tint and not the one ink, Shift-click and hold anywhere along the slider bar, and then move your mouse until the sliders all move to some legal position.
- And, as you can in any palette, you can advance from one option box to the next by pressing the Tab key. Or you can move in reverse order by pressing Shift-Tab. If you wish to apply a new value and keep that option box active (allowing you to quickly test a number of different settings), press Shift-Return.
- If you're an adept Photoshop user and you're wondering whether you can use the up and down arrow keys to modify option box values as you can in the fab image editor, the answer is no. Where slider bars are concerned, the two programs go their own ways.

Creating a Color Swatch

The Swatches palette is ideal for applying colors on the fly and saving colors as swatches. But if you intend to use a color on a regular basis, you'll want to give it a name and save it along with your illustration for quick and easy retrieval. You can use these colors as both process and spot colors. You can even print a color as a spot color one time and as a process color the next. (See the section "Process Color or Spot?" later in this chapter.)

You create and modify colors in the Swatch Options dialog box, shown in Figure 14-4, which you can access in four ways:

- To create a new color, choose New Swatch from the pop-up menu in the Swatches palette. The Swatch Options dialog box opens with the default name—New Color Swatch—selected.
- Option-click on the New Swatch button in the Swatches palette and the dialog box opens.

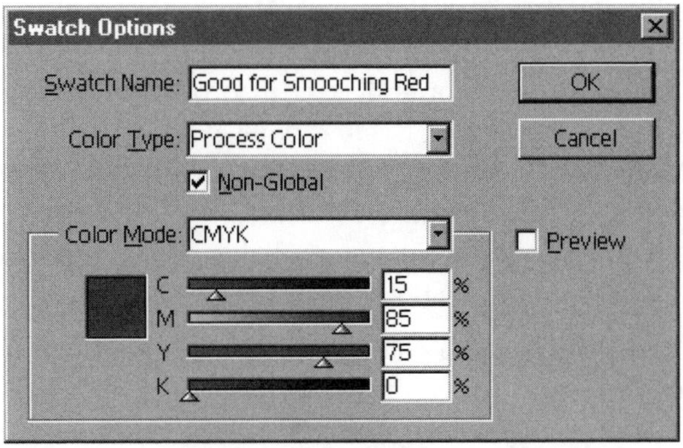

Figure 14-4: You can create and edit swatch colors—whether process colors or spot colors—in the Swatch Options dialog box.

- You can edit a specific swatch color. Click on the swatch that you want to rename. Then choose Swatch Options from the pop-up menu in the Swatches palette.
- Double-click on an existing swatch to display the dialog box.

In the Swatch Options box, you can change a color's name, decide whether it should be a spot or process color, and even readjust the color.

- First and foremost, give your color a name. After all, the right name for your random color is of the utmost importance. (OK, actually it doesn't matter in the least whether your color has a special name. You can knock yourself out and dub it indubitably, or if that's not worth your time, go ahead and use the name that Illustrator assigns it—New Color Swatch number whatever.)
- From the Color Type menu, you can decide whether your newly created color should be a process color or a spot color. The big thing to remember here is that when you designate a color as a spot color, you are indicating that you expect your print house to dip into the vat of specially created inks to perfectly match the color. After all, you can't expect your personal printer to come stocked with this new spot color, and, as you've undoubtedly guessed, no print house has any reserve of the special color you've just created.

  In the end, it's a little silly that Illustrator even provides this option. The typical Illustrator user has neither the resources nor the inclination to create a spot color. I know that I certainly don't. When you save a color as a swatch, you should leave it as a process color. If you find that you're using a preexisting spot color and want it to print as a process color, you can switch its orientation after you've added it to the Swatches palette. Moreover, if you decide that you want all the spot colors in your illustration to print as process colors, you can select the Convert to Process check box in the Separation dialog box, as discussed in the upcoming "Process Color or Spot?" section.

- It used to be that when you saved a color as a swatch, the color of the swatch was written in stone (or, as least, in very durable pixels). Nowadays, you can change the color any time the Swatch Options dialog box is open. Simply adjust the slider bars as you would in the Color palette when you're first creating a color. You can even switch the color's model via the Color Model pull-down menu. If you want to see how the changes look in your document, check the Preview check box. All selected paths that use that color will reflect you modification.
- After you've dragged your color onto the Swatches palette, all paths that use the color can be updated automatically to reflect any changes you make to the colors swatch in the future. To have Illustrator do this, uncheck the Non-Global check box. From that point on, any and all paths that you create using this color will be chromatically linked and will automatically reflect any changes that you make to the color. To break this link for future paths, open the Swatch Options dialog box and check the Non-Global option.

Organizing Swatches

The Swatches palette provides a handful of options for organizing swatches. For example, you can choose to display the swatches by name or by icon (large or small). Once the Swatches palette is in focus—you've ⌘-Option-clicked on a swatch to surround the swatch list with a heavy border—you can scroll around the swatches by pressing the arrow keys.

From the Swatches palette, you can control the organization of the swatches by the following methods:

- To sort the swatches by either name or kind, choose the appropriate command from the pop-up menu in the Swatches palette. Sorting by kind groups similar swatches together. All the process colors appear first, followed by the spot colors, gradients, and finally the pattern swatches.
- Choose the appropriate command from the pop-up menu to view swatches by their name or simply by an icon that samples their color.

- Use the four buttons along the bottom left of the Swatches palette to control which type of swatches display. Click on the second, third, or fourth button to restrict the display of swatches only to colors, gradients, or patterns, respectively. Click on the first button to show all swatches.

The Swatches palette offers another function that helps you organize your swatches. From the pop-up menu, choose the Select All Unused command to select all swatches that are not applied to paths or text blocks in any open illustration. Once the swatches are selected, you can drag them to a new location in the swatch list or delete them all by Option-clicking on the Delete button. You can even duplicate them if you so choose.

Spot Color Swatches

In the Swatches palette, a white triangle with a dot covers the lower right corner of a spot color swatch and distinguishes it from process color swatches. If you display the swatches by name, a square with an inscribed circle appears to the right of a spot color (vs. a grayed square that appears for process color).

When you click on a spot color swatch, the Color palette displays the color and a tint slider bar, as shown in Figure 14-5. You can modify the intensity of a color by changing the Tint value. Again, all the standard techniques discussed a few pages back in the "Using the Slider Bars" section apply to the Tint slider bar as well.

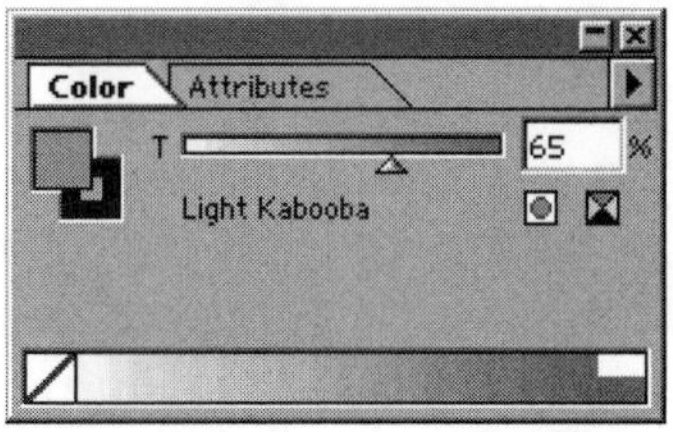

Figure 14-5: After selecting a spot color swatch from the Swatches palette, you can modify the intensity of the color using the Tint slider bar that appears in the Color palette.

Process Color or Spot?

Generally speaking, you decide whether to convert a color to CMYK separations or use it as a spot color during the printing process. To specify how you want to print a color, choose File » Separation Setup (⌘-Option-P) to display the great big Separation dialog box, partially shown in figure 14-6.

If this is the first time you've used this dialog box, most of the options will appear dimmed. You must first open a printer description file using the Open PPD button to enable these options. Assuming that you've installed the AdobePS 8.5 driver or its Windows equivalent, AdobePS 4.1—I explain why that's a good idea in Chapter 18—you'll find the printer description files in the Printer Descriptions folder inside the Extensions folder in your System Folder (or in the PPD folder in the Utilities folder on the Windows side).

The all-important process and spot color options are in the bottom left corner and in the color list of the Separation dialog box. I've spotlighted these options in Figure 14-6. By default, the Convert to Process check box is turned on, which automatically converts all spot colors to their process color ingredients. If that suits you fine, press the Return key and continue illustrating. If you prefer to print one or more colors as spot colors, turn the check box off, as shown in the figure.

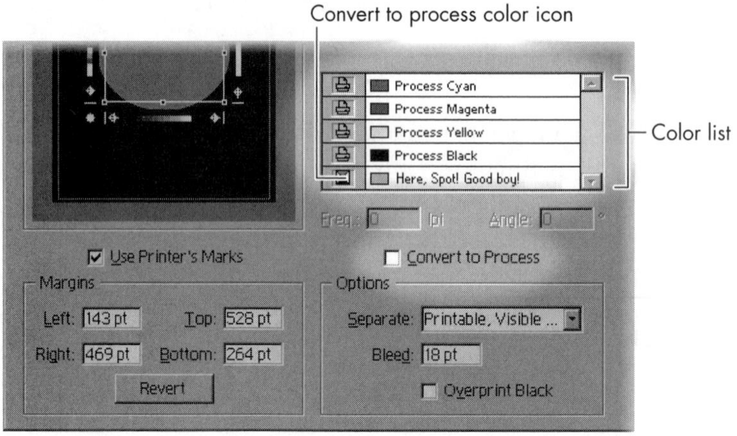

Figure 14-6: You can select color options in the Separation dialog box after choosing File » Separation Setup.

After you turn off the Convert to Process check box, the icon boxes in the color list (labeled in Figure 14-6) come to life. The list contains the names of the four process colors, plus all spot colors used to fill and stroke objects in the illustration. To the left of the color names is a column of small icons. Click on an icon box to specify how the color will print:

- To prevent a particular color from printing, click several times on the icon until the icon disappears. If you use only black and a spot color, for example, Illustrator automatically turns off the Process Cyan, Process Magenta, and Process Yellow items.
- To change a process color to a spot color, click on the icon until a little printer appears. This icon ensures that Illustrator prints the color to a separate page or sheet or film, which is what spot colors are all about.

- To break down a color into its process ingredients, click on the icon until the four-color icon (which looks like a tiny CMYK target) appears. This icon is used exclusively for custom colors. You can't convert cyan, magenta, yellow, or black to a process color since it already is one.

Don't fret too much if you don't immediately understand how these options work. This section is meant merely as an introduction to the color printing process to help you understand where custom colors fit in. I explore printing is much more detail in Chapter 18.

Converting Spot to Process on the Fly

If you want to convert a spot color assigned to an object to its process ingredients, select the object and click on the color model of choice from the pop-up menu in the Color palette. When you do this, Illustrator keeps the color of the object intact but breaks the link between the spot color and the object. With no more effort than this, your object will automatically print to process color separations regardless of the settings in the Separation dialog box.

Using Predefined Color Libraries

Illustrator ships with several libraries filled with predefined colors from Pantone, Trumatch, and others who make their money from this most intangible of all possible intellectual properties. Adobe supplies the libraries as documents in the Swatches Libraries folder.

You can open one of these files using the standard File » Open command. Illustrator will load all the colors from the library and dump them in the Swatches palette for your open Illustrator file. But loading all those colors can prove a tad overwhelming, and they needlessly increase the size of an illustration on disk. Moreover, these swatches will be available only to that single document. So don't do it this way. Illustrator provides a much better method.

You can open third-party swatch libraries as independent palettes. Simply choose the appropriate library from the Window » Swatch Library submenu. A new palette will appear chock-full of all the library's swatches. This palette will be available to all open illustrations. Now, to save disk space (and not to mention RAM), find and ⌘-click on each color that you need and choose the Add To Swatches command from the palette's pop-up menu. The new swatches appear in the Swatches palette. You can do this for each open illustration that requires any of these swatches. Close the library by clicking on the palette's close box. When you next save your illustration, the new swatches are saved with it, whether or not they are used to fill or stroke objects.

TIP

If you want a particular library to open every time you launch Illustrator, first choose the library from the Swatch Library submenu and then, after the palette displays, select the Persistent command from the palette's pop-up menu. The next time you start-up Illustrator, that library will be part of your Illustrator window.

TIP

If, on the other hand, you use a small cache of colors on a regular basis, you can add them to the Adobe Illustrator Startup file. For example, if one of your clients sells lawn flamingos, you might want to keep Pantone 225 pink on hand at all times. Just open the Startup file (in the Plug-ins folder), open the appropriate swatch library (via the Windows »Swatches Libraries command), select from the library's palette the color that you want to use on a regular basis, and choose Add to Swatch from the palette's pop-up menu. Be sure to then close the library's palette. After you save the Startup file, the color will be available to all illustrations, whether old or new.

The following items briefly introduce the color brands in reverse order of their impact on the American market—if you'll pardon me for being so unscrupulously ethnocentric—from smallest impact to greatest:

- **Focoltone, DIC color and Toyo:** Both Focoltone and Dianippon Ink and Chemical (DIC) and Toyo fall into the negligible-impact category. All are foreign standards with followings abroad. Focoltone is based in England, while DIC and Toyo hails from Japan. None have many subscribers here in the States and their basic purpose is to satisfy foreign clientele.
- **Trumatch:** Designed entirely using a desktop system and with desktop publishers in mind, the Trumatch Colors file contains more than 2,000 process colors, organized according to hue, saturation, and brightness. The colors correspond to the Colorfinder swatch book that I mentioned earlier. Trumatch happens to be my favorite process color collection, and I keep a copy of the Colorfinder close at hand at all times.
- **Pantone:** The largest color vendor in America is Pantone. It offers three libraries in the Swatch Libraries submenu—Pantone Coated, Pantone Process, and Pantone Uncoated. If you're interested in printing Pantone spot colors, the Pantone Coated and Process Uncoated libraries are for you. Coated and uncoated refer to the paper used in printing. These

colors correspond to Color Formula Guide 1000 swatch book. The Pantone Process library contains process colors that match printed colors in the Process Color System Guide swatch book.

Strictly speaking, it's not a good idea to separate spot colors from the Pantone Coated file into their supposed CMYK ingredients. The whole reason Pantone spot colors exist, after all, is to fill in the considerable gaps left by the four basic process colors. That said, some Pantone colors convert to process colors better than others. For example, you can simulate Pantone 129 yellow quite well using 15 percent magenta and 76 percent yellow. And 100 percent cyan plus 9 percent magenta is a dead ringer for Pantone 2995 blue. (Who can figure out this numbering scheme?) But close-by Pantone 2935 blue bears about as much resemblance to 100 percent cyan, 47 percent magenta as royal blue bears to mud. If you want to see exactly how Pantone spot colors convert to process, you need to purchase yet another swatch book, the Process Color Imaging Guide 1000.

If the palette doesn't seem to respond correctly as you type in numbers, it's probably because you're typing too fast. If you slow it down a little, it should work just fine.

Applying the Overprint Options

A few color-related options appear in locations that might surprise you. The first two of these are the Overprint check boxes in the Attributes palette, spotlighted in Figure 14-7. These options control whether the color applied to the fill or stroke of the selected object mixes with the colors of the objects behind it. When the Fill or Stroke check box is turned on, the fill or stroke color overprints the colors behind it, provided that the fill or stroke color is printed to a different separation from the background colors.

For example, suppose you've created a Mardi Gras illustration consisting of three spot colors, Pantones 2592, 3405, and 1235, which any resident of Louisiana can tell you are purple, green, and gold. Purple can overprint green, green can overprint purple, and either can overprint or be overprinted by gold, because Pantones 2592, 3405, and 1235 print to their own separations. However, a 30 percent tint of purple cannot overprint a 70 percent tint of purple, because all purple objects print to the same Pantone 2592 separation.

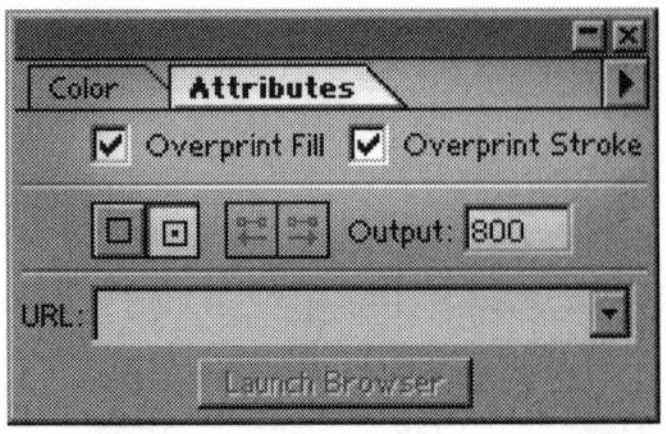

Figure 14-7:
Use the Overprint check boxes in the Attributes palette to mix colors in overlapping objects, as long as the colors print to different separations.

When one color overprints onto another color, the two colors mix together. You could overprint purple onto gold, for example, to get a deep brown color.

If the Overprint check boxes are turned off, as they are by default, any portion of an object that is covered by another object is knocked out and the object on top prints; that is, the covered object doesn't print, even when the two objects are output to different separations. This ensures that colors from different separations do not mix. For nonblack paths, unless you are absolutely sure that you want a path to overprint another (and thus you want its colors to mix with the colors of any other path that it touches), you should leave these controls alone.

Overprinting Process Colors

The Overprint options have no influence over black-and-white illustrations that don't require separations. If the selected object is filled with one or more process colors, only those colors on different separations overprint. For example, suppose you have two objects, one filled with 30 percent magenta and 75 percent yellow (gold) and another filled with 70 percent cyan and 95 percent magenta (purple). If you select the gold object and turn on the Overprint Fill check box, the intersection of the two objects is printed with 70 percent cyan, 30 percent magenta, and 75 percent yellow. The magenta value from the gold object wins out—even though it's lighter than the magenta value in the purple object—because overprinting doesn't affect colors placed on the same separation.

The downside of overprinting is that an overprinted color doesn't show up correctly on screen, nor does it proof correctly to color printers. There's no way to tell by looking at an object whether it overprints or not. So you have to keep an eye on the Overprint check boxes in the Attributes palette.

TIP: If you want to mix the colors in overlapping objects and see the results on screen, choose Object » Pathfinder » Hard. As explained back in Chapter 9, the Hard filter splits the intersection of two selected objects into a separate path and fills the intersection with a mix of the objects' colors. If I applied the Hard filter to our gold and purple objects, the Hard filter would fill the intersection with 70 percent cyan, *95 percent* magenta, and 75 percent yellow. So it displays the darkest of the two magenta values, which is slightly different than overprinting. But quite frankly, in most cases, the darker value is preferable. And, of course, you can always edit the color of the intersection if you aren't satisfied with the result.

The only problem with using the Hard filter is that it always converts spot colors to their process color equivalents. So if you want to mix two spot colors, and you want them to remain spot colors, you have no choice but to use the Overprint check boxes.

Overprinting Black Ink

Although you may occasionally use the Overprint options to mix spot colors, most professionals apply overprinting primarily to black ink to anticipate printing problems. Because black is opaque—and it's typically the last ink applied during the printing process—it covers up all other inks. So it doesn't look much different when printed over, say, cyan than it looks when printed directly onto the white page. But while overprinting has little affect on the appearance of black ink, it prevents gaps from occurring between a black object and a different-colored neighbor. Even if the paper shifts on the printing press, the black ink comes out looking fine.

Illustrator provides two means for overprinting black ink—the Filter » Colors » Overprint Black command and the Overprint Black check box in the Separation dialog box. For complete information on both of these time-saving features, read Chapter 18. This is where I discuss the more nitty-gritty sides of overprinting, color separations, and registration problems in their proper context.

Transferring Colors Between Objects and Images

Any illustration program worth its salt permits you to transfer a color from one object to another. Transferring colors means that you don't have to scribble down notes about how different objects are colored when you want to create new objects that match exactly. As mentioned earlier, you can drag colors from palettes and drop them onto objects, but you can also lift colors with the eyedropper tool and plunk them down with the paint bucket. This approach is equally convenient and more flexible in the long run, as you'll soon see.

Using the Paint Bucket

The paint bucket tool—the alternate tool in the eyedropper tool slot—applies colors from the Color palette to objects in the illustration window. To use the tool, specify the desired fill and stroke attributes in the palettes, and then click on the target object that you want to color. If the object has no fill, you'll need to click on the outline, as demonstrated in Figure 14-8. Although it used to automatically select the path when it filled and stroked it with the paint bucket tool, Illustrator now simply changes the fill and stroke colors of paths that you click on with the paint bucket tool. This means that you can change an object's attributes without altering its selection status (or the selection status of any other path in your illustration).

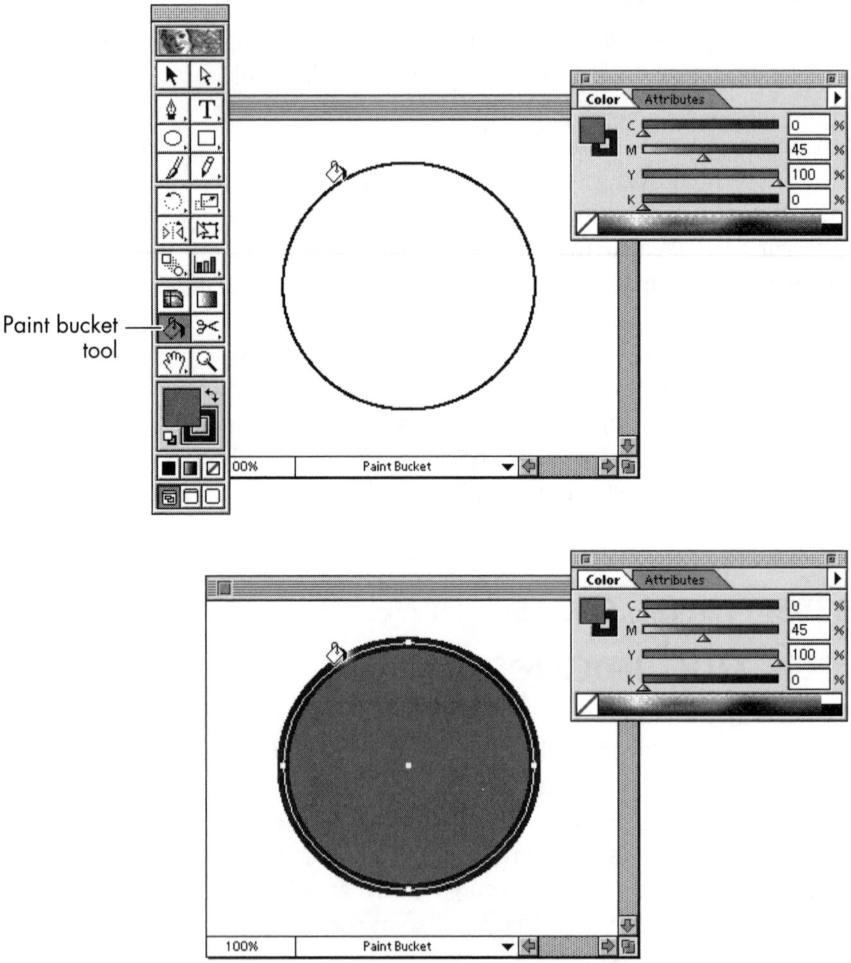

Figure 14-8: Click on the outline of a path (top) or inside a filled path to color the path with the attributes specified in the Color palette (bottom).

You can also use the paint bucket on text and black-and-white images. But to color type, you have to click on the alignment point, baseline, or text path, just as you do when selecting text with the arrow tool. You can't click directly on the letters unless the Type Area Select option in the Type & Auto Tracing Preferences dialog box is selected. When you click on a black-and-white image (in which the white pixels are transparent), the paint bucket fills the black pixels with color.

Remember, when it comes to type, you can use the paint bucket to transfer character and paragraph attributes between text objects. For a quick review of this topic, see Chapter 6.

Using the Eyedropper

The eyedropper is the paint bucket's opposite. It lifts colors from objects and puts them inside the Color palette. (It also displays all the stroke's information in the Stroke palette, as discussed in Chapter 16. If the object contains text, both the Character and Paragraph palettes are updated to reflect the object's type attributes.) To use the eyedropper, click on or inside a path or click on the alignment point, baseline, or path belonging to a text object. The eyedropper cursor becomes partially black to show that you're lifting color.

TIP: One of the best kept secrets of the eyedropper tool is that you can transfer the color of a path's stroke to the Fill icon in the Color palette. Just click on the very edge of the stroke—as shown in the bottom example of Figure 14-9—where it exceeds the boundary of the path. This technique works best when working with fat strokes. The Stroke icon will adopt the None paint style to indicate that no stroke color is selected.

TIP: Tips abound for using the eyedropper. If you click on an object with the eyedropper with other objects selected, you not only lift the colors from the object but you also apply the colors to all selected objects. This enables you to transfer a fill and stroke from one object to multiple selected objects in one fell swoop.

TIP: If you Shift-click with the eyedropper, it will transfer color only to the active icon while leaving the other icon unaffected. This means that only the corresponding attribute of the selected object will change.

You can lift colors from any image in Illustrator, whether placed or parsed, imported or rasterized. The color on which you click becomes the fill color in the Color palette and toolbox.

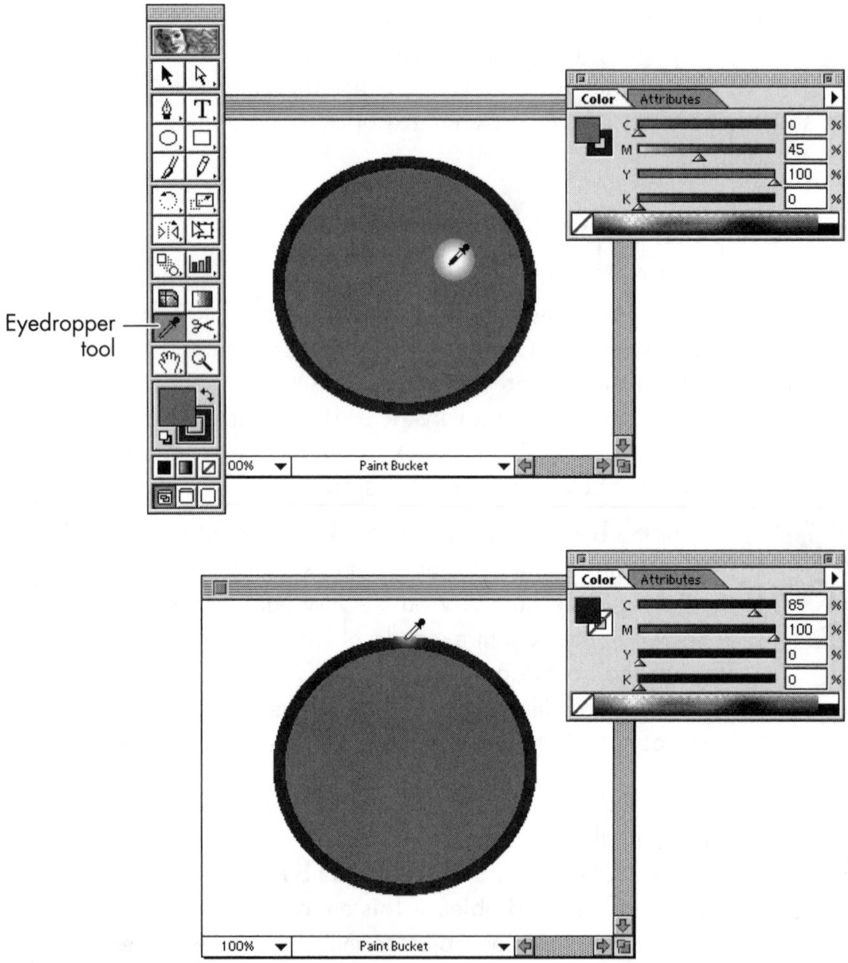

Figure 14-9: Click inside a path to lift both the fill and stroke (top). Click on the edge of a stroke to lift the stroke color and use it as a fill (bottom).

TIP

You can lift colors from background windows, including an image open inside Photoshop, or from the Finder desktop. But you can't just click outside the illustration window; that merely switches applications. You have to click and hold inside the illustration window and then drag outside the window. As you drag, the color of the Fill icon perpetually changes to reflect the color under your cursor. When you get to the color you like, release the mouse.

More Suck-and-Dump Trivia

Double-click on either the paint bucket or the eyedropper icon in the toolbox to display the dialog box full of check boxes, shown in Figure 14-10. You can select these options to apply and lift specific attributes with the paint bucket and eyedropper. The options are grouped according to fill and stroke attributes. Deselecting the Fill or Stroke check box turns off and dims all corresponding options below it.

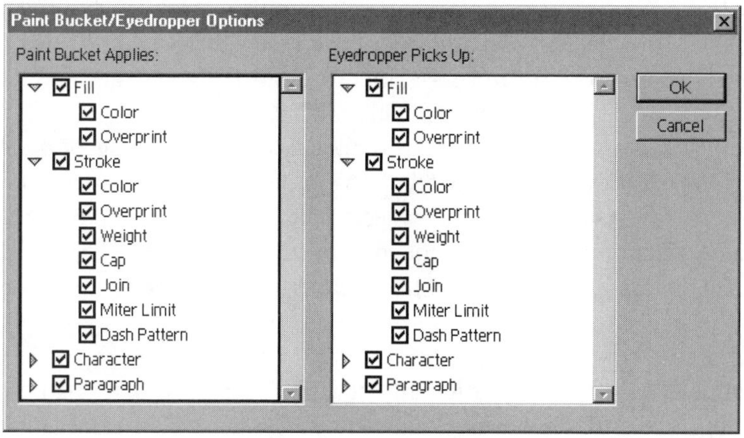

Figure 14-10: Double-click on the bucket or dropper icon in the toolbox to access these check boxes.

TIP

And one more thing: You can toggle between the paint bucket and the eyedropper by pressing the Option key. If the bucket is selected, pressing Option gets you the eyedropper. When the eyedropper is selected, press Option to get the bucket. As a pal of mine from Adobe likes to say, the Option key allows you to alternately "suck and dump" colors without changing tools. (Now if they'd only put that into the manual!)

Applying Automated Color Manipulations

The Filter » Colors submenu contains a total of ten filters that affect the colors of selected objects and imported images. You can use these filters to increase or decrease the intensity of primary inks and, in some cases, spot colors. While the filters aren't nearly as capable or sophisticated as similar color correction commands found in Photoshop, they do make it possible to edit multiple objects and colors simultaneously, which can save you a significant amount of time.

I already mentioned that I'll be discussing the Filter » Colors » Overprint Black command in Chapter 18. I discuss the remaining nine color correction commands in the following sections.

Adjusting Colors

The Filter » Colors » Adjust Colors command is Illustrator's most capable color correction command. You can vary the amount of ink assigned to a CMYK or an RGB object, convert spot colors to process colors, or colorize grayscale objects. You can also modify the colors of placed RGB and CMYK images.

Choose the Adjust Colors filter to display the Adjust Colors dialog box, as shown in Figure 14-11. From the Color Mode pop-up menu, choose which type of colors you wish to adjust. If the selected objects contain both spot colors and CMYK colors, choose Custom to alter the spot colors without changing the CMYK colors. To affect all colors at once, check the Convert check box (mentioned below).

Once you've chosen a color mode, you can adjust the percentage composition of the colors in the selected objects by adjusting the slider bars or by entering new values in the option boxes. Enter positive values to add ink, and enter negative values to reduce the ink intensity.

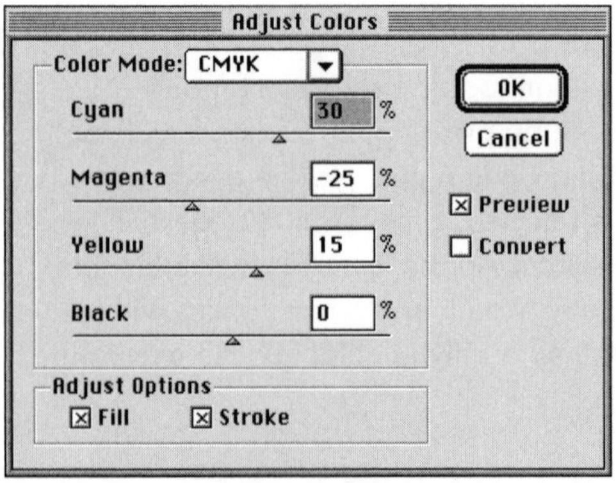

Figure 14-11: The Adjust Colors dialog box allows you to increase or decrease the percentage of colors assigned to selected objects.

NOTE

Note that the values in the Adjust Colors dialog box represent absolute values. In other words, each value raises or lowers an ink intensity by exactly that percent. For example, if I were to apply the values shown in Figure 14-11 to an object with a 100 percent magenta fill, Illustrator would change the fill to 30 percent cyan, 75 percent magenta, and 15 percent yellow. This is different—and decidedly less useful—than the way most of Photoshop's color commands work. Photoshop's best color-correction functions—Levels, Curves, and Variations—change the relative coloring of images. For example, these functions permit you to increase or decrease the intensity of medium cyan values within a selection, without affecting noncyan colors or full-intensity cyans. Only one command in Illustrator, Filter » Colors » Saturate, permits relative color modifications, but even it doesn't begin to compare to Photoshop's capabilities.

The Adjust Colors dialog box also offers the following check boxes:

- **Fill:** Select this option if you want to modify the fills of selected objects. Turn off the option if you want to change only strokes.
- **Stroke:** Same thing as Fill, only opposite. Turn on the check box if you want to adjust strokes; turn it off if you want to affect only fills.
- **Convert:** Select this check box to modify all colors of the selected objects according to the option box values. If you turn off this check box, you can adjust a color only in terms of its original color model.
- **Preview:** Select this check box to keep apprised of the effects of your color modifications as you work inside the Adjust Colors dialog box. Keep this option on to avoid surprises.

TIP

To colorize a grayscale image, your best bet is to first convert it to the RGB or CMYK color model using Filter » Colors » Convert To RGB or Filter » Colors » Convert To CMYK. Then use the Adjust Colors filter to add red, blue, and green or cyan, magenta, and yellow to the image.

Switching Between Color Models

Not only does Illustrator support RGB colors throughout the program, but it lets you switch between the RGB and CMYK color models. Choose either Filter »

Colors » Convert To RGB or Filter » Colors » Convert To CMYK and all the colors of the selected objects will change to their RGB or CMYK equivalents. No rasterizing involved. Be aware that these filters will also convert spot colors to process colors without the slightest warning.

Illustrator provides a similar filter that converts all colors to grayscale: Filter » Colors » Convert To Grayscale. This filter is especially handy for dealing with any clip art that you may use. Most clip art these days is created in color, while often Illustrator graphics are printed in black-and-white to keep costs down. Converting your illustration to grayscale is also useful for draft printing.

Changing the Overall Ink Intensity

If you want to apply relative adjustments to the colors of selected objects, choose Filter » Colors » Saturate. The Saturate command displays a small dialog box with a single slider bar and a corresponding option box:

- Enter a negative value to decrease the intensity of the colors in selected objects filled or stroked with process colors. This value also reduces the tints of selected objects filled or stroked with spot colors. (The Saturate command does not convert colors to process, so spot colors remain intact.)
- Enter a positive value to increase the intensity of the colors or the tint of colors.

Unlike the Adjust Colors command, Saturate makes relative color adjustments. If you apply a Saturate value of 50 percent to an object filled with 20 percent cyan and 50 percent magenta, Illustrator changes the fill to 30 percent cyan and 75 percent magenta. That's a 50 percent increase in the previous intensities of both inks.

The command isn't entirely consistent. For example, it changes white absolutely; while a 50 percent Saturate increases a 10 percent black fill to 15 percent black, it changes a white fill to 50 percent black. And the Saturate command becomes completely unpredictable when applied to grayscale images.

After everything is said and done, Filter » Colors » Saturate is best suited to lightening or darkening the colors of several objects at once (as I did when lightening the mosaic tiles in the "Converting an Image to Squares" section of Chapter 13). You can use the command to establish highlights or shadows, whether the selected objects are filled and stroked with gray values or colors.

Inverting Selected Colors

After you choose Filter » Colors » Invert Colors, Illustrator changes the colors of all selected objects to their opposites. The result is the same as choosing Invert from the Color palette's pop-up menu (a color composed of 100 red, 150 blue, and 200 green inverts to 155 red, 105 blue, and 55 green) except that the filter affects all color of all the selected objects.

The Invert command also inverts objects filled and stroked with gray values. Black inverts to white, white inverts to black—it's just like a photographic negative.

Creating Color Blends

The remaining three commands in the Filter » Colors submenu—Blend Front to Back, Blend Horizontally, and Blend Vertically—create continuous color blends between three or more selected objects. Each command uses two extreme objects as base colors and recolors all other selected objects between the extremes.

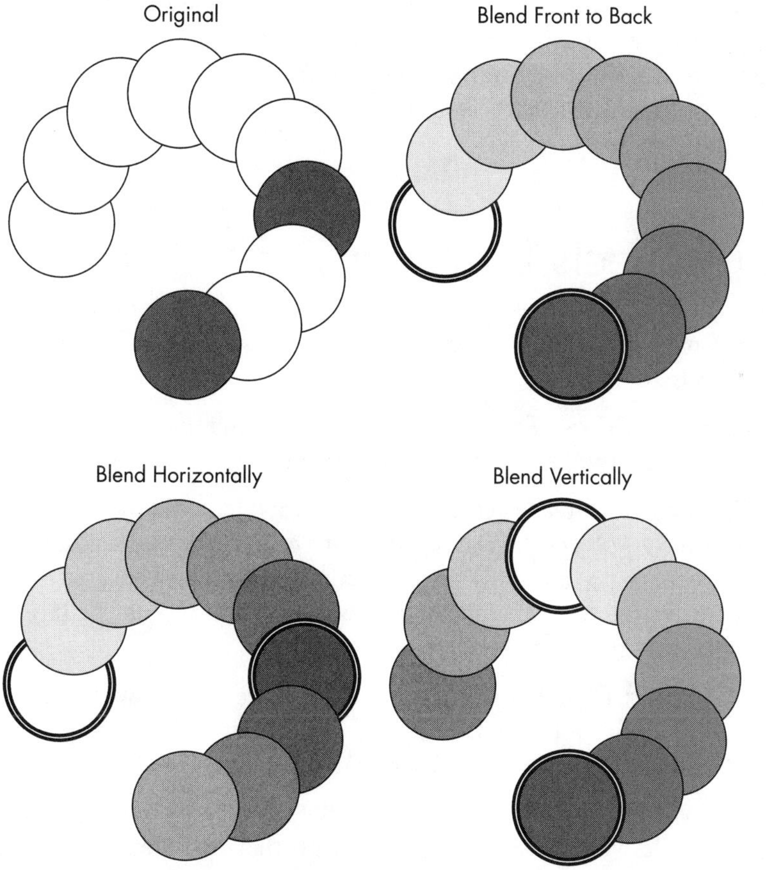

Figure 14-12: The results of applying each of the three Blend filters to the original collection of circles shown at upper left.

In the first example in Figure 14-12, I created a series of circles by Option-dragging a circle with the rotate tool and pressing ⌘-D several times in a row. I filled two of the circles with medium gray. Then I selected all of the circles and applied the various Blend filters to get the results shown in the other examples in the figure.

In each case, Illustrator used different circles for the base colors. (I've stroked the extreme circles with heavy outlines in each Blend example.) When I chose Blend Front to Back, Illustrator used the back and front circles as extremes and recolored the circles stacked in between. The Blend Horizontally command blended between the left and right extremes; and Blend Vertically blended between the top and bottom circles.

All three Blend filters affect gray values as well as CMYK and RGB colors just fine. But you can't use them on spot colors. Strokes are completely ignored.

The Blend filters are great for modifying the colors in a series of objects created with the transformation tools and Arrange » Repeat Transform (as in Figure 14-12). You can also use them to recolor a series of objects created with the blend tool, as I discuss in Chapter 17.

Selecting Objects by Color

The last color commands I cover in this chapter allow you to select objects according to the way that you've colored them. These commands are available from the Edit » Select submenu:

- **Same Paint Style:** Choose this filter to select any paths that share the exact same fill and stroke attributes as a selected object.
- **Same Fill Color:** This filter selects all paths that are filled with the same color as the selected object. In versions prior to 8, this filter refused to select text objects as do (and did) the other filters I discuss here. These days, though, this filter selects text objects along with any other paths that share the same fill color.
- **Same Stroke Color:** This filter selects all paths that are stroked with the same color as the selected object. This filter ignores line weight, caps, joins, and all other stroke attributes except color.
- **Same Stroke Weight:** If you want to select all objects that are stroked with a certain line weight, select an object with that line weight and choose the Same Stroke Weight filter. This filter ignores color, caps, joins, and everything else except line weight. (See Chapter 16 for the lowdown on strokes.)

The color selection filters are essential for making global changes to objects filled or stroked with gray values and colors. For example, in Figure 14-13, I decided that the two darkest grays in the illustration on the left were interfering with the black of the letter M. I selected one of the objects filled with the darkest gray, chose Select » Same Fill Color to select the others, and entered a new Tint value in the Color palette. After repeating this process for the objects filled with the next darkest shade of gray, I arrived at the more intelligible illustration on right.

Figure 14-13: Using Same Fill Color, I easily changed all the occurrences of the two darkest gray fills in the left-hand illustration.

To quickly reselect all objects that fulfill the requirements of the last selection filter you used, press ⌘-6 or choose Edit » Select » Select Again. So, for example, if you choose Edit » Select » Same Fill Color to select all objects with a royal purple fill, later select an object with a sky blue fill, and then press ⌘-6, Illustrator will select all objects that have that same sky blue fill.

None of the color selection filters will work properly if you have selected more than one object and those objects have different fill or stroke colors. For the best results, select just one object and then choose a filter.

CHAPTER 15

GRADATIONS AND OTHER FAB FILLS

In Illustrator, you can fill the interior of any path with a single color, a blend of colors, or a custom pattern. Though it may not sound like much, fill is one of Illustrator's most essential capabilities. If Illustrator couldn't fill objects with opaque colors, your paths and character outlines would be without form or substance. You'd be able to see through each and every path to the path behind it, like some kind of chaotic Miro-inspired scribble art. In fact, fill and stroke are all that separate the preview mode from the wireframe artwork mode. If you ever wonder what the world would be like without fill, just press ⌘-Y. (Lordy, imagine presenting *that* to a client! It gives me the willies just thinking about it.)

If push came to shove, you could live without stroke. You could draw thin shapes and fill them. In fact, I know many artists who barely use strokes. But there's no getting around fill. It enables you to design complex illustrations, create shadows and highlights, or simply add color to a document. Fill is the skin wrapped around the skeleton of a path, the airbrushing inside the frisket, the drywall over the studs. Fill permits you to show viewers exactly what you want them to see.

Figure 15-1:
In the artwork mode, the fill of a closed path is invisible (top). But in the preview mode, the fill permeates the shape (bottom).

Filling Closed and Open Paths

Before I explain how you can define and apply cool fills like gradations, I'd like to clarify a few basic principles. First of all, you can fill any kind of path, whether open or closed. When you fill a closed path, the entire interior of the path is affected. Figure 15-1 shows a closed path as it appears selected in the artwork mode and the same path filled in the preview mode. The shape acts like a malleable water balloon—the fill seeps into every nook and cranny of the outline.

Following that same logic, new users sometimes worry that a fill will leak out an open path and get all over the page. (Don't laugh—that's exactly what happens in a painting program.) But in Illustrator, the fill is held in check by an imaginary straight segment drawn between the two endpoints. Figure 15-2 shows an open path in the artwork and preview modes. I've added a thick stroke so you can see that the path is open. The straight segment without a stroke is the imaginary segment Illustrator adds to keep the fill from pouring out.

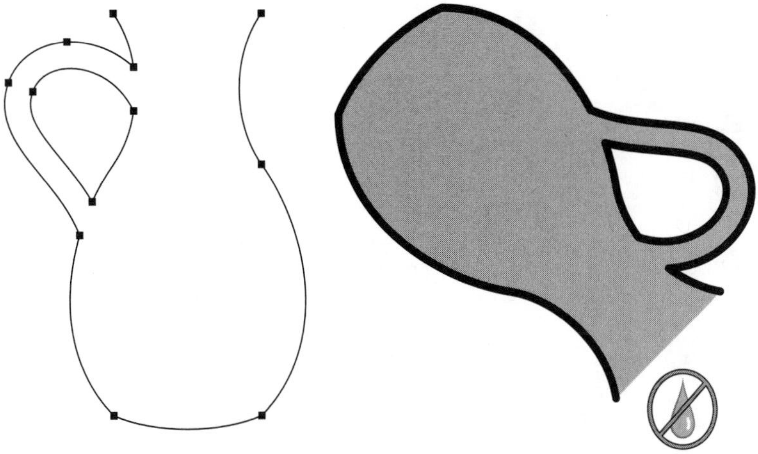

Figure 15-2: After drawing an open path (left), I filled it and tipped it upside down (right). And yet, by the miracle of the imaginary straight segment, not a drop of fill is spilled.

Filled open paths can be very useful for creating indefinite boundaries in a graphic. The paths with the thick outlines in Figure 15-3 demonstrate this technique. For example, because the forward wing is an open path, it is not stroked where it connects with the body of the rocket. And because the wing and body are filled with the same shade of gray, the fill of one path appears to flow into the fill of the other. The path around the body of the rocket is also an open path. It opens at the base, creating another indefinite boundary.

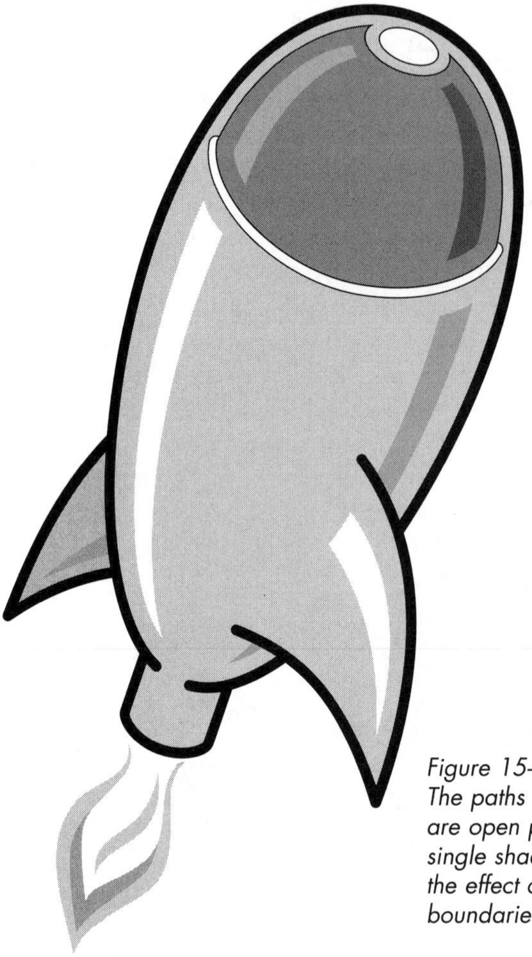

Figure 15-3:
The paths with thick strokes are open paths filled with a single shade of gray, creating the effect of indefinite boundaries.

Filling Type and Text Blocks

You can also fill text objects to change the colors of individual characters or to change the background color of a text block. If you select a text object with the arrow tool and apply a fill, the fill affects all the type in the text object and leaves the associated path unchanged.

For instance, the first example in Figure 15-4 shows a text block selected with the arrow tool. If you fill the object with a light gray, the type becomes filled, as shown in the second example in the figure. The result is gray type against a white background.

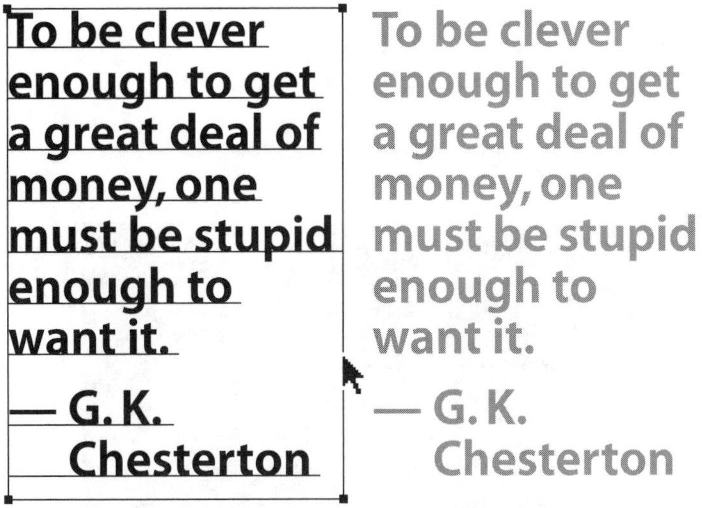
To be clever enough to get a great deal of money, one must be stupid enough to want it.
— G. K. Chesterton
To be clever enough to get a great deal of money, one must be stupid enough to want it.
— G. K. Chesterton

Figure 15-4: If you apply a fill color to a text block selected with the arrow tool (left), Illustrator fills the text (right).

But if you select the path around the text block with the direct selection tool and apply a fill, Illustrator fills just the path. The characters inside the text block remain filled as before, as demonstrated in Figure 15-5.

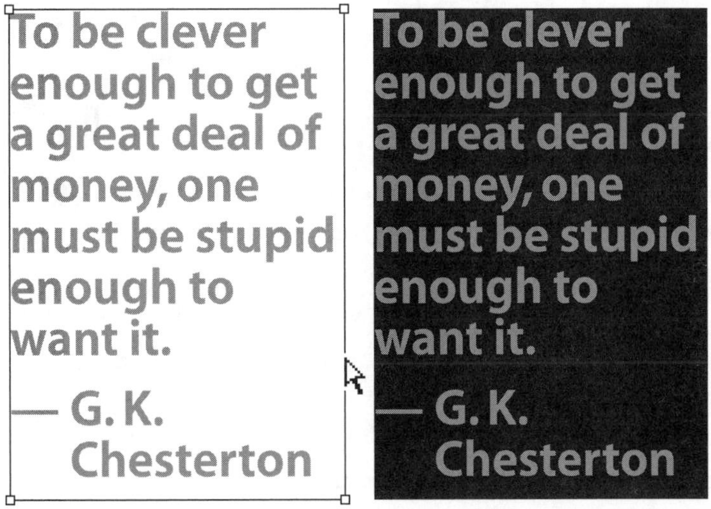
To be clever enough to get a great deal of money, one must be stupid enough to want it.
— G. K. Chesterton
To be clever enough to get a great deal of money, one must be stupid enough to want it.
— G. K. Chesterton

Figure 15-5: If you select the path of a text object with the direct selection tool (left) and then apply a fill, Illustrator fills the path only (right).

To fill single characters and words, you have to select the text with the type tool. Like any character-level formatting attribute, such as font or type size, fill affects only the highlighted characters, as demonstrated in Figure 15-6. In this way, Illustrator allows you to apply several different fills to a single text object.

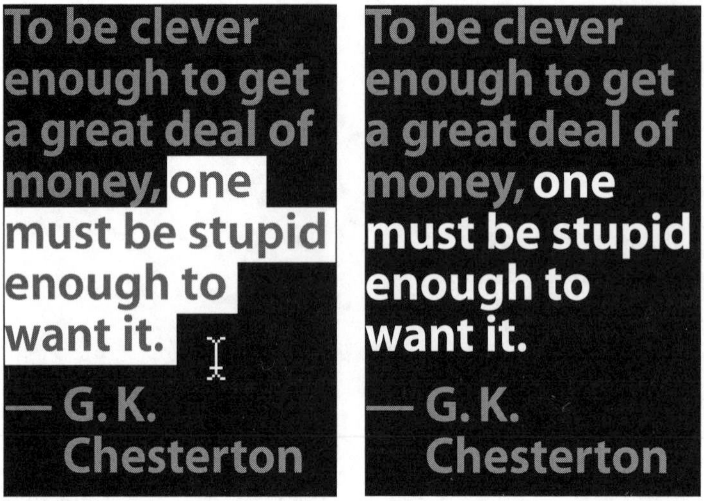
To be clever enough to get a great deal of money, one must be stupid enough to want it.
— G. K. Chesterton
To be clever enough to get a great deal of money, one must be stupid enough to want it.
— G. K. Chesterton

Figure 15-6: By selecting text with the type tool (left), you fill only the highlighted characters (right).

General Method for Applying a Fill

Whether you're filling paths or text blocks, follow these steps:

1. **Select the path or characters that you want to fill.**

   You can use the arrow, direct selection, or type tool. In fact, you can be in the middle of drawing a path with the pen tool and still fill a path. As long as you can see selection handles or highlighted text in the illustration window, you can apply a fill.

   If no object is selected, modifying the fill changes the default settings.

2. **Click on the Fill icon in the toolbox.**

   Or, if the Stroke icon is active—overlapping the Fill icon—press X. The X key toggles between the two icons.

3. Display the Color, Swatches, or Gradient palette.

That is, if it's not already displayed. Press F6 for the Color palette, F5 for the Swatches palette, or F9 for the Gradient palette.

4. Select a fill from the appropriate palette.

Or you can press the comma key (,) for the last used solid color or pattern or press the period key (.) for the last used gradient. Press the slash key (/) to be done with all this filling and have a transparent object. You can also click on the corresponding buttons in the lower portion of the toolbox, shown in Figure 15-7.

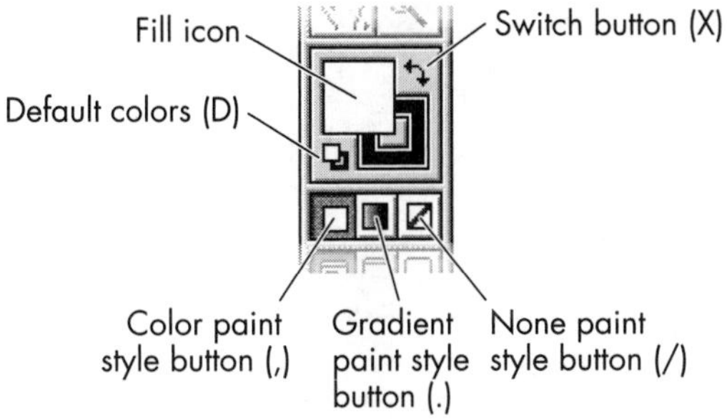

Figure 15-7: The fill related controls in the toolbox.

5. Edit the fill in the Color palette as desired.

For example, you can adjust the slider bars to change a process color. Or you can select a color from a gradient and change it.

Gradients in the Key of Life

Figure 15-8 demonstrates the power of gradations. I drew these relatively simple structured paths to represent RCA cables for the book *Mac Multimedia & CD-ROMs for Dummies* (IDG Books Worldwide). The left pair of cables shows the paths filled with flat gray values; the right pair is filled with gradations. As you can see, the gradations make all the difference in the world, single-handedly transforming the paths from cardboard cutouts into credible representations of three-dimensional objects.

Flat fills such as gray values, process colors, and named colors—all covered in the previous chapter—are very well and good. But if you're serious about imitating real life or giving your illustration a sense of depth, you'll appreciate

Illustrator's unparalleled gradations. A gradation (or gradient fill) is a fill pattern that fades from one color into another. Illustrator lets you assign lots of colors to a single gradation—the number of colors that you can use is limited only by the amount of RAM you have in your machine, but you can have at least 32 colors. You can even fade between spot colors.

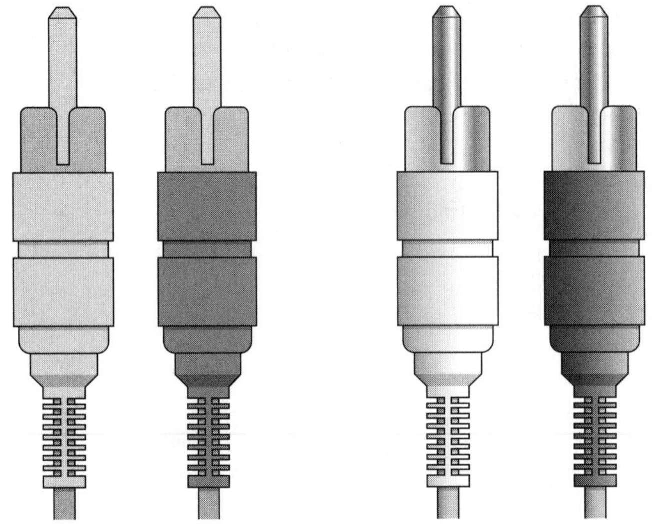

Figure 15-8: The only difference between the objects on left and their counterparts on right is that the latter objects are filled with gradations, which lends them the air of three-dimensionality.

You can create one of two types of gradient fills:

- A linear gradation is one in which the color transition follows a straight line. All of the gradations in Figure 15-8 are linear, flowing horizontally from left to right.
- A radial gradation starts with a pinpoint of color and fades outward in concentric circles.

Figure 15-9 shows examples of linear and radial gradations. A linear gradation can flow in any angle, so long as it flows in a straight line. And a radial gradation can begin at any location inside a shape as long as it flows outward in a circular pattern.

If you want to create a gradation that doesn't quite fall into either of these camps—such as the wavy-line pattern at the bottom of Figure 15-9—you can create a custom blend using the aptly named blend tool and then mask the blend inside a shape. Chapter 17 discusses blends, masks, and other extraordinary fill options.

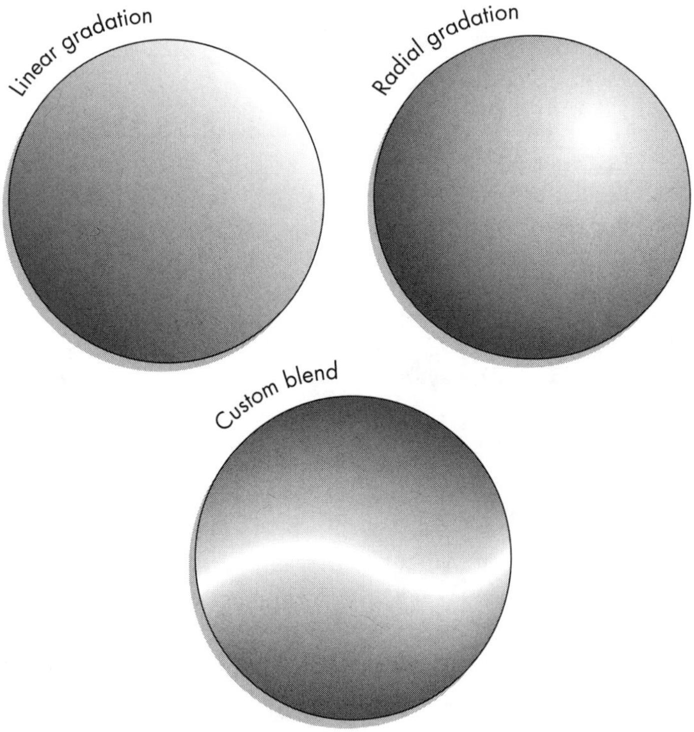

Figure 15-9: The two top fills are varieties of Illustrator automated gradations. To create the bottom fill, I used the blend tool.

Applying and Modifying Gradations

To apply a gradient fill to a selected path, select the fill box or the fade bar in the Gradient palette. (To apply a gradation to text, first choose Type » Create Outlines.) If you prefer, press the period key (.) to select the last used fill and display the Gradient palette. You can even click on one of the gradient swatches in the Swatches palette—the predefined gradients contained in the Adobe Illustrator Startup file (assuming you haven't added any gradations of your own).

The problem with Illustrator's predefined gradations is that you probably won't find much use for them (except as a starting point for a new gradation). It's not Adobe's fault; the predefined collection represents a healthy variety. It's just that gradations aren't particularly versatile creatures. A gradation created for one illustration is unlikely to be useful in another. Figure 15-8, for example, contains eight gradations, none of which come from Illustrator's default collection, and none of which I've used more than once.

So you'll spend a lot of time designing new gradations in Illustrator. The Gradient palette, shown in Figure 15-10, is an ideal place to create and edit gradient fills (especially since it's the only place to do this).

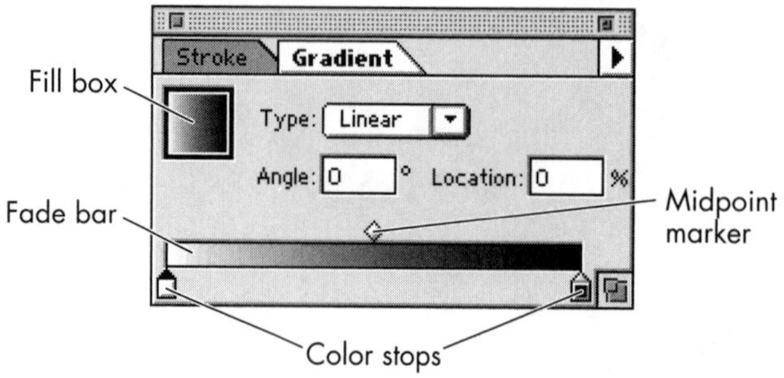

Figure 15-10: Add gradients to your world with the help of the Gradient palette.

The Gradient Fade Bar

Along the bottom of the Gradient palette is the fade bar. The starting color appears as a square color stop on the far left; the ending color is the square stop on the far right. The diamond in the middle, called the midpoint marker, represents the spot at which the two colors mix in exactly equal amounts. You can change the location of any stop or marker by dragging it. Or you can click on a stop or marker to select it and then enter a value into the Location percentage option box above and to the right of the fade bar. When a stop is selected, the little triangle on top of it changes from white to black. A selected marker appears in black.

- When numerically positioning a selected color stop, a value of 0 percent indicates the left end of the fade bar and 100 percent indicates the right end. Even if you add more color stops to the gradation, the values represent absolute positions along the fade bar.
- When repositioning a midpoint marker, the initial setting of 50 percent is smack dab between the two color stops; 0 percent is all the way over to the left stop, and 100 percent is all the way over to the right. Midpoint values are therefore measured relative to color stop positions. In fact, when you move a color stop, Illustrator moves the midpoint marker along with it to maintain the same relative positioning.

Figure 15-11 shows a gradation from light to dark gray subjected to various color stop and midpoint marker settings. As you can see, moving the color stops compresses the area in which the colors fade. In the second example in the figure, for example, the colors fade exclusively between the 30 percent and 90 percent stops. The areas to the left of the 30 percent stop and right of the 90 percent stop are filled with flat colors.

Meanwhile, moving the midpoint marker changes the rate at which colors fade. In the third example in Figure 15-11, the colors fade very quickly between the 0 percent color stop and the 25 percent marker, but they fade more slowly on their way to the 100 percent stop. The opposite is true in the fourth example: the colors fade slowly at first and then speed up at the end. The last example in the figure shows the result of moving both the color stops and the midpoint marker.

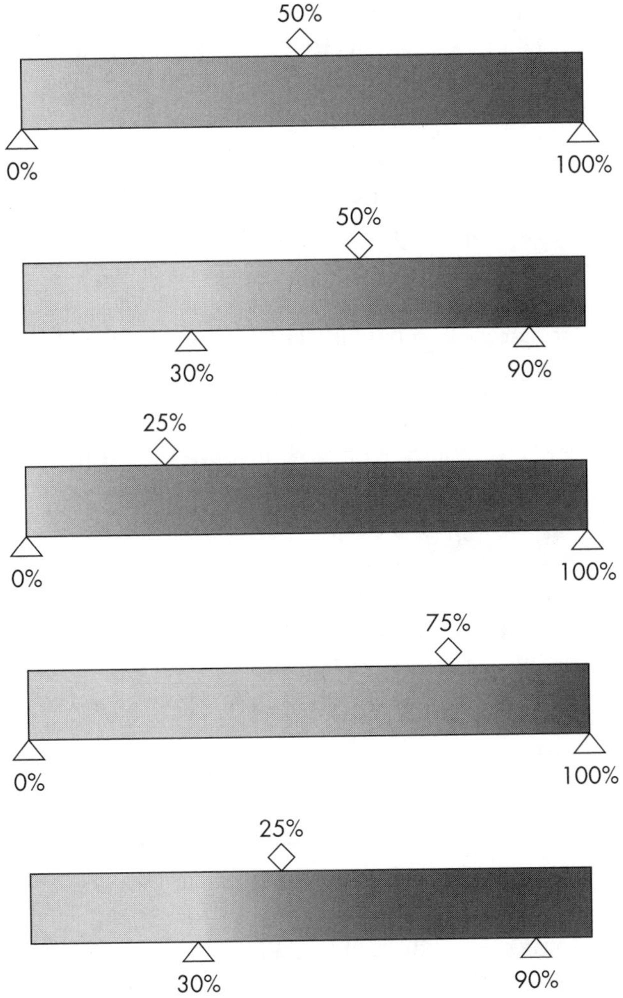

Figure 15-11: The results of applying different color stop and midpoint marker values to a single gradation.

Adjusting the Colors in a Gradation

You can change the colors in a gradation by selecting a color stop in the Gradient palette and by editing the color options in the Color palette (as discussed in Chapter 14). When a color stop is selected, the fill box in the Color palette displays a color stop right below it. This signifies that the color that you're modifying is part of a gradient. If you accidentally click on the color box (in the Color palette) while trying to edit a gradient color, the color stop icon will disappear and you will change the fill of the selected objects to a solid color. Press ⌘-Z to undo and return the gradations.

You can also drag a color swatch from the Swatches palette onto a color stop in the Gradient palette to change the color of the color stop. If you prefer not to drag, Option-click on the color swatch of you choice. Remember, if you simply click on a swatch, you will change the fill of the selected items to a solid color. You can, of course, remedy any such misclick by pressing ⌘-Z.

TIP: Have you ever wished you could lift a color from an object in the illustration window while working in the Gradient palette? As it turns out, you can. First, select the color stop you want to modify. Then select the eyedropper tool and Shift-click on an object with a flat fill. Illustrator applies the fill color to the selected color stop.

As I mentioned in the previous chapter, Illustrator is one of the few applications that lets you blend between spot colors without converting them to their process color ingredients. This can be a real advantage when creating two- and three-color documents. To create a gradation between two spot colors, drag the spot color swatches onto the color stops. Then, after applying the gradation to a few shapes, print the illustration to spot-color separations (as detailed in the "Process Color or Spot?" section of Chapter 14). Illustrator will print a black-to-white gradation on one separation and a white-to-black gradation on the other, so that the two spot colors fade into each other in the final color reproduction.

Adding, Deleting, and Swapping Color Stops

Congratulations, you are now four bullet points away from knowing everything there is to know about color stops:

- Two color stops make for a two-color gradation. But you can have tons of colors (as many as your RAM permits) per gradient fill. To add a color stop, click anywhere along the bottom of the fade bar. A new color stop appears right where you click. Illustrator also adds a midpoint marker between the new color stop and its neighbor. You can move the color stop, assign a different color to it, or reposition the midpoint marker, just as before.

- You can also add a color stop by dragging a color swatch from the Swatches palette to anywhere along the fade bar in the Gradient palette. Illustrator will force this new color into the gradation and add another marker.
- To remove a color stop, drag the triangle down into the lower portion of the Gradient palette. The triangle vanishes and the fade bar automatically adjusts as defined by the remaining color stops.

TIP: To switch the colors of any two color stops, Option-drag one color stop onto the other. Illustrator swaps the colors and automatically updates the gradation. Illustrator automatically shifts the position of the midpoint marker to compensate for the reversed color stops.

Other Gradient Options

The fade bar is easily the most important part of the Gradient palette. But I would be remiss if I didn't also mention the following options:

- If you want to work from an existing gradation, select it from the swatch in the Swatches palette. When the list is active (with a heavy border around it), you can select a gradation by typing in the first few letters in its name.
- To create a new gradation based on a selected one, click on the Duplicate Swatch command in the Swatches palette's pop-up menu. Illustrator creates a clone of the gradation. You can now edit it as usual.
- To create a new gradient swatch, drag the gradient that appears in the fill icon in the Gradient palette onto the Swatches palette or click on the New Swatch button in the Swatches palette. To display the Swatches Options dialog box (in which you can name the gradient swatch), Option-click on the New button or choose the New Swatch command in the Swatches palette.
- To change the name of a gradient, double-click on its swatch or choose the Swatch Options command in the Swatches palette. When the Swatches Option dialog box displays, enter a new name.

- Click on the Delete button to delete a gradation from all open illustrations. Illustrator warns you that this action cannot be undone. (As with color swatches, clicking the Delete button does not affect illustrations that you open in the future. If you delete Green & Blue from one illustration, and then open an illustration that uses Green & Blue, Green & Blue is back in business.) Option-click to delete the swatch and bypass the warning.
- In the Gradient palette is the Type pop-up menu—containing Linear and Radial commands—that lets you specify whether you want to create a linear or radial gradation. If this doesn't ring a bell, refer back to Figure 15-9.
- When creating a radial gradation, the left color stop represents the center color in the fill; the right color stop represents the outside color. If you want the gradation to produce a highlighting effect, as in the left example in Figure 15-12, make the first color lighter than the last one. If you make the first color darker than the last, the edges of the shape are highlighted, as in the right example in the figure.

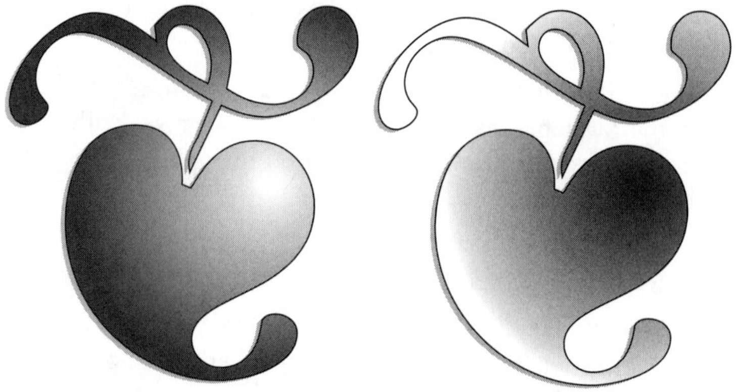

Figure 15-12: Two radial gradations, one in which the first color is white and the last color is dark gray (left) and the other in which the colors are reversed (right).

- If you create a gradient that you think should win the Nobel Prize for really super pretty color thing, preserve it for all time. Open the Adobe Illustrator Startup file (found in the Plug-ins folder) and draw a square. Fill it with your precious gradient and hit Save. Next time you boot-up Illustrator, that gradient will be at your disposal.

Finally, you can choose the only command offered in the Gradient palette's pop-up menu. Choose Hide Options to contract the Gradient palette so that just the fade bar is visible. Click again to expand the palette. It's difficult to edit gradations when the palette is collapsed, but you can store the collapsed palette when it's not in use.

Adjusting a Gradient Fill to Fit Its Path

When you first assign a linear gradation to a path, Illustrator orients the gradation horizontally so it fades from left to right. When you assign a radial gradation, the gradation starts in the center of the shape. Because neither of these two settings is very interesting, Illustrator lets you change the angle of a linear gradation and reposition colors inside any gradation.

Changing the Angle Value

One way to change the angle of a linear gradation is to enter a value into the Angle option box in the Gradient palette. This is useful if you want to match the angle of an object ascertained with the measure tool.

For example, in the top example of Figure 15-13, I've assigned the predefined Steel Bar gradation to a star. To make the angle of the fill match the angle of the shape, I first drag with the measure tool from the base of the star to its tip, as the arrow in the figure shows. The Info palette informs me that the angle is 112.792 degrees. (Oh sure, I could tell it was 112 degrees just by looking at it, but I wasn't sure about that 0.792.)

The bottom example in Figure 15-13 shows the result of entering a new Angle value of 112.792 and pressing Return. (Illustrator rounds off the value to 112.79 because the Angle value is accurate only to 0.01 degree.) The angle of the gradation now matches the angle of the star precisely.

The Angle value is also useful for matching the angles of multiple gradations to one another. Select the object that contains the properly angled gradation and note the Angle value in the Gradient palette. Then select the objects that you want to match and replace their Angle values with the new one.

Keep an eye on the Angle value, however. Each time you change it, it becomes the default setting for the next object. Even if you select a different gradation, the Angle value remains intact until you manually enter a new value or select an object filled with a different gradation.

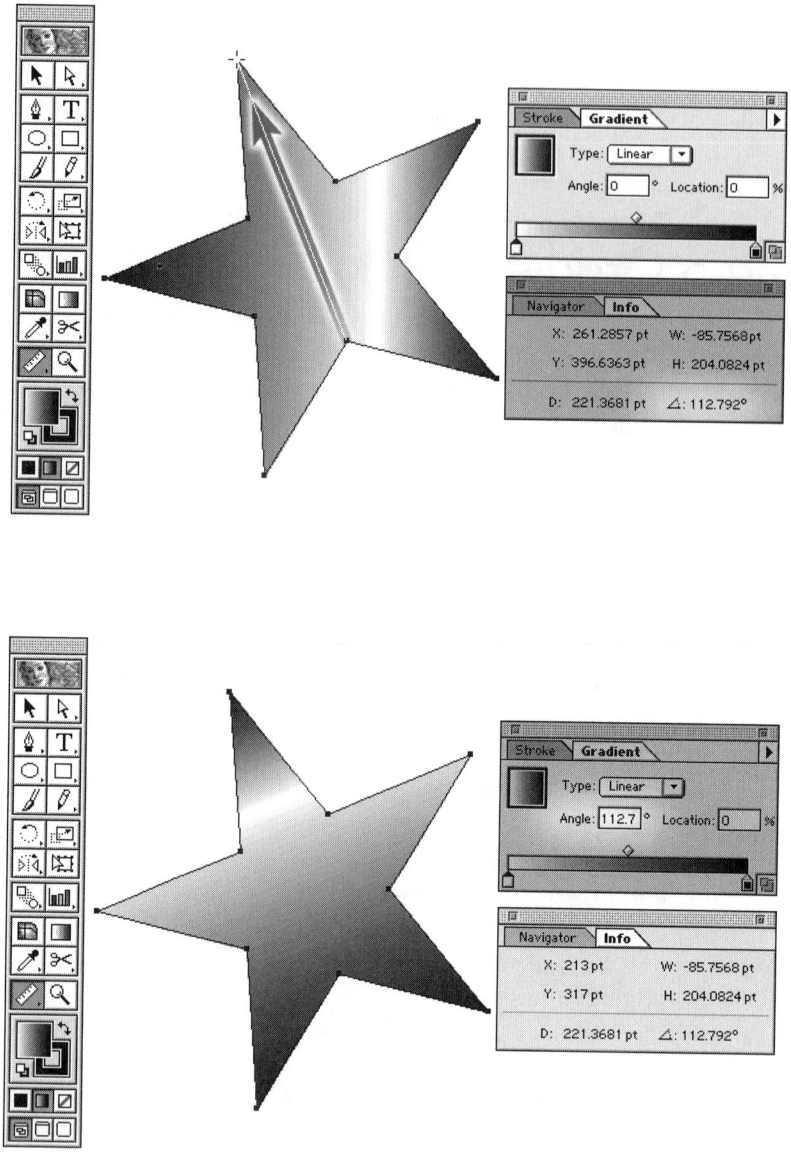

Figure 15-13: After measuring the angle of a shape filled with a gradation (top), I entered the measured value into the Angle option box in the Gradient palette (bottom).

Using the Gradient Tool

For those times when you want to reposition colors in a gradation, Illustrator offers the gradient tool. You can also use the tool to change the angle of a gradation, which is frequently more convenient than entering a numerical Angle value.

Adjusting a Linear Gradation

If a selected object is filled with a linear gradation, you can drag across the object with the gradient tool to change the angle of the gradation. The first color appears at the point where you start your drag and the last color appears where you release the mouse button. The angle of the gradation matches the angle of the drag, as demonstrated in Figure 15-14.

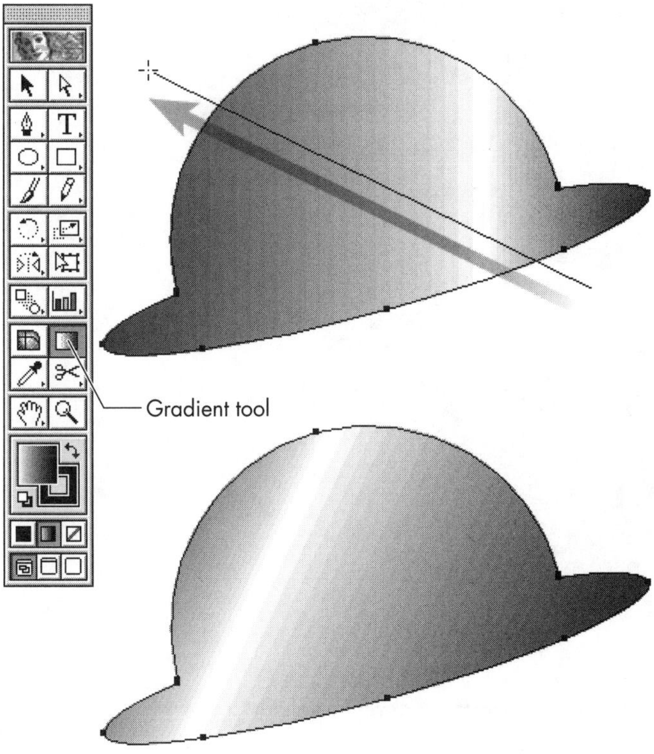

Figure 15-14: Drag with the gradient tool (top) to change the angle of the gradation inside a selected object (bottom).

Figure 15-15 shows a single light-to-dark gray gradation set to different angles with the gradient tool. The white lines show the direction of the drag for each shape. The black dots show where I started dragging, and the white dots show where I stopped.

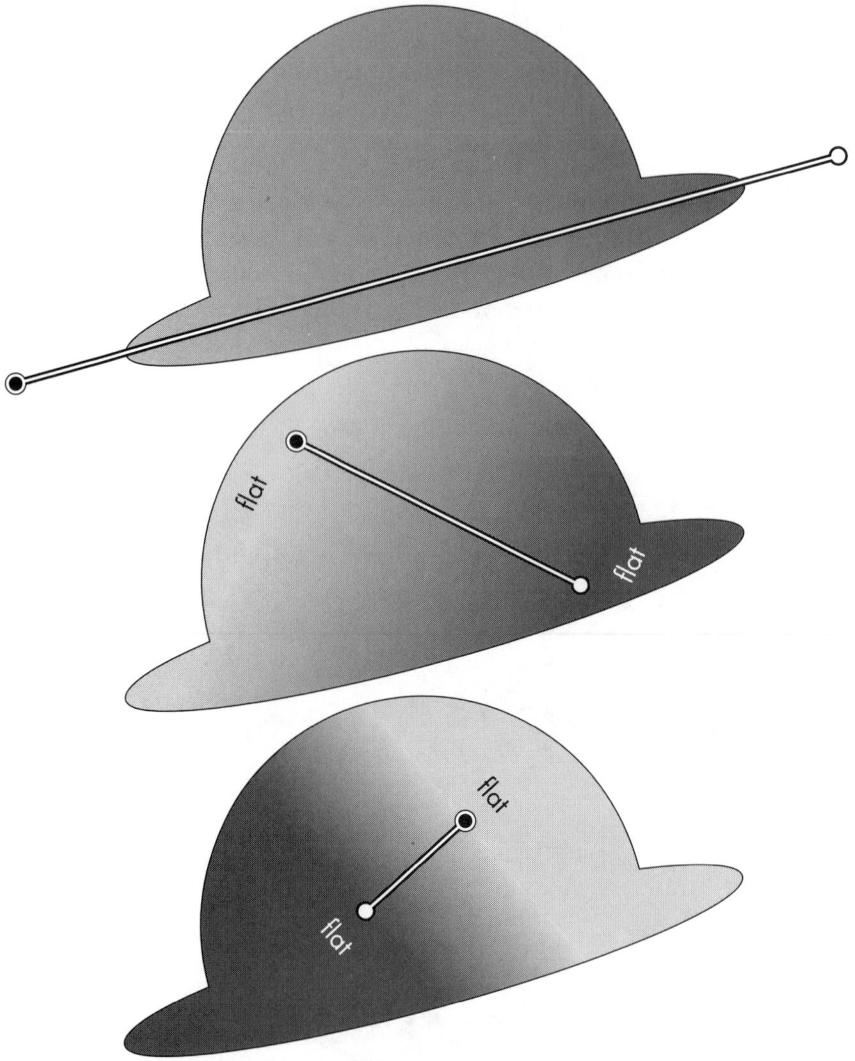

Figure 15-15: Three examples of the effect of the gradient tool on a gradation. The black dots show where I started dragging; the white dots show where I released the mouse.

- In the first example, the start and stop points lie well outside the shape, so the first and last colors fall outside the shape as well. This draws out the gradation and attenuates the range. Though the gradation runs from 15 to 70 percent black, you can only see 25 to 60 percent black inside the shape.

- The start and stop points fall inside the second shape. Now you can see the full range of the gradation. But when a gradation doesn't fully traverse a path, you get areas of flat color, as labeled in the figure.
- Too much flat color can interrupt the rhythm of the gradation. In the last example, I dragged across a very short distance with the gradient tool. The resulting gradient fill flies by quickly, leaving large areas of flat color inside the shape.

It's especially unwise to leave flat areas of white inside a gradient fill. The transition from printed ink to no ink is harsh enough without accentuating the problem by magnifying the size of the no-ink area. To give you a sense of what I'm talking about, check out Figure 15-16, which shows examples of four black-to-white gradations, each ending earlier inside its shape. Without much effort, most folks can see a sharp cutoff point where the last shade of gray gives way to white. The funny thing is, the transition frequently appears more abrupt when the illustration is output from a high-resolution imagesetter than when it's output from a laser printer. If in doubt, I suggest you run your own tests.

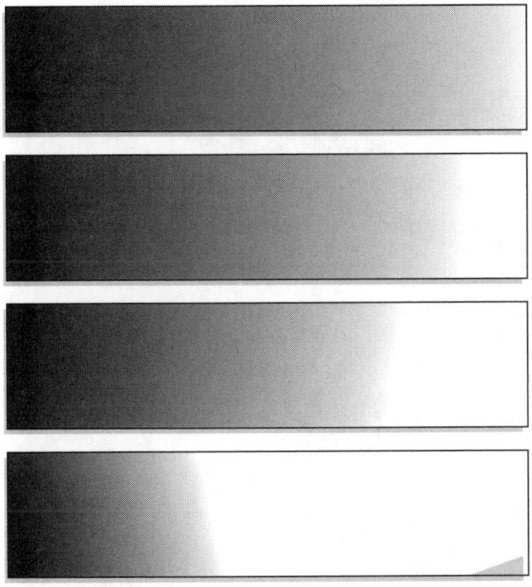

Figure 15-16: Leaving large flat areas of white can ruin the effect of a gradation and result in a crisp boundary between ink and no ink.

TIP

To avoid this effect, substitute 5-percent black (or some other very light shade) in place of white in your linear gradations. This way, you always have a little ink coverage in the gradation, no matter how slight. (This assumes you're using a properly calibrated printer, of course. If the printer is a little off, 5-percent black can turn white. Again, print a few tests to be sure.)

Modifying a Radial Gradation

Using the gradient tool on an object filled with a radial gradation changes the balance of the gradation and repositions its center. If you drag across a selected radial gradation, Illustrator repositions the first color to the point at which you start dragging. It extends the outer ring to the point at which you release.

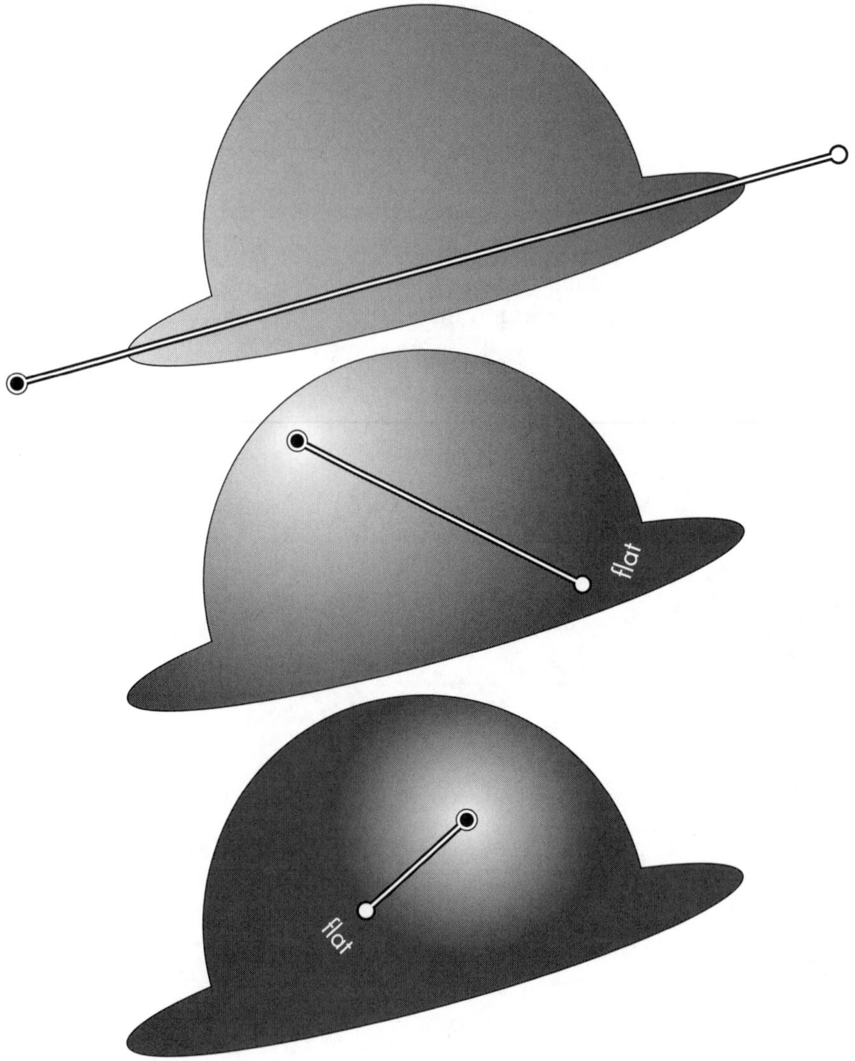

Figure 15-17: Here I converted the fill from Figure 15-15 to a radial gradation. The black and white dots show where I started and stopped dragging with the gradient tool.

In Figure 15-17, I took the linear gradation from Figure 15-15 and selected the Radial option to convert it into a radial gradation. I also changed the first color to white. As before, the black dot shows where I started dragging and the white dot shows where I stopped.

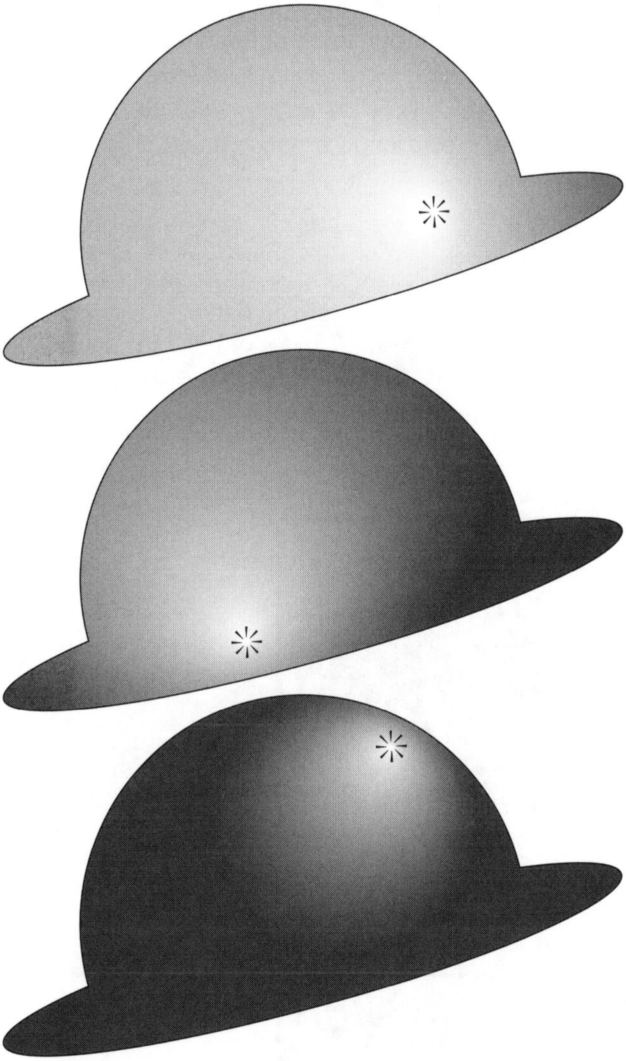

Figure 15-18: I clicked at each of the sparkles to offset the first color in the radial gradation independent of the last color.

In a radial gradation, the first color is never flat, no matter where you start dragging in an object (which is why white doesn't tend to create problems for radial gradations the way it does for linear ones). But the last color can go flat, because Illustrator fills the area beyond the drag with the last color (as indicated by the word flat in the figure).

TIP: If you click in a radial gradation with the gradient tool, Illustrator repositions the first color in the gradation independently of the outer ring formed by the last color. Figure 15-18 shows the result of clicking inside each of the shapes from Figure 15-17. In each case, Illustrator moved the first color, white, to the point at which I clicked (as indicated by a sparkle) and offset the gradation to produce a sort of spotlight effect.

Dragging through Multiple Paths

The gradient tool also allows you to apply a single gradation across multiple selected objects. In this way, all objects appear lit by a single light source. To accomplish this effect, select several objects, fill them with a gradation, and drag across them with the gradient tool. Illustrator creates one continuous gradation across all the selected shapes.

Figure 15-19: After applying a five-color gradient fill to a few converted letters (top), I dragged over the letters with the gradient tool (bottom).

Figure 15-19 shows two lines of text converted to path outlines. In the first line, I selected the characters and filled them with a five-color gradient. Illustrator filled each letter independently. In the second line, I dragged across the selected characters with the gradient tool, resulting in one continuous, angled gradation.

TIP The background rectangle in Figure 15-19 is filled with a slightly lighter duplicate of the five-color gradation set to the same angle as the bottom line of text. Truth be told, both the rectangle and the bottom characters were selected when I dragged with the gradient tool. This shows that you can angle and position multiple gradient fills at the same time, so that the fills lighten and darken at precisely the same points.

More Gradient Vector Trivia

Finally, just for the record, here are a few more tidbits of gradient tool information you might want to sock away inside that incredibly full brain of yours:

- Like so many other tools in Illustrator, you can Shift-drag with the gradient tool to create a gradation that flows horizontally, vertically, or at a 45-degree angle.
- You can modify the angle of a Shift-drag by rotating the constraint axes. For example, back in Figure 15-13, I set the angle of a gradation to 112.79 degrees using the Angle value. But had I wanted to reposition the first and last colors as well as rotate the gradation, I could have entered 112.79 into the Constrain Angle option box in the General Preferences dialog box and then Shift-dragged with the gradient tool. (If you do this, you need to remember to set the Constrain Angle value back to 0 when you're done.)
- Assuming the View » Snap to Point command is in effect (that is, a checkmark appears next to it in the View menu), the gradient tool snaps to points and guides in the illustration window.

Slanting Gradations

So far I've showed you three ways to transform gradations. You can change the angle of a linear gradation, which is the same as rotating the gradation inside its shape. You can move the first and last colors around, which is the same as scaling the gradation. (As I explained in Chapter 11, relative movement is what scaling is all about.) And if you reverse the first and last colors in a gradation, you flip the fill. That leaves just one transformation unexplored—slanting.

Because the rows of color in a linear gradation stretch off into infinity, you can effectively slant a linear gradation by dragging with the gradient tool. (Try dragging slightly against the direction of the path and you'll see the rows of color slant. Skip ahead to Figure 15-22 to see an example of this technique.) To slant a radial gradation, however, you have to use the shear tool, as explained below.

As it turns out, every one of the transformation tools transforms the gradient fill inside a path as well as the path. Therefore, to slant a radial gradation, you can select the path with the arrow tool and then use the shear tool to slant it. For example, Figure 15-20 begins with a rectangle filled with a radial gradation. After selecting the rectangle, I double-clicked on the shear tool icon in the toolbox to display the Shear dialog box. Then I entered a value of 60 degrees with Horizontal selected from the Axis options. The result is the second example in the figure. As you can see, Illustrator has slanted both the object and the circular rings inside the gradient fill.

Now at this point, I had two options. I could restore the rectangle to its original orientation and leave the gradation slanted. Or I could apply the slanted gradation to a different sets of paths.

To restore the rectangle, I could select all of the segments in the shape—without selecting any of the points—by clicking and Shift-clicking on each segment with the direct selection tool. Then I could double-click again on the shear tool icon and enter an opposite slant value (–60 degrees in this case) to reverse the transformation. Because the path is only partially selected—all segments but no points—Illustrator slants the object but not the fill. Very cool.

The problem with this technique is that it works properly only if the selected object is made up entirely of straight segments. A single curved segment ruins the effect. Also, it involves an awful lot of clicking and Shift-clicking, which can prove rather monotonous after a while.

That's why I prefer to apply the slanted gradation to one or more different paths using the Intersect filter. In the third example of Figure 15-20, I selected the upper left and lower right corner points in the skewed rectangle and slanted them –70 degrees to widen the shape. Then I positioned three stars in front of the rectangle and combined the stars into a single compound path (⌘-8). I next sent the stars to back by pressing ⌘-Option-[(left bracket), Shift-clicked on the rectangle with the arrow tool to add it to the selection, and then chose Filter » Pathfinder » Intersect. Illustrator found the intersection of the compound stars and rectangle and applied the fill from the forward shape, which was the slanted gradation.

TIP

Some artists like to use Illustrator's masking function (discussed in Chapter 17) to fill an object with a slanted gradation. But masks can cause printing problems, especially when applied to gradations. And at the very least, they increase the print time. By contrast, the Intersect filter creates a clean, cookie-cutter effect that takes no more time to print than the original slanted object.

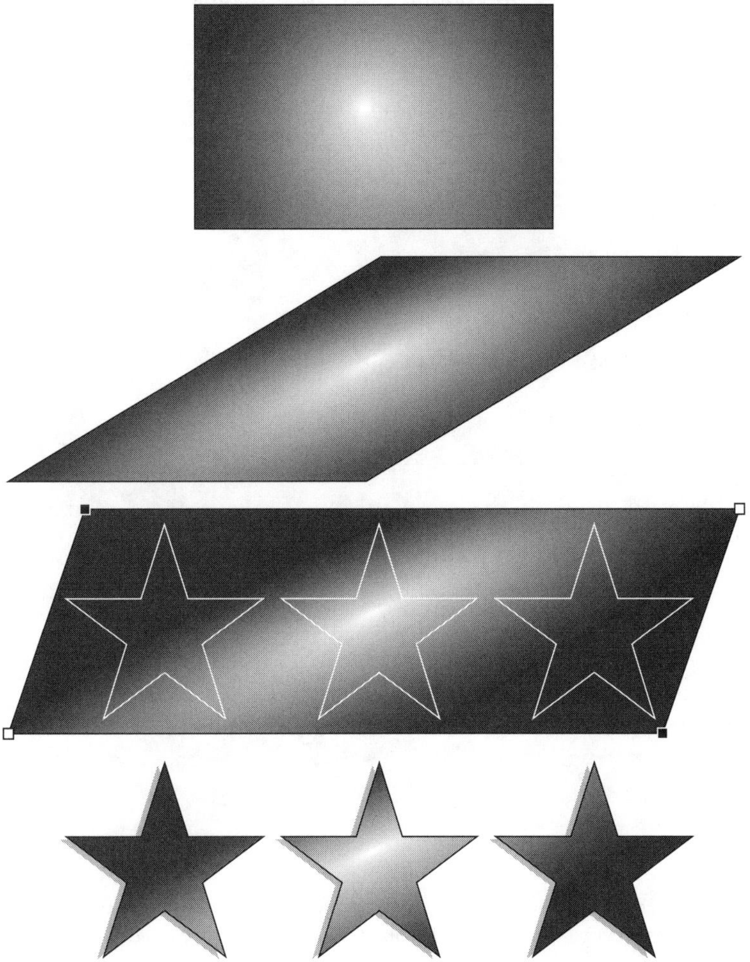

Figure 15-20: After filling a rectangle with a gradation (top), I slanted the shape (second), selected two points and slanted them in the opposite direction (third), and intersected the rectangle with some compound stars (bottom).

If you know exactly how far you want to slant a gradation, you can engage in a little preemptory slanting. Before applying the gradation, slant the object in the opposite direction of how you'd like to slant the gradient fill. Then apply the gradient fill and slant the object back to its normal orientation. In Figure 15-21, for example, I started with the gray spade (a converted Zapf Dingbats character). Then I double-clicked on the shear tool and entered –60 degrees with a horizontal axis. After applying the radial gradation, I again double-clicked on the shear tool and entered 60 degrees. The result is an upright shape with a slanted fill.

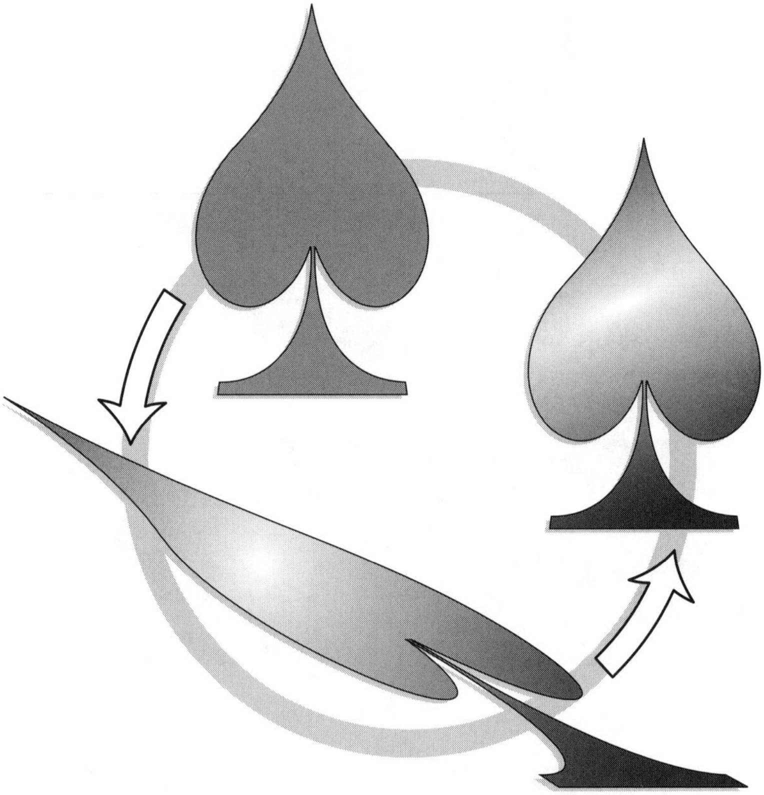

Figure 15-21: Another way to slant a gradation is to slant the shape in the opposite direction, apply the gradation, and then reverse the slant.

Resetting a Gradation

After transforming a gradation—whether with the transformation tool or the gradient tool—you may find that you've modified a fill too much and you're better off restoring the default orientation. Thought there are several way to accomplish this, the easiest method is to press the comma key (,) and then the period key (.). This changes the fill to the last used color or pattern and then back to the original form of the gradation. If the gradation remains rotated, enter 0 into the Angle option box in the Gradient palette and press Return.

Creating Gradient Shadows

Gradations lend themselves naturally to shadows. When you shine a light source on an object in real life, the shadow fades away from the object. This is a function of ambient light, which reflects around the object to progressively lighten the shadow.

Figure 15-22 shows what I mean. Created entirely in Illustrator—using the four old-school transformation tools and the brand spanking new free transform tool (on the 8)—this illustration exploits gradations to produce a photo-realist effect. I filled the 8 ball with a black-to-white radial gradation. I set the midpoint marker for the gradation to 87 percent to exaggerate the black and leave just a slim lining of white. The hint of horizon is a slanted rectangle filled with a very short light gray-to-white linear gradation. The shadow is also filled with a linear gradation. To get the skewed fill effect, I dragged almost straight down with the gradient tool. (This is what I meant by dragging against the direction of the path back in the "Slanting Gradations" section.)

Gradient shadows require more work when they cross different colored shapes. Though the shadow shown in the first example of Figure 15-23 is filled with a gradation, it doesn't look even remotely plausible because it fails to take the background shapes and colors into account. But by defining some additional gradations and taking advantage of the Intersect filter, I'm able to arrive at the top-notch work of Zot art shown in the second example.

The following steps tell how to mix a gradient shadow with background objects that contain flat fills:

1. **Create a new gradation swatch for each background shape and add the colors from each object to the shadow.**

   The gradient shadow in the top example in Figure 15-23 ranges from 35 percent to 15 percent black. The darker of the two background shapes is filled with flat 40 percent black and the lighter contains 20 percent black. Therefore, I created two duplicates of the original gradation (using the Duplicate button in the Gradient palette). Then I colored one gradation with 75 percent to 55 percent black (that's 40 percent + 35 percent to 40 percent + 15 percent); and the other with 55 percent to 35 percent black (20 percent + 35 percent to 20 percent + 15 percent). As in any option box, you can let Illustrator do the math. So, you can enter the new numbers into the Swatch palette's Location percentage option box or you can just add +40 for the first gradation and +20 for the second.

Figure 15-22: Real-life shadows almost always fade slightly, just as this gradient shadow becomes lighter as it slants away from the eight ball.

It's even easier if the background shapes contain CMYK colors and the shadow is exclusively black. Then you just mix the CMYK values with the black; no adding is necessary. For example, suppose the darker of the two shapes in Figure 15-23 is filled with 100 percent cyan, and the other is filled with 100 percent yellow. The first of the two new gradations would range from 100 percent C, 35 percent K to 100 percent C, 15 percent K; the second would range from 100 percent Y, 35 percent K to 100 percent Y, 15 percent K.

2. **If the shadow is made up of many shapes, you need to combine them into a single compound path.**

   The shadow in Figure 15-23 comprises three converted characters, known the world around as *Z*, *O*, and *T*. Since the letters don't overlap, you won't be able to find the intersection of the letters with the background objects in Step 6. By selecting the letters and pressing ⌘-8, I instruct Illustrator to consider these shapes as a single compound path. Now I can apply the Intersect filter with impunity.

Figure 15-23: A gradient shadow laid over different colored background shapes looks nasty (top). But if you mix the shadow and background shapes, you can achieve a highly realistic effect (bottom).

3. **Send the shadow behind the background shapes.**

   Press ⌘-Option-[(left bracket). The first example in Figure 15-24 shows our progress so far. It doesn't look like much, but it's full of promise.

4. **Select the shadow and one of the background shapes.**

   Since the shadow is already selected, you can just Shift-click on the first shape with the arrow tool.

5. **Copy the selection and paste it in front.**

   That's ⌘-C, ⌘-F. This prevents you from harming your original paths.

6. **Click the Pathfinder's palette Intersect button.**

   Illustrator draws new paths around the regions where the shadow and background shape overlap.

7. **Fill the selected paths with the first gradation.**

   I filled my paths with the 75 percent to 55 percent black gradation, as in the second example in Figure 15-24.

8. **Repeat Steps 4 through 7 for each additional background shape.**

   I have only one more background shape, so I selected it and the original shadow, copied them and pasted them in front, applied the Intersect filter, and filled the resulting paths with the 55 percent to 35 percent gradation. The last example in Figure 15-24 shows what I got.

9. **Make sure the gradations flow in the same direction.**

   Select all the shadow shapes and drag across them with the gradient tool. This ensures that the shadows go in a consistent direction and the colors change at a consistent rate.

You may have noticed that the strokes in Figure 15-24 aren't quite where they ought to be. Because my background shapes had strokes, the Intersect filter assigned strokes to my new shadows as well. To arrive at the finished effect in Figure 15-23, I had to delete these strokes. Then I copied one of the background shapes, selected the corresponding shadow, pasted the shape in front, and made the fill transparent. This restored the stroke around the shape without interfering with the shadow. I then repeated the process on the remaining background shapes. (For complete information on this technique, read the "Stroke on Fill" section of Chapter 16.)

Figure 15-24:
After sending the original shadow to back (top), I found the intersection of the shadow with the first shape (middle) and then found the intersection of the shadow and the second shape (bottom).

Strictly speaking, it is possible to mix a gradient shadow with a gradient background object, but I think it's more trouble than it's worth. To do this, you have to convert both gradients to blends using Object » Expand Fill and then mix all the objects together using Filter » Pathfinder » Soft. Illustrator needs a ton of memory to pull this off—calculating tens of thousands of path intersections is nothing to sneeze at. And even if it works, you're left with a sufficient number of objects to clog the mightiest printer. Meanwhile, the simplified approach demonstrated in Figure 15-23 looks great and prints like a dream.

Gradient Mesh

Illustrator 8 gives you another method for creating gradients. You can convert an object into a *gradient mesh object*. A gradient mesh object is a strokeless path filled with a series of lines. The lines follow along the outline of the path. Wherever the lines cross, you have a node that you can assign a different color. Each node has four control handles that dictate the curve of the lines that leave the node from each of the four directions.

Creating a Gradient Mesh

Although you can create a gradient mesh object by manually adding the lines and nodes with the gradient mesh tool, it's easier to let Illustrator convert an object to a gradient mesh and then remove any node and line you don't want with the tool. To do so, follow these steps:

1. **Select a path.**

   Although the path you select can be open or closed, Illustrator will automatically close an open path when it applies the gradient mesh. The gradient mesh will work with any flat fill but will convert a gradient fill or a pattern to a black and white gradient mesh. It ignores any stroke and will not work until you remove any brush associated with the path.

2. **Choose the Object » Create Gradient Mesh command.**

   This displays the Create Gradient Mesh dialog box, as shown in Figure 15-25. As with all good dialog boxes, it has a Preview check box. Be sure to activate this option so that you can see how the gradient mesh looks in your path.

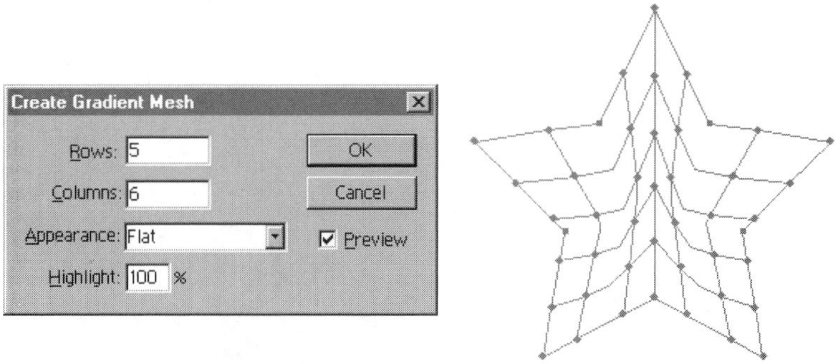

Figure 15-25: In this dialog box, you decide the number of lines Illustrator adds to a path when it creates the gradient mesh.

3. **Choose the number of rows and columns you want in your gradient mesh.**

   Enter an integer value in both the Rows and Columns option boxes. For the sake of simplicity, enter only as many as you need. In Figure 15-25, I gave my star five rows and six columns. This means that Illustrator added four row lines and five column lines resulting in five row divisions and six column divisions.

4. **Choose the appearance of the gradient.**

   In the Appearance pop-up menu, you have the option of a flat fill or one in which the fill color of the object fades to a tint of that same color.

5. **Adjust the tint value.**

   Enter a value into the Highlight option box. By default, this value is 100 percent. This means that if you selected either of the Fade To commands from the Appearance pop-up menu, the fade to color will be white. If you lower this value, the fade will be less dramatic. Lower the value to 0 percent and you won't see any difference.

Modifying Your Mesh

Once you created your gradient mesh, you'll need to adjust the color of each node. To do so, click with the direct selection tool on the node that you want to recolor. If you want to switch a number of the nodes to the same color, click and Shift-click on all the nodes you want to change. Then, simply make sure that the Fill icon is active in the Color palette and select the new color. As shown on the left of Figure 15-26, I selected a number of the nodes with the direct selection tool. This can be a bit confusing on first glance since all the nodes' numerous control handles also select. But for the sake of coloring, the handles aren't important. I then filled the nodes with black, resulting in a very unique gradation.

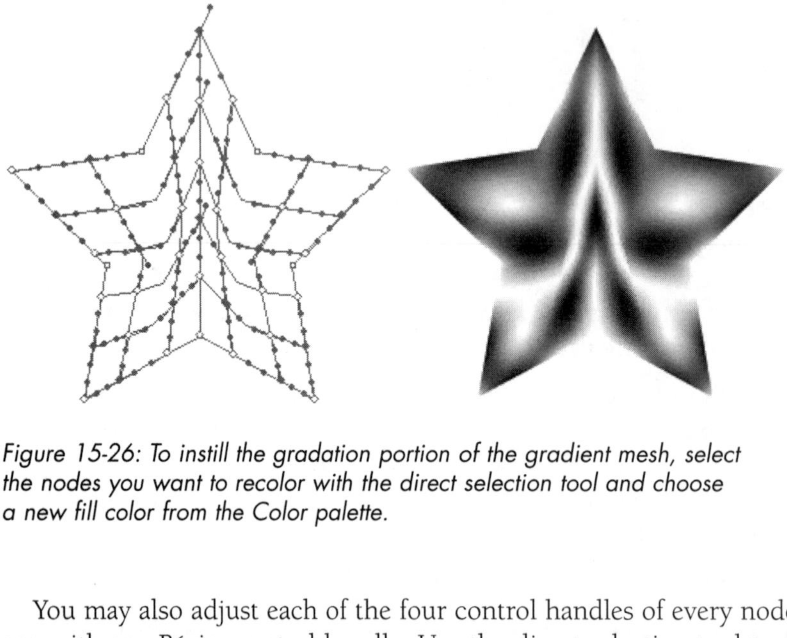

Figure 15-26: To instill the gradation portion of the gradient mesh, select the nodes you want to recolor with the direct selection tool and choose a new fill color from the Color palette.

You may also adjust each of the four control handles of every node just as you can with any Bézier control handle. Use the direct selection tool to adjust opposite control handles like levers or use the convert point tool to manipulate them independently. If you need to, flip back to Chapter 5 to brush up on all the point-conversion techniques.

Illustrator also provides a gradient mesh tool. Click with it to add individual nodes. If you click a regular path, you convert the path into a gradient mesh object with one node. Click on a gradient mesh object to add another node. To remove a gradient mesh node, Option-click on the node with the gradient mesh tool. To remove only one of the lines going into a node, Option-click with the gradient mesh tool on that line you want to remove.

Filling Objects with Tiles

In Illustrator, you can fill both paths and text objects with tile patterns, which are rectangular patterns that repeat over and over inside a shape. The patterns are just like the tiles on a kitchen floor, only you don't have to gets your hands all messy when applying the mortar. You can create your own tile patterns or select from the vast library included on the Illustrator CD-ROM.

WARNING

Tile patterns are perhaps the most difficult kind of object to print from Illustrator. In fact, you can pretty much guarantee that if you use more than three different tile patterns in a single illustration, it doesn't stand a snowball's chance in a microwave of printing. To prevent heartbreak and frustration, apply tile patterns to simple objects, and don't use more than two or three per illustration. Your nervous system thanks you.

Applying and Modifying Tile Patterns

Apply tile patterns from the Swatches palette by clicking on the pattern swatch of choice. As always, these represent patterns stored in the Adobe Illustrator Startup file.

But if Illustrator's default collection of gradations isn't particularly useful, the default patterns are even worse. These are some of the dullest patterns I've ever seen. Heck, I wouldn't allow these tiles in my guest bathroom.

NOTE

Incidentally, the pattern names with numbers and periods—like *DbLine1.2.outer* and *Laurel.inner*—aren't meant to be used as tile patterns. Though they show up in the tile pattern list, they're actually path patterns, which are specifically designed to follow the stroke of a path. I examine path patterns in Chapter 16.

Creating a New Tile Pattern

To create a tile pattern in Illustrator, you simply select a bunch of objects and choose Edit » Define Pattern. If you like, drag the selected items onto the Swatches palette, as shown in Figure 15-27. It's that easy. Illustrator automatically incorporates the objects into a rectangular tile. Really, that's it.

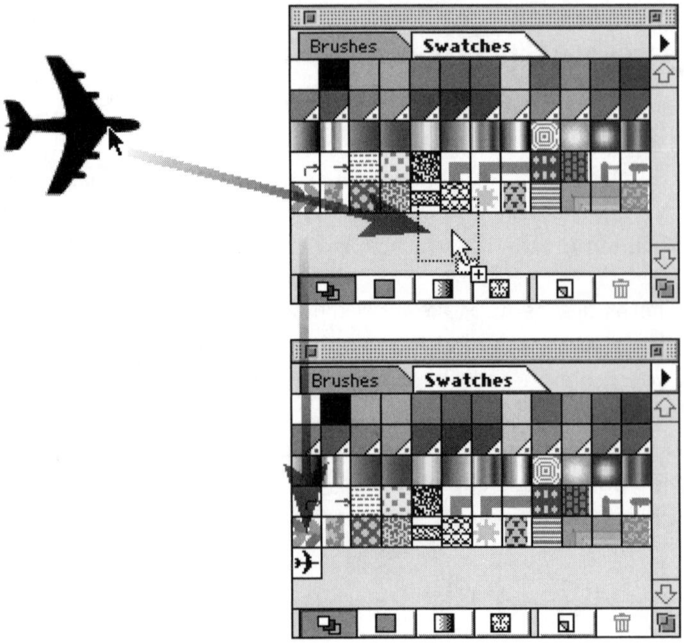

Figure 15-27: Drag the selected objects onto the Swatches palette (top) to create a new pattern swatch (bottom).

Ah, but if you want to create something that looks halfway decent, you have to do a little more work. As with many other operations in Illustrator, so many nuances are involved in creating a tile pattern that you can learn only by making one yourself. To this end, the following steps walk you through the task of designing a cool-looking tile pattern:

1. **Create a new illustration.**

   Even if you ultimately intend to apply the tile pattern to an existing object, it's a good idea to start off with a new document. You will have to drag-and-drop it between illustration windows, but this gives you more room to work.

2. **Assemble a few objects to create a basic design.**

   In the first example in Figure 15-28, I took an airplane character from the Zapf Dingbats font and converted it to path outlines. (If you have Zapf Dingbats—named for influential type designer Hermann Zapf—press Shift-9 to get the plane.) Then I rotated a clone of the plane 90 degrees and pressed ⌘-D twice to create two more rotated clones.

3. **Draw a rectangle around the design with the rectangle tool.**

   This rectangle represents a single tile in the tile pattern. The rectangle should cut slightly into the design, as it does in Figure 15-28. Objects that overlap one edge of the rectangle will repeat at the opposite edge. This helps to interrupt the rectangular rhythm of the pattern and create a more free-form appearance.

4. **Copy the rectangle, and then convert it to a guide.**

   Press ⌘-C, ⌘-5. If you've created a tile pattern before, this may sound like an odd step. But it permits you to align portions of the pattern to ensure invisible transitions from one tile to the next.

5. **Paste the rectangle in front, and then separate its edges.**

   Press ⌘-F, and then click on each of the four corners of the pasted rectangle with the scissors tool. You now have four straight segments that you can use to align objects to the tile.

6. **Select the top edge and all objects that overlap the top edge.**

   I selected both the top edge and the upward-pointing plane.

7. **Option-drag the selected edge downward until it snaps to the bottom of the rectangle.**

   By pressing the Option and Shift keys, you clone the object and constrain your drag to straight lines; and by dragging the edge instead of the object itself, you ensure a snug fit with the rectangular guide. The second example in Figure 15-28 shows me snapping a clone of the plane along the bottom edge. Just as the nose of the plane extends out of the tile past the top edge, it now extends into the tile from the bottom edge. This ensures that the plane will flow smoothly from one tile into the next.

8. **Next select the bottom edge and the objects that overlap that edge, and clone them onto the top edge.**

   In my case, I selected and cloned the downward-pointing plane.

9. **Repeat Step 8 for the objects that overlap the left and right edges as well.**

   After completing this step, I had a total of eight planes. The nose of each plane overlapped a side of the rectangle. And the same plane that overlapped one side also overlapped the opposite side. As a result, all of the planes will enter and exit the tiles in precise alignment.

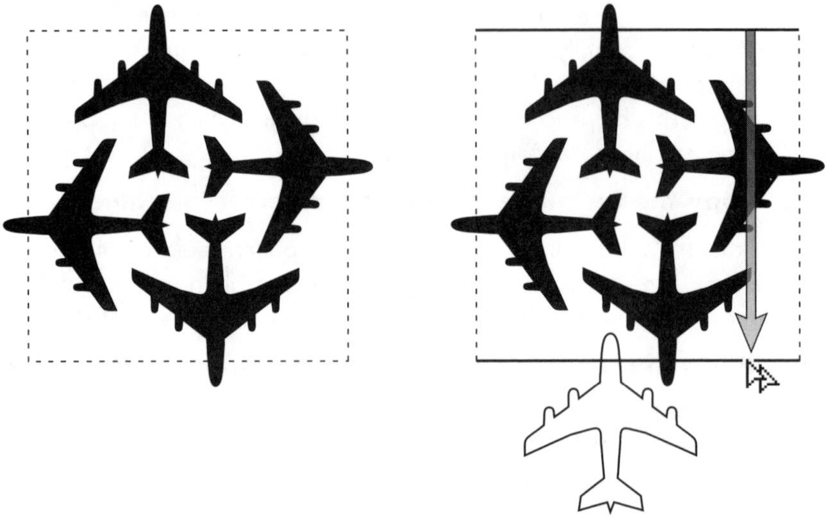

Figure 15-28: First, I created a design and drew a rectangular guide around it (left). Then I Option-Shift-dragged the plane that overlaps the top of the rectangle to clone it and snap it into position along the bottom of the rectangle (right).

10. Edit the objects as needed.

It's unlikely that you'll get your design exactly right on the first try. You may need to tweak it here and there. But pay careful attention to what you do. If you change the way one object overlaps an edge of the rectangle, you have to modify the matching object along the opposite edge in kind.

For my part, my plane pattern left gaps at each of the four corners of the tile. So I took another Zapf Dingbats character—the one that looks like a steering wheel (which you get by pressing the quote key)—and converted it to outlines. Then I selected the inner circle of the character with the direct selection tool and clicked the Show Center button in the Attributes palette. I next selected the entire character with the arrow tool and dragged it by the center point so it snapped into alignment with one of the corners of the rectangle. Finally, I Option-dragged the character a total of three times to snap it to the remaining corners. Figure 15-29 shows the objects in my completed design. As you can see, one quarter of each steering wheel lies inside the rectangle, so that a single wheel will appear each time four tiles meet.

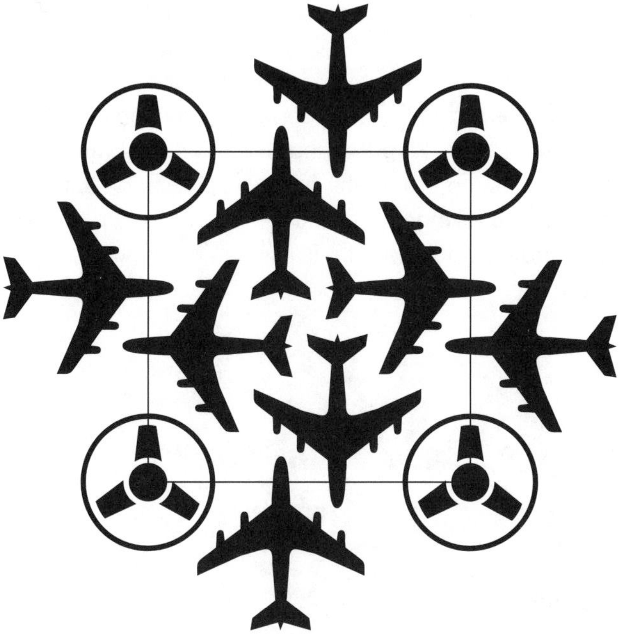

Figure 15-29: After cloning and snapping the planes into place, I added steering wheels to fill in the corners of the tile.

11. Select all the straight segments around the edges of the rectangle and delete them.

Their work is done.

12. Unlock the guide and convert it back into a normal object.

Assuming the guide is locked, press ⌘-Option-semicolon (;) to unlock it. Then select the guide and press ⌘-Option-5 to convert it to an object.

13. Fill and stroke the objects—including the background rectangle—as desired.

When filling objects, use flat colors only. The Edit » Define Pattern command cannot accommodate objects filled with gradations or tile patterns.

I used a popular embossing technique to create the effect shown in Figure 15-30. First, I selected and grouped all objects except the rectangle to make them easier to edit. Then I filled the rectangle with 30 percent black and the grouped objects with 25 percent, so that the rectangle and group were nearly identical in color. I also gave all the objects a transparent stroke—I clicked on the Stroke icon in the toolbox and then pressed slash (/). To create the shadow for the embossing effect, I selected the group, copied it, and pasted it in back. Then I nudged it down 1 point and to the left 1 point, and filled it with 55 percent black. To create the highlight, I selected the original group and pressed ⌘-B again. Then I nudged the copy up 1 point and to the right 1 point, and filled it with white. The result is what you see in Figure 15-30.

Figure 15-30: I cloned and filled the plane and wheel shapes to create this common embossing effect.

14. Select the rectangle and copy it.

It's now time to get rid of all the junk that's exceeding the boundaries of the rectangle. Illustrator wants a clean, rectangular edge, or it'll make one for you (and you don't want that).

15. Paste the rectangle in front of everything.

The easiest way to do this is to press ⌘-Shift-A to deselect everything, and then press ⌘-F to paste the rectangle at the front of the illustration.

If the rectangle is filled, it will cover up some stuff, but don't worry about it. The rectangle dies a fiery death in the next step.

16. Select everything and apply the Crop filter.

Press ⌘-A, and then choose Filter » Pathfinder » Crop. After a few moments of intense calculating, Illustrator crops away all portions of the selected objects that lie outside the frontmost rectangle. The rectangle also gets gobbled up, leaving behind a perfect tile.

17. Open the illustration that requires the tile.

You should probably save the current illustration first. Then open the tile's destination file and drag-and-drop the tile from the old window to the new window.

18. Choose Edit » Define Pattern.

Or drag the tile onto the Swatches palette. Since the Crop filter leaves the tile selected, you're ready to add it to your collection of pattern swatches, just like back in Figure 15-27.

19. Name the pattern.

Choose the Swatches Options command from the Swatches palette and name your pattern. I named my pattern "Drive that Plane Well, Sonny Chuck."

Well done! You have successfully completed a tile pattern that would make your dear mother's heart swell with unmitigated pride. You can now select an object inside your illustration and apply your new tile pattern from the Swatches palette.

Just to make more work for myself, I created a couple of variations on my Drive that Plane Well, Sonny Chuck tile pattern and applied the patterns to the shapes shown in Figure 15-31. The patterns are identical except in color. After creating the first pattern, I cloned the original objects and used Filter » Colors » Saturate to create lighter and darker variations. (I entered a value of 30 percent to darken one set of objects and –30 percent to lighten the other set.) Then I used the Edit » Define Patter command to save each of these variations as yet another pattern. In Figure 15-31, I filled the plane with the light pattern, the shadow with the dark pattern, and the background rectangle with the very first pattern. Notice how the objects in all three patterns align precisely, making for seamless transitions.

WARNING

Figure 15-31 is an example of an illustration that may be too complex to print. After creating the figure, I couldn't get it to print to my LaserWriter IINTX for the life of me. (Granted, the NTX is an aging machine equipped with Level 1 PostScript, but it's a reliable workhorse of a printer.) I converted the tile patterns to elaborate masks using Object » Expand Fill, but the page still wouldn't print. Ultimately, I broke up the masks (by choosing Object » Masks » Release) and used the Crop filter to carve the shapes into the expanded patterns. I had to assign a whopping 30MB of RAM to Illustrator to get the crop filter to work, and even then it took several minutes per shape. Total time lost: 2 hours.

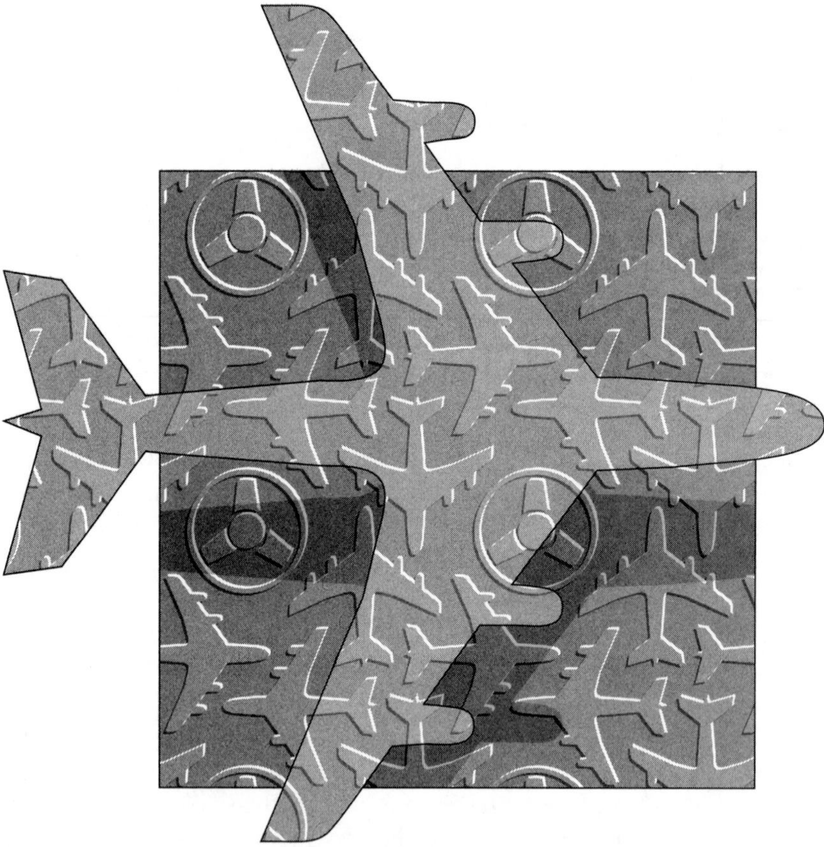

Figure 15-31: This illustration contains three objects filled with three different tile patterns. The patterns vary only in color.

I keep hoping Illustrator is going to resolve its pattern printing problems once and for all, but my experience suggests that Illustrator still has a ways to go. So let my wasted efforts be a lesson. Filling an intricate outline like the large foreground plane with a relatively complex tile pattern may be enough to break the camel's back. Use tile patterns conservatively, or stay the heck away from them.

Transforming Tiles Inside Objects

I mentioned earlier that Illustrator always transforms a gradient fill along with its object. But things are more flexible where tile patterns are concerned. You can transform an object and its pattern fill together or transform just the object or just the pattern. Here's how it works:

- To transform tile patterns with their objects, press ⌘-K to display the General Preferences dialog box and turn on the Transform Patterns Tiles check box. This option affects all transformations, including movements made with the arrow tool.
- If you want a tile pattern to remain unmolested no matter how much you may molest the filled object, leave the Transform Patterns Tiles check box off. Back in Figure 15-31, for example, I was able to freely move the plane, shadow, and background rectangle without jarring the patterns out of perfect alignment.
- The Move, Scale, Rotate, Reflect, and Shear dialog boxes are all equipped with two check boxes—Objects and Patterns. By default, just the Objects check box is active. This transforms the selected objects without transforming any pattern fills. If you select both Objects and Patterns, Illustrator transforms both items. You can also turn off the Objects check box and turn on Patterns to transform the tiles without affecting the objects at all.

  Figure 15-32 shows examples of pattern tiles transformed independently of their objects. Rotating and slanting are particularly useful for camouflaging the linear appearance of a pattern. Scaling is handy for showing off more or less of a pattern at a time. Though I don't show it, you can move a pattern to align tiles with the edges of an object. And flipping...well, flipping isn't all that useful, but it's good to have around just in case.
- If you turn on the Patterns check box in addition to the Objects check box inside any dialog box, Illustrator activates the check box in all dialog boxes. It also selects the Transform Patterns Tiles option inside the General Preferences dialog box. The arrow tool and all transformation tools will affect both objects and pattern fills until you turn off one of these options.

- On the other hand, if you turn on the Patterns check box but turn off the Objects check box, Illustrator transforms the pattern fill one time only. Adobe was worried that it might be confusing to find yourself transforming only tile patterns—particularly since most objects aren't filled with patterns—so this particular combination of options is not saved as a default.

Scaled 50 percent

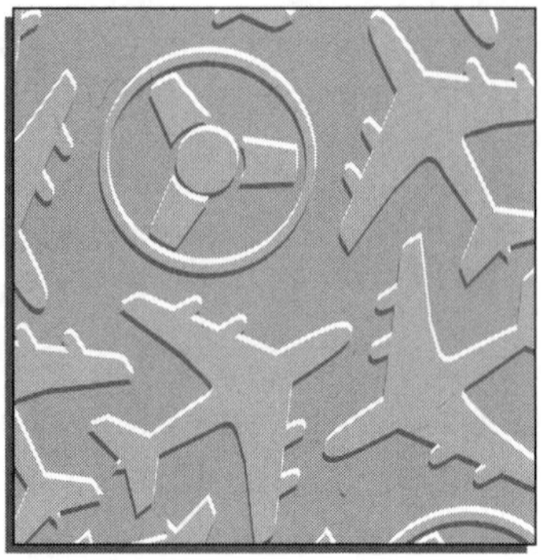

Rotated 30 degrees

Slanted 40 degrees

Scaled, slanted, and rotated

Figure 15-32: You can manipulate a pattern fill independently of its object by turning off the Objects option and turning on the Patterns option inside any transformation dialog box.

TIP

I learned this very cool tip from Luanne Seymour Cohen, one of the Illustrator developers at Adobe. It turns out that you don't have to use a dialog box to transform a pattern fill independently of an object; you can also do it by dragging with a tool. Press the tilde key—you know, the little flying worm, ~, at the upper left of the keyboard—while dragging with the arrow tool or any transformation tool to modify the tile pattern inside a shape and leave the shape unchanged. Just be sure to press the ~ key *before* you start dragging.

CHAPTER 16

STROKES AND BRUSHES

Stroke is a gizmo in the PostScript printing language that controls the appearance of the outline of a path. Strokes share many similarities with fills. A stroke can be any gray value or color. A stroke is equally applicable to path and text objects (though you can't stroke imported images). And you apply stroke attributes from the Stroke palette. But unlike fill, you can't stroke a path with a gradation. Stroked tile patterns don't look right on screen. And stroke includes a handful of unique attributes for which fill has no use (as we will naturally explore in this chapter).

Brushes are similar to strokes in that they control the appearance of the outline of a path. But instead of merely stripping the edges of a path, brushes let you add a variety of enhancements to the outline, making the outline part the artwork itself. I cover brushes in all their glory in the second half of this chapter.

Strokes and brushes are secondary attributes in Illustrator—sort of a Park Place to fill's Boardwalk—for the very same reasons that editable text is sometimes less useful than text converted to paths:

- You can't just click any old place on a stroke or a brush to select the path. You click precisely on the path outline—which runs through the center of the stroke—much like you click on the baseline to select type.
- Some of Illustrator's functions are downright stroke and brush–unfriendly. The knife tool, for example, destroys strokes, as do many of the Pathfinder filters—namely Divide, Trim, Merge, Crop, Hard, and Soft. You can't find the intersection of two path outlines or unite them. The Blend filters ignore strokes and unconverted brushes and Object » Expand Fill misinterprets them.
- You have to rely on Illustrator to display the stroke properly on screen. Illustrator is nearly always right on target, but at times the on-screen stroke and the printed stroke may not exactly match. To see what I mean, try to make two curves with thick strokes exactly touch each other (without overlapping) and then print the curves to a high-resolution imagesetter. Eyeballing simply isn't nearly as reliable as snapping the points in two unstroked paths, which absolutely guarantees alignment.
- The stroke of a path is always uniform in thickness. If you want to create a line of variable thickness, you have to draw it as a filled path, just like "lines" drawn with the paintbrush tool.

Some artists don't stroke or brush paths. Or they use strokes as interim measures, ultimately converting the strokes to path outlines using Object » Path » Outline Path (as explained later in this chapter). I'm not saying you shouldn't use strokes and brushes. I use them, and most of the illustrations in this book contain strokes—cripes, some of my best friends have strokes! But you should be aware of their limitations as you are mesmerized by their potential.

Stroking Paths

A stroke strides the outline of a path, just as a monorail strides its electric track. In Figure 16-1, I've applied a couple of different strokes to an open path and a closed path. In each case, I've drawn in the path itself as a thin white line to show how the path always runs through the center of its stroke. This is important for you to keep in mind as you're selecting and aligning stroked paths. You can also exploit this feature to create overlay effects, as you will in the "Stacked Stroke and Fill Effects" section later in this chapter.

You can use strokes to exaggerate or mitigate the corners of a path. In Figure 16-2, I applied two different kinds of "joins" to identical starbursts. The black joins look sharp enough to pierce rocks. The gray joins are soft and stubby. You can also create an absolutely inexhaustible supply of dashed strokes and even round off the dashes if you want.

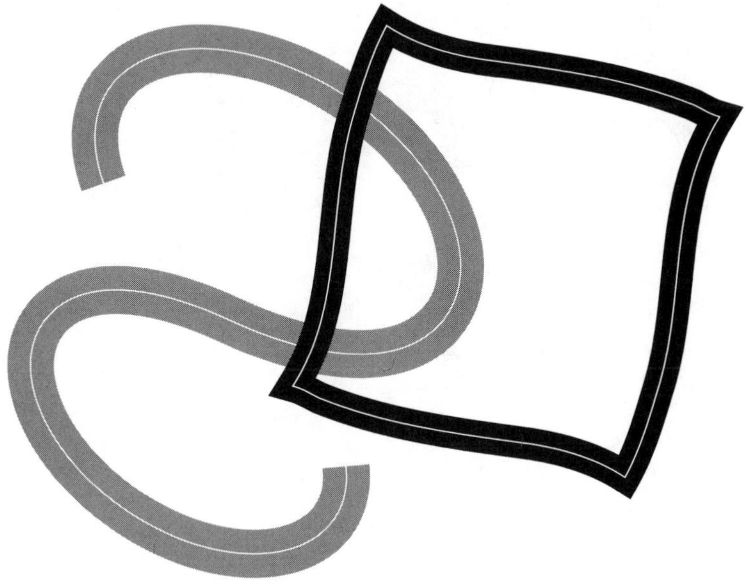

Figure 16-1: These open and closed paths are stroked with heavy outlines. The paths themselves are shown in white.

WARNING

Watch out for straight lines that look like they're stroked when they're not. If you draw a straight line by clicking at two points with the pen tool and then add a black fill with no stroke, the fill follows the line on screen, creating the appearance of a thin stroke. The problem is, however, that the false stroke won't print accurately, particularly to a high-resolution imagesetter. Be sure to manually assign a stroke using the options in the Stroke palette, and never accept a thin stroke applied to a straight line at face value.

Figure 16-2: Strokes can be sharp or soft or even dashed. I've drawn the paths in white to show how the strokes build up the corners.

Stroking Type and Text Paths

Like fill, stroke affects type differently depending on how the type is selected:

- If you select a text object with the arrow tool, applying a stroke affects all type along the path. The first example in Figure 16-3 shows selected path text. In the second example, I applied a transparent fill and a thin black stroke. As you can see, Illustrator stroked the type but not the path.
- If you select the path with the direct selection tool, you can apply a stroke to the path only, leaving the text as is. In Figure 16-4, I used the direct selection tool to apply a thick gray stroke to the path. You can also select the rectangle around a text block or the path around area text.

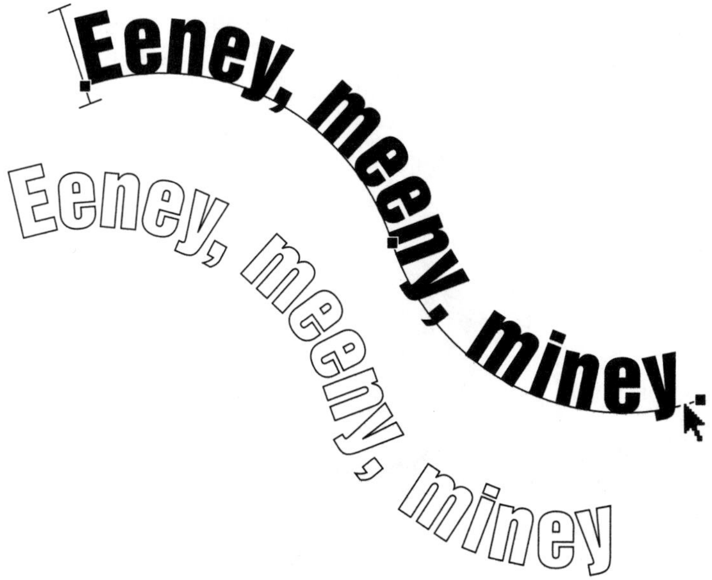

Figure 16-3: If you stroke a text block that was selected with the arrow tool (top), only the text becomes stroked (bottom).

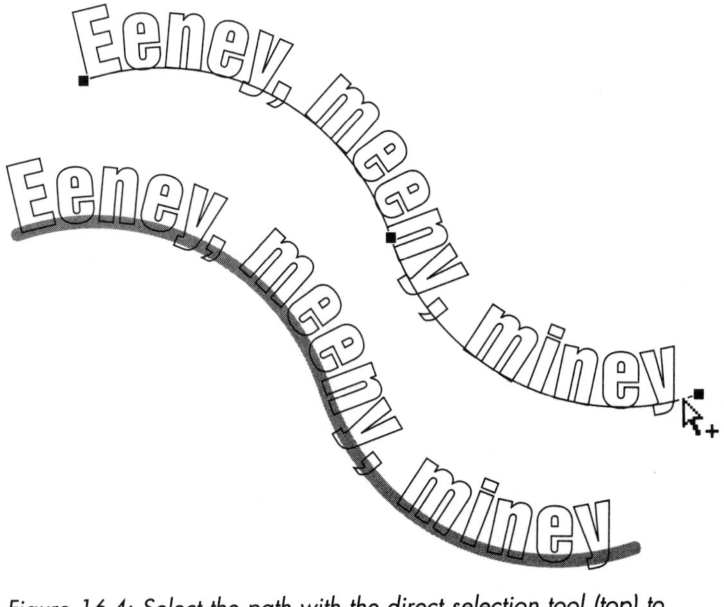

Figure 16-4: Select the path with the direct selection tool (top) to stroke just the path and leave the text unchanged (bottom).

- Select text with the type tool to stroke single characters or words. In this case, stroke is just another character-level formatting attribute that affects selected characters independently of deselected ones, as demonstrated in Figure 16-5. Using the type tool, you can apply several different strokes to a single text object.

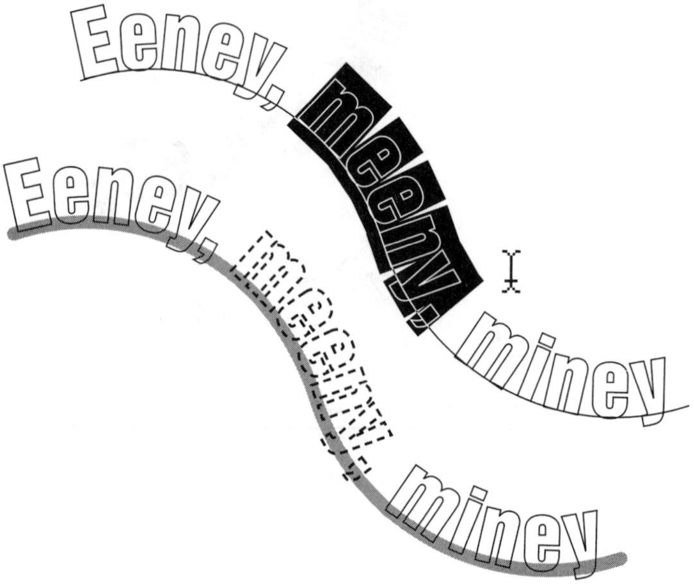

Figure 16-5: By selecting text with the type tool (top), you stroke only the highlighted type (bottom).

Applying a Stroke from the Stroke Palette

The following steps explain how to use these options to apply a stroke to a selected path or text object:

1. **Select the objects that you want to stroke.**

   If no object is selected, editing the stroke changes the default settings.

2. **Click on the Stroke icon in the Color palette or the toolbox.**

   Or press X if the Stroke icon is not active. When active, the Stroke icon overlaps the Fill icon as shown in Figure 16-6.

3. Choose a paint style.

To color a stroke, choose a color from the Color palette. Make sure that the Stroke icon is active (that is, that the Stroke icon overlaps the Fill icon in the palette). To remove the stroke, make it transparent by clicking on the None paint style button or use the keyboard shortcut, press the slash key (/).

4. Specify the color in the Color palette.

You can choose the color of a stroke exactly as described in Chapter 14. Although stroking a path with a tile pattern is just begging for trouble if you want them to print, you are certainly welcome to apply a pattern as directed in Chapter 15.

TIP

You can also drag a swatch from the swatch list in the Swatches palette and drop it onto the Stroke icon in the toolbox. The Stroke icon doesn't have to be selected.

5. Change the Weight value.

The Weight value determines the thickness of the stroke (also known as stroke weight).

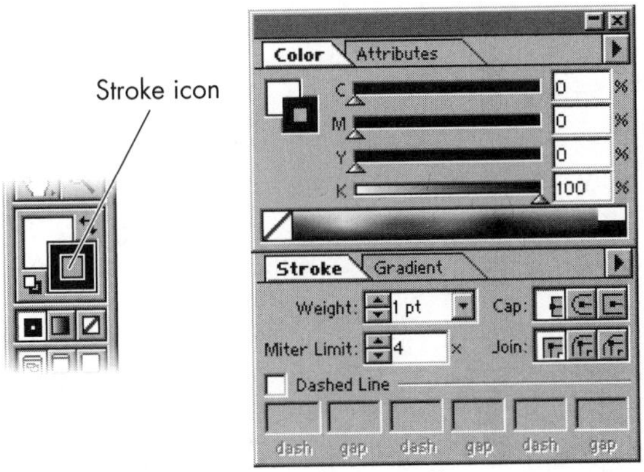

Figure 16-6: Select the Stroke icon in the toolbox and play around with the options in the Stroke palette to modify the stroke of selected objects.

6. Select icons from the Cap and Join options.

These option buttons appear in the upper-right corner of the Stroke palette, as shown in Figure 16-6. You use the Cap icons to determine how the stroke wraps around the ends of an open path. You use the Join icons to control the appearance of the stroke at corner points. The Miter Limit option box appears to the left of the options only when the first Join icon is selected. Otherwise, the option box is dimmed. (I'll explain this option in a few moments.)

7. Select the Dashed Line check box to create a dashed outline.

Then enter values into the Dash and Gap option boxes along the bottom of the dialog to specify the length of each dash and each gap between dashes. (This option, too, will be explained just up ahead, good and trusting reader.) If you don't want a dashed stroke, leave it unchecked.

8. Press the Return key.

Illustrator returns its focus to the illustration window.

Many options that affect stroke are available anytime a stroke has been assigned, even if the Fill icon is selected. (If the stroke is set to None, all stroke options are dimmed.) This means you can modify these stroke attributes regardless of which icon is active. You need to select the Stroke icon only if you want to change the color of a stroke, and even then you can drag a color swatch and drop it onto the dimmed Stroke icon if you prefer.

Weight, cap, join, and dash pattern are all powerful stroke attributes that bear further explorations. That's why I discuss each one in some detail in the following sections.

Line Weight

The Weight values control the thickness of a stroke. Folks who spent their formative years laying down lines of sticky black ruling tape with X-acto knives prefer the term "line weight," so that's the term I'll use in my discussions. In Illustrator, line weight is always measured in points, even if the ruler units are set to inches or millimeters. Of course, if you want to create a stroke one inch thick, you can enter 1 in and press Return. But stroke—like text—is best served by a tiny and precise unit of measurement: the point.

You can enter any number between 0 and 1000 (which is longer than a foot), accurate to 0.01 point. However, I advise against specifying a line weight value smaller than 0.1. A 0.3-point line weight is commonly considered a hairline, so 0.1 point is about as thick as dandruff. Figure 16-7 shows several line weights applied to a frilly path. The 0.1-point line is barely visible. Any thinner simply will not reproduce.

WARNING: Do *not* enter a line weight of 0. This tells Illustrator to print the thinnest line available from the output device. The thinnest line printable by a 300-dpi laser printer is 0.24-point thick. However, high-resolution imagesetters easily print lines as thin as 0.03-point, or 10 times thinner than a hairline. Such a line cannot possibly survive the reproduction process.

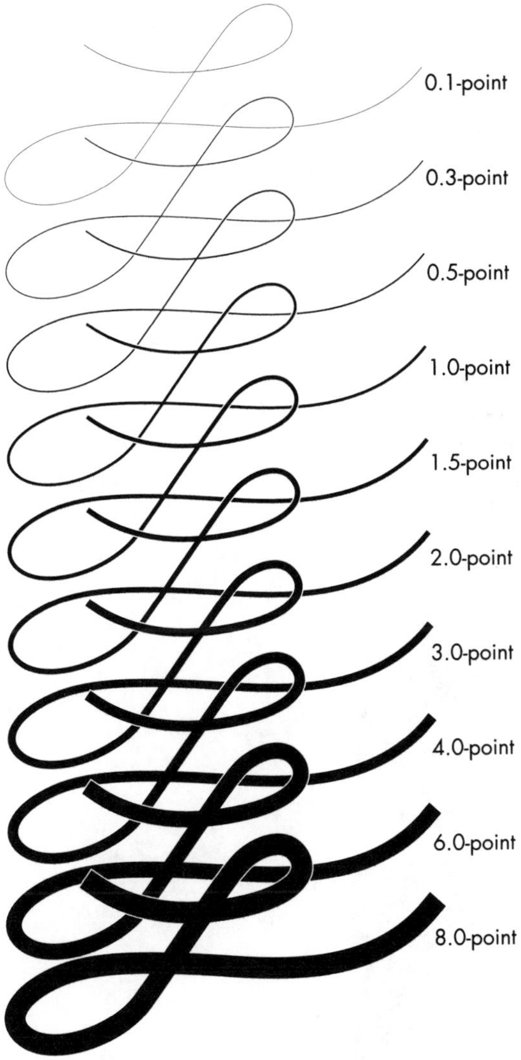

Figure 16-7:
Here are several examples of line weights printed from Illustrator. The top line is barely visible; anything thinner than 0.1 point is essentially invisible.

Line Caps

You can select from three types of line caps, which determine the appearance of a stroke at its endpoint. Line caps are generally useful only when you're stroking an open path. The only exception to this is when you use line caps in combination with dash patterns, in which case Illustrator applies the cap to each and every dash, as I explain later in this chapter.

The three Cap icons in the Stroke palette work as follows:

- **Butt cap:** The first Cap icon is the butt cap option, the default setting and the most commonly used line cap. (Whether it's fit for polite company I can't say, but butt is the official PostScript term for this kind of cap.) Notice the black line that runs through the center of each of the Cap icons. This indicates the position of the path relative to the stroke. When the butt cap option is selected, the stroke ends immediately at an endpoint and is perpendicular to the final course of the path, as shown in the top diagram in Figure 16-8.

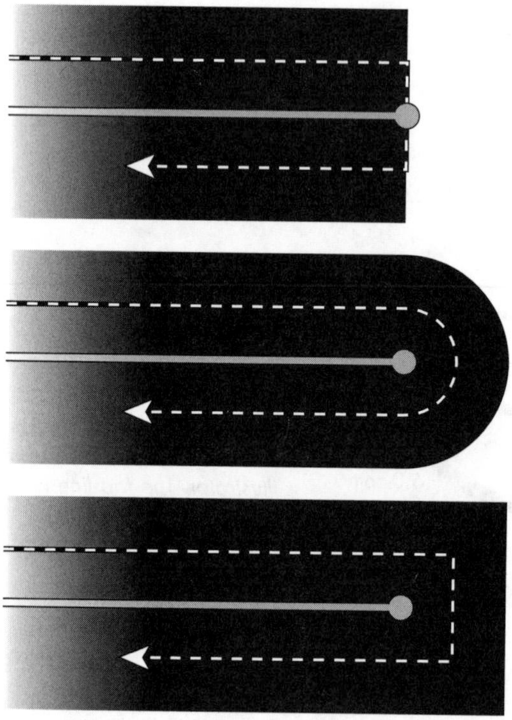

Figure 16-8: Diagrams of the three kinds of line caps—butt (top), round (middle), and square (bottom). The gray line indicates the path, while the dotted line shows the stroke moving around the path.

- **Round cap:** The second icon represents a round cap, which wraps the stroke around the path to circle the endpoint. The radius of the circle is half the line weight, as demonstrated by the second diagram in Figure

16-8. If you have a 4-point line weight, for example, the round cap extends exactly 2 points out from the endpoint.

Round caps are used to soften the appearance of a line. The line appears to taper, rather than abruptly end. I frequently apply round caps when using thick strokes.

- **Square cap:** Last and least is the square cap icon—Illustrator calls it the Projecting Cap. Here, a square is attached to the end of a line; the endpoint is the center of the square. Like the round cap, the square cap sticks out half the line weight from the endpoint, as the bottom diagram in Figure 16-8 shows. The only difference is that the square cap has very definite corners, making it appear to jut out more dramatically.

  Use square caps when you want to close a gap. For example, if you want the stroke from an open path to meet with the edge of another stroked path, the square cap gives the open path a little extra length.

Figure 16-9 shows a collection of seven open paths repeated three times, each with different line caps. In the first eye, the lines with butt caps either clear each other or barely touch. In the round cap eye, the caps close many gaps, but you can plainly see that the touching lines are not part of the same path. (See, don't round caps look better? I just love them.) In the third eye, the square caps completely eliminate even the hint of gaps in the corner of the lids and the spot where the top iris path meets the top lid. The square caps give the paths a more substantial appearance all around.

Figure 16-9: I drew each of these eyes using the same collection of open paths. The only difference is the line caps—butt on the left, round in the middle, and square on the right.

Line Joins

The Stroke palette offers three line joins, which determine the appearance of a stroke at the corners of a path. The stroke always forms a continuous curve at each smooth point in a path, but you can use line joins to clip away the stroke at corner points and cusps. Here's how each of the Joins icons work:

Miter join: The first Join icon represents a miter join, which is the default setting. If a corner has a miter join, the outside edges of the stroke extend all the way out until they meet to form a crisp corner. The first star in Figure 16-10 is stroked with miter joins. Compare its perfect spikes to the rounded and chopped off corners in the other stars. Watch out, though. Illustrator may cut a miter join short according to the Miter Limit value, explained in the next section.

Figure 16-10: Each of these stars is stroked with a different line join—miter (top), round (middle), and bevel (bottom). Notice that the joins affect all corners in the paths, whether they point out or in.

Round join: The second icon is the round join option, which is identical in principle to the round cap. Half of the line weight wraps around the corner point to form an arc, as shown in the second star in Figure 16-10. Round joins and round caps are so similar, in fact, that they are almost exclusively used together. The only time you should avoid using round joins is when a dash pattern is involved. Because round joins actually form complete circles around corner points, they can interrupt the flow of the dashes.

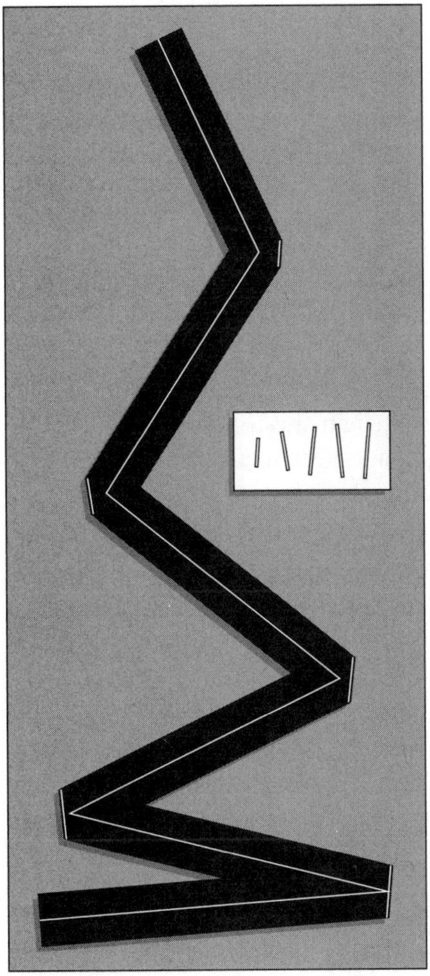

Figure 16-11:
As segments meet at sharper angles, the bevel joins lengthen. Each bevel is repeated in the inset for side-by-side comparison.

Bevel join: Use the third and last icon to apply a bevel join. Very similar to a butt cap, the bevel join shears the stroke off at the corner point.

As shown in the bottom star in Figure 16-10, the bevel join creates a flat edge at each corner point. The length of this flat edge varies depending on the angle of the segments. A gradual angle results in a short bevel; a sharp angle results in a longer one. Figure 16-11 shows a path made up of segments that meet at progressively sharper angles. I've traced the bevels with white lines to demonstrate their increasing lengths. For comparison's sake, the inset shows the five bevels arranged in a row, with the top bevel on the left and the bottom bevel on the right.

Giving Excessive Miter Joins the Ax

Directly to the left of the Joins icons in the Stroke palette is the Miter Limit option box. This value tells Illustrator when to chop off excessively long miter joins. The Miter Limit value represents a ratio between the length of the miter—from inside to outside corner—and the line weight, both diagrammed in Figure 16-12. In other words, as long as the miter length is shorter than the line weight multiplied by the Miter Limit value, Illustrator creates a miter join. But if the miter length is longer than the line weight times the Miter Limit value, Illustrator chops off the miter and makes it a bevel join.

The length of a miter grows as its segments move closer together. If I had applied miter joins to the path in Figure 16-11, for example, the bottom joins would be more likely to get chopped off than the top joins. A miter can grow especially long when two curved segments meet to form a cusp. As shown in Figure 16-13, two inward-curving segments create a serious Pinocchio effect. What's worse, the join doesn't curve along with the segment; it straightens out after the corner point. The result is an unbecoming spike that looks completely out of place with the rest of the path.

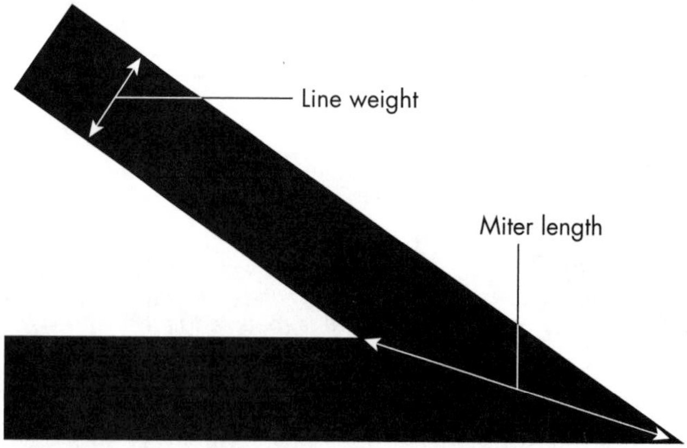

Figure 16-12: The miter length grows as the angle between two segments shrinks.

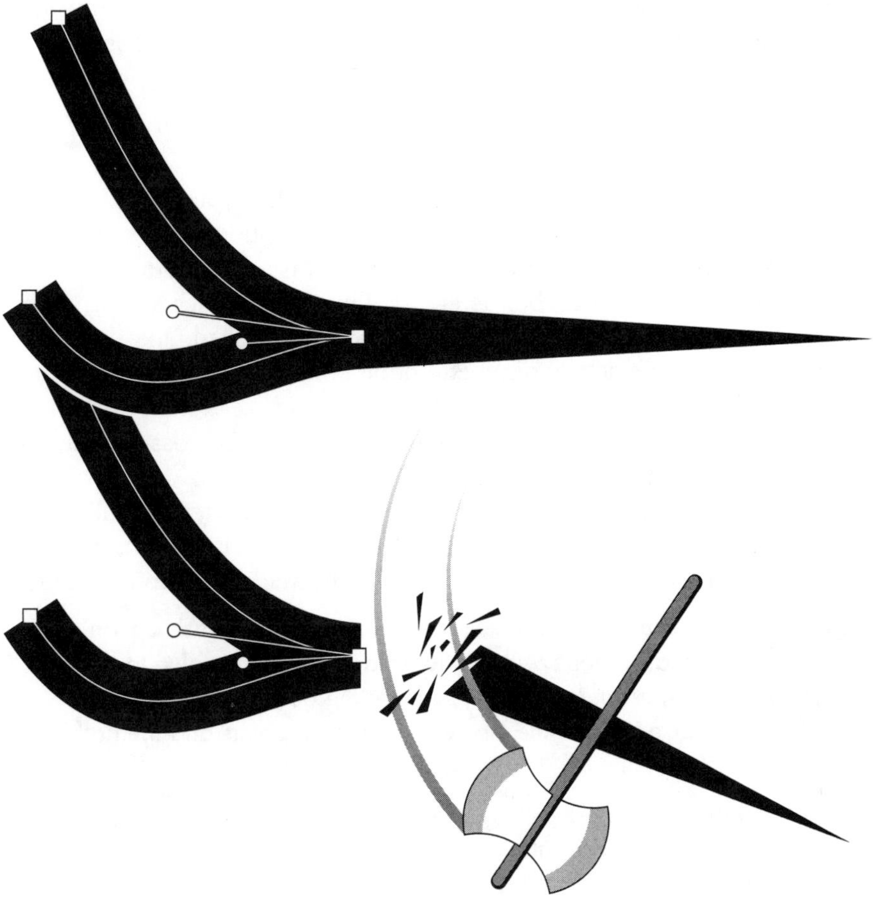

Figure 16-13: It is truly a shame that miter joins lose control when applied to curved segments (top, extending off to the right), but is chopping them clean off (bottom) really the best solution?

But the solution of hacking away the join (as so painfully illustrated in the second example of Figure 16-13) is a harsh compromise. In fact, it's not a compromise at all. Illustrator either gives you a ridiculously long miter or it bevels it completely. If you want to preserve the precise quality of a miter join without allowing it to take on a life of its own—and a rather lewd one at that—you should manually adjust your path to increase the angle between segments, which in turn reduces the length of the miter. The Miter Limit option should be considered a last resort.

The Miter Limit value can range from 1 to 500, provided that the value multiplied by the line weight doesn't exceed 1800 points. The default value is 4. A miter limit of 1 tells Illustrator to lop off every join and is therefore identical to selecting the bevel join icon. If either the round or bevel join icon is selected, the Miter Limit option appears dimmed.

Dash Patterns

The options along the bottom of the Stroke palette allow you to apply a dash pattern to a stroke. Dash patterns are repetitive interruptions in a stroke. For example, a standard coupon border in a newspaper ad is a dash pattern.

When the Dashed Line check box is empty, Illustrator creates a solid stroke with no interruptions. To create a dash pattern, select the Dashed Line check box, which brings to life six previously dimmed option boxes. Each option box represents an interval, measured in points, during which the stroke is on or off over the course of the path. The Dash values determine the length of the dashes; the Gap values determine the length of the gaps between the dashes.

You don't have to fill all Dash and Gap options with values. In fact, most folks simply fill in the first pair of option boxes and leave the rest blank. Whatever you do, Illustrator repeats the values you enter and ignores the empty option boxes.

TIP: If you like, you can enter a value into the first Dash option box and be done with it. Illustrator applies the value to both the dashes and gaps. If you enter the default Dash value of 12, for example, the stroke is on for 12 points and then off for 12 points.

The ghost grid in Figure 16-14 shows a sampling of dashes created using only the first pair of Dash and Gap options. These horrifying members of the spirit world are arranged into columns and rows according to their Dash and Gap values.

If you scrutinize the phantoms carefully—a task best left to the stout of heart, I admit—you may notice that the dashes pile up at the point where the path starts and stops. For example, each eerie eye begins at the bottom of the shape, which is why you sometimes see an extra long dash at this point. Each macabre mouth begins at the top, and every spectral shroud starts in the bottom left corner.

When stroking a closed path, you ideally want the sum of the dash and gap to divide evenly into the length of the path outline. This way, you don't have any dash pileups. Unfortunately, Illustrator provides no mechanism for telling you how long a path is, so even if math is your friend, you can't figure it out. So your only recourse is trial and error. In the first ghoul in Figure 16-15, I applied a Dash value of 6 and a Gap of 3 to the eyes. But as the white circles show, I ended up with an extra long dash at the bottom of each shape. The solution? I gradually raised the Gap value in 0.01-point increments until the dash shrunk back to the proper size. A Gap value of 3.11 finally did the trick.

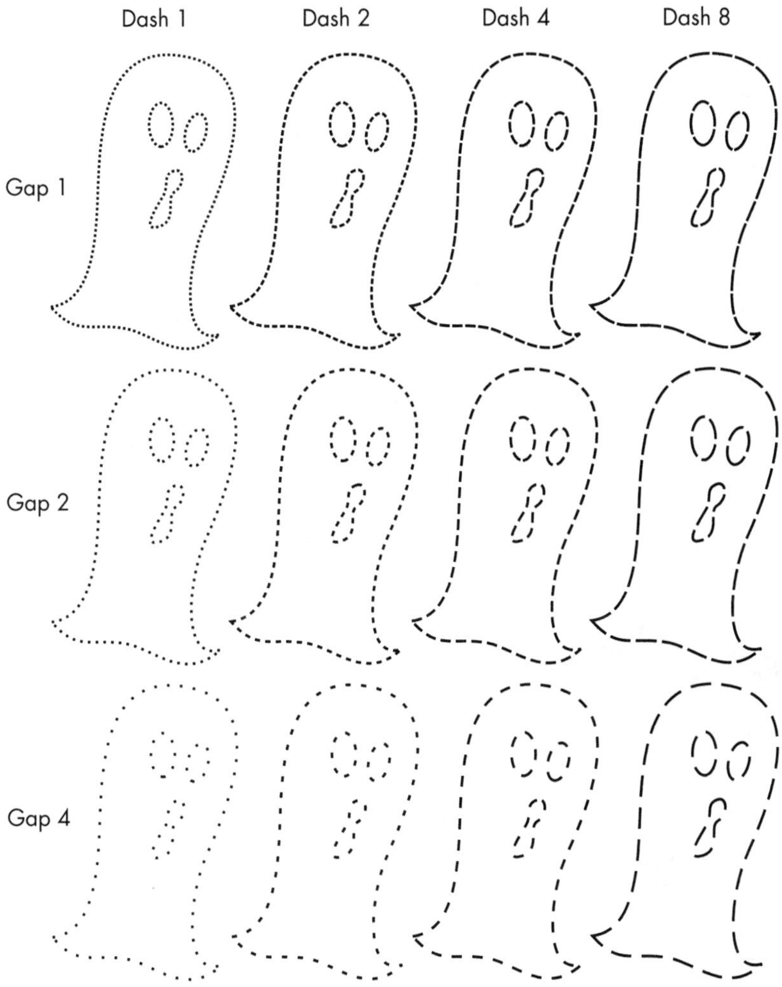

Figure 16-14: A grid of dash patterns demonstrating 12 combinations of Dash and Gap values.

TIP

In addition to their predictable uses, dash patterns are great for creating sparkles. The sparkles in the hair and on the ear of the woman in Figure 16-16 are actually circles—drawn with the ellipse tool—stroked with dash patterns. The Dash values range from 1 to 3 points, with Gap values from 2 to 7. The length of the sparkles is a function of the line weights, which run as high as 18 points. As you can see, the dashes actually flair as they go around the circle, thickening up toward the outer edge. It's a simple, elegant effect.

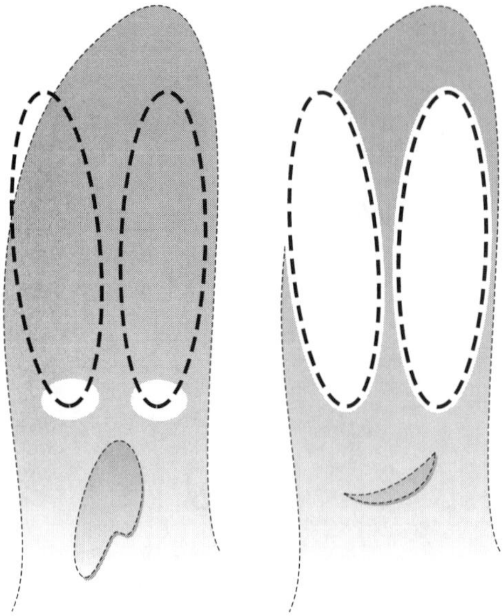

Figure 16-15:
After applying a stroke with 6-point dashes and 3-point gaps (left), I gradually raised the gap value to eliminate any dash pileups (right).

Figure 16-16:
Before boarding the Orient Express, this temptress adorned herself with several fetching (but surprisingly cheap) dash-pattern sparkles.

Using Line Caps with Dash Patterns

Another thing to consider when applying a dash pattern is the effect of the active line cap. Illustrator treats the beginning and ending of each dash in a pattern as a start and stop in the stroke. Therefore, both ends of a dash are affected by the selected line cap, which makes it possible to create round dashes.

I stroked each of the three lines in Figure 16-17 with a 16-point line weight that included a dash pattern and round caps. I entered 0—yes, 0—for the Dash value and 26 for the Gap. When you specify the length of each dash as 0, you instruct Illustrator to allow no distance between the round cap at the beginning of the dash and the round cap at the end of the dash. The two round caps therefore meet to form a complete circle.

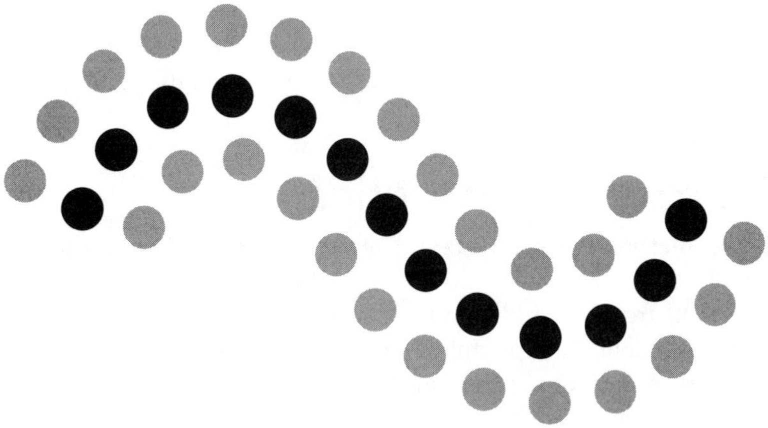

Figure 16-17: Three lines stroked with the same dash pattern in two different colors. I selected the round cap icon and set the Dash value to 0, resulting in circular dots.

Figure 16-18 shows a diagram of two dashes set to 0 with round caps. The path appears in gray; the dotted lines show the round cap wrapping around the 0-point dash. Notice that the only thing separating the circles is the Gap value. The Gap value defines the distance from the center of one circle to the center of the next, while the line weight determines the diameter of each circle. Therefore, to prevent one circular dot from touching the next, the Gap value must be larger than the Weight value. In Figure 16-17, for example, the 26-point gap is greater than the 16-point line weight, creating a 10-point break between each pair of dots. If the Gap and Weight values are equal, the dots just barely touch. And if the gap is smaller than the line weight, the dots overlap.

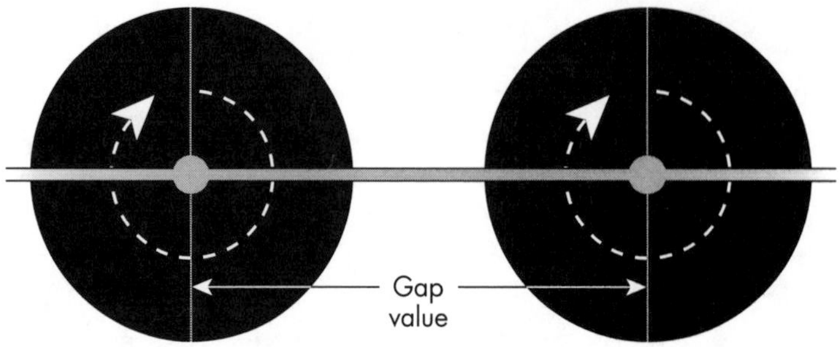

Figure 16-18: A diagram of a dash pattern with a 0-point dash and round caps. The thick gray line represents the path, while the dotted line shows the stroke wrapping around each dash.

Raising the Dash value above 0 elongates the dashes so they're no longer circular. The larger the Dash value, the more the dashes look like little submarines.

Stacked Stroke and Fill Effects

You can achieve alternatively practical and remarkable effects by cloning an object in place and varying stroke and fill attributes from one clone to the next. By stacking a series of strokes and fills on top of each other, you cover up some portions of the strokes and fills and permit other portions to show through. It may sound weird, but it's merely another technique for getting precisely what you want out of this powerful program.

Fill on Stroke

The problem with stroke is that you can't scoot it side to side on a path, the way you can scoot type along the baseline using baseline shift. The stroke always straddles the path, so that one half of the stroke lies on one side and one half lies on the other.

Why is this a problem? Well, suppose you want to draw a thick outline around some important text. In the top example in Figure 16-19, I've applied a 3-point stroke. This means the stroke cuts 1.5 points into the letters, making them illegible and terribly ugly.

Ideally, you'd simply ask Illustrator to move the stroke to the outside of the path. But, ask though you may, Illustrator will ignore you. The following, nonverbal solution is much more productive:

1. Set the stroke to twice the desired line weight. I set my stroke weight to twice 3-point, or 6-point.
2. Clone the text. You can either press ⌘-C and ⌘-F or choose Option-↑, ↓.
3. Remove the stroke by selecting the None icon in the toolbox or by pressing the / (slash) key.
4. If the selected object is not already filled, assign a fill. I filled the letters with white.

The result is the second example in Figure 16-19. The white clone blocks out the portion of the stroke that intrudes into the letters. Half of the stroke from the original letters appears outside the filled clone. Because I doubled the line weight to 6-point, I'm left with the same 3-point outline used in the previous example. But this time, it looks way the heck better.

Figure 16-19: Type with a 3-point stroke (top) and then type the same text with a 6-point stroke topped off by a filled clone with no stroke (bottom).

TIP In addition to permitting you to scoot the stroke outside your letters, this fill-on-stroke technique increases your range of options. For example, you can offset the filled clone to create a slightly three-dimensional look, as shown in Figure 16-20. In the first example in the figure, I nudged the clone up and to the right 1 point. The black stroke is now 2 points thick above and to the right of the letters and 4 points thick below and to the left. In the second example in the figure, I nudged the clone another point up and to the right. I also selected the original letters and applied round joins to smooth away the corners.

Figure 16-20: The result of nudging the cloned letters 1 point (top) and 2 points (bottom) up and to the right. I also rounded off the stroked letters in the second example.

TIP

If you want to scoot the stroke to the *inside* of a path—exactly the opposite effect demonstrated in Figure 16-19—you have to use Illustrator's masking function. First stroke the path with twice the desired line weight. Then clone the path, select both the clone and the original, and choose Object » Masks » Make. For more information on using and abusing masks, see Chapter 17.

Stroke on Fill

The opposite of fill on stroke is—you guessed it—stroke on fill. You clone a path, make the fill transparent, and then apply a stroke. The purpose of this technique is to reinstate a stroke that gets covered up or appears partially obscured.

In Figure 16-21, I started with my flashy News logo positioned in front of a stripe (which is actually a slanted rectangle). I wanted to make the logo appear translucent, so that the white of the letters and the gray of the stripe mixed together. After converting the letters to path outlines, I combined them into a single compound path (⌘-8). Then I selected both the letters and the stripe, cloned the shapes, chose the Pathfinder palette's Intersect filter to retain the overlap area, and applied a light gray fill. (I could have used the Soft filter instead of Intersect, but that would have destroyed the original letter outlines, which I still need.) I also set the stroke to None, because I wanted to stroke only the letters, not the light gray area. If I stroked the gray area, unwanted lines would appear inside the white letters.

The problem with the result—shown in the second example in the figure—is that the light gray overlap obscures some of the stroke. So to re-establish the stroke, I applied the stroke-on-fill technique. I selected the original white-letter outlines, copied them (⌘-C), selected the light gray shapes, and pasted the letters in front (⌘-F). Then I set the fill to None to achieve the effect shown in the bottom example of Figure 16-21. This creates a separate stroke above the fray, making it appear as if the letters have multiple fills. It's a simple and extremely useful effect.

Figure 16-21: I created a translucent effect by assembling white letters and a gray stripe (top) and adding a light gray overlap with the Intersect filter (middle). Then I pasted the stroked letters in front with a transparent fill (bottom).

Stroke on Stroke

Now we leave the realm of the practical and ascend to the plane of pure special effects. You can stack differently stroked clones onto each other to create parallel lines, outlined lines, hollow dashes, and lines with depth. Although these aren't what I would call strictly practical techniques, they can be a lot of fun. And no matter how many pages I devote to sharing a few of my effects with you, you'll be able to come up with twice as many of your own an hour later.

First the basics. The top example in Figure 16-22 shows two identical lines—both without fill, one in front of the other. The first line has a 12-point black stroke, while the clone in front of it has an 8-point white stroke. The white stroke clears a path through the black one, leaving what appears to be two parallel 2-point lines.

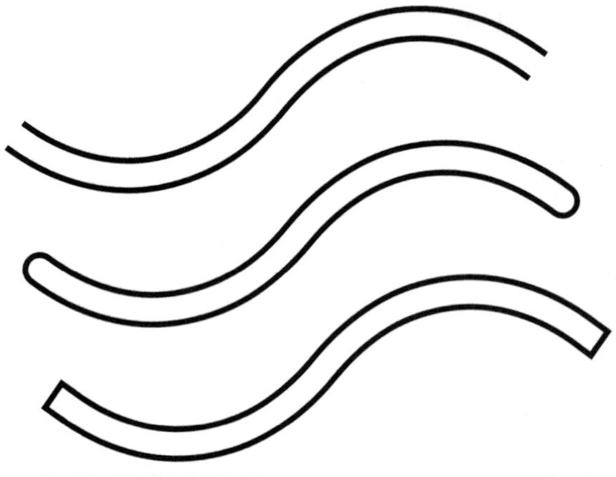

Figure 16-22: Three sets of stacked paths, each with a 12-point black stroke in back and an 8-point white stroke in front. I assigned butt caps to the top lines, round caps to the middle, and square caps to the bottom.

Both of the strokes in the top example include butt caps. But if you want to connect the ends of the paths to create a single, continuous outline, you'd apply a round cap or square cap. In fact, this is precisely how I arrived at the other lines in Figure 16-22. I applied round caps to produce the second example and square caps to get the third.

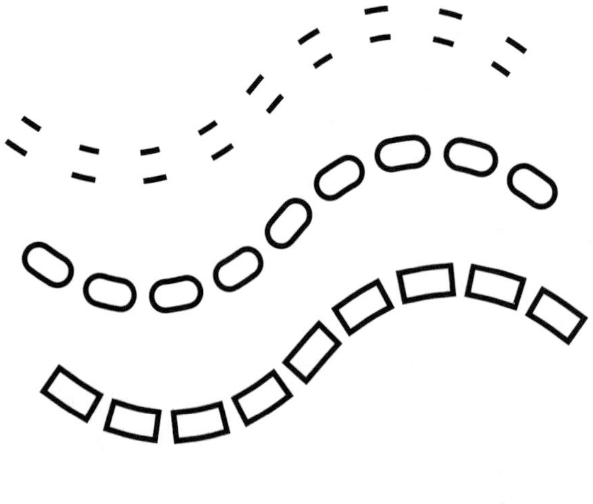

Figure 16-23: The paths from Figure 16-22, subjected to dash patterns with a Dash value of 8 and a Gap of 16.

Figure 16-23 shows the same three sets of lines from Figure 16-22, but this time I've used dash patterns. In every case, the Dash value was set to 8 and the Gap to 16. In the butt cap example at top, this resulted in a series of fragmented dashes, almost like a pattern of equal signs. But with round and square caps applied, each dash turns into an identifiable unit with either curved or straight edges.

Now you know everything there is to know. From here on, you can take off in a million different directions. You can add as many clones as you want, stroking each clone with a progressively thinner line weight to reveal portions of lower clones and cover up other portions. You can alternate line caps and experiment with the Dash and Gap values.

Figure 16-24 shows the evolutionary progression of a squad of flying sushi rolls. Starting from the second example in Figure 16-23, I selected the top line and changed the Dash and Gap values to 0 and 24 respectively. This not only resulted in absolutely circular white dollops of rice, but it maintained the rhythm—or periodicity—of the pattern. Before, the Dash and Gap values were 6 and 18, which add up to 24. Now, they still add up to 24. So long as I maintain this total, the dashes remain in alignment. Also worth noting, the stroke starts on the left side of the figure. This is why the rice circles appear on the left sides of the black seaweed wrappers. I didn't do anything special to achieve this effect; Illustrator did it for me. What a wonderful sushi chef Illustrator would have been.

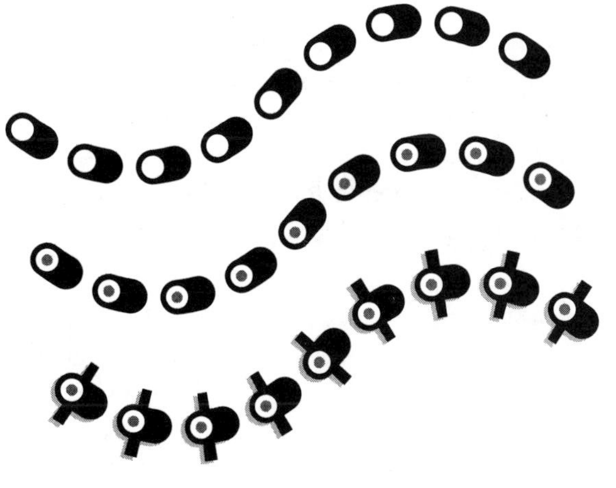

Figure 16-24: I kept cloning the line and adjusting the line weights, dash patterns, and colors to create the feared flying sushi squadron.

To create the bits of avocado in the second line of rolls, I cloned the white path and changed the color to gray and the line weight to 4 points. Finally, I copied the original black path and pasted it in back of the white path. I then set the line weight to 24 points, selected the butt cap, and set the Dash and Gap values to 4 and 20. This created the all-important wings shown in the last row in Figure 16-24. To create the shadows behind the sushi, I selected both the wings and the seaweed wrappers. Then I copied both shapes, pasted them in back, nudged them down and to the right, and colored them with light gray. Sushi squadron, you are ready to fly.

Selecting Stacked Strokes

Selecting from a bunch of identical cloned lines can prove very confusing. You can always select the path on top, but how do you select the others? One way is to periodically lock paths with Object » Lock (⌘-2). For example, to select the black path in the second row of sushi in Figure 16-24, you could click on the line with the arrow tool, press ⌘-2, click again, press ⌘-2, and click a third time. This would select the front line of avocado, lock it, select the next line of white rice, lock it, and then select the black seaweed wrappers. When you finish editing the path, unlock everything by pressing ⌘-Option-2.

TIP: Locking requires that you count your way down. To select a path in back of three others, you have to click and lock three times, and then click a fourth. If you need more visual feedback to prevent your brain from inverting, use Object » Hide Selection (⌘-3) instead of Lock. Select the front path and then press ⌘-3 to hide it. The path disappears temporarily, showing you that it's now out of your way. When you finish with your edits, press ⌘-Shift-3 to bring back the hidden paths.

NEW 8: Illustrator now offers you another way to create individual paths that are perfectly overlapped by other paths. In fact, in the Object » Select submenu inside the context-sensitive pop-up menu (the one that displays when you Control-click) are four commands exclusively devoted to this task. I know this might seem a little weird, but this is the only place that these commands appear.

Choose the Next Object Above—⌘-Option-] (right bracket)—and the Next Object Below—⌘-Option-[(left bracket)—commands to deselect the current path and select the one directly above or below it. In the Figure 16-24 sushi example, you could select the back black path by selecting the front gray path and pressing ⌘-Option-] twice. This would select the avocado, deselect it and select the rice, deselect the rice and, finally, select the desired seaweed.

You can use the other two commands in the context-sensitive Select submenu, First Object Above—⌘-Option-Shift-] (right bracket)—and Last Object Below—⌘-Option-Shift-[(left bracket)—for selecting the foremost and rearmost objects in a stack. This means that I could have selected the back black path by selecting the gray top path and pressing ⌘-Option-Shift-[.

When you're using these commands, keep in mind that the only visual feedback you get when the two paths change their selection status is that the Fill and Stroke icons in the Color palette and the Toolbox update to reflect the second path's attributes.

Making Deep Strokes

I don't know If you remember back this far, but in Figure 11-20—I know, that was several chapters ago—I created an emblem using stacked strokes to produce depth effects. Well no matter, I'm going to show you how to produce similar effects in this section.

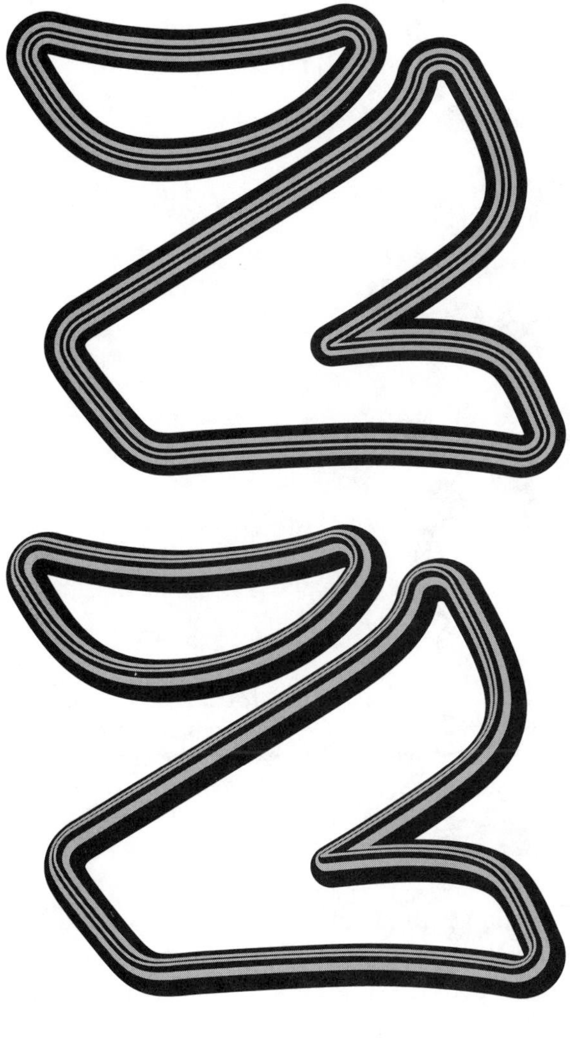

Figure 16-25: A simple collection of four identical stacked paths with progressively thinner strokes (top) and the same paths and strokes slightly offset from each other (bottom).

After stacking a few strokes on top of each other, all you have to do to produce the effect of depth is nudge the paths slightly. The top two shapes in Figure 16-25 originate from a modified letter Z from the Sho font. (There are two Z's in the figure, in case you're having problems focusing.) The letter is repeated a total of four times, stroked from back to front with 16-point black, 8-point gray, 4-point black, and 2-point gray. It just looks like a bunch of strokes on top of each other, moderately interesting if you're a stripe enthusiast, but that's about it.

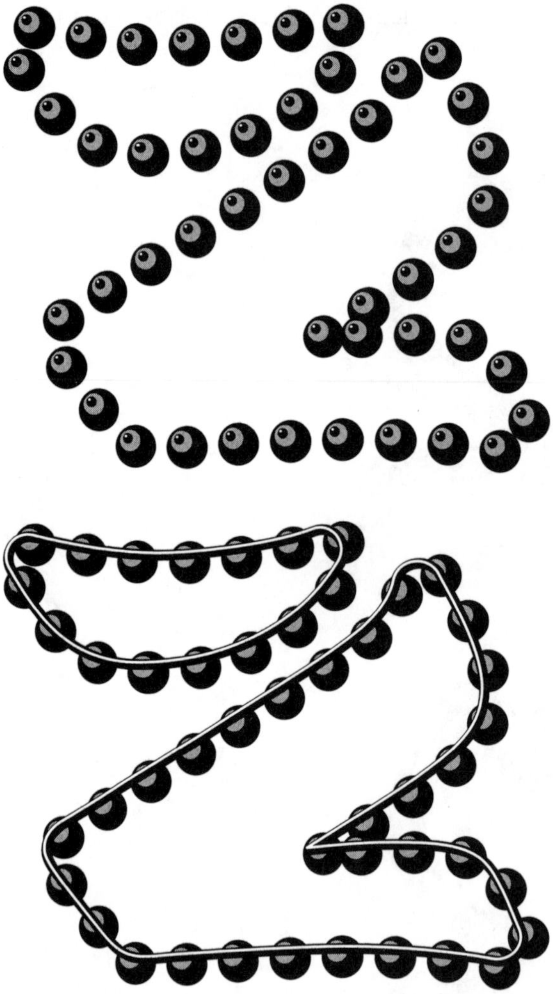

Figure 16-26: Two variations on the Z from the previous figure created using dash patterns with a Dash value of 0 and a Gap of 20.

But look what happens when I nudge the paths. In the second example in Figure 16-25, I have nudged each path up and to the left with respect to the path behind it. In each case, I nudged the path as far as I could without having it go outside the boundaries set by the 16-point black path in back. This way, there's always a hint of black around the edge of each stroke, enough to suggest depth without pushing the illusion too far.

This effect also works with dash patterns. In the first example of Figure 16-26, I took the second Z from Figure 16-25 and applied a dash pattern with a Dash value of 0 and a Gap of 20. It looks like a bird's-eye view of a bunch of truffles. In the second example, I returned the top two paths to solid lines. Now we have a track mounted on top of a layer of suction feet. If you can dream it up, you can create it.

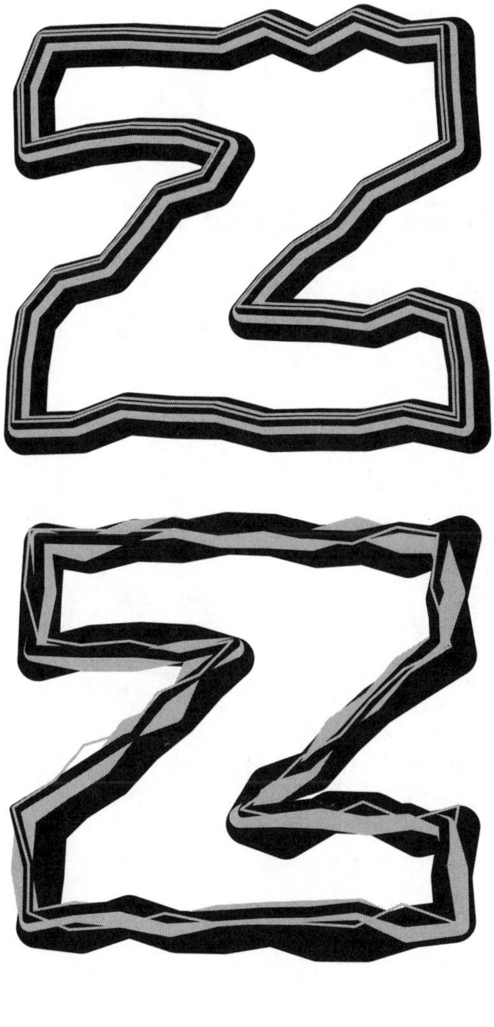

Figure 16-27:
The result of applying the Roughen filter and then cloning the path and stacking the strokes (top) compared to what happens if you apply Roughen after you clone and stroke (bottom).

TIP

Sho is a calligraphic, almost primitive looking typeface that lends itself to weird depth effects. Since you probably don't have a copy of Sho lying around, you might be wondering how you can come up with a primitive font of your own to experiment with. The answer, of course, is to make one. In Figure 16-27, I took a character set in Helvetica Bold and converted it to paths using Type » Create Outlines (⌘-Shift-O). Then I used Filter » Distort » Roughen to pound some bumps and dents into the path. If you do this, be sure to apply the Roughen filter before you start cloning and stroking the path. If you apply Roughen to several paths at a time, you'll get a random effect like the one show at the bottom of Figure 16-27.

Fashioning Arrowheads without Flint

That's it for the stroke options in the Stroke palette. From here on out, I'll be discussing a few commands that specifically affect strokes. First among these is Filter » Stylize » Add Arrowheads, which permits you to add arrowheads to the ends of open paths.

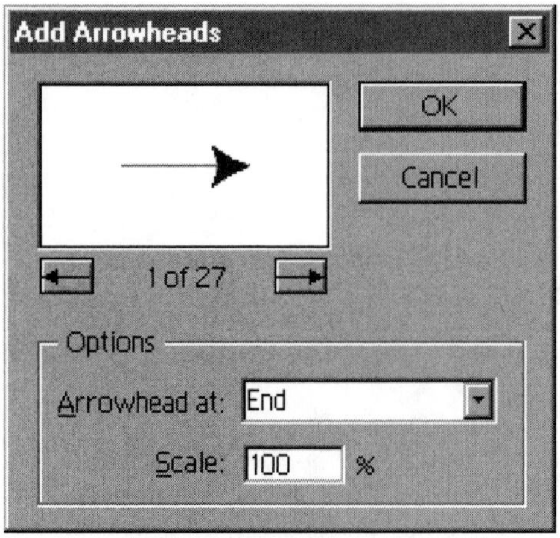

Figure 16-28: The Add Arrowheads dialog box lets you select from 27 different arrowheads that you can add to either end of an open path.

After selecting an open path—the filter doesn't work on closed paths or text objects—choose Filter » Stylize » Add Arrowheads to display the Add Arrowheads dialog box shown in Figure 16-28. The size of the arrowhead is dependent upon two factors—the line weight of the selected path and the percentage value in the

Scale option box. Figure 16-29 shows five paths with different line weights, varying from 0.5 to 6 points, each with the Scale value set to 100 percent. Illustrator's default scaling generally suits 1-point and 2-point lines, but you'll want to raise or lower the Scale value if the line is thinner or thicker, respectively.

Illustrator lets you specify whether you want to apply the arrowhead to one end, the other, or both ends of the open path. Which end is which depends on how you drew the path. Generally, you'll just make a guess and go for it. If it turns out to be the wrong end, press ⌘-Z and ⌘-Option-E to undo and redisplay the Add Arrowheads dialog box. Then try the other end.

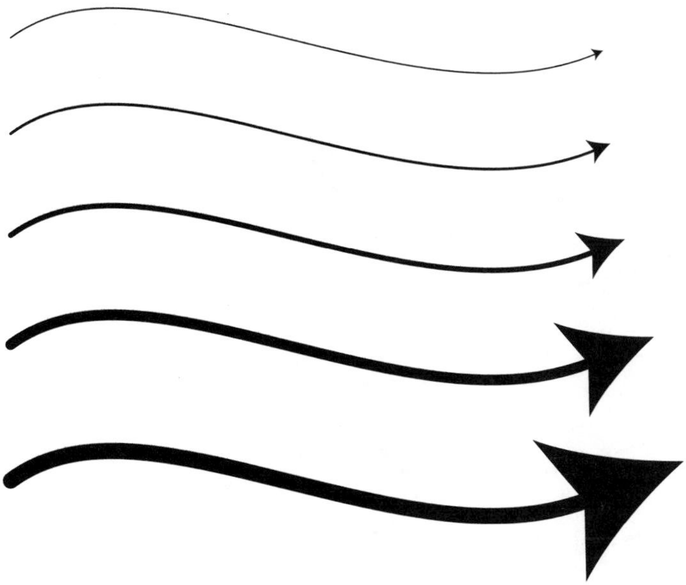

Figure 16-29: The first arrowhead option as it appears when applied to lines 0.5, 1, 2, 4, and 6 points thick. For all lines, the Scale value was set to 100 percent.

You can choose from among 27 arrowheads. Scroll through the collection by clicking on one of the two arrow icons that appear below the big arrow. Figure 16-30 shows 26 of the arrowheads in order—numbers 2 through 14 down the left side and 15 through 27 down the right. (Arrowhead number 1 appears in Figure 16-29.) Note that you can assign only one variety of arrowhead at a time. If you want to assign an arrow to one end of a path and a tail to the other, you have to choose the Add Arrowheads command twice.

After you press the Return key, Illustrator assigns the arrowhead to the path. The arrowhead is a separate path—or in some cases, several paths—that Illustrator groups with the original open path. This is important for you to keep in mind when transforming the path. If you scale the path disproportionately, for example, you'll squish or stretch the arrowhead. If this happens, select the arrowhead with the direct selection tool, delete it, and then apply a new arrowhead.

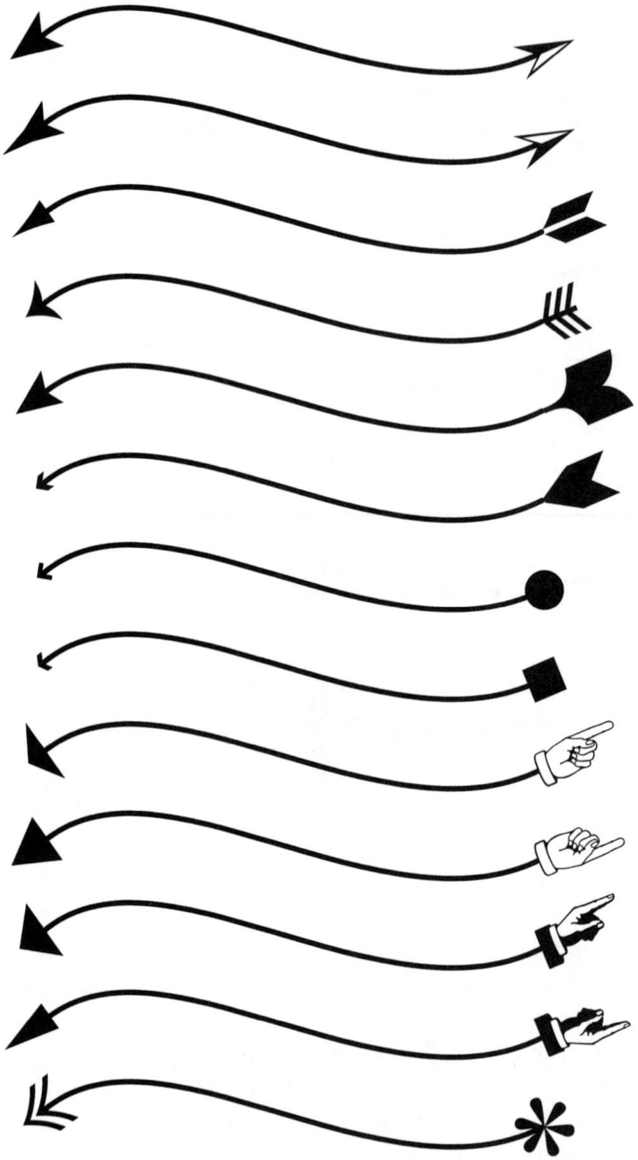

Figure 16-30: You can apply any of these festive arrowheads using the Add Arrowheads filter. In each case, the line weight is 2 points and the Scale value is set to 100 percent.

If you select the line and arrowhead with the arrow tool, the Color palette and the toolbox display question marks for both the Fill and Stroke icons. This is because the line is stroked but presumably not filled, while the arrowhead is filled but not stroked. If you want to change the fill or stroke of either portion of the object, use the direct selection tool to select either line or arrowhead independently.

TIP

If you've already positioned the open path exactly where you want it, you'll notice that Illustrator appends the arrowhead to the end of the path, elongating it. To move the arrowhead back to the proper position, try this: Marquee around the entire arrowhead with the direct selection tool. This selects both the arrowhead and the endpoint of the line. Then drag the arrowhead by its tip and snap it onto the previous location of the endpoint. This technique doesn't always do the trick when working with curved lines, but it fixes straight lines without a hitch.

Converting Strokes to Filled Paths

You can choose the Object » Path » Outline Path command to convert stroked lines to filled shapes based on the path's line weight. Choose the command to instruct Illustrator to trace around the stroke of a selected object. Figure 16-31 shows a star that used to be stroked with a 6-point outline. Illustrator actually traced two paths around the stroke, one along the inside and the other along the outside, resulting in a compound path.

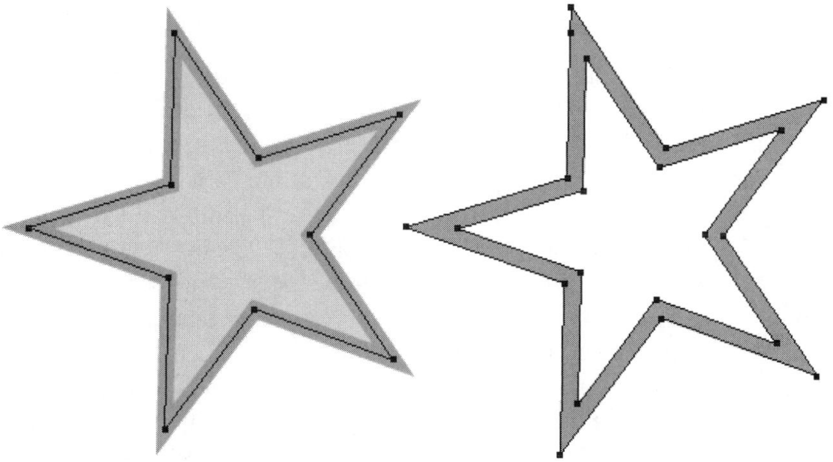

Figure 16-31: Starting with a star with no fill and a 6-point stroke, I applied the Outline Path filter (left). The new path appears directly above the original.

The Outline Path filter has been improved in Illustrator 8. In previous versions, at least one of the paths that the filter created would overlap itself in places, which required that you apply the Unite filter to remove overlapping segments and simplify the path. Adobe has seen fit to change this fault of the Outline Path filter and spare you this tedium. Now only non-overlapping paths are created when you use this filter.

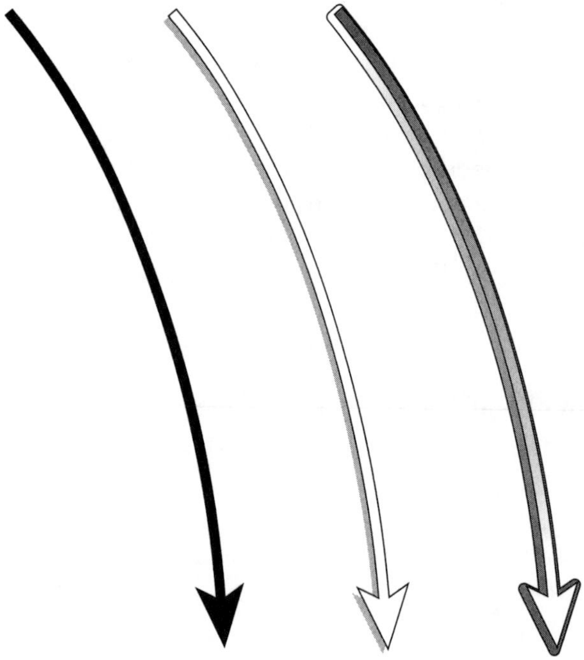

Figure 16-32: After adding an arrowhead to a line (left), I converted the line to a closed path and united it with the arrowhead (middle). Then I applied the Offset Path filter and filled both paths with gradations (right).

Why is the Outline Path filter so gosh-darn wonderful? Take, as examples, the arrows in Figure 16-32. I started with a 4-point line with a nondescript arrowhead. Then I selected the line independent of the arrowhead with the direct selection tool and converted it to a closed path using the Outline Path command. I next selected both the converted path and the arrowhead and combined them into a single shape using the Pathfinder palette's Unite option. To get the result shown in the second example in the figure, I filled the arrow shape with white, stroked it with a thin black outline, and cloned the path to create a light gray drop shadow. Without the Outline Path filter, this would have been very difficult to pull off.

But while the second example in Figure 16-32 would have been difficult to create without Outline Path, the third example would have been impossible to make. Here I used our old friend Object » Path » Offset Path to create a larger version of the arrow path. (I set the Offset value to 2 and the Line Join option to Round.) Then I nudged the first arrow up and to the right a little and filled both paths with the same gray-to-white gradation. Finally, I used the gradient vector tool to point one gradation in one direction and the other in the opposite direction.

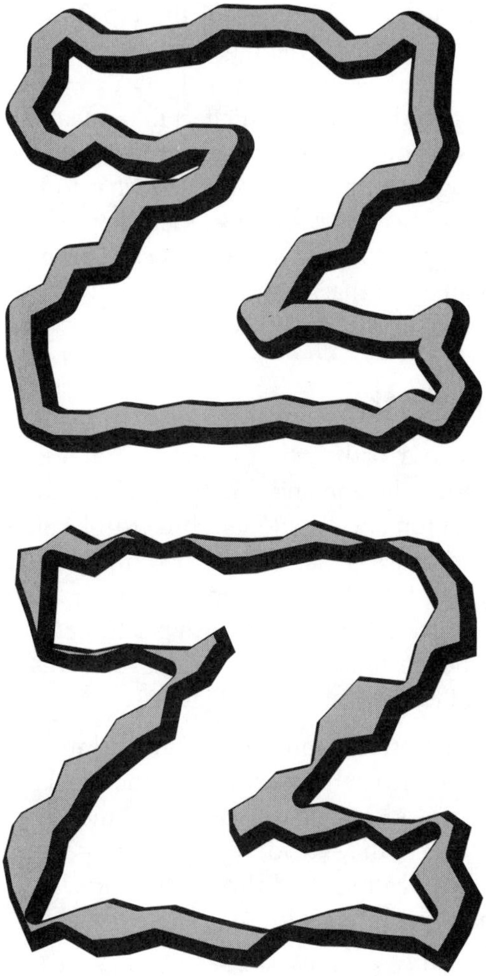

Figure 16-33:
The effect of the Roughen filter on a couple of stroked paths (top) compared with its effect on a few filled shapes created with the Outline Path command (bottom).

Figure 16-33 demonstrates another of the Outline Path filter's miracles—it lets you create variable-width lines. In the top example, I took a converted letter with a 16-point black stroke, abused it with Filter » Distort » Roughen, cloned and nudged the beleaguered path, and applied an 8-point gray stroke to the clone. It's very similar to what I did back in Figure 16-27.

In the second example, I introduced a new element—Outline Path—and arrived at a significantly different result. I started with the same 16-point Z but immediately converted the stroke with the Outline Path filter. Then I applied the same settings as before with the Roughen filter. But this time, the Roughen command modified both edges of the compound path around the Z, randomly altering the thickness of the outline. (By contrast, the outline of the top Z, while random in shape, is uniformly thick.) Since applying the filter had created a new shape, I could no longer clone the path and change its stroke, so I chose the Offset Path filter and entered a value of –4. This produces a similar effect to reducing the stroke by 8 points since the filter shaves 4 points off either side of the path. The Offset command produced a lot of garbage, so I manually decided what to keep and what to throw away with the direct selection tool and Delete key. Then I nudged the path up and to the left and applied a gray fill. As you can see, using Outline Path and Offset Path, I created an effect that's more prehistoric than ever.

Brushing Up on Your Paths

Instead of adding a simple outline to your paths, you can now brush a path. The brush follows the path, perfectly fitting the ebb and tide of the path's curve. Any path you create with the brush tool automatically adopts a brushstroke along its length. One of the great things about brushes is that they are not limited to the paths created with the brush tool. The fact is that you can apply a brush to any selected path. Simply select the path and click on one of the Brush palette's entries.

There are four different type of brushes in Illustrator. By default, the Brushes palette contains a number of examples of each, as shown in Figure 16-34.

- **Calligraphic Brushes:** A calligraphic brush simulates the lines created with a fountain pen. You have control over the roundness of the brush tip, the angle of the tip and its size. Although you can use a mouse when drawing with a calligraphic brush, they are ideal for pressure sensitive tablets. With such a tablet, you can vary all three of the brush's attributes as a function of how hard you press with the tablet's stylus.
- **Scatter Brushes:** A scatter brush takes a single object or a group of objects and repeats them a number of times along the length of the path. You can control the size of the objects, the spacing (or the distance between the objects along the path), the scattering (or the distance the objects stray to the side of the paths), and the rotation of the objects.
- **Art Brushes:** An art brush takes a single drawing and stretches it the length of the path. You can decide in which direction the brush will

follow the path, the width of the brush, and whether the brush will flip across the path.

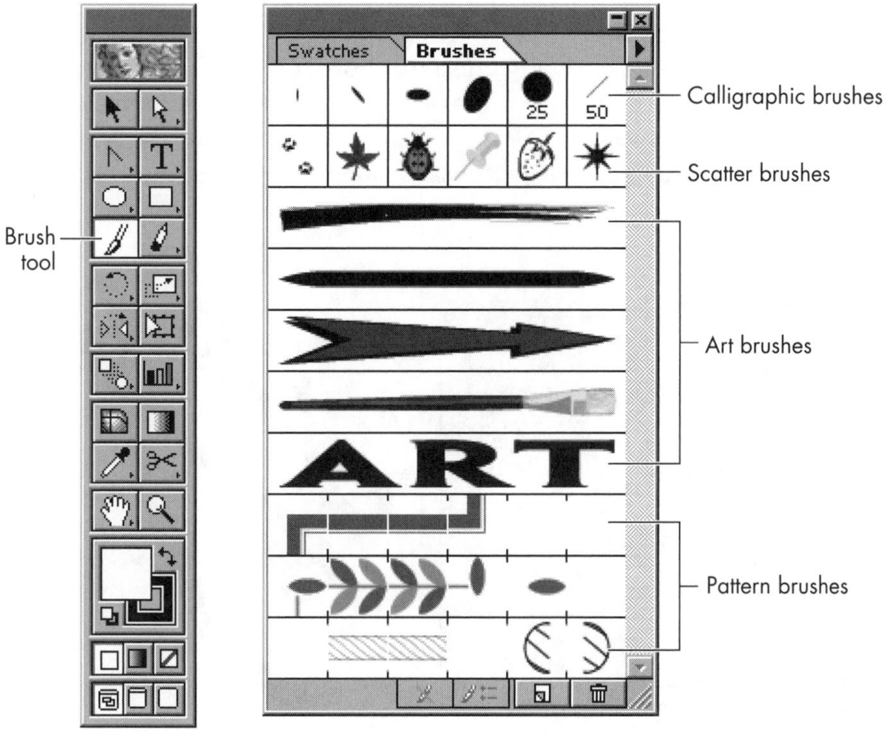

Figure 16-34: The standard Brushes palette contains several versions of each of the four brush types.

- **Pattern Brushes:** A pattern brush is a compilation of individual blocks that link together to form a continuous chain. They are ideal for borders since you can specify the design of the both the beginning and the end of the path, the appearance of the inner and outer corners, and all the parts that make up all the pieces in between.

Creating Brushes

To design a new brush, you need to assemble all its components and choose New Brush from the Brushes palette's pop-up menu. Illustrator then gives you the option of creating any one of the four types of brushes. Illustrator is rather fussy about what kinds of graphic elements it will allow you to use in a brush. A candidate for a new brush cannot contain gradients, live blends, rasterized objects, other brushes, or unconverted type. You can, however, use regular old paths with flat fills and strokes. These paths can't be masked or part of compound path. The best rule of thumb when creating brushes is to keep it simple.

Calligraphic Brushes

The calligraphic brush is the only brush that doesn't require you to create part of the brush before you design a new brush. Choose New Brush from the Brush palette's pop-up menu and choose New Calligraphic Brush from the New Brush dialog box. The Calligraphic Brush options dialog box will display, as shown in Figure 16-35.

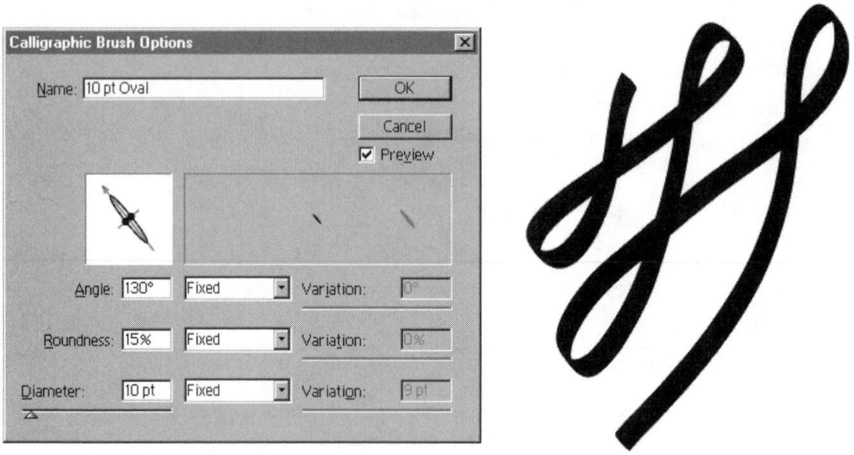

Figure 16-35: A calligraphic brush simulates a real-world pen. All you need to do is decide on the specifics of the pen's tip.

- **Angle:** You can choose how many degrees from the horizontal the tip will deflect. Either enter a value into the Angle option box or drag the arrow in the example box to change the angle.
- **Roundness:** Here you decide how round you want the tip, whether you want a nice round tip or a more oblong one, like the tip of an old felt marker. Enter a value into the Roundness dialog box or drag one of the black circles in the example box to change the roundness.
- **Diameter:** Enter a value that reflects the size of the brush that you want.

All three of the options come with their own pop-up menus that give you control over how Illustrator will apply the options.

- **Fixed:** This means that the pen will use the value in a consistent way.

- **Random:** This means that Illustrator will vary the value as you apply the brush. A second slider bar to the right of the pop-up menu will appear. Here you decide the amount that the original value can vary.
- **Pressure:** If you use a pressure-sensitive drawing tablet, you can opt to have Illustrator take this into account. When selected, a second slider bar will activate to the right of the pop-up menu. With it you decide how much more or less the original value will vary to reflect the pressure you apply to the tablet.

Scatter Brushes

For a new scatter brush, you first need to design the objects you want to appear along your brush stroke. You can start with a very simple design, such as a rectangle or ellipse. With your paths selected, choose New Brush from the Brushes palette's pop-up menu and select the New Scatter brush. The Scatter Brush Options dialog box will appear, as shown in Figure 16-36.

- **Size:** Enter a percentage between 0 and 100. This dictates how large the individual objects will appear along the brush.
- **Spacing:** Here you choose how far apart you want the objects to space themselves along the path.

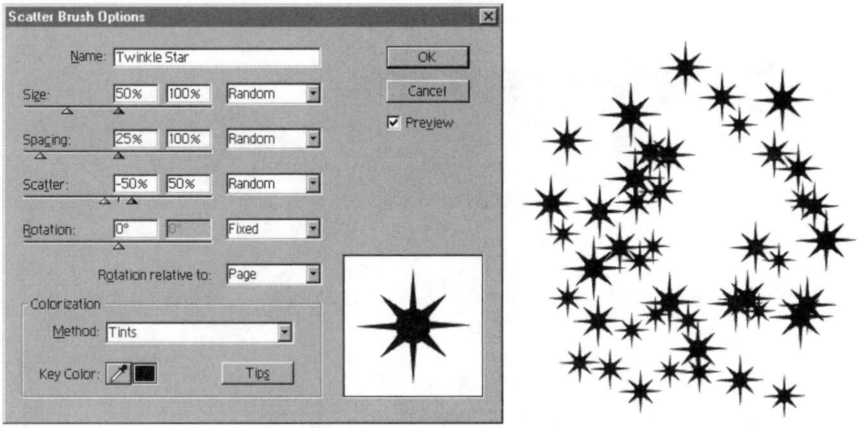

Figure 16-36: With a scatter brush, small objects repeat across the path's outline. Here I used a scatter on a spiral.

- **Scatter:** This is the distance that the objects will appear above and below the path. In Figure 16-36, the stars scatter a healthy 50 percent above and below the path making it slightly difficult to make out the spiral nature of the original path. Keep these values small if you want to stress the shape of the path.

- **Rotation:** The scatter brush objects can rotate as they appear along the path. Also you decide whether the objects will rotate relative to the page or the path.

All of these options come with the same pop-up menus as occur in the options for the New Calligraphic Brush. You can choose to have the scatter objects appear uniformly along the path or vary them, either randomly or as dictated by the pressure you apply to your drawing tablet.

Art Brushes

Once again, you need to design the brush first. Select all the paths, choose New Brush from the Brushes palette's pop-up menu, and select the New Art Brush option. The Art Brush Options dialog box will appear, as shown in Figure 16-37. The pencil I made consists of four rectangles, three rounded rectangles, and two triangles. All the paths use flat fills and stroke.

- **Direction:** This determines the direction that the brush will lie with respect to the path and the direction in which it was drawn.
- **Size:** Enter a value to set the thickness of the brush. If you want to uniformly change the size, click the Proportional check box.
- **Flip:** You can choose to flip the object along the axis of the path or across its axis.

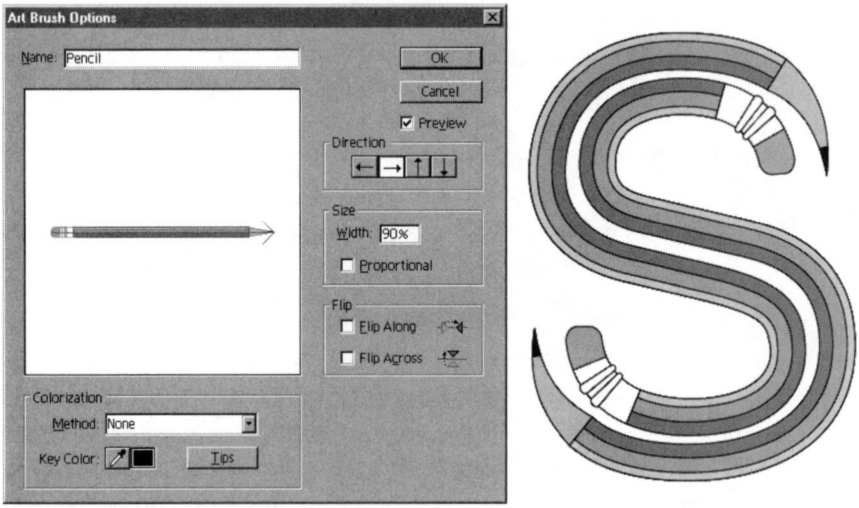

Figure 16-37: I created a new art brush from a collection of nine paths and applied it to a converted and slightly modified letter S.

Art brushes work well with converted text. The only thing is that you will need to break the converted paths apart to get the best results. In Figure 16-37, I converted an S into a path, cut away the two small pieces that capped the ends and applied my new art brush to the remaining paths. Illustrator brushed both path simultaneously. Since the two pieces were drawn in different directions, the brushes flow up one and down the other.

Pattern Brushes

You don't need to design a pattern brush entirely from scratch, but if you don't, you're stuck with Illustrator's lame design choices. The design elements for a pattern brush come from pattern swatches in the Swatches palette. You can design the elements of your new pattern brush one at a time and add them to the brush individually via the New Brush command, but it's easier to design a bunch of patterns swatches and add them to the Swatches palette first and then assemble them with the New Brushes command. Either way, when you choose New Brush from the Brushes palette's pop-up menu and select the New Pattern Brush option, the Pattern Brush Options dialog box will appear, as shown in Figure 16-38.

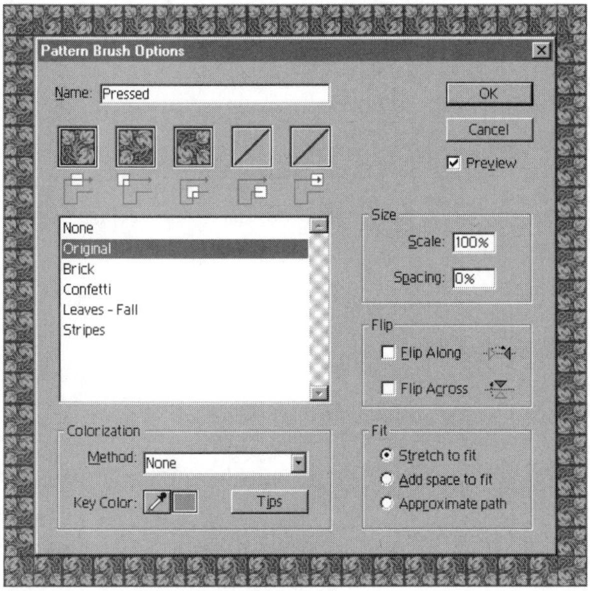

Figure 16-38: With this brush, you form a seamless chain of graphics. I used a pattern brush on a path that's the same size as the dialog box. The brush forms a lovely border for the dialog box, making the dialog box suitable for hanging.

- **Size:** Choose the thickness of the brush. If you want to uniformly change the size, click the Proportional check box.

- **Flip:** You can choose to flip the object along the axis of the path or across its axis.
- **Fit:** Unlike with the other brushes, the pattern brushes are blocks that link together to form a smooth pattern along the path. This means that the bits of the pattern may not always fit exactly. You have three choices of how Illustrator will fit the brush to the path. Stretch to Fit will stretch the brush elements as needed to just fit the brush to the path. This means that Illustrator will need to distort the brush elements. Add Space to Fit means that Illustrator will add tiny spaces to the brush as necessary. It won't distort any brush elements, but it may give a disjointed appearance to you path. With Approximate Path, Illustrator changes the actual size of the path so that it fits the brush perfectly.

Changing a Brush's Appearance

You can change the attributes of a brush globally or on a case-by-case basis. To change the appearance of all occurrences of a particular brush, either double-click on the brush in the Brushes palette or choose the Brush Options from the palette's pop-up menu. The same Brush Options dialog box that appears when you create a new brush will display. After you make you changes to a brush and click the OK button, Illustrator displays an alert box. Click the Apply to Stroke button to apply your changes to all current and future uses of the brush. Click the Leave Stroke button to apply change to only future uses of the brushes.

To change only the appearance of the selected objects, choose the Option of Selected Objects from the Brushes palette's pop-up menu. The selected path must use the same brush if you want to use this option. This will display a slightly reduced version of the appropriate Brush Options dialog box. Any changes you make will affect only the selected paths and not impact any future use of the brush.

Removing a Brush

Brushing a path converts the path into an object that is less versatile than a regular stroked object. You cannot add a brushed path to a compound path. You can brush paths that are currently part of a compound path, but these paths must start off as normal objects. You can't convert a brushed path into a gradient mesh object. You can't blend between brushed paths, and you can't apply the Pen and Ink Hatch Effects filter to a brushed path.

In most cases, you can first remove a brush from a path, modify the path, and then reapply the brush. To remove a brush, select a brushed path and choose the Remove Brush Stroke from the Brushes palette's pop-up menu.

CHAPTER 17

BLENDS, MASKS, AND SPECIAL INKS

Blends and masks continue to be two of Illustrator's most powerful and flexible capabilities. They are truly tools of the advanced user. One permits you to create custom gradations and shape morphings; the other permits you to clip those gradations—or any other collection of objects—inside a path. These are not tools for the timid; the blend tool takes skill, effort, and time to master, and the mask function can choke the printer if used unwisely or in excess. But if you value control and versatility, blends and masks are for you.

This chapter offers another method to create a custom gradation. For example, you can create two or more paths, fill them with different colors, and then blend them to create a host of incremental color bands. Were you to blend two colors using a gradient fill or a multicolor fill, the resulting fill would contain only a dithering of the two colors. (Dithering is a visual effect that arranges two colors in a pattern to give the appearance of a broader range of colors.) Only the blending of two colors gives you incremental color bands.

This chapter concludes with the Pen and Ink filter. This unusual and exceptionally complex feature combines the powers of blending and masking to create cross-hatch, line, and dot patterns. Unlike tile patterns, Pen and Ink patterns can change over the course of the shape, becoming progressively lighter and darker like gradations. You need a strong will to put up with the Pen and Ink Hatch Effects dialog box—easily the most daunting collection of options inside all of Illustrator—but your labor will not go unrewarded.

In other words, welcome to the hard stuff in Illustrator. When you finish with this chapter, you'll fully deserve to stick a gold star on your monitor.

Blending Paths

Blending is one of Illustrator's most exotic and oldest capabilities. Back when every one of its competitors offered automated gradations, Illustrator allowed you to design your own custom gradations. Illustrator's blend tool wasn't easy to use, but it yielded an unlimited range of results. There wasn't a single gradation you couldn't create if you put your mind to it.

Now, Illustrator offers what is undoubtedly the finest automatic gradient fill function of any drawing program (as discussed in Chapter 15) and a blend tool that's simply unrivaled. Anytime you want to go beyond linear and radial gradations, the blend tool is at your beck and call.

Blending is part duplication, part distribution, and part transformation. It creates a series of intermediate paths, called *steps*, between two selected free-form paths. I say that it's part duplication because the Blend command creates as many clones of a path as you like. It's part distribution because the steps are evenly distributed between the two original objects. And it's part transformation because FreeHand automatically adjusts the shape of each step depending on where it lies. Steps near the first of the two original paths resemble the first path; steps near the second path more closely resemble the second path.

Blending creates a metamorphic transition between one shape and another. For example, suppose that you create two paths, one that represents a man and one that represents a lycanthropic alter ego. By blending these two paths, you create several steps that represent metamorphic stages between the two life forms, as shown in Figure 17-1. The first intermediate path is shaped much like the man. Each intermediate path after that becomes less like the man and more like the wolf.

Figure 17-1: Blending between these extremes creates a series of transformed and distributed duplicates between the two objects.

Illustrator also blends the fills and strokes between two paths. If one path is white and the other is black, for example, the steps between the paths are filled with a fountain of transitional gray values. Though each step is filled with a solid color (assuming that you're blending objects with flat fills), the effect is that of a gradation. To create the steps shown in Figure 17-1, for example, I used opposite fill and stroke colors in each path. After I created the blend, I expanded the blends (discussed later), brought the wolfen to the front, and applied heavier strokes to both the man and wolfman.

Creating a Blend

To create a blend, you must first select two or more free-form paths. You can blend between paths that are by themselves, part of groups, or even composite paths. (Selecting only a single path from a group or compound path forces the entire path to join in the blend.) Although it is possible to blend an open path to a closed path, the results are often rather ugly. Paths should be filled and stroked similarly. For example, if one path is stroked with a 6-point line weight, you can't blend it with a path that has a transparent stroke.

TIP

You can, however, blend between a path stroked with a 6-point line weight and one stroked with a 0-point line weight. Because a 0-point line weight results in the thinnest line that your printer can create, the stroke is practically transparent when printed to a high-resolution imagesetter.

To blend paths you can either let Illustrator automatically decide the best blending arrangement or you can choose which point you want to blend. To use Illustrator's blending instincts, select the paths and choose Object » Blends » Make, or press ⌘-Option-B to create a series of steps. Illustrator treats the front-most path of the originals as the first path in the blend and the rear path as the last path. The steps are layered between the first and last paths, descending in stacking order—one in back of another—as they approach the last. For a bit more control, click with the blend tool on one point in the first path and then click on a point in another path. In either case, Illustrator automatically combines original paths and steps into a grouped object that has special properties (which are discussed in later sections). This object is a blend. Alternatively, you can select one (and only one) point in each path. Selecting points allows you more control over the blend. If the paths are open, you must select an endpoint in each path. (See "Deciding Which Points to Select" later in this chapter.)

To create a simple blend, follow these steps:

1. **Specify the fill and stroke of the paths you want to blend.**

   Illustrator can blend any two colors, including gray values and spot colors. It can even blend gradations or a flat fill and a gradient. Illustrator can also blend strokes and line weights, but don't expect to be able to blend two different line caps, joins, or dash patterns. Also, Illustrator can't use brushes in blends.

2. **Select the paths.**

   Illustrator can blend numerous paths at a time. In fact, your machine's RAM is the only limiting factor. For now, it's best to keep it simple and use only a few paths.

TIP

Although Illustrator is not restricted to blending paths that have the same number of points, they do work best for blending. But if one path has more points than the other, you can even things out by selecting all points in one path and the same number of points in the other path. (See the upcoming section "Deciding Which Points to Select.")

3. Choose Object » Blends » Make.

Or press ⌘-Option-B. Illustrator will produce what it thinks is the smoothest possible blend between the selected paths. If you prefer to specify the points that you want Illustrator to blend around, click on one point in each selected path with the blend tool. First click on one point, and then click on another. If you miss a point, Illustrator tries its best to guess which point you were going after. You can blend only two paths at a time with the blend tool. After the first two paths blend, click again with the blend tool on another path's point and Illustrator will add that path to the blend.

The points on which you click have a big impact on the final blend. If possible, click on similar points in both paths. In Figure 17-2, for example, I clicked on the lower left point in the outside cone and then on the lower left point on the inside cone. (See the section "Deciding Where to Click" later in this chapter for more info.)

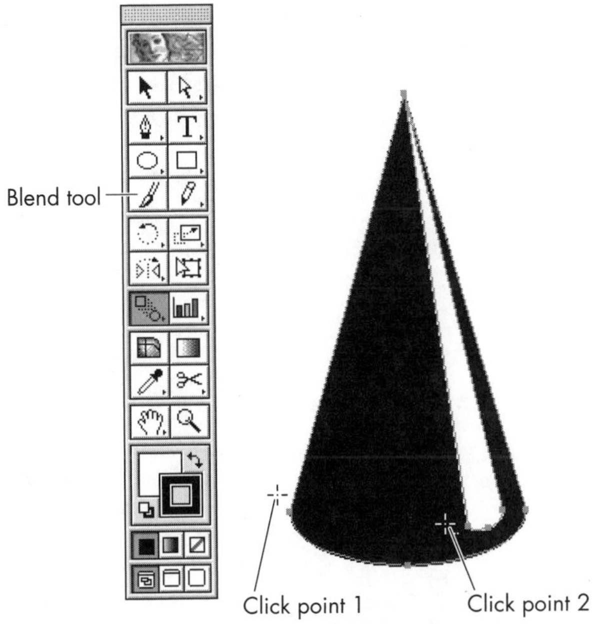

Figure 17-2: After selecting the blend tool, I clicked on the lower left point in each of two selected shapes.

4. Specify the blend spacing.

Choose Object » Blends » Blend Options. The Blend Options dialog box will display, as shown in Figure 17-3. By default, Illustrator uses the smooth color spacing scheme to decide how many intermediate paths are needed to produce the best blend.

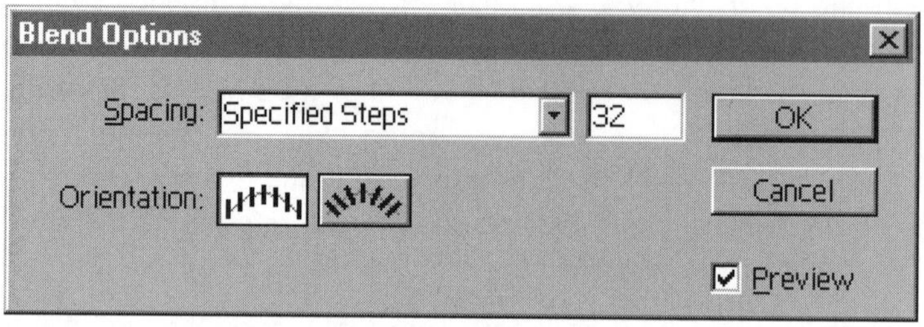

Figure 17-3: The Blend Options dialog box lets you choose the number of steps that make up your blend.

If you find that Illustrator has not added enough steps, or if Illustrator has included more steps than you think are necessary, you can change the number of steps by choosing either the Specified Steps or the Specified Distance from the Spacing pop-up menu. Deciding how many steps to use can be a difficult proposition. (For a technical evaluation of steps, with some numerical recommendations, read the "Deciding the Number of Steps" section later in this chapter.)

5. Change the Orientation.

...Only if you want to, that is. The orientation of the blend steps is limited to aligning to the page and aligning to the path. Figure 17-4 shows the difference.

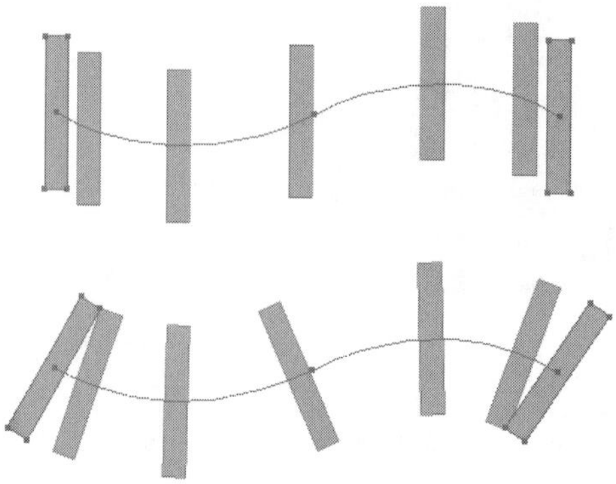

Figure 17-4: The example on the top is the standard Align to Page orientation that Illustrator applies by default. On the bottom, we see that with the Align to Path icon selected, the rectangles are not square to the page but instead curve around with the path.

Deciding Which Points to Select

If you choose to use the blend tool to manually select the points that you want Illustrator to consider in the blend, you'll have no problem when both paths contain the same number of points. Illustrator merely takes a point in Path A, finds its buddy in Path B, and creates a blend between them. But if the paths are so much as one point different, Illustrator gets mixed up. It tries to blend between pairs of points at first but then gives it up about midway through.

Figure 17-5 is a perfect example of a bad blend. Here I've blended between a five-sided polygon and a five-pointed star. You'd think Illustrator would be able to figure out what close cousins these paths are, but all Illustrator knows is that the star contains ten points and the pentagon contains only five. If you look closely, you can see a clear progression of steps between the bottom three points in the star and the bottom three points in the pentagon. But the rest of the blend is chaos and confusion. The steps eke outside the star, twist all over the place, and generally make a mockery out of any semblance of an orderly gradation.

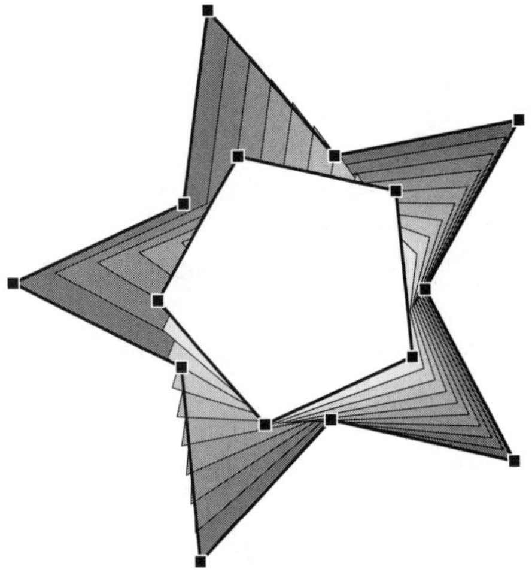

Figure 17-5: Selecting all points in paths with different numbers of points results in a crazy, mixed up blend.

The solution to this problem is to carefully select the points you want to blend with the direct selection tool. For example, in this case, I'd select all five points in the pentagon and then select five corresponding points in the star. The points that make the most sense are the five spike points, selected in the first example of Figure 17-6. This causes the corners of the pentagon to blend into the spikes in the star. But I could also select the five crease points, as in the right example in the figure. This also results in a logical, constant blend, though the effect is somewhat unusual. Either way, I told Illustrator exactly what I wanted and Illustrator delivered.

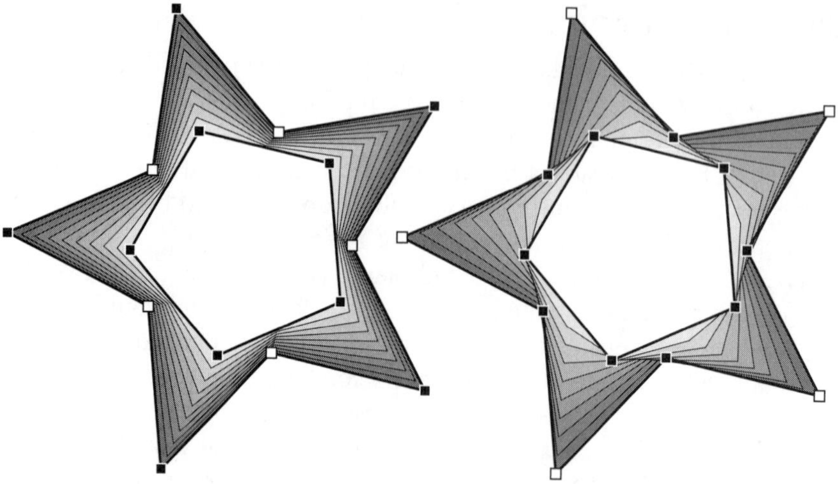

Figure 17-6: If you select the same number of points in each shape—in this case, five points apiece—the blend become orderly. (The selected points appear black.)

Deciding Where to Click

When clicking with the blend tool, you have to click on a selected point, and if the path is open, you have to click on an endpoint. Those are the only hard-and-fast rules. But merely following the rules doesn't ensure good results. Which points you click on can make or break a blend.

The two click points tell Illustrator the locations of the first pair of points it should blend. The program then wanders around the shapes in a clockwise direction and pairs up the other points. Figure 17-7 shows the results of blending two five-pointed stars after clicking on different points in the two shapes. I always clicked on the lower right point in the small star, but I clicked on a total of six different points in the larger star. As you can see, this has a profound effect on how the blend progresses.

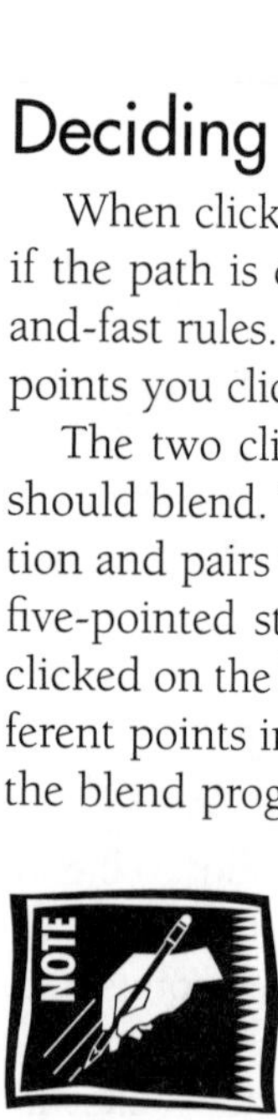

Each small star in Figure 17-7 was originally filled with white. I changed the fills to None after blending the shapes to permit you to see the steps in back, some of which would have been covered up if I had left the star white.

Though many of the effects in Figure 17-7 are interesting, only the first three are suitable for creating gradations, as demonstrated in Figure 17-8. And even then, the third example is a mighty unusual gradation with harsh edges. Your safest bet is to click on a matching point in each object, as in the first example in Figure 17-8. This results in the smoothest possible progression.

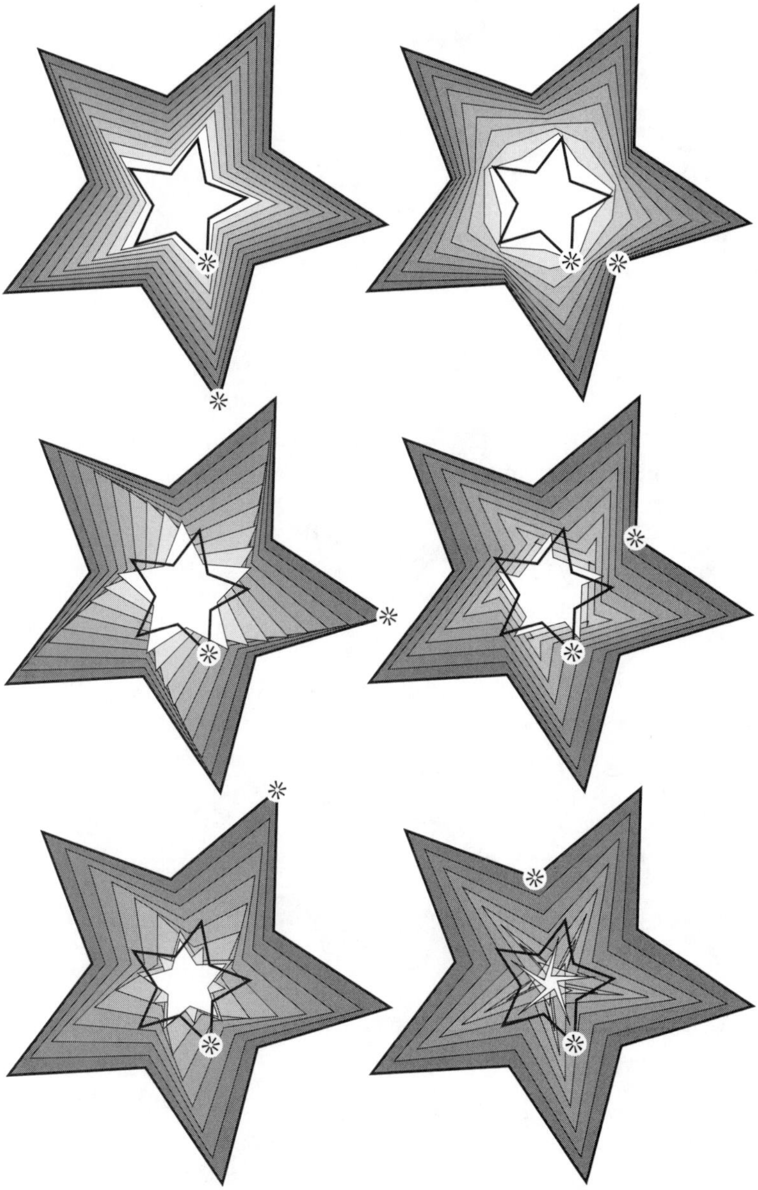

Figure 17-7: The sparkles show the points where I clicked on each pair of shapes with the blend tool.

Figure 17-8: Here I used the same click points used for Figure 17-7, but I got rid of the strokes and increased the number of steps to 88 per blend.

Recognizing When You Need More Points

Although it may seem unfair, you can still end up with harsh edges after taking the precautions of selecting an equal number of points in both shapes and clicking on similar points. Consider the first example in Figure 17-9. Both shapes contain four points (all selected) and I clicked on the lowest point in each shape. And yet, as the second example shows, I ended up with harsh edges. The top and bottom of the white shape look like they're thrusting forward from the black ellipse. No, no, no, we simply cannot have this!

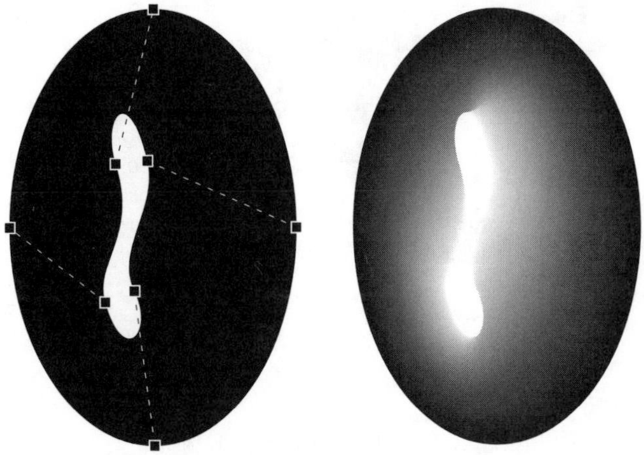

Figure 17-9: If you can't draw straight lines between the paired points in your shapes without running over segments (left), you'll end up with harsh edges in your final blend (right).

The problem is that two of the paired points in the two shapes aren't properly aligned. That is, if a crow were to fly from one point to another, it would smack into a segment. I've drawn dotted lines between the paired points in the first example. The lines between the left and right pairs of points are unobstructed, but the lines between the top and bottom pairs intersect the smaller shape. These intersections are precisely the areas in which our problems occur.

TIP

The solution is to add more points. If you add a point to every segment in each shape, you can ensure that all points are in line. Use the add point tool, not the automated Add Anchor Points command. As shown in Figure 17-10, you don't want the points to be spaced consistently. What matters is that you can draw a straight line between every pair of points in the shapes and not come in contact with any segments. As the dotted lines show, this is precisely what I've accomplished in Figure 17-10. Then I selected all points and blended between them, creating the silky smooth gradation shown in the second example.

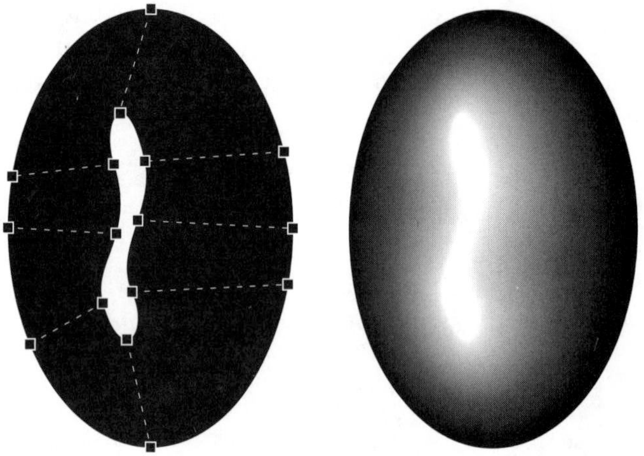

Figure 17-10: Use the add point tool to add points to both shapes so that all straight lines drawn between the paired points are unobstructed (left). This ensures a fluid gradation (right).

Deciding the Number of Steps

Another problem that plagues blends is a pesky printing phenomenon called *banding*. Rather than printing as a seamless gradation, the blend exhibits distinct bands of color. When banding occurs, gradient credibility goes out the window. Figure 17-11 offers an exaggerated example of banding. In the first blend, I created 13 steps, hardly enough to produce smooth shading. You can see almost every step in the shape, resulting in lots of bands. The second blend is much smoother, but it also contains 198 steps.

Unfortunately, while using very few steps practically guarantees banding, having lots of steps doesn't necessarily prevent it. You have to print enough steps to take advantage of your printer's ability to generate gray values, but not so many that one or more steps appear out of sync with their neighbors. In an ideal blend, each printed step corresponds to a unique gray value and varies from its neighbors by a consistent amount. Illustrator creates unique, consistent steps automatically, no matter how many steps you assign, but this doesn't mean they'll necessarily print correctly. It all hinges on the answers to two questions:

- Is the printer properly calibrated?
- What is the resolution and screen frequency of the printer?

You can't anticipate bad calibration. You just have to hope that your service bureau or commercial printer has its machinery in top condition. But you can account for resolution and screen frequency. Very briefly—I cover both topics in more detail in Chapter 18—resolution is the number of pixels the printer can print per inch (just like screen resolution). And screen frequency is the number of halftone dots that print per inch. Printer resolution is measured in dots per inch (dpi), and screen frequency is measured in lines per inch (lpi). The resolution is fixed, but the screen frequency can change. For example, a typical LaserWriter prints at 300 dpi, but the lpi can be set to 60 or 53.

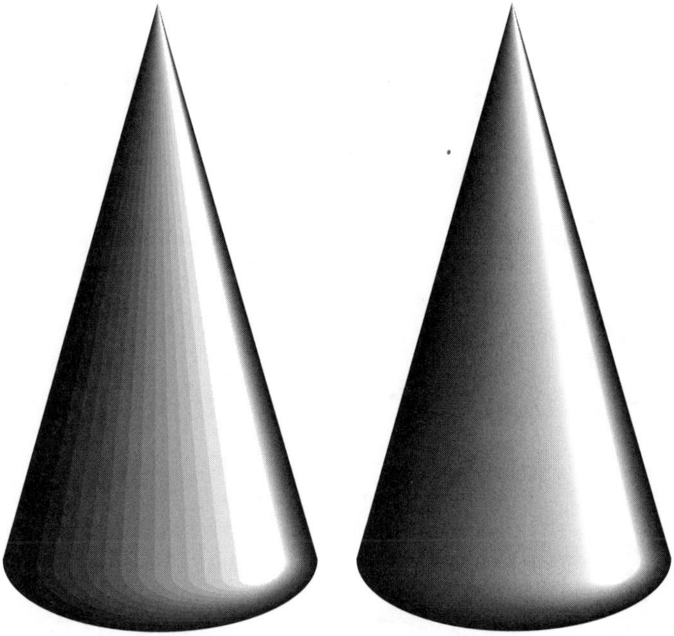

Figure 17-11: A blend with banding (left) and one with seamless color transitions (right).

If you print a 60-lpi screen from a 300-dpi LaserWriter, each halftone dot measures 5 pixels wide by 5 pixels tall. (That's because 300 ÷ 60 = 5.) And a 5-by-5 dot contains a total of 25 pixels. If all pixels are turned off, the halftone dot is white. All pixels turned on produces black, and turning on 1 to 24 pixels produces a shade of gray. Including black and white, that's a total of 26 gray values, which is the absolute maximum number of shades a 300 dpi, 60 lpi LaserWriter can print.

That's just one example. Printers vary from model to model. But if you know the dpi and lpi values, you can calculate the number of printable gray values using this formula:

$(\text{dpi} \div \text{lpi})^2 + 1$

Take a top-of-the-line Linotronic imagesetter, for example. The resolution is 2540 dpi, and the default screen frequency is 133 lpi. When you divide 2540 by 133, you get 19.097. Then you multiply 19.097 by itself and add 1 to get 365 gray values, quite a few more than the LaserWriter.

I hate to make you do too much math, so here are the maximum number of gray values associated with a few popular resolutions and screen frequencies:

Resolution	Screen frequency	Maximum shades of gray
300	53	33
300	60	26
400	60	45
400	75	29
600	60	101
600	75	65
600	90	45
1200	75	256
1200	90	179
1200	120	101
1200	133	82
1270	75	256
1270	90	200
1270	120	113
1270	133	92
2400	up to 150	256
2540	up to 150	256

After you find the maximum number of gray values, you need to factor in the range of colors in your blend. A black-to-white blend requires all the gray levels your printer can produce. Just take the value in the last column of the table and subtract 2—black and white. For example, if you're creating a black-to-white blend for a 1270 dpi, 90 lpi printer, you want 200 – 2 = 198 steps.

If the color range is smaller, there's no sense in using all those steps because your printer won't be able to print them. So multiply the maximum printable gray values by the percentage change in color and then subtract 2. The range of grays in a blend from 70 percent black to 20 percent black is 50 percent. If you plan to print this to our 1270 dpi, 90 lpi printer, you'd multiply 200 by 0.5 (50 percent), which is 100. Then subtract 2 to get 98 steps.

When creating color blends that you intend to print, look for the biggest CMYK difference. For example, let's say you want to blend between a shape filled with 40%C 30%M 20%Y 10%K and one filled with 100%C 40%M 30%Y 20%K. The biggest variation between any of the process colors is 100%C minus 40%C, which is 60 percent. So you'd multiply 200 by 0.6 (60 percent) to get 120, and then subtract 2 to calculate 118 steps in the blend.

Lastly, factor in size. If the blend covers the whole page, you have to use all the steps you can (according to the above calculations). But if it's a small gradation, you may be able to get away with fewer. For example, a blend that's 1-inch wide doesn't merit 118 steps. You can probably get away with half that many, or 59. If you decide to decrease the number of steps, always divide by an whole number, like 2, 3, or 4.

After all this, you may be thinking it's just easier to accept the Steps value Illustrator gives you and call it a day. And certainly you can do that if you like. But if you notice banding inside your printed illustrations, come back to this section and give it another try.

On the other hand, if this brief introduction to banding has only whetted your appetite, check out *Real World Scanning and Halftones* (Peachpit Press) by David Blatner and Steve Roth. Tough topic, smart guys, ideal combination.

Cool Blend Tool Tricks

I've droned on about the blend tool for quite a while now, but I haven't even begun to tell you all the great things you can do with it. Though I can't share every blend tool and custom gradation trick I've invented or gleaned over the years, I will suggest a handful of what I consider to be the most interesting tips and tricks in the following sections. With any luck, they'll inspire you to develop more sophisticated techniques of your own.

Morphing Path Outlines

In addition to generating custom gradations, the blend tool is a shape-modification tool. Much like the Pathfinder filters, you can use the tool to take two paths and combine them into a third. This technique is known as *morphing*.

In Figure 17-12, I've taken a series of shapes and morphed between them. Each column in the figure represents a separate morph, with the original shapes in gray at the top and bottom. In each case, I created three steps between the two original shapes. That way, I created an instant library of intermediate shapes to choose from; no other path-combination feature provides such a range of alternatives.

But I should warn you, it's not quite as easy as it looks. I had to spend a few minutes on each pair of original paths, making sure the two had the same number of points. For example, the pair of stars in the first column each have 20 points, even though the top star has half as many spikes as the bottom one. The circle and star in the second column each have 16 points, and so on. I inserted most of the points with Object » Path » Add Anchor Points, but I had to add a few manually with the add point tool.

Figure 17-12: A series of morphings, arranged in columns, created between a shape at the top and its counterpart at the bottom.

You can also use the blend tool to morph type converted to path outlines. In Figure 17-13, I started with a line of type in Bookman Light Italic and another in Bookman Bold Italic. (Both are widely available LaserWriter Plus fonts.) I created the three rows of white letters with the blend tool. If you're a type enthusiast, you'll love this technique because it permits you to generate your own custom styles and weights without purchasing more fonts. But it takes some skill and effort. When converted to path outlines, the light and bold characters contain different numbers of points—not wildly different but enough to keep you on your toes. There's no room for automation here; you have to insert points manually with the add point tool.

Figure 17-13:
Three character morphs created by blending between the top row of Bookman Light Italic and the bottom row of Bookman Bold Italic.

You won't even have to worry about the compound paths used to create the *B*, *e*, and *d*. It used to be the case that you would have to blend between each subpath in a separate operation. Now, Illustrator is smart enough to do all the blending without having to bother you one iota.

If you're feeling extra brave, you can even blend between character outlines and standard shapes. In Figure 17-14, I tried my hand at blending between three converted characters of Helvetica and a modified star, figure 8, and spiral. As you can see, I modified the letters slightly before morphing by changing the compound paths of the *A* and *B* into continuous outlines. I also abused the shapes at the bottom of the figure fairly significantly. The shapes in the middle of the figure were culled from a series of eight steps (shown in the background in gray). I can't claim that these type/path crossbreeds are in any way beautiful—in fact, they're almost comically ugly—but they possess a certain mutated quality that I wouldn't have achieved without the free-spirited blend tool.

Figure 17-14: I blended between three Helvetica characters (top) and some basic shapes (bottom) to create a series of morphs that are at once utterly abstract and recognizable as letters (middle).

Creating Multi-Color Blends

You know you've earned your blend tool black belt when you can successfully tackle multi-color gradations. By creating a series of colored shapes and blending between them in succession, you can create photo-realistic graphics with sharp outlines and exact edges, the Holy Grail of commercial artwork.

Figure 17-15 shows eight shapes I created to represent a cat's eye. All but one of these shapes is designed to function as the beginning or end of a blend. The medium gray path through the middle of the eye served as the end of one blend and the beginning of another. Only the lozenge-shaped pupil is not part of a blend but was instead designed to crop the blend. (If you can't wait to see how the finished cat's eye turned out, sneak a peek at Figures 17-17 and 17-18.)

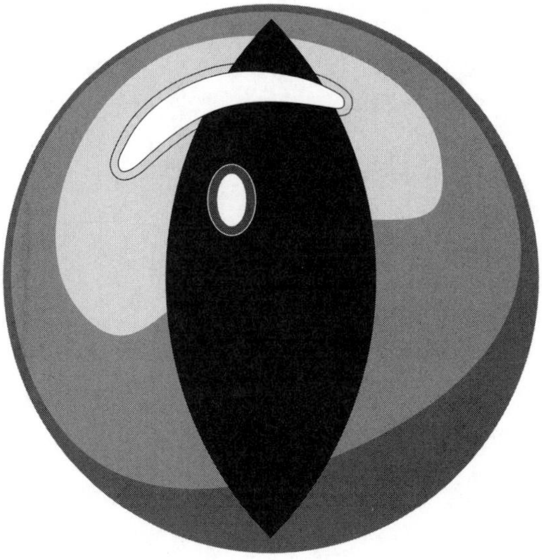

Figure 17-15:
These eight shapes were the only ones I had to draw to create a realistic cat's eye. I generated all others in Figures 17-16 and 17-17 with the blend tool.

Notice in Figure 17-15 that other than the pupil, no two paths overlap. This ensures that I don't have to blend a path with the bits and pieces from another blend, which would be a real nightmare.

The white shapes in the figure represent highlights. The rings around the white shapes were created with the Offset Path command and are both filled with the same colors as the shapes behind them. I used the shapes to soften the highlights. (The strokes in the figure are there just so you can see the shapes. None of the paths were actually stroked when I blended them.)

First, I wanted to emulate the shades of light and dark inside the pupil. So I copied the outer circle, the light gray shape, and the two highlight shapes that intersect the lozenge and pasted them in back of the shape. I filled the outer circle with black, kept the highlight white, and filled the other two shapes with 70 percent black. Then I blended between the two large shapes and the two highlight shapes to get the effect shown on the left side of Figure 17-16. I next selected all of my new shapes and the lozenge and chose Object » Pathfinder » Crop. The command took a minute or so to finish, leaving behind the gradient lozenge that appears on the right side of Figure 17-16.

In the first example of Figure 17-17, I blended between the three eye shapes. First I blended from the dark gray shape to the medium gray shape. Then I blended from the medium gray shape to the light gray one. All that remained was to blend the highlights, which I did to get the right example in Figure 17-18. I also added a stroked path behind the large circle of the eye to give it a little more definition.

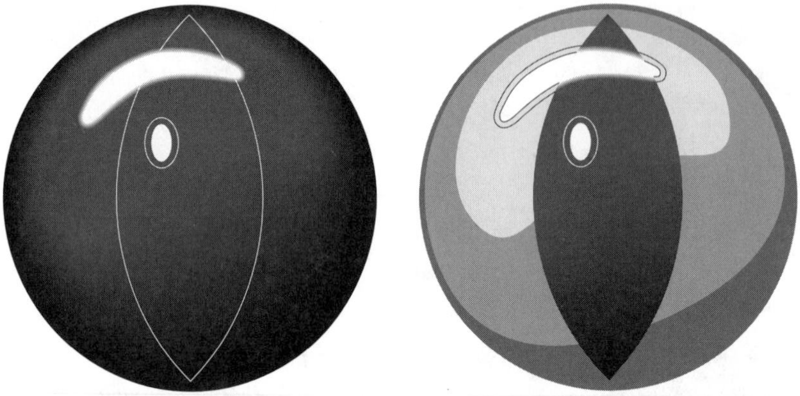

Figure 17-16: I copied a few shapes, pasted them behind the lozenge, filled them with dark colors, and blended between them (left). Then I used the crop filter to cut away portions of the blend outside the pupil (right).

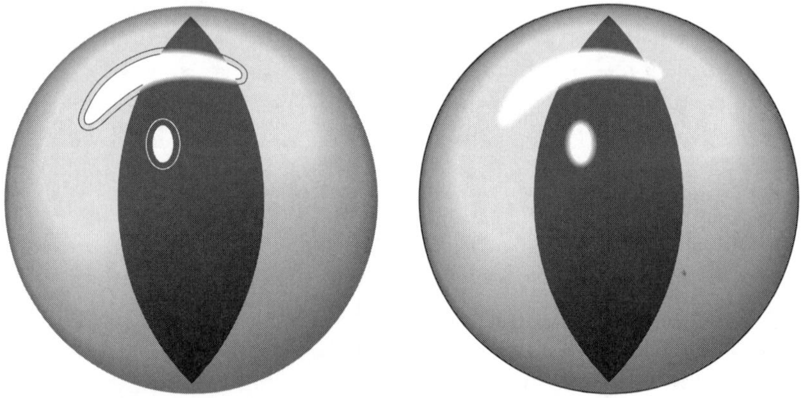

Figure 17-17: I blended the large gray shapes behind the pupil (left) and then blended the two sets of highlight paths (right).

The hardest part is deciding what kinds of paths to draw in the first place. The trick is to pay careful attention to what you see in the real world and simplify the forms enough to prevent one gradation from overlapping another. In Figure 17-19, I added a few elements that I saw in my cat's eye, notably the white membrane over the iris and the dark skin around the eye. (I positioned the thin, upper eyelid in front of the eye and the dark skin blend behind the eye. And I used the Crop filter to slice the shape of the membrane into the blend shapes, just as I did for the pupil.) Multi-color blending demands that you balance realism with stylization in roughly equal portions.

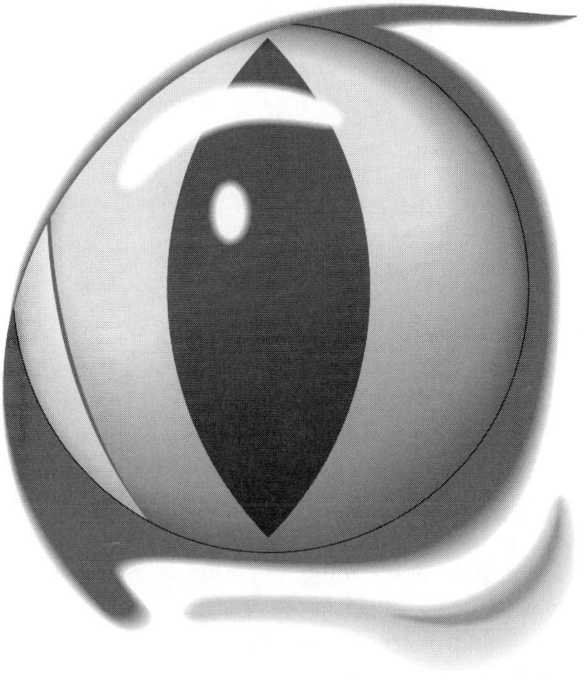

Figure 17-18: The finished cat's eye includes five additional blends, the large one in back of the eye and the other four in front.

Blending Between Gradations

Have I mentioned that Illustrator's blending capability is the best around? No? Well, it is. If you don't believe me, here's proof: In Illustrator, you can blend between two paths filled with directional and radial gradations. That's right, the program can actually create gradations between gradations. I should warn you, though, that doing so can be time-consuming.

The top example in Figure 17-19 features two slim paths filled with linear gradations. (I've outlined the paths so that you can see them.) Both gradations flow in the same direction, but one flows from 80 percent black to white and the other flows from white to 80 percent black. Blending between them creates a four-point gradation that flows from 80 percent black in the upper left and lower right corners and from white in the lower left and upper right corners. The second example in the figure shows the blend masked inside a letter converted to paths.

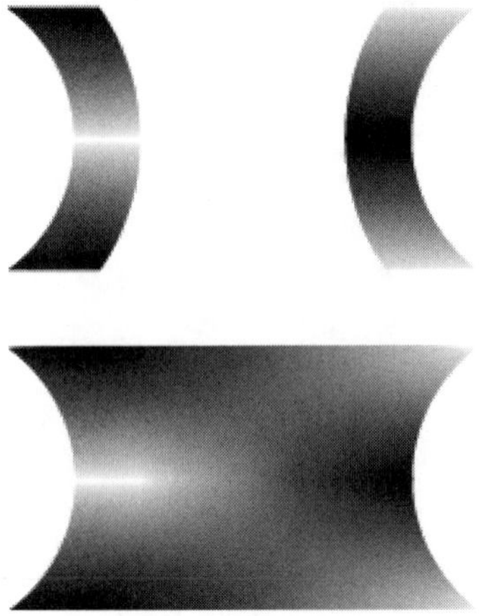

Figure 17-19: The result of blending two paths with gradient fills.

Blending gradations is a great way to create even more stupendous gradations—try it out in color!—but it can be a little tricky. For the best results, use linear gradations. Although radial gradations do blend, they don't work nearly as well. Also, you can't blend between a graduated gradation and a radial gradation. For linear blends, make sure that the gradations in both paths flow in the same direction. In other words, don't assign different Angle values in the Gradient palette. Assign different colors for the two gradations. Illustrator blends these colors, so you get the most mileage out of the effect if all the colors are different. And, finally, you must have the same number of color stops on both of the two gradients—refer back to Chapter 15 for gradient info.

Blending Strokes

Back when I began this chapter, I mentioned that the blend tool incrementally varies two stroke attributes—color and line weight. This last fact is very important since it means that you can blend a thick stroke with a thin one to create a softened edge.

Figure 17-20 demonstrates one of the common stroke-blending effects, the old neon text trick. I started by converting some text to paths and splitting and joining the letters with the scissors tool and Join command to combine all letters into a single, open path. (After all, in a real neon sign, one tube forms all the letters.) I assigned the line an 8-point black stroke. Then I cloned the line, nudged it upward a couple of points, and gave it a 0.5-point white stroke. The result appears at the top of Figure 17-20.

NOTE

Although nudging the top path is mostly for effect, it's necessary if you want to blend via the blend tool. If one path exactly overlaps the other, you can't click on the back path with the blend tool. Even when the paths are a couple of points apart, you'll probably need to zoom in to a very magnified view size (say, 400 percent or more) before you can click on the points.

After setting up my paths, I zoomed in and clicked on an endpoint in each path. (You have to click on an endpoint in an open path, remember.) Then I specified 14 steps, enough to ensure that each step changed by exactly 0.5 point. The second example in Figure 17-20 shows the result.

TIP

You don't need many steps when working with strokes because the distances are so small. A line weight variation of 0.5 point means that you can see only about 0.25 point of color around each side of the stroke. (With the strokes offset, the color bands may be as wide as 0.3 point, but that's about the maximum.) To ensure a 0.5-point line weight variation between your steps, use this simple formula. Of the two strokes you want to blend, subtract the thinner line weight from the thicker one. Then multiply that number by 2 and subtract 1. For example, I subtracted 0.5 from 8 to get 7.5. Multiplying that number by 2 produced 15, and subtracting 1 gave me 14. For the record, the line weight of these 14 steps are 1, 1.5, 2, 2.5, 3, 3.5, 4, 4.5, 5, 5.5, 6, 6.5, 7, and 7.5. You can't go wrong.

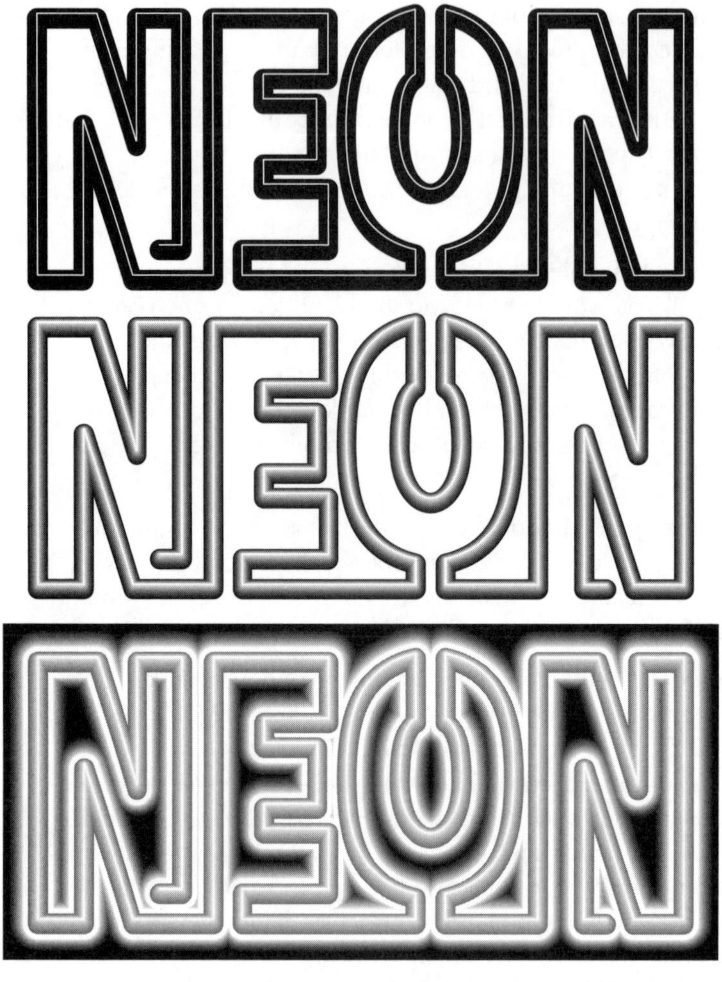

Figure 17-20: Here I've taken two stroked paths (top) and blended between them to create a neon effect (middle). Then I blended between a 12-point white stroke and a 24-point black one to create the glow (bottom).

To create the glow in the last example in Figure 17-20, I first copied the rear path. Then I hid the neon letters to get them out of my way (⌘-U), pasted the path in back (⌘-B), and changed the stroke to 12-point white. To create the blend-to path, I pasted to back again, nudged the pasted path up 2 points, and changed its stroke to 24-point black. Then I blended between the two paths with the blend tool. (To calculate the number of steps, I subtracted 12 from 24 to get 12; multiplied that by 2 and subtracted 1 to get 23.) To make the background black, I drew a black rectangle behind the whole thing. And I pressed ⌘-Shift-U to bring the neon letters back from hiding.

TIP

Notice that the strokes in Figure 17-20 have round joins. The same is true for the blended strokes in Figure 17-21. Round joins invariably blend best because they smooth out the transitions at the corner points. Miter and bevel joins result in harsh corners that rarely benefit a gradation.

Neon isn't the only effect you can produce by blending strokes. You can also create soft shadows. In Figure 17-21, I started by converting some letters from the typeface Eras to paths. Then I stroked the letters with 1-point medium gray and made the fill transparent. I cloned the letters, nudged them down and left, and sent them to back. I stroked the clone with 12-point white. Because each letter is an independent path, I had to use the blend tool a total of five times, and once for the inside of the O and another for the outside. (The letters have no fill, so I didn't have to worry about recombining each of the 21 O steps into compound paths.) Finally, I cloned the letters again, changed the fill to white, and removed the stroke to create the white letters up front.

Figure 17-21: Soft shadows created using blended strokes work only when the shadows are spread apart (top). If the shadows overlap, they develop distinctly un-shadow-like edges (bottom).

An important point to remember when creating soft stroke shadows is that each shadow has to completely clear the shadows around it. That's why the letters in the top example of Figure 17-21 are spread far apart from each other. If a stroke from one shadow cuts into a stroke from a neighbor shadow, it ruins the effect, as shown in the bottom example.

You can even blend between strokes with dash patterns. The blend tool can interpret between different dash patterns, and it can maintain a consistent dash pattern throughout all steps. And by virtue of its ability to incrementally change line weights, it can change the size of dashes with round caps, as demonstrated in Figure 17-22.

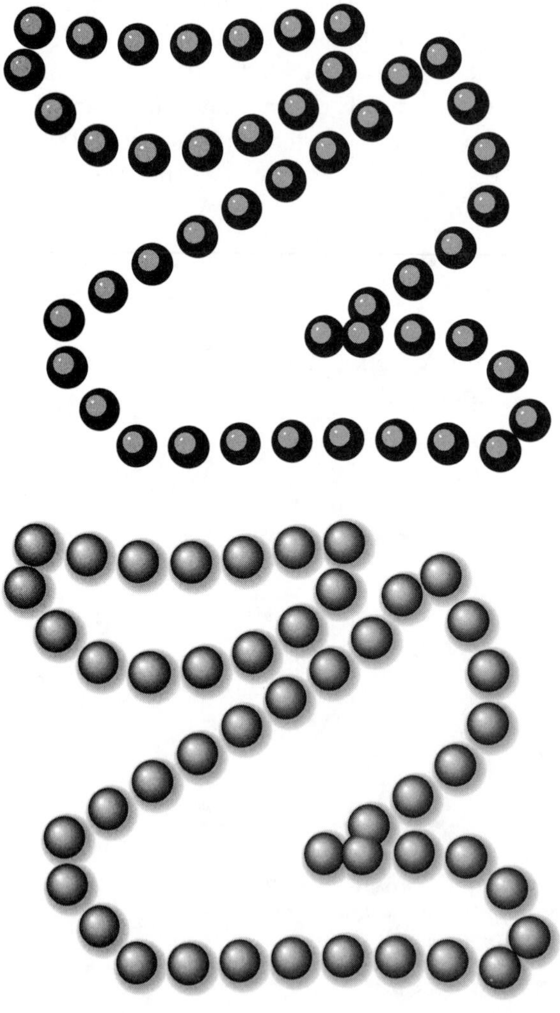

Figure 17-22: I started with three sets of paths (top), stroked with different colors and line weights but all having the same dash pattern. Blending between these paths resulted in a series of three-dimensional beads (bottom).

I started with three copies of my Z paths from Chapter 16, each stroked with the same dash pattern (Dash: 0, Gap: 20) but with different colors and line weights. Blending between these paths results in the luminous beads shown in the second example in the figure. I also added soft drop shadows, again varying the line weight and color but leaving the dash pattern unchanged.

Reblending Blends

It used to be the case that many Illustrator users coveted their FreeHand-using neighbors. In FreeHand, you've always been able to edit either of the extreme paths in a blend and the program will automatically update the steps in between accordingly. Well, covet your neighbor's FreeHand no longer, brethren (and sisteren, tooeth). For, now with Illustrator 8's live blending capabilities, if you decide to change the shape of one path or the other, you need only select one of the blend's original path with the direct selection (or group selection) tool and change it to your heart's content.

For example, you can change the color of one extreme path or the other and Illustrator will automatically update the blend. In the top example of Figure 17-23, for instance, I've blended between two stars, the back one filled with black and the front one filled with white. Then I edited the extreme paths, changing the back one to white and the front one to gray. The second example is not a true representation of the intermediate steps since it shows both of these changes simultaneously. In reality, Illustrator would update the blend after each of the changes. The last example, at the bottom right of Figure 17-23, shows the final result.

TIP

If you think the number of steps in your blend might be sufficient, but you can't quite remember how many steps there are, select the blend with the arrow tool and choose File » Selection Info. Then select Objects from the Info pop-up menu. The first item in the list tells you exactly how many paths are selected. This number includes the number of original paths in the blend. To get the number of steps, you have to take the number shown in the Selection Info dialog box and subtract the number of original paths in the blend. This will leave you with the number of steps.

Figure 17-23: After blending between two stars (top), I changed the colors of the front and back shapes (left) and Illustrator automatically updated the colors of the steps (right).

Editing a Gradient Fill

Now that I've told you nearly everything there is to know about blends, I'd like to share one more little secret. Every gradation in Illustrator is actually a blend. That's right, Illustrator calculates each color in a gradient fill as a separate step in a blend. It hides the details from you to keep things tidy. But as far as Illustrator and the printer are concerned, gradations and blends are all variations on the same theme.

Illustrator gives you the power to tear down the walls. At a moment's notice, you can convert any object filled with a gradation to an object filled with a blend. Just select the object and choose Object » Expand Fill. An alert box comes up, asking you how many steps you would like to create. Ignore the nonsense about 40 steps for the screen and 255 for the printer that Illustrator recommends in the alert box and follow my advice from the "Deciding the Number of Steps" section earlier in this chapter. That is, take the number of gray values your printer can print and multiply it by the percentage color range. Just one difference—don't subtract 2. The first and last colors are part of the gradation, so you don't want to delete them from the Steps value.

When you expand a gradation, Illustrator converts it to steps inside a mask. The shape that was previously filled with the gradation serves as the mask. Illustrator selects the mask and all rectangular steps inside the mask, as shown in the right half of Figure 17-24.

TIP: If you want to simplify the mask into a series of cropped steps, choose Object » Mask » Release, and then choose Object » Pathfinder » Crop. That's all it takes. You lose the flexibility of a mask—which I describe at length in the next section—but cropped steps are tidier on the screen and you can be sure the steps will print.

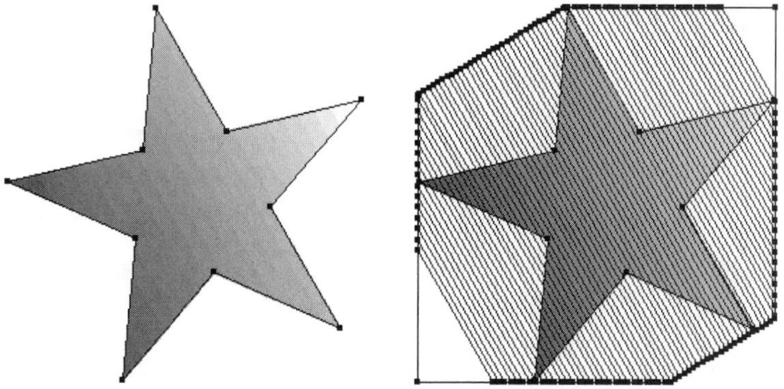

Figure 17-24: Choose Object » Expand Fill to convert a shape filled with a gradient fill (left) to a mask filled with colored steps (right).

One of the best reasons to convert a gradation to steps is to pinpoint exactly the locations of colors inside a shape. For example, in Figure 17-25, I've drawn two intersecting stars, each filled with gradations that converge at a common color. To achieve the effect, I split one star in half using the scissors tool and sent the left half to back. To make the transition between the forward half and the full star (with the heavy outline) as seamless as possible, I wanted both stars to intersect at precisely the same shade of gray. But there's no way to find the exact color in a gradation at a specific point. So I had to convert the full star to a blend using Object » Expand Fill. Next I opened the Gradient palette and Control-clicked with the eyedropper tool on the band of gray where the stars meet. (I've surrounded this band with a dotted line in Figure 17-25.) This gray value became the first color in the gradient fill assigned to the forward half star.

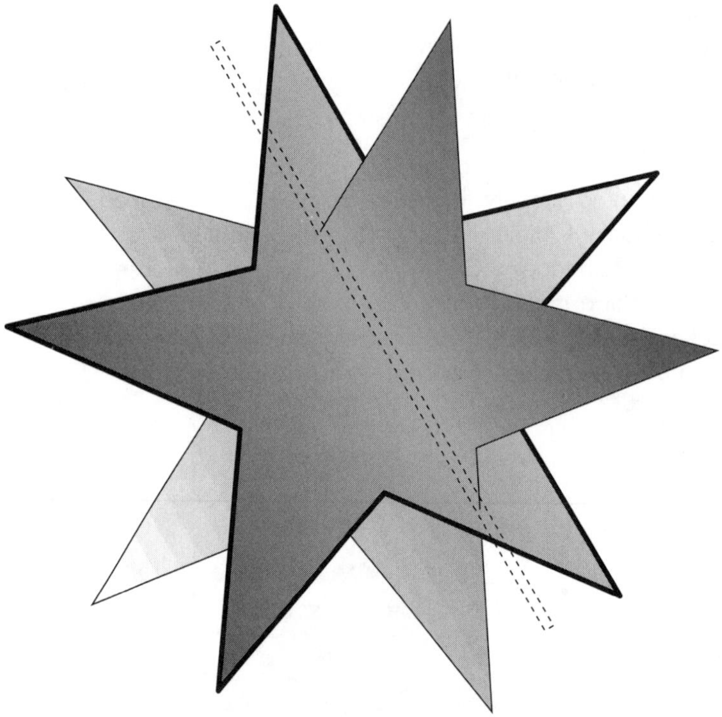

Figure 17-25: After converting the full star (heavy outline) to a blend, I lifted the band of color where the full and half stars meet (dotted line) and used it as the first color in the gradient fill of the half star.

Filling Objects with Objects

Illustrator's masking feature allows you to take one group of objects and put it inside of a selected path. The path becomes the mask, and the objects inside the mask are the content element. The mask clips away all portions of the content elements that fall outside the boundaries of the mask. Most artists use the masking feature to fill a path with a blend, but content elements can be stroked paths, text, or imported images. The mask itself must be a path. To create a mask, do the following:

1. Bring the mask to front.

Select the path you want to fill with other objects, and bring it to front by pressing ⌘-Shift-[(left bracket). A mask must be in front of its content elements.

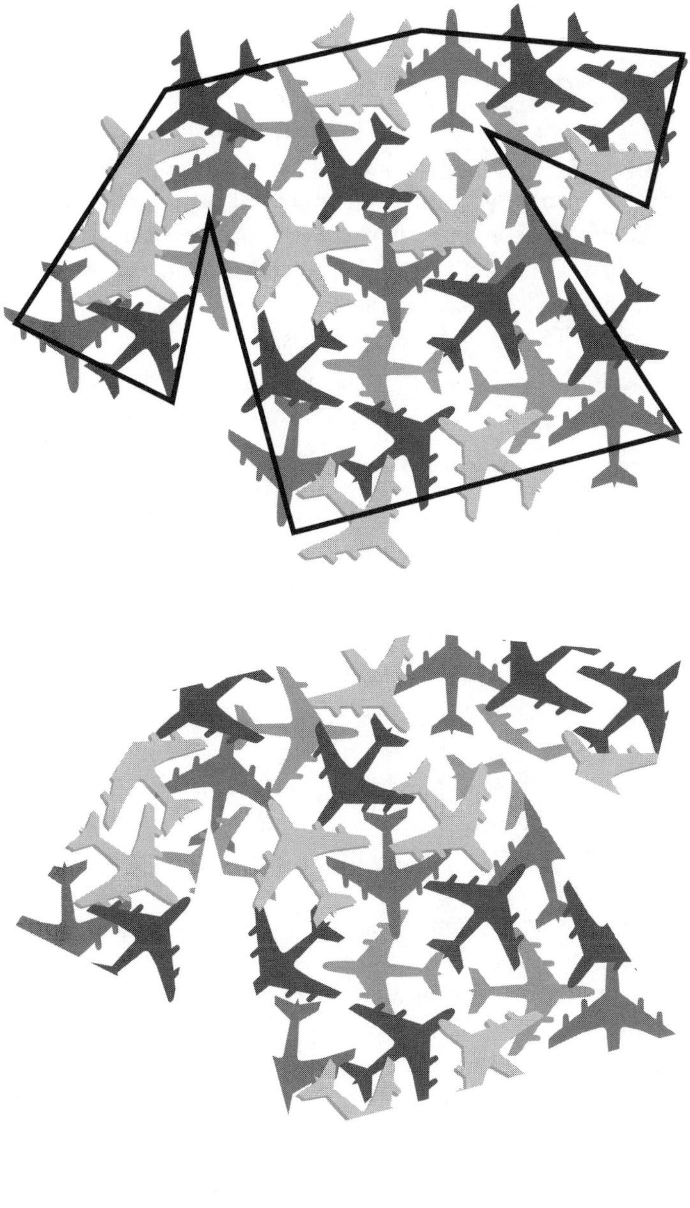

Figure 17-26: After selecting the planes and shirt outline (top), I chose Object » Mask » Make to mask the planes inside the shirt (bottom).

2. **Select the path and all objects that you want to put inside it, and choose Object » Masks » Make.**

   Or press ⌘-7. If you select objects inside different groups, compound paths, or masks, Illustrator will complain. So it's best to select the objects with the arrow tool prior to choosing the command. When successful, Illustrator clips away all portions of the content element that fall outside the frontmost path in the selection.

3. **Choose Object » Group.**

   Or press ⌘-G. This groups the mask and its contents together. Though this step is not absolutely necessary, it makes your illustration a little tidier. See, unless you group, you can select the mask and each and every object inside the mask independently of its neighbors using the arrow tool. If you take a moment to group, you can use the arrow tool to select the entire mask—including its contents—and use the direct selection tool to dig around inside the mask.

Figure 17-26 shows an example of a mask. Here I've assembled a completely random collection of Zapf Dingbats planes, made even more random using Object » Transform » Transform Each. (I couldn't have achieved this effect with tile patterns.) Then I positioned a stylized shirt outline in front of the planes, as the top example shows. I next selected all paths and chose Object » Mask » Make. (I also pressed ⌘-G to keep things tidy.) The result is the bottom example in the figure. Voila, instant pajama top.

Restoring a Mask's Fill and Stroke

Notice that Illustrator has dispensed with the stroke around my shirt in the bottom example of Figure 17-26. Illustrator assumes that you do not want your masking path to include a fill or stroke. Masks are traditionally dummy objects used to stencil the content elements, and that's all. Illustrator used to provide a filter that would allow you to automatically reinstate the fill and stroke of a mask. It's not part of the Illustrator 8 repertoire.

Instead, the option to fill and stroke your mask is built into the latest model of Illustrator. Even though Illustrator still deletes the path's fill and stroke when it transforms the path into a mask, you can now reinstate the mask's original color attributes as you can with any other object. Option-click the mask outline with the direct selection tool. If you ignored my words of wisdom and neglected to group the mask—do I have to come over there and make you to do it?—then you can select the mask outline with the arrow tool. Now simply assign a fill and stroke (including stroke weight) as you normally would. The stroke will appear in front of all the content elements and the fill will appear behind them. Figure 17-27 shows the result of applying a fill and stroke to the shirt outline. As far as I'm concerned, this is a great little addition to Illustrator.

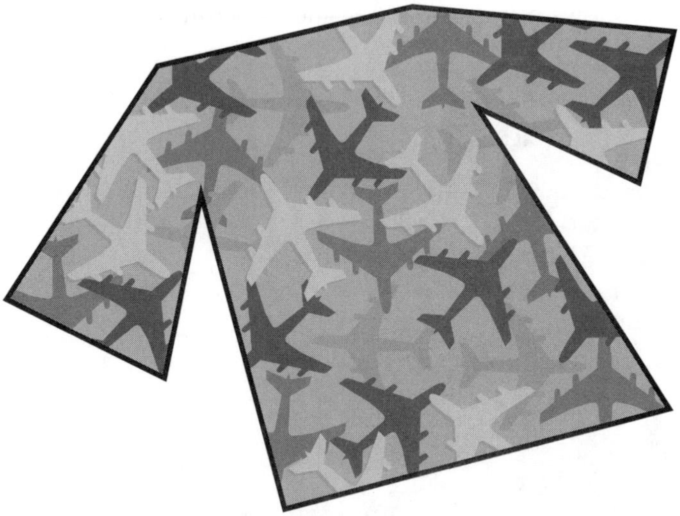

Figure 17-27: The result of applying Filter » Create » Fill & Stroke for Mask to the shirt outline, which adds a stroke and a fill.

Selecting Inside Grouped Masks

Here's something to keep in mind when editing the mask in the future. If you choose to add a fill to a masking path, you will not be able to select the content elements independently of the mask. To select the content elements masked by a filled path, you'll need to select the masking path and lock or hide it (⌘-2 or ⌘-3). You can also remove the fill temporarily while you go about selecting the content elements and then reinstate the mask's fill after you all done. Here's how to select objects inside a grouped mask with the direct selection tool, provided that the mask has no fill:

- To select a point or segment inside any content element, just click on it. To select an entire path, Option-click. (No surprises there.)
- To select a point or segment on the mask, click on it, or Option-click to select the entire thing.
- To select the entire mask—including mask outline, stroked and filled paths, and content elements—Option-click twice on an object in the mask.

When you select the entire mask, you see the outlines of all objects. Many of the outlines extend outside the mask, like the planes in Figure 17-28. This is because every one of these objects is still fully available. If I were to drag one of the clipped planes back inside the mask, I could again see the whole thing. The mask is a live stencil that shows you everything inside its perimeter and nothing outside.

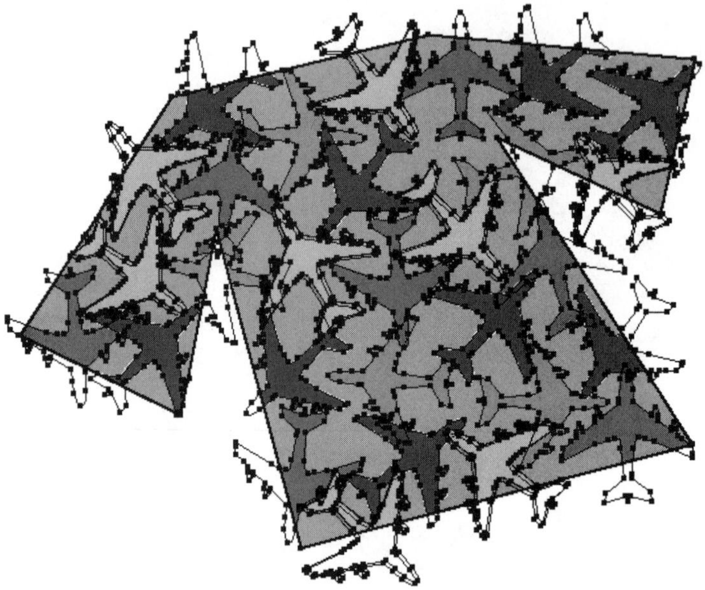

Figure 17-28: Option-click twice with the direct selection tool on any object inside a grouped mask to select everything.

Masking Versus Cropping

This live quality is the primary factor that distinguishes Object » Masks » Make from the somewhat similar Crop filter (of the Pathfinder palette fame). The Masks » Make command and Crop filter work similarly—in both cases, the front path clips all selected paths behind it. If you were to apply the two to identical collections of filled paths, the results would even look the same.

But where masking is a live operation that permits changes, cropping does permanent damage. Masking hides portions of content elements that extend outside the mask; cropping deletes them. Also worth noting, the Crop command deletes strokes and is not applicable to text or imported images. Masking, meanwhile, can accommodate any kind of object.

But where cropping results in a simple collection of filled objects, masking requires more work on the part of the printer. Masks take longer to print than cropped paths—several times longer in some cases—and a sufficiently complicated mask that contains lots of complex objects can prevent your illustration from printing.

So use masks when you need them and apply Crop when you don't. In Figure 17-29, for example, I used the Crop filter to stencil the shadows out of the arms, neck, face, and ears. But I used masks for the hair and shirt. I retained the mask for the shirt because I wanted to preserve the ability to edit the planes later on down the line. And I used a mask for the hair because of the white stroke from the head that extends up into the hair. The Crop filter would have deleted this stroke. If I had reapplied it, I wouldn't have gotten the white head line to align with the black head line precisely at the hair line.

Figure 17-29: The shirt and hair were created using masking. I created the other stenciled shapes using Crop.

TIP

A mask is a special kind of combined object, like a group or a compound path. This means you can use the Paste In Front and Paste In Back commands to introduce additional elements to the mask. In Figure 17-29, I created the black line around the hair by cloning the mask outline and pasting it in back. I then applied a 4-point stroke to the clone. Since I pasted the clone in back of the original mask outline, Illustrator added it to the mask and masked away the half of the stroke that rides along the outside of the path, leaving what looks like a 2-point line weight. Then I selected the white head line with the direct selection tool and pressed ⌘-Shift-] (right bracket). This placed the white head line in front of the other content elements but not in front of the masking path. This is due to the masks' special nature. The white line overlaps the black one, giving the head an inverted appearance inside the hair—a look that I think we've all wanted at one time or another in our lives.

Compound Masks

If you want a collection of content elements to continue through multiple masks, you should assemble the mask shapes into a compound path before applying the Masks » Make command. In Figure 17-30, for example, I created two identical star blends, one from white to gray (no strokes) and the other from gray to black (with strokes). Then I drew the paths for the goofy face—the four circles, the eyebrows, and the two mouth shapes—and combined them into a compound path. (I also had to use direction buttons in the Attributes palette to reverse the direction of one of the pupils, thus making it transparent.) Then I took the compound path and combined it with the white-to-gray star blend using Object » Masks » Make. The result is a single star blend that progresses uniformly from one path to another.

Although compound masks are very powerful, they demand still more work than regular masks. Figure 17-30 didn't give me any printing problems—it took a while, but that's only to be expected—but you should be aware that you're potentially treading into dangerous territory when you flirt with compound masks.

Figure 17-30: The shapes in this face all are members of a single compound path that I turned around and used as a mask. His expression arises out of fear that he might not print.

Disassembling a Mask

You can return a mask into a standard, everyday collection of objects by choosing Object » Masks » Release or by pressing ⌘-Option-7. If you grouped your mask, you should also ungroup the objects to make them independent. (It doesn't matter whether you release the mask first or ungroup first; either order is okay.) The content elements become entirely visible again.

Designing a Custom Cross-Hatch

Illustrator's Pen and Ink filters let you take a simple object called a *hatch pattern* (or just plain *hatch*) and repeat it over and over inside a path at different sizes, angles, and densities. In principle, it's the same thing as defining a custom halftone pattern. Instead of printing little round halftone dots, you print little crosses, straight lines, or squiggles.

Figure 17-31 shows a big X filled with a bunch of tiny X's. The tiny X's are the hatches. Notice how the little X's change in size and angle throughout the big X. If you squint your eyes, this produces an effect very much like a gradation, starting off light in the lower left corner and becoming darker toward the upper right.

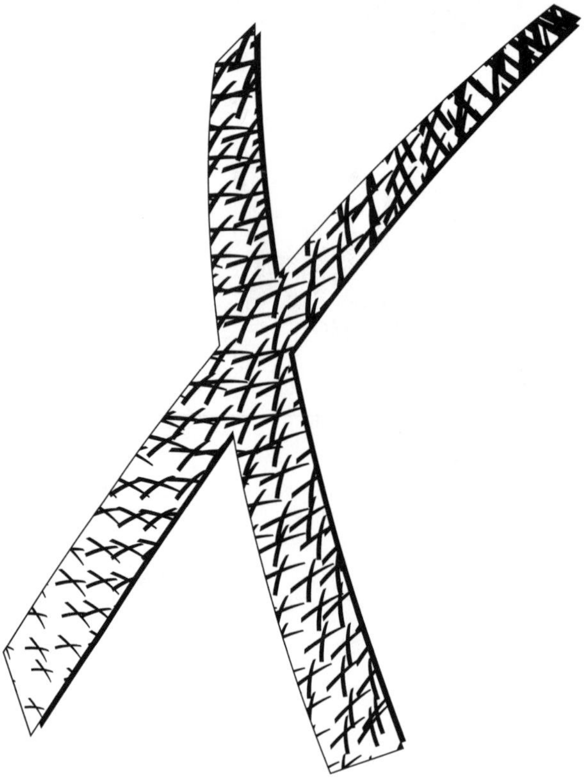

Figure 17-31: A big X filled with little X's using the Pen and Ink filters. The little X's grow, shrink, and twirl around over the course of the shape.

You define a hatch using Filter » Pen and Ink » New Hatch. Then you fill a path with the hatch pattern using Filter » Pen and Ink » Hatch Effects. The latter filter converts a selected path into a mask, and fills the mask with several hundred hatches. In Figure 17-31, for example, the big X is the mask and the little X's are content elements. This means that after applying the hatch pattern, you can edit the individual hatches as much as you want.

The following sections explain how these two Pen and Ink filters work.

Creating a Custom Hatch Pattern

To create a hatch, follow these steps:

1. **Draw a few simple objects.**

   Keep them very simple. The best hatches contain anywhere from 2 to 20 anchor points and only one to three paths. After all, simple objects mean faster and more reliable printing. This is one time where you want to leave the razzle-dazzle to Illustrator. In Figure 17-32, I've drawn an X using a minimal 12 points, which is more complicated than any of Illustrator's predefined hatches.

2. **Assign fills and strokes to the objects as desired.**

   Whatever fill color you use will show up when you apply the hatch pattern to a path using Filter » Pen and Ink » Hatch Effects. But don't get too hung up on it; you can always override the fill color so you might as well just use black.

TIP

Stroke is more important than fill color. It doesn't matter particularly what color or line weight you use, just whether or not you assign a stroke. If you do, you'll be able to tell Illustrator to vary the thickness of the stroke over the course of the mask. If you set the stroke to None, you won't be able to vary the thickness, but the final effect will print a little faster.

3. **Choose Filter » Pen and Ink » New Hatch.**

   The prospective hatch objects should be selected when you choose this filter. The New Hatch dialog box comes up on screen, looking something like Figure 17-32.

4. **Click on the New button.**

   Illustrator asks you to name the pattern. Enter a name and press Return. In Figure 17-32, I named my pattern *Slim X*. The name appears in the Hatch pop-up menu, and a preview of the hatch appears in the left side of the dialog box.

5. **Click on the OK button or press Return.**

   Illustrator closes the New Hatch dialog box and stores the hatch pattern with the foreground illustration.

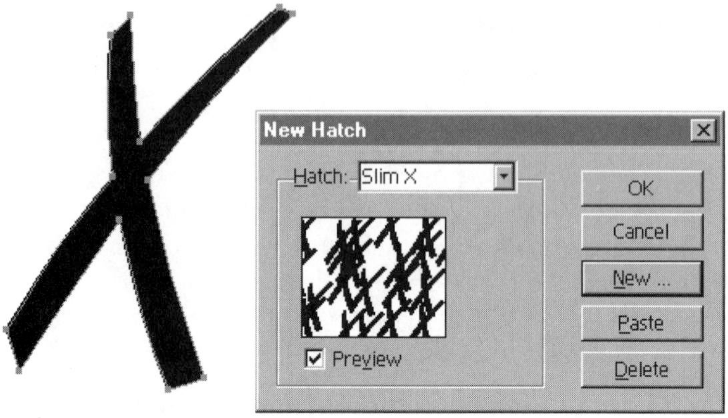

Figure 17-32: I select the X path and choose Filter » Pen and Ink » New Hatch to convert it to a hatch.

You can also use the buttons in the New Hatch dialog box to delete a hatch from the illustration or paste the selected hatch in the illustration window so you can edit it. You can also import a hatch saved to disk or save a selected hatch to disk.

Applying a Hatch Pattern to a Path

Creating a hatch is easy. Filling a selected path with a hatch pattern is significantly more complicated. But if you take it slow and give it some time, you can generate some pretty interesting effects. Here's the rub, in step-by-step form:

1. **Select the path you want to fill with a hatch pattern.**

   It has to be a path. No text blocks or imported images allowed.

TIP: If you want the hatches to match a certain color or gradation, assign that color or gradation to the path from the appropriate palette.

2. **Choose Filter » Pen and Ink » Hatch Effects.**

   Illustrator displays the massive dialog box shown in Figure 17-33. Isn't that something? When I first saw it, I moaned audibly. But having spent some quality time with it, I now look on it as an old friend—a ridiculously fussy, outrageously inflated, exasperatingly difficult old friend.

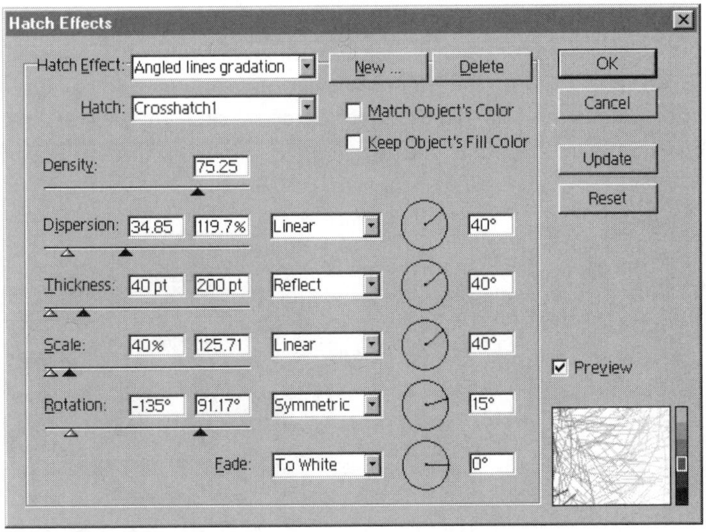

Figure 17-33: Although it contains more options than just about every other dialog box in Illustrator put together, the Hatch Effects dialog box is well organized and exceedingly capable.

3. **Select the hatch pattern you want to apply from the Hatch pop-up menu.**

   The Hatch pop-up menu is the most important option in the dialog box.

4. **Use the Color and Fade options to change the color of the hatches.**

   If you want to change the color of the hatches to match the colors in the selected path in the illustration window, select the Match Object's Color check box. In the first example in Figure 17-34, I applied the Match Object's Color option to an object filled with a gradation. Illustrator used the colors from the gradation to fill the individual hatches.

   To place the hatches in front of the fill assigned to the selected path, select the Keep Object's Fill Color option. In the second example in Figure 17-34, I selected the Keep Object's Fill Color option to keep the original gradation in the background.

   You can also choose to fade the colors of the hatches to white or to black by selecting options from the Fade pop-up menu. For example, assigning the To White option to a bunch of black hatches creates a black-to-white gradation. You can set the angle of the gradation using the Fade Angle value. A fourth option, Use Gradient, matches the colors of the hatches to the gradient fill assigned to the selected path. This option produces the very same effect demonstrated in the first example in Figure 17-34, except that you can modify the angle of the gradation using the Fade Angle option.

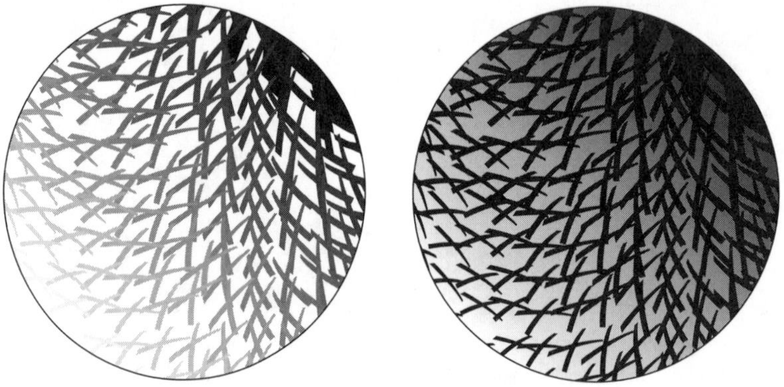

Figure 17-34: Paths filled with hatches using the Match Object's Color (left) and Keep Object's Fill Color (right) options.

5. Specify the density of the hatch pattern.

The Density slider bar changes the number of hatches that are packed into the shape. Raise the Density value or drag the slider triangle to the right to increase the hatch population; you can reduce the value or drag the triangle to the left to nuke those hatches till there are barely any of the suckers left alive.

In the lower right corner of the dialog box, you can keep an eye on the effects of raising or lowering the hatch population in the preview box. To the right of the preview box is a density adjustment bar. Click on a light swatch in the bar to decrease the number of hatches; click on a dark swatch to raise the number. What's the difference between this bar and the Density slider bar? The little density adjustment bar works in big, clunky increments, but otherwise, they're the same. One merely compounds the effects of the other.

6. Modify the Dispersion, Thickness, Scale, and Rotation options until the men in the white suits come to take you away.

These options, all contained in the same pop-up menu as the Density command, are at the heart of what makes the Pen and Ink feature so cool, but learning how to use them is no small task. Each of these options includes a pop-up menu, a couple of Range option boxes, an angle option box and icon, and a slider bar with one or two triangles.

- **Dispersion:** These options control how far Illustrator is allowed to move hatches up, down, and sideways inside the selected path.
- **Thickness:** The Thickness options let you modify the line weights of stroked hatches. If the selected hatch doesn't include a stroke, the Thickness options are dimmed.
- **Scale:** These options enlarge and reduce the hatches.
- **Rotation:** Use these options to rotate hatches inside the selected path.

All four sets of options are actually transformations—Dispersion is move, Thickness scales the stroke, and Rotation and Scale are what they say they are. They work much like the options inside the Transform Each dialog box is discussed back in Chapter 11, except that they affect hatches instead of selected objects.

All four of these pop-up menus include an identical collection of six options. They permit Illustrator to transform the hatches within a set range or to apply constant transformations. Figure 17-35 shows each option as it affects the Scale settings. The hatch pattern used in the figure is a simple black circle.

- **None:** Select this option to prevent the transformation from working at all. Throughout Figure 17-35, Dispersion, Thickness, and Rotation were all set to None. In the first example, Scale is set to None as well.
- **Constant:** This option applies a constant transformation value to all hatches. You are permitted just one option box and one slider triangle. In the Constant example in Figure 17-35, the single Scale value is set to 75 percent.
- **Linear:** Select this option if you want to create a gradation of transformations. You enter two Range values to specify the minimum and maximum transformations, and Illustrator varies between them at a constant rate from one end of the selected path to the other. You also specify the angle of the variation using the option box and icon at the right side if the slider bar. It's like a linear gradation. In the Linear example in the figure, the Range values were 50 and 150 percent and the angle was set to 45 degrees (as they were for the remaining examples as well).

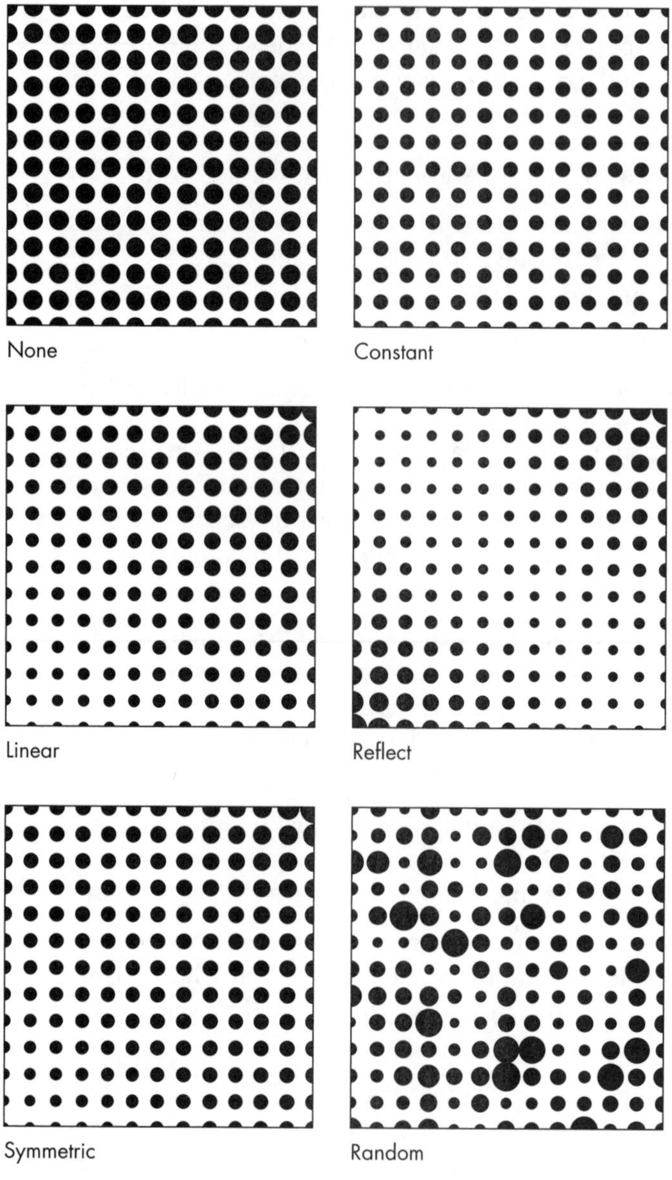

Figure 17-35: The six pop-up menu options, each applied to the Scale setting. To keep things as clear as possible, Dispersion, Thickness, and Rotation were all set to None.

- **Reflect:** The Reflect option varies the transformation from the center of the shape outward. Therefore, it starts with the second Range value, gradually varies to the first, and then varies back to the second, as the Reflect example in the figure demonstrates.
- **Symmetric:** At first glance, the Symmetric and Linear examples in Figure 17-35 appear identical. But there is a subtle difference. The hatches in the Linear example increase in size at a constant rate from the lower left corner to the upper right corner of the square. Not so in the Symmetric example. The hatches grow quite a bit at first, flatten out somewhat in the middle, and grow briskly again at the end. The Symmetric option is supposed to simulate shading around a cylinder—changing quickly, flattening out, and changing quickly again. But the effect is so slight, I doubt most viewers will notice. Oh well, at least the Adobe engineers gave it the extra effort.
- **Random:** If you want Illustrator to transform the hatches ad hoc, select the Random option. In the Random example in the figure, for example, Illustrator has randomly scaled the hatches from 50 to 150 percent. The angle options are dimmed when you select Random because, well, an angle would imply order and Random directly opposes order. (You can have a random angle, but you can't have an angled Random.)

TIP

If you're interested in producing a gradient effect, set the Thickness and/or Scale settings to Linear, Reflect, or Symmetric. This allows the hatches to grow and shrink, just like the halftone dots in a standard gradation. It doesn't matter how you set the Dispersion or Rotation options. Neither of these options simulates a gradation, although they can be used to enhance the effect.

7. **Press the Return key to apply the hatch pattern.**

   As I said, Illustrator converts the selected path in the illustration window to a mask and fills it with hatch objects. The mask and its contents are automatically grouped. Each hatch is a separate path, so you can edit it with the direct selection tool (among others). And if you prefer to crop the hatches into independent paths that are easier to print, choose Object » Mask » Release and click the Pathfinder palette's Crop button.

The only Hatch Effects options I ignored in the preceding steps are those at the very top and down the right side of the Hatch Effects dialog box. Because this dialog box contains so many options, Illustrator lets you store settings for later use. To store all settings in the Hatch Effects dialog box, click on the New button and enter a name for the settings. You can retrieve a collection of settings by selecting an option from the Settings pop-up menu. If you modify a few settings, you can assign them to the named item in the pop-up menu by clicking on the Update button. And, of course, you can trash a collection of settings by clicking on the Delete button.

CHAPTER 18

PRINTING YOUR ILLUSTRATIONS

A lot of programs out there print high-resolution, object-oriented type and graphics. PageMaker, QuarkXPress, FreeHand, and others describe type and graphics using a series of mathematically positioned points and mathematically defined curves. But if I had to cast a vote for the most reliable printing program of the bunch, it would have to be Illustrator. Although PageMaker, QuarkXPress, and FreeHand are all well-versed in the art of output, Illustrator outperforms them all, printing objects exactly as you see them on screen with the lowest likelihood of error (though, as I have warned throughout previous chapters, printing errors are possible). Where printing is concerned, Illustrator is the model by which all other programs are judged.

Illustrator's one nagging printing problem in previous versions was merely a convenience issue. To print color separations, you had to run a separate utility called, aptly enough, Separator. Adobe long defended this strange requirement by boasting that the Separator utility, while a bother to use, was the best color separation program out there. But back in Illustrator 6, Adobe finally bit the bullet and integrated all of Separator into the core Illustrator application. To print color separations, you press ⌘-P, just as in every other program. And what do you know? There's no loss of functionality whatsoever. We truly live in an age of miracles.

This chapter explains how to print your illustrations to a PostScript-compatible printer (also called an *output device*). Although Illustrator is capable of printing to non-PostScript printers, such as StyleWriters and other inexpensive ink-jet devices, this is not its forté. I don't mean to be a PostScript elitist—heck, I own one of those little Hewlett-Packard DeskWriters—but every high-resolution, professional-quality device includes a PostScript interpreter. If you want to proof your artwork to another kind of printer, fine. You'll find the process works very much like I describe it in this chapter. But when it comes time to print the finished artwork, PostScript is the only way to go.

Printing Composite Pages

A composite is a one-page representation of an illustration. A black-and-white composite, printed from a standard laser printer or professional imagesetter (which I describe in a few pages), translates all colors of an illustration to gray values. A color composite, printed from a color printer or film recorder, prints the illustration in full color. Composites are useful when you want to reproduce the illustration in black-and-white, proof an illustration, or fire off a few color photocopies. But you can't use them for professional-quality color reproduction. For that, you need to print color separations, which I discuss later in the section "Printing Color Separations."

Printing a composite illustration is a five-step process (Windows users can skip to Step 2):

1. If your computer is hooked up to a network, use the Network control panel to select the network that the printer is connected to.
2. Use the Chooser desk accessory to activate the AdobePS driver and select the network printer. (Windows users choose from the list of available printers in the Print Setup dialog box.)

3. Choose File » Document Setup (⌘-Option-P). Press the Page Setup button (or the Print Setup button in Windows) to determine the size of the printed page. Close the dialog box when you're finished.
4. If needed, position the page-size boundary in the drawing area with the hand tool.
5. Choose File » Print (⌘-P) to print the illustration to the desired output device.

I explain each of these steps in detail in the following sections.

Selecting a Network on a Mac

Most Macintosh computers sold in the last several years include two kinds of printing ports: the serial LocalTalk port and the EtherTalk port. The LocalTalk port connects directly to a printer or to an AppleTalk network. The EtherTalk port connects to an Ethernet printer or a large-scale Ethernet network. If you work in a large office, you're probably connected to other computers via Ethernet, which is the standard networking protocol used throughout corporate America. If you work in a small office or at home, you probably print by way of the LocalTalk port.

If you have access to multiple networks, you can switch from one network to another using either the Network or the AppleTalk control panel. Choose Apple » Control Panels » Network or Apple » Control Panels » AppleTalk to bring up the appropriate window. The AppleTalk control panel is shown in Figure 18-1. Depending on your model of computer, you'll probably find at least two options —LocalTalk and EtherTalk. You may see a third icon, Remote Only, which allows you to print through your modem to a remote network. (This is a function of Apple Remote Access, which freelancers like me have to use to communicate with distant editors.) Select the kind of network that contains the printer you want to use, and then click in the close box in the upper left corner of the window.

Your Mac can communicate over several different kinds of networks, but it can access only one network at a time. So if you are sharing files, say, over Ethernet and you switch to a LocalTalk printer, an error message tells you that the Ethernet connection is about to be broken. This is the price one pays for connectivity.

NOTE

If you are connected to a single network—or no network at all—you can probably point the Network or the Apple Talk control panel to the proper network once and ignore it from that point on. But EtherTalk sometimes requires a little extra attention. In order to initialize EtherTalk, your Mac sends out a signal to the network. If it doesn't get a response—whether it's because no machine is turned on at the other end of the network or because the hub is down—the system automatically switches over to LocalTalk. This is especially a problem for small businesses like mine that rely on EtherWave or a similar transceiver; if you don't have two transceivers or adapters up and running at once, you can't activate EtherTalk. This means that every so often you may have to go back to the control panel and turn the darn thing on again.

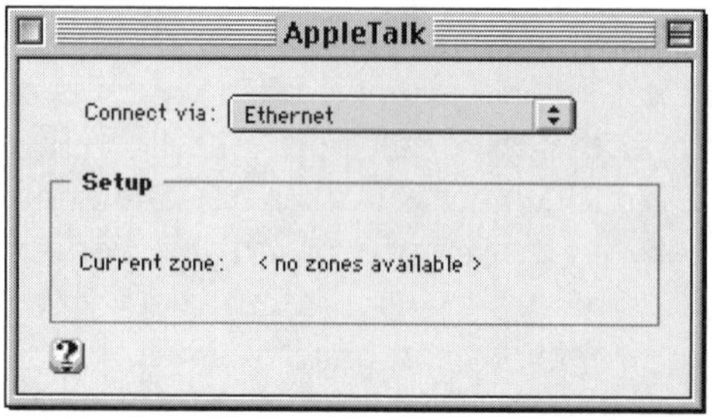

Figure 18-1:
If your computer is hooked up to multiple networks, use the Network control panel to select the network that includes the printer you want to use.

If you find yourself schlepping a PowerBook from one client's office to the next and connecting to various company networks to print proofs, you'll have to visit the Network control panel quite frequently. In fact, it's not a bad idea to keep an EtherWave AAUI Transceiver or a PowerBook Adapter (both from Farallon, 510/814-5000 or http://www.farallon.com) in your bag in case you need to connect into a corporate network in which the general mood does not run in favor of Macs.

Choosing a PostScript Printer on a Mac

To select a printer on a Macintosh, locate the Chooser desk accessory in the list of items under the Apple menu. The Chooser dialog box comes up, as shown in Figure 18-2. The dialog box is split into two halves, with the left half devoted to a scrolling list of printer driver icons and network zones and the right half devoted to specific printer options.

Select the AdobePS icon, spotlighted in Figure 18-2. AdobePS is the most recent PostScript printer driver direct from Adobe, the inventor and custodian of PostScript. It helps Illustrator and the system software translate the contents of an illustration to the output device.

If AdobePS is not available in the list of printer driver icons, or if you haven't yet installed the newest version, AdobePS 8.5, insert the CD-ROM that came with your copy of Illustrator and open the Adobe Products folder. Inside, you'll find the AdobePS 8.5 subfolder. Open it and double-click on the Installer program. This installs the AdobePS driver as well as lots of PostScript printer description files, which I'll describe in a moment. Together, they make Illustrator print at peak form. If you prefer, you can visit the Adobe product Web page at http://www.adobe.com/prodindex/printerdrivers/main.html. Here you can get the most recent printer drivers and PostScript printer description (PPD) files.

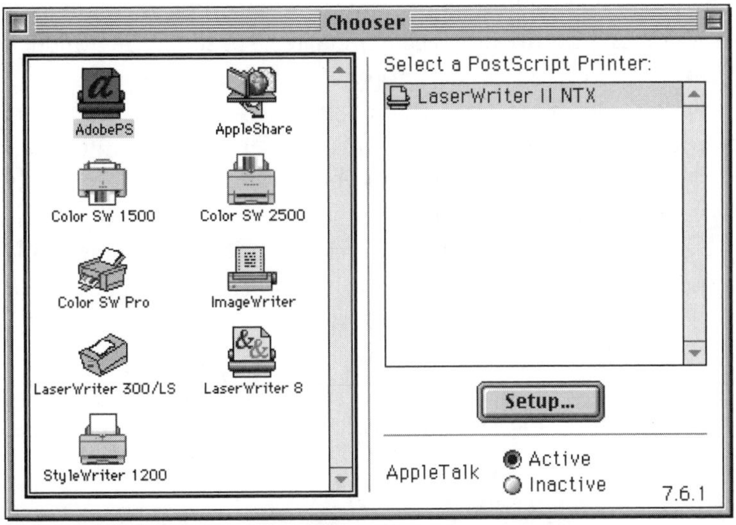

Figure 18-2: Select the AdobePS icon in the Chooser window to select and initialize a PostScript printer.

If the network includes multiple AppleTalk zones, you'll see two scrolling lists on the left side of the Chooser dialog box: one with icons and one with text. Select the zone that contains the desired printer from the lower list. If no zones appear, don't worry about it. They exist only to keep us all at the mercy of network administrators who bandy about mystical terms like "bandwidth" and "gateway" to dull our minds and keep us docile.

After you select the required printer driver and, if necessary, gain access to the proper zone, you can select the name of your printer from the scrolling list on the right side of the dialog box. Under the list are two sets of radio buttons for Background Printing and AppleTalk. The latter refers to the communications protocol required to hook up your Mac to a network. If you turn it off, you won't be able to access your printer anymore, so by all means leave it turned on.

Background Printing isn't quite so cut and dry. When enabled, this option quickly spools an illustration and lets you resume working without a lot of waiting around. Illustrator describes the illustration to a system-level program called PrintMonitor. When it finishes spooling, the software frees up and lets you get back to business while the system software prints the illustration in the background. Unfortunately, spooling can interrupt foreground tasks and increase the likelihood of printing errors. Although it succeeds more often than it fails, PrintMonitor can drop code, which may result in some very strange problems. If perfect output is more important than fast output, turn off Background Printing.

The AdobePS driver supports PPD files. AdobePS can't account for the tiny differences among different models of PostScript printers, so each PPD serves as a little guidance file, customizing the driver to accommodate a specific printer model. After selecting a printer, you can access the proper PPD by clicking on the Setup button. (Or just double-click on the printer name in the list.) A new dialog box claws its way onto your screen, as shown in Figure 18-3. Click on the Auto Setup button to instruct the system software to talk to your printer and automatically determine the proper PPD. If the system fails, or if it selects the dreaded Generic option, click on the Select PPD button and try to locate the proper PPD file inside the Printer Descriptions folder in the Extensions folder in your System folder. When you finish, click on the OK button or press Return.

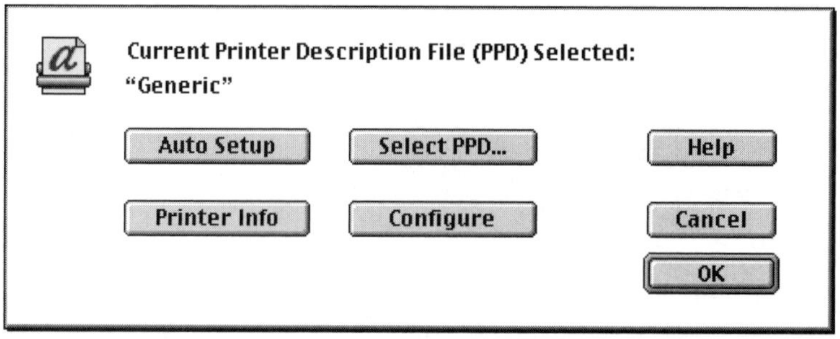

Figure 18-3: Use this dialog box to select the proper printer description file for your particular brand of PostScript printer.

Back in the Chooser dialog box, at the top of the list of printers is a pop-up menu labeled Type. By default, it's set to PostScript Printer. But if you prefer, you can select the Virtual Printer option, which lets you prepare an illustration for output to a PostScript printer when no such printer is currently hooked up to your computer. For example, you might select this option prior to submitting an illustration to be printed from an imagesetter at a service bureau. Use the Setup button to select the PPD file for the kind of printer you think the service bureau will be using, and then press Return.

When you finish selecting options in the Chooser dialog box, click on the close box in the upper left corner of the title bar. If you've changed the printer, the system delivers an alert box telling you that you have to visit the Page Setup dialog box. Tell it to go away and leave you alone; everything is already in hand.

Choosing a PostScript Printer in Windows

If you're using the Windows 95 or Windows 98 operating system, you select a printer from the Start menu by choosing the Settings » Printers command. Click on the Add Printer icon and follow the instructions in the Install Wizard. If you don't have the most current PostScript printer driver, go to the Adobe product Web page (http://www.adobe.com/prodindex/printerdrivers/main.html). Download AdobePS 4.1 for Windows 95 or AdobePS 4.2 for both Windows 95 and Windows 98. (The latter will not work with Level 1 PostScript printers.) After you've downloaded it on your hard drive, use the Setup program to install it onto your system. You'll be asked to specify a default PPD during the installation. The Illustrator 8 CD comes with a number of PPDs, and you can also find some additional ones at the Adobe Web site.

After you have installed the printer drivers you want, choose the File » Document Setup command (⌘-Option-P) in Illustrator. Click on the Print Setup button and choose the printer you want to use from the Name pop-up menu inside the Print Setup dialog box. If you want to change to another printer, one for which you've already installed a driver, choose it from the Name pop-up menu whenever the mood strikes you while using Illustrator.

Setting the Various Print Options in Windows

As I've mentioned in earlier chapters, this book is primarily geared toward Macintosh users, since the majority of Illustrator owners are also Mac owners. As such, the printing-related options covered in the following sections are presented in an order that is consistent with how these options appear in the various dialog boxes found on the Mac version of Illustrator. Unfortunately, due to the difference in the operating systems, many of the printing-related options appear in completely different locations on the Windows side. If one of the options discussed below does not appear in the dialog box with the same name (or at least a similar name) on the Windows side, you will have to look elsewhere (assuming the option exists in Windows).

One place you can look for the equivalent options in the Windows version of Illustrator is in the Properties dialog box. You open this dialog box by clicking on the Properties button in the Print Setup dialog box. If you can't find an option in one of the many panels that appear in the Properties dialog box within Illustrator, try accessing this dialog box from the desktop level. From the Start menu, choose

Settings » Printers. Right-click on the same printer that you chose in the Print Setup dialog in Illustrator. Usually, more panels and thus more options are included in the desktop-level version of the Properties dialog box.

Keep in mind that when you make changes to the Properties dialog box at the desktop level, you affect how things print in all applications. Changes made in the Properties dialog box found in Illustrator, on the other hand, affect items appearing and printed in Illustrator only.

For the various print options described in the following sections, if an equivalent exists in Windows, I include a reference to which panel inside the Properties dialog box most likely contains the equivalent option and, when necessary, the appropriate name for the option.

Setting Up the Page

Your next step is to define the size of the page on which you intend to print your illustration. Choose the File » Document Setup command or press ⌘-Option-P. After the Document Setup dialog box displays, click on the Page Setup button (or the Print Setup button) to display the AdobePS Page Setup dialog box shown in Figure 18-4, which contains the following options:

- **Paper:** Select the size of the paper on which you want to print. The specific options available from this pop-up menu depend on which PPD file you selected in the Chooser. For example, I selected the PPD file for the Linotronic 530 imagesetter using the Virtual Printer option in the Chooser dialog box. Then, when I selected MaxMeasure from the long list of Paper options in the Page Setup dialog box, the page icon on the left side of the dialog box kindly explained the dimensions of this page, as you can see in Figure 18-4. (Most PPDs don't provide this handy feedback; instead, the page icon contains a big, useless letter a.) The Linotronic 530 can print a page 18 inches wide and more than 3 feet tall, which is suitable for a small poster. I could also select a Custom option and enter my own page dimensions in the page icon area.
- **Formatted for:** This option—found in the Paper panel on the Windows side—lets you print multiple miniaturized versions of your Illustrator pages on each sheet of paper. You can print 2 or 16 pages at increasingly more drastic reductions. It saves paper and cuts down on print time. But it makes sense only if your illustration contains multiple pages, which most illustrations don't.

- **Scale:** To scale your illustration as you print it, enter any value from 25 to 400 percent in this option box—Windows users will find the Scaling option box in the Graphics panel. Generally, you'll use this option to reduce large artwork when proofing it on a laser printer or on another device that's limited to letter-sized pages.

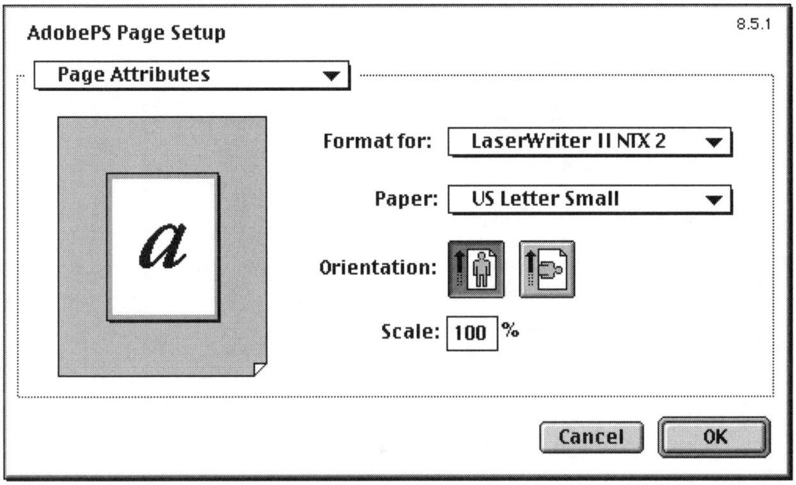

Figure 18-4: You can specify the size and orientation of the printed page in the Page Setup dialog box.

- **Orientation:** The Page Setup dialog box has two Orientation options—Windows users will find similar options in the Paper panel. By default, the page is positioned upright in the Portrait position. But if you want to print a wide illustration, you can select the Landscape option. You Win-folks need to select the Rotated check box in conjunction with the Landscape radio button. This lets you print illustrations onto pages that already have holes punched into the margins.

Click on the Options button to open the dialog box shown in Figure 18-5. Click the check boxes in this dialog box to perform a few printing effects that you generally don't need to bother with, but that sometimes come in handy. The sample page on the left side of the dialog box demonstrates the effect of the selected options. The big letter a represents the illustration on the page, and the dotted line represents the margin size.

The options in the PostScript Options dialog box are most useful when printing an illustration to a midrange output device, such as a laser printer. If you're printing to a color thermal-wax or dye-sublimation device or an imagesetter, some of the options—particularly Flip Horizontal, Flip Vertical, and Invert Image—may duplicate or nullify settings in the more important Print Options dialog box, described in the "Printing Pages" section. Be sure to read that section to learn more.

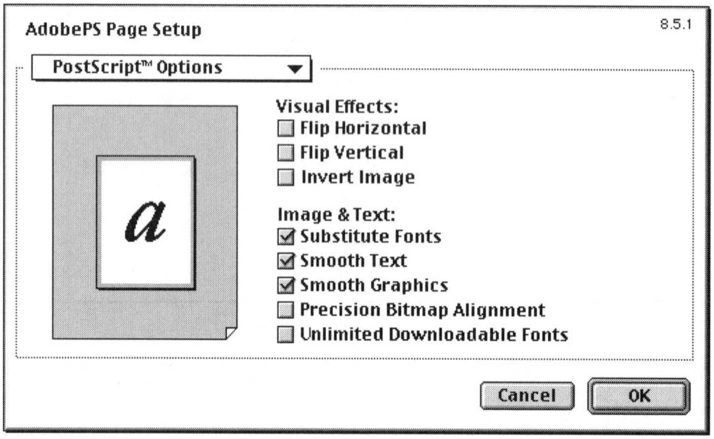

Figure 18-5: The PostScript Options dialog box lets you perform certain printing effects, which range from moderately useful to nonfunctioning.

The check boxes in the PostScript Options dialog box work as follows:

- **Flip Horizontal:** Select this option (called Print as a Mirror Image in the Graphics panel for Windows users) to flip the objects in an illustration horizontally on the printed page. When printing film negatives, select this check box to print the illustration so the emulsion side of the film is away from the viewer, which is called emulsion down. Turn off the check box to face the emulsion side toward the view, which is called emulsion up. I explain film negatives more thoroughly in the "Printing Color Separations" section later in this chapter.
- **Flip Vertical:** Select this check box to flip the illustration vertically on the printed page. You can use this option instead of Flip Horizontal to specify the emulsion side of a film negative. However, if you select both Flip Horizontal and Flip Vertical, you nullify the effect, returning the

emulsion side up. Selecting both options also causes the illustration to print upside down.

- **Invert Image:** Select this option (called Print as a Negative Image in the Graphics panel for Windows users) to change all blacks to white and all whites to black. Select this check box to print a photographic negative of the illustration, primarily when printing to film. Most commercial printers prefer film negatives when transferring artwork to printing plates.
- **Substitute Fonts:** This check box—similar to the options found in the Windows Fonts panel—supposedly substitutes the fonts Geneva, Monaco, and New York with their respective PostScript equivalents of Helvetica, Courier, and Times. But if you try to use the option with Illustrator, the program automatically turns off the check box and prints the TrueType versions of Geneva, Monaco, and New York. In other words, you can ignore this option.
- **Smooth Graphics:** Here's another one to ignore. Back in the old days, when MacPaint was a hot program, folks were bound and determined to get their jagged black-and-white images to print with smooth edges. The Smooth Graphics check box did just that, averaging pixels to give them smooth, though gummy, edges. Well, it doesn't matter how you have this option set in Illustrator. Imported black-and-white images always have jagged edges, just as Mother Nature meant them to have.
- **Precision Bitmap Alignment:** This option reduces a typical 72-ppi image dragged over from Photoshop to 96 percent of its original size, making it compatible with a 300-dpi laser printer. This increases the resolution of a 72-ppi image to 75 ppi, which is evenly divisible into 300. Unless the laser printer is your final output device, I recommend that you leave this option unchecked.
- **Unlimited Downloadable Fonts in a Document:** This check box, which is similar to the options found in the Windows Fonts panel, is designed to help moron applications that don't know how to properly download fonts. Some programs try to download every font in a document at the same time, which can overwhelm the printer's memory. This check box tells the program to wise up. Illustrator manages its fonts just fine without this silly option.

Adjusting the Page Size

You can modify the page boundaries in the artboard by selecting one of the View radio buttons inside the Document Setup dialog box, which I introduced back in Chapter 3. To display the dialog box, choose File » Document Setup or press ⌘-Option-P. Then select the desired radio button:

- **Tile Imageable Areas:** Select this radio button to subdivide the artboard into multiple partial pages, called tiles. I talk more about tiling large artwork in the "Tiling Oversized Illustrations" section later in this chapter.
- **Tile Full Pages:** Select this radio button to display as many whole pages as will fit inside the artboard. Use this check box to print a multipaged document like a flier or a two-page ad.
- **Single Full Page:** Select this radio button to display a single page size inside the artboard. This ensures that you will print just one page for the entire illustration.

After you select one of these options and press the Return key, you can use the page tool to position the page size relative to the objects in your illustration. If the dotted page boundaries are not visible, choose View » Show Page Tiling. If you selected the Tile Imageable Areas option in the Document Setup dialog box, the page number of each tile is listed in the lower left corner of the tile. This way, you can specify the particular pages that you want to print when outputting the illustration.

Printing Pages

To initiate the printing process, choose File » Print or press the trusty keyboard equivalent, ⌘-P. The General Printer dialog box appears, as shown in Figure 18-6. Most of the options are the same as those you see when printing from any Macintosh application, but a few are unique to Illustrator. The Windows Print dialog box offers most of the same options. Here's how they work:

- **Copies:** Enter the number of copies you want to print in the Copies option box. You can print 999 copies of an illustration, but if you want to print more than 10, you're better off having them commercially reproduced. Commercial reproduction provides better quality for less money, and it ensures less wear and tear on your printer.
- **Pages:** Specify a range of pages using the Pages options. By default, the All radio button is selected. If the drawing area displays a single page size, Illustrator will print just that page. If the drawing area contains

multiple pages or tiles, Illustrator prints all pages that contain objects. To define a specific range of pages or tiles to be printed, enter the page numbers in the From and To option boxes. These numbers should correspond to the page numbers displayed in the lower left corners of pages in the drawing area.

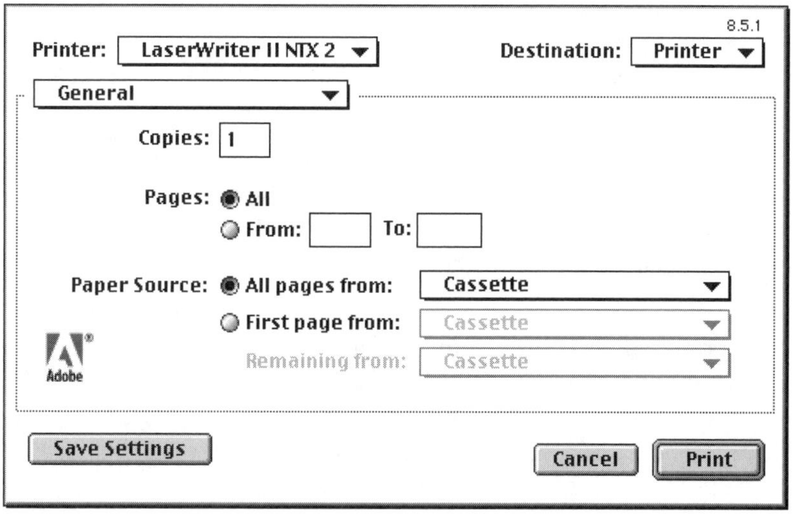

Figure 18-6: You can print the pages in your illustration to a PostScript-compatible printer from the Printer dialog box.

- **Paper Source:** If you want to print your illustration on a letterhead or other special piece of paper that you manually feed into the printer, select the First From radio button, and then select Manual Feed from the accompanying pop-up menu. The Windows equivalent option appears in the Print Setup dialog box. You can then print the remaining pages in the illustration to pages in the paper tray using the Remaining From pop-up menu.
- **Destination:** This option—called Print to File in the Windows Print dialog box—allows you to generate a PostScript-language definition of the file on disk rather than printing it directly to your printer. Select the Printer option to print the image to an output device as usual. Select File to write a PostScript-language version of the image to disk. You can then submit the file to a service bureau and have the printer technician download the file. This way, the technician can't accidentally (or purposely) modify the illustration when he or she opens it in Illustrator.

If you selected the Virtual Printer option in the Chooser, the Printer option is dimmed, leaving File as your only option. For more information on saving PostScript language files, read the "Printing to Disk" section later in this chapter.

The Printer dialog box gives you access to other print-related dialog boxes. You drag from the main pop-up menu to choose between them, just as you choose from the different preference boxes in the General Preferences dialog box. The various Printer dialog boxes contain straightforward options that don't need explanation, but I should take a couple of minutes and explain those of the Adobe Illustrator 8.0 Printer dialog box, shown in Figure 18-7. Here's how the options work.

- **Output:** Select the Composite option from the Output pop-up menu to print a black-and-white or color composite of your illustration. Select the Separate option to print color separations. I explain the latter option in more detail in the next section.
- **PostScript:** Select Level 1, Level 2, or Level 3, depending the kind of PostScript that's built into your output device. PostScript printers made in the last 12 months are very likely to be Level 3 devices. Most PostScript printers manufactured in the previous three years are Level 2, while most older machines are Level 1. (For what it's worth, Adobe introduced Level 2 in 1991, but it took a while to catch on.) Apple's Printer Utility will tell you Mac users the PostScript capabilities of your printer. If you don't know, leave it set to Level 2 and hope for the best.
- **Data:** If your network doesn't support binary encoding, select the ASCII option to transfer data in the text-only format. The printing process takes much longer to complete, but at least it's possible. When in doubt, however, leave this option set to Binary.
- **Selection Only:** If you just want to print the selected objects in the illustration, select this check box. When the option is turned off—as by default—Illustrator prints all objects, whether selected or not.
- **Separation Setup:** This button displays the Color Separation dialog box that allows you to specify settings for printing color separations. I explain this humongous dialog box from A to Z in the next section.

One other Printer dialog box that may give you some trouble is the PostScript Errors Printer dialog box. It gives you access to the options that control how the system reports PostScript printing errors. The default option, No Special Reporting, reports errors in passing in the progress window at the top of your screen. If the Background Printing option in the Chooser is turned off, you can select Summarize on Screen to report the error message on screen. (Too bad this isn't the default setting, but too many folks print in the background to make that feasible.) Or you can select Print Detailed Report to print the error message. This last option is generally a waste of paper and is to be used only if you can't get a satisfactory response from your printer using any other method.

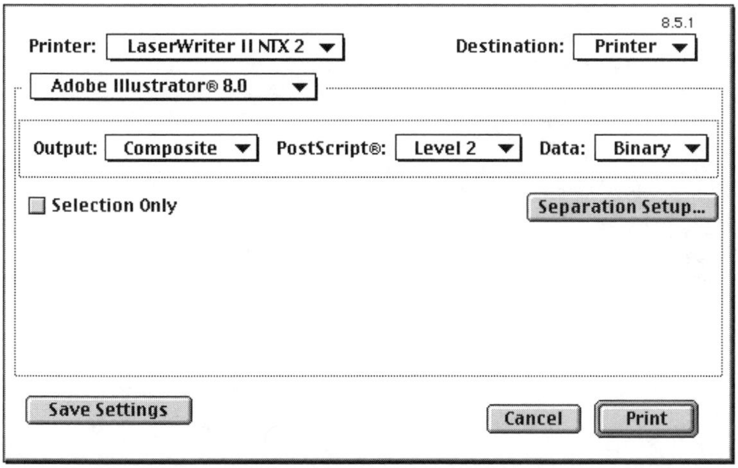

Figure 18-7: The options in this dialog box vary from one PPD to the next.

To discover the meaning and uses for the options unique to your printer, consult the documentation that came with your printer. If you're printing a file to disk with the intention of taking it to a service bureau, consult the service bureau about these options. If you want to lock these settings in as defaults for future illustrations—so you don't have to mess with them every time you print—click on the Save Settings button. (This button is available only when additional options appear below the dotted line.) When you finish, click on the OK button or press Return.

Click on the Print button in the Printer dialog box (or press Return) to initiate the printing process. Two small windows appear: a progress window at the top of the screen and a cancel instruction window slightly lower (both pictured in Figure 18-8). If you want to cancel the print job, you should be able to press ⌘-period, but Illustrator is rarely paying close enough attention to recognize such a subtle gesture. As anyone who prints for a living can tell you, you have to whack ⌘-period 10 to 15 times in a row to get the program's attention. No joke.

You lucky Windows owners are provided with a Cancel button. If you're quick, you can cancel the operation before all the code has spooled to the printer. If the print is underway and you still want it terminated, from the Start menu, choose

Settings » Printers. In the resulting Printers dialog box, double-click on the printer icon that corresponds to the device that's printing your document. A dialog box named after that printer will display. Right-click on the document that you don't want printed and choose Cancel Printing. After a few seconds, Window dumps the code and the document's name will disappear from the dialog box.

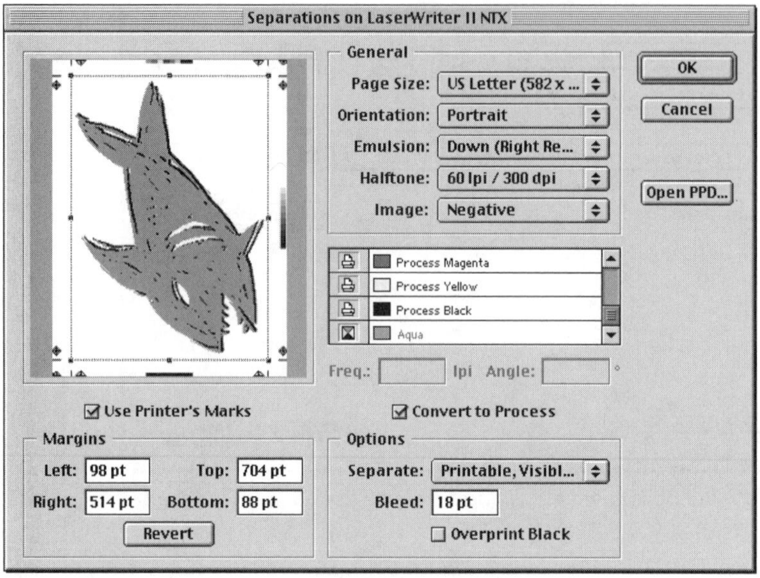

Figure 18-8: The only way to cancel a print job is to repeatedly hit ⌘-period with the persistent fury of a desperate pugilist.

Printing Color Separations

Professional color reproduction requires that you print an illustration to color separations, which means that you print a separate sheet of paper or film for each of the process color primaries—cyan, magenta, yellow, and black—or for each spot color used in the illustration. You can even add spot colors to the four process primaries to enhance the range of colors in the final document or target the colors in a logo or another color-sensitive element. But keep in mind that every additional separation you print incurs additional cost—additional ink has to be applied to the pages, and extra labor costs are charged for making the plates and running the plates and paper through the press.

There is little point in printing color separations from a laser printer, and certainly no reason to print from any kind of color device. The only category of printer up to the job of color separations is an *imagesetter*, which is a typesetter that's equipped with a graphics page-description language like PostScript. An imagesetter prints photosensitive paper or film by exposing it to light, much like a camera. (Some imagesetters output directly to printing plates, eliminating the middleman.) But unlike a camera, an imagesetter knows only two colors, black and white. The colors are applied with inks on the printing press.

You can also print color separations of an illustration in one of the following ways:

- Take the Illustrator file to a service bureau or commercial printer and let a qualified technician deal with it.
- Import the illustration as an EPS file into PageMaker or QuarkXPress. Then take the PageMaker or QuarkXPress file to a service bureau and let these folks do their jobs.
- Print the separations directly from PageMaker or QuarkXPress to an in-house imagesetter.

The last option—printing the color separations directly from Illustrator on your own—either to an in-house imagesetter or to a file that you can later deliver to a service bureau—is perhaps the most unlikely scenario of them all. But it is the reason that Illustrator integrates color separation capabilities, which is why I explain it in great detail in the next few pages.

To print color separations from Illustrator, do the following:

1. Prepare the illustration just as you did when printing the composite, using the Chooser, the Page Setup command, and the page tool.
2. Choose File » Print or press ⌘-P to display the Printer dialog box.
3. Select the Separate option from the Output pop-up menu.
4. Click on the Separation Setup button to display the Color Separation dialog box. Modify the settings as desired and press the Return key to return to the Printer dialog box.
5. Press Return again to start printing.

Only Step 4 requires much effort, and it requires quite a bit. Figure 18-9 shows the Color Separation dialog box in full regalia. The dialog box is divided into two parts—the separation preview, as well as a few options above and below the preview, on the left side of the box and a series of separation options along the right.

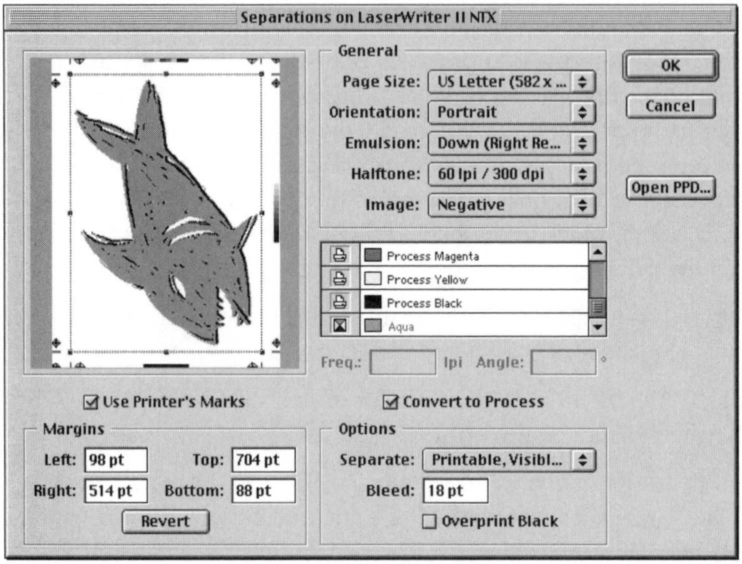

Figure 18-9: You can access this dialog box either by clicking on the Separation Setup button inside the Printer dialog box or by choosing File » Separation Setup.

If this is the first time you've opened this dialog box (most of the options will be dimmed), you need to select a PPD file. Click on the Open PPD button, and then locate the desired PPD file inside the Printer Descriptions folder in the Extensions folder in your Utilities folder. The PPD file you select will determine which options are available in the pop-up menus throughout the Color Separation dialog box. In Figure 18-9, I've selected the Linotronic 530—a top-of-the-line imagesetter—as listed at the top of this dialog box.

The other options in the Color Separation dialog box work as follows:

- **Page Size:** This pop-up menu lists the page sizes available for your output device, based on the active PPD. Next to the common name of each page size is the imageable area of the page, measured in points. Keep an eye on the preview to make sure the illustration and all the printer marks around the illustration fit on the page. In Figure 18-9, for example, the printer marks are getting slightly cut off. If I upgrade my Page Size choice to Letter.Extra (684 x 864) Points, I can avoid this problem.

  Assuming you've selected the PPD file for an imagesetter, you can define your own page size by selecting the Custom option from the

Page Size pop-up menu. This displays the dialog box shown in Figure 18-10. The default values for the Width and Height options are the dimensions of the smallest page that will hold all the objects in your illustration. The Offset option allows you to add space between your illustration and the right edge of the paper or film. If the Offset value is left at 0, the output device will automatically center the illustration on the page.

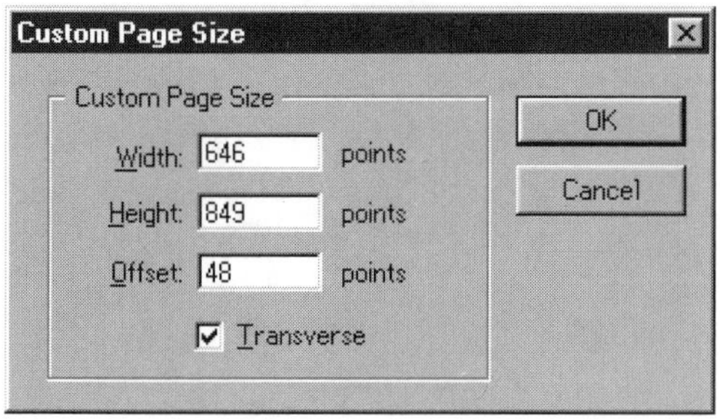

Figure 18-10: This dialog box allows you to specify a custom page size as well as a distance between pages.

The Transverse check box controls the orientation of your custom page relative to the paper or film. By default, the printer places the long side of a portrait illustration parallel to the long edge of the film. You can reduce paper or film waste by rotating the illustration so its short side is parallel to the long edge of the film, known as transverse orientation. Then use the Offset value to specify the amount of space that lies between your illustration and any printed image that follows it.

And now back to the Color Separation dialog box:

- **Orientation:** Set this option to Portrait or Landscape, just as you have inside the Page Setup dialog box. This option works independently of the Transverse check box; if the Orientation option is set incorrectly, you'll cut off part of your illustration. In Figure 18-9, for example, I've drawn my fish on a horizontal artboard, so I selected Landscape to make sure every scale on the creature prints.
- **Emulsion:** The Emulsion options control how the illustration prints relative to the emulsion side of photosensitive film. The names given to the options, Up and Down, refer to the sides of the film on which the emulsion is located. When printing film negatives, you probably want to select Down from the pop-up menu; when printing on paper, Up is usually the correct setting. (Be sure neither Flip Horizontal or Flip Vertical is selected in the AdobePS Options dialog box—shown back in

Figure 18-5—since either option will nullify the Emulsion setting.) Consult your commercial printer to confirm which option you should select.

- **Halftone:** Weird as it may sound, traditional printing presses aren't capable of applying shades of color to paper. They can apply solid ink or no ink at all. That's it. So to represent different light and dark values, imagesetters generate thousands of little black halftone dots, as illustrated in Figure 18-11. The halftone dots grow and shrink to represent respectively darker and lighter shades of color.

  You can specify the density of the halftone dots by selecting an option from the Halftone pop-up menu in the Color Separation dialog box. The first value before the slash represents the screen frequency, which is the number of halftone dots per linear inch. The second value represents the printer resolution, which is the number of tiny printer pixels that print in a linear inch. You can figure out the number of printer pixels that fit inside the largest possible halftone dot by dividing the second number by the first. For example, in this book, all illustrations are printed at a resolution of 2,540 dpi and a screen frequency of 120 lpi. If you divide 2,540 by 120, you get a little more than 21, which means that a halftone dot inside a very dark shade of gray is 21 printer pixels tall and 21 pixels wide.

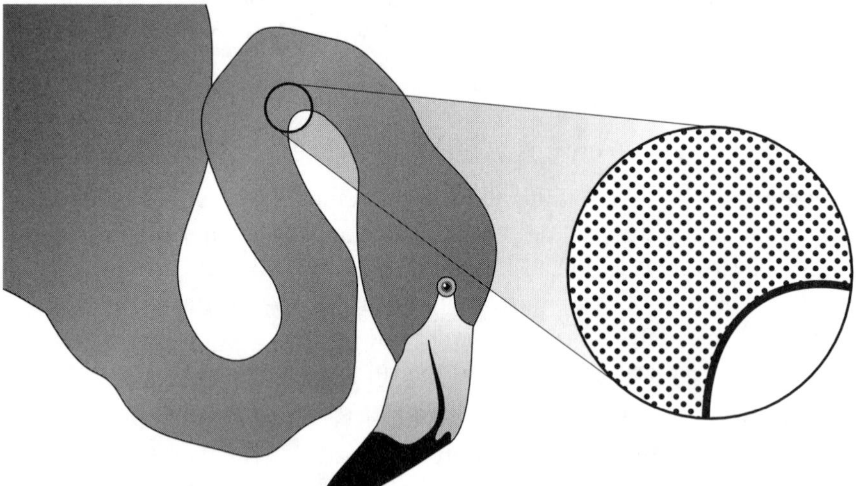

Figure 18-11: A gray value is printed as thousands of little halftone dots. The dots can grow and shrink to imitate different shades.

Fascinating as this may be, the real question is, as always, which option should you use? Unless you have a specific reason for doing otherwise, set the printer resolution (the second value) as high as it will go. If you're printing to paper, you probably don't want to set the screen frequency (the first value) any higher than 120 lpi, since the dots may grow and clog up as the illustration is transferred to film and then to plates. When printing to film, screen frequencies of 133 lpi and higher are acceptable. Consult your commercial printer if you are at all unsure.

- **Image:** The Image option controls whether the illustration prints as a positive or a negative image. If you're printing to paper, the default Positive is usually the correct setting. However, when printing to film, you'll probably want to select Negative. (The Invert check box in the AdobePS Options dialog box should be turned off; otherwise, it will interfere with the Image setting.)
- **Color list:** The scrolling list of colors that appears below the Image pop-up menu allows you to specify exactly which colors you want to print to independent separations. The process colors are listed first followed by any spot colors (which appear dimmed by default). A couple of different icons may appear in front of the colors and are labeled in Figure 18-12. These icons specify whether a color gets its own separation, whether a spot color is converted to its process ingredients, or whether the color gets printed at all.

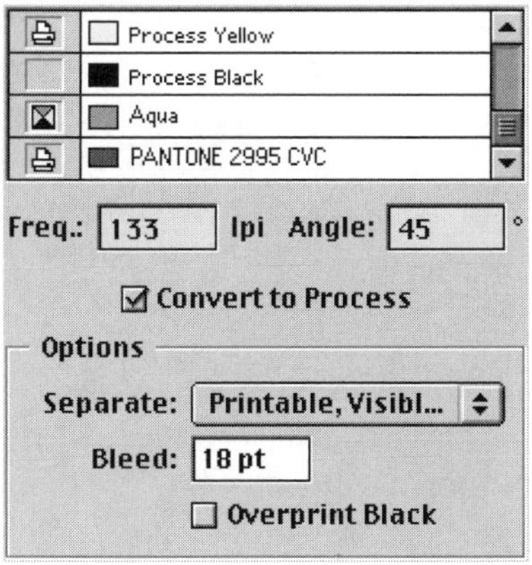

Figure 18-12:
To decide which spot colors you want to separate and which you want to convert to their CMYK ingredients, turn off the Convert to Process check box.

By default, Illustrator is ready to convert all spot colors to their process ingredients. If you want to print at least one spot color to its own separation, turn off the Convert to Process check box. The spot colors in the list should immediately change from dimmed to black. Then click in front of the color on the icon until it changes to the little printer icon to print that color to its own separation. For all other spot colors that you want to convert to CMYK, leave the Convert to Process icon intact. For example, in Figure 18-12, I've set Aqua to convert to CMYK colors because no printer in the world stocks an ink called Aqua. But I've set Pantone 2995, an ink readily available at just about every print shop in the country, to print to its own separation.

- **Frequency and Angle:** In addition to changing the overall screen frequency of the illustration, you can modify the frequency of a single separation. You can also change the angle of the halftone dots. Back in Figure 18-11, for example, you can see that the halftone angle is 45 degrees—that is, each dot is angled 45 degrees from its closest neighbor. To change either the frequency or angle, select a color from the list and enter a new value in the Frequency or Angle option box.

  Why would you want to change either of these values? To avoid creating weird patterns (called moirés) between the halftone dots from different separations. See, by default, all process colors are set to the same frequency. Black is angled at 45 degrees, cyan is set to 15 degrees, magenta is 75 degrees, and yellow is 0 degrees. Rotations of 90 degrees or more are repetitive, because the halftone dots extend in all different directions. This means that cyan, magenta, and black are each rotated 30 degrees from each other; only yellow is closer—measuring only 15 degrees from cyan and magenta—but yellow is so light, its halftone dots don't create a patterning effect.

  So far, so good. There's no reason to change the process colors. The problem is, how do you prevent a spot color from clashing? Unless you know exactly what you're doing, you shouldn't mess around with the Frequency value. And there aren't really any good angles left. This leaves you with the following frequency and angle options:

TIP

If you're printing an illustration that contains one or two spot colors and black—but not cyan, magenta, or yellow—leave black set to 45 degrees and set the spot colors to 15 and 75 degrees. It doesn't matter which color you set to which value. If you have only one spot color, pick an angle—15 or 75—and go with it. When printing a spot color in addition to CMYK, pick a color—black, cyan, or magenta—that the spot color never overlaps. (If the spot color overlaps all three, return to your illustration and modify it so the overlap no longer exists.) Then mimic the angle of that color. For example, if the spot color and cyan never mix—you don't blend between the two colors, mix them together in a gradation, or overprint one on top of the other—then you would set the angle of the spot color to 15 degrees.

- **Use Printer's Marks:** The old Separator utility used to allow you to specify exactly which kinds of printer marks you wanted to use and even position them on the printed page. But this isn't the case in Illustrator. Now you can either print or not print a predefined collection of printer marks. Turn on this check box to print the marks; turn it off to hide them.

  The printer marks include star targets and registration marks to aid in registration. To register plates is to get them into exact alignment, so one color doesn't appear out of sync with another. Illustrator also prints crop marks around the entire illustration and different types of progressive color bars along the edges. Most important, Illustrator labels each separation according to the ink it goes with. There is no good reason to turn off this option. But I sure do wish Illustrator still let you customize the marks.

- **Convert to Process:** I already covered this check box in the "Color list" item. When on, it converts all spot colors to their process ingredients. When off, you can select which colors you want to print as spot color and which you want to convert to CMYK.

- **Separate:** Use this pop-up menu to specify which layers you want to print inside your illustration. (If the file contains just one layer, skip this option and move on.) Choose the Printable Layers option to print just those layers that you have set to print; if you turn off the Print check box for a layer in the Layer Options dialog box (as discussed in the "Modifying Your Layers" section of Chapter 10), the layer won't print. Select the Visible Layers option to print all layers that are visible on screen, even if the Print check box is off. And select the All option to print all layers, whether hidden or turned off. The preview shows the results of the option you select.

- **Overprint Black:** Select this check box to overprint all black ink inside the illustration. Overprinting black is a common way of anticipating registration problems. Also, it permits you to create so-called "saturated blacks." Although black is theoretically as dark as dark can be, you can create colors that are visibly darker by adding cyan, magenta, or yellow to solid black. The result is a rich, glossy black. But overprinting every black in your illustration has its drawbacks. If a black rectangle is positioned on top of a dark CMY object, for example, you can end up applying more ink than the page can absorb. Most paper stocks max out at about 300 percent saturation. If you go over that—for example, 90%C 80%M 70%Y 100%K, which adds up to 340 percent saturation—the ink can actually puddle or run, creating some messy results. Unless you're sure your illustration is safe from oversaturation, I would avoid the Overprint Black check box and use the more selective Filter » Colors » Overprint Black command, as I explain near the end of this chapter.

- **Margin and Bounding box:** The Margin options—Left, Right, Top, and Bottom—allow you to adjust the size of the area Illustrator allots to the illustration. The default values represent the smallest bounding box that can be drawn around the illustration. Printer marks appear in the margins around the bounding box in the preview; the bounding box itself appears as a rectangle.

  You can modify the bounding box either by dragging the corner handles in the preview or by changing the values in the Left, Right, Bottom, and Top Margin option boxes. These values represent the distance from the edge of the page size (specified with the Page Size pop-up menu) and the edge of the bounding box. Therefore, entering smaller values increases the size of the bounding box; entering larger values shrinks the bounding box. Illustrator automatically moves the printer marks so they stay outside the bounding box inside the preview.

- **Bleed:** Though this last option may sound like a practice that died with medieval barbers, it actually controls the distance from the edge of the bounding box to the beginning of the crop marks. In printing, a bleed is the distance that an image extends off the printed page. For example, a bleed of 18 points ensures that even if the page shifts ¼ inch on the press or the trim is ¼ inch off, the illustration still fills the entire page and extends off the sides. How you set the bounding box affects the amount of illustration that is permitted to bleed off the edge. The Bleed value (which can vary from 0 to 18 points) determines how much of this bleed gets printed and offsets the crop marks and other printer marks so they don't overlap too much of the printed artwork. Unless you're running out of room on the film, you're better off leaving the Bleed value set to its default and highest value, 18 points.

Printing to Disk

When you print a illustration to a PostScript printer, Illustrator downloads a PostScript-language version of the file to the printer. The printer reads the file and creates your illustration according to its instructions. Illustrator also lets you print an illustration to disk; that is, you can write the PostScript-language file to your hard drive. This way, you can control how an illustration will print, even though you don't have direct access to the output device. You can then send the file off to your service bureau over a modem or copy the file to disk and drop it off on your way home from work.

Printing to disk is easy. Use the Virtual Printer option in the Chooser to select the PPD file for the printer that you intend to use. (Windows people need only select the Print to File option in the Print dialog box.) Then press ⌘-P, fiddle with the desired options, and hit the Return key, which activates not the OK button but the Save button.

In return, you'll be greeted by the dialog box shown in Figure 18-13. (The Print to File dialog box that Windows users encounter provides only options for naming the file and for deciding its destination.) You can name the file and specify its destination, just as in any Save dialog box. You can also select from a few other options:

- **Format:** Select the format that you want to use to save the illustration from this pop-up menu. The pop-up menu offers three EPS options, but there's no reason to select any of them. You can create an editable EPS file in Illustrator. To create a file you can download to a printer, select the PostScript Job option, which is the default setting.

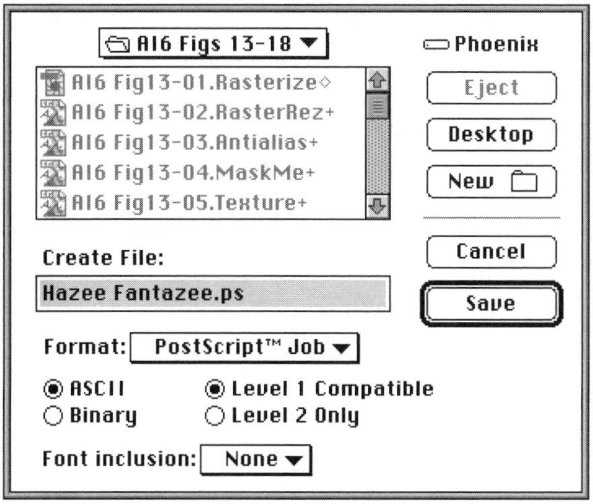

Figure 18-13: This dialog box allows you to print a illustration to disk and save font definitions along with the file.

- **ASCII or Binary:** If the folks at the service bureau will be downloading this file from a Mac, select the Binary option. Binary encoding is much faster, much more efficient, and results in smaller files. Select the ASCII option only if you'll be giving the file to a Windows or DOS user.
- **Level 1, 2, or 3:** You'll have to consult with your service bureau on this one. If the service bureau uses an imagesetter equipped with Level 3 PostScript, by all means select the Level 3 Only option. Otherwise, select Level 1 or Level 2 as required.
- **Font inclusion:** If you used any special fonts in your illustration—anything besides Times, Helvetica, Courier, and Symbol—select the All But Standard 13 option. This tells Illustrator to include printer font definitions for every font that you use, except Times and the others. If the intended printer includes the LaserWriter Plus family of fonts—including Palatino, Bookman, Avant Garde, Gothic, New Century Schoolbook, Zapf Chancery, and Zapf Dingbats—select the All But Standard 35 option. Adding font definitions to your file greatly increases the size of the illustration on disk, but it also prevents your text from printing incorrectly. If you're sure that your service bureau is already equipped with the correct version of all the fonts you're using, select the None option to minimize the size of the illustration on disk.

Click on the Save button or press Return to save the file. Illustrator will deposit a file on your disk, ready for downloading to the printer.

Unusual Printing Considerations

So much for the huge array of printing options that are crammed into the major printing dialog boxes. Although these options are very important—some clearly more important than others—you'll spend most of your time pressing ⌘-P, hitting the Return key, and going off to get some coffee.

Unfortunately, things don't always go according to plan. Sometimes you have to spend a few minutes massaging your illustration to get it ready to deliver the most ideal results in less than ideal conditions. Most problems can be overcome using the options that I've already described, but others can't. Those that can't are the subject of the remaining pages in this chapter.

The following sections explain all the preparatory alternatives that Illustrator permits prior to printing your artwork. Though none of these measures is obligatory—or even customary—they are the sorts of options that you'll want to be at least vaguely familiar with. For example, you can slice and dice large illustrations, insert your own crop marks or trim marks, overcome printing errors, and anticipate registration problems using tools and commands that are spread out from one end of the illustration window to the other. These are the fringe printing features, out of touch with the common illustration and miles away from the automated worlds of the Page Setup and Print commands. But when things turn slightly uncommon, you may be very glad to have them around.

Tiling an Oversized Illustration

By virtue of the Page Setup dialog box, Illustrator provides access to various common page sizes. But many artists require custom page sizes that mid-range printers can't accommodate. So how do you proof oversized artwork using a typical laser printer?

To proof your artwork to letter-sized pages, choose File » Document Setup (⌘-Option-P) and select the Tile Imageable Areas radio button. Illustrator automatically sections your illustration into separate tiles as indicated by the dotted lines in the drawing area. If these breaks will not permit you to easily reassemble your artwork, use the page tool to manually reposition the dotted lines.

Even after you meticulously set up and print the tiles, your pages may not fit together properly. Most notably, the tiles may fade toward the outside of the paper, so that the pasted artwork appears to have gutters running through it. The only solution is to adjust the tiles with the page tool, print a page, adjust the tiles again, print another page, and so on until you get it right. Illustrator doesn't provide any automated means for creating an overlap from one tile to the next.

Creating Crop Marks and Trim Marks

Crop marks indicate the boundaries of an illustration. Most imagesetters print pages between 12 and 24 inches wide, regardless of the actual size of the illustration. When you have the illustration commercially reproduced, the printer will want to know the dimensions of the final page size and how the illustration should be positioned on the page. Crop marks specify the boundaries of the reproduced page, and properly positioned crop marks help to avoid miscommunication and additional expense.

Illustrator automatically creates crop marks around an entire illustration when you print color separations (as I discussed in the "Printing Color Separations" section). But what if you want to print a grayscale composite? Or perhaps you want to more precisely control the placement of the crop marks in the illustration window. In either case, you can take advantage of Object » Cropmarks » Make, which lets you manually position crop marks inside the illustration window.

To create crop marks, draw a rectangle that represents the size of the final reproduced sheet of paper. Then, with the rectangle selected, choose Object » Cropmarks » Make. Illustrator converts the rectangle into crop marks. For example, in Figure 18-14, I drew a business card. Then I drew a rectangle around the card in the first example and converted the rectangle to crop marks in the second example. Notice that the marks are positioned well outside the rectangular boundary, preventing them from appearing on the final card. The objects that extend outside the crop marks—including the gray bars and my personal insignia, the elegant yet meaningless Smiley Cyclops—will bleed off the edge of the business cards.

TIP

If no object is selected and a single page is displayed in the drawing area (i.e., the Single Full Page radio button is active in the Document Setup dialog box), choose Object » Cropmarks » Make to create crop marks around the page. This is an ideal way to add crop marks to a black-and-white illustration.

Unfortunately, only one set of crop marks can exist in an illustration. When you choose Object » Cropmarks » Make, you delete any previous crop marks while creating new ones. Also, you can't move crop marks after you create them. You have to convert the crop marks back to a rectangle by choosing Object » Cropmarks » Release, edit the rectangle as desired, and then choose Object » Cropmarks » Make again to move the crop marks.

When you display the Color Separation dialog box—whether by clicking on the Separation Setup button in the Printer dialog box or by choosing File » Separation Setup—Illustrator automatically sizes the bounding box in the preview to the exact size of the area surrounded by the crop marks. This is a handy method for sizing the boundary, typically more accurate and easier to manipulate than the bounding box controls inside the Color Separation dialog box.

Illustrator 8 also offers the trim marks filter that adds printable guides to your illustration. Trim marks are similar to crop marks in appearance. They differ from crop marks in that they print inside the page boundary (provided they appear within the printable area), they don't affect printing boundaries (or impact any other printing considerations), you can use as many sets of them as you wish in a single illustration, and they can encompass any shape.

Trim marks are intended to help you or your printer cut your final print into its components. Say you wanted to print a number of the business cards shown in the bottom portion of Figure 18-14. Instead of using crop marks, you would select the rectangle that surrounds the card and choose Filter » Create » Trim Marks to have Illustrator add eight little lines that look just like crop marks. These trim marks will surround the rectangle. Since the trim marks filter doesn't modify the rectangle (like the Cropmarks » Make command does), you will need to delete the rectangle around the card. If you don't like the placement of the marks, you can move them—something that's not possible to do with crop marks without first releasing them. To move a trim marks, simply select the marks by Option-clicking on them with the direct selection tool, and then move them to their new locale.

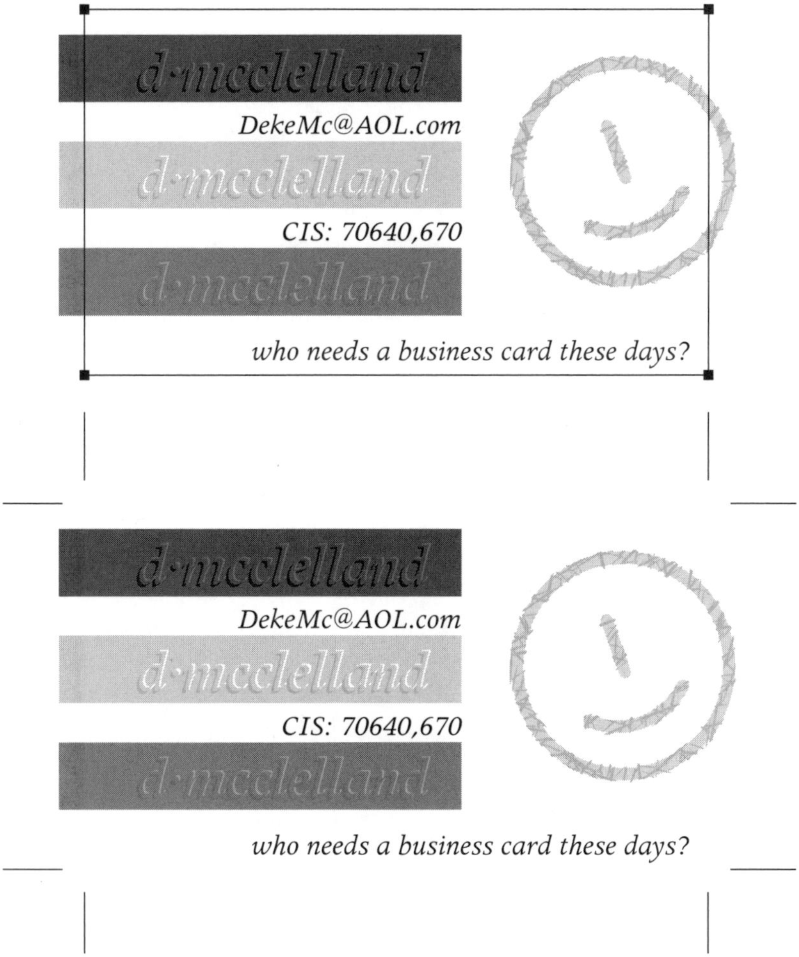

Figure 18-14: After drawing a rectangle to specify the size of the trimmed illustration (top), choose Object » Cropmarks » Make to convert the rectangle to crop marks (bottom).

Select the all the card elements and the trim marks and cut and paste them so that you fit as many as you can into the printable area. After you print your drawing, you can cut along the trim marks to form several individual cards.

Flatness and Path Splitting

You can encounter a fair number of errors when printing an illustration, but one of the most common is the limitcheck error, which results from a limitation in your printer's PostScript interpreter. If the number of points in the mathematical representation of a path exceeds this limitation, the illustration will not print successfully.

Unfortunately, the "points" used in this mathematical representation are not the anchor points you used to define the object. Instead, they're calculated by the PostScript interpreter during the printing process. When presented with a curve, the interpreter has to plot hundreds of tiny straight lines to create the most accurate possible rendering. So rather than drawing a perfect curve, your printer creates an approximation with hundreds of flat edges. The exact number of edges is determined by a variable known as flatness, which is the maximum distance a flat edge can vary from the mathematical curve, as illustrated in Figure 18-15.

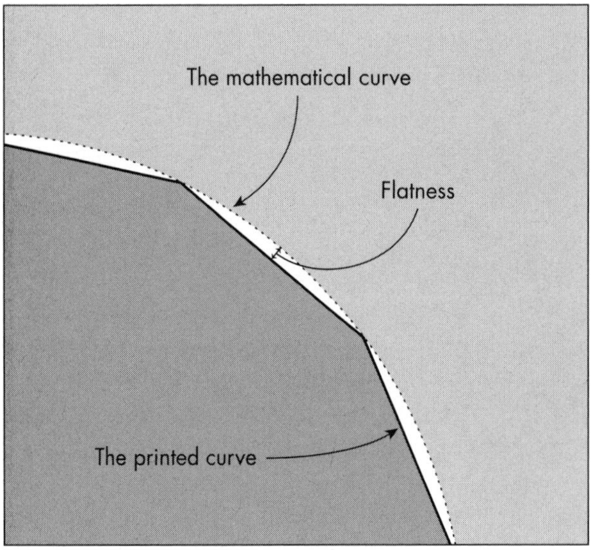

Figure 18-15: The flatness value determines the greatest distance between the center of a flat edge and the closest point along the true mathematical curve.

The default flatness value for a typical laser printer is 1 pixel, or 1/300 inch. This means the center of any flat edge of the printed curve can be at most 1/300 inch from the closest point along the perfect, mathematical curve. If you were to raise the flatness value, the printer could draw fewer flat edges, which quickens the print time but results in more blocky curves.

Each tiny line in the polygon rendering is joined at a point. If the number of points exceeds your printer's built-in path limit, you'll see the telltale words "limitcheck error" in the progress area on your screen, and the illustration will fail to print. The path limit for the original LaserWriter was 1500, seemingly enough flat edges to imitate any curve. But when you factor in such path variations as compound paths and masks, both of which merge shapes with hundreds or thousands of flat edges together, things can get extremely complicated.

You can overcome limitcheck errors in three ways:

- Select the Split Long Paths check box in the Document Setup dialog box (⌘-Option-P). Then enter the resolution for the final output device into the Output Resolution option box. (Higher resolutions produce less dramatic results.) The next time you save or print the current illustration, Illustrator will automatically break up every path that it considers to be at risk into several smaller paths. In most cases, this won't affect the printed appearance of your illustration.

WARNING: Unfortunately, there's no way to automatically reassemble paths after Illustrator splits them apart. If you ever need to join them back together, you have to do so manually, which complicates the editing process. So be sure to save your illustration before selecting the Split Long Paths check box, and then use File » Save As to save a copy of the split illustration under a different name.

Another problem is that Illustrator's automated path-splitting feature only accounts for the complexity of a single path. It doesn't consider masks, tile patterns, or other factors that are more likely to cause limitcheck errors.

- If path splitting doesn't suit your needs, you can change the flatness of individual paths. Select the path that seems responsible for the error—bearing in mind that tile patterns, masks, and compound paths are the most likely culprits—and display the Attributes palette by pressing F11. Then lower the value in the Output option box. This raises the flatness value, which equals the resolution of your printer divided by the Output value. For example, when printing to a 2,540-dpi imagesetter, changing the Output value to 635 changes the flatness of the selected path to 2540 ÷ 635 = 4. This further flattens out the path and increases its likelihood of printing correctly.

- The best solution is to use masks and tile patterns wisely, as I encouraged you to do in Chapters 15 and 17. If a complex mask isn't printing, for example, choose Object » Mask » Release to release the mask and click the Pathfinder palette's Crop button to permanently crop the content elements. Though this may necessitate some manual edits on your part, it will almost always solve the printing problem, and it allows you to print smooth curves without worrying about strange printing issues like flatness.

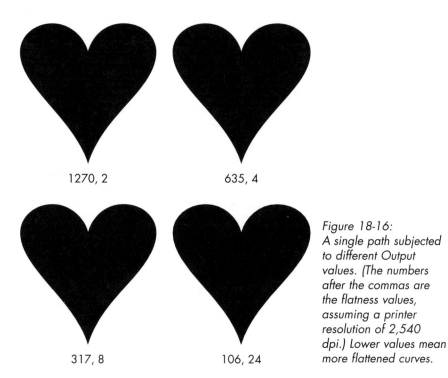

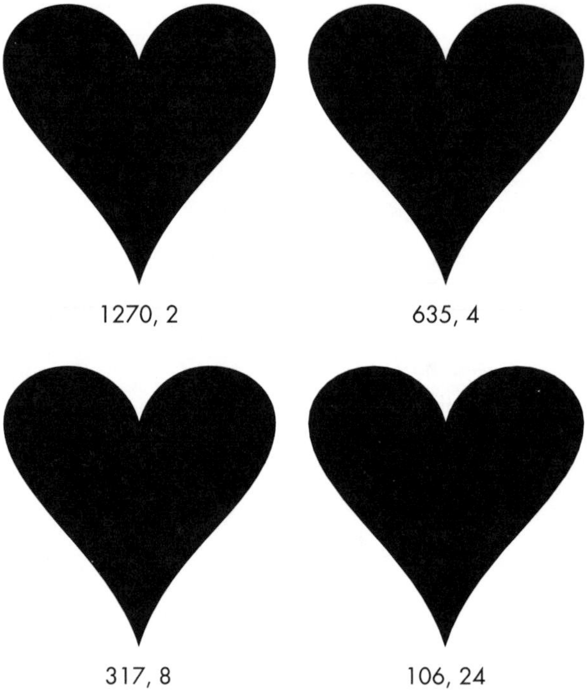

Figure 18-16: A single path subjected to different Output values. (The numbers after the commas are the flatness values, assuming a printer resolution of 2,540 dpi.) Lower values mean more flattened curves.

NOTE: Many of the Pathfinder filters have a habit of producing alert boxes when they complete, warning you that they may have generated paths that are too complicated to print. Ignore these messages! They are almost always inaccurate. Wait until you encounter a limitcheck error before you worry about an overly long path.

The default output resolution for every illustration you create is 800 dpi. This means that curves printed to a 2,540-dpi imagesetter will be treated to a flatness of approximately 3, while lower resolution printers will use lower flatness values. You can print a test version of an illustration by lowering the Output Resolution in the Document Setup dialog box to, say 300, and leaving the Split Long Paths check box turned off. This will significantly speed up the print time at the expense of the curves.

NOTE: All Output Resolution values are saved with an EPS file and included with the illustration even if you import it into another application. So don't expect an illustration to print better from PageMaker or QuarkXPress than it does directly from Illustrator.

Printing Pattern Tiles

As I mentioned more than once in the previous section, tile patterns can cause limitcheck errors. But more commonly, they can cause out-of-memory errors by overwhelming the amount of RAM available to your printer. (Yes, like computers, PostScript printers have RAM.) See, Illustrator downloads the tile as if it were a font to your printer's memory. In this way, the printer accesses tile definitions repeatedly throughout the creation of an illustration. So if the illustration contains too many tile patterns or if a single tile is too complex, the printer's memory may fill up, in which case the print job is canceled and you see an out-of-memory error on screen. (If your printer just stops working on a job, even though Illustrator seems to have sent the illustration successfully, this is likewise an indication of an out-of-memory error.)

Out-of-memory errors are not as common when you're printing to modern, high-resolution imagesetters, because these machines tend to include updated PostScript interpreters and have increased memory capacity. Therefore, you will most often encounter an out-of-memory error when proofing an illustration to a mid-range laser printer or to another low-memory device. Try one of these techniques to remedy the problem:

- Change all typefaces in the illustration to Times, Helvetica, or some other printer-resident font. Or, better yet, convert all characters to paths using Type » Create Outlines. This way, Illustrator won't have to download both tile and font definitions.
- Print objects filled with different tile patterns in separate pages. Then use traditional paste-up techniques to combine the patterns into a composite proof.

When you print the illustration to an imagesetter, it will probably print successfully because of the imagesetter's increased memory capacity. But if the illustration still encounters an out-of-memory error, you'll have to delete some patterns or resort to traditional paste-up techniques, as suggested in the second item above.

Trapping Selected Paths

Mainstream applications like PageMaker, QuarkXPress, FreeHand, and (alas) Illustrator are still in the stone age when it comes to trapping, which is used to help cover up registration problems that sometimes occur when printing full-color documents. If your commercial printer's plates are slightly out of register—as they frequently are—gaps may form between high-contrast edges. It's always a good idea to employ a professional printing company that has lots of experience in color printing and guarantees its work. But even the most conscientious printers may be off by as little as a half point, enough to cast a shadow of shoddiness across your artwork.

Full-service (read mega-expensive) printers will trap your work for you using dedicated systems from Scitex or Crosfield. Other printers may charge you a little extra to trap your illustration with software such as TrapWise or IslandTrapper. If your printer does not provide trapping services, however, you may want to create your own traps in Illustrator.

Illustrator's Trap command works by creating a new path of a specified thickness that overprints the neighboring paths below it. The result is a slight darkening of colors where two paths meet, an imperfect solution that is nevertheless much preferable to a white gap.

You can't trap an entire illustration. Instead, you trap two or more neighboring paths at a time. Also, the filter works only on paths with flat fills. It can't handle gradations, tile patterns, strokes, text, or imported images.

TIP: If you want to trap a stroke, first convert it to a filled path by choosing Object » Path » Outline Path. To trap text, convert the characters to paths with Type » Create Outlines. You'll want to trap only large text, such as headlines or logos. Traps around small letters can make the text gooey and illegible.

The trick when using the Trap filter is to recognize which paths need trapping and which do not. Here are a few instances where trapping may be helpful:

- Two paths filled with different spot colors.
- A path filled with a spot color next to a path filled with a process color.
- Two paths filled with process colors that don't share any primary color in common. For example, an 80 percent cyan path next to a 50 percent yellow, 40 percent magenta path needs to be trapped.

If two neighboring paths are both filled with process colors, and they share one or more primary colors in common, trapping is not necessary. For example, if a 50 percent cyan, 20 percent magenta path overlaps a 70 percent cyan, 30 percent yellow path, a continuous screen of cyan will occur between the two paths even if the magenta and yellow plates are incorrectly registered. Likewise, you don't have to trap between two paths filled with different tints of a spot color. Registration problems have no effect on paths printed from the same plate.

NOTE The Trap filter is pretty smart about telling you when you need and don't need to trap. If the filter refuses to work, it means that the paths are too similar to require trapping. (This assumes that the paths are filled with flat colors; gradations, strokes, and other attributes can trip up the Trap filter as well.)

To trap two or more selected paths, choose Object » Pathfinder » Trap, which displays the Pathfinder Trap dialog box shown in Figure 18-17. The options in this dialog box work as follows:

- **Thickness:** This is the key option in the dialog box. Here you specify the width of the overprinting path created by the filter. The default value, 0.25 point, is awfully small, only sufficient to remedy extremely slight registration problems. If your commercial printer is a top-of-the-line operation, this is sufficient. If your printer is more the workaday, get-the-job-out variety, a value of 0.5 or 1 might be more appropriate.

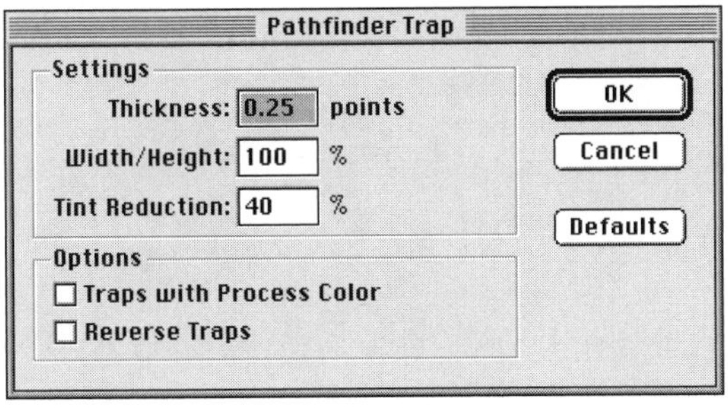

Figure 18-17: From this dialog box, you can create a sliver of a path that traces the border between a pair of selected paths.

- **Width/Height:** This value represents the ratio between the vertical and horizontal thickness of the trapping path. A value of 100 percent means that the trap will be the same thickness—as specified in the previous option—throughout its length. Raise the value to increase the vertical thickness of the trap; lower the value to decrease the vertical thickness. The horizontal thickness is always the exact width entered into the

Thickness option box. The purpose of this option—in case you're wondering—is to account for differences in vertical and horizontal misregistration. Check with your printer to find out if any compensation is needed.

- **Tint reduction:** When trapping paths filled with spot colors, Illustrator fills the trap with a tint of the lightest color. So if a selected yellow path neighbors a selected brown path, the trap is filled with a tint of yellow. The light yellow trap looks lighter than either of the neighboring paths on screen, but because it overprints, the trap leaves the yellow path unaffected and slightly darkens the brown path.

  When trapping process-color paths (or if you convert the trap applied to spot colors to a process color using the Convert Custom Colors to Process check box), Illustrator mixes a 100-percent tint of the darker color with a lighter tint of the lighter color.

  Whether you're trapping spot or process colors, the Tint Reduction value determines the tint of the lighter color. A light tint appears less intrusive than a dark one, so the default 40 percent is a good value for most jobs.

- **Traps with Process Color:** Choose this check box to fill the trap with a process color regardless of whether the trapped paths are filled with spot or process colors. Generally, you'll want to leave this option off. If the lighter color is a spot color, it stands to reason that the trap should be a tint of that spot color. Only if the darker of two neighboring paths is filled with a process color and the screen angle of the spot color might interfere with those of the process colors should you select this option. Never select it when trapping two neighboring paths filled with spot colors.

- **Reverse traps:** Select this option to change the fill of the trap to favor the darker color instead of the lighter one, when you disagree with Illustrator over which of two neighboring colors is lighter. For example, when trapping a red path and a blue path, Illustrator will most likely see the blue path as lighter, while you may see it as darker. If you don't like the way Illustrator fills the trap, undo the operation and reapply it with Reverse Traps selected.

After you press Return, Illustrator creates a trapping path along the border between each pair of neighboring selected shapes. Figure 18-18 shows two trapping scenarios (converted to grayscale for purposes of this book). In each case, just the outlined paths were selected. As you can see, Illustrator creates traps around the neighboring borders of the selected paths only; portions of selected paths that do not neighbor other selected paths are ignored.

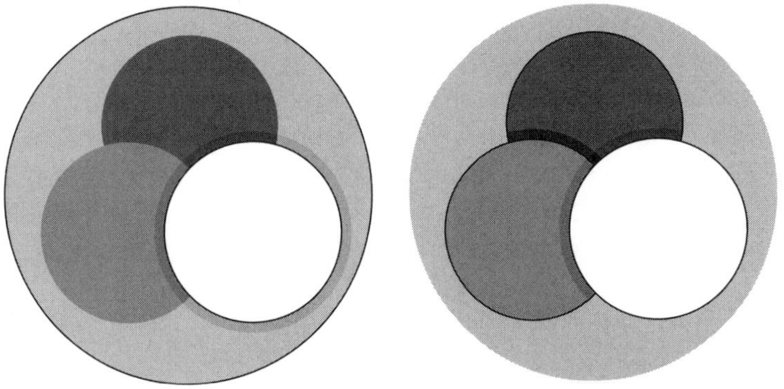

Figure 18-18: The results of two trapping operations. In each case, the outlined paths were selected, paths without outlines were not. The dark strips are the traps.

This system works great when trapping spot colors, but it gets a little weird when trapping process colors. For example, suppose in the first example in Figure 18-18 that the small selected circle is yellow and the large selected circle is deep purple. The overprinting trap will have hints of both yellow and purple, even when it overlaps the deselected circles, which may be green, orange, or any other color. The fact is, the purple of the background circle has no business being there.

TIP

To avoid this problem, remove the tint of the background path from the trap. In the case of my example, I would simply remove the purple from the trap and leave the yellow intact. A yellow trap surrounding a yellow path is always acceptable, regardless of the paths it overprints.

Overprinting Black Paths

Another way to trap two objects is to overprint one on top of the other. If a text block is full of small black type, you'll probably want to select the Overprint Fill check box in the Attributes palette. This way, Illustrator prints the text on top of any background colors to ensure that no gaps appear between character outlines and neighboring colors.

Overprinting black is such a common practice that Illustrator provides a filter to automate the process. This filter allows you to overprint a specific percentage of black through the fills and strokes of all selected objects. Select all the objects you might want to overprint, and then choose Filter » Colors » Overprint Black. Illustrator displays the Overprint Black dialog box shown in Figure 18-19.

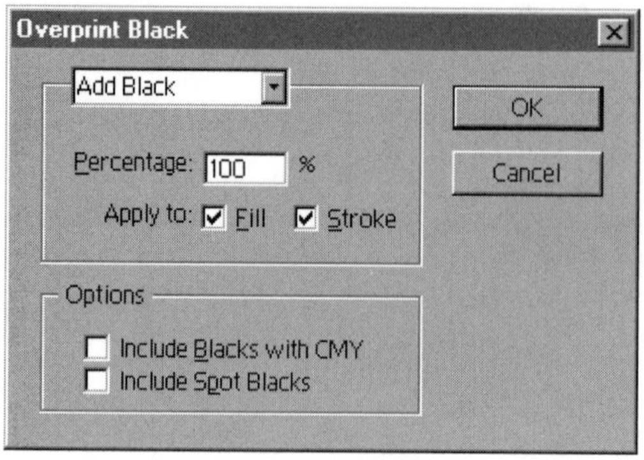

Figure 18-19: Use the Overprint Black filter to overprint all selected objects that contain a specific percentage of black.

The options in this dialog box work as follows:

- **Add Black and Remove Black:** If you want to overprint colors, select the Add Black command in the pop-up menu. If you want to remove overprinting from selected objects—so that they knock out the colors behind them—select Remove Black.
- **Percentage:** Enter the intensity of black ink that you want to overprint. All objects with that exact percentage of black will overprint.
- **Apply to Fill and Stroke:** Use these check boxes to overprint—or to remove the overprinting from—fills, strokes, or both fills and strokes. By default, both check boxes are selected.
- **Include Blacks with CMY:** To overprint CMYK objects that contain a specific percentage of black, select this check box. For example, if you set the Percentage Black value to 40, and a selected object is filled with 30%C 20%M 10%Y 40%K, this check box must be turned on for the filter to affect the object.
- **Include Spot Blacks:** When this check box is on, any spot blacks in you document will also overprint. If you intend for your objects to print as spot colors, you should check this option. (Since the CMYK values are for screen display purposes only, the Black value in a spot color has nothing to do with the printed ink.) But if you plan on converting all spot colors to CMYK, you don't have to worry about this option.

This filter would be better if it would allow you to change a range of blacks at a time (an oversight that I'm still hoping Adobe might fix in the future). And it would be nice if the filter could automatically detect oversaturations and make sure that overprinted blacks don't smudge on the printed page. Still, it's safer than simply selecting the Overprint Black check box in the Separation dialog box.

APPENDIX

Taking Illustrator's Shortcuts

As with any drawing program, you'll spend much of your time interacting with Illustrator by clicking and dragging with your mouse or some other input device. However, a number of commands and other operations can also be executed by way of the keyboard or via keyboard-and-mouse combinations. The tables that appear throughout this appendix explain keyboard equivalents applicable to Illustrator 8, categorized by function.

For each keyboard equivalent listed in the following charts, key names are separated by hyphens. For example, the keyboard equivalent for Edit » Select All is ⌘-A. This means that you should press both the ⌘ key and the A key *at the same time* to perform the Select All command.

Mouse actions are a little more complicated. If one or more key names precede a mouse action, you should press the key(s), perform the action, and then release the key(s). For example, Shift-click means that you press and hold down the Shift key, click on the item, and then release the Shift key; the Shift key is down throughout the mouse operation.

In an attempt to make Illustrator look and feel like Photoshop, Adobe has evolved most of Illustrator's keyboard shortcuts to more closely match those in the popular image editor. To ease your transition, I've divided the tables on the following pages into columns, listing both the old Illustrator 6 and 7 shortcuts and the new Illustrator 8 counterparts side by side by side. If you're adept at using Illustrator 6 and earlier, the sheer quantity of changes may overwhelm you at first. But remember that the method behind this seeming madness is greater productivity in the long run. If all goes according to plan, you'll be able to switch between Illustrator and Photoshop with approximately equal proficiency in both programs. If, on the other hand, you're accustomed to the shortcuts of Illustrator 7, you'll find it easy to acclimate to those in version 8 since only a few have changed.

Bear in mind that these aren't *all* the weird little tricks you can perform in Illustrator; they're just the hottest little doodads that I can communicate in the shortest order. I don't include the drawing tricks—like the myriad pen tool tricks and cloning options—because they require more detailed descriptions and are better explained in proper context in the book.

One last thing: These tables are geared toward the Macintosh user. For you Windows users, the shortcuts differ only slightly. When you see a reference to the ⌘ key or Option key, you'll need to substitute the Ctrl key or Alt key, respectively. The table's Macintosh orientation is not a reflection of platform bias on my part—in fact, I spent my first week using Illustrator 8 on the Windows side. It's just that, for now, the vast majority of Illustrator users work with Macintosh computers. Illustrator is still mainly a Mac application and since this book has its space constraints, only the Mac equivalents are listed.

Choosing Menu Commands

The following list shows how to access most of the menu commands included in Illustrator 8 using keystrokes and the occasional secret mouse trick. For the sake of continuity with previous versions of Illustrator, I've included a few commands that no longer exist but still offer keyboard shortcuts. Any command that is not listed cannot be accessed from the keyboard and must be chosen from a menu.

Command	Illustrator 6 shortcut	Illustrator 7 shortcut	Illustrator 8 shortcut
Actual Size	⌘-H or double-click on zoom tool icon	⌘-1 or double-click on zoom tool icon	⌘-1 or double-click on zoom tool icon
Average	⌘-L	⌘-Option-J	⌘-Option-J
Average (and Join)	⌘-Option-J or ⌘-Option-L	⌘-Option-Shift-J	⌘-Option-Shift-J
Artwork mode	⌘-E	⌘-Y when in preview mode	⌘-Y when in preview mode
Bring Forward	*none*	⌘-]	⌘-]
Bring To Front	⌘-plus (+)	⌘-Shift-]	⌘-Shift-]
Center (alignment)	⌘-Shift-C	⌘-Shift-C	⌘-Shift-C
Character	⌘-T	⌘-T	⌘-T
Clear	Delete or Backspace	Delete or Backspace	Delete or Backspace
Close	⌘-W	⌘-W	⌘-W

Command	Illustrator 6 shortcut	Illustrator 7 shortcut	Illustrator 8 shortcut
Copy	⌘-C	⌘-C	⌘-C or F3
Create Outlines	*none*	⌘-Shift-O	⌘-Shift-O
Cut	⌘-X	⌘-X	⌘-X or F2
Deselect All	⌘-Shift-A	⌘-Shift-A	⌘-Shift-A
Document Setup	⌘-Shift-D	⌘-Shift-P	⌘-Option-P
Exit (or Quit)	⌘-Q	⌘-Q	⌘-Q
Filter, repeat last	⌘-Shift-E	⌘-E	⌘-E
Filter, repeat with new settings	⌘-Option-Shift-E	⌘-Shift-E	⌘-Option-E
Fit In Window	⌘-M or double-click on hand tool icon	⌘-0 (zero) or double-click on hand tool icon	⌘-0 (zero) or double-click on hand tool icon
General Preferences	⌘-K	⌘-K	⌘-K
Grid, show or hide	*none*	⌘-"	⌘-"
Group	⌘-G	⌘-G	⌘-G
Guides, show or hide	*none*	⌘-;	⌘-;
Hide Selection	⌘-3	⌘-U (and ⌘-3 on the Mac)	⌘-3
Hide Edges	⌘-Shift-H	⌘-H	⌘-H
Join	⌘-J	⌘-J	⌘-J
Join (first Average)	⌘-Option-J or ⌘-Option-L	⌘-Option-Shift-J	⌘-Option-Shift-J
Justify (alignment)	⌘-Shift-J	⌘-Shift-J	⌘-Shift-J
Justify Last Line	⌘-Shift-B	⌘-Shift-F	⌘-Shift-F
Left (alignment)	⌘-Shift-L	⌘-Shift-L	⌘-Shift-L
Link Blocks	⌘-Shift-G	⌘-3 (Windows only)	*none*
Lock (selected objects)	⌘-1	⌘-L (and ⌘-2 on the Mac)	⌘-2
Lock Guides	⌘-7	⌘-Option-;	⌘-Option-;
Make Blends	*none*	*none*	⌘-Option-B
Make Compound Paths	⌘-8	⌘-8	⌘-8
Make Guides	⌘-5	⌘-5	⌘-5
Make Masks	*none*	⌘-7	⌘-7
Move	⌘-Shift-M or Option-click on arrow tool	Double-click on arrow tool	Double-click on arrow tool
New	⌘-N	⌘-N	⌘-N
New View	⌘-Control-N	*none*	*none*
Other Type Size	⌘-Shift-S	*none*	*none*
Open	⌘-O	⌘-O	⌘-O
Paragraph	⌘-Shift-T	⌘-M	⌘-M
Paste	⌘-V	⌘-V	⌘-V or F4
Paste In Back	⌘-B	⌘-B	⌘-B

continued on next page

continued from previous page

Command	Illustrator 6 shortcut	Illustrator 7 shortcut	Illustrator 8 shortcut
Paste In Front	⌘-F	⌘-F	⌘-F
Preferences	⌘-K	⌘-K	⌘-K
Preview Mode	⌘-Y	⌘-Y	⌘-Y
Preview Selection	⌘-Option-Y	⌘-Shift-Y	⌘-Shift-Y
Print	⌘-P	⌘-P	⌘-P
Print Setup	*none*	*none*	⌘-Shift-P
Quit	⌘-Q	⌘-Q	⌘-Q
Redo	⌘-Shift-Z	⌘-Shift-Z	⌘-Shift-Z
Release Blend	*none*	*none*	⌘-Option-Shift-B
Release Compound Paths	⌘-9	⌘-Option-8	⌘-Option-8
Release Guides	⌘-6 or Shift-Control-double-click on guide	⌘-Option-5	⌘-Option-5 or ⌘-Shift-double-click on guide
Release Masks	*none*	⌘-Option-7	⌘-Option-7
Repeat Pathfinder	*none*	⌘-4	⌘-4
Revert	*none*	F12	F12
Right (alignment)	⌘-Shift-R	⌘-Shift-R	⌘-Shift-R
Rulers, show or hide	⌘-R	⌘-R	⌘-R
Save	⌘-S	⌘-S	⌘-S
Save a Copy	*none*	⌘-Option-S	⌘-Option-S
Save As	*none*	⌘-Shift-S	⌘-Shift-S
Select Again	*none*	*none*	⌘-6
Select All	*none*	⌘-A	⌘-A
Send Backward	*none*	⌘-[	⌘-[
Send To Back	⌘-minus (-)	⌘-Shift-[	⌘-Shift-[
Separation Setup	*none*	⌘-Option-P	*none*
Show All (hidden objects)	⌘-4	⌘-Shift-U (and ⌘-Option-3 on the Mac)	⌘-Option-3
Smart Guides	*none*	*none*	⌘-U
Snap to Grid	*none*	⌘-Shift-"	⌘-Shift-"
Snap to Point	*none*	*none*	⌘-Option-"
Tab Ruler	⌘-Shift-T	*none*	⌘-Shift-T
Template, show or hide	*none*	*none*	⌘-Shift-W
Transform Again	⌘-D	⌘-D	⌘-D
Undo	⌘-Z	⌘-Z	⌘-Z
Ungroup	⌘-U	⌘-Shift-G	⌘-Shift-G
Unlink Blocks	⌘-Shift-U	⌘-Option-3 (Windows only)	*none*
Unlock All (locked objects)	⌘-2	⌘-Shift-L (and ⌘-Option-2 on the Mac)	⌘-Option-2

Command	Illustrator 6 shortcut	Illustrator 7 shortcut	Illustrator 8 shortcut
Vertical Tab Ruler	*none*	*none*	⌘-Option-Shift-T
Zoom In	⌘-]	⌘-plus (+)	⌘-plus (+)
Zoom Out	⌘-[	⌘-minus (-)	⌘-minus (-)

Displaying and Hiding Palettes

The following table explains how to show and hide palettes from the keyboard. Most of these straightforward shortcuts are not listed in any menu.

Palette	Illustrator 6 shortcut	Illustrator 7 shortcut	Illustrator 8 shortcut
Attributes palette	⌘-Control-A	F11 or ⌘-Shift-I	F11 or ⌘-Shift-I
Brushes palette	*none*	*none*	F5
Character palette	⌘-T	⌘-T	⌘-T
Color palette	⌘-I	F6 or ⌘-I	F3 or ⌘-I
Gradient palette	*none*	F9	F9
Info palette	⌘-Control-I	F8	F8
Layers palette	⌘-Control-L	F7	F7
Paragraph palette	⌘-Shift-P	⌘-M	⌘-M
Stroke palette	⌘-I	F10	F10
Swatches palette	*none*	F5	*none*
Tab Ruler palette	⌘-Shift-T	*none*	⌘-Shift-T
All palettes, including toolbox	Tab	Tab	Tab
All palettes *except* toolbox	*none*	Shift-Tab	Shift-Tab
Toolbox only	⌘-Control-T	*none*	*none*

Selecting Tools

In Illustrator 8, you can access every tool directly from the keyboard. This is a great time saver; it means you can spend less time hunting down a tool with the mouse and more time creating and editing your drawing. Some shortcuts activate the tool only so long as you hold down the key; releasing the key returns you to the previously selected tool. These temporary equivalents are distinguished by the word "hold." The other keys select the last used tool in that tool slot just as if you had clicked on its icon. If the tool you're looking for is not the last used tool in its tool slot, you'll need to also press the Shift key along with the other key to cycle through the tools in that slot. The tools are listed in the order they appear in the toolbox.

Tool	Illustrator 6 shortcut	Illustrator 7 shortcut	Illustrator 8 shortcut
Last selection tool used	Hold ⌘ when any tool is active	Hold ⌘ when any tool is active	Hold ⌘ when any tool is active
Selection (arrow) tool	⌘-Tab when direct-selection or group-selection tool is active	⌘-Tab when direct-selection or group-selection tool is active, or press V	⌘-Tab when direct-selection or group-selection tool is active, or press V or Shift-V
Direct selection tool	⌘-Tab when selection tool is active	⌘-Tab when selection tool is active, or press A	⌘-Tab when selection tool is active, or press A or Shift-A
Group selection tool	Hold Option when direct selection tool is active	Hold Option or press A when direct selection tool is active	Hold Option or press Shift-A when direct selection tool is active
Pen tool	Hold Control when freehand tool is active	Press P	Press P or Shift-P
Add anchor point tool	Hold Option when scissors or delete anchor point tool is active	Hold Option when scissors or delete anchor point tool is active or press P when pen is active	Hold Option when scissors anchor point tool is active or press Shift-P when pen is active
Delete anchor point tool	Hold Option when add anchor point tool is active	Hold Option or press P when add anchor point tool is active	Hold Option or press Shift-P when add anchor point tool is active
Convert point tool	Hold Control when selection tool is active; hold Control-Option when pen tool is active	Hold ⌘-Option when selection tool is active; hold Option when pen tool is active; or press P when delete anchor point tool is active	Hold ⌘-Option when selection tool is active; hold Option when pen tool is active; or press Shift-P when delete anchor point tool is active
Type tool	Hold Control when area or path type tool is active	Press T or hold Shift when vertical type tool is active	Press T or Shift-T or hold Shift when vertical type tool is active
Area type tool	Click on closed path or Option-click on open path when type tool is active	Click on closed path, Option-click on open path, or press T when type tool is active	click on closed path, Option-click on open path, or press Shift-T when type tool
Path type tool	Click on open path or Option-click on closed path when type tool is active	Click on open path or Option-click on closed path when type tool is active; or press T when area type tool is active	Click on open path or Option-click on closed path when type tool is active; or press Shift-T when area type tool is active
Vertical type tool	*new tool*	Hold Shift when type tool is active; or press T when path style tool is active	Hold Shift when type tool is active; or press Shift-T when path style tool is active
Vertical area type tool	*new tool*	Shift-click on closed path or Option-Shift-click on open path when type tool is active;or press T when vertical type tool is active	Shift-click on closed path or Option-Shift-click on open when type tool is active; or press Shift-T when vertical type tool is active

Tool	Illustrator 6 shortcut	Illustrator 7 shortcut	Illustrator 8 shortcut
Vertical path type tool	*new tool*	Shift-click on open path or Option-Shift-click on closed path when type tool is active; or press T when vertical area type tool is active	Shift-click on open path or Option-Shift-click on closed path when type tool is active; or press Shift T when vertical area type tool is active
Ellipse tool	*none*	Press N	Press N or Shift-N
Centered Ellipse tool	Hold Option when ellipse tool is active	Hold Option or press N when ellipse tool is active	Hold Option when ellipse tool is active
Regular polygon tool	*none*	Press N when centered ellipse tool is active	Press Shift-N when ellipse tool is active
Star tool	*none*	Press N when regular polygon tool is active	Press Shift-N when regular polygon tool is active
Spiral tool `	*none*	Press N when star tool is active	Press Shift-N when star tool is active
Rectangle tool	*none*	Press M	Press M or Shift-M
Rounded rectangle tool	*none*	Press M when rectangle tool is active	Press Shift-M when rectangle tool is active
Centered rectangle tool	Hold Option when rectangle tool is active	Hold Option when rectangle tool is active or press M when rounded rectangle tool is active	Hold Option when rectangle tool is active
Centered rounded rectangle tool	Hold Option when rounded rectangle tool is active	Hold Option when rounded rectangle tool is active or press M when centered rectangle tool is active	Hold Option when rounded rectangle tool is active
Paintbrush tool	*none*	Press Y when pencil tool is active	Press B
Pencil (freehand) tool	*none*	Press Y	Press Y or Shift-Y
Smooth tool	*new tool*	*new tool*	Hold Option when pencil or erase tool is active; press Shift-Y when pencil tool is active
Erase tool	*new tool*	*new tool*	Press Shift-Y when smooth tool is active
Rotate tool	*none*	Press R	Press R or Shift-R
Twirl tool	*none*	Press R when rotate tool is active	Press Shift-R when rotate tool is active
Scale tool	*none*	Press S	Press S or Shift-S
Reshape tool	*new tool*	Press S when scale tool is active	Press Shift-S when scale tool is active
Reflect tool	*none*	Press O	Press O or Shift-O
Shear tool	*none*	Press W	Press Shift-O when reflect tool is active

continued on next page

continued from previous page

Tool	Illustrator 6 shortcut	Illustrator 7 shortcut	Illustrator 8 shortcut
Free Transform tool	*new tool*	*new tool*	Press E
Blend tool	*none*	Press B	Press W or Shift-W
Autotrace tool	*none*	Press B when blend tool is active	Press w when blend tool is active
Graph tool	*none*	Press J	Press J or Shift-J
Gradient Mesh tool	*new tool*	*new tool*	Press U
Gradient tool	*none*	Press G	Press G
Eyedropper tool	Hold Option key when paint bucket tool is active	Hold Option key when paint bucket tool is active or press I	Hold Option key when paint bucket tool is active or press I or Shift-I
Paint bucket tool	Hold Option key when eyedropper tool is active	Hold Option key when eyedropper tool is active or press K	Hold Option key when eyedropper tool is active or press Shift-I
Scissors tool	*none*	Press C	Press C or Shift-C
Knife tool	*none*	Press C when scissors tool is active	Press Shift-C when scissors tool is active
Hand tool	Hold spacebar when any tool is active	Hold spacebar when any tool is active or press H	Hold spacebar when any tool is active or press H or Shift-H
Page tool	*none*	Press H when hand tool is active	Press Shift-H when hand tool is active
Measure tool	*none*	Press U	Press Shift-H when page tool is active
Zoom tool	Hold ⌘-spacebar when any tool is active	Hold ⌘-spacebar when any tool is active or press Z	Hold ⌘-spacebar when any tool is active or press Z

Activating Toolbox Controls

You can also press keys to access the paint style and window size controls located in the bottom portion of the toolbox. These paint style controls are the same as those located in the Color palette.

Control	Illustrator 6 shortcut	Illustrator 7 shortcut	Illustrator 8 shortcut
Revert to default colors	*none*	Press D	Press D
Switch focus between fill and stroke	*none*	Press X	Press X
Switch fill and stroke colors	*new feature*	*new feature*	Press Shift-X
Cycle through window sizes	*new feature*	Press F	Press F

Control	Illustrator 6 shortcut	Illustrator 7 shortcut	Illustrator 8 shortcut
Select flat color paint style	*none*	Press , (comma)	Press , (comma)
Select gradient paint style	*none*	Press . (period)	Press . (period)
Select transparent paint style	*none*	Press / (slash)	press / (slash)

Creating and Manipulating Type

This list explains how to create, select, flow, and reposition type. Unless otherwise indicated, you perform all techniques using any of the six type tools.

Operation	Illustrator 6 shortcut	Illustrator 7 shortcut	Illustrator 8 shortcut
Create single line of type	Click with type tool	Click with type tool or vertical type tool	Click with type tool or vertical type tool
Create new text block	Drag with type tool	Drag with type tool or vertical type tool	Drag with type tool or vertical type tool
Create type inside path	Click on shape with type or area type tool	Click on shape with type tool, area type tool, or vertical type counterpart	Click on shape with type tool, area type tool, or vertical type counterpart
Create type on path	Click on line with type or path type tool	Click on line with type tool, path type tool, or vertical type counterpart	Click on line with type tool, path type tool, or vertical type counterpart
Insert type in text block	Click inside block	Click inside block	Click inside block
Select type in text block	Drag across characters	Drag across characters	Drag across characters
Select word	Double-click on word	Double-click on word	Double-click on word
Select paragraph	Triple-click in paragraph	Triple-click in paragraph	Triple-click in paragraph
Flow text into new column	Option-drag outline of column with direct-selection tool	Option-drag outline of column with direct-selection tool	Option-drag outline of column with direct-selection tool
Move text along path	Drag I-beam with selection tool	Drag I-beam with selection tool	Drag I-beam with selection tool
Flip direction of text on path	Double-click on I-beam with selection tool	Double-click on I-beam with selection tool	Double-click on I-beam with selection tool

Formatting Type

This next list spells out the formatting functions that you can access from the keyboard, as well as a few that offer special mouse shortcuts. Many keyboard formatting controls rely on increments set using the Size/Leading, Baseline Shift, and Tracking options in the Type & Auto Tracing Preferences dialog box. All shortcuts assume that text is selected with one of the selection or type tools.

Operation	Illustrator 6 shortcut	Illustrator 7 shortcut	Illustrator 8 shortcut
Insert line break	Enter (on the keypad)	Enter (on the keypad)	Enter (on the keypad)
Highlight Font option	⌘-T; ⌘-Shift-F; or ⌘-Option-Shift-M	⌘-Option-Shift-M	⌘-Option-Shift-M
Increase type size by Preferences increment	⌘-Shift->	⌘-Shift->	⌘-Shift->
Decrease type size by Preferences increment	⌘-Shift-<	⌘-Shift-<	⌘-Shift-<
Increase type size by 5x Preferences increment	*none*	*none*	⌘-Option-Shift->
Decrease type size by 5x Preferences increment	*none*	*none*	⌘-Option-Shift-<
Highlight Size option	⌘-Shift-S	*none*	*none*
Reset type to 12 points	*none*	*none*	⌘-click on the size symbol in the Character palette
Increase leading	Option-down arrow	Option-down arrow	Option-down arrow
Decrease leading	Option-up arrow	Option-up arrow	Option-up arrow
Solid leading	Click on word *Leading* in Character palette	double-click on the leading symbol in the Character palette	double-click on the leading symbol in the Character palette
Auto leading	*none*	*none*	⌘-click on the leading symbol in the Character palette
Kern together by Preferences increment	Option-left arrow	Option-left arrow	Option-left arrow
Kern apart by Preferences increment	Option-right arrow	Option-right arrow	Option-right arrow
Kern together by 5x Preferences increment	⌘-Option-left arrow	⌘-Option-left arrow	⌘-Option-left arrow
Kern apart by 5x Preferences increment	⌘-Option-right arrow	⌘-Option-right arrow	⌘-Option-right arrow
Reset kerning to 0	Click on word *Kerning* in the Character palette	⌘-Shift-Q	⌘-Shift-Q or ⌘-click on the kerning symbol in the Character palette
Highlight Kerning option	⌘-Shift-K	⌘-Option-K	⌘-Option-K
Raise baseline shift by Preferences increment	Option-Shift-up arrow	Option-Shift-up arrow	Option-Shift-up arrow
Lower baseline shift by Preferences increment	Option-Shift-down arrow	Option-Shift-down arrow	Option-Shift-down arrow
Raise baseline shift by 5x Preferences increment	*none*	⌘-Option-Shift-up arrow	⌘-Option-Shift-up arrow
Lower baseline shift by 5x Preferences increment	*none*	⌘-Option-Shift-down arrow	⌘-Option-Shift-down arrow
Reset baseline shift to 0	Click on words *Baseline Shift* in Character palette	*none*	⌘-click on the baseline symbol in the Character palette

Operation	Illustrator 6 shortcut	Illustrator 7 shortcut	Illustrator 8 shortcut
Reset horizontal scale to 100%	Click on words *Horizontal Scale* in Character palette	⌘-Shift-X	⌘-Shift-X or ⌘-click on the horizontal scale symbol in the Character palette
Reset vertical scale to 100%	*none*	*none*	⌘-click on the vertical scale symbol in the Character palette
Force hyphenate word	⌘-Shift-hyphen (-)	⌘-Shift-hyphen (-)	⌘-Shift-hyphen (-)
Left-align paragraph	⌘-Shift-L	⌘-Shift-L	⌘-Shift-L
Center-align paragraph	⌘-Shift-C	⌘-Shift-C	⌘-Shift-C
Right-align paragraph	⌘-Shift-R	⌘-Shift-R	⌘-Shift-R
Justify paragraph	⌘-Shift-J	⌘-Shift-J	⌘-Shift-J
Force justify entire paragraph, including last line	⌘-Shift-B	⌘-Shift-F	⌘-Shift-F
Move multiple tab stops at a time	Shift-drag tab stop in Tabs palette	Shift-drag tab stop in Tabs palette	Shift-drag tab stop in Tabs palette
Change type of tab stop	Option-click on tab stop in Tabs palette	Option-click on tab stop in Tabs palette	Option-click on tab stop in Tabs palette
Change tab measurement	Click on measurement in Tabs palette	Click on measurement in Tabs palette	Click on measurement in Tabs palette
Align Tabs palette with selected paragraph	Click on size box on right side of title bar	Click on size box on right side of title bar	Click on size box on right side of title bar
Lift character and paragraph attributes from one block and apply them to all selected blocks	*new feature*	*new feature*	Click with eyedropper tool in desired block

Working with Colors

FreeHand users boast that their program lets you drag and drop colors onto objects. Illustrator 8 not only mimics some of FreeHand's capabilities, but it also provides more hidden shortcuts for trading colors between objects and palettes. The only trick is remembering them all.

Operation	Illustrator 6 shortcut	Illustrator 7 shortcut	Illustrator 8 shortcut
Switch focus from fill to stroke (or vice versa)	*none*	Press X	Press X
Swap fill and stroke color	*new feature*	*new feature*	Press Shift-X
Change fill or stroke to flat color	*none*	Press , (comma)	Press , (comma)

continued on next page

continued from previous page

Operation	Illustrator 6 shortcut	Illustrator 7 shortcut	Illustrator 8 shortcut
Make fill or stroke transparent	*none*	Press / (slash)	Press / (slash)
Apply stroke color when fill is active (or vice versa)	*none*	Option-click on color bar at bottom of Color palette	Option-click on color bar at bottom of Color palette
Apply swatch color to any object	*none*	Drag color from Swatches palette and drop onto object	Drag color from Swatches palette and drop onto object
Apply color to stroke of object when fill is active (or vice versa)	*none*	Drag color from Swatches and Shift drop onto object palette	Drag color from Swatches and Shift drop onto object palette
Copy colors from target object to selected objects	Double-click on target object with eyedropper	Click on target object with eyedropper	click on target object with eyedropper
Raise or lower active value in Color palette by 1 percent	Option-click on slider in any color palette or dialog box	*none*	*none*
Raise or lower active value in Color palette by 5 percent	Option-Shift-click on slider in any color palette or dialog box	*none*	*none*
Create tint of color	Shift-drag any slider triangle in Paint Style palette	Shift-drag any slider triangle in Color palette	Shift-drag any slider triangle in Color palette
Cycle through color bars (CMYK to grayscale palette RGB)	*none*	Shift-click on color bar at bottom of Color palette	Shift-click on color bar at to bottom of Color
Choose the compliment of a selected color	*new feature*	*new feature*	⌘-click on color bar at bottom of Color palette
Choose the inverse of a selected color	*new feature*	*new feature*	⌘-Shift-click on color bar at bottom of Color palette
Add color to Swatches palette	Option-click on empty swatch at end of list	Drag color from other palette and drop into Swatches	Drag color from other palette and drop into Swatches
Replace color in Swatches palette	Option-click on swatch	Drag color from other palette and Option-drop into Swatches	Drag color from other palette and Option-drop into Swatches
Duplicate color in Swatches palette	Option-drag swatch from one location to another	Drag swatch onto page icon at bottom of palette	Drag swatch onto page icon at bottom of palette
Delete swatch without warning	⌘-Option-click on swatch	Option-click on trash icon at bottom of Swatches palette	Option-click on trash icon at bottom of Swatches palette
Select range of swatches	Shift-click on color in Swatches palette	Shift-click on color in Swatches palette	Shift-click on color in Swatches palette
Select multiple swatches in random order	⌘-click on color in Swatches palette	⌘-click on color in Swatches palette	⌘-click on color in Swatches palette
Shift focus to color list so you can select color by typing name	*none*	⌘-Option-click in Swatches palette	⌘-Option-click in Swatches palette
Change fill to gradation	*none*	Press . (period)	Press . (period)

Operation	Illustrator 6 shortcut	Illustrator 7 shortcut	Illustrator 8 shortcut
Add color in Gradient palette	Click below fade bar	Click below fade bar	click below fade bar
Clone color in Gradient palette	Option-drag color stop	Option-drag color stop	Option-drag color stop
Apply swatch to selected color in Gradient palette	*none*	Option-click on color in Swatches palette	Option-click on color in Swatches palette
Lift color from illustration and apply to selected color in Gradient palette	Control-click with eyedropper tool in drawing area	Shift-click with eyedropper tool in drawing area	Shift-click with eyedropper tool in drawing area
Reset gradation to default black and white	*none*	⌘-click on grad preview box	⌘-click on grad preview box
Return fill and stroke to default white and black	*none*	Press D	Press D

Transforming Objects

Covered in Chapter 11, transformations are a category of loosely related operations that include moving, scaling, rotating, and a few others. You can transform an object using a special tool, or you can enter numeric values into the Transform palette. Adobe has made only modest changes to Illustrator's transformation capabilities over the years, but there are a few differences in version 8.

Operation	Illustrator 6 shortcut	Illustrator 7 shortcut	Illustrator 8 shortcut
Position origin point	Click with transformation tool	Click with transformation tool or drag origin point	click with transformation tool or drag origin point
Restore origin to center of selection	Drag with transformation tool	Double-click on a transform tool, click Cancel, and then reselect transformation tool	Double-click on a transform tool, click Cancel, and then reselect transformation tool
Transform from previous tool origin point	*none*	Drag with transformation tool	Drag with transformation
Display transformation dialog box	Option-click with transform tool or double-click on transform tool icon	Option-click with transform tool or double-click on transform tool icon	Option-click with transform tool or double-click on transform tool icon
Display Move dialog icon	⌘-Shift-M or Option-click on arrow tool icon	Double click on arrow tool icon	Double click on arrow tool
Clone selected objects with transformation tool	Press and hold Option before releasing mouse button	Press and hold Option before releasing mouse button	Press and hold Option before releasing mouse button
Scale non-proportionally from Transform palette	*none*	Enter percentage value into W or H, press Return	Enter percentage value into W or H, press Return
Scale proportionally from Transform palette	Enter new Scale value, press Return	Enter percentage value into W or H, press ⌘-Return	Enter percentage value into W or H, press ⌘-Return

continued on next page

continued from previous page

Operation	Illustrator 6 shortcut	Illustrator 7 shortcut	Illustrator 8 shortcut
Clone from Transform palette	Enter value, press Option-Return	Enter value, press Option-Return	Enter value, press Option-Return
Transform pattern fill independently of object	Press and hold P before releasing mouse button	Press and hold ~ before releasing mouse button	Press and hold ~ before releasing mouse button

Using Layers

Layers have been a part of Illustrator since version 5. This makes them old hat to Mac folks, but they might be new to the Windows crowd. Illustrator 8 has made a few changes to the once-familiar Layers palette, lifting the look and feel from Photoshop. Every one of the following shortcuts takes advantage of an icon in the Layers palette.

Operation	Illustrator 6 shortcut	Illustrator 7 shortcut	Illustrator 8 shortcut
Create new layer at top of stack, bypass dialog box	*none*	Click on page icon at bottom of palette	⌘-click on page icon
Create new layer, display dialog box	*none*	Option-click on page icon	Option-click on page icon
Create new layer behind active layer	*none*	⌘-click on page icon	⌘-Option-click on page icon
Create new layer above active layer	*none*	⌘-Option-click on page icon	Click on page icon
Duplicate layer	*none*	Drag layer onto page icon	Drag layer onto page icon
Select all objects on layer	*none*	Option-click on layer	Option-click on layer
Move selected objects to different layer	Drag colored square on right x different layer	Drag colored square on right side of palette	Drag colored square on right side of palette
Copy selected objects to different layer	*none*	Option-drag colored square to a different layer	Option-drag colored square to a different layer
Move selected objects to a locked layer	*none*	*none*	⌘-drag colored square to a locked layer
Copy selected objects to a locked layer	*none*	*none*	⌘-Option-drag colored square to a locked layer
Hide a layer	Click on dot in eyeball column	Click on eyeball icon	Click on eyeball icon
View one layer and hide all others	*none*	Option-click on eyeball icon in Layers palette	Option-click on eyeball icon in Layers palette
Set layer to artwork mode	Option-click on dot in eyeball column	⌘-click on eyeball icon	⌘-click on eyeball icon
Preview one layer and set all others to artwork mode	*none*	⌘-Option-click on eyeball icon	⌘-Option-click on eyeball icon

Operation	Illustrator 6 shortcut	Illustrator 7 shortcut	Illustrator 8 shortcut
Lock a layer	Click in pencil column	Click in pencil column (to the right of eyeballs)	Click in pencil column (to the right of eyeballs)
Lock all layers except one	*none*	Option-click in pencil column	Option-click in pencil column
Select range of layers	*none*	Shift-click on layer name	Shift-click on layer name
Select multiple layers in random order	Shift-click on layer name	⌘-click on layer name	⌘-click on layer name
Delete layer without displaying warning	*none*	Option-click on trash icon	Option-click on trash icon

Entering Graph Data

The Graph Data dialog box operates differently from all other dialog boxes in Illustrator. The good news is that these shortcuts have remained the same since their introduction.

Operation	Illustrator 6 shortcut	Illustrator 7 shortcut	Illustrator 8 shortcut
Select cell data	Click in cell	Click in cell	Click in cell
Select multiple cells	Drag over cells	Drag over cells	Drag over cells
Select all cells with values	⌘-A	⌘-A	⌘-A
Clear selected cells	Clear	Clear	Clear
Return character in cell data	Shift-\ (vertical line character, |)	Shift-\ (vertical line character, |)	Shift-\ (vertical line character, |)
Use numerical value as label	Straight quotes (") around numbers	Straight quotes (") around numbers	Straight quotes (") around numbers
Move one cell right	Press right arrow or Tab	Press right arrow or Tab	Press right arrow or Tab
Move one cell left	Press left arrow	Press left arrow	Press left arrow
Move one cell up	Press up arrow	Press up arrow	Press up arrow
Move one cell down	Press down arrow or Return	Press down arrow or Return	Press down arrow or Return
Change width of cell	Drag column handle	Drag column handle	Drag column handle
OK button	Press Enter	Press Enter	Press Enter
Cancel change to cell data	⌘-Z	⌘-Z	⌘-Z
Cancel all changes	Click close box, D (N under Windows)	Click close box, D (N under Windows)	Click close box, D (N under Windows)

Miscellaneous

As an added bonus, here are a few extra shortcuts that don't fit neatly into any particular category.

Operation	Illustrator 6 shortcut	Illustrator 7 shortcut	Illustrator 8 shortcut
Change Units on the fly	⌘-Control-U	⌘-Control-U (Macs only)	⌘-Control-U (Macs); Ctrl-click on a ruler (Windows)
Move panel out of palette	*new feature*	Drag panel tab	Drag panel tab
Fully collapse palette	*new feature*	Double-click on panel tab or click on collapse box	Double-click on panel tab or click on collapse box
Advance to next option box	Press Tab	Press Tab	Press Tab
Return to previous option box	Press Shift-Tab	Press Shift-Tab	Press Shift-Tab
Apply palette value and return focus to illustration	Press Return	Press Return	Press Return
Apply palette value but keep value active	*none*	Press Shift-Return	Press Shift-Return
Cancel button	⌘-Period or Escape	⌘-Period or Escape	⌘-Period or Escape
OK button	Press Return or Enter	Press Return or Enter	Press Return or Enter
Copy button	Option-Return	Option-Return	Option-Return
Don't Save button (No button under Windows)	Press D (N under Windows)	Press D (N under Windows)	Press D (N under Windows)

Other Shortcut Sources

A company called Key Finder (800/290-4584, http://www.keyfinder.com) creates a series of mousepad inserts that include shortcuts for Illustrator, Photoshop, and other major programs. They're especially useful if you're new to the program—you can just look at the mousepad to see how to perform an operation more quickly. Key Finder also offers inserts that show how to access special text characters, including the weird stuff in the Symbol and Zapf Dingbats fonts. You can order Key Finders that include one, three, or five different inserts ranging in price from $18 to $35.

Illustrator Actions

Photoshop has included an Actions palette for a while now and Adobe has decided that Illustrator should also have one. The Action palette, aptly enough, stores actions—groups of steps that are designed to complete a specific procedure.

The Actions palette shown in Figure A-1 allows you to display its actions in either the default mode or the button mode. In the default mode, the palette lists the sets, the actions within the sets, and the steps that make up the different actions. With the Actions palette in this mode, you can see every detail of each entry by expanding the set, action, or step by clicking on its expander triangle. You can also fiddle with its settings by turning on or off the Item toggle or the Dialog toggle. In the Button mode, only the different actions are displayed, as shown on the right of Figure A-1. Though you are given details of the actions in the Button mode, you can list more actions at once.

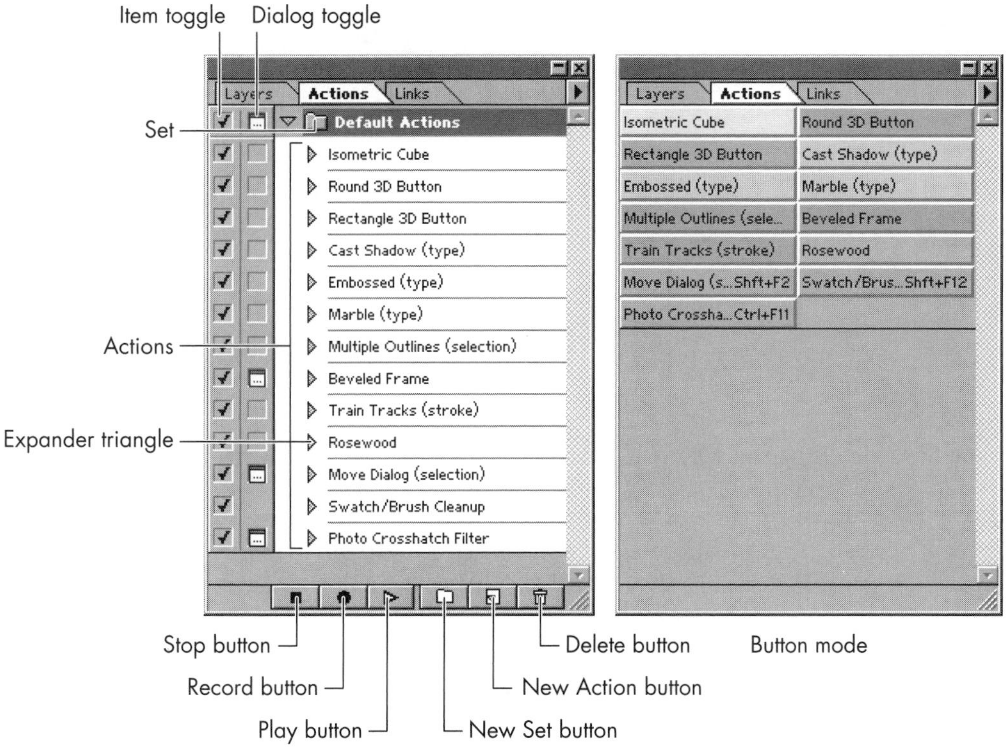

Figure A-1: Within the Actions palette, you can choose to display the actions and set hierarchies or just display the action buttons.

Understanding Actions

The best way for you to understand actions and what they can do is to look at an action. Illustrator ships with a number of preset actions. To see them, display the Actions palette (if hidden) by choosing the Windows » Show Actions command and then clicking on the expander triangle just to the left of the Default Actions set. The Default Actions set stores several actions, as shown in Figure A-1.

The Round 3D Button action is a good example of something an action can create. The action is self-contained and doesn't require that you do any prep work. Click on the Round 3D Button action in the Action palette and press the Play button. Illustrator will execute the steps that make up the action, creating two concentric circles. Figure A-2 shows the steps in the Round 3D Button action and the button that they are designed to make.

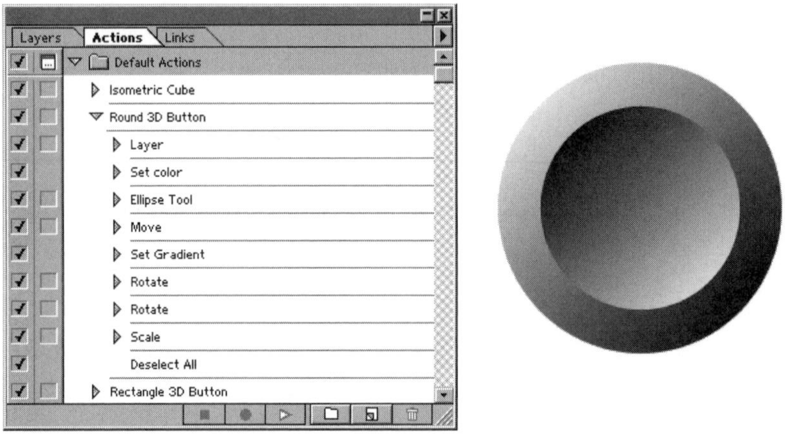

Figure A-2: The steps executed when you press the Round 3D Button action and its final result.

The Round 3D Button action consists of nine steps. All of the steps, except for the last one, have an expander triangle that lets you see exactly what tasks each step is intending to do. First, a new layer is created specifically for the button that the action creates. Click on the Layer step's expander triangle and you'll see the new layer's name and all the layer's settings. The layer it creates is a regular previewing and printing layer that's named Round 3D Button. Next, the Set Color step changes the current stroke to none. This means that any paths created now will have no stroke. The third step creates a circle, 45 points across. The circle has no stroke, as expected, but its fill is entirely dependent on the current fill setting selected in your copy of Illustrator—none of the steps in the Round 3D Button action has yet addressed the issue of fill color. With the execution of the fourth step, the newly created circle is moved (rather arbitrarily, in my opinion) to a specific locale on your page. The fifth step back pedals a bit and sets the fill to the standard black-and-white gradient. The sixth step rotates the filled circle 180 degrees. (This step is actually unnecessary.) In the last Set Color step, the one that fills the circle with the black-and-white gradient, the angle of the gradient was set to 135 degrees. Rotating the circle by 180 degrees produces the same result that would be produced if the gradient had simply been set to –55 degrees (135-180) or 315 degrees (135+180). Of course, this Rotate step is harmless; it just means that Illustrator will take slightly longer to complete the action. On first glance, the seventh step appears to be a repeat of the previous step. But, in fact, this Rotate step rotates and clones the original circle, creating a second circle on top of the first. The next step scales this clone, reducing it uniformly to 70 percent of its original size. The final step simply deselects everything, leaving you with the completed button on its own layer.

Creating a New Action

Now that you've seen what an action can do, it's time to create a new action. Before you construct an action anew, you should give some thought to what kind of action you want to make. Illustrator lets you create two types of actions: the *construction action* and the *modifying action*. The construction action is a self-contained action that creates objects from scratch and requires nothing of you except your desire to use the action. The Round 3D Button action explored above is a construction action. Conversely, the modifying action is designed to make changes to an existing path. Before you execute the action, you must first create the path that you want the action to modify and select that path before you play the action.

I like the modifying actions more because they are more flexible and allow me to consistently transform whatever path I choose to use as a starting point. In the example below, I design an action that's intended to give selected text a spiky effect.

Organizing your Action

The Actions palette is your headquarters for action design, but it also lets you organize your actions into folders or directories called *sets*. As I mentioned, Illustrator's preset actions are all stored in the set called Default Actions. When you create a new action, you can choose to add it to the other actions in the Default Action set or first create a new set that better reflects the nature of your new action. To create a new set, either click the New Set button located at the bottom of the Actions palette or choose the New Set command from the palette's pop-up menu.

The New Set dialog box will display. You have but one decision to make with this dialog box: what to name the set. Since the action that I'm going to create is one that modifies text, I'll call the new set "My Text Modifiers."

Recording an Action

In *recording* an action, you show Illustrator all the steps you want it to follow. Since this action is going to modify some text, I first create a line of point text and then select it with the arrow tool. Figure A-3 show the text I'm using as my starting object. The content and font of the text is completely open-ended since it has no bearing on the action. But since the action I'm going to make will be designed for 72-point type, I'll set its size to 72pt in the Character palette.

Figure A-3: This 72-point text is the starting point for the action that I'm about to record. I'll modify this text to show Illustrator the steps involved in the action.

With all the groundwork for my new action out of the way, it's time to start designing or recording my new action.

1. **Click the New Action button, or choose the New Action command from the pop-up menu.**

   The New Action dialog box will display, as shown in Figure A-4. Here you name the action and choose the set in which it should reside. I named this action "Spike Effect 72pt" and directed it to the set I created above, My Text Modifiers. If you think you're going use the action often and want it to have its own keyboard shortcut, you can assign it a function key. Bear in mind that Illustrator already has shortcuts for all the function keys, so if you choose a shortcut for your action, be sure to also check either or both the Shift and Command check boxes. Otherwise, you could lose a preset shortcut. If you display your Action palette in the button mode, you can choose a color for the action's button.

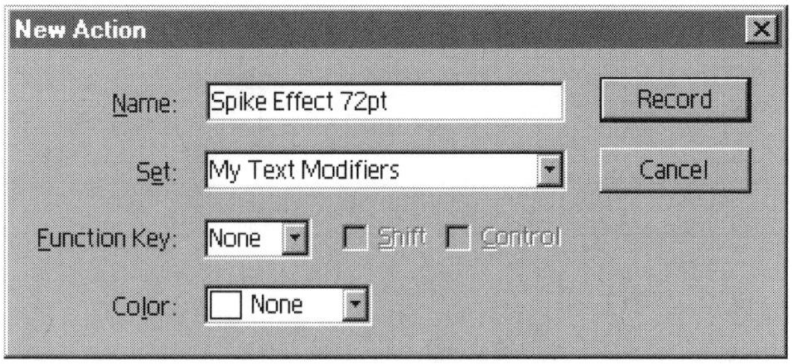

Figure A-4: In the New Action dialog box, you can name your action and choose the set to which it belongs.

2. **Click the Record button, or press Return.**

   Illustrator will add your new action to the set you specified and activate the Record button, as shown in Figure A-5. When Illustrator is recording, the Record button changes from black to red. Now any changes I make will become part of the Spike Effect 72pt action.

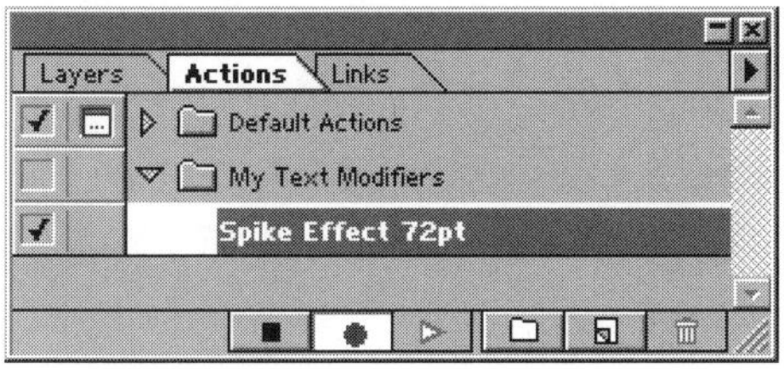

Figure A-5: The Actions palette is ready to record the new Spike Effect 72pt action.

3. **Set the fill to none and give it an 8-point black stroke.**

   The number of steps that Illustrator assigns to this task and the nature of the individual steps depend entirely on how you go about changing the fill and stroke. Don't worry about it, since you can streamline the action after you're done recording it. I discuss this in an upcoming section, "Changing an Action."

4. **Covert the text to paths by choosing the Type » Create Outline command.**

   Or press ⌘-Shift-O. I could have started with this step. After I'm done recording the action, if I decide that this should be the starting point, I can move this step, as discussed in the "Changing an Action" section.

5. **Choose Object » Transform » Move.**

   I entered *–0.5* into the Move Horizontal and *1* into the Move Vertical option boxes. This nudges the paths up 1 point and to the left 0.05 point.

6. **Click the Copy button.**

   A slightly displaced clone appears in front of the original.

7. **Change the stroke attributes.**

   I changed the stroke to a dash pattern with a 0-point dash and a 10-point gap and selected round caps and joins.

8. **Change the color to 90 percent black.**

   Now I have my 90 percent black clones covering the original 8-point black paths.

9. **Choose Object » Transform » Transform Again.**

   Or simply press ⌘-D to repeat the move and copy transformation.

10. **Reduce the stroke to 7 and change the stroke's color to 80 percent black.**

    This second copy is slightly lighter and smaller than the first.

11. **Repeat the last two steps six more times.**

    This means that each time I pressed ⌘-D, I reduced the stroke by 1 point and lightened its color by 10 percent.

12. **Click on the Stop button located at the bottom of the Actions palette.**

    The action is complete.

The top example of Figure A-6 shows the modifications that I made to my original path. To repeat all these steps by hand to a new bit of point text would take me almost as long as it took to create the Spike Effect 72pt action. But now that it's recorded, the actions will re-create the effect in just a few seconds. In the bottom portion of Figure A-6, I created a new line of text and applied the Spike Effect 72pt action. It took Illustrator about 6 seconds to spike up this new line.

Figure A-6: The top line is the end result of all the changes I made to the original line of text. The bottom line is the result of Illustrator applying the action that I just created.

Changing an Action

After you create an action, you'll probably find that it contains more steps than necessary or that you want to add a step or two. Fortunately, Illustrator allows you to make changes to an action with relative ease.

Streamlining an Action

After I created my Spike Effect 72pt action, I noticed that it took more steps than I wanted. For example, in the beginning, I had simply deleted the paths' fill and changed the stroke to 8-point black. By my count, this should take three steps—two Set Color steps and one Set Stroke step. Illustrator recorded six Set Color steps and two Set Stroke steps, and some of the steps that Illustrator recorded were not needed. For example, look at the two steps shown in Figure A-7. (I clicked on the expansion triangles so that I could see the contents of each step.) The first Set Color step tells Illustrator to bring the Fill icon into focus but does nothing to the fill's color. The second step tells Illustrator to bring the Fill icon into focus and change it to none. The first step in not necessary and I can delete it. Before I make any changes, though, I copy the entire action by selecting it and choosing Duplicate from the Actions palette's pop-up menu. Then in the copy, I select the first Set Color step (the one that doesn't change the fill's color) and choose Delete from the palette's pop-up menu. Illustrator displays a warning box to confirm my changes. I could also remove the step by selecting it and clicking the Delete button. (To bypass the warning, Option-click the Delete button.) If

I find that an entire action is not up to snuff, I can use the Delete command or button to remove the action.

After going through all the steps in the action, I found that nine of the steps that Illustrator recorded were not necessary and I deleted them. Then, to make sure that I didn't remove any critical steps, I applied the altered copy of the action to a new line of text. It worked fine, so I deleted the original action. Streamlining the action results in a faster action and one that is easier to read and, thus, easier to further modify.

If you like an action as is, but you can see how it may be more useful in some cases with a couple of the steps removed, you can temporarily turn off steps. To do so, click on the Item Toggle box located at the far left of the step. The check mark will disappear from the box, indicating that Illustrator will bypass the step when it next carries out the action. To turn the step back on, click on the Item Toggle box again and the check mark will return.

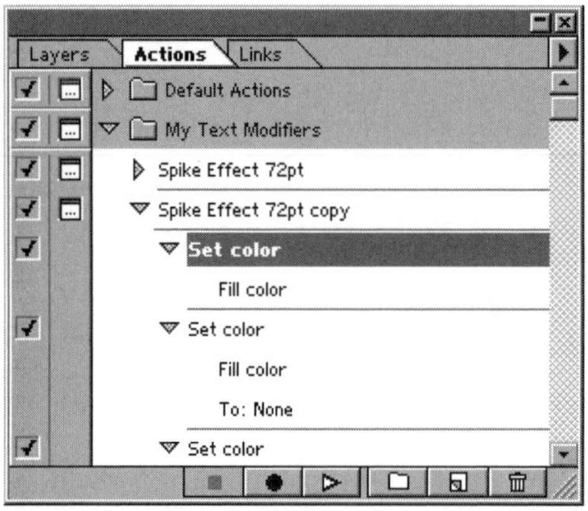

Figure A-7:
In an effort to streamline my action, I first duplicated the entire action and then looked through it step by step to see which steps were unnecessary.

Reordering an Action

You can switch the order of an action's steps by dragging a step to a new position. As I mentioned in the steps above, I could have applied the Create Outline command before I made any changes to the path's color. To move the Create Outline step to the head of the stack, I merely dragged it to the top. Once again, I first made my changes to a copy of the action and tested the modified action to confirm that I didn't overlook anything.

You can also move multiple steps at once. Select the first step and then ⌘-click on each additional step you want to move. When you've selected all the steps you want, drag them to their new location. Illustrator will drop them as a contiguous block in which the original order of the steps is preserved.

Adding to an Action

Just as you can easily delete steps from an action, you can easily add steps. To add steps, select the action in the Actions palette and click the Record button. Define the desired steps, and then click the Stop button when you're done. Illustrator will tack the new steps onto the end of the action and you can then move them to their proper position.

For example, say I want to add two steps to my Spike Effect 72pt action: a Roughen command that should follow the Create Outline step and a Deselect All command at the end. First I would create a new bit of point text and convert it to path by pressing ⌘-Shift-O. (I need to convert new point text to path so that I can apply the Roughen filter.) Then, with this path selected, I select the action and click the Record button. Then I choose the Filter » Distort » Roughen command, set the options to my liking, click OK, and then choose the Edit » Deselect All command. After applying these two new commands, I click on the Stop button. Illustrator records two new steps at the end of my action. Since I want the Deselect All command at the end of the action to inform me that the action is complete, I leave it where it is. The Roughen step needs to follow the Create Outline step, so I drag the new step into place.

Making Actions More Interactive

For the most part, Illustrator needs your input only at the beginning of an action and doesn't bother you while it completes all the steps. You can allow for user input in two ways. The first relies on commands that you recorded and that have dialog boxes associated with them. If a step requires the use of a dialog box, Illustrator records this along with the step and inserts a Dialog Toggle box to the left of the command. For example, every time I used the Move command in my Spike Effect 72pt action, a Dialog Toggle box appeared with the step. By default, Illustrator turns all of these boxes off when you record your action. This means that Illustrator will apply your original settings without asking you for new input. If you want Illustrator to pause at a step that uses a dialog box and display the box, you must click the Dialog Toggle box. The box will be filled with a small icon. While the Dialog Toggle is active, Illustrator will display the appropriate dialog box when it comes to that step. You can then make changes to the box's settings or choose to go with the original settings. Before Illustrator moves to the next step, you will have to close the dialog box.

Another way to allow for user input in the execution of an action is to add a *stop* to the action. A stop forces Illustrator to stop the execution of an action, and it won't resume the action until you tell it to do so. To add a stop to an action while you're creating it, choose Insert Stop from the Action palette's pop-up menu. To add a stop to an existing action, select the step that you want the stop to precede and choose Insert Stop from the pop-up menu. In either case, the Record Stop dialog box will display, as shown in Figure A-8. In the Message field, you can explain to the user why Illustrator is pausing here. (This could be a simple explanation of what the following step is about to do, or it could be instructions to the user about what the user needs to do.) For example, I could insert a stop at the beginning of my Spike Effect 72pt action to explain to a user that the action works best for 72-point text or to explain that the action adds eight new paths.

When Illustrator encounters a stop, it displays a warning box complete with your instructions, also shown in Figure A-8. Depending on whether you activated the Allow Continue option in the Record Stop dialog box, the warning may include a Continue button in addition to the standard Stop button. In cases in which you only want to provide information and you want the user to be able to quickly move on, be sure to check the Allow Continue check box. This will allow the user simply to click the Continue button and Illustrator will resume the next step in the action. If the user clicks the Stop button, Illustrator terminates the action at that point, but it remembers where it is in the action. At this point, for example, the user could apply some changes to the artwork and, when finished, have Illustrator complete the rest of the action by clicking the Play button.

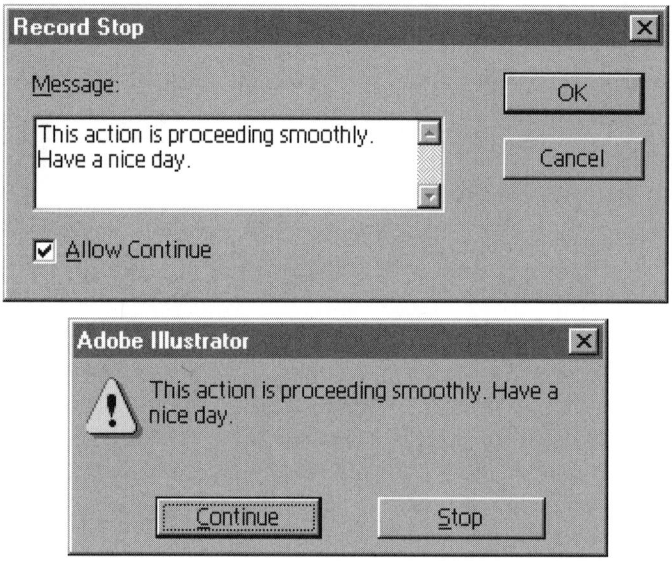

Figure A-8: When you insert a stop, Illustrator will prompt you for a message with the Record Stop dialog box. When Illustrator comes across a stop while playing an action, it will display a warning box with your message.

INDEX

A

B

C

D

E

F

H

I

L

M

N

O

P

Q

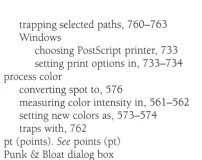

R

S

T

U

V

W

X

Y

Z